DICTIONARY
OF PERSONNEL MANAGEMENT
AND LABOR RELATIONS

DICTIONARY
OF PERSONNEL MANAGEMENT
AND LABOR RELATIONS

JAY M. SHAFRITZ
University of Colorado at Denver

MOORE PUBLISHING COMPANY, INC.
OAK PARK, ILLINOIS

Library of Congress Cataloging in Publication Data

Shafritz, Jay M
    Dictionary of personnel management and labor relations.

    1. Personnel management—Dictionaries. 2. Industrial
relations—Dictionaries. I. Title.
HF5549.A23S52   658.3'003   79-24632

ISBN 0-935610-09-X

Moore Publishing Company, Inc.
701 South Gunderson Avenue, Oak Park, Illinois 60304

CONTENTS

SPECIAL FEATURES

ILLUSTRATIONS

PREFACE

This dictionary is a tool for all those who must be knowledgeable about the theory, concepts, practices, laws, institutions, literature, and people of the academic disciplines and professional practices of personnel management and labor relations. In short, it is a tool—a source of expertise—for all those who are faced with, or concerned about, the managing of people in organizations.

A dictionary is inherently a "work in progress." Unless a subject is a dead language or an expired technology, its terminology is constantly changing and evolving into its future state. This is certainly true of personnel management and labor relations. Each year, for example, new Supreme Court decisions, new labor legislation, new advances in examination validation, and new personnel management processes change the language of personnel management and labor relations and advance (or impede depending upon one's perspective) the professional practice. This dictionary seeks to capture and codify the language of personnel management and labor relations fully aware that when finished it will be incomplete. A living language does not wait on publisher's deadlines.

While this effort may be incomplete by its nature, it is nevertheless comprehensive by design. Contained herein are all of the words, terms, phrases, processes, names, laws, and court cases with which personnel management and labor relations specialists should be familiar. And then some. Some because they are historically important. Some just for fun. The criteria for including definitions had to be rather loosely defined because the boundaries of personnel management and labor relations, both as academic disciplines and professional practices, are so wide that they overlap many other fields. It was the author's judgment that determined just how far to go into related fields such as law, economics, psychology, statistics, management, history, and medicine, among others. As a rule of thumb, if a term was found in any of several score personnel management or labor relations textbooks, it is included here. Generally excluded were any terms whose meaning in the context of personnel management and labor relations did not differ from definitions to be found in any standard dictionary of the English language.

This dictionary is generic. It neither favors nor discriminates against the private or public sector. Everything that the author found relevant to either sector was included. In the end, it turned out that 95 percent of the definitions were relevant to the private sector and 95 percent were relevant to the public sector. This seems to be a mathematical impossibility until you consider that 90 percent of the definitions are relevant to both sectors. Each sector can then claim 5 percent of the definitions as uniquely its own. The differences between personnel management and labor relations in the private sector and public personnel management and labor relations continue to grow less significant with the passing of each year and with the passing of each new wave of federal legislation.

In addition to the entries that the reader might expect to find in a dictionary concerned with personnel management and labor relations, there are some special kinds of entries that warrant a word of explanation:

● **BIOGRAPHICAL ENTRIES**. There are hundreds of identifications of individuals, both living and dead, who have been significant in the history, writing, and practice of personnel management and labor relations. Such entries are designed to merely identify an individual; that being the purpose of a dictionary. The author readily concedes that some notable individuals may have been excluded or that other individuals may have been described in words too brief to do them justice. Remember, the object was identification, not justice.

● **COURT CASES**. There are hundreds of legal decisions on issues relevant to personnel management and labor relations, including *every* major U.S. Supreme Court ruling in this area. Such judicial decisions are usually many pages long for good reason. So be cautious! A brief summary of a case, no matter how succinct, may not be sufficient information upon which to base formal action. These summaries were written to identify the case and its significance, not necessarily to make less work for lawyers. The full legal citation is given with each entry of this type so that the reader may readily locate the full text of any of these court cases.

● **JOURNALS**. A list of *all* of the journals and magazines that bear upon personnel management and labor relations would be almost as large as this entire dictionary. So the author included only those periodicals that most consistently address the concerns of personnel and labor relations specialists. Each periodical entry contains a statement of purpose as well as an appropriate address. A master list of all journal entries is found under the entry "personnel journals."

● **LAWS**. All federal laws that directly impact upon personnel and labor relations practices are summarized. The reader should be aware that these entries are necessarily brief summaries of complicated laws that are constantly subject to ammendment.

● **ORGANIZATIONS**. All of the major governmental agencies, private organizations, and professional societies that bear upon personnel management and labor relations have been included. All such entries contain a statement of the purposes of the organization as well as its address and phone number.

● **TESTS**. Included are descriptions of the most commonly used commercial tests used in personnel selection and employee counseling. A master list of all commercial test entries is found under the entry for "personnel tests."

● **UNIONS**. Listed under "labor organization" are the names, addresses, phone numbers, and memberships of all of the major unions in the United States.

In general, those items which are more central to the concerns of personnel management and labor relations tend to be given more detailed coverage than those that are more on the periphery of the subject. There are basically two types of definitions: (1) those that are given brief glossary descriptions and (2) those that are given more comprehensive descriptions. The references given at the end of the latter serve to give an example of the usage of the term as well as to provide sources for further information. Because such references have been given as often as is possible or practical, they are in their totality a comprehensive bibliography.

No one writes a dictionary alone. My various intellectual debts are acknowledged throughout this book by the bibliographic references that follow many of the entries. On a more personal level many individuals encouraged me along the way. Dan Oran, a childhood friend and the author of *Law Dictionary for Non-Lawyers* (St. Paul, Minn.: West Publishing, 1975) first suggested I do this dictionary after I admiringly examined his then new law dictionary and asked, "Was it hard to do?" He replied, "No, even you could do one." This inspired me onward. I then went to my frequent collaborator, Albert C. Hyde, and said, "Let's write a dictionary together!" But Hyde said, "That doesn't sound like much fun. You'll have to do it yourself." Happily, Hyde was wrong in both instances. Parts of this dictionary were great fun to do and I was able to get help. Where does any professor go for help when his friends forsake him? To his students! Over a several year period while I was on the faculty of the University of Houston at Clear Lake City, at least one graduate course each semester was concerned with defining personnel management and labor relations. I am very much indebted to the following students for bringing to my attention much material that I surely would have otherwise missed: Donna Anderson, John Arnold, Michael Bernstein, Warren Brasher, Robert Bryden, Helen Cahill, Mary Cook, Kenneth Demel, Thomas Brubbs, Charles Haines, Jon Harpold, Carmen Jackson, Lonnie Jenkins, Lawrence King, John Knochel, Robert Lewis, Donald Mitchell, Donald Mullen, Susan Needle, Ishmael Paul, Tony Redding, Mylie Reid, Jose Reyes, Donald Simanton, Fred Spross, Richard Stewart, and Robert Stults.

Two students were so helpful in gathering materials and went so far beyond what might normally be expected of students that I owe Dawn G. Hoyle and Joseph D. Atkinson (both of NASA's Johnson Space Center) a special debt.

In one fashion or another I am indebted to the following colleagues for offering advice, assistance and encouragement: Wayne Boss, University of Colorado at Boulder; Philip Burgess, University of Colorado at Denver; Jean J. Couturier, Northwestern University; Elizabeth J. Mitchell, M. D. Anderson Hospital and Tumor Institute of Houston; Thomas H. Patten, Jr., Michigan State University; David H. Rosenbloom, Syracuse University; Frank J. Thompson, University of Georgia; Philip H. Whitbeck, NASA's Johnson Space Center; and Robert Wilcox, University of Colorado at Denver. Ginger Ware is the gracious lady who spent more than a year typing and retyping this manuscript.

Finally some domestic acknowledgements. My wife, Luise, was my most severe critic, ever reminding me that the dictionary would get done sooner if I would turn off the television. At such times I always assured her that I was in fact diligently thinking about a complex definition. My sons, Todd and Noah, assisted me enormously by advising me of when I violated the laws of alphabetical order, by telling me to "hurry up and finish so we can play," and by ever reminding me of how difficult it is to manage the personnel of even a single household.

JAY M. SHAFRITZ

A

AA: *see* AFFIRMATIVE ACTION.

AAA: *see* AMERICAN ARBITRATION ASSOCIATION.

AAAA: *see* LABOR ORGANIZATION. Actors and Artistes of America, Associated.

AACSB: *see* AMERICAN ASSEMBLY OF COLLEGIATE SCHOOLS OF BUSINESS.

AACSE: *see* LABOR ORGANIZATION, Classified School Employees, American Association of.

AAG: *see* AFFIRMATIVE ACTION GROUPS.

AAO: *see* AFFIRMATIVE ACTION OFFICER.

AAP: *see* AFFIRMATIVE ACTION PLAN or AFFIRMATIVE ACTION PROGRAM.

AAUP: *see* LABOR ORGANIZATION, University Professors, American Association of.

abandonment of position, quitting a job without formally resigning.

Abel, I. W. (1908-   ), full name IORWITH WILBER ABEL, president of the United Steel Workers of America from 1965 to 1977. For biographical information, *see:* John Herling, *Right to Challenge: People and Power in the Steelworkers Union* (N.Y.: Harper & Row, 1972).

ability, the present power to perform a physical or mental function.

ability test, performance test designed to reveal a measure of present ability (*e.g.*, a typing test).

ability to pay, concept from collective bargaining referring to an employer's ability to tolerate the costs of requested wage and benefit increases. Factfinders and arbitrators frequently use the "ability to pay" concept in justifying their decisions.

    See also NATIONAL LABOR RELATIONS BOARD V. TRUITT MANUFACTURING.

Abood v. *Detroit Board of Education*, 431 U.S. 209 (1977), U.S. Supreme Court case, which held that public sector agency shops requiring nonunion employees to pay a service fee equivalent to union dues were constitutional. The court declared unconstitutional a union's use of such service fees for political and ideological purposes unrelated to collective bargaining.

abrogation of agreement, formal cancellation of a collective bargaining agreement or portion thereof.

absence, short-term unavailability for work, lasting at least one day or normal tour of duty.

Incidence of Absence from Work for Fulltime Wage and Salary Workers Except Farm, by Reason (May 1973-76)

(Numbers in thousands)

Item	1973	1974	1975	1976
Total reporting	55,283	56,248	54,700	56,414
Total absent	3,614	3,499	3,332	3,630
Incidence rate:				
For all reasons ..	6.5	6.2	6.1	6.4
For illness or injury	4.1	3.7	3.7	4.0
For personal & civic reasons ..	2.4	2.5	2.4	2.5

(Because of rounding, detail may not equal totals.)

SOURCE: Janice Neipert Hedges, "Absence from Work—Measuring the Hours Lost," *Monthly Labor Review* (October 1977).

If an employee is absent from the job for a lesser period, it is usually considered a lateness. For relationship between absence and job satisfaction, *see* Nigel Nicholson, Colin A. Brow, and J. K. Chadwick-Jones, "Absence From Work and Job Satisfaction," *Journal of Applied Psychology* (December 1976). *See also* Donald L. Hawk, "Absenteeism and Turnover," *Personnel Journal* (June 1976).

For some comparative statistics, *see* Janice Neipert Hedges, "Absence from Work—A Look at Some National Data," *Monthly Labor Review* (July 1973).

See also ABSENCE RATE.

absence rate, amount of absence, calculated by the U.S. Bureau of Labor Statistics using the following formula:

$$\text{absence rate} = \frac{\text{work days lost (per month)}}{\text{days worked plus days lost}} \times 100$$

absence without leave, absence without prior approval.

absentee, any worker not present for one or more scheduled days of work. *see* John Scherba and Lyle Smith, "Computerization of Absentee Control Programs," *Personnel Journal* (May 1973).

absenteeism, as defined by the U.S. Bureau of Labor Statistics:

> the failure of workers to appear on the job when they are scheduled to work. It is a broad term which is applied to time lost because sickness or accident prevents a worker from being on the job, as well as unauthorized time away from the job for other reasons. Workers who quit without notice are also counted as absentees until they are officially removed from the payroll.

Generally, "absenteeism" is associated with unnecessary, unexcused, or habitual absences from work. For an academic analysis of the problem, *see* R. Oliver Gibson, "Toward a Conceptualization of Absence Behavior of Personnel in Organizations," *Administrative Science Quarterly* (June 1966). For a "nuts-and-bolts" presentation of the problem, *see* Frederick J. Gaudet, *Solving the Problem of Employee Absence* (N.Y.: American Management Associations, 1963). For a bibliography, *see* Paul M. Muchinsky, "Employee Absenteeism: A Review of the Literature," *Journal of Vocational Behavior* (June 1977).

See also REINFORCEMENT.

Academy of Management, nonprofit organization with primary objectives of advancing research, learning, teaching, and practice in the field of management and encouraging the extension and unification of knowledge pertaining to management. The Academy, most of whose members are college teachers, views itself as America's academic "voice" in U.S. management.

Academy of Management Journal, quarterly that publishes articles in the fields of business policy and planning, international management, management consulting, management education and development, management history, manpower management, organizational behavior, organization and management theory, organization development, production-operations management, social issues in management, organizational communication, and health care administration.

The *Journal* publishes original research of an empirical nature either in the form of articles or as research notes. Although studies which serve to test either theoretical propositions or hypotheses derived from practice are of particular interest, exploratory work and survey research findings are also included. The *Journal* does not publish purely conceptual papers which do not contain any original data. Conceptual articles of this kind are published in the *Academy of Management Review*.

Academy of Management Journal
P.O. Box KZ
Mississippi State University
Mississippi State, MS 39762

Academy of Management Review, quarterly that publishes articles in the field of business policy and planning, international management, management consulting, management education and development, management history, personnel/human resources, organizational behavior, organization and management theory, organization development, production–operations management, social issues in management, organizational communication, and health care administration.

The *Review* seeks distinguished original manuscripts which (a) move theoretical conceptualization forward in the field of management, and/or (b) indicate new theoretical linkages that have rich potential for theory and research in management, and (c) provide clear implications of theory for problem-solving in administrative and organizational situations.

Academy of Management Review
P.O. Box KZ
Mississippi State University
Mississippi State, MS 39762

accelerating premium pay, bonus incentive system in which pay rates rise as production standards are exceeded. For example, an employee who exceeds standard production by two percent may get just a two percent bonus, while an employee who exceeds by five percent may get a ten percent bonus.

acceptable level of unemployment, An acceptable level of unemployment means that the individual to whom it is acceptable still has a job.

acceptance theory of authority: *see* ZONE OF ACCEPTANCE.

accession, any addition to the workforce of an organization.

accession rate, also called HIRING RATE, number of employees added to a payroll during a given time period, usually expressed as a percentage of total employment. The accession rate is a significant indicator of economic growth—an increase (decrease) tends to indicate economic recovery (recession). Statistics on the accession rates of major industries are gathered monthly by the Bureau of Labor Statistics of the U.S. Department of Labor. Accession rates can be computed using the following formula:

$$\text{accession rate} = \frac{\text{total accessions} \times 100}{\text{total number of workers}}$$

accidental death benefit, feature found in some life insurance policies that provides for payment of additional amounts to the beneficiary if the insured party dies as a result of an accident. When such provisions allow for an accidental death benefit that is twice the normal value of the policy, they are known as "double-indemnity" provisions.

accident and sickness benefits, variety of regular payments made to employees who lose time from work due to off-the-job disabilities occasioned by accidents or sickness.

accident frequency rate, as computed by the Bureau of Labor Statistics, the accident frequency rate is the total number of disabling injuries per million hours worked.

accident prevention, total planned effort on the part of labor, management, and government regulators to eliminate the causes and severity of industrial injuries and accidents. For a text, *see* Willie Hammer, *Occupational Safety Management and Engineering* (Englewood Cliffs, N.J.: Prentice-Hall, 1976).

accident-proneness, concept that implies that certain kinds of personalities are more likely to have accidents than others. However, psychological research supports the assertion that accident-proneness is more related to situational factors than personality factors. For the classic analysis on the subject, *see* A. G. Arbous and J. E. Kerrich, "The Phenomenon of Accident-Proneness," *Industrial Medicine and Surgery* (April 1953). Nevertheless, Joseph T. Kunce established a relationship between "Vocational Interest and Accident Proneness," in the *Journal of Applied Psychology* (June 1967).

accident severity rate, generally computed as the number of work days lost because of accidents per thousand hours worked.

accountability, extent to which one is responsible to higher authority—legal or organizational—for one's actions in society at large or within one's particular organizational position. For discussion in a public administration context, *see* Jerome B. McKinney and Lawrence C. Howard, *Public Administration: Balancing Power and Accountability* (Oak Park, Ill.: Moore Publishing Co., 1979). For a private sector context, *see* Robert Albanese, *Managing: Toward Accountability for Performance* (Homewood, Ill.: Richard D. Irwin, rev. ed., 1978).

accreditation: *see* AMERICAN SOCIETY FOR PERSONNEL ADMINISTRATION ACCREDITATION INSTITUTE.

achievement battery: *see* ACHIEVEMENT TEST.

achievement drive, also called ACHIEVEMENT NEED, motivation to strive for high standards of performance in a given area of endeavor. For the classic work on achievement motivation, *see* David C. McClelland, *The Achieving Society* (Princeton, N.J.: Van Nostrand Rinehold Co., 1961). *Also see* David C. McClelland, "Achievement Motivation Can be Developed," *Harvard Business Review* (November–December 1965).

achievement need: *see* ACHIEVEMENT DRIVE.

achievement test, test designed to measure an individual's level of proficiency in a specific subject or task. A collection of achievement tests designed to measure levels of skill or knowledge in a variety of areas is called an achievement battery. *See* Norman E. Gronlund, *Constructing Achievement Tests* (Englewood Cliffs, N.J.: Prentice-Hall, 2nd ed., 1977).

ACIPP: *see* ADVISORY COUNCIL ON INTER-GOVERNMENTAL PERSONNEL POLICY.

across-the-board increase, increase in wages, whether expressed in dollars or percentage of salary, given to an entire workforce.

ACT: *see* LABOR ORGANIZATION, Technicians, Association of Civilian.

act, written bill formally passed by a legislature, such as the U.S. Congress. An act becomes law when it is signed, by a chief executive, such as the U.S. President.

actionable, an act or occurance is actionable if it provides adequate reason for a grievance or lawsuit.

action research, in its broadest context, the application of the scientific method to practical problems. As the basic model underlying organization development, action research, according to Wendell L. French and Cecil H. Bell, Jr., in *Organization Development: Behavioral Science Interventions for Organization Improvement* (Englewood Cliffs, N.J.: Prentice-Hall, 1973), is:

> the process of systematically collecting research data about an ongoing system relative to some objective, goal, or need of that system; feeding these data back into the system; taking actions by altering selected vari-

ables within the system based both on the data and on hypotheses; and evaluating the results of actions by collecting more data. This definition characterizes action research in terms of the activities comprising the process: first a static picture is taken of an organization; on the basis of "what exists," hunches and hypotheses suggest actions; these actions typically entail manipulating some variable in the system that is under the control of the action researcher (this often means doing somthing differently from the way it has always been done); later, a second static picture is taken of the system to examine the effects of the actions taken.

For a book length study of action research in action, *see* William F. Whyte and Edith L. Hamilton, *Action Research for Management* (Homewood, Ill.: Irwin–Dorsey Press, 1964). *See also* Mark A. Frohman, Marshall Sashkin, and Michael J. Kavanagh, "Action Research As Applied to Organization Development," *Organization and Administrative Sciences* (Spring/Summer 1976).

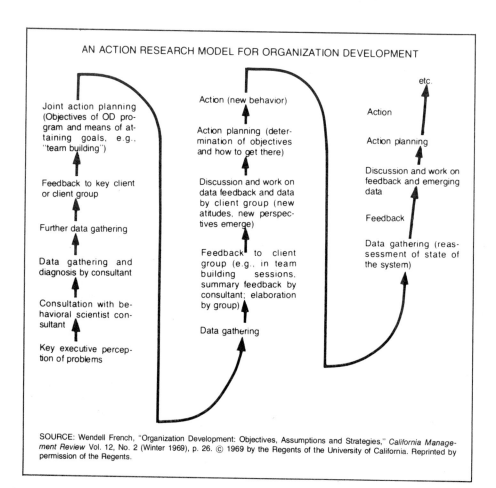

AN ACTION RESEARCH MODEL FOR ORGANIZATION DEVELOPMENT

SOURCE: Wendell French, "Organization Development: Objectives, Assumptions and Strategies," *California Management Review* Vol. 12, No. 2 (Winter 1969), p. 26. © 1969 by the Regents of the University of California. Reprinted by permission of the Regents.

active listening, counseling technique in which the counselor listens to both the facts and the feelings of the speaker. Such listening is called "active" because the counselor has the specific responsibilities of showing interest, of not passing judgment, and of helping the speaker to work out his problems. For a discussion, *see* Carl R. Rogers and Richard E. Farson, "Active listening," *Readings in Management: An Organizational Perspective*, edited by C. R. Anderson and M. J. Gannon (Boston: Little, Brown and Co., 1977).

Actors and Artistes of America, Associated: *see* LABOR ORGANIZATION.

Actors' Equity Association: *see* LABOR OR-GANIZATION, under Actors and Artistes of America, Associated.

actuarial projections, mathematical calculations involving the rate of mortality for a given group of people. *See* Howard E. Winklevoss, *Pension Mathematics with Numerical Illustrations* (Homewood, Ill: Richard D. Irwin, 1977).

actuary, specialist in the mathematics of insurance.

ACTWU: *see* LABOR ORGANIZATION, Clothing and Textile Workers Union, Amalgamated.

Adair v. United States: *see* ERDMAN ACT OF 1898.

Adamson Act of 1916, federal law that provided the eight-hour day for interstate railroad employees. Its constitutionality was upheld by the U.S. Supreme Court in *Wilson v. New*, 243 U.S. 332 (1917).

Adams v. Tanner, 224 U.S. 590 (1917), U.S. Supreme Court case that held private employment agencies could be regulated by the states but could not be prohibited.

Adaptability Test, The, mental ability test designed specifically for use in industrial job placements. This 35-item, spiral-omnibus test is used primarily with clerical workers and first-line supervisors. TIME: 15 minutes; AUTHORS: Joseph Tiffin and C. H. Lawshe; PUBLISHER: Science Research Associates, Inc. (*see* TEST PUBLISHERS).

addiction: *see* DRUG ADDICTION.

ad hoc arbitrator, arbitrator selected by the parties involved to serve on one case. Nothing prevents the arbitrator from being used again if both parties agree. *Ad hoc* or temporary, single-case arbitration is distinguished from "permanent" arbitration where arbitrators are named in an agreement to help resolve disputes about the agreement that may arise during the life of the agreement.

ad hoc committee, committee created for a specific task or purpose, whose existance ceases with the attainment of its goal.

ad-hocracy, Alvin Toffler's term, in *Future Shock* (N.Y.: Random House, 1970), for "the fast-moving, information-rich, kinetic organization of the future, filled with transient cells and extremely mobile individuals." Ad-hocracy is obviously a contraction of ad hoc (Latin for "to this" or temporary) and bureaucracy.

See also FUTURE SHOCK.

Adkins v. Children's Hospital: *see* WEST COAST HOTEL V. PARRISH.

adjusted case, according to the National Labor Relations Board, cases are closed as "adjusted" when an informal settlement agreement is executed and compliance with its terms is secured. A central element in an "adjusted" case is the agreement of the parties to settle differences without recourse to litigation.

Administration & Society, quarterly that seeks to further the understanding of public and human service organizations, their administrative processes, and their impacts upon the larger society. Most articles are written by academics and government employees.

Administration & Society
Sage Publications, Inc.
275 South Beverly Drive
Beverly Hills, CA 90212

administrative agency, in the context of labor relations, any impartial private or governmental entity that maintains lists of available labor arbitrators. The American Arbitration Association is an example of a private administrative agency. The federal government, as well as almost all state governments, have agencies that provide lists of qualified arbitrators.

Administrative Conference of the United States, a permanent independent agency established by the Administrative Conference Act of 1964. The purpose of the Administrative Conference is to develop improvements in the legal procedures by which federal agencies administer regulatory, benefit, and other government programs. As members of the Conference, agency heads, other federal officials, private lawyers, university professors, and other experts in administrative law and government are provided with a forum in which they can conduct continuing studies of selected problems involving administrative procedures and combine their experience and judgment in cooperative efforts toward improving the fairness and effectiveness of such procedures.

> Administrative Conference of the United
> States
> 2120 L Street, N.W.
> Washington, DC 20037
> (202) 254-7020

administrative law, as defined by the man who has written the standard texts on the subject, Kenneth Culp Davis:

> Administrative law is the law concerning the powers and procedures of administrative agencies, including especially the law governing judicial review of administrative action. An administrative agency is a governmental authority, other than a court and other than a legislative body, which affects the rights of private parties through either adjudication, rulemaking, investigating, prosecuting, negotiating, settling, or informally acting. An administrative agency may be called a commission, board, authority, bureau, office, officer, administrator, department, corporation, administration, division or agency. Nothing of substance hinges on the choice of name, and usually the choices have been entirely haphazard. When the President, or a governor, or a municipal governing body exercises powers of adjudication or rulemaking, he or it is to that extent an administrative agency.

See Kenneth Culp Davis, *Administrative Law Text*, 3rd ed. (St. Paul, Minn.: West Publishing Co. 1972).

administrative law judge, also called HEARING EXAMINER and HEARING OFFICER, governmental official who conducts hearings in the place of and in behalf of a more formal body, such as the National Labor Relations Board or the Merit Systems Protection Board.

Administrative Management, monthly trade magazine dealing with current topics in management.

> Administrative Management
> Geyer-McAllister Publication, Inc.
> 51 Madison Avenue
> New York, NY 10010

Administrative Procedures Act of 1946, basic law of how U.S. Government agencies must operate in order to provide adequate safeguards for agency clients and the general public.

Administrative Science Quarterly, this quarterly, the premier scholarly journal of its kind, is dedicated to advancing the understanding of administration through empirical investigation and theoretical analysis. Articles cover all phases of management, human relations, organizational behavior, and organizational communications.

> Administrative Science Quarterly
> Graduate School of Business and
> Public Administration
> Cornell University
> Malott Hall
> Ithaca, NY 14853

admonition, simple reproval of an employee by a supervisor.

See also REPRIMAND.

ADO: *see* ALLEGED DISCRIMINATORY OFFICIAL.

Advanced Management Journal: see SAM ADVANCED MANAGEMENT JOURNAL.

Advanced Personnel Test (APT), test of verbal reasoning ability used by business and industry for employment and upgrading of management and research personnel. TIME: Untimed. AUTHOR: W. S. Miller. PUBLISHER: Psychological Corporation (*see* TEST PUBLISHERS).

advance on wages, wages/salaries drawn in advance of work performance or earned commissions. Also applies to payments in advance of the regular pay day for sums already earned.

adverse action personnel action considered unfavorable to an employee, such as discharge, suspension, demotion, etc.

See also DISCIPLINARY ACTION.

adverse effect, differential rate of selection (for hire, promotion, etc.) that works to the disadvantage of an applicant subgroup, particularly subgroups classified by race, sex, and other characteristics on the basis of which discrimination is prohibited by law.

See also WASHINGTON V. DAVIS.

adverse impact, when a selection process for a particular job or group of jobs results in the selection of members of any racial, ethnic, or sex group at a lower rate than members of other groups, that process is said to have adverse impact. Federal EEO enforcement agencies generally regard a selection rate for any group that is less than four fifths (4/5) or eighty percent of the rate for other groups as constituting evidence of adverse impact. *See* John Klinefelter and James Thompkins, "Adverse Impact in Employment Selection," *Public Personnel Management* (May-June 1976).

See also SYSTEMIC DISCRIMINATION and WASHINGTON V. DAVIS.

adverse-inference rule, an analytical tool used by the Equal Employment Opportunity Commission (EEOC) in its investigations. The EEOC holds that when relevant evidence is withheld by an organization when the EEOC feels that there is no valid reason for such a withholding, the EEOC may presume that the evidence in question is adverse to the organization being investigated. The EEOC Compliance Manual permits use of the adverse-inference rule only if "the requested evidence is relevant," the evidence was requested "with ample time to produce it and with notice that failure to produce it would result in an adverse inference," and the "respondent produced neither the evidence nor an acceptable explanation."

advisory arbitration, arbitration that recommends a solution of a dispute but is not binding upon either party.

Advisory Council on Intergovernmental Personnel Policy (ACIPP), organization created to advise the President on intergovernmental personnel matters. It was established on January 5, 1971 by President Nixon's Executive Order 11607, in accordance with the requirements of the Intergovernmental Personnel Act of 1970 (Public Law 91 - 648). The Council was abolished June 25, 1974 by Executive 11792.

AEA: *see* LABOR ORGANIZATION, Actors' Equity Association, under Actors and Artistes of America, Associated.

Aeronautical Examiners, National Association of: *see* LABOR ORGANIZATION.

Aeronautical Production Controllers, National Association of: *see* LABOR ORGANIZATION.

AFA: *see* LABOR ORGANIZATION, Association of Flight Attendants, under Air Line Pilots Association.

affected class, according to the U.S. Department of Labor's Office of Federal Contract Compliance:

persons who continue to suffer the present effects of past discrimination. An employee or group of employees may be members of an affected class when, because of discrimination based on race, religion, sex, or national origin, such employees, for example, were assigned initially to less desirable or lower paying jobs, were denied equal opportunity to advance to better paying or more desirable jobs, or were subject to layoff or displacement from their jobs.

Employees may continue to be members of an "affected class" even though they may have been transferred or advanced into more desirable positions if the effects of past discrimination have not been remedied. For example, if an employee who was hired into a lower paying job because of past discriminatory practices has been subsequently promoted, further relief may be required if the employee has not found his or her "rightful place" in the employment structure of a federal government contractor.

affidavit, written statement made under oath before a person permitted by law to administer such an oath (e.g., a notary public). Such statements are frequently used in labor arbitration and other formal hearings.

affirmative action, when the term first gained currency in the 1960s, it meant the removal of "artificial barriers" to the employment of women and minority group members. Toward the end of that decade, however, the term got lost in a fog of semantics and came out meaning the provision of compensatory opportunities for hitherto disadvantaged groups. In a formal, legal sense, affirmative action now refers to specific efforts to recruit, hire, and promote disadvantaged groups for the purpose of eliminating the present effects of past discrimination. For an official treatment, *see* U.S. Equal Employment Opportunity Commission, *Affirmative Action and Equal Employment: A Guidebook for Employers* (Washington, D.C., U.S. Government Printing Office, 1974). For a hostile critique, *see* Nathan Glazer, *Affirmative Discrimination: Ethnic Inequality and Public Policy* (N.Y.: Basic Books, 1975). *Also see* Margery M. Milnick, "Equal Employment Opportunity and Affirmative Action: A Managerial Training Guide," *Personnel Journal* (October 1977) and Diane P. Jackson, "Affirmative Action for the Handicapped and Veterans: Interpretative and Operational Guidelines," *Labor Law Journal* (February 1978).

See also the following entries:

DEFUNIS V. ODEGAARD
EQUAL EMPLOYMENT OPPORTUNITY
PHILADELPHIA PLAN

Affirmative Action Compliance Manual for Federal Contractors, publication of the Bureau of National Affairs, Inc., which includes a "News and Developments" report, plus the manual used by the Office of Federal Contract Compliance Programs (OFCCP), the OFCCP Construction Compliance Program Operations Manual, and material taken from the official compliance manuals used by the Department of Defense, the Department of the Treasury, the Department of Housing and Urban Development, and the Department of Health, Education, and Welfare—with appropriate excerpts from other official compliance manuals.

affirmative action groups also called PRO-TECTED GROUPS, segments of the population that have been identified by federal, state, or local laws to be specifically protected from employment discrimination. Such groups include women, identified minorities, the elderly, and the handicapped.

affirmative action officer, individual in an organization who has the primary responsibility for the development, installation, and maintenance of the organization's affirmative action program.

affirmative action plan, an organization's written plan to remedy past discrimination against, or underutilization of, women and minorities. The plan itself usually consists of a statement of goals, timetables for achieving milestones, and specific program efforts.

affirmative action program, formal course of action undertaken by employers to hire and promote women and minorities in order to remedy past abuses or maintain present equity. The most basic tool of an affirmative action program is the affirmative action plan.

affirmative discrimination: *see* AFFIRMATIVE ACTION.

affirmative order, order issued by the National Labor Relations Board (NLRB) or similar state agency demanding that an employer or union take specific action to cease performing and/or undo the effects of an unfair labor practice. For example, the NLRB might issue an affirmative order to a company to "make whole" a wrongfully discharged employee by reinstating the employee with full back pay and reestablishing the employee's seniority and other rights.

affirmative recruitment, recruiting efforts undertaken to assure that adequate numbers of women and minorities are represented in applicant pools for positions in which they have been historically underutilized.

AFGE: *see* LABOR ORGANIZATION, Government Employees, American Federation of.

AFGM: *see* LABOR ORGANIZATION, Grain Millers, American Federation of.

AFGW: *see* LABOR ORGANIZATION, Glass Workers' Union of North America, American Flint.

AFL: *see* AMERICAN FEDERATION OF LABOR.

AFL–CIO: *see* AMERICAN FEDERATION OF LABOR–CONGRESS OF INDUSTRIAL ORGANIZATIONS.

AFM: *see* LABOR ORGANIZATION, Musicians, American Federation of.

AFSA: *see* LABOR ORGANIZATION, School Administrators, American Federation of.

AFSCME: *see* LABOR ORGANIZATION, State, County, and Municipal Employees, American Federation of.

AFT: *see* LABOR ORGANIZATION, Teachers, American Federation of.

AFTRA: *see* LABOR ORGANIZATION, American Federation of Television and Radio Artists, under Actors and Artistes of America, Associated.

age discrimination, disparate or unfavorable treatment of an individual in an employment situation because of age. The Age Discrimination in Employment Act of 1967 makes most age discrimination illegal, except where a bona fide occupational qualification (BFOQ) is involved. Executive Order 11141 prohibits age discrimination in the federal government. For a critique of the problem, *see* W. L. Kendig, *Age Discrimination in Employment* (N.Y.: American Management Associations, 1978) or Frank P. Doyle, "Age Discrimination and Organizational Life," *Industrial Gerontology* (Summer 1973).

See also RETIREMENT AGE.

Age Discrimination in Employment Act of 1967, U.S. federal statute that prohibits employment discrimination against individuals between 40 and 65 years of age by employers (with 25 or more employees) engaged in interstate commerce and makes it illegal to refuse to hire, discharge, or otherwise discriminate against an individual in compensation or privileges of employment because of age. As amended in 1974, it applies to state and local governments with 20 or more employees. As amended in 1978, it raises to 70 years the minimum mandatory retirement age for workers in private companies and state and local governments and bans forced retirement at any age for federal workers. Tenured college teachers are exempt from coverage until July 1, 1982. Business executives with private annual pensions over $27,000 are also exempt from the higher retirement age. In cases where mandatory retirement is part of a collective bargaining agreement in effect on Sept. 1, 1977, the new age will not apply until Jan. 1, 1980, or the expiration of the contract, whichever comes first.

See also the following entries:

OSCAR MAYER & CO. V. EVANS
RETIREMENT AGE
UNITED AIRLINES V. MCMANN

ageism, in the tradition of racism and sexism, ageism is discrimination against those who are considered old.

agency, employment: *see* EMPLOYMENT AGENCY.

agency shop, union security provision, found in some collective bargaining agreements, which requires that non-union employees of the bargaining unit must pay the union a sum equal to union dues as a condition of continuing employment. The agency shop was designed as a compromise between the union's desire to eliminate "free riders" by means of compulsory membership and management's wish that union membership be voluntary. Its constitutionality was upheld by the U.S. Supreme Court in *Abood* v. *Detroit Board of Education.* For a legal analysis, *see* Norman E. Jones, "Agency Shop," *Labor Law Journal* (November 1959).

See also ABOOD V. DETROIT BOARD OF EDUCATION and NATIONAL LABOR RELATIONS BOARD V. GENERAL MOTORS.

agent, person who is formally designated to act on behalf of either an employer or a union.

See also BARGAINING AGENT and BUSINESS AGENT.

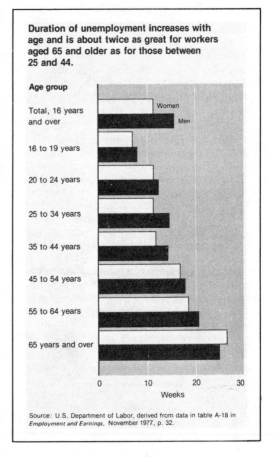

Duration of unemployment increases with age and is about twice as great for workers aged 65 and older as for those between 25 and 44.

Age group

Total, 16 years and over — Women / Men
16 to 19 years
20 to 24 years
25 to 34 years
35 to 44 years
45 to 54 years
55 to 64 years
65 years and over

0   10   20   30
Weeks

Source: U.S. Department of Labor, derived from data in table A-18 in *Employment and Earnings,* November 1977, p. 32.

agent provocateur, individual who is specifically hired by an organization to create trouble for a rival organization by inducing its members to perform acts that are in the best interest of the opposition.

aggregate cost method also called AGGREGATE METHOD, projected funding technique that computes pension benefits and costs for an entire plan rather than for its individual participants.

AGMA: *see* LABOR ORGANIZATION, American Guild of Musical Artists, under Actors and Artistes of America, Associated.

AGPA: *see* AMERICAN GROUP PSYCHOTHERAPY ASSOCIATION.

agreement: *see* the following entries:

BLANKET AGREEMENT
FAIR-SHARE AGREEMENT
GENTLEMEN'S AGREEMENT
INDEX OF AGREEMENT
INDIVIDUAL AGREEMENT
INTERIM AGREEMENT
LABOR AGREEMENT

MASTER AGREEMENT
MODEL AGREEMENT
OPEN-END AGREEMENT
SWEETHEART AGREEMENT

AGVA: *see* LABOR ORGANIZATION, American Guild of Variety Artists, under Actors and Artistes of America, Associated.

AIM: *see* AMERICAN INSTITUTE OF MANAGEMENT.

Air Line Dispatchers Association: *see* LABOR ORGANIZATION.

Air Line Employees Association: *see* LABOR ORGANIZATION, under Air Line Pilots Association.

Air Line Pilots Association: *see* LABOR ORGANIZATION.

Air Traffic Controllers Organization, Professional: *see* LABOR ORGANIZATION, under Marine Engineers Beneficial Association, National.

Air Traffic Specialists, Inc., National Association of: *see* LABOR ORGANIZATION.

AIU: *see* LABOR ORGANIZATION, Atlantic, Independent Union.

AIW: *see* LABOR ORGANIZATION, Industrial Workers of America, International Union Allied.

Alabama Labor Council: *see* AMERICAN FEDERATION OF LABOR–CONGRESS OF INDUSTRIAL ORGANIZATIONS.

Alabama Power Co. v. Davis, 431 U.S. 581 (1977), U.S. Supreme Court case, which held that employers who rehire a returning veteran are required to credit the employee's military service toward the calculation of pension benefits. A unanimous court concluded that "pension payments are predominantly rewards for continuous employment with the same employer," rather than deferred compensation for services rendered. Thus, the purpose of Section 9 of the Selective Service Act, as explained by Justic Thurgood Marshall for the Court, is to protect veterans "from the loss of such rewards when the break in their employment resulted from their response to the country's military needs."

Alabama State Employees Association: *see* LABOR ORGANIZATION.

Alaska Public Employees Association: *see* LABOR ORGANIZATION.

Alaska State Federation of Labor: *see* AMERICAN FEDERATION OF LABOR–CONGRESS OF INDUSTRIAL ORGANIZATIONS.

Albemarle Paper Co. v. Moody, 422 U.S. 405 (1975), U.S. Supreme Court case, that established the principle that once discrimination has been proven in a Title VII (of the Civil Rights Act of 1964) case, the trial judge ordinarily does not have discretion to deny back pay. For analyses, *see* William H. Warren, "*Albemarle* v. *Moody:* Where It All Began," *Labor Law Journal* (October 1976) and Thaddeus Holt, "A View from Albemarle," *Personnel Psychology* (Spring 1977).

alcoholism, detrimental dependency on alcoholic beverages. It was only in 1956 that the American Medical Association first recognized alcoholism as a disease. However, it is still not universally recognized as such. Almost all large organizations have some program to deal with alcoholic employees. For the most comprehensive reference on employee alcoholism, *see* Joseph F. Follman, Jr., *Alcoholics and Business: Problems, Costs, Solutions* (N.Y.: Amacom, 1976).

Major national organizations offering information on alcoholism include:

1. *Alcoholics Anonymous*
   P.O. Box 459
   Grand Central Station
   New York, NY 10017

2. *National Clearinghouse
   for Alcohol Information*
   Box 2345
   Rockville, MD 20852

3. *National Council on Alcoholism*
   1424 16th Street, N.W.
   Washington, DC 20036

4. *National Institute on Alcohol
   Abuse and Alcoholism*
   5600 Fishers Lane
   Rockville, MD 20852

ALEA: *see* LABOR ORGANIZATION, Air Line Employees Association, under Air Line Pilots Association.

Alexander v. Gardner-Denver Company, 415 U.S. 36 (1974), U.S. Supreme Court case, that held the prior submission of a claim to find arbitration under the nondiscrimination clause of a collective bargaining agreement does not foreclose an employee from subsequently exercising his right to a trial *de novo* under title VII of the Civil Rights Act of 1964. For analyses, *see* Gary R. Siniscalco, "Effect of the Gardner-Denver Case on title VII Disputes," *Monthly Labor Review* (March 1975); Sanford Cohen and Christian

Eaby, "The Gardner-Denver Decision and Labor Arbitration," *Labor Law Journal* (January 1976).

ALGOL, acronym for ALGORITHMIC LANGUAGE, computer language made up of both algebraic and English components.

aliens: *see* the following entries:
AMBACH V. NORWICK
CITIZENSHIP, U.S.
FOLEY V. CONNELIE
HAMPTON V. MOW SUN WONG
SUGARMAN V. DOUGALL

Alien Registration Act of 1940, also called the SMITH ACT, U.S. law that requires the annual registration of aliens. It also prohibits advocating the violent overthrow of the U.S. government.

alleged discriminatory official (ADO), individual charged in a formal equal employment opportunity complaint with having caused or tolerated discriminatory actions. For an analysis of the due process procedures to which ADOs are entitled, *see* Glenn E. Schweitzer, "The Rights of Federal Employees Named as Alleged Discriminatory Officials," *Public Administration Review* (January-February 1977).

Alliance for Labor Action, title given to the United Auto Workers' efforts from 1969 to 1972 to organize workers in industries where the AFL-CIO was only slightly represented.

Allied Chemical Workers* v. *Pittsburgh Plate Glass Co., 404 U.S. 157 (1971), case in which the U.S. Supreme Court held that unions have no right to bargain over retirees' benefits because retired persons are neither employees nor members of a bargaining unit.

Allied Workers International Union, United: *see* LABOR ORGANIZATION.

***Allis-Chalmers* decision:** *see* NATIONAL LABOR RELATIONS BOARD V. ALLIS-CHALMERS.

allocate, also REALLOCATE, to assign a position or class to a particular salary grade in the salary schedule, based on an evaluation of its relative worth. To reallocate is to change the existing allocation of a position or class to a different salary grade in the schedule.

allowance, financial payment to compensate an employee for the extra expense of living at a hardship post, for special clothing (such as uniforms), or for some other benefit that personnel policy allows.
See also the following entries:
CLOTHING ALLOWANCE

COST-OF-LIVING ALLOWANCE
FAMILY ALLOWANCE
FATIGUE ALLOWANCE
HARDSHIP ALLOWANCE
HOUSING ALLOWANCE
MILEAGE ALLOWANCE
RELOCATION ALLOWANCE
SUBSISTENCE ALLOWANCE
TAX-REIMBURSEMENT ALLOWANCE

allowed time, also called NORMAL TIME, time given an employee to perform a task. Normally includes an allowance for fatigue and personal and/or unavoidable delays.

ALO: *see* LABOR ORGANIZATION, Lace Operatives of America, Amalgamated.

ALPA: *see* LABOR ORGANIZATION, Air Line Pilots Association.

alphabetism, discrimination against those whose names begin with letters at the end of the alphabet.

alternate form, also called EQUIVALENT FORM or COMPARABLE FORM, any of two or more versions of a test that are the same with respect to the nature, number, and difficulty of the test items and that are designed to yield essentailly the same scores and measures of variability for a given group.

alternate-form reliability, measure of the extent to which two parallel or equivalent forms of a test are consistent in measuring what they purport to measure.

alternation ranking, technique, used in job evaluation and performance appraisal, that ranks the highest and the lowest, then the next highest and the next lowest, etc., until all jobs have been ranked.

Aluminum Workers International Union: *see* LABOR ORGANIZATION.

AMACOM: *see* AMERICAN MANAGEMENT ASSOCIATIONS.

Amalgamated Association of Street, Electric Railway, and Motor Coach Employees of America* v. *Lockridge, 403 U.S. 274 (1971), case in which the U.S. Supreme Court held that a complaint from a union member that his union had wrongfully interfered with his employment (he was suspended from his union because of dues arrearage) was a matter within the exclusive jurisdiction of the National Labor Relations Board.

Amalgamated Clothing and Textile Workers Union: *see* LABOR ORGANIZATION, Clothing and Textile Workers Union, Amalgamated.

Amalgamated Lace Operatives of America: *see* LABOR ORGANIZATION, Lace Operatives of America, Amalgamated.

Amalgamated Meat Cutters and Butcher Workmen of North America: *see* LABOR ORGANIZATION, under Food and Commercial Workers International Union, United.

Amalgamated Transit Union: *see* LABOR ORGANIZATION, Transit Union, Amalgamated.

Ambach v. *Norwick*, 60 L.Ed. 2d 49 (1979), U.S. Supreme Court decision, which held that barring aliens from permanent certification as public school teachers did not violate the 14th Amendment's equal protection clause. The ruling upheld the New York Education Law's citizenship requirement for public (but not private) school teachers.

See also the following entries:

CITIZENSHIP, U.S.
FOLEY V. CONNELIE
HAMPTON V. MOW SUN WONG
SUGARMAN V. DOUGALL

American Arbitration Association (AAA), formed in 1926, a public service, nonprofit organization dedicated to the resolution of disputes of all kinds through the use of arbitration, mediation, democratic election and other voluntary methods. The AAA does not act as arbitrator. Its function is to submit to parties selected lists from which disputants may make their own choices and to provide impartial administration of arbitration. The association's National Panel of Arbitrators consists of some 40,000 men and women, each an expert in some field or profession, who have been nominated for their knowledge and reputation for impartiality. In non-labor cases, these arbitrators serve without compensation except under unusual circumstances. They offer their time and skill as a public service. AAA's panels also include impartial experts in labor–management relations for arbitrating disputes arising out of the application and interpretation of collective bargaining agreements.

The AAA's access to impartial experts, its reputation for impartiality, and its experience in dispute-settling techniques of all kinds are put at the disposal of the public in ways other than the administration of arbitrations. Its Community Dispute Services division applies the techniques of arbitration, mediation, and factfinding to the solution of conflicts of all kinds in urban areas. AAA's Election Department conducts impartial polls to choose union officers, to determine the appropriate representatives for school teachers, to select committee members in local anti-poverty programs, and for many other purposes.

The AAA is the most important single center of information, education and research on arbitration. Among the association's periodicals are three monthly publications summarizing labor arbitration awards in private industry, in schools, and in other agencies of government; a monthly news bulletin for members and arbitrators; a quarterly journal, *The Arbitration Journal*, containing reports of arbitration court cases and authoritative articles on arbitration; a bimonthly report of no-fault automobile arbitration awards; a quarterly law letter on arbitration; various specialized pamphlets on arbitration practice and procedure; and outlines for teaching labor-management arbitration and arbitration law courses. The AAA's library serves other educational institutions as a clearing house of information and answers the research inquiries of AAA members and of students.

Although headquartered in New York, the AAA has regional offices throughout the United States. For further information, *see* Robert Coulson, *Labor Arbitration—What You Need To Know* (N.Y.: American Arbitration Association, 2nd ed., 1978).

American Arbitration Association
140 West 51st Street
New York, NY 10020
(212) 977-2000

See also NATIONAL ACADEMY OF ARBITRATORS.

American Assembly of Collegiate Schools of Business (AACSB), an organization of institutions devoted to higher education for business and administration, formally established in 1916. Its membership has grown to encompass not only educational institutions but business, government, and professional organizations as well, all seeking to improve and promote higher education for business and working to solve problems of mutual concern. Through its accrediting function, the AACSB provides guidelines to educational institutions in program, resource, and faculty planning. The Accreditation Council of AACSB is recognized by the Council on Postsecondary Accreditation and by the U.S. Office of Education, Department of Health, Education, and Welfare, as the sole accrediting agency for bachelors and masters programs in business and administration.

11500 Olive Street Road
Suite 142
St. Louis, MO 63141
(314) 872-8481

American Assembly of Collegiate Schools of Business

1755 Massachusetts Avenue, N.W.
Suite 308
Washington, DC 20036
(202) 667-9109

The following colleges and universities have graduate or undergraduate programs that have been accredited by the AACSB as of 1978:

UNIVERSITY OF AKRON
UNIVERSITY OF ALABAMA
UNIVERSITY OF ALABAMA IN
  BIRMINGHAM
UNIVERSITY OF ALBERTA
APPALACHIAN STATE UNIVERSITY
UNIVERSITY OF ARIZONA
ARIZONA STATE UNIVERSITY
UNIVERSITY OF ARKANSAS
UNIVERSITY OF ARKANSAS AT LITTLE
  ROCK
ATLANTA UNIVERSITY
AUBURN UNIVERSITY
BALL STATE UNIVERSITY
THE BERNARD M. BARUCH COLLEGE OF
  THE CITY UNIVERSITY OF NEW YORK
BAYLOR UNIVERSITY
BOSTON COLLEGE
BOSTON UNIVERSITY
BOWLING GREEN STATE UNIVERSITY
BRADLEY UNIVERSITY
UNIVERSITY OF BRIDGEPORT
BRIGHAM YOUNG UNIVERSITY
UNIVERSITY OF CALIFORNIA, BERKELEY
UNIVERSITY OF CALIFORNIA, LOS
  ANGELES
CALIFORNIA STATE COLLEGE,
  BAKERSFIELD
CALIFORNIA STATE UNIVERSITY, CHICO
CALIFORNIA STATE UNIVERSITY,
  FRESNO
CALIFORNIA STATE UNIVERSITY,
  FULLERTON
CALIFORNIA STATE UNIVERSITY,
  HAYWARD
CALIFORNIA STATE UNIVERSITY, LONG
  BEACH
CALIFORNIA STATE UNIVERSITY, LOS
  ANGELES
CALIFORNIA STATE UNIVERSITY,
  NORTHRIDGE
CALIFORNIA STATE UNIVERSITY,
  SACRAMENTO
CANISIUS COLLEGE
CARNEGIE-MELLON UNIVERSITY
CASE WESTERN RESERVE UNIVERSITY
UNIVERSITY OF CHICAGO
UNIVERSITY OF CINCINNATI
CLARKSON COLLEGE
CLEMSON UNIVERSITY
CLEVELAND STATE UNIVERSITY
UNIVERSITY OF COLORADO
COLORADO STATE UNIVERSITY
COLUMBIA UNIVERSITY
UNIVERSITY OF CONNECTICUT
CORNELL UNIVERSITY
CREIGHTON UNIVERSITY
DARTMOUTH COLLEGE
UNIVERSITY OF DELAWARE
UNIVERSITY OF DENVER
DePAUL UNIVERSITY
UNIVERSITY OF DETROIT
DRAKE UNIVERSITY
DREXEL UNIVERSITY
DUQUESNE UNIVERSITY
EAST CAROLINA UNIVERSITY
EAST TEXAS STATE UNIVERSITY
EASTERN MICHIGAN UNIVERSITY
EASTERN WASHINGTON UNIVERSITY
EMORY UNIVERSITY
UNIVERSITY OF FLORIDA
FLORIDA ATLANTIC UNIVERSITY
FLORIDA STATE UNIVERSITY
FLORIDA TECHNOLOGICAL UNIVERSITY
FORDHAM UNIVERSITY
FORT LEWIS COLLEGE
THE GEORGE WASHINGTON

UNIVERSITY
UNIVERSITY OF GEORGIA
GEORGIA INSTITUTE OF TECHNOLOGY
GEORGIA SOUTHERN COLLEGE
GEORGIA STATE UNIVERSITY
HARVARD UNIVERSITY
UNIVERSITY OF HAWAII
HOFSTRA UNIVERSITY
UNIVERSITY OF HOUSTON
HOWARD UNIVERSITY
IDAHO STATE UNIVERSITY
UNIVERSITY OF ILLINOIS AT CHICAGO
  CIRCLE
UNIVERSITY OF ILLINOIS AT URBANA -
  CHAMPAIGN
INDIANA UNIVERSITY
UNIVERSITY OF IOWA
JOHN CARROLL UNIVERSITY
UNIVERSITY OF KANSAS
KANSAS STATE UNIVERSITY
KENT STATE UNIVERSITY
UNIVERSITY OF KENTUCKY
LEHIGH UNIVERSITY
LOUISIANA STATE UNIVERSITY
LOUISIANA TECH UNIVERSITY
LOYOLA UNIVERSITY, CHICAGO
LOYOLA UNIVERSITY, NEW ORLEANS
UNIVERSITY OF MAINE AT ORONO
MARQUETTE UNIVERSITY
UNIVERSITY OF MARYLAND
UNIVERSITY OF MASSACHUSETTS
MASSACHUSETTS INSTITUTE OF
  TECHNOLOGY
MEMPHIS STATE UNIVERSITY
UNIVERSITY OF MIAMI
MIAMI UNIVERSITY
THE UNIVERSITY OF MICHIGAN
MICHIGAN STATE UNIVERSITY
MIDDLE TENNESSEE STATE UNIVERSITY
UNIVERSITY OF MINNESOTA
UNIVERSITY OF MISSISSIPPI
MISSISSIPPI STATE UNIVERSITY
UNIVERSITY OF MISSOURI-COLUMBIA
UNIVERSITY OF MISSOURI-KANSAS CITY
UNIVERSITY OF MISSOURI-KANSAS CITY
UNIVERSITY OF MISSOURI-ST. LOUIS
UNIVERSITY OF MONTANA
MURRAY STATE UNIVERSITY
UNIVERSITY OF NEBRASKA-LINCOLN
THE UNIVERSITY OF NEBRASKA AT
  OMAHA
UNIVERSITY OF NEVADA-RENO
THE UNIVERSITY OF NEW MEXICO
NEW MEXICO STATE UNIVERSITY
UNIVERSITY OF NEW ORLEANS
NEW YORK UNIVERSITY
UNIVERSITY OF NORTH CAROLINA
UNIVERSITY OF NORTH FLORIDA
NORTH TEXAS STATE UNIVERSITY
NORTHEAST LOUISIANA UNIVERSITY
NORTHEASTERN UNIVERSITY
NORTHERN ARIZONA UNIVERSITY
NORTHERN ILLINOIS UNIVERSITY
NORTHWESTERN UNIVERSITY
UNIVERSITY OF NOTRE DAME
OHIO STATE UNIVERSITY
OHIO UNIVERSITY
UNIVERSITY OF OKLAHOMA
OKLAHOMA STATE UNIVERSITY
OLD DOMINION UNIVERSITY
UNIVERSITY OF OREGON
OREGON STATE UNIVERSITY
PACIFIC LUTHERAN UNIVERSITY
UNIVERSITY OF PENNSYLVANIA
THE PENNSYLVANIA STATE UNIVERSITY
UNIVERSITY OF PITTSBURGH
UNIVERSITY OF PORTLAND

PORTLAND STATE UNIVERSITY
PURDUE UNIVERSITY
RENSSELAER POLYTECHNIC INSTITUTE
UNIVERSITY OF RHODE ISLAND
UNIVERSITY OF RICHMOND
UNIVERSITY OF ROCHESTER
ROOSEVELT UNIVERSITY
RUTGERS-THE STATE UNIVERSITY OF
  NEW JERSEY
SAINT CLOUD STATE UNIVERSITY
ST. JOHN'S UNIVERSITY
SAINT LOUIS UNIVERSITY
SAN DIEGO STATE UNIVERSITY
UNIVERSITY OF SAN FRANCISCO
SAN FRANCISCO STATE UNIVERSITY
SAN JOSE STATE UNIVERSITY
UNIVERSITY OF SANTA CLARA
SEATTLE UNIVERSITY
SETON HALL UNIVERSITY
UNIVERSITY OF SOUTH ALABAMA
UNIVERSITY OF SOUTH CAROLINA
UNIVERSITY OF SOUTH DAKOTA
UNIVERSITY OF SOUTH FLORIDA
UNIVERSITY OF SOUTHERN CALIFORNIA
SOUTHERN ILLINOIS UNIVERSITY AT
  CARBONDALE
SOUTHERN ILLINOIS UNIVERSITY AT
  EDWARDSVILLE
SOUTHERN METHODIST UNIVERSITY
UNIVERSITY OF SOUTHERN MISSISSIPPI
STANFORD UNIVERSITY
STATE UNIVERSITY OF NEW YORK AT
  ALBANY
STATE UNIVERSITY OF NEW YORK AT
  BUFFALO
STEPHEN F. AUSTIN STATE UNIVERSITY
SYRACUSE UNIVERSITY
TEMPLE UNIVERSITY
UNIVERSITY OF TENNESSEE,
  KNOXVILLE
TENNESSEE TECHNOLOGICAL
  UNIVERSITY
THE UNIVERSITY OF TEXAS AT
  ARLINGTON
THE UNIVERSITY OF TEXAS AT AUSTIN
TEXAS A & M UNIVERSITY
TEXAS CHRISTIAN UNIVERSITY
TEXAS SOUTHERN UNIVERSITY
TEXAS TECH UNIVERSITY
THE UNIVERSITY OF TOLEDO
TULANE UNIVERSITY
UNIVERSITY OF TULSA
UNIVERSITY OF UTAH
UTAH STATE UNIVERSITY
VILLANOVA UNIVERSITY
UNIVERSITY OF VIRGINIA
VIRGINIA COMMONWEALTH UNIVERSITY
VIRGINIA POLYTECHNIC INSTITUTE AND
  STATE UNIVERSITY
UNIVERSITY OF WASHINGTON
WASHINGTON AND LEE UNIVERSITY
WASHINGTON STATE UNIVERSITY
WASHINGTON UNIVERSITY
WAYNE STATE UNIVERSITY
WEST VIRGINIA UNIVERSITY
WESTERN ILLINOIS UNIVERSITY
WESTERN MICHIGAN UNIVERSITY
WICHITA STATE UNIVERSITY
COLLEGE OF WILLIAM AND MARY
UNIVERSITY OF WISCONSIN-MADISON
UNIVERSITY OF WISCONSIN-
  MILWAUKEE
UNIVERSITY OF WISCONSIN-OSHKOSH
UNIVERSITY OF WISCONSIN-
  WHITEWATER
WRIGHT STATE UNIVERSITY
UNIVERSITY OF WYOMING

13

American Association of Classified School Employees: *see* LABOR ORGANIZATION, Classified School Employees, American Association of.

American Association of University Professors: *see* LABOR ORGANIZATION, University Professors, American Association of.

American Federation of Government Employees: *see* LABOR ORGANIZATION, Government Employees, American Federation of.

American Federation of Grain Millers: *see* LABOR ORGANIZATION, Grain Millers, American Federation of.

American Federation of Labor (AFL), organized in 1881 as a federation of craft unions, the Federation of Organized Trade and Labor Unions, it changed its name to the American Federation of Labor in 1886 after merging with those craft unions that had become disenchanted with the Knights of Labor. In 1955, the AFL merged with the Congress of Industrial Organizations to become the AFL–CIO (*see* AMERICAN FEDERATION OF LABOR–CONGRESS OF INDUSTRIAL ORGANIZATIONS).

American Federation of Labor–Congress of Industrial Organizations (AFL-CIO), a voluntary federation of over 100 national and international unions operating in the United States. The AFL–CIO is itself not a union; it does no bargaining. It is perhaps best thought of as a union of unions. The affiliated unions created the AFL–CIO to represent them in the creation and execution of broad national and international policies and in coordinating a wide range of joint activities.

Each member union of the AFL–CIO remains autonomous, conducting its own affairs in the manner determined by its own members. Each has its own headquarters, officers and staff. Each decides its own economic policies, carries on its own contract negotiations, sets its own dues and provides its own membership services. Each of the affiliated unions is free to withdraw at any time. But through its voluntary participation, it plays a role in establishing over-all policies for the U.S. labor movement, which in turn advance the interests of every union.

The AFL-CIO serves its constituent unions by:

1). Speaking for the whole labor movement before Congress and other branches of government.

2). Representing U.S. labor in world affairs, through its participation in international labor bodies and through direct contact with the central labor organizations of free countries throughout the world.

3). Helping to organize the unorganized workers of the United States.

4). Coordinating such activities as community services, political education and voter registration for greater effectiveness.

While retaining control over their own affairs member unions have ceded a degree of authority to the AFL–CIO in certain matters. These include:

1). *Ethical practices.* Every affiliated union must comply with the AFL–CIO Ethical Practices Codes, which established basic standards of union democracy and financial integrity.

2). *Totalitarian domination.* No union controlled by Communists, fascists or other totalitarians can remain in the AFL–CIO.

3). *Internal disputes.* Each union has agreed to submit certain types of disputes with other affiliated unions to the mediating and judicial processes of the AFL–CIO.

> AFL–CIO
> 815 16th Street, N.W.
> Washington, DC 20006
> (202) 637-5000

A listing of AFL–CIO state labor organizations follows:

Alabama Labor Council
231 West Valley Avenue
Birmingham, AL 35209
(205) 942-5260

Alaska State Federation of Labor
4251 Warwick Drive
Anchorage, AK 99504
(907) 279-6311

Arizona State AFL-CIO
520 West Adams St.
Phoenix, AZ 85003
(602) 258-3407

Arkansas State AFL-CIO
1115 Bishop Street
Little Rock, AR 72202
(501) 375-9101

California Labor Federation
995 Market St., Suite 310
San Francisco, CA 94103
(415) 986-3585

Colorado Labor Council
360 Acoma St., Room 300
Denver, CO 80223
(303) 733-2401

Connecticut State Labor Council, AFL-CIO
9 Washington Avenue
Hamden, CT 06518
(203) 288-3591

Delaware State AFL-CIO
922 New Road, Elsmere
Wilmington, DE 19805
(302) 998-8801

Florida AFL-CIO
P.O. Box 1836
135 South Monroe Street
Tallahassee, FL 32302
(904) 224-6926

Georgia State AFL-CIO
501 Pulliam St., Room 549
Atlanta, GA 30312
(404) 525-2793

Hawaii State Federation of Labor
547 Halckauwila St., Suite 216
Honolulu, HI 96813
(808) 536-4945

Idaho State AFL-CIO
225 N. 16th
Boise, ID 83706
(208) 345-8582

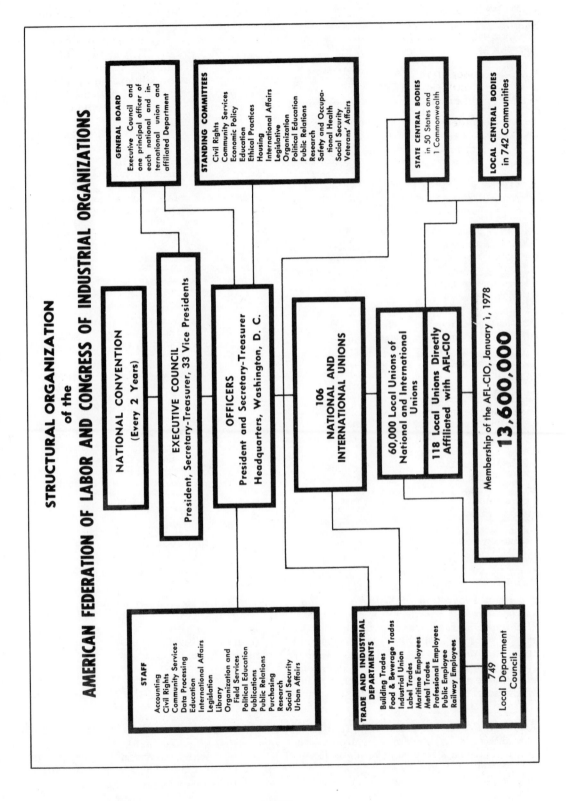

STRUCTURAL ORGANIZATION
of the
AMERICAN FEDERATION OF LABOR AND CONGRESS OF INDUSTRIAL ORGANIZATIONS

GENERAL BOARD
Executive Council and one principal officer of each national and international union and affiliated Department

STANDING COMMITTEES
Civil Rights
Community Services
Economic Policy
Education
Ethical Practices
Housing
International Affairs
Legislative
Organization
Political Education
Public Relations
Research
Safety and Occupational Health
Social Security
Veterans' Affairs

STATE CENTRAL BODIES
in 50 States and 1 Commonwealth

LOCAL CENTRAL BODIES
in 742 Communities

NATIONAL CONVENTION
(Every 2 Years)

EXECUTIVE COUNCIL
President, Secretary-Treasurer, 33 Vice Presidents

OFFICERS
President and Secretary-Treasurer
Headquarters, Washington, D. C.

106 NATIONAL AND INTERNATIONAL UNIONS

60,000 Local Unions of National and International Unions

118 Local Unions Directly Affiliated with AFL-CIO

Membership of the AFL-CIO, January 1, 1978
13,600,000

STAFF
Accounting
Civil Rights
Community Services
Data Processing
Education
International Affairs
Legislation
Library
Organization and Field Services
Political Education
Publications
Public Relations
Purchasing
Research
Social Security
Urban Affairs

TRADE AND INDUSTRIAL DEPARTMENTS
Building Trades
Food & Beverage Trades
Industrial Union
Label Trades
Maritime Employees
Metal Trades
Professional Employees
Public Employee
Railway Employees

749 Local Department Councils

15

Illinois State AFL-CIO
300 North State St.
Chicago, IL 60610
(312) 222-1414

Indiana State AFL-CIO
P.O. Box 385
1000 N. Madison Avenue
Greenwood, IN 46142
(317) 881-6773

Iowa Federation of Labor
2000 Walker St., Suite A
Des Moines, IA 50317
(515) 262-9571

Kansas State Federation of Labor
110 W. 6th, P.O. Box 1455
Topeka, KS 66601
(913) 357-0396

Kentucky State AFL-CIO
706 East Broadway
Louisville, KY 40202
(502) 584-8189

Louisiana AFL-CIO
P.O. Box 3477
429 Government Street
Baton Rouge, LA 70821
(504) 383-5741

Maine AFL-CIO
72 Center Street
Brewer, ME 04412
(207) 989-3630

Maryland State and District of Columbia
AFL-CIO
305 West Monument St.
Baltimore, MD 21201
(301) 727-7307

Massachusetts State Labor Council
6 Beacon Street, Suite 720
Boston, MA 02108
(617) 227-8260

Michigan State AFL-CIO
419 South Washington Avenue
Lansing, MI 49806
(517) 487-5966

Minnesota AFL-CIO
175 Aurora Avenue
St. Paul, MN 55103
(612) 227-7647

Mississippi AFL-CIO
2826 North West St.
Jackson, MS 39205
(601) 948-0517

Missouri State Labor Council
P.O. Box 1086
208 Madison Street
Jefferson City, MO 65101
(314) 634-2115

Montana State AFL-CIO
P.O. Box 1176
Lundy Shopping Center
Helena, MT 59601
(406) 442-1708

Nebraska State AFL-CIO
1821 California St.
Omaha, NE 68102
(402) 345-2500

Nevada State AFL-CIO
P.O. Box 2999
Reno, NV 89505
(702) 329-1508

New Hampshire State Labor Council
P.O. Box 1305
Portsmouth, NH 03801
(603) 625-8941

New Jersey State AFL-CIO
106 West State St.
Trenton, NJ 08608
(609) 989-8730

New Mexico State AFL-CIO
6303 Indian School Road, N.E.
Albuquerque, NM 87110
(505) 292-2911

New York State AFL-CIO
30 East 29th St.
New York, NY 10016
(212) 689-9320

North Carolina State AFL-CIO
P.O. Box 10805
Raleigh, NC 27605
(919) 833-6678

North Dakota AFL-CIO
RR 01
Bismarck, ND 58501
(701) 223-0784

Ohio AFL-CIO
271 East State St.
Columbus, OH 43215
(614) 224-8271

Oklahoma State AFL-CIO
501 N.E. 27th Street
Oklahoma City, OK 73105
(405) 528-2409

Oregon AFL-CIO
530 Center Street
Salem, OR 97301
(503) 585-6320

Pennsylvania AFL-CIO
101 Pine Street
Harrisburg, PA 17101
(717) 238-9351

Puerto Rico Federation of Labor (AFL-CIO)
Avenida Central 274
Bajos, Hyde Park
Rio Piedras, Puerto Rico 00918
(809) 764-4980

Rhode Island AFL-CIO
357 Westminister St.
Providence, RI 02903
(401) 751-7100

South Carolina Labor Council, AFL-CIO
7420 North Main St.
Columbia, SC 29203
(803) 754-8205

South Dakota State Federation of Labor
515 South Dakota Avenue, Room 6
Sioux Falls, SD 57102
(605) 338-3811

Tennessee State Labor Council
226 Capitol Blvd., Rm. 203
Nashville, TN 37219
(615) 256-5687

Texas State AFL-CIO
1106 Lavaca St., Suite 200
P.O. Box 12727
Austin, TX 78711
(512) 477-6195

Utah State AFL-CIO
2261 South Redwood Road
Salt Lake City, UT 84119
(801) 972-2771

Vermont State Labor Council AFL-CIO
149 State St., Box 858
Montpelier, VT 05602
(802) 223-5229

Virginia State AFL-CIO
3315 West Broad St.
Richmond, VA 23230
(804) 355-7444

Washington State Labor Council, AFL-CIO
2701 First Avenue, Room 300
Seattle, WA 98121
(206) 682-6002

West Virginia Labor Federation, AFL-CIO
1018 Kanawha Blvd., East, Suite 1200
Charleston, WV 25301

Wisconsin State AFL-CIO
6333 West Bluemound Road
Milwaukee, WI 53213
(414) 771-0700

Wyoming State AFL-CIO
1904 Thomes Avenue
Cheyenne, WY 82001
(307) 635-5149

American Federation of Labor v. National Labor Relations Board, 308 U.S. 401 (1940), U.S. Supreme case, which held that the National Labor Relations Board under Section 9 (d) of the National Labor Relations (Wagner) Act of 1935 had the discretion to determine appropriate bargaining units and that such a certification is not subject to review by federal appellate courts.

American Federation of Labor v. Swing, 312 U.S. 321 (1941), U.S. Supreme Court case, which held that stranger picketing is lawful. Justice Felix Frankfurter wrote that "a State cannot exclude working men from peacefully exercising the right of free communication by drawing the circle of economic competition between employers and workers so small as to contain only an employer and those directly employed by him."

American Federation of Musicians: *see* LABOR ORGANIZATION, Musicians, American Federation of.

American Federation of Musicians v. Wittstein, 379 U.S. 171 (1964), U.S. Supreme Court case, which held that Section 101 (a) (3) (B) of the Labor–Management Reporting and Disclosure (Landrum–Griffin) Act of

1959 permits a weighted-voting system under which delegates cast a number of votes equal to the membership of their local union.

American Federation of School Administrators: see LABOR ORGANIZATION, School Administrators, American Federation of.

American Federation of State, County, and Municipal Employees: see LABOR ORGANIZATION, State, County, and Municipal Employees, American Federation of.

American Federation of Teachers: see LABOR ORGANIZATION, Teachers, American Federation of.

American Federation of Television and Radio Artists: see LABOR ORGANIZATION, under Actors and Artistes of America, Associated.

American Flint Glass Workers' Union of North America: see LABOR ORGANIZATION, Glass Workers' Union of North America, American Flint.

American Group Psychotherapy Association (AGPA), professional association organized to provide a forum for the exchange of ideas among qualified professional persons interested in group psychotherapy; to publish and to make publication available on all subjects relating to group psychotherapy; to encourage the development of sound training programs in group psychotherapy for qualified mental health professionals; to establish and maintain high standards of ethical, professional group psychotherapy practice; and to encourage and promote research in group psychotherapy.

American Group Psychotherapy Association
1995 Broadway
New York, NY 10023
(212) 787-2618

American Guidance Services, Inc.: see TEST PUBLISHERS.

American Guild of Musical Artists: see LABOR ORGANIZATION, under Actors and Artistes of America, Associated.

American Guild of Variety Artists: see LABOR ORGANIZATION, under Actors and Artistes of America, Associated.

American Institute of Management (AIM), founded in 1948 to conduct studies in management research and to enhance the development of the managerial sciences as an educational discipline, AIM serves as a professional association for managers. Its purpose is to improve management thinking, practices, performance, and results through pertinent comments, studies, meetings, and publications that contribute to managerial knowledge, skill, and theory.

American Institute of Management
607 Boylston Street at Copley Square
Boston, Massachusetts, 02116
(617) 536-2503

American Management Associations (AMA), with over 58,000 members the AMA is by far the largest organization for professional managers. AMA programs operate principally through its 12 divisions: Finance, General Management, Insurance & Employee Benefits, Manufacturing, Marketing, Management Systems, Research and Development, Human Resources, Packaging, International Management, Purchasing, and General Administrative Services. AMACOM is it's in-house publishing division.

American Management Associations
135 West 50th Street
New York, NY 10020
(212) 586-8100

American Municipal Association: see NATIONAL LEAGUE OF CITIES.

American Newspaper Publishers Association v. National Labor Relations Board, 345 U.S. 100 (1953), U.S. Supreme Court case, in which it was held that requiring employers to pay printers for setting "bogus" type was not an unfair labor practice on the part of the union under Section 8(b) (6) of the National Labor Relations Act. The court said that Section 8(b) (6) "condemned only the exactment by a union of pay from an employer in return for services not performed and not to be performed, but not the exactment of pay for work done by an employee with the employer's consent."

See also FEATHERBEDDING.

American Nurses' Association: see LABOR ORGANIZATION, Nurses' Association, American.

American Personnel and Guidance Association (APGA), professional association with over 40,000 members organized into 13 national divisions, spanning personnel and guidance work at all educational levels from kindergarten through higher education, in community agencies, correction agencies, rehabilitation programs, government, business/industry and research facilities.

American Personnel and Guidance Association
1607 New Hampshire Ave., N.W.
Washington, DC 20009
(202) 483-4633

American Plan, term used by employers in the early part of this century to encourage open or non-union shops. By implication, the closed or union shop was portrayed as alien to the nation's individualistic spirit, restrictive of industrial efficiency, and generally "un-American."

American Postal Workers Union *see* LABOR ORGANIZATION, Postal Workers Union, American.

American Productivity Center, Inc., created in 1977, a privately funded, nonprofit organization dedicated to strengthening the free enterprise system by developing practical programs to improve productivity and the quality of working life in the United States.

American Productivity Center, Inc.
1700 West Loop South
Houston, TX 77027
(713) 961-7740

American Psychological Association (APA), founded in 1892 and incorporated in 1925, the APA is the major psychological organization in the United States. With more than 46,000 members in 1978, it includes most of the qualified psychologists in the country.

The purpose of the APA is to advance psychology as a science and a profession and as a means of promoting human welfare by the encouragement of psychology in all its branches in the broadest and most liberal manner. It does so by the promotion of research in psychology and the improvement of research methods and conditions; by the continual improvement of the qualifications and competence of psychologists through high standards of ethical conduct, education, and achievement; and by the dissemination of psychological knowledge through meetings, psychological journals, and special reports.

American Psychological Association
1200 Seventeenth Street, N.W.
Washington, DC 20036
(202) 833-7600

American Radio Association: *see* LABOR ORGANIZATION, Radio Association, American.

American Railway and Airway Supervisors Association, The: *see* LABOR ORGANIZATION, Railway and Airway Supervisors Association, The American.

American Shipbuilding Co. v. National Labor Relations Board, 380 U.S. 300 (1965), U.S. Supreme Court case, which held that an employer, in the face of a bargaining impasse, could temporarily shut down his plant and lay off his employees for the sole purpose of bringing pressure to bear in support of his bargaining position.

See also LOCKOUT.

American Society for Personnel Administration (ASPA), a nonprofit, professional association of personnel and industrial relations managers. Founded in 1948, ASPA today serves over 20,000 members with 300 chapters in the United States and 37 other countries. It is the largest professional association devoted exclusively to human resource management.

ASPA's purpose is (1) to provide assistance for the professional development of members, (2) to provide international leadership in establishing and supporting standards of excellence in human resource management, (3) to provide the impetus for research to improve management techniques, (4) to serve as a focal point for the exchange of authoritative information, and (5) to publicize the human resource management field to create a better understanding of its functions and importance.

*American Society for Personnel
    Administration*
19 Church Street
Berea, OH 44017
(216) 234-2500

American Society for Personnel Administration Accreditation Institute, a personnel accreditation program sponsored by the American Society for Personnel Administration, which is designed to raise and maintain professional standards in the field. Through testing and peer reviews, the program identifies persons who have mastered the various functions and levels of personnel and industrial relations. There are four levels of ASPA accreditation: (1) Accredited Personnel Specialist, (2) Accredited Personnel Manager, (3) Accredited Personnel Diplomate, (4) Accredited Executive in Personnel.

AASPA Accreditation Institute
Box F
Berea, OH 44017

American Society for Personnel Administration Code of Ethics: *see* CODE OF ETHICS.

American Society for Public Administration (ASPA), a nationwide, nonprofit educational and professional organization dedicated to improved management in the public service through exchange, development, and dissemination of information about public administration. ASPA has over 20,500 members and subscribers representative of all governmental levels, program responsibilities, and administrative interests. Its membership includes government administrators, teachers, researchers, consultants, students, and civic leaders. In addition, government agencies, universities, and other organizations are affiliated with the Society on an institutional basis. Since its inception in 1939, ASPA has provided national leadership in advancing the "science, processes, and art" of public administration. It is the only organization of its kind in the U.S. aiming broadly to improve administration of the public service at all levels of government and in all functional and program fields. Society members are located in every state as well as overseas. Many activities are carried out through more than 90 chapters in major governmental and educational centers. The ASPA program includes publications, meetings, education, research, and various special services, all aimed at improved understanding and strengthened administration of the public service.

American Society for Public Administration
1225 Connecticut Avenue, N.W.
Washington, DC 20036
(202) 785-3255

American Society for Training and Development (ASTD), national professional society for persons with training and development responsibilities in business, industry, government, public service organizations, and educational institutions. ASTD is the only organization devoted exclusively to the comprehensive education, development, and expansion of the skills and standards of professionals in training and human resource development.

American Society for Training and
Development
P.O. Box 5307
Madison, WI 53705
(608) 274-3440

American Steel Foundries v. *Tri-City Central Trades Council*, 257 U.S. 184 (1921), U.S. Supreme Court case, which held that the right of pickets are restricted to "observation, communication and persuasion;" and required that strikebreakers be given "clear passage."

American Train Dispatchers Association: *see* LABOR ORGANIZATION, Train Dispatchers Association, American.

American Watch Workers Union: *see* LABOR ORGANIZATION, Watch Workers Union, American.

amicus curiae, literally, "friend of the court";

any person or organization allowed to participate in a lawsuit who would not otherwise have a right to do so. Participation is usually limited to filing a brief on behalf of one side or the other. *See* Samuel Krislov, "The *Amicus Curiae* Brief: From Friendship to Advocacy," *Yale Law Journal* (March 1963).

ANA: *see* LABOR ORGANIZATION, Nurses' Association, American.

analogies test, test that asks a whole series of questions such as: a foot is to a man as a paw is to what? The examinee is usually given four or five answers to choose from.

analogue, individual's counterpart or opposite number in another organization.

analysis of variance, statistical procedure for determining whether the change noted in a variable that has been exposed to other variables exceeds what may be expected by chance.

analytical estimating, work measurement technique whereby the time required to perform a job is estimated on the basis of prior experience.

Anderson v. *Mt. Clemens Pottery*, 328 U.S. 680 (1946), U.S. Supreme Court case, which held that employers were liable for "portal-to-portal" pay claims under the provisions of the Fair Labor Standards Act. This decision led to the passage of the Portal-to-Portal Pay Act of 1947, which established a cutoff date for back claims.

See also FAIR LABOR STANDARDS ACT and PORTAL-TO-PORTAL PAY ACT OF 1947.

androgy, science of adult learning. For books by the leading authority on the theory and process of androgy, *see* Malcolm S. Knowles, *The Modern Practice of Adult Education* (N.Y.: Association Press, 1969); Malcolm S. Knowles, *The Adult Learner: A Neglected Species* (Houston: Gulf Publishing, 1973).

annual earnings, employee's total compensation during a calendar year—includes basic salary or wages, all overtime and premium pay, vacation pay, bonuses, etc.

annualized cost, cost of something for a 12-month period. Annualized costs may be figured on the calendar year, the fiscal year, the date a contract becomes effective, etc.

annuitant, one who is the recipient of annuity

benefit payments.

See also RE-EMPLOYED ANNUITANT.

annuity, annual sum payable to a former employee who has retired.

See also the following entries:
DEFERRED ANNUITY
DEFERRED LIFE ANNUITY
FIXED ANNUITY
GROUP ANNUITY
TAX-DEFERRED ANNUITY

Anti-Kickback Act of 1934: *see* KICKBACK.

anti-labor legislation, any law at any level of government that organized labor perceives to be to its disadvantage and to the disadvantage of prime union interests—better hours, wages, and working conditions. Leading examples would be "right-to-work" laws and "anti-strike" laws.

Anti-Racketeering Act of 1934, also called the HOBBS ACT, a federal law that, as amended, prohibits the use of extortion or violence that in any way obstructs, delays, or affects interstate commerce. Thus, it is a federal crime for union leaders to either blackmail employers or accept bribes for not calling strikes.

See also LABOR RACKETEER.

Anti-Strikebreaker Act of 1936, also called the BYRNES ACT, federal statute that prohibits employers from transporting strikebreakers across state lines. As amended in 1938, it also forbids the interstate transportation of persons for the purpose of interfering with peaceful picketing (common carriers excluded).

Anti-Trust Act of 1914: *see* CLAYTON ACT.

APA: *see* AMERICAN PSYCHOLOGICAL ASSOCIATION.

APEA: *see* LABOR ORGANIZATION, [1]Alaska Public Employees Association, [2]Arizona Public Employees Association.

Apex Hosiery Company* v. *Leader, 310 U.S. 469 (1940), U.S. Supreme Court case, which held that strikes did not constitute a restraint of interstate commerce merely because a strike caused a decline in the volume of goods moving in interstate commerce.

APGA: *see* AMERICAN PERSONNEL AND GUIDANCE ASSOCIATION.

apparatchik, Russian word for a bureaucrat, now used colloquially to refer to any administrative functionary. The word as used in English seems to have no political connotations; it merely implies that the individual referred to mindlessly follows orders.

appeal, any proceeding or request to a higher authority that a lower authority's decision be reviewed.

appellant, one who appeals a case to a higher authority.

appellate jurisdiction, power of a tribunal to review cases that have previously been decided by a lower authority.

apple polishers, as defined in Edward M. Cook, "The High Cost of Promoting Apple Polishers," *Personnel Administration* (May-June 1966):

There are two major categories of apple polishers: (a) *Hard-Core Apple Polisher*—The Compulsive yes man; never known to disagree with a superior; seldom supports his subordinates if conflict develops; pleasant personality; has many good qualities but close study of performance reveals the apple polishing syndrome. He seldom seeks real responsibility, contributes little that is creative, has seldom actually fought for his ideas or grasped a nettlesome problem with his bare hands; he may be valuable on the lower rungs of the corporate ladder, dangerous as he ascends, murder if allowed to select, cultivate, and proliferate subordinates in his own image. (2) *Skin-Deep Apple Polisher*—This category includes many younger people who are ambitious and have been led to believe that polishing is somehow almost as important as performance; many of these individuals are salvageable if the right kind of supervisor influences them in time. Unfortunately, some may become hard-core eventually, depending on organization climate; included in this group are many good, creative men of integrity who don't enjoy polishing and eventually move on to organizations which don't require it.

applicant, an individual seeking initial employment or an in-house promotional opportunity.

applicant pool, all those individuals who have applied for a particular job over a given period.

applicant population, the set of individuals within a geographical area, with identifiable characteristics or a mix of such characteristics, from which applicants for employment are obtained. Changes in recruiting practices may change certain characteristics of those who apply for work and therefore may change the nature of the applicant population.

applicant tally, tally system by which the EEO status of applicants is recorded at the time of application or interview. By periodically comparing applicant tally rates with rates of appointment and/or rejection, the progress of affirmative action recruitment efforts can be measured.

application blank, frequently the first phase of the selection process. Properly completed it can serve three purposes: (1) it is a formal request for employment; (2) it provides information that indicates the applicants fitness for the position; and (3) it can become the basic personnel record for those applicants who are hired. Application Blanks must conform to all EEOC guidelines; requested information must be a valid predictor of performance. For additiona information, *see* C. C. Kessler and G. J. Gibbs, "Getting the Most from Application Blanks and References," *Personnel* (January-February 1975).
See also WEIGHTED APPLICATION BLANK.

applied psychology, generally, the practical use of the discoveries and principles of psychology.

appointing authority: *see* APPOINTING OFFICER.

appointing officer, also APPOINTING AUTHORITY, person having power by law, or by lawfully delegated authority, to make appointments to positions in an organization.

appointment, non-elective government job. Most jurisdictions offer several different kinds of appointments. For example, the federal government offers the following four varieties in its merit system:

1. *Temporary appointment*—does not ordinarily last more that 1 year. A temporary worker can't be promoted and can't transfer to another job. Temporary employees are not under the retirement system. Persons over 70 can be given only temporary appointments, but the appointments can be renewed.
2. *Term appointment*—made for work on a specific project that will last more than 1 year but less than 4 years. A term employee can be promoted or reassigned to other positions within the project for which that employee was hired. He is not under the retirement system. If you accept a temporary or term appointment, your name will stay on the list of eligibles from which you were appointed. This means that you will remain eligible for permanent jobs that are normally filled by career-conditional or career appointments.
3. *Career-conditional appointment*—leads after 3 years' continuous service to a career appointment. For the first year, the employee serves a probationary period. During this time, it must be demonstrated that the employee can do a satisfactory job and he or she may be dismissed for failure to do so. Career-conditional employees have promotion and transfer privileges. After career-conditional employees complete their probation, they cannot be removed except for cause. However, in reduction-in-force (layoff) actions, career-conditional employees are dismissed ahead of career employees.
4. *Career appointment*—employee serves a probationary period, as described above, and has promotion and transfer privileges. After completion of the probation, this type of employee is in the last group to be affected in layoffs.

See also NONCOMPETITIVE APPOINTMENT and PROVISIONAL APPOINTMENT.

apportionment, a requirement, written into the Pendleton Act of 1883, that all federal government merit system jobs in headquarters offices of agencies in the metropolitan Washington, D.C., area are to be distributed among the residents of the states, territories and the District of Columbia. Each state or territory is allocated a certain number of these competitive positions on the basis of population. Residents of states which have not filled their allocations are considered for appointment to these apportioned positions ahead of residents of states which have exceeded their allocations.

apprentice, according to the U.S. Department of Labor's *Dictionary of Occupational Titles* (Fourth Edition, 1977):

. . . a worker who learns, according to written or oral contractual agreement, a recognized skilled craft or trade requiring one or more years of on-the-job training through job experience supplemented by related instruction, prior to being considered a qualified skilled worker. High school or vocational school education is often a prerequisite for entry into an apprenticeship program. Provisions of apprenticeship agreement regularly include length of apprenticeship; a progressive scale of wages; work processes to be taught; and amount of instruction in subjects related to the craft or trade, such as characteristics of materials used, physics, mathematics, estimating, and blueprint reading. Apprenticeability of a particular craft or trade is best evidenced by its acceptability for registration as a trade by a State apprenticeship agency or the Federal Bureau of Apprenticeship and Training. Generally, where employees are represented by a union, apprenticeship programs come under the guidance of joint apprenticeship committees composed of representatives of the employers or the employer association and representatives of the employees. These committees may determine need for apprentices in a locality and establish minimum apprenticeship standards of education, experience, and training. In instances where Committies do not exist, apprenticeship agreement is made between apprentice and employer, or an employer group.

While the title, "apprentice," is often loosely used as a synonym for any beginner, helper, or trainee, this is technically incorrect. For an evaluation of current practices, *see* Norman Parkin, "Apprenticeships: Outmoded or Undervalued?" *Personnel Management* (May 1978).

apprentice rate, also APPRENTICE SCALE, usually a schedule of rates for workers in formal apprenticeship programs that gradually permits the attainment of the minimum journeyman rate.

apprentice scale: *see* APPRENTICE RATE.

Apprenticeship Act of 1937, also called the FITZGERALD ACT, Public Law 77-308, law that authorized the Secretary of Labor to formulate and promote the furtherance of labor standards necessary to safeguard the welfare of apprentices and to cooperate with the states in the promotion of such standards.

Apprentice Information Centers: *see* UNITED STATES EMPLOYMENT SERVICE.

apprentice training: *see* APPRENTICE.

APT: *see* ADVANCED PERSONNEL TEST or AUTOMATICALLY PROGRAMMED TOOL SYSTEM.

aptitude, capacity to acquire knowledge, skill, or ability with experience and/or a given amount of formal or informal education or training.

Aptitude Classification Test, Flanagan: *see* FLANAGAN APTITUDE CLASSIFICATION TEST.

aptitude test, usually a battery of separate tests designed to measure an individual's overall ability to learn. A large variety of specialized aptitude tests have been developed to predict an applicant's performance on a particular job or in a particular course of study. *See* Edwin E. Ghiselli, *The Validity of Occupational Aptitude Tests* (N.Y.: John Wiley & Sons, 1966).

APWU: *see* LABOR ORGANIZATION, Postal Workers Union, American.

ARA: *see* LABOR ORGANIZATION, Radio Association, American.

ARASA: *see* LABOR ORGANIZATION, Railway and Airway Supervisors Association, The American.

arbiter, one chosen to decide a disagreement.

arbitrability, whether or not an issue is covered by a collective bargaining agreement and can be heard and resolved in arbitration. The U.S. Supreme Court held, in *United Steelworkers* v. *Warrior & Gulf Navigation Co.*, 363 U.S. 574 (1960), that any grievance is arbitrable unless there is an express contract provision excluding the issue from arbitration; doubts "should be resolved in favor of coverage."
See also UNITED STEELWORKERS OF AMERICA V. WARRIOR AND GULF NAVIGATION CO.

arbitration, means of settling a labor dispute by having an impartial third party (the arbitrator) hold a formal hearing and render a decision that may or may not be binding on both sides. The arbitrator may be a single individual or a board of three, five, or more. When boards are used, they may include, in addition to impartial members, representatives from both of the disputants. Arbitrators may be selected jointly by labor and management or recommended by the Federal Mediation and Conciliation Service, by a state or local agency offering similar referrals, or by the private American Arbitration Association. For a summary of the "state-of-the-art," *see* Frank Elkouri and Edna Asper Elkouri, *How Arbitration Works* (Washington, D.C.: Bureau of National Affairs, Inc., 3rd ed., 1973).
See also the following entries:
BINDING ARBITRATION
COMPULSORY ARBITRATION
EXPEDITED ARBITRATION
FINAL OFFER ARBITRATION
GRIEVANCE ARBITRATION
INTEREST ARBITRATION
OBLIGATORY ARBITRATION
TERMINAL ARBITRATION
TEXTILE WORKERS V. LINCOLN MILLS
UNITED STEELWORKERS OF AMERICA V. AMERICAN MANUFACTURING CO.
UNITED STEELWORKERS OF AMERICA V. ENTERPRISE WHEEL AND CAR CORP.
VOLUNTARY ARBITRATION
WAGE ARBITRATION
ZIPPER CLAUSE

arbitration clause, provision of a collective bargaining agreement stipulating that disputes arising during the life of the contract over its interpretation are subject to arbitration. The clause may be broad enough to include "any dispute" or restricted to specific concerns.

Arbitration Journal, quarterly journal of the American Arbitration Association, Inc., includes articles written by practitioners and academics on all phases of arbitration and labor relations as well as reviews of related legal decisions.

> *Arbitration Journal*
> American Arbitration Association, Inc.
> 140 West 51st Street
> New York, NY 10020

arbitration tribunal, panel created to decide a dispute that has been submitted to arbitration.

arbitrator, one who conducts an arbitration.
> *See also* NATIONAL ACADEMY OF ARBITRATORS and PERMANENT ARBITRATOR.

architectural barriers, physical aspects of a building that might hinder or prevent the employment of a physically handicapped person. The lack of a ramp, for example, may prevent a person in a wheelchair from entering a building having only stairways for access. The Architectural Barriers Act of 1968 (Public Law 90-480), as amended, requires that buildings constructed with federal funds be accessible to and usable by the physically handicapped. In addition, the U.S. Department of Health, Education and Welfare requires that organizations receiving HEW funds provide free access to their buildings for all citizens.

Architectural Barriers Act of 1968: *see* ARCHITECTURAL BARRIERS.

archives, permanently available records created or received by an organization for its formal/official purposes.

area agreement, collective bargaining agreement that covers a variety of employers and their workers in a large geographical area.

area of consideration, geographic area within which all candidates who meet the basic requirements for promotion to a position are given the opportunity to be considered.

area wage differences, differing pay rates for various occupations in differing geographic areas.

area wage survey: *see* WAGE SURVEY.

area-wide bargaining, collective bargaining between a union and the representatives of an industry in the same city or locality.

ARF: *see* ASSOCIATION OF REHABILITATION FACILITIES.

Argyris, Chris (1923-   ), one of the most influential advocates of the use of organization development (OD) techniques. His writings have provided the theoretical foundations for innumerable empirical research efforts dealing with the inherent conflict between the personality of a mature adult and the needs of modern organizations. Major works include: *Personality And Organization* (N.Y.: Harper & Row, 1957); *Understanding Organizational Behavior* (Homewood, Ill.: Dorsey, 1960); *Interpersonal Competence And Organization Effectiveness* (Homewood, Ill.: Dorsey, 1962); *Integrating the Individual and the Organization* (N.Y.: Wiley, 1964); *Intervention Theory and Method* (Reading, Mass.: Addison-Wesley 1970); *Management and Organizational Development* (N.Y.: McGraw-Hill, 1971).
> *See also* PSEUDO-EFFECTIVENESS.

arithmetic mean: *see* MEAN.

Arizona Public Employees Association: *see* LABOR ORGANIZATION.

Arizona State AFL–CIO: *see* AMERICAN FEDERATION OF LABOR–CONGRESS OF INDUSTRIAL ORGANIZATIONS.

Arkansas State AFL–CIO: *see* AMERICAN FEDERATION OF LABOR–CONGRESS OF INDUSTRIAL ORGANIZATIONS.

Army Alpha and Beta Tests, in 1917 a special committee of the American Psychological Association was convened to develop tests that would help the U.S. Army classify the abilities of its recruits. The committee developed the Army Alpha Intelligence Test (a verbal test for literate recruits) and the Army Beta Intelligence Test (a nonverbal test suited for illiterate and foreign-born recruits). After World War I, the tests were released for civilian use and became the progenitors of modern industrial and educational group intelligence/aptitude testing.

Arnett v. Kennedy, 416 U.S. 134 (1974), U.S. Supreme Court case, which held that the administrative procedures afforded federal employees discharged "for such cause as will promote the efficiency of the service" neither violated the due process rights of such employees nor were unconstitutionally vague.

Arnold Co. v. Carpenters District Council of Jacksonville: *see* WILLIAM E. ARNOLD CO. V. CARPENTERS DISTRICT COUNCIL OF JACKSONVILLE.

Asbestos Workers, International Association of Heat and Frost Insulators and: *see* LABOR ORGANIZATION.

ASCS County Office Employees, National Association of: *see* LABOR ORGANIZATION.

ASCSE: *see* LABOR ORGANIZATION, ASCS County Office Employees, National Association of.

ASEA: *see* LABOR ORGANIZATION, Alabama State Employees Association.

Ashurst–Sumners Act of 1935, federal law that forbids the interstate shipping of goods produced by convict labor into states that prohibit convict labor.

ASPA: *see* AMERICAN SOCIETY FOR PERSONNEL ADMINISTRATION or AMERICAN SOCIETY FOR PUBLIC ADMINISTRATION.

ASPA Accreditation Institute: *see* AMERICAN SOCIETY FOR PERSONNEL ADMINISTRATION ACCREDITATION INSTITUTE.

ASQ: *see* ADMINISTRATIVE SCIENCE QUARTERLY.

assembly line, production method requiring workers to perform a repetitive task on a product as it moves along on a conveyor belt or tract. Although much has been written about the "inhuman" demands of machine-paced work, the classic study remains Charles R. Walker and Robert H. Guest's *The Man on the Assembly Line* (Cambridge, Mass.: Harvard University Press, 1952).

assertiveness training, training program designed to help less assertive people communicate and express their ideas and feelings more effectively. The ideal level of assertiveness lies midway between passivity and aggressiveness. The concept was pioneered by J. Wolpe in his *Psychotherapy by Reciprocal Inhibition* (Stanford, Calif.: Stanford University Press, 1958). For a general discussion, *see* Harold H. Dawley, Jr., and W. W. Wenrich, *Achieving Assertive Behavior: A Guide to Assertive Training* (Belmont, Calif.: Wadsworth Publishing Co., 1976). For the obverse, *see* Michael D. Ames, "Non-Assertion Training Has Value Too," *Personnel Journal* (July 1977).

assessment center, the term "assessment center" does not refer to a particular place. Rather, it is a process consisting of the intense observation of a subject undergoing a variety of simulations and stress situations over a period of several days. Assessment centers have proven to be an increasingly popular way of identifying individuals with future executive potential so that they may be given the appropriate training and development assignments.

As the assessment center concept is more widely adopted, one question will become more and more commonplace: If the door to management development and advancement goes through the assessment center, who will be the gatekeeper? Unless the organization can afford to process its entire management cadre through assessment centers, those individuals not selected for attendance might justifiably conclude they have been negatively evaluated. The decision, or nondecision, not to send an individual to an assessment center while peers are being sent could even have considerable legal ramifications. Because management development funds will continue to a scarce resource, any organization implementing an assessment center program must also be concerned with designing an equitable nomination process.

For accounts of assessment center methodologies, *see* Douglas W. Bray, "The Assessment Center Method," *Training and Development Handbook*, Robert L. Craig, ed. (N.Y.: McGraw-Hill, 2nd ed., 1976) and William C. Byham and Carl Wettengel, "Assessment Centers for Supervisors and Managers: An Introduction and Overview," *Public Personnel Management* (September - October 1974).
See also IN-BASKET EXERCISE.

assessments, amounts paid by union members in addition to their regular dues when a union needs funds urgently in order to support a strike or some other union endorsed cause. The amount of these assessments are usually limited by a union's constitution and/or bylaws.

asset-linked annuity: *see* VARIABLE ANNUITY.

assignment of wages, also called ATTACHMENT OF WAGES, procedure that has an employer, upon the authorization of the employee, automatically deduct a portion of the employee's wages and pay it to a third party, usually a creditor. When this is ordered by a court, the process is known as garnishment.
See also GARNISHMENT.

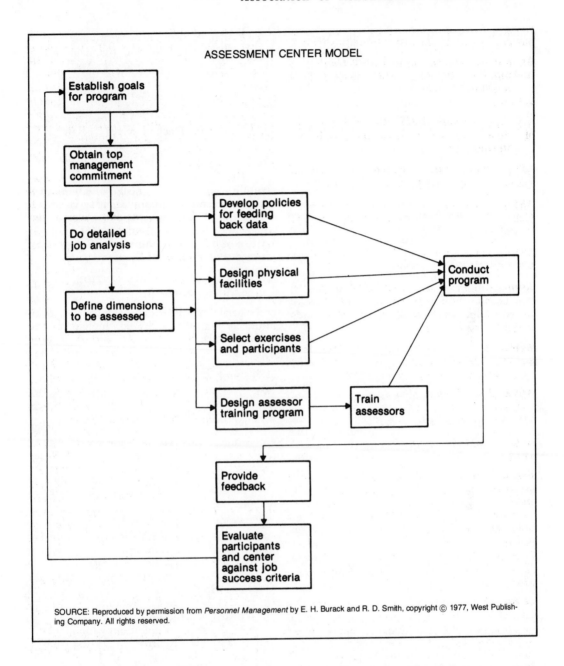

ASSESSMENT CENTER MODEL

Associated Actors and Artistes of America: *see* LABOR ORGANIZATION, under Actors and Artistes of America, Associated.

association, employer: *see* EMPLOYERS' ASSOCIATION.

association agreement, model or standarized collective bargaining agreement put forth by an employer's association.

Association of Civilian Technicians: *see* LABOR ORGANIZATION, Technicians, Association of Civilian.

Association of Flight Attendents: *see* LABOR ORGANIZATION, under Air Line Pilots Association.

Association of Rehabilitation Centers: *see* ASSOCIATION OF REHABILITATION FACILITIES.

Association of Rehabilitation Facilities (ARF),

formed in 1969 by the merger of the Association of Rehabilitation Centers and the National Association of Sheltered Workshops and Homebound Programs, the ARF is organized to strengthen the resources of rehabilitation facilities so that through effective operation they may provide high-quality services to handicapped persons and the community at large.

Association of Rehabilitation Facilities
5530 Wisconsin Ave. Suite 955
Washington, DC 20015
(301) 654-5882

Association of Western Pulp and Paper Workers: *see* LABOR ORGANIZATION, Pulp and Paper Workers, Association of Western.

assumption-of-risk doctrine, common-law concept that an employer should not be held responsible for an accident to an employee if the employer can show that the injured employee had voluntarily accepted the hazards associated with a given job.

ASTD: *see* AMERICAN SOCIETY FOR TRAINING AND DEVELOPMENT.

ATDA: *see* LABOR ORGANIZATION, Train Dispatchers Association, American.

Atkins v. *Kansas*, 191 U.S. 207 (1903), U.S. Supreme Court decision that established the right of government to regulate the hours of private contractors working for the government.

Atlantic Independent Union: *see* LABOR ORGANIZATION.

attachment of wages: *see* ASSIGNMENT OF WAGES.

attendance bonus, also called ATTENDANCE MONEY, possible payment to an employee that serves as inducement to regular attendance.

attitude, learned predisposition to act in a consistent way toward particular persons, objects, or conditions.

attitude scale, any series of attitude indices that have given quantitative values relative to each other.

attitude survey, questionnaire, usually anonymous, that elicits the opinion of employees. Once completed they are summarized and analyzed to determine compliance with and attitudes towards current personnel management policies. *See* Martin Fishbein (ed.), *Readings in Attitude Theory and Measurement* (N.Y.: John Wiley, 1967);

Price Pritchett, "Employee Attitude Surveys: A Natural Starting Point for Organization Development," *Personnel Journal* (April 1975); Stuart M. Klein, Allen I. Kraut, and Alan Wolfson, "Employee Reactions to Attitude Survey Feedback: A Study of the Impact of Structure and Process," *Administrative Science Quarterly* (December 1971); Randall B. Dunham and Frank J. Smith, *Organizational Surveys* (Glenview, Ill.: Scott, Foresman and Co., 1979).

attrition, reduction in the size of a workforce through normal processes, such as voluntary resignations, retirements, discharges for cause, transfers, and deaths. *See* Jack Frye, "Attrition in Job Elimination," *Labor Law Journal* (September 1963).

ATU: *see* LABOR ORGANIZATION, Transit Union, Amalgamated.

audio-visual media, those things that communicate information through human sight or sound sensors—films, slides, recordings, maps, etc.

audit, desk/job: *see* DESK AUDIT.

au pair, British term which usually refers to a foreigh girl who does light domestic chores for a family in exchange for room and board.

authoritarian theory: *see* THEORY X.

authority, power inherent in a specific position or function that allows an incumbent to perform assigned duties and assume assigned responsibilities.
See also FUNCTIONAL AUTHORITY.

authorization card, form signed by a worker to authorize a union to represent the worker for purposes of collective bargaining. The U.S. Supreme Court held, in *National Labor Relations Board* v. *Gissel Packing Co.*, 395 U.S. 575 (1969), that the National Labor Relations Board had the power to require an employer to bargain with a union which had obtained signed authorization cards from a majority of the employees. In such circumstances a secret ballot election is considered unnecessary.
See also SHOWING OF INTEREST.

authorization election, or REPRESENTATION ELECTION, polls conducted by the National Labor Relations Board (or other administrative agency) to determine if a particular group of employees will be represented by a particular union or not. *See* Dean S. Ellis, Laurence Jacobs, and Cary Mills, "A Union Authorization Election: The Key to Winning," *Personnel Journal* (April 1972) and Julius G. Getman, Stephen B. Goldberg, and Jeanne B. Herman, *Union Representation Elections: Law and Reality* (N.Y.: Russell Sage Foundation, 1976).

See also the following entries:

JOY SILK MILLS V. NATIONAL LABOR RE-
LATIONS BOARD
NATIONAL LABOR RELATIONS BOARD V. EX-
CHANGE PARTS
RUN-OFF ELECTION
SHOWING OF INTEREST

automatically programmed tool system (APT), computer language that describes the operations to be performed in English-like terms.

automatic checkoff, also called COMPULSORY CHECKOFF, illegal procedure whereby the employer deducts union dues and assessments from the pay of all employees in the bargaining unit without the prior consent of each individual employee. Section 302 of the Labor–Management Relations (Taft–Hartley) Act of 1947 provides that checkoffs must be voluntary and initiated only upon the written authorization of each employee on whose account such deductions would be made.

automatic wage adjustment, raising or lowering of wage rates in direct response to previously determined factors such as an increase/decrease in the Consumer Price Index or the company's profits.

automation, sometimes called MECHANIZATION, use of machines to do work that would otherwise have to be done by humans. While examples of automation go back to ancient times, the term itself was only coined in the mid 1930s by D. S. Harder, then of General Motors. As a word, automation has a considerable emotional charge since its manifestations have tended to create technological unemployment.

Automation tends to be popularly used interchangeably with mechanization—the use of machines. However, a production system is not truly automated unless the machinery is to some degree self regulated—that is, capable of adjusting itself in response to feedback from its earlier outputs. This attribute lessens the need for human attendants. According to Herbert A. Simon, in *The Shape of Automation for Men and Management* (N.Y.: Harper & Row, 1965),

the term "mechanization" has nearly been replaced by its newer synonym, "automation." Automation is nothing new; it is simply the continuation of that trend toward the use of capital in production that has been a central characteristic of the whole Industrial Revolution. What is possibly new, if anything, is the extension of mechanization to wider and wider ranges of productive processes, and the growing prospect of complete mechanization—that is, the technical feasibility of productive processes that do not require human participation.

automaton, person acting mechanically in a monotonous routine without the need to use any intellectual capacities. The thrust of the scientific management movement was to make workers the most efficient possible automatons. A significant portion of modern industrial unrest is directly related to the workforce's resentment at being treated in such a manner.

Automobile, Aerospace, and Agricultural Implement Workers of America International Union, United: *see* LABOR ORGANIZATION.

auxiliary agency, also called HOUSEKEEPING AGENCY or OVERHEAD AGENCY, administrative unit whose prime responsibility is to serve other agencies of the greater organization. Personnel agencies are usually auxiliary, housekeeping, or overhead agencies.

average deviation, also called MEAN DEVIATION, measure of dispersion that provides information on the extent of scatter, or the degree of clustering, in a set of data.

average earned rate, total earnings for a given time period divided by the number of hours worked during the period.

average hourly earnings, wages earned by an employee per hour of work during a specific time period. The average hourly earnings are computed by dividing total pay received by the total hours worked.

average incumbents, average workforce strength figure found by adding the workforce strengths at the beginning and end of a specified report period and dividing this sum by two. This type of computation is widely used in turnover analysis.

average straight-time hourly earnings, average wages earned per hour exclusive of premium payments and shift differentials.

award, at the end of the arbitration process, the final decision of the arbitrator(s) when such arbitration is binding on both parties.

award, incentive: *see* INCENTIVE AWARD.

AWIU: *see* LABOR ORGANIZATION, Allied Workers International, United.

AWOL, absent without official leave. This term is usually restricted to the military.

AWPPW: *see* LABOR ORGANIZATION, Pulp and Paper Workers, Association of Western.

AWU: *see* LABOR ORGANIZATION, Aluminum Workers International Union.

AWWU: *see* LABOR ORGANIZATION, Watch Workers Union, American.

B

Babbage, Charles (1792-1871), English mathematician and inventor. Best known as the "father" of the modern computer, he is also acclaimed for building upon the assembly line concepts of Adam Smith and anticipating the scientific management techniques of Frederick W. Taylor. Major works include: *On the Economy of Machinery and Manufactures* (London: Charles Knight, 1832); *Passages from the Life of a Philosopher* (London: Longman & Green, 1864). For modern biographies, *see* Maboth Moseley, *Irascible Genius: A Life of Charles Babbage, Inventor* (London: Hutchinson & Co., 1964); Philip and Emily Morrison, eds., *Charles Babbage and His Calculating Engines* (N.Y.: Dover Publications, 1961).

Babbitt v. United Farm Workers, 60 L. Ed. 2d 895 (1979), U.S. Supreme Court case, which held that a state's regulation of union election procedures did not violate First Amendment rights.

Babcock and Wilcox decision: *see* NATIONAL LABOR RELATIONS BOARD V. BABCOCK AND WILCOX.

Baby Wagner Acts, state labor laws that parallel the federal Wagner–Connery Act of 1935.

back pay, delayed payment of wages for a particular time period.

back-to-work movement, striking employees returning to their jobs before their union has formally ended the strike.

Baer, Fred William (1884-1946), president of the International Association of Fire Fighters from 1919 to 1946.

Bakery and Confectionery Workers' International Union of America (AFL–CIO): *see* LABOR ORGANIZATION.

Bakke, E. Wight (1903-1971), social scientist most noted for his pioneering empirical research on the problemsolving behavior of groups in organizations. Major works include: *Bonds of Organization* (N.Y.: Harper & Row, 1950); *The Fusion Process* (New Haven, Conn.: Labor and Management Center, Yale University, 1953).

Bakke decision: *see* REGENTS OF THE UNIVERSITY OF CALIFORNIA V. ALLAN BAKKE.

band curve chart or CUMULATIVE BAND CHART, chart on which the bands of a graph are plotted one above the other.

bank holiday, any of the traditional legal holidays or other special occasions when banks as well as most, but not all, other businesses remain closed. The six essentially "standard" paid holidays are: Christmas Day, Thanksgiving Day, New Year's Day, Independence Day, Labor Day, and Memorial Day. Many business and government jurisdictions offer as many as twice this number of paid holidays for their employees, but the specific days vary with local customs. In addition to the six listed above, all federal employees have paid holidays for Washington's Birthday, Columbus Day, and Veteran's Day.

Bankruptcy Act: *see* WAGE EARNER PLAN.

bar examination, written test that new lawyers must pass in order to practice law.

bargaining: *see* the following entries:
  BLUE SKY BARGAINING
  COALITION BARGAINING
  COLLECTIVE BARGAINING
  CRISIS BARGAINING
  GOOD-FAITH BARGAINING
  INDIVIDUAL BARGAINING
  INDUSTRY-WIDE BARGAINING
  JOINT BARGAINING
  MULTIEMPLOYER BARGAINING
  PATTERN BARGAINING
  PRODUCTIVITY BARGAINING
  REGIONAL BARGAINING
  SUNSHINE BARGAINING

bargaining agent, the union organization (not an individual) that is the exclusive repre-

29

sentative of all the workers, union as well as non-union, in a bargaining unit. Employers may voluntarily agree that a particular union will serve as the bargaining agent for their employees, or the decision on representation can be settled by secret ballot election conducted by the federal National Labor Relations Board or a counterpart state agency.

bargaining agreement: *see* LABOR AGREEMENT.

bargaining item, illegal: *see* ILLEGAL BARGAINING ITEM.

bargaining rights, legal rights that all workers have to bargain collectively with their employers.
See also EXCLUSIVE BARGAINING RIGHTS.

bargaining strength, relative power that each of the parties holds during the negotiating process. The final settlement often reflects the bargaining power of each side.

bargaining theory of wages, theory that wages are based on the supply and demand for labor, that wages can never be higher than a company's break-even point or lower than bare subsistence for the workers, and that the actual "price" of labor is determined by the relative strengths—the bargaining power—of employers and workers. While the bargaining theory does not explain wage determination over the long run, it is generally accepted as the most pragmatic explanation of short-run wage determination. The beginnings of the bargaining theory are found in Adam Smith's *The Wealth of Nations* (1776), but its modern formulation dates from John Davidson's *The Bargaining Theory of Wages* (N.Y.: G.P. Putnam's Sons, 1898). *Also see* John T. Dunlop, (ed.), *Theory of Wage Determination* (N.Y.: St. Martin's Press, 1957).

bargaining unit, or simply UNIT, group of employees, both union members as well as others, that an employer has recognized and/or an administrative agency has certified as appropriate for representation by a union for purposes of collective bargaining. All of the employees in a bargaining unit are subsequently covered in the labor contract that the union negotiates on their behalf. Bargaining units may be as small as the handful of workers in a local shop or as large as the workforce of an entire industry. The size of a bargaining unit is important in that it significantly affects the relative bargaining strength of both labor and management.
See also the following entries:

AMERICAN FEDERATION OF LABOR V. NATIONAL LABOR RELATIONS BOARD
NATIONAL LABOR RELATIONS BOARD V. MAGNAVOX
UNION SECURITY

Barnard, Chester I. (1886-1961), a Bell System executive closely associated with the Harvard Business School, best known for his sociological analyses of organizations that encouraged and foreshadowed the post World War II behavioral revolution. Barnard viewed organizations as cooperative systems where "the function of the executive" was to maintain the dynamic equilibrium between the needs of the organization and the needs of its employees. In order to do this, management had to be aware of the interdependent nature of the formal and informal organization. Barnard's analysis of the significance and role of informal organizations provided the theoretical foundations for a whole generation of empirical research. Major works include: *The Functions of the Executive* (Cambridge, Mass.: Harvard University Press, 1938); *Organization and Management: Selected Papers* (Cambridge, Mass.: Harvard University Press, 1948). For a biography, *see* William B. Wolf, *How to Understand Management: An Introduction to Chester I. Barnard* (Los Angeles: Lucus Brothers Publishers, 1968).

Barry, Leonora (**Marie Kearney**) (1849-1930) also known as MOTHER LAKE, led the women's division of the Knights of Labor from 1886 to 1890. Acquired her nickname following her marriage to O. R. Lake in 1890.

BARS: *see* BEHAVIORALLY ANCHORED RATING SCALES.

base period, time that an employee must work before becoming eligible for state unemployment insurance benefits.

base points, minimum point values given to the factors in a job evaluation system.

base rate: *see* BASE SALARY.

base salary, or BASE RATE, standard earnings before the addition of overtime or premium pay.

base time, time required for an employee to perform an operation while working normally with no allowance for personal/unavoidable delays or fatigue.

BASIC, acronym for Beginners' All-purpose Symbolic Instruction Code. An introductory computer language.

basic rate of pay, employee's hourly wage.

The regular rate of pay upon which overtime and other wage supplements would be computed.

basic workday, number of hours in a normal workday, as established by collective bargaining agreements or statutory law. Premium payments must usually be paid for time worked in excess of the basic workday. The eight-hour day is widely accepted as the standard basic workday.

basic workweek, number of hours in a normal workweek, as established by collective bargaining agreements or statutory law. Premium payments must usually be paid for time worked in excess of the basic workweek. The 40-hour week is widely accepted as the standard basic workweek.

See also FAIR LABOR STANDARDS ACT.

Batterton v. Francis, 432 U.S. 416 (1977), U.S. Supreme Court case, which held that a state could deny welfare benefits for families of unemployed fathers if the father is unemployed as a result of a strike.

battery, or TEST BATTERY, two or more tests administered together and standardized on the same population so that the results on the various tests are comparable. The term battery is also used to refer to any tests administered as a group. *See* W. Considine, *et al.*, "Developing a Physical Performance Test Battery for Screening Chicago Fire Fighter Applicants," *Public Personnel Management* (January-February 1976).

Bay Ridge Company v. Aaron, 334 U.S. 446 (1948), U.S. Supreme Court case, which held that premium payments provided for in collective bargaining agreements had to be considered in computing the "regular rate" of pay for overtime computations.

BCW: *see* LABOR ORGANIZATION, Bakery and Confectionery Workers' International Union of America.

Beck, Dave (1894-), president of the International Brotherhood of Teamsters (1952–1957) who was sentenced to prison in 1958 because of income tax evasion. Under Beck's leadership, the Teamsters grew so corrupt that they were expelled from the AFL–CIO in 1958. As a direct result of the notoriety of the Beck case, the U.S. Congress passed the Labor–Management Reporting and Disclosure (Landrum–Griffin) Act of 1959, which created safeguards against irresponsible and corrupt union leadership.

Bedaux Plan also BEDAUX POINT SYSTEM, wage incentive plan introduced in 1916 by Charles E. Bedaux, which provided that the bonus earned for incentive effort be divided between the employee and management.

Bedford Cut Stone Company v. Journeymen Stone Cutters' Association, 174 U.S. 37 (1927), U.S. Supreme Court case, which held that union members cannot, without being in violation of the Sherman Anti-Trust Act of 1890, refuse to work on work that had previously been worked on by non-union labor.

beginner's rate, or TRAINEE RATE, wage rate for an inexperienced employee. Once a previously established training period is completed, an employee is entitled to the regular rate of pay for the job.

behaviorally anchored rating scales (BARS), performance evaluation technique that is premised upon the scaling of critical incidents of work performance. For the methodology, *see*, Donald Schwab, Herbert Heneman III, and Thomas DeCotiis, "Behaviorally Anchored Scales: A Review of the Literature," *Personel Psychology*, Vol. 28 (1975); Frank J. Landy, *et al.*, "Behaviorally Anchored Scales for Rating the Performance of Police Officers," *Journal of Applied Psychology* (December 1976).

behavior modeling, training, usually for first or second line supervisors, that uses videotapes and/or role-playing sessions to give supervisors an opportunity to improve their supervisory abilities by imitating "models" who have already mastered such skills. For a summary of the technique, *see* Bernard L. Rosenbaum, "New Uses for Behavior Modeling," *The Personnel Administrator* (July 1978).

behavior modification (BMod), use of positive or negative reinforcements to change the behavior of individuals or groups. *See* C. E. Schneider, "Behavior Modification: Training the Hard Core Unemployed," *Personnel* (May-June 1973); C. Ray Gullett and Robert Reisen, "Behavior Modification: A Contingency Approach to Employee Performance," *Personnel Journal* (April 1975); W. Clay Hamner and Ellen P. Hamner, "Behavior Modification on the Bottom Line," *Organizational Dynamics* (Spring 1976).

behavioral sciences, general term for all of the academic disciplines that study human and animal behavior by means of experimental research.

See also NATIONAL TRAINING LABORA-TORIES INSTITUTE FOR APPLIED BEHAVIOR-AL SCIENCE.

behavioral technology, emerging discipline that seeks to meld together both the technical and human aspects of the workplace. It places equal emphasis on the social as well as the technological sciences in order to foster the individual's fullest use as both a human and technical resource. *See* James G. Brianas "Behavioral Technology: A Challenge to Modern Management," *Public Personnel Management* (July-August 1973).

behaviorism, school of psychology which holds that only overt behavior is the proper subject matter for the entire discipline. According to the foremost exponent of behaviorism, B. F. Skinner, "behaviorism is not the science of human behavior; it is the philosophy of that science." *About Behaviorism* (N.Y.: Alfred A. Knopf, 1974).

Bell, Daniel (1919-), sociologist whose critiques of modern industrial societies have touched upon their politics and their management. Bell is considered to be both a major critic of the "machine civilization" of the scientific management era and a pioneer in social forecasting. Major works include: *Work and Its Discontents: The Cult of Efficiency in America* (Boston: Beacon Press, 1956); *The End of Ideology* (Glencoe, Ill.: The Free Press, 1960); *The Coming of Post-Industrial Society* (N.Y.: Basic Books, 1973).

benchmark, any standard that is identified with sufficient detail so that other similar classifications can be compared as being above, below, or comparable to the "benchmark" standard.

benchmark position, position used as a frame of reference in the evaluation of other positions.

beneficiary, person, group, or organization to whom an insurance policy is payable.

benefit, death: *see* DEATH BENEFIT.

benefit–cost analysis: *see* COST–BENEFIT ANALYSIS.

benefit plans, welfare programs administered by a union for its members and paid for out of dues, voluntary contributions, or special assessments.
See also the following entries:
CAFETERIA BENEFITS PLAN
FLAT-BENEFIT PLAN

FRINGE BENEFITS
HEALTH BENEFITS

benefit seniority, use of seniority in computing an employee's economic fringe benefits such as pensions, vacations, bonuses, etc.

Benge, Eugene J. (1896-), generally credited with having "invented" the factor-comparison method of job evaluation in the 1920s. Major works include: *Manual of Job Evaluation* with S. Burk and E. N. Hay (N.Y.: Harper Bros., 1941); *How To Manage for Tomorrow* (Homewood, Ill.: Dow Jones-Irwin, 1975); *Elements of Modern Management* (N.Y.: AMACOM, 1976).

Bennett Mechanical Comprehension Test (BMCT), paper-and-pencil test that uses pictures to test the individual on basic understanding of mechanical principles and facts. TIME: 30/35 minutes. AUTHOR: George K. Bennett. PUBLISHER: Psychological Corporation (*see* TEST PUBLISHERS).

Bennis, Warren G. (1925-), a leading proponent of organization development, is perhaps best known for his continuous sounding of the death knell of bureaucratic institutions. Bennis has indicted most present organizational formats as inadequate for a future that will demand rapid organizational and technological changes, participatory management, and the growth of a more professionalized workforce. Organizations of the future, Bennis maintains, will be more responsive to these needs and in consequence, decidedly less bureaucratic, less structured, and less rigid. Major works include: *Changing Organizations* (N.Y.: McGraw-Hill, 1966); *The Temporary Society*, with Philip E. Slater (N.Y.: Harper & Row, 1968); *Organization Development: Its Nature, Origins, and Prospects* (Reading, Mass.: Addison-Wesley, 1969); *The Leaning Ivory Tower*, with P. W. Biederman (N.Y.: Jossey-Bass, 1973).
See also POSTBUREAUCRATIC ORGANIZATIONS.

bereavement leave: *see* FUNERAL LEAVE.

Berne, Eric (1910-1970), born ERIC LENNARD BERNSTEIN, the psychoanalyst who founded the field of transactional analysis. Major works include: *Games People Play: The Psychology of Human Relationship* (N.Y.: Grove Press, 1964); *Principles of Group Treatment* (N.Y.: Oxford University Press, 1966); *What Do You Say After You Say Hello?* (N.Y.: Grove Press, 1972); *Intuition & Ego States: The Origins of Transactional*

Analysis (N.Y.: Harper & Row, 1977). For biography, *see* Warren D. Cheney, "Eric Berne: Biographical Sketch," in Eric Berne, *Beyond Games and Scripts* (N.Y.: Grove Press, 1976).

Bernreuter Personality Inventory (BPI), personality inventory commonly used in business and industry to measure six personality traits (neurotic tendency, self-sufficiency, intro–extroversion, dominance/submission, self confidence, and sociability). TIME: 25-30 minutes. AUTHOR: Robert G. Bernreuter. PUBLISHER: Consulting Psychologists Press, Inc. (*see* TEST PUBLISHERS).

Bernstein, Eric Lennard: *see* BERNE, ERIC.

Bertalanffy, Ludwig von (1901-1972), Austrian–Canadian biologist considered to be the "father of general systems theory." His basic statement on the subject is: *General System Theory: Foundations, Development, Applications* (N.Y.: George Braziller, rev. ed., 1968).

bespoke work, archaic term for special orders. In the olden days master craftsmen would produce products either on speculation (hoping that they would later find a buyer for them) or in response to a specific order. These latter products were bespoke work—they had literally been spoken for.

Beth Israel Hospital v. National Labor Relations Board, 57 L. Ed. 2d 370 (1978), U.S. Supreme Court case, which upheld a National Labor Relations Board determination that employees seeking to organize a bargaining unit of hospital employees could not be prohibited from distributing leaflets in a hospital cafeteria patronized predominantly by hospital employees. To a limited extent, the court gave its approval to the NLRB's attempt to permit a substantial range for union communication to actual and potential members, provided such communication does not disrupt employer's business activities.

BFOQ: *see* BONA FIDE OCCUPATIONAL QUALIFICATION.

bias, tendency of a selection device to err in a particular direction.
See also CULTURAL BIAS.

biased sample, sample that does not truly represent the total population from which it was selected.

bidding, means by which an employee of an organization makes known his or her interest in a vacant position in that same organization.

Big Eight, slang term for the eight largest public accounting firms: Arthur Anderson and Co.; Coopers and Lybrand; Ernst and Ernst; Haskins and Sells; Peat, Marwick, Mitchell and Company; Price Waterhouse and Company; Touche Ross and Company, and Arthur Young and Company.

bigotry: *see* DISCRIMINATION.

Big Steel, and LITTLE STEEL, historically "big steel" has referred to just the United States Steel Corporation, and "little steel" was all others. More recently, "big steel" has been used to refer collectively to all of the largest steel makers.

Big Three, the three largest American auto makers: General Motors, Ford, and Chrysler.

bill: *see* ACT.

bimodal distribution, frequency distribution in which there are two modes—two most frequently occurring scores. A graphic presentation would show two peaks.

binding arbitration, actually a redundancy! Arbitration, unless it is advisory, is by its nature binding upon the parties.

Binet, Alfred (1857-1911), French psychologist who originated the first modern intelligence test.

bi-partite board, labor–management committee established as part of a grievance process in order to resolve a dispute short of arbitration.

birth leave, paid time off upon the birth of a child. This is generally available only to men. Women, should the occasion warrant, would necessarily take maternity leave.
See also MATERNITY LEAVE.

biserial correlation, correlation between the score on a particular item and the total test score.

Bishop v. Wood, 426 U.S. 341 (1976), U.S. Supreme Court case, which held that an employee's discharge did not deprive him of a property interest protected by the Due Process Clause of the U.S. Constitution's 14th Amendment. The court further asserted that even assuming a false explanation for the employee's discharge, he was still not deprived of an interest in liberty protected by the clause if the reasons for his discharge were not made public.

Bituminous Coal Act Of 1937, federal law that regulates the sale of bituminous coal in interstate commerce and provides collective bargaining rights for coal miners.

black leg: *see* SCAB.

black list, originally lists prepared by merchants containing the names of men who had gone bankrupt. The early union movement found that employers were using "don't hire" lists of men who joined unions. But the National Labor Relations (Wagner) Act of 1935 made such blacklisting illegal. In the 1950s, many in the entertainment industry were "blacklisted" and thus denied employment for alleged "un-American" activities. For a history of this period, *see* David Caute, *The Great Fear: The Anti-Communist Purge Under Truman and Eisenhower* (N.Y.: Simon & Schuster, 1978).

black-lung disease, scientific name PNEUMO-CONIOSIS, chronic and disabling occupational disease (mostly of miners) resulting from the inhalation of dusts over a long period of time. Its popular name results from the tendency of the inhaled dusts to blacken lung tissue. *See* Carvin Cook, "The 1977 Amendments to the Black Lung Benefits Law," *Monthly Labor Review* (May 1978).

See also USERY V. TURNER ELKHORN MINING CO.

Blake, Robert R. (1918-   ) **and Jane S. Mouton.** (1930-   ), industrial psychologists best known for their conceptualization of the "managerial grid"—a graphic description of the various managerial approaches. The grid itself represents leadership styles that reflect two prime dimensions, "concern for people" on the vertical axis, and "concern for produc-

tion" on the horizontal axis. For a complete presentation of the grid concept, see any of their books: *The Managerial Grid* (Houston, Texas: Gulf Publishing, 1964); *Corporate Excellence Through Grid Organization Development* (Houston, Texas; Gulf Publishing, 1968); *Building a Dynamic Organization Through Grid Organization Development* (Reading, Mass.: Addison-Wesley, 1969).

blanket agreement, collective bargaining agreement that is based on industrywide negotiations or negotiations covering a large geographic area within an industry.

Blau, Peter M. (1918-   ), sociologist who has specialized in the study of formal organizations and bureaucracies and produced pioneering empirical as well as theoretical analyses of organizational behavior. Major works include: *The Dynamics of Bureaucracy* (Chicago: University of Chicago Press, 1955, revised 1963); *Bureaucracy in Modern Society* (N.Y.: Random House, 1956); *Formal Organizations*, with W. Richard Scott (San Francisco: Chandler Publishing, 1962); *Exchange and Power in Social Life* (N.Y.: Wiley, 1964); *The American Occupational Structure* (N.Y.: Wiley, 1967); *The Structure of Organizations* (N.Y.: Basic Books, 1971); *The Organization of Academic Work* (N.Y.: Wiley, 1973).

Blaylock, Kenneth T. (1935-   ), became president of the American Federation of Government Employees in 1976.

BLE: *see* LABOR ORGANIZATION, Locomotive Engineers, Brotherhood of.

NO. 547. BLACK LUNG BENEFIT PROGRAM—BENEFICIARIES AND BENEFIT PAYMENTS, 1970 TO 1977, AND BY SELECTED STATES, 1977

[Benefits currently payable by the Social Security Administration to miners totally disabled because of pneumoconiosis and to their dependents and survivors under the "Black Lung" program established by the Federal Coal Mine Health and Safety Act of 1969]

BENEFICIARIES AND PAYMENTS	1970	1973	1974	1975	1976	1977 Total	Selected States						
							Pa.	W. Va.	Ky.	Ohio	Ill.	Va.	Ala.
Beneficiaries [1]___1,000__	112	461	487	482	470	457	138.0	80.6	55.8	26.8	25.6	25.9	20.0
Miners_____1,000__	44	160	169	165	158	149	44.0	27.0	18.2	8.6	8.2	8.7	6.6
Widows_____1,000__	25	124	135	139	143	145	47.9	21.2	12.8	9.1	10.4	6.4	6.5
Dependents [2]__1,000__	43	178	183	177	169	164	46.2	32.3	24.8	9.1	6.9	10.8	6.9
Payments_____mil. dol__	110	1,045	952	948	963	942	287	160	103	56	58	52	43
Avg. mo. payment: [2]													
Miner's family_____	$200	$253	$267	$282	$294	$317	$310	$319	$318	$311	$316	$334	$322
Widow's family_____	$150	$188	$197	$207	$216	$231	$227	$237	$239	$232	$226	$239	$234

[1] As of end of year.   [2] Dependent wife or child or surviving child, parent, brother, or sister.

SOURCE: Bureau of the Census, *Statistical Abstract of the United States* (Washington, D.C., Government Printing Office, 1978), p. 346.

Employment in nonfarm occupations
(Seasonally adjusted)

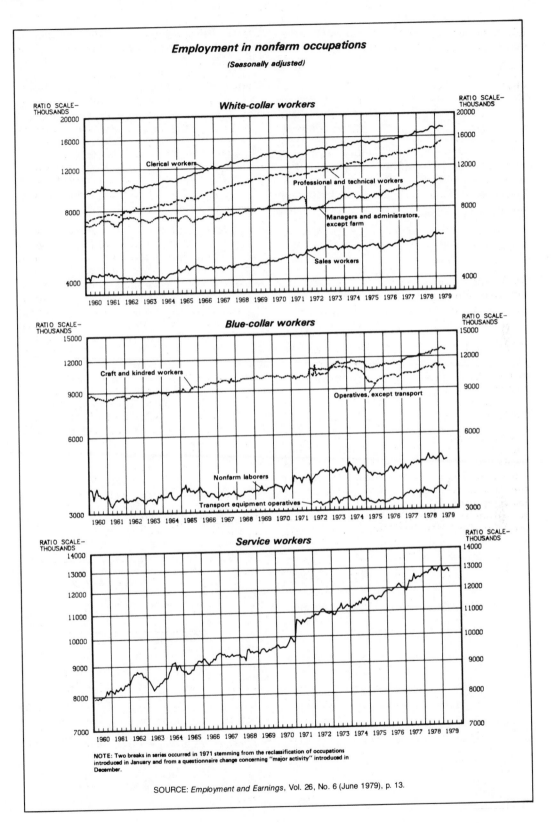

White-collar workers

RATIO SCALE—THOUSANDS

Clerical workers

Professional and technical workers

Managers and administrators, except farm

Sales workers

1960 1961 1962 1963 1964 1965 1966 1967 1968 1969 1970 1971 1972 1973 1974 1975 1976 1977 1978 1979

Blue-collar workers

RATIO SCALE—THOUSANDS

Craft and kindred workers

Operatives, except transport

Nonfarm laborers

Transport equipment operatives

1960 1961 1962 1963 1964 1965 1966 1967 1968 1969 1970 1971 1972 1973 1974 1975 1976 1977 1978 1979

Service workers

RATIO SCALE—THOUSANDS

1960 1961 1962 1963 1964 1965 1966 1967 1968 1969 1970 1971 1972 1973 1974 1975 1976 1977 1978 1979

NOTE: Two breaks in series occurred in 1971 stemming from the reclassification of occupations introduced in January and from a questionnaire change concerning "major activity" introduced in December.

SOURCE: *Employment and Earnings*, Vol. 26, No. 6 (June 1979), p. 13.

BLS: *see* BUREAU OF LABOR STATISTICS.

blue-circle rate: *see* GREEN-CIRCLE RATE.

blue-collar workers, those workers, both skilled and unskilled, engaged primarily in physical labor. For example, the U.S. Bureau of the Census considers all craftsmen, construction workers, machine operators, farm workers, transportation equipment operators, factory production and maintenance workers to fit into the blue-collar category. The proportion of blue-collar workers in the U.S. economy has been steadily declining. In 1950, there were 31 million. By 1971, the number had dropped to 26 million, over a time when total employment grew by about 20 million. For an analysis of blue-collar angst, *see* Irving Howe (ed.), *The World of the Blue-Collar Worker* (N.Y.: Quadrangle Books, 1972).

See WHITE-COLLAR WORKERS for unemployment rates.

Blue Cross and Blue Shield, nonprofit group health insurance plans for, respectively, hospital and physician's fees.

Blue Eagle: *see* NATIONAL INDUSTRIAL RECOVERY ACT OF 1933.

blue flu, when police officers informally strike by calling in sick, they are said to be suffering from a disease so unique that it affects only police—the blue flu.

Blue Shield: *see* BLUE CROSS AND BLUE SHIELD.

blue sky bargaining, unreasonable and unrealistic negotiating demands by either side, made usually at the beginning of the negotiating process. The only "useful" purposes of such bargaining are to (1) satisfy an outside audience that their concerns are being attended to, (2) delay the "real" negotiations because such a delay is thought to hold a tactical advantage, and (3) provide a basis for compromise as the negotiations progress.

BMCT: *see* BENNETT MECHANICAL COMPREHENSION TEST.

BMod: *see* BEHAVIOR MODIFICATION.

BMWE: *see* LABOR ORGANIZATION, Maintenance of Way Employees, Brotherhood of.

BNA: *see* BUREAU OF NATIONAL AFFAIRS, INC.

BNA Pension Reporter, Bureau of National Affairs, Inc., information service that provides weekly notification of developments under the Employee Retirement Income Security Act of 1974, including enforcement actions, court decisions, labor and industry activities, and employee benefit trust fund regulation; activities of the Department of Labor, the Internal Revenue Service, the Pension Benefit Guaranty Corporation, and Congress; and state and local government actions.

BNA Policy and Practice Series, "commonsense" guide on the handling of employer-employee relations published by the Bureau of National Affairs, Inc. Covers personnel management, labor relations, fair employment practices, wages and hours, and compensation.

Board of Regents v. Roth, 408 U.S. 564 (1972), U.S. Supreme Court case, which established the principle that a dismissed or nonrenewed public employee had no general constitutional right to either a statement of reasons or a hearing. However, both of these might be constitutionally required, the court ruled, in individual instances where any of the following four conditions existed:

1. Where the removal or nonrenewal was in retaliation for the exercise of constitutional rights such as freedom of speech or association.

2. Where the adverse action impaired the individual's reputation.

3. Perhaps not fully distinguishable from the above, where a dismissal or nonrenewal placed a stigma or other disability upon the employee which foreclosed his or her freedom to take advantage of other employment opportunities.

4. Where one had a property right or interest in the position, as in the case of tenured or contracted public employees.

Bobbs-Merrill Company, Inc.: *see* TEST PUBLISHERS.

bod biz, slang term for sensitivity training programs.

body chemistry, nebulous concept that refers to the fact that strangers, upon meeting, react to a variety of irrational and subliminal signals, which, in turn, determine whether they like each other or not.

Boeing decision: *see* NATIONAL LABOR RELATIONS BOARD V. BOEING.

bogey, easily exceeded informal standard that employees may establish in order to restrict production.

Bommarito, Peter (1915-   ), became president of the United Rubber, Cork, Linoleum and Plastic Workers of America in 1966.

bona fide occupational qualification (BFOQ or BOQ), *bona fide* is a Latin term meaning "in good faith," honest, or genuine. A BFOQ, therefore, is a *necessary* occupational qualification. Title VII of the Civil Rights Act of 1964 allows employers to discriminate against applicants on the basis of religion, sex, or national origin, when being considered for certain jobs if they lack a BFOQ. However, what constitutes a BFOQ has been interpreted very narrowly by the EEOC and the federal courts. Legitimate BFOQ's include female sex for a position as an actress or male sex for a sperm donor. There are no generally recognized BFOQ's with respect to race or color. Overall, a BFOQ is a job requirement that would be discriminatory and illegal were it not for its necessity for the performance of a particular job. For analyses, *see* Jeffery M. Shaman, "Toward Defining and Abolishing the Bona Fide Occupational Qualification Based on Class Status," *Labor Law Journal* (June 1971); Thomas Stephen Neuberger, "Sex as a Bona Fide Occupational Qualification Under Title VII," *Labor Law Journal* (July 1978).
   See also DOTHARD V. RAWLINSON.

bona fide union, union that was freely chosen by employees and that is not unreasonably or illegally influenced by their employer.

bonus, also called SUPPLEMENTAL COMPENSATION, any compensation that is in addition to regular wages and salary. Because "bonus" has a mildly paternalistic connotation, it has been replaced in some organizations by "supplemental compensation."
   See also the following entries:
   DANGER-ZONE BONUS
   NONPRODUCTION BONUS
   PRODUCTION BONUS
   STEP BONUS

boondoggle, slang term for any wasteful and/or unproductive program.

Booster Lodge No. 405, Machinists v. National Labor Relations Board, 412 U.S. 84 (1973), U.S. Supreme Court case, which held that a union's attempt to collect fines from strikers who had resigned from the union before crossing picket lines was an unfair labor practice.

Boot and Shoe Workers' Union: *see* LABOR ORGANIZATION, Food and Commercial Workers International Union, United.

bootleg wages, wages above union scale that an employer might pay in a tight labor market in order to retain and attract employees, as well as wages below union scale that an employee might accept in lieu of unemployment.

BOQ: *see* BONA FIDE OCCUPATIONAL QUALIFICATION.

Boren, James H.: *see* INTERNATIONAL ASSOCIATION OF PROFESSIONAL BUREAUCRATS.

***Borg-Warner* case:** *see* NATIONAL LABOR RELATIONS BOARD V. WOOSTER DIVISION OF BORG-WARNER CORP.

boss, slang term used by subordinates to refer to anyone from whom they are willing to take orders.

bottom-line concept, in the context of equal employment opportunity, the bottom-line concept suggests that an employer whose total selection process has no adverse impact can be assured that EEO enforcement agencies will not examine the individual components of that process for evidence of adverse impact. However, not all EEO enforcement agencies subscribe to the concept.

bottom-up management, catch-phrase describing a philosophy of participative management designed "to release the thinking and encourage the initiative of all those down from the bottom up." For the original presentation, *see* W. B. Given, Jr., *Bottom Up Management* (N.Y.: Harper & Row, 1949).

Boulding, Kenneth E. (1910-   ), economist, social scientist, and prolific author best known to organizational analysts for his classic article, "General Systems Theory—The Skeleton of Science," *Management Science* (April 1956), and his book *The Organizational Revolution* (N.Y.: Harper & Row, 1953), which deal with the relationships between organizations and ethical systems.

Boulwareism, approach to collective bargaining in which management makes a final "take-it-or-leave-it" offer that it believes is both fair and is the best it can do. The concept is named for Lemuel R. Boulware, a vice president of the General Electric Company, who pioneered the tactic in the 1950s. If the final offer is rejected by the union, management grants the benefits of the offer to all non-union workers and assures the union that there will be no retroactive benefits when the union finally accepts the "final" offer. Because this tactic called for management to communicate directly to the workers, circumventing the union, it was challenged as an unfair practice. Boulwareism, as used by General Electric, was found in violation of the National Labor Relations Act in a 1969 ruling of the U.S. Circuit Court of Appeals in New York. The company's appeal to the U.S. Supreme Court was denied. The major defense of Boulwareism is: Lemuel R. Boulware, *The Truth About Boulwareism: Trying To Do Right Voluntarily* (Washington, D.C.; Bureau of National Affairs, 1969).

bounded rationality: *see* SATISFICING.

boycott, during the mid-19th century, Charles C. Boycott, a retired English army captain, was in Ireland managing the estate of an absentee owner. His methods were so severe and oppressive that the local citizens as a group refused to deal with him in any manner. When Captain Boycott was forced to flee home to England, the first boycott or nonviolent intimidation through ostracism was a success.

In the context of labor relations, a boycott is any refusal to deal with or buy the products of a business as a means of exerting pressure in a labor dispute. The U.S. Supreme Court has consistently held that boycotts are an illegal "restraint of trade" under the Sherman Antitrust Act of 1890.

See also the following entries:

LAWLOR V. LOEWE
NATIONAL WOODWORK MANUFACTURES ASSOCIATION V. NATIONAL LABOR RELATIONS BOARD
PRIMARY BOYCOTT
SECONDARY BOYCOTT
UNITED STATES V. HUTCHESON

Boyle, (W. A.) "Tony" (1904-), John L. Lewis' handpicked successor, president of the United Mine Workers from 1963 to 1972. After conspiring to kill "Jock" Yablonski, a union rival, he was convicted on three counts of first degree murder for the 1969 deaths of Yablonski, his wife, and daughter.

Boys Market* v. *Retail Clerks' Local 770, 398 U.S. 235 (1970), U.S. Supreme Court case, which held that when a labor contract has a no-strike provision and provides an arbitration procedure, a federal court may, upon the request of an employer, issue an injunction to terminate a strike by employees covered by such a contract. This reversed an earlier decision, *Sinclair Refining* v. *Atkinson*, 370 U.S. 195 (1962), that forbade federal courts from issuing injunctions to stop a strike in violation of a no-strike clause. For an analysis, *see*

John A. Relias, "The Developing Law Under Boys Markets," *Labor Law Journal* (December 1972).

BPI: *see* BERNREUTER PERSONALITY INVENTORY.

bracero program, or BRACERO SYSTEM, during World War II, the farm manpower shortage was so great that Mexican field hands or braceros were imported as seasonal farm workers. The practice, sanctioned by law in 1951, was long opposed by organized labor and was terminated by Congress in 1964. Since that time, however, an informal and unofficial bracero program has evolved from the large numbers of illegal aliens coming into the United States from Mexico.

See also UNDOCUMENTED WORKERS.

Bradford, Leland P. (1905-), director of the National Training Laboratories from 1947 to 1967, who pioneered the development of "sensitivity" training. Major Works include: *T-Group Theory and Laboratory Method: Innovation in Re-Education*, co-editor (N.Y.: John Wiley, 1964); *Making Meetings Work: A Guide for Leaders & Group Members* (San Diego, Calif.: University Associates, 1976).

brain drain, pejorative term referring to the unfortunate flow of human capital—talent—from a country or an organization. While historically used to describe the exodus of doctors, scientists, and other professionals from a particular country, it is colloquially used to refer to the departure of any valued employee or group of employees. *See* Walter Adams (ed.), *The Brain Drain* (N.Y.: Macmillan, 1968).

brainstorming, frequently used to describe any group effort to generate ideas. It has a more formal definition—a creative conference for the sole purpose of producing suggestions or ideas that can serve as leads to problem solving. The concept has been most developed by Alex Osborn. See his *Applied Imagination* (N.Y.: Charles Scribner's Sons, 1963). For a how-to-do-it account, *see* Ronald H. Gorman and H. Kent Baker, "Brainstorming Your Way to Problem-Solving Ideas," *Personnel Journal* (August 1978).

BRASC: *see* LABOR ORGANIZATION, Railway, Airline and Steamship Clerks, Freight Handlers, Express and Station Employees, Brotherhood of.

brass, slang term of military origin which now refers to the key executives in an organization.

BRC: *see* LABOR ORGANIZATION, Railway Carmen of the United States and Canada, Brotherhood of.

breach of contract, violation of a collective bargaining agreement by either party. If established grievance machinery is not adequate to deal with the dispute, traditional lawsuits remain as a remedy.

bread-and-butter unions: *see* BUSINESS UNIONS.

breakdown: *see* NERVOUS BREAKDOWN.

Brennen, Peter J. (1918-   ), Secretary of Labor from 1973 to 1975.

Brick and Clay Workers of America, The United (AFL-CIO): *see* LABOR ORGANIZATION.

Bricklayers and Allied Craftsmen, International Union of (AFL-CIO): *see* LABOR ORGANIZATION.

bridge job, position specifically designed to facilitate the movement of individuals from one classification and/or job category to another classification and/or category. Such bridge jobs are an integral part of many career ladders and upward mobility programs.

Bridges, Harry (1901-   ), full name ALFRED BRYANT RENTON BRIDGES, president of the International Longshoremen's and Warehousemen's Union since 1937, who has, because of suggested Communist leanings, been one of the most controversial of U.S. labor leaders. For a biography, *see* Charles P. Larrowe, *Harry Bridges: The Rise and Fall of Radical Labor in the U.S.* (N.Y.: Lawrence Hill and Co., 2nd ed. rev., 1977).

Broadcast Employees and Technicians, National Association of (AFL-CIO): *see* LABOR ORGANIZATION.

Brookings Institution, nonprofit organization devoted to research, education, and publication in economics, government, foreign policy, and the social sciences generally. In its research, it functions as an independent analyst and critic, committed to publishing its findings for the information of the public. In its conferences and other activities, it serves as a bridge between scholarship and public policy, bringing new knowledge to the attention of decision makers and affording scholars a better insight into policy issues. The Institution's Advanced Study Program is devoted to public policy education of leaders in both government and business.

Brookings Institution
1775 Massachusetts Avenue, N.W.
Washington, DC 20036
(202) 797-6000

broken time, or SPLIT SHIFT, daily work schedule that is divided by a length of time considerably in excess of the time required for a normal meal break. For example, a school bus driver may work from 6 to 10 a.m. and then from 2 to 6 p.m.

brotherhood, term used by some of the older unions as an indication of solidarity and common interests. For example, the Brotherhood of Railroad Signalmen.

Brotherhood of Locomotive Engineers: *see* LABOR ORGANIZATION, Locomotive Engineers, Brotherhood of.

Brotherhood of Maintenance of Way Employees: *see* LABOR ORGANIZATION, Maintenance of Way Employees, Brotherhood of.

Brotherhood of Railroad Signalmen: *see* LABOR ORGANIZATION, Railroad Signalmen, Brotherhood of.

Brotherhood of Railway, Airline and Steamship Clerks, Freight Handlers, Express and Station Employees: *see* LABOR ORGANIZATION, Railway, Airline and Steamship Clerks, Freight Handlers, Express and Station Employees, Brotherhood of.

Brotherhood of Railway Carmen of the United States and Canada: *see* LABOR ORGANIZATION, Railway Carmen of the United States and Canada, Brotherhood of.

Brotherhood of Shoe and Allied Craftsmen: *see* LABOR ORGANIZATION, Shoe and Allied Craftsmen, Brotherhood of.

Brotherhood of Sleeping Car Porters: *see* LABOR ORGANIZATION, Sleeping Car Porters, Brotherhood of.

Brotherhood of Utility Workers of New England, Inc.: *see* LABOR ORGANIZATION, Utility Workers of New England, Inc., Brotherhood of.

Brown v. *General Services Administration*, 425 U.S. 820 (1976), U.S. Supreme Court case, which held that Congress intended Title VII of the Civil Rights Act of 1964 to provide the sole statutory protection against employment discrimination for federal employees—even though it is not the sole protection for workers in the private sector.

brown lung disease, scientific name BYSSINOSIS, chronic and disabling lung disease that affects workers in cotton mills. *See* Mary Lee Gosney, "Whatever Happened to Brown Lung? Compensation for Difficult to Diagnose Occupational Diseases," *Industrial Relations Law Journal*, Vol. 3, No. 1 (1979).

BRS: *see* LABOR ORGANIZATION, Railroad Signalmen, Brotherhood of.

BSAC: *see* LABOR ORGANIZATION, Shoe and Allied Craftsmen, Brotherhood of.

BSCP: *see* LABOR ORGANIZATION, Sleeping Car Porters, Brotherhood of.

BSIW: *see* LABOR ORGANIZATION, Iron Workers, International Association of Bridge and Structural.

BSW: *see* LABOR ORGANIZATION, Food and Commercial Workers International Union, United.

buckology, basic technique for evading responsibility. *See* R. C. Burkholder, "Buckology: The Art and Science of Passing the Buck," *Supervision* (March 1978).

buddy system, on-the-job training technique that has a trainee assigned to work closely with an experienced worker until the trainee has gained enough experience to work alone.

budget, financial plan serving as a pattern for and control over future operations—hence, any estimate of future costs or any systematic plan for the utilization of the workforce, material, or other resources. Budgets are short-range segments of action programs that set out planned accomplishments and estimate the resources to be applied for the budget periods in order to attain those accomplishments.

budgeting, the process of translating planning and programming decisions into specific projected financial plans for relatively short periods of time.

Buffalo Forge Co. v. United Steelworkers, 423 U.S. 911 (1976), U.S. Supreme Court case, which held that federal courts were permitted to enjoin a strike over a nonarbitrable issue pending an arbitrator's decision on whether the strike violates a no-strike pledge in a collective bargaining contract.

buggin's turn, British phrase for promotion based on seniority rather than merit.

bump, or BUMPING, layoff procedure that gives an employee with greater seniority the right to displace or "bump" another employee. Sometimes bumping rights are restricted to one plant, office, or department. Because of legally guaranteed bumping rights, the laying off of a single worker can lead to the sequential transfers of a dozen others.

burden of proof, requirement that a party to an issue show that the weight of evidence is on his or her side in order to have the issue decided in his or her favor.

bureau, government department, agency or subdivision of same.

bureaucracy, while bureaucracy is used as a general invective to refer to any inefficient organization, its more formal usage has it referring to a specific set of structural arrangements. The dominant structural definition of bureaucracy, indeed the point of departure for all further analyses on the subject, is that of the German sociologist, Max Weber. Drawing upon studies of ancient bureaucracies in Egypt, Rome, China, and the Byzantine Empire, as well as on the more modern ones emerging in Europe during the 19th and early part of the 20th centuries, Weber used an "ideal type" approach to extrapolate from the real world the central core of features that would characterize the most fully developed bureaucratic form of organization. This "ideal type" is neither a description of reality nor a statement of normative preference. It is merely an identification of the major variables or features that characterize bureaucracy. The fact that such features might not be fully present in a given organization does not necessarily imply that the organization is "non-bureaucratic." It may be an immature rather than a fully developed bureaucracy. At some point, however, it may be necessary to conclude that the characteristics of bureaucracy are so lacking in an organization that it could neither reasonably be termed bureaucratic nor be expected to produce patterns of bureaucratic behavior.

Weber's "ideal type" bureaucracy possesses the following characteristics:

1. The bureaucrats must be personally free and subject to authority only with respect to the impersonal duties of their offices.
2. They are arranged in a clearly defined hierarchy of offices.
3. The functions of each office are clearly specified.
4. Officials accept and maintain their appointments freely—without duress.
5. Appointments are made on the basis of

technical qualifications which ideally are substantiated by examinations—administered by the appointing authority, a university, or both.

6. Officials should have a money salary as well as pension rights. Such salaries must reflect the varying levels of positions in the hierarchy. While officials are always free to leave the organization, they can be removed from their offices only under previously stated specific circumstances.

7. An incumbent's post must be his sole or at least his major occupation.

8. A career system is essential. While promotion may be the result of either seniority or merit, it must be premised on the judgment of hierarchical superiors.

9. The official may not have a property right to his position nor any personal claim to the resources which go with it.

10. An official's conduct must be subject to systematic control and strict discipline.

While Weber's structural identification of bureaucratic organization (first published in 1922) is perhaps the most comprehensive statement on the subject in the literature of the social sciences, it is not always considered satisfactory as an intellectual construct. For example, Anthony Downs, in *Inside Bureaucracy* (Boston: Little, Brown, 1967), argues that at least two elements should be added to Weber's definition. First, the organization must be large. According to Downs, "any organization in which the highest ranking members know less than half of the other members can be considered large." Second, most of the organization's output cannot be "directly or indirectly evaluated in any markets external to the organization by means of voluntary *quid pro quo* transactions."

Definitions of bureaucracy apply equally to organizations in the public as well as the private sector. However, public sector bureaucracies tend to operate in a somewhat different climate from those in the private sector. What has come to be known as the "third sector"—not-for-profit organizations such as hospitals, universities, and foundations—would analytically be classed with public organizations because of the lack of free-market forces upon them. In short, bureaucracy is best conceptualized as a specific form of organization, and public bureaucracy should be considered a special variant of bureaucratic organization.

For further information, *see* M. Albrow, *Bureaucracy* (New York: Praeger, 1970); Peter Blau, and M. Meyer, *Bureaucracy in Modern Society* (New York: Random House, 2nd ed., 1971); R. Fried, *Performance in*

American Bureaucracy (Boston: Little, Brown, 1976); H. H. Gerth, and C. Wright Mills (eds.), *From Max Weber: Essays in Sociology* (New York: Oxford University Press, 1958).

See also the following entries:

NATIONAL ASSOCIATION OF PROFESSIONAL BUREAUCRATS
POSTBUREAUCRATIC ORGANIZATIONS
REALPOLITIK
REPRESENTATIVE BUREAUCRACY
WEBER, MAX

bureaucrat, denizen of a bureaucracy.
See also APPARATCHIK.

Bureau of International Labor Affairs, agency of the Department of Labor that assists in formulating international economic and trade policies affecting U.S. workers. It administers the trade adjustment assistance program under the Trade Act of 1974, which provides special benefits for workers adversely affected by import competition. It helps represent the U.S. in multilateral and bilateral trade negotiations and on such international bodies as the General Agreement on Tariffs and Trade, the International Labor Organization and the Organization for Economic Cooperation and Development. The Bureau also helps provide direction to U.S. labor attaches at embassies abroad, carries out technical assistance projects overseas, and arranges trade union exchange and other programs for foreign visitors to the U.S.

Bureau of International Labor Affairs
Department of Labor
200 Constitutional Ave. N.W.
Washington, DC 20210
(202) 523-8165

Bureau of Labor Statistics (BLS), agency responsible for the economic and statistical research activities of the Department of Labor. The BLS is the government's principal factfinding agency in the field of labor economics, particularly with respect to the collection and analysis of data on manpower and labor requirements, labor force, employment, unemployment, hours of work, wages and employee compensation, prices, living conditions, labor–management relations, productivity and technological developments, occupational safety and health, structure and growth of the economy, urban conditions and related socio-economic issues, and international aspects of certain of these subjects.

It has no enforcement or administrative functions. Practically all of the basic data it collects from workers, businesses, and from other governmental agencies are supplied by voluntary cooperation based on their interest in and need for the analyses and summaries that result. The research and statistical projects planned grow out of the needs of these groups, as well as the needs of Congress and the federal and state governments. The information collected is issued in monthly press releases, in special publications, and in its official publication, the *Monthly Labor Review*. Other major BLS periodicals include: *The Consumer Price Index, Wholesale Prices and Price Indexes, Employment and Earnings, Current Wage Developments, Occupational Outlook Handbook*, and *Occupational Outlook Quarterly*. For a history, *see* Jonathan Grossman and Judson MacLaury, "The Creation of the Bureau of Labor Statistics," *Monthly Labor Review* (February 1975).

Bureau of Labor Statistics
441 G Street N.W.
Washington, DC 20210
(202) 523-1221

Bureau of National Affairs, Inc. (BNA), the largest private employer of information specialists in the nation's capital. Its function is to report, analyze, and explain the activities of the federal government and the courts to those persons who are directly affected—educators, attorneys, labor relations practitioners, business executives, accountants, union officials, personnel administrators, and scores of others. The BNA organization is universally recognized as a leading source of authoritative information services. It's labor information reports and services include:

> Affirmative Action Compliance Manual for Federal Contractors
> BNA Pension Reporter
> BNA Policy and Practice Series
> Collective Bargaining Negotiations & Contracts
> Construction Labor Report
> Daily Labor Report
> EEOC Compliance Manual
> Employment and Training Reporter
> Fair Employment Practice Service
> Government Employee Relations Report
> Government Manager, The
> Labor Arbitration Reports
> Labor Relations Reporter
> Retail/Services Labor Report
> Union Labor Report
> White Collar Report

BNA Communications, Inc. produces employee communication, motivational, and supervisory and sales training films, case studies for management development, and related instructional materials.

Bureau of National Affairs, Inc.
1231 25th Street, N.W.
Washington, DC 20037
(202) 452-4500

bureaupathology, term used by Victor A. Thompson, in *Modern Organization* (N.Y.: Knopf, 1960), to describe the pathological or dysfunctional aspects of bureaucracy. According to Thompson, the

> bureaupathic official usually exaggerates the official, non-technical aspects of relationships and suppresses the technical and the informal. He stresses rights, not abilities. Since his behavior stems from insecurity, he may be expected to insist on petty rights and prerogatives, on protocol, on procedure—in short, on those things least likely to affect directly the goal accomplishment of the organization. For example, a rather functionless reviewing officer will often insist most violently on his right of review and scream like an injured animal if he is by-passed. He will often insist on petty changes, such as minor changes in the wording of a document. If he has a counterpart at a higher organizational level, he will probably insist on exclusive contact with that higher clearance point. By controlling this particular communication channel he protects his authority and influence.

***Burns* decision:** *see* NATIONAL LABOR RELATIONS BOARD V. BURNS INTERNATIONAL SECURITY SERVICES.

business agent, full-time officer of a local union, elected or appointed, who handles grievances, helps enforce agreements, and otherwise deals with the union's financial, administrative, or labor–management problems.

business games: *see* MANAGEMENT GAMES.

business necessity, the major legal defense for using an employment practice that effectively excludes women and/or minorities. The leading court case, *Robinson v. Lorrilard Corp.*, 444 F.2d 791 (4th Cir. 1971); *cert. denied*, 404 U.S. 1006 (1971), holds that the test of the business necessity defense

> is whether there exists an overriding legitimate business purpose such that the practice is necessary to the safe and efficient operation of the business. Thus, the business purpose must be sufficiently compelling to override any racial impact; the challenged practice must effectively carry out the business purpose it is alleged to serve; and there must be available no acceptable alternative policies or practices which would better accomplish the business purpose advanced, or accomplish it equally well with a lesser differential racial impact.

business unions also called BREAD-AND-BUTTER UNIONS, the conservative U.S. trade unions have been called "bread-and-butter" or "business" unions because they have tended to concentrate on gaining better wages and working conditions for their members rather than devote significant efforts on political action as many European unions have done. For a historical analysis, *see* Philip Taft, "On the Origins of Business Unionism," *Industrial and Labor Relations Review* (October 1963).

buzz group, device that seeks to give all the individuals at a large meeting an equal opportunity to participate by breaking the larger meeting into small groups of from six to eight persons each. These "buzz groups" then designate one person each to report on their consensus (and dissents if any) when the total group reconvenes.

buzzwords, Robert Kirk Mueller, in *Buzzwords: A Guide to the Language of Leaderships* (N.Y.: Van Nostrand Reinhold Co., 1974), credits the late Professor Ralph Hower of Harvard for first using "buzzwords" to mean "those phrases that have a pleasant buzzing sound in your ears while you roll them on your tongue and that may overwhelm you into believing you know what you're talking about when you don't." In spite of this "formal" definition, the technical vocabularies of any occupational specialty are often referred to as buzzwords.

Byrnes Act: *see* ANTI-STRIKEBREAKER ACT OF 1936.

byte, in computer terminology, a byte is usually the smallest possible unit of information storage.

C

cafeteria benefits plan, also called SMOR-GASBORD BENEFITS PLAN, any program that allows employees to choose their fringe benefits within the limits of the total benefit dollars for which they are eligible. This allows each employee to have, in effect, his own individualized benefit program. Because such programs cost more to administer, they tend to exist mainly as part of high-level, managerial compensation packages. However, increasing computer capabilities will make it increasingly likely that such plans will be more widely offered. See George W. Hettenhouse, "Compensation Cafeteria for Top Executives," *Harvard Business Review* (September-October 1971); Robert V. Goode, "Complications at the Cafeteria Checkout Line," *Personnel* (November-December 1974).

Cahan, Abraham (1860-1951), journalist, novelist, and socialist, who was one of the most powerful voices for the union movement during the early part of this century.

California Labor Federation: *see* AMERICAN FEDERATION OF LABOR–CONGRESS OF INDUSTRIAL ORGANIZATIONS.

California Management Review (CMR), quarterly that seeks to serve as a bridge between creative thought about management and executive action. An authoritative source of information and ideas contributing to the advancement of management science, it is directed to active managers, scholars, teachers, and others concerned with management.

> *California Management Review*
> Graduate School of Business Administration
> 350 Barrows Hall
> University of California
> Berkeley, CA 94720

COPSystem: *see* CALIFORNIA OCCUPATIONAL PREFERENCE SURVEY.

California Occupational Preference Survey, also called COPSYSTEM, self-report inventory of job activity interest. Scores used in vocational guidance and counseling. Areas of interest measured include science, technology, business, outdoors, clerical, arts, communication, and service-oriented professions. TIME: 30/40 minutes. AUTHORS: R. R. Knopp, Bruce Grant, G. D. Demos. PUBLISHER: Educational and Industrial Testing Service (*see* TEST PUBLISHERS).

California Psychological Inventory (CPI), 480-item true/false questionnaire that measures the personality characteristics of normal (non-psychiatrically disturbed) individuals. TIME: 45/60 minutes. AUTHOR: Harrison G. Gough. PUBLISHER: Consulting Psychologists Press, Inc.

California Short Form Test of Mental Maturity (CTMM/SF), intelligence test that measures functional capacities basic to learning, problemsolving, and responding to new situations. It is a shortened version of the California Test of Mental Maturity (CTMM) and omits the measure of spatial relationships. TIME: 45 minutes. AUTHORS: Elizabeth Sullivan, Willis W. Clark, and Ernest Tiegs. PUBLISHER: California Test Bureau/McGraw-Hill (*see* TEST PUBLISHERS).

California State Employees' Association: *see* LABOR ORGANIZATION.

California Test Bureau: *see* TEST PUBLISHERS.

California Test of Mental Maturity (CTMM), intelligence test that measures functional capacities basic to learning, problemsolving, and responding to new situations (*i.e.*, logical reasoning, spatial relationships, numerical reasoning, verbal concepts, and memory). TIME: 90 minutes. AUTHORS: Elizabeth Sullivan, Willis W. Clark, and Ernest W. Tiegs. PUBLISHER: California Test Bureau/McGraw-Hill.

call-back pay, compensation, often at premium rates, paid to workers called back on the job after completing their normal shift. Contract provisions often provide for a minimum number of hours of call-back pay regardless of the number of hours actually worked.

call-in pay, wages or hours of pay guaranteed to workers (usually by contract provision) who, upon reporting to work, find no work to do.

CAL-SEA: see LABOR ORGANIZATION, California State Employees' Association.

Campbell, Alan K. (1923-   ), nickname SCOTTY, the last chairman of the U.S. Civil Service Commission, who became the first director of the Office of Personnel Management in 1979.

Canadian Labour Congress (CLC), Canadian counterpart of the AFL-CIO.

candidate, applicant for a position.

candidate population, all of the individuals who apply for a particular position.

Cannon v. Guste, 423 U.S. 918 (1975), U.S. Supreme Court case, which held that a Louisiana statute requiring state civil service employees to retire at age 65 violated neither the due process nor the equal protection clause of the 14th Amendment.

capacity building, term used to refer to any system, effort, or process—including a federal grant or contract—which includes among its major objectives strengthening the capability of elected chief executive officers, chief administrative officers, department and agency heads, and program managers in general purpose government to plan, implement, manage or evaluate policies, strategies or programs designed to impact on social conditions in the community. For a discussion, see William A. Jones, Jr., and C. Bradley Doss, Jr., "Local Officials' Reaction to Federal 'Capacity Building'," *Public Administration Review* (January–February 1978).

CAPE: see COALITION OF AMERICAN PUBLIC EMPLOYEES.

captive shop, any production unit whose output is used almost entirely by the company owning it.

career, total work history of an individual. Harold L. Wilensky has defined career in structural terms as "a succession of related jobs, arranged in a hierarchy of prestige,

through which persons move in an ordered (more - or - less predictable) sequence," in his article, "Orderly Careers and Social Participation: The Impact of Work History on Social Integration in the Middle Mass" from the *American Sociological Review*, (August 1961). For an analysis of the career interactions between individuals and their organizations, see Edgar H. Schein, "The Individual, the Organization, and the Career: A Conceptual Scheme," *Journal of Applied Behavioral Science* (July–August 1971)

career appointment: see APPOINTMENT.

career change, occurs when individuals break with their present careers in order to enter other fields. For analyses, see Marie R. Haug and Marvin B. Sussman "The Second Career—Variant of a Sociological Concept," *Journal of Gerontology*, Vol. 23 (1967); Dale L. Hiestand, *Changing Careers after Thirty-five* (New York: Columbia University Press, 1971); Rimantas Vaitenas and Yoash Weiner, "Developmental, Emotional, and Interest Factors in Voluntary Mid-Career Change," *Journal of Vocational Behavior*, Vol. 11 (1977).

career-conditional appointment: see APPOINTMENT.

career counseling, guidance provided to employees in order to assist them in achieving occupational training, education, and career goals. See Andrew H. Souerwine, *Career Strategies: Planning for Personal Achievement* (N.Y.: AMACOM, 1978).

career curve: see MATURITY CURVE.

career decisionmaking, or OCCUPATIONAL DECISIONMAKING, evaluation process that leads to a choice of an occupation for an individual to pursue. See Martin Katz, "A Model of Guidance for Career Decision-Making," *Vocational Guidance Quarterly* (September 1966); Donald R. Kaldor and Donald G. Zytowski, "A Maximizing Model of Occupational Decision-Making," *Personnel and Guidance Journal* (April 1969).

career ladder, series of classifications in which an employee may advance through training and/or on-the-job experience into successively higher levels of responsibility and salary.

career management, aspect of personnel management that is concerned with the occupational growth of individuals within an organization. See Marion S. Kellogg, *Career*

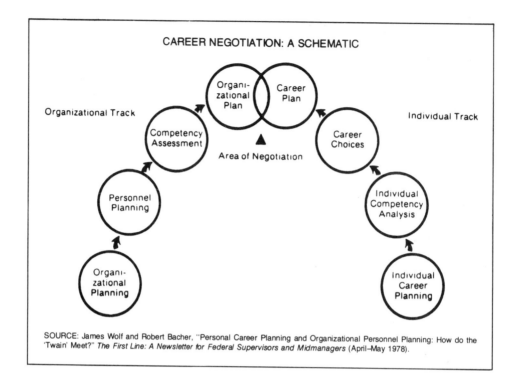

CAREER NEGOTIATION: A SCHEMATIC

Organizational Track

Individual Track

Organi-zational Plan

Career Plan

Competency Assessment

Career Choices

Area of Negotiation

Personnel Planning

Individual Competency Analysis

Organi-zational Planning

Individual Career Planning

SOURCE: James Wolf and Robert Bacher, "Personal Career Planning and Organizational Personnel Planning: How do the 'Twain' Meet?" *The First Line: A Newsletter for Federal Supervisors and Midmanagers* (April–May 1978).

Management (N.Y.: American Management Association, Inc., 1972); Douglas T. Hall and Francine S. Hall, "What's New in Career Management," *Organizational Dynamics* (Summer 1976); Edward O. Joslin, "Career Management: How to Make it Work," *Personnel* (July–August 1977).

career negotiation, that aspect of career planning that has both the individual employee and the organization, in the light of their respective interests and needs, develop (negotiate) a career plan that serves both parties.

career path, direction of an individual's career as indicated by career milestones. An employee following a career path may proceed up a single career ladder and then beyond it into supervisory or executive position, or an employee may move from one career ladder to another. *See* Joseph J. Wnuk, Jr., "Career Paths," *Training and Development Journal* (May 1970); James W. Walker, "Let's Get Realistic About Career Paths," *Human Resource Management* (Fall 1976); Donald Grass, "A Guide to R & D Career Pathing," *Personnel Journal* (April 1979).

career pattern, sequence of occupations of an individual or group of individuals. The study of career patterns has spawned the theory

that an individual's work history is good predictor of future vocational behavior. For the pioneering research, *see* William H. Form and Delbert C. Miller, "Occupational Career Pattern as a Sociological Instrument," *American Journal of Sociology* (January 1949); Donald E. Super, "Career Patterns as a Basis for Vocational Counseling," *Journal of Counseling Psychology*, Vol. 1, No 1 (1954).

career planning, according to James W. Walker, "Does Career Planning Rock the Boat," *Human Resources Management* (Spring 1978), career planning

> is the personal process of planning one's life work. It entails evaluating abilities and interests, considering alternative career opportunities, establishing career goals and planning practical development activities. The process results in decisions to enter a certain occupation, join a particular company, accept or decline job opportunities (relocations, promotions or transfers, etc.) and ultimately leave a company for another job or for retirement.

Also see Charles E. Okosky, "Career Planning," *Personnel Journal* (November 1973); Sam Gould, "Career Planning in the Organization," *Human Resource Management* (Spring 1978).

career promotion, promotion made on the

basis of merit, but without competition with other employees. An example is the promotion of an employee who, as he or she learns more about the job, can do more difficult kinds of work and assume greater responsibility, so that he or she is performing duties classified at a higher grade level.

career system, sequence of progressively more responsible positions in the same general occupation that an organization makes available to qualified individuals.

Carpenters and Joiners of America, United Brotherhood of: *see* LABOR ORGANIZATION.

Cary v. *Westinghouse Electric Corp.*, 375 U.S. 261 (1964), U.S. Supreme Court case, which held that disputes involving work assignments were arbitrable.

Case Co. v. *National Labor Relations Board:* *see* J. I. CASE CO. V. NATIONAL LABOR RELATIONS BOARD.

casual labor, employees that are (1) essentially unskilled, (2) used only a few days at a time, or (3) needed seasonally.

catalyst: *see* CHANGE AGENT.

Cattell Culture Fair Intelligence Test, basic general intelligence test. Scores are relatively free of educational and cultural influences, desirable where environmental factors may unduly influence conventional test scores. Particularly useful for relating intelligence to achievement, educational, and vocational guidance, testing of foreign-speaking/ bilingual subjects, immigrant testing and cross-cultural studies. TIME: 30/60 minutes. AUTHORS: Raymond B. and A. K. S. Cattell. PUBLISHER: Bobbs-Merrill Company, Inc. (*see* TEST PUBLISHERS).

cause, short form of "just cause," reason given for removing someone from an office or job. The cause cited may or may not be the real reason for the removal.

CCH: *see* COMMERCE CLEARING HOUSE, INC.

CEA: *see* COUNCIL OF ECONOMIC ADVISERS.

cease-and-desist order, ruling, frequently issued in unfair labor practice cases, which requires the charged party to stop conduct held to be illegal and take specific action to remedy the unfair labor practice.

ceiling, upper limit of ability measured by a test. A test has a low ceiling for a given population if many examinees obtained perfect scores; it has a high ceiling if there are few or no perfect scores.

ceiling, job or position: *see* JOB CEILING.

Cement, Lime and Gypsum Workers International Union, United: *see* LABOR ORGANIZATION.

Center for Political Studies: *see* INSTITUTE FOR SOCIAL RESEARCH.

Center for Research on Utilization of Scientific Knowledge: *see* INSTITUTE FOR SOCIAL RESEARCH.

Central Hardware Co. v. *National Labor Relations Board*, 407 U.S. 539 (1972), U.S. Supreme Court case, which held that nonemployee organizers seeking to solicit on an employer's private property must show that the property has assumed some of the characteristics of public property and that no reasonable alternative means of reaching the employees is available.

central hiring hall: *see* HIRING HALL.

central labor union, association of local labor unions in a specific geographic region.

central tendency, series of statistical measures that provide a representative value for a distribution, or, more simply, refer to how scores tend to cluster in a distribution. The most common measures of central tendency are the mean, median, and the mode.

CEO: *see* CHIEF EXECUTIVE OFFICER.

Ceramic Workers of North America: *see* LABOR ORGANIZATION, Glass and Ceramic Workers of North America, United.

certification, formal determination by the National Labor Relations Board or other administrative agency that a particular union is the majority choice, and thus the exclusive bargaining agent, for a group of employees in a given bargaining unit. *Decertification* is the opposite process where an administrative agency withdraws a union's official designation as the exclusive bargaining agent. In both cases, these actions are usually preceded by a formal polling of the union membership.

See also OCCUPATIONAL CERTIFICATION.

certification of eligibles, procedure whereby those who have passed competitive civil service examinations have their names ranked in order of score and placed on a list of those eligible for appointment. When a government agency has a vacancy, it requests its personnel arm to provide a list of eligibles for the class to which the vacant position has been allocated. The personnel agency then "certifies" the names of the highest ranking eligibles to the appointing authority for possible selection. Usually, only a limited number of the qualified eligibles are certified. When a jurisdiction requires that three eligibles be certified to the appointing authority, this is referred to as the "rule of three". For an overview, *see* Carmen D. Saso and Earl P. Tanis, *Selection and Certification of Eligibles: A Survey of Policies and Practices* (Chicago: International Personnel Management Association, 1974).

certification proceeding, process by which the National Labor Relations Board discovers whether or not the employees of an organization want a particular union to represent them.

certified employee organization, union that an administrative agency has certified as the official representative of the employees in a bargaining unit for the purpose of collective negotiations. Such certification is usually the direct result of a representation election.

Certified Public Accountant (CPA), accountant certified by a state government as having met specific educational and experience requirements.

certiorari, order or writ from a higher court demanding that a lower court send up the record of a case for review. Except for a few instances of original jurisdiction, most cases that reach the U.S. Supreme Court do so because the Supreme Court itself has issued such a writ or "granted certiorari." If certiorari is denied by the Supreme Court, it means that the justices are content to let the lower-court decision stand.

CETA: *see* COMPREHENSIVE EMPLOYMENT AND TRAINING ACT OF 1973.

CFI: *see* WLW CULTURE FAIR INVENTORY.

CFR: *see* CODE OF FEDERAL REGULATIONS.

Chaikin, Sol C. (1918-   ), became president of the International Ladies' Garment Workers' Union in 1975.

chain picketing, continuous, moving human chain sometimes formed by striking workers to prevent anyone from crossing their picket line.

chance score, score that has a significant probability of occurring on the basis of random selection of answers.

Chandler v. *Roudebush*, 425 U.S. 840 (1976), U.S. Supreme Court case, which held federal employees, after exhausting all administrative remedies concerning a claim of sexual and/or racial discrimination, have the same right to a trial *de novo* in the federal courts as is enjoyed by other employees under the Civil Rights Act of 1964 as amended.

change agent, or CATALYST, descriptive ways of referring to organization development consultants or facilitators. *See* Lee Grossman, *The Change Agent* (N.Y.: AMACOM, 1974).

charging party, any individual who formally asserts that he or she is aggrieved because of an unlawful employment practice.

charismatic leadership, leadership that is based on the compelling personality of the leader rather than upon formal position.

Chavez, Cesar (Estrada) (1927-   ), leader of the United Farm Workers' Union and its predecessor organization (the National Farm Workers Association) since 1962, who is nationally known for his tactic of calling for grape and lettuce boycotts. For biographies, *see* Joan London and Henry Anderson, *So Shall Ye Reap: The Story of Cesar Chavez and the Farm Workers Movement* (N.Y.: Crowell 1970); George D. Horwitz, *La Causa: The California Grape Strike* (N.Y.: Macmillan, 1970); Ronald B. Taylor, *Chavez and the Farm Workers* (Boston: Beacon Press, 1975).

checkoff, union security provision, commonly provided for in the collective bargaining agreement, that allows the employer to deduct union dues, assessments, and initiation fees from the pay of all union members. The deducted amounts are delivered to the union on a prearranged schedule. The Labor–Management Relations (Taft–Hartley) Act of 1947 requires that union members must give written permission for these fees to be deducted.

checkoff, compulsory: AUTOMATIC CHECKOFF.

Chemical Workers Union, International: *see* LABOR ORGANIZATION.

Chesser, Al H. (1914-   ), became president of the United Transportation Union in 1971.

chief executive officer (CEO), individual who is personally accountable to the board of directors or the electorate for the activities of the organization or the jurisdiction. *See* Chris Argyris, "The CEO's Behavior: Key to Organizational Development," *Harvard Business Review* (March-April 1973); Robert H. Rock, *The Chief Executive Officer* (N.Y., D.C. Heath-Lexington Books, 1977).

chief steward, union representative who supervises the activities of a group of shop stewards.

chi-square, statistical procedure that estimates whether the observed values in a distribution differ from the expected distribution and thus may be attributable to the operation of factors other than chance. Particular values of chi-square are usually identified by the symbol χ^2.

childbirth: *see* PREGNANCY.

child labor, employment of children below the legal age limit. The Fair Labor Standards Act of 1938 (as amended) contains strong child-labor prohibitions. For histories of the horrendous conditions that led to the passage of federal and state child labor prohibitions, *see* Jeremy P. Felt, *Hostages of Fortune: Child Labor Reform in New York State* (Syracuse, N.Y.: Syracuse University Press, 1965); Walter I. Trattner, *Crusade for the Children: A History of the National Child Labor Committee and Child Labor Reform in America* (Chicago: Quadrangel Books, 1970); Ronald B. Taylor, *Sweatshops in the Sun: Child Labor on the Farm* (Boston: Beacon Press, 1973).

See also FAIR LABOR STANDARDS ACT and WORKING PAPERS.

chilling effect, employment practices, government regulations, court decisions, or legislation (or the threat of these) may create an inhibiting atmosphere or chilling effect that prevents the free exercise of individual employment rights. A "chilling" effect tends to keep minorities and women from seeking employment and advancement in an organization even in the absence of formal bars. Other chilling effects may be positive or negative, depending upon the "chillee's" perspective. For example, even discussion of proposed regulations can "chill" employers or unions into compliance.

Christian Labor Association of the United States of America: *see* LABOR ORGANIZATION.

Christmas bonus: *see* NONPRODUCTION BONUS.

chronic unemployment, unemployment lasting longer than six months.

CIO: *see* (1) CONGRESS OF INDUSTRIAL ORGANIZATIONS and (2) AMERICAN FEDERATION OF LABOR-CONGRESS OF INDUSTRIAL ORGANIZATIONS.

circuit court of appeals: *see* COURT OF APPEALS.

citizenship, U.S., a requirement for public employment in some jurisdictions. For a discussion of recent court rulings, *see* Arnold L. Steigman, "Public Administration by Litigation: The Impact of Court Decisions Concerning Citizenship on Public Personnel Management," *Public Personnel Management* (March–April 1979).

See also the following entries:
AMBACH V. NORWICK
FOLEY V. CONNELIE
HAMPTON V. MOW SUN WONG
SUGARMAN V. DOUGALL

City of Los Angeles, Department of Water & Power* v. *Manhart, 55 L.Ed.2d 657 (1978), U.S. Supreme Court case, which held that a pension plan requiring female employees to contribute more from their wages to gain the same pension benefits as male employees was in violation of Title VII of the Civil Rights Act 1964. While the actual statistics were undisputed (women live longer than men), the court reasoned that Title VII prohibits treating individuals "as simply components of a racial, religious, sexual or national class."

CIU: *see* LABOR ORGANIZATION, (1) Coopers' International Union of North America and (2) Independent Unions, Congress of.

civilian labor force: *see* LABOR FORCE.

Civilian Technicians, Association of: *see* LABOR ORGANIZATION, Technicians, Association of Civilian.

civil rights, generally, the protections and privileges given to all citizens by the U.S. Constitution. However, "civil rights" frequently is used to refer to those positive acts of government that seek to make constitutional guarantees a reality for all citizens.

Civil Rights Act of 1964, the most far-reaching regulations of labor relations since the National Labor Relations Act of 1935. Designed to eliminate racial and sexual discrimination in most areas of U.S. life, it affected employers of 15 or more employees engaged in interstate commerce by providing for the withholding of federal funds from programs administered in a discriminatory manor and establishing a right to equal employment opportunity without regard to race, color, religion, sex or national origin. It also created the Equal Employment Opportunity Commission (EEOC) to assist in implementing this right. Its provisions were extended to public sector employers in 1972 (*see* EQUAL EMPLOYMENT OPPORTUNITY ACT OF 1972).

See also EQUAL EMPLOYMENT OPPORTUNITY COMMISSION and TITLE VII.

Civil Rights Acts of 1866, 1870, and 1971, insure equality before the law in a variety of functional areas (ability to enter into contracts, sue, give evidence, and secure equal protection of persons and property) and establish that individuals or governments denying any rights or privileges shall be liable for legal action. These acts are often used in conjunction with, but are not replaced by, the Civil Rights Act of 1964 as the basis for suits.

Civil Rights Acts of 1957 and 1960, the Civil Rights Act of 1957 (Public Law 85-135) is generally considered to be the beginning of contemporary civil rights legislation. It established the U.S. Commission on Civil Rights and strengthened the judiciary's ability to protect civil rights. The Civil Rights Act of 1960 (Public Law 86-449) served mainly to plug legal loopholes in the 1957 law. For a broad history of the civil rights movement, *see* Richard Bardolph (ed.), *The Civil Rights Record: Black Americans and the Law, 1849-1970* (N.Y.: Thomas Y. Crowell Co. 1970).

Civil Rights Commission: *see* COMMISSION ON CIVIL RIGHTS.

civil service, collective term for all of those employees of a government who are not members of the military services. For histories of the U.S. civil service, *see* Paul P. Van Riper, *History of the United States Civil Service* (Evanston, Ill: Row, Peterson, 1958); Jay M. Shafritz, *Public Personnel Management: The Heritage of Civil Service Reform* (N.Y.: Praeger, 1975).

See also INTERNATIONAL CIVIL SERVICE.

Civil Service Assembly of the United States and Canada: *see* INTERNATIONAL PERSONNEL MANAGEMENT ASSOCIATION.

civil service commission, government agency charged with the responsibility of promulagating the rules and regulations of the civilian personnel management system. Depending upon its legal mandate, a civil service commission may hear employee appeals and take a more active (or passive) role in the personnel management process. *See* Donald R. Harvey, *The Civil Service Commission* (N.Y.: Praeger, 1970); Winston W. Crouch, *A Guide for Modern Personnel Commissions* (Chicago: International Personnel Management Association, 1973).

See also GRANT'S CIVIL SERVICE COMMISSION.

Civil Service Commission, U.S.: *see* GRANT'S CIVIL SERVICE COMMISSION, MERIT SYSTEMS PROTECTION BOARD, OFFICE OF PERSONNEL MANAGEMENT, and UNITED STATES CIVIL SERVICE COMMISSION.

Civil Service Commission v. National Association of Letter Carriers: *see* UNITED STATES CIVIL SERVICE COMMISSION V. NATIONAL ASSOCIATION OF LETTER CARRIERS.

Civil Service Employees Association, Inc.: *see* LABOR ORGANIZATION.

Civil Service Journal, official quarterly of the U.S. Civil Service Commission. It ceased publication in 1979.

Civil Service Reform Act of 1978, on March 2, 1978, President Carter, with the enthusiastic support of his Civil Service Commission leadership, submitted his civil service reform proposals to Congress. On that same day, before the National Press Club, he further called his proposals to Congress' attention by charging that the present federal personnel system had become a "bureaucratic maze which neglects merit, tolerates poor performance, and permits abuse of legitimate employee rights, and mires every personnel action in red tape, delay, and confusion."

The reform bill faced considerable opposition from federal employee unions (who thought the bill was too management oriented) and from veterans' groups (who were aghast at the bill's curtailment of veterans' preferences). The unions lost. The veterans won. The bill passed almost totally intact. The major exception was the deletion of strong veterans' preference curtailments. The Senate passed the bill by voice vote and the House endorsed it with the wide margin of 365 to 8. On October 13, 1978—only six months after he had submitted it to the Congress—President Carter signed the Civil Service Reform Act of 1978 into law.

The act mandated that (in January of 1979) the U.S. Civil Service Commission would be divided into two agencies—an Office of Personnel Management (OPM) to serve as the personnel arm of the chief executive and an independent Merit Systems Protection Board (MSPB) to provide recourse for aggrieved employees. In addition, the act created a Federal Labor Relations Authority (FLRA) to oversee federal labor–management policies.

While the act includes provisions for new performance appraisal systems, mandates new adverse action and appeals procedures, and requires a trial period for new managers and supervisors, probably its greatest management innovation is the creation of the Senior Executive Service (SES). The SES will pool the most senior-level managers (GS 16 and up) into an elite 11,000-member executive corps that the Office of Personnel Management will have wide latitude in rewarding and punishing. Unfortunately, this elite group is bound to be known, perhaps with some affection, as the "SES pool."

See also (1) FEDERAL LABOR RELATION AUTHORITY, (2) MERIT SYSTEMS PROTECTION BOARD, (3) OFFICE OF PERSONNEL MANAGEMENT, and (4) SENIOR EXECUTIVE SERVICE.

Civil Service Retirement and Disability Fund, the accumulation of money held in trust by the U.S. Treasury for the purpose of paying annuity, refund, and death benefits to persons entitled to them. The Fund's funds come from five main sources: (1) deductions from the pay of employees who are members of the Civil Service Retirement System; (2) contributions by the employing agencies in amounts which match the deductions from their employees' (3) payments from the U.S. Treasury for interest on the existing unfunded liability of the system and for the cost of allowing credit for military service; (4) appropriations to meet liabilities that result from changes in the system; and (5) interest earned through investment of money received from the first four sources. How is the money invested? It is invested by the U.S. Treasury in government securities.

CJA: *see* LABOR ORGANIZATION, Carpenters and Joiners of America, United Brotherhood of.

CLA: *see* LABOR ORGANIZATION, Christian Labor Association of the United States of America.

class, unique position or a group of positions sufficiently similar in respect to duties and responsibilities that the same title may be used to designate each position in the group, the same salary may be equitably applied, the same qualifications required, and the same examination used to select qualified employees.

See also the following entries:
GROUP OF CLASSES
SERIES OF CLASSES
SPECIFICATION
TITLE

class action, search for judicial remedy that one or more individuals may undertake on behalf of themselves and all others in similar situations. Rule 23(b) of the Federal Rules of Civil Procedure establishes the technical legal requirements for the definition of a class in federal court proceedings:

> One or more members of a class may sue or be sued as representative parties on behalf of all only if (1) the class is so numerous that joinder of all members is impractical, (2) there are questions of law or facts common to the class, (3) the claims or defenses of the representative parties are typical of the claims or defenses of the class, and (4) the representative parties will fairly and adequately protect the interests of the class.

classical organization theory: *see* ORGANIZATION THEORY.

classification: *see* POSITION CLASSIFICATION.

Classification Acts: *see* POSITION CLASSIFICATION.

Classification and Compensation Society, founded in 1969 to promote and improve classification and compensation as a professional field. The Society's goals are to provide for the exchange of ideas, information, and experiences for the benefit of members and employing organizations; provide perspective on events and problems; and stimulate creative efforts to improve or develop concepts, techniques, programs, and systems. Advancement of these objectives is accomplished through work study groups; open forums such as seminars and conferences; and publication of articles, studies, reports, and technical papers.

Classification and Compensation Society
National Press Building
Suite 976
Washington, DC 20045
(202) 638-1290

classification standards, descriptions of classes of positions that distinguish one class from another in a series. They are, in effect, the yardstick or benchmark against which positions are measured to determine the proper level within a series of titles to which a position should be assigned.

Classified School Employees, American Association of: *see* LABOR ORGANIZATION.

classified service, all those positions in a governmental jurisdiction that are included in a formal merit system. Excluded from the classified service are all exempt appointments. Classified service is a term that predates the concept of position classification and has no immediate bearing on position classification concepts or practices.

classify, group positions according to their duties and responsibilities and assign a class title. To reclassify is to reassign a position to a different class, based on a re-examination of the duties and responsibilities of the position.

Clay Workers of America: *see* LABOR ORGANIZATION, Brick and Clay Workers of America, The United.

Clayton Act, also called the ANTI-TRUST ACT OF 1914, hailed at the time as labor's "Magna Carta," the Clayton Act sought to exempt labor unions from antitrust laws and to limit the jurisdiction of courts in issuing injunctions against labor organizations. Subsequent judicial construction limited its effectiveness and new laws were necessary to achieve its original intent.
See also LAWLOR V. LOEWE.

CLC: *see* CANADIAN LABOUR CONGRESS.

clean-up time, time during the normal work day when employees are allowed to cease production in order to clean themselves, their clothing, or their workplace. Clean-up-time allowances are frequently written into union contracts.

cleansing period, the Labor–Management Reporting and Disclosure (Landrum–Griffin) Act of 1959 required, under Section 504, that a person previously a member of the Communist party or convicted of criminal acts must undergo a "cleansing period" of five years before he can hold a union office. However, the U.S. Supreme Court, in *United States* v. *Archie Brown*, 381 U.S. 437 (1965), declared Section 504 unconstitutional as a bill of attainder.

Cleveland Board of Education* v. *Lafleur, 414 U.S. 632 (1974), U.S. Supreme Court case, which held that arbitrary mandatory maternity leaves were unconstitutional. The court held that requiring pregnant teachers to take unpaid maternity leave five months before expected childbirth was in violation of the due process clause of the 14th Amendment.

CLGW: *see* LABOR ORGANIZATION, Cement, Lime and Gypsum Workers International Union, United.

clique, organizational sub-group whose members prefer to associate with each other on the basis of common interests. Melville Dalton, in *Men Who Manage* (N.Y.: Wiley, 1959), offers an extensive analysis of organizational cliques and concludes that they

> are both an outgrowth and instrument of planning and change. They fall into recognizable types shaped by, and related to, the official pattern of executive positions. Cliques are the indispensable promoters and stabilizers—as well as resisters—of change; they are essential both to cement the organization and to accelerate action. They preserve the formalities vital for moving to the goal, and they provoke but control the turmoil and adjustment that play about the emerging organization.

clock card, form designed to be used with a time clock.

closed anti-union shop, work organization that will not hire current or prospective union members. Such a tactic is illegal if the organization is engaged in interstate commerce.

closed shop, union security provision that would require an employer to only hire and retain union members in good standing. The Labor–Management Relations (Taft–Hartley) Act of 1947 made closed shops illegal.

closed union, union that formally bars new members or makes becoming a member practically impossible in order to protect the job opportunities of its present members.

closing date, when a civil service examination is announced, applications are accepted as long as the announcement is "open." The closing date is the deadline for submitting applications and is usually stated on the announcement.

clothing allowance, funds provided by employers to employees so that they can buy special clothing, such as uniforms or safety garments.

Clothing and Textile Workers Union, Amalgamated: *see* LABOR ORGANIZATION.

cluster laboratory, laboratory training experience for a group of people from the same organization. The group consists of several subgroups of individuals whose work in the larger organization is related.

CMR: *see* CALIFORNIA MANAGEMENT REVIEW.

CMT: *see* CONCEPT MASTERY TEST.

coaching, also COACHING ANALYSIS, face-to-face discussions with a subordinate in order to effect a change in his or her behavior. *Coaching analysis* consists of analyzing the reasons why unsatisfactory performance is occurring. According to Ferdinard F. Fournies, in *Coaching for Improved Work Performance* (N.Y.: Van Nostrand Reinhold, 1978), there are five steps in the coaching technique:

1. Getting the employee's agreement that a problem exists.
2. A mutual discussion of alternative solutions.
3. Mutual agreement on the action to be taken to solve the problem.
4. Measuring the results of subsequent performance.
5. Recognize achievement and improved performance when it occurs.

coaching analysis: *see* COACHING.

coalition bargaining, also COORDINATED BARGAINING, in coalition bargaining an employer negotiates with a group of unions whose goal is to gain one agreement covering all or identical agreements for each. *Coordinated bargaining* differs only in that bargaining sessions take place simultaneously at differing locations. *See* George H. Hildebrand, "Cloudy Future for Coalition Bargaining," *Harvard Business Review* (November-December 1968); Stephen B. Goldberg, "Coordinated Bargaining: Some Unresolved Questions," *Monthly Labor Review* (April 1969).

Coalition of American Public Employees (CAPE), formed in 1972 by leaders of public employees organizations in an effort to coordinate programs of political, legal, and legislation action and public education at the national and state level. Members include the American Federation of State, County and Municipal Employees (AFSCME); the National Education Association (NEA); the American Nurses Association (ANA); the Physicians National Housestaff Association (PNHA); and the National Association of Social Workers (NAWS). Representing nearly 4 million workers, CAPE is the largest organization of public employees in the nation.

> CAPE
> 1126 16th Street, N.W.
> Washington, DC 20036
> (202) 223-2267

Coal Mine Health and Safety Act of 1969: *see* USERY V. TURNER ELKHORN MINING CO.

COBOL, acronym for "Common Business Oriented Language," a procedure-oriented computer language that resembles standard business English.

code of ethics, statement of professional standards of conduct to which the practitioners of many professions say they subscribe. For example, the Code of Ethics of the American Society for Personnel Administration offers the following nice thoughts:

As a member of the American Society for Personnel Administration, I acknowledge my responsibility to strive for personal growth in my chosen career field and commit myself to observe the following ethical practices:

- I will respect the dignity of the individual as one of the essential elements of success in any enterprise.
- I will demonstrate and promote a spirit of cooperative effort between owners, managers, employees and the general public, directly or indirectly connected with the enterprise.
- I will advance those ethical employee relations concepts in personnel administration and labor relations which contribute to the objectives of the enterprise.
- I will reveal the facts in any situation where my private interests are in conflict with those of my employer or other principals.
- I will not permit considerations of religion, nationality, race, sex, age, party politics, or social standing to influence my professional activities.
- I will strive to attain and demonstrate a professional level of competence within the body of knowledge comprising the management field.
- I will encourage and participate in research to develop and advance new and improved management methods, skills and practices, sharing the productive results of such research with others.
- I will never use the Society or its membership for purposes other than those for which they were designed.

See also ETHICS and STANDARDS OF CONDUCT.

Code of Federal Regulations (CFR), annual cumulation of executive agency regulations published in the daily *Federal Register*, combined with regulations issued previously that are still in effect. Divided into 50 titles, each representing a broad subject area, individual volumes of the CFR are revised at least once each calendar year and issued on a staggered quarterly basis. An alphabetical listing by agency of subtitle and chapter assignments in the CFR is provided in the back of each volume under the heading "Finding Aids" and is accurate for the revision date of that volume.

codetermination, in German MITBESTIM-MUNGSRECHT, union participation in all aspects of management even to the extent of having union representatives share equal membership on an organization's board of directors. In Germany, where codetermination is often legally required, the process is called *Mitbestimmungsrecht*, literally meaning "the right of codetermination." *See* Svetozar Pejovich (ed.), *The Codetermination Movement in the West: Labor Participation in the Management of Business Firms* (Lexington, Mass.: Lexington Books, 1978).

coefficient of correlation: *see* CORRELATION COEFFICIENT.

coffee break, also called TEA BREAK, popular term for any brief rest period for workers. While work breaks for refreshments and socializing go back to ancient times, it wasn't until after World War II that coffee breaks became a national institution: first, because millions of workers brought the custom with them from World War II military service and, second, because by this time considerable research on worker fatigue had consistently shown that beverage breaks reduce fatigue while improving alertness and productivity. The British, of course, have tea breaks. For a brief history of the coffee break, *see* William J. Tandy, "Tempest in a Coffee Pot," *Public Personnel Review* (October 1953). *See also* Steven Habbe, "Coffee, Anyone?" *The Conference Board Record* (July 1965).

cognitive dissonance, theory first postulated by Leon Festinger, in *A Theory of Cognitive Dissonance* (Evanston, Ill.: Row, Peterson Co., 1957), which holds that when an individual finds himself in a situation where he is expected to believe two mutually exclusive things, the subsequent tension and discomfort generates activity designed to reduce the dissonance or disharmony. For example, an employee who sees himself in an inequitable wage situation could experience cognitive dissonance. The theory of cognitive dissonance assumes that a worker performing the same work as another but being paid significantly less will do something to relieve his dissonance. Among his options are asking for a raise, restricting output, or seeking another job. For studies on wage inequity, *see* J. Stacy Adams, "Wage Inequities, Productivity and Work Quality," *Industrial Relations* (October 1963); William M. Evan and Roberta G. Simmons, "Organizational Effects of Inequitable Rewards in Two Experiments in Status Inconsistency," *Administrative Science Quarterly* (June 1969). For further studies in cognitive dissonance, *see* J. W. Brehm and A. R. Cohn, *Explorations in Cognitive Dissonance* (N.Y.: John Wiley, 1962).
See also INEQUITY THEORY.

COINS, acronym for the classes of people for whom affirmative action data must usually be collected. It stands for "Caucasian, Oriental, Indian, Negro, and Spanish."

COLA: *see* COST-OF-LIVING ADJUSTMENT.

COL-APE: *see* LABOR ORGANIZATION, Colorado Association of Public Employees.

cold-storage training, the preparation of employees for jobs in advance of the need for them in these particular jobs.

Cole v. Richardson, 405 U.S. 676 (1971), U.S. Supreme Court case, which upheld the right of Massachusetts to exact from its employees a promise to "oppose the overthrow of the government of the United States of America or of this Commonwealth by force, violence or by any illegal or unconstitutional method." A public employer may legitimately require employees to swear or affirm their allegiance to the Constitution of the United States and of a particular state. Beyond that, the limits of constitutional loyalty oaths are unclear.

collective bargaining, a comprehensive term that encompasses the negotiating process that leads to a contract between labor and management on wages, hours, and other conditions of employment as well as the subsequent administration and interpretation of the signed contract. Collective bargaining is, in effect, the continuous relationship that exists between union representatives and employers. The four basic stages of collective bargaining are: (1) the establishment of organizations for bargaining, (2) the formulation of demands, (3) the negotiation of demands, and (4) the administration of the labor agreement.

Collective bargaining is one of the keystones of the National Labor Relations Act, which declares that the policy of the United States is to be carried out

> by encouraging the practice and procedure of collective bargaining and by protecting the exercise by workers of full freedom of association, self-organization, and designation of representatives of their own choosing, for the purpose of negotiating the terms and conditions of their employment or other mutual aid or protection.

No. 688. Major Collective Bargaining Settlements—Average Percent Change in Wages and Benefits Negotiated: 1969 to 1977

[In percent, except as indicated. Data represent private nonfarm industry settlements affecting production and related workers in manufacturing and nonsupervisory workers in nonmanufacturing industries. Data exclude possible adjustments in wages under cost-of-living escalator clauses, except increases guaranteed by the contract. Includes all settlements, whether wages and benefits were changed or not]

ITEM	1969	1970	1971	1972	1973	1974	1975	1976	1977
Wage-rate adjustments: [1]									
All industries:									
First year changes	9.2	11.9	11.6	7.3	5.8	9.8	10.2	8.4	7.8
Contracts with escalator clauses	(NA)	(NA)	12.9	7.9	5.7	9.5	12.2	8.4	8.0
Contracts without escalator clauses	(NA)	(NA)	10.3	7.2	5.8	10.2	9.1	8.3	7.6
Over life of contract [2]	7.6	8.9	8.1	6.4	5.1	7.3	7.8	6.4	5.8
Contracts with escalator clauses	(NA)	7.3	7.1	5.7	4.9	6.1	7.1	5.7	5.0
Contracts without escalator clauses	(NA)	10.1	9.2	6.5	5.3	9.1	8.3	7.3	6.9
Manufacturing:									
First year changes	7.9	8.1	10.9	6.6	5.9	8.7	9.8	8.9	8.4
Over life of contract [2]	6.0	6.0	7.3	5.6	4.9	6.1	8.0	6.0	5.5
Nonmanufacturing: [3]									
First year changes	10.8	15.2	12.2	7.8	5.7	10.5	10.4	7.7	7.4
Over life of contract [2]	9.3	11.5	8.9	6.9	5.3	8.0	7.8	6.8	6.0
Number of workers affected ____ 1,000	2,836	4,675	3,978	2,424	5,320	5,139	2,890	4,050	4,010
Percent of civilian labor force	3	6	5	3	6	6	3	4	4
Manufacturing ____ 1,000	1,459	2,184	1,913	913	2,403	1,854	778	2,075	1,638
Nonmanufacturing [3] ____ 1,000	1,377	2,491	2,066	1,510	2,917	3,285	2,112	1,975	2,372
Wage and benefit adjustments: [4]									
First year changes	10.9	13.1	13.1	8.5	7.1	10.7	11.4	8.5	9.6
Over life of contract [2]	8.2	9.1	8.8	7.4	6.1	7.8	8.1	6.6	6.2

NA Not available.   [1] Covers only contracts in which each settlement involved 1,000 or more workers.
[2] Average annual rate of change.   [3] Includes construction.
[4] Covers only contracts in which each settlement involved 5,000 or more workers.

SOURCE: Bureau of the Census, *Statistical Abstract of the United States* (Washington, D.C.: Government Printing Office, 1978), p. 425.

For texts, *see* Neil W. Chamberlain and James W. Kuhn, *Collective Bargaining* (N.Y.: McGraw-Hill, 2nd ed., 1965); Harold W. Davey, *Contemporary Collective Bargaining* (Englewood Cliffs, N.J.: Prentice-Hall, 3rd ed., 1972); Edwin F. Beal, Edward D. Wickersham, and Philip K. Kienast, *The Practice of Collective Bargaining* (Homewood, Ill.: Richard D. Irwin, 1976). For a public sector perspective, *see* J. Joseph Loewenberg and Michael H. Moskow, *Collective Bargaining in Government* (Englewood Cliffs, N.J.: Prentice-Hall, 1972). For a scathing attack, *see* Merryle Stanley Rukeyser, *Collective Bargaining: The Power to Destroy* (N.Y.: Delacorte Press, 1968).

See also the following entries:

H. J. HEINZ CO. V. NATIONAL LABOR RELATIONS BOARD
INLAND STEEL CO. V. NATIONAL LABOR RELATIONS BOARD
PORTER CO. V. NATIONAL LABOR RELATIONS BOARD
PRODUCTIVITY BARGAINING
REGIONAL BARGAINING
REOPENER CLAUSE
RETIREMENT AGE
REVERSE COLLECTIVE BARGAINING
SPLIT-THE-DIFFERENCE
SUNSHINE BARGAINING
TEXTILE WORKERS V. LINCOLN MILLS

UNFAIR LABOR PRACTICES (EMPLOYERS)
UNFAIR LABOR PRACTICES (UNIONS)
UNION SECURITY CLAUSE
WELFARE FUNDS
ZIPPER CLAUSE

Collective Bargaining Negotiations & Contracts, biweekly reference service published by the Bureau of National Affairs, Inc., which presents comprehensive coverage of wage rates and data, and cost-of-living figures; bargaining issues, demands, counterproposals, and significant settlements; strategy, techniques, industry facts and figures; equal employment opportunity activities as they affect collective bargaining.

collective negotiations, in the public sector "collective bargaining" may sometimes be legally and/or semantically unacceptable; so "collective negotiations" is available as an alternative.

College Placement Annual: see COLLEGE PLACEMENT COUNCIL, INC.

College Placement Council, Inc., nonprofit corporation that provides professional services to career planning and placement directors at four-year and two-year colleges and universities in the United States, as well as to employers who hire graduates of these institutions. Each year the Council publishes the *College Placement Annual* which includes the occupational needs anticipated by approximately 1,300 corporate and governmental employers who normally recruit college graduates.

College Placement Council, Inc.
P.O. Box 2236
Bethlehem, PA 18001

College and University Personnel Association (CUPA), international organization dedicated to providing current methodology, models, studies, and other references to human resource professionals associated with higher education around the world.

College and University Personnel Association
11 Dupont Circle
Washington, DC 20036
(202) 462-1038

Collyer **doctrine**, the predisposition of the National Labor Relations Board to defer to arbitral awards in disputes involving unfair labor practices if certain conditions are met—one of them being that the arbitrator must have considered and resolved the statutory issues, if any, present in the case. This was first enunciated in the case of *Collyer Insulated Wire*, 192 NLRB 837 (1971).

Colorado Association of Public Employees: *see* LABOR ORGANIZATION.

Colorado Labor Council: *see* AMERICAN FEDERATION OF LABOR–CONGRESS OF INDUSTRIAL ORGANIZATIONS.

Columbia Journal of World Business, quarterly published by Columbia University that seeks to present analyses of the major currents and issues that are shaping today's international business, and that will shape tomorrow's. Articles are selected on the basis of their utility to business executives, the academic community, and government officials with responsibilities and interests in international business.

Columbia Journal of World Business
Columbia University
408 Uris
New York, NY 10027

comer, slang term for younger managers who seem to have the potential of assuming top management responsibilities. For how to find and best use your organization's "comers," *see* Robert A. Pitts, "Unshackle Your 'Comers,'" *Harvard Business Review* (May–June 1977).

Commerce, Department of, created in 1913 when the Congress split the Department of Commerce and Labor (founded in 1903) into two cabinet level departments, encourages, serves, and promotes the nation's economic development and technological advancement. It offers assistance and information to

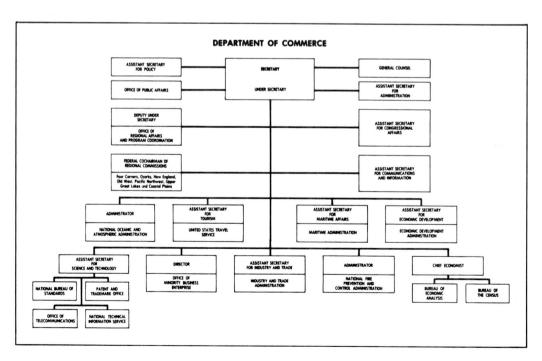

domestic and international business; provides social and economic statistics and analyses for business and government planners; assists in the development and maintenance of the U.S. merchant marine; provides research for and promotes the increased use of science and technology in the development of the economy; provides assistance to speed the development of the economically underdeveloped areas of the nation; seeks to improve understanding of the earth's physical environment and oceanic life; promotes travel to the United States by residents of foreign countries; assists in the growth of minority businesses; and seeks to prevent the loss of life and property from fire.

Department of Commerce
14th St. Between Constitution Ave. and E
   Street N.W.,
Washington, DC 20230
(202) 377-2000

Commerce Clearing House, Inc. (CCH), publishers of a variety of loose leaf information services concerned with law, taxes, business, urban affairs, etc.

Commerce Clearing House, Inc.
4025 W. Paterson Ave.
Chicago, IL 60646
(312) 267-9010

commission earnings, compensation to sales personnel that is based on a percentage of the value of the sales for which they are individually credited.

Commissioners of Conciliation: *see* CONCILIATION.

Commission on Civil Rights, also called CIVIL RIGHTS COMMISSION, the role of the Commission on Civil Rights is to encourage constructive steps toward equal opportunity for minority groups and women. The Commission investigates complaints, holds public hearings, and collects and studies information on denials of equal protection of the laws because of race, color, religion, sex, or national origin. Voting rights, administration of justice, and equality of opportunity in education, employment, and housing are among the many topics of specific Commission interest.

The Commission on Civil Rights, created by the Civil Rights Act of 1957, makes findings of fact but has no enforcement authority. Findings and recommendations are submitted to both the President and the Congress. More than 60 percent of the Commission's recommendations have been enacted, either by statute, executive order, or regulation. The Commission evaluates federal laws and the effectiveness of government equal opportunity programs. It also serves as a national clearinghouse for civil rights information.

Commission on Civil Rights
1121 Vermont Avenue N.W.
Washington, DC 20425
(202) 254-6758

commission plan, any of a varity of compensation programs for sales employees where wages or salary are established totally or in part as a percentage of the total dollar value of sales made over a given period of time. *See* John P. Steinbrink, "How to Pay Your Sales Force," *Harvard Business Review* (July-August 1978).

Committee for Industrial Organization, committee established within the American Federation of Labor in 1935 that grew to be the Congress of Industrial Organizations in 1938. *See* (1) CONGRESS OF INDUSTRIAL ORGANIZATIONS and (2) AMERICAN FEDERATION OF LABOR–CONGRESS OF INDUSTRIAL ORGANIZATIONS.

committeeman, or COMMITTEEWOMAN, worker (usually) elected by co-workers to represent the union membership in the handling of grievances and the recruitment of new union members among other duties.

Committee on Political Education (COPE), nonpartisan organization of the AFL–CIO, made up of members of the AFL–CIO's Executive Council, has the responsibility spelled out in the AFL–CIO Constitution of "encouraging workers to register and vote, to exercise their full rights and responsibilities of citizenship, and to perform their rightful part in the political life of the city, state and national communities."

COPE is not a political party, nor is it committed to the support of any particular party. From the first convention of the AFL–CIO (in 1955) to the most recent, COPE has been instructed to work in support of candidates who support issues of concern to the AFL–CIO regardless of the party affiliation of the candidate. The policies of COPE are determined by its national committee in line with the policies and programs adopted by the AFL–CIO conventions.

COPE reports facts about issues and candidates. It publishes voting records of elected officials to help AFL–CIO members inform themselves in order to vote intelligently. Candidates for political offices are recommended to the membership in the appropriate area by state and local COPE bodies, representing affiliated unions at the local and state level. The basis for the endorsement is the record and the program of the candidates compared to the policies of the AFL–CIO.

For a critical review of COPE's activities, see: Terry Catchpole, *How to Cope with COPE: The Political Operations of Organized Labor* (New Rochelle, N.Y.: Arlington House, 1968).

Committee on the Civil Services: *see* FULTON COMMITTEE.

Common Business Oriented Language: *see* COBOL.

common labor rate, wage rate for the least skilled physical or manual labor in an organization. This is usually an organization's lowest rate of pay.

common law of the shop, or INDUSTRIAL RELATIONS COMMON LAW, common law is the total body of law established by judicial precedent. The *common law of the shop* or *industrial relations common law* is that portion of the common law that applies to the workplace.

common situs picketing, picketing of an entire construction site by members of a single union to increase their strike's impact and to publicize a dispute with one or more contractors or subcontractors. In 1976, President Ford vetoed a bill that would have made common situs picketing legal. *See* Paul A. Brinker, "Common Situs Picketing in Construction Unions Since 1958," *Labor Law Journal* (June 1972).

Commonwealth v. Hunt: *see* SHAW, LEMUEL.

communication, process of exchanging information, ideas, and feelings between two or more individuals or groups. *Horizontal communication* refers to such an exchange among peers or people at the same organizational level. *Vertical communication* refers to such an exchange between individuals at differing levels of the organization. For a text, *see* William V. Haney, *Communications and Interpersonal Relations* (Homewood, Ill.: Richard D. Irwin, 4th ed., 1979).

See also NONVERBAL COMMUNICATION.

Communications Workers of America: *see* LABOR ORGANIZATION.

Community Dispute Services: *see* AMERICAN ARBITRATION ASSOCIATION.

community of interest, criterion used to determine if a group of employees make up an appropriate bargaining unit.

community wage survey, any survey whose purpose is to ascertain the structure and level of wages among employers in a local area.

company doctor, slang term for an expert brought in to save a company or organization from severe difficulties. The "doctor" could be a new chief executive, a consultant, a lawyer, an accountant, or other person with special expertise.

company fellowship plan, formal arrangement under which a particular company provides one or more graduate students with nonrepayable monetary allowances to help them attend universities, on a full-time basis, in pursuit of a master's or a doctoral degree. Specific details of such plans vary widely. *Company scholarship plans* differ in that they are restricted to undergraduate study. For a survey of company fellowship/scholarship plans, *see* J. Roger O'Meara, *Combating Knowledge Obsolescence: Company Fellowship Plans* (New York: The Conference Board, 1968).

company loans, loans made to employees by a company. Such loans are usually in response to an emergency, usually of short duration, and usually without interest.

company scholarship plan: *see* COMPANY FELLOWSHIP PLAN.

company spy, also called LABOR SPY, someone hired by an employer to report on what is happening within a union.

company store, store operated by an organization for the exclusive use of employees and their families. The largest company store in the world is the U.S. military's PX (Post Exchange) system.

company town, slang term for any community whose economy is dominated by one employer. True company towns, where the company literally owned all of the land, buildings, and stores are practically nonexistent in the modern U.S.—with the possible exception of remote areas of Alaska. For history, *see* James B. Allen, *The Company Town in the American West* (Norman, Okla.: University of Oklahoma Press, 1966); Christopher Norwood, "The Bittersweet Story of the First Company Town," *Business and Society Review* (Summer 1976).

company union, an historical term that described unions organized, financed, or otherwise dominated by an employer. The National Labor Relations (Wagner) Act of 1935 outlawed employer interference with unions, thus relegating company unions to history.

See also TEXAS AND NEW ORLEANS RAILWAY V. BROTHERHOOD OF RAILWAY AND STEAMSHIP CLERKS and UNFAIR LABOR PRACTICES (EMPLOYERS).

comparable form test: *see* ALTERNATE FORM.

comparative-norm principle, as defined in Arthur A. Sloane and Fred Witney, *Labor Relations* (Englewood Cliffs, N.J.: Prentice-Hall, 3rd ed., 1977):

> To a great extent, company and union negotiators make use of the "comparative-norm principle" in wage negotiations. The basic idea behind this concept is the presumption that the economics of a particular collective bargaining relationship should neither fall substantially behind nor be greatly superior to that of other employer-union relationships; that, in short, it is generally a good practice to keep up with the crowd, but not necessarily to lead it.

compassionate leave, any leave granted for urgent family reasons. This term, which is mainly used by the military, is sometimes informally abbreviated to "passionate leave."

compensable factors, various elements of a job that, when put together, both define the job and determine its value to the organization.

compensable injury, work injury that qualifies an injured worker for workers' compensation benefits.

compensation, also PAY or REMUNERATION, generic terms that encompass all forms of organizational payments and rewards. For general discussions, *see* Patrick R. Pinto and Benjamin H. Lowenberg, "Pay: A Unitary View," *Personnel Journal* (June 1973); Edward E. Lawler III, "New Approaches To Pay: Innovations That Work," *Personnel* (September-October 1973); Thomas A. Mahoney (ed.), *Compensation and Reward Perspectives* (Homewood, Ill.: Richard D. Irwin, Inc., 1979).

See also the following entries:

BONUS
DEFERRED COMPENSATION
EXECUTIVE COMPENSATION
INDIRECT WAGES
UNEMPLOYMENT BENEFITS

compensation management, that facet of management concerned with the selection, development, and direction of the programs that implement an organization's financial reward system. For the two best surveys of the subject, *see* Richard I. Henderson, *Compensation Management: Rewarding Performance in the Modern Organization* (Reston, Va.: Reston Publishing Co., 1976); Thomas H. Patten, Jr., *Pay: Employee Compensation and Incentive Plans* (N.Y.: The Free Press, 1977).

Compensation Review, quarterly journal covering all aspects of employee compensation. Also contains "condensations of noteworthy articles" from other business and professional publications that relate to compensation.

Compensation Review
Editorial Adress:
AMACOM
Division of American Management Associations
135 West 50th Street
New York, NY 10020

Subscriptions:
Compensation Review
Box 319
Saramac Lake, NY 12983

compensatory time, time off in lieu of overtime pay.

competence, ability to consistently perform a task or job to an acceptable standard.

See also INTERPERSONAL COMPETENCE.

competitive area, during layoffs or reductions-in-force employees of large organizations are sometimes restricted to competing for retention in their competitive area—the commuting area to which they are assigned.

competitive level, all positions of the same grade within a competitive area which are sufficiently alike in duties, responsibilities, pay systems, terms of appointment, requirements for experience, training, skills, and aptitudes that the incumbent of any of them could readily be shifted to any of the other positions without significant training or undue interruption to the work program. In the federal government, the job to which an employee is officially assigned determines his competitive level.

competitive promotion, selection for promotion made from the employees rated *best* qualified in competition with others, all of whom have the *minimum* qualifications required by the position.

competitive seniority, use of seniority in determining an employee's right, relative to other employees, to job related "rights" that cannot be supplied equally to any two employees.

competitive service, general term for those civilian positions in a governmental jurisdiction that are not specifically excepted from merit system regulations.

competitive wages, rates of pay that an employer, in competition with other employers, must offer if he or she is to recruit and retain employees.

compliance agency, generally, any government agency that administers laws and/or regulations relating to equal employment opportunity. Specifically, a federal agency delegated enforcement responsibilities by the U.S. Department of Labor's Office of Federal Contract Compliance Programs (OFCCP) to ensure that federal contractors adhere to EEO regulations and policies.

complaint examiner, official designated to conduct discrimination complaint hearings.

completion item, text question that calls for the examinee to complete or fill in the missing parts of a phrase, sentence, etc.

complimentary interview, according to Joseph P. Cangemi and Jeffrey C. Claypool, "Complimentary Interviews: A System for Rewarding Outstanding Employees," *Personnel Journal* (February 1978),

> the general purpose of a complimentary interview is to positively evaluate personnel and to give them performance feedback, recognition and praise, to highlight potential, and to enhance organizational planning.

Composers & Lyricists Guild of America: *see* LABOR ORGANIZATION.

composite score, score derived by combining scores obtained by an applicant on two or more tests or other measures.

Comprehensive Employment and Training Act of 1973 (CETA), as amended, CETA establishes a program of financial assistance to state and local governments to provide job training and employment opportunities for economically disadvantaged, unemployed, and underemployed persons. CETA provides funds for state and local jurisdictions to hire unemployed and underemployed persons in public service jobs. In 1978, over 725,000 people were employed in CETA-funded public service jobs. *See* William Mirengoff and Lester Rindler, *The Comprehensive Employment and Training Act: Impact on People, Places, Programs—An Interim Report* (Washington, D.C.: National Academy of Sciences, 1976). For an indictment, *see* Juan Cameron, "How CETA Came to be a Four-Letter Word," *Fortune* (April 9, 1979).

> *See also* UNITED STATES EMPLOYMENT SERVICES.

compressed time, the same number of hours worked in a week spread over fewer days than normal.

comp time: *see* COMPENSATORY TIME.

compulsory arbitration, negotiating process whereby the parties are required by law to arbitrate their dispute. Some state statutes concerning collective bargaining impasses in the public sector mandate that parties who have exhausted all other means of achieving a settlement must submit their dispute to an arbitrator. The intent of such requirements for compulsory arbitration is to induce the parties to reach agreement by presenting them with an alternative that is both certain and unpleasant. *See* Carl M. Stevens, "Is Compulsory Arbitration Compatible with Bargaining," *Industrial Relations* (February 1966); Mollie H. Bowers, "Legislated Arbitration: Legality, Enforceability, and Face-Saving," *Public Personnel Management* (July-August 1974).

> *See also* LOCAL 174, TEAMSTERS V. LUCAS FLOUR CO.

compulsory checkoff: *see* AUTOMATIC CHECK-OFF.

compulsory retirement, ceasation of employment at an age specified by a union contract or company policy.

computer, machine that solves problems by manipulating large amounts of information at high speed. *See* Marion J. Ball, *What Is a Computer?* (Boston: Houghton Mifflin, 1972).

Concept Mastery Test (CMT), intelligence test that measures ability to deal with ideas or concepts by sampling two kinds of verbal problems: synonyms–antonyms and the completion of analogies. Questions draw on concepts from physical and biological sciences, mathematics, history, geography, literature, music, etc. Measures power or capacity rather than speed. TIME: 35/40 minutes. AUTHOR: L. M. Terman. PUBLISHER: Psychological Corporation (*see* TEST PUBLISHERS).

conciliation: *see* MEDIATION.

Conciliation, Commissioners of: *see* MEDI-ATION.

conciliator, individual who is assigned or who assumes the responsibility for maintaining disputing parties in negotiations until they reach a voluntary settlement. The Federal Mediation and Conciliation Service (FMCS) has Commissioners of Conciliation located in its various regional offices available to assist parties in the settlement of labor–management disputes.

concurrent validity, to assess the concurrent validity of a prospective employment examination, it must be given to individuals already performing successfully on the job. Each incumbent must also be independently rated by supervisors on actual job performance. Then the test scores and the ratings are correlated. If the better workers also obtain the better test scores, then the examination can be said to have concurrent validity. *See* Bruce A. Fournier and Paul Stager, "Concurrent Validation of a Dual-Task Selection Test," *Journal of Applied Psychology* (October 1976).

Confectionery Workers' International Union of America: *see* LABOR ORGANIZATION, Bakery and Confectionery Workers' International Union of America.

Conference Board, Inc., The, independent, nonprofit business research organization. For more than 60 years it has continuously served as an institution for scientific research in the fields of business economics and business management. Its sole purpose is to promote prosperity and security by assisting in the effective operation and sound development of voluntary productive enterprise. The Board has more than 4,000 associates and serves 40,000 individuals throughout the world. It does continuing research in the fields of economic conditions, marketing, finance, personnel administration, international activities, public affairs, antitrust, and various other related areas.

> *The Conference Board, Inc.*
> 845 Third Ave.
> New York, NY 10022

confidence testing, testing approach that allows the subject to express his or her attraction to or confidence in possible answers in percentage terms. *See* Ernest S. Selig, "Confidence Testing Comes of Age," *Training and Development Journal* (July 1972).

conflict of interest, any situation where a decision that may be made (or influenced) by an office holder may (or may appear to) be to that office holder's personal benefit.

conflict resolution, according to Kenneth E. Boulding, in *Conflict and Defense: A General Theory* (N.Y.: Harper & Bros., 1962), the objective of conflict resolution is to see that conflicts, which are inevitable, remain constructive rather than destructive. Traditional administrative theory, having been based on the models provided by the military and the Catholic Church, viewed organizational conflict as deviancy. But the growing recognition that reasonable conflict can produce organizational benefits is leading to changes in administrative structure that will permit and control conflict. Since it has been the hierarchical structure of organizations that has commonly suppressed the potential value of conflict, that hierarchical structure must be altered before conflict can come into its full beneficent flower. The implications of this for the future of personnel management are awesome.

confrontation meeting, organization development technique that has an organizational group (usually the management corps) meet for a one-day effort to assay their organizational health. *See* Richard Beckhard, "The Confrontation Meeting," *Harvard Business Review* (March-April 1967).

congressional exemption, exclusion of the approximately 18,000 congressional staff employees from coverage of the large variety of laws regulating working conditions that the U.S. Congress has passed throughout the years. Each member of Congress has complete autonomy over the pay and working conditions of his or her staff and need not comply with laws on labor relations, equal pay, civil rights, occupational safety, etc.

See also DAVIS V. PASSMAN.

Congress of Independent Unions: *see* LABOR ORGANIZATION, Independent Unions, Congress of.

Congress of Industrial Organizations (CIO), labor organization that originated in 1935, when the Committee for Industrial Organization was formed within the American Federation of Labor (AFL) to foster the organization of workers in mass production industries. The activities of the Committee precipitated a split in the AFL because many of the older union leaders refused to depart from the craft union concept. In 1937, those unions associated with the committee were formally expelled from the AFL. One year later, those unions formed their own federation—the Congress of Industrial Organizations—with John L. Lewis as its first president. In 1955, the CIO formally merged with the AFL to form the present AFL–CIO. For a history of the split, *see* Walter Galenson, *The CIO Challenge to the AFL: A History of the American Labor Movement, 1935–1941* (Cambridge, Mass.: Harvard University Press, 1960). *See also* AMERICAN FEDERATION OF LABOR–CONGRESS OF INDUSTRIAL ORGANIZATIONS.

Connecticut Employees Union: *see* LABOR ORGANIZATION.

Connecticut State Employees Association: *see* LABOR ORGANIZATION.

Connecticut State Labor Council, AFL–CIO: *see* AMERICAN FEDERATION OF LABOR–CONGRESS OF INDUSTRIAL ORGANIZATIONS.

Connell v. *Higginbotham*, 403 U.S. 207 (1971), U.S. Supreme Court case, which held that it was unconstitutional to require public employees to swear that they "do not believe in the overthrow of the Government of the United States or of the State of Florida by force or violence." The court reasoned that at the very least, the Constitution required that a hearing or inquiry be held to determine the reasons for refusal.

See also LOYALTY OATH.

CONN-EU: *see* LABOR ORGANIZATION, Connecticut Employees Union.

CONN-SEA: *see* LABOR ORGANIZATION, Connecticut State Employees Association.

consensual validation, procedure of using mutual agreement as the criterion for validity.

consent decree, approach to enforcing equal employment opportunity involving a negotiated settlement that allows an employer to not admit to any acts of discrimination yet agree to greater EEO efforts in the future. Consent decrees are usually negotiated with the Equal Employment Opportunity Commission or a federal court. *See* Lewis J. Ringler, "EEO Agreements and Consent Decrees may be Booby-Traps," *The Personnel Administrator* (February 1977).

conspiracy doctrine: *see* SHAW, LEMUEL.

construct, an idea or concept created or synthesized ("constructed") from available information and refined through scientific investigation. In psychological testing, a construct is usually dimensional, an attribute of people that varies in degree from one person to another. Tests are usually intended to be measures of intellectual, perceptual, psychomotor, or personality constructs (*e.g.,* a clerical test may measure the construct known as "perceptual speed and accuracy" or the performance of invoice clerks may be measured in terms of "ability to recognize errors").

construct validity, measure of how adequate a test is for assessing the possession of particular psychological traits or qualities.

Construction Labor Report, weekly report on union–management developments in the construction labor field published by the Bureau of National Affairs, Inc. Covers bargaining issues, settlements, job-safety and health developments under the Occupational Safety and Health Administration, equal employment opportunity activities, union policies and activities, agency and court decisions, arbitration awards, and state and federal legislative developments. Also supplies economic data, such as industry earnings, hours of work, cost of living, and employment figures.

constructive discharge theory, if an employer makes conditions of continued employment so intolerable that it results in a "constructive discharge" whereby the employee "voluntarily" leaves, the employer may still be subject to charges that the employer violated Title VII of the Civil Rights Act of 1964, which generally prohibits employers from discharging employees because of their race, color, sex, or national origin.

Consulting Psychologists Press, Inc.: *see* TEST PUBLISHERS.

Consumer Credit Protection Act of 1970, limits the amount of an employee's disposable income which may be garnisheed and protects employees from discharge because of one garnishment.

Consumer Price Index (CPI), also called COST-OF-LIVING INDEX, monthly statistical measure of the average change in prices in a fixed market basket of goods and services. Effective with the January 1978 CPI, the Bureau of Labor Statistics began publishing CPI's for two groups of the population. One index, a new CPI for "All Urban Consumers," covers 80 percent of the total noninstitutional population. The other index, a revised CPI for "Urban Wage Earners and Clerical

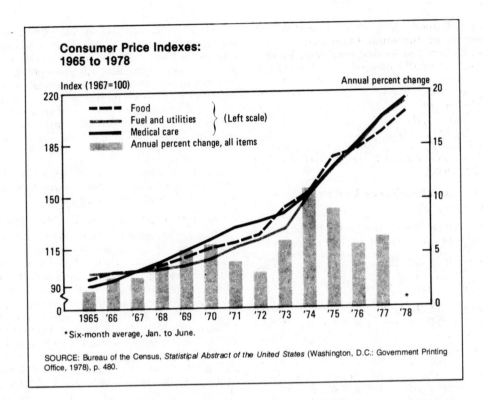

Consumer Price Indexes: 1965 to 1978

Index (1967=100)   Annual percent change

- - - Food
········· Fuel and utilities } (Left scale)
──── Medical care
▓▓▓ Annual percent change, all items

1965 '66 '67 '68 '69 '70 '71 '72 '73 '74 '75 '76 '77 '78

*Six-month average, Jan. to June.

SOURCE: Bureau of the Census, *Statistical Abstract of the United States* (Washington, D.C.: Government Printing Office, 1978), p. 480.

Workers," covers about half the new index population. The "All Urban Consumers" index includes, in addition to urban wage earners and clerical workers, professional, managerial, and technical workers, the self-employed, short-term workers, the un-employed, retirees, and others not in the labor force.

The CPI is based on prices of food, cloth-ing, shelter, fuel, drugs, transportation fares, doctor's and dentist's fees, and other goods and services that people buy for day-to-day living. The quantity and quality of these items is kept essentially unchanged between major revisions so that only price changes will be measured. Prices are collected from over 18,000 tenants, 24,000 retail establish-ments, and 18,000 housing units for property taxes in 85 urban areas across the country. All taxes directly associated with the purchase and use of items are included in the index.

Though the CPI is often called the *Cost-of-Living Index*, it measures only price change, which is just one of several important factors affecting living costs. Area indexes do not measure differences in the level of prices

Consumer Price Index for Urban Wage Earners and Clerical Workers, annual averages and changes, 1967–77

[1967 = 100]

Year	All items Index	Percent change	Food and beverages Index	Percent change	Housing Index	Percent change	Apparel and upkeep Index	Percent change	Transportation Index	Percent change	Medical care Index	Percent change	Entertainment Index	Percent change	Other goods and services Index	Percent change
1967	100.0	......	100.0	......	100.0	......	100.0	......	100.0	......	100.0	......	100.0	......	100.0	......
1968	104.2	4.2	103.6	3.6	104.0	4.0	105.4	5.4	103.2	3.2	106.1	6.1	105.7	5.7	105.2	5.2
1969	109.8	5.4	108.8	5.0	110.4	6.2	111.5	5.8	107.2	3.9	113.4	6.9	111.0	5.0	110.4	4.9
1970	116.3	5.9	114.7	5.4	118.2	7.1	116.1	4.1	112.7	5.1	120.6	6.3	116.7	5.1	116.8	5.8
1971	121.3	4.3	118.3	3.1	123.4	4.4	119.8	3.2	118.6	5.2	128.4	6.5	122.9	5.3	122.4	4.8
1972	125.3	3.3	123.2	4.1	128.1	3.8	122.3	2.1	119.9	1.1	132.5	3.2	126.5	2.9	127.5	4.2
1973	133.1	6.2	139.5	13.2	133.7	4.4	126.8	3.7	123.8	3.3	137.7	3.9	130.0	2.8	132.5	3.9
1974	147.7	11.0	158.7	13.8	148.8	11.3	136.2	7.4	137.7	11.2	150.5	9.3	139.8	7.5	142.0	7.2
1975	161.2	9.1	172.1	8.4	164.5	10.6	142.3	4.5	150.6	9.4	168.6	12.0	152.2	8.9	153.9	8.4
1976	170.5	5.8	177.4	3.1	174.6	6.1	147.6	3.7	165.5	9.9	184.7	9.5	159.8	5.0	162.7	5.7
1977	181.5	6.5	188.0	6.0	186.5	6.8	154.2	4.5	177.2	7.1	202.4	9.6	167.7	4.9	172.2	5.8

SOURCE: *Monthly Labor Review* (August 1978), p. 81.

among cities; they only measure the average change in prices for each area since the base period. For a brief history, *see* Julius Shiskin, "Updating the Consumer Price Index—An Overview," *Monthly Labor Review* (July 1974).

contact counseling, according to Len Sperry and Lee R. Hess, *Contact Counseling: Communication Skills for People in Organizations* (Reading, Mass.: Addison-Wesley, 1974), contact counseling "is the process by which the manager aids the employee to effectively problem-solve and develop."

content validity, a selection device has content validity if it measures the specific abilities needed to perform the job. Examinations that require applicants to perform an actual, representative sample of the work done on the job would obviously have content validity. *See* Stephen Wollack, "Content Validity: Its Legal and Psychometric Basis, *Public Personnel Management* (November-December 1976); Lyle F. Schoenfeldt *et al.*, "Content Validity Revisited," *Journal of Applied Psychology* (October 1976); Erich P. Prien, "The Function of Job Analysis in Content Validation," *Personnel Psychology* (Summer 1977); Stephen J. Mussio and Mary K. Smith, *Content Validity: A Procedural Manual* (Chicago: International Personnel Management Association, 1973).

contextual variable, a condition that may affect the validity of a test.

contingency management, also called SITUATIONAL MANAGEMENT, any management style that recognizes that the application of theory to practice must necessarily take into consideration, and be contingent upon, the given situation. *See* Henry L. Tosi and W. Clay Hamner, *Organizational Behavior and Management: A Contingency Approach* (Chicago, Ill.: St. Clair Press, 1974).

contingency model of leadership effectiveness, Fred E. Fiedler's theory of leadership effectiveness. According to Fiedler, the appropriate leadership style is determined by three critical elements in the leader's situation: (1) the power position of the leader; (2) the task structure; (3) the leader–member personal relationships. The nature of these three factors determines the "favorableness" of the situation for the leader, which in turn requires a particular leadership style. Fiedler views leader behavior as a single dimension ranging from "task-oriented" to "relationship-oriented." He contends that task-oriented leaders perform best in very favorable or very unfavorable situations, whereas relationship-oriented leaders are best in mixed situations. Fiedler suggests that it may be to an organization's advantage to try to design jobs to fit leaders' styles rather than attempting to change leaders' behavior to fit the situation. For the original presentation, *see* Fred E. Fiedler, *A Theory of Leadership Effectiveness* (N.Y.: McGraw-Hill, 1967). For a critique of Fiedler's concepts, *see* George Green, James Orris, and Kenneth M. Alvares, "Contingency Model of Leadership Effectiveness: Some Methodological Issues," *Journal of Applied Psychology* (June 1971).

continuing education, general term that usually refers to graduate or undergraduate course work undertaken on a part-time basis in order to keep up to date on new developments in one's occupational field, learn a new field, or contribute to one's general education. *See* Irwin M. Rubin and Homer G. Morgan, "A Projective Study of Attitudes Toward Continuing Education," *Journal of Applied Psychology*, Vol. 51, No. 6 (1967); Philip T. Crotty." "Continuing Education and the Experienced Manager," *California Management Review* (Fall, 1974); Richard Morano, "Continuing Education in Industry," *Personnel Journal* (February 1973).

continuous negotiating committee, labor–management committee established to review a collective bargaining agreement on a continuous basis.

contract: *see* the following entries:
BREACH OF CONTRACT
EMPLOYMENT CONTRACT
INCENTIVE CONTRACT
INDIVIDUAL CONTRACT
IRON-CLAD OATH
LABOR AGREEMENT
MASTER AGREEMENT
SWEETHEART CONTRACT
TERMINATION CONTRACT
YELLOW-DOG CONTRACT

contract bar, an existing collective bargaining agreement that bars a representation election sought by a competing union.

contracting-out, having work performed outside an organization's own work force. Contracting-out has often been an area of union–management disagreement. While many unions recognize management's right to occasionally subcontract a job requiring specialized skills and equipment not possessed by the company or its employees, they oppose the letting of work that could be done by the organization's own work force. In particular, unions are concerned if work normally performed by its members is contracted to firms having inferior wages or working conditions or if such action may result in reduced earnings or layoffs of regular employees.

contract labor, workers imported from a foreign country for employment with a specific employer.

contributory pension plan, any pension program that has employees contributing a portion of the cost.

convalescent leave, federal government agencies have the right to grant convalescent leave to civilian employees on duty abroad who are injured as a result of "war, insurgency, mob violence, or other similar hostile action." Such leave with pay is completely separate from an employee's sick-leave benefits.

convergent validity, in testing, evidence that different measures of a construct will produce similar results.

converted score, general term referring to any of a variety of "transformed" scores, in terms of which raw scores on a test may be expressed for such reasons as facilitating interpretation and permitting comparison with scores on other tests forms. For example, the raw scores obtained by candidates on the various College Board tests are converted to scores on a common scale that ranges from 200 to 800.

convict labor: *see* ASHURST–SUMNERS ACT OF 1935.

coolie labor, originally a term for unskilled Asian labor in the 19th-century U.S., the phrase is now applied—typically in a jocular or derisive manner—to any cheap labor.

cooling-off period, Any legal provision that postpones a strike or lockout for a specific period of time in order to give the parties an additional opportunity to mediate their differences. While the device has great popular appeal, it has proven to be of doubtful value because "more time" will not necessarily resolve a labor dispute. The first federal requirements for a cooling-off period were set forth in the War Labor Disputes (Smith–Connally) Act of 1943. This was superceded by the national emergency provisions of the National Labor Relations (Taft–Hartley) Act of 1947, which called for an 80-day cooling-off period in the event of a "national emergency."

cooperative education, an educational process wherein students alternate formal studies with actual work experiences. It is distinguished from other part-time employment in that successful completion of the off-campus experiences becomes a prerequisite for graduation. For an account of one company's experiences over twenty years, *see* Jack J. Phillips, "Is Cooperative Education Worth It? One Company's Answer," *Personnel Journal* (October 1977). For a text, *see* Ronald W. Stadt and Bill G. Gooch, *Cooperative Education* (Indianapolis: Bobbs-Merrill Co., Inc., 1977).

Cooperative School and College Ability Test (SCAT), test designed to measure basic verbal and mathematical abilities. Most commonly used to yield an estimate of academic potential in college, this test is also used by manager assessment centers. TIME: 40/50 minutes. PUBLISHER: Cooperative Tests and Services, Educational Testing Service (*see* TEST PUBLISHERS).

Cooperative School Program: *see* UNITED STATES EMPLOYMENT SERVICE.

Coopers' International Union of North America: *see* LABOR ORGANIZATION.

Cooper v. Delta Airlines, 274 F.Supp. 781 (1967), case in which a U.S. district court invalidated the practice of firing women stewardesses who were either married or more than 32 years old.

cooptation, efforts of an organization to bring and subsume new elements into its policymaking process in order to prevent such elements from being a threat to the organization or its mission. The classic analysis of cooptation is found in Philip Selznick's *TVA and the Grass Roots* (Berkeley, Calif.: University of California Press, 1949).

coordinated bargaining: *see* COALITION BARGAINING.

COPE: *see* COMMITTEE ON POLITICAL EDUCATION.

Copeland Act: *see* KICKBACK.

Corning Glass Works v. Brennan, 417 U.S. 188 (1974), U.S. Supreme Court case, which held that it was a violation of the Equal Pay Act of 1963 to continue to pay some men at a higher rate ("red circle") than women for the same work even though all new hires for these same positions would receive the same salary regardless of sex.

Coronado Coal v. United Mine Workers, 268 U.S. 295 (1925), U.S. Supreme Court case, which held that unincorporated organizations such as labor unions could be sued and held liable for damages.

corporation headhunter: *see* HEADHUNTER.

corporation man, concept, developed by Anthony Jay, in *Corporation Man: Who He Is, What He Does, Why His Ancient Tribal Impulses Dominate the Life of the Modern Corporation* (N.Y.: Random House, 1971), which holds man's primative instincts as a hunter prevail in the corporate world.

correction for guessing, reduction in a test score for wrong answers—sometimes applied in scoring multiple-choice questions—that is intended to discourage guessing and to yield more accurate ranking of examinees in terms of their true knowledge.

correlation, relationship or "going-togetherness" between two sets of scores or measures; the tendency of one score to vary concomitantly with the other.

correlation, biserial: *see* BISERIAL CORRELATION.

correlation coefficient, number expressing the degree to which two measures tend to vary together. A correlation coefficient can range from -1.00 (a perfect negative relationship) to $+1.00$ (a perfect positive relationship). When there is no correlation between two measures, the coefficient is 0. A correlation coefficient only indicates concomitance; it does not indicate causation.

The values of the correlation coefficient are easily misinterpreted since they do not fall along an ordinary, absolute scale. For example, a correlation coefficient of .20 does not signify twice as much relationship as does one of .10, nor can a correlation coefficient be interpreted as a percentage statement. A correlation coefficient is a mathematical index number, which requires for its interpretation some knowledge of that branch of mathematical statistics known as correlation theory. As a very rough guide to interpretation, however, a correlation between a single employment test and a measure of job performance of approximately .20 often is high enough to be useful (such correlations rarely exceed .50), a correlation of .40 is ordinarily considered very good, and most personnel research workers are usually pleased with a correlation of .30.

The mathematical symbol for the correlation coefficient is: r.

cosmic search, in the context of equal employment opportunity, the cosmic search refers to an endless search by an employer for an alternative selection procedure with less adverse impact.

cosmopolitan–local construct, two latent social roles that manifest themselves in organizational settings, according to Alvin W. Gouldner. The first role, *cosmopolitan*, tends to be adopted by true professionals. It assumes a small degree of loyalty to the employing organization, a high commitment to specialized skills, and an outer-reference group orientation. The second role, *local*, tends to be adopted by nonprofessionals. It assumes a high degree of loyalty to the employing organization, a low commitment to specialized skills, and an inner-reference group orientation. These role models are extremes and represent the two ends of a continuum. *See* Alvin W. Gouldner, "Cosmopolitans and Locals: Toward an Analysis of Latent Social Roles—I," *Administrative Science Quarterly* (December 1957). While Gouldner's construct has received substantial empirical testing and criticisms, its value as a general model remains evident. For a critical examination of the construct, *see* Andrew J. Grimes and Philip K. Berger, "Cosmopolitan–Local: Evaluation of a Construct," *Administrative Science Quarterly* (December 1970).

cost–benefit analysis, also BENEFIT–COST ANALYSIS, any process by which organizations seek to determine the effectiveness of their spending, in relation to costs, in meeting policy objectives. *See* E. J. Mishan, *Cost–Benefit Analysis*, new and expanded edition (N.Y.: Praeger Publishers, 1976); Logan Cheek, "Cost Effectiveness Comes to the Personnel Function," *Harvard Business Review* (May-June 1973).

cost effectiveness: *see* COST–BENEFIT ANALYSIS.

cost-of-living adjustment (COLA), also COST-OF-LIVING ALLOWANCE, a *cost-of-living adjustment* is an increase in compensation in response to increasing inflation. A *cost-of-living allowance* is additional compensation for accepting employment in high costs-of-living areas. *See* Robert J. Thorton, "A Problem with the 'COLA' Craze," *Compensation Review* (Second Quarter 1977).

cost-of-living escalator: *see* ESCALATOR CLAUSE.

costing-out, determining the actual cost of a

contract proposal (wages and fringe benefits). *See* W. D. Heisel and Gordon S. Skinner, *Costing Union Demands* (Chicago: International Personnel Management Association, 1976).

Cost of Living Council, federal agency, authorized by the Economic Stabilization Act of 1970, which monitored inflation. Created by Executive Order 11615 in 1971, it was abolished by Executive Order 11788 in 1974.

Cost-of-Living Index: *see* CONSUMER PRICE INDEX.

Council of Economic Advisers (CEA), established in the Executive Office of the President by the Employment Act of 1946, the CEA consists of three economists (one designated chairman) appointed by the president by and with the advice and consent of the Senate who formulate proposals to "maintain employment, production and purchasing power." The CEA, as the president's primary source of economic advice, assists the president in preparing various economic reports.

Council of Economic Advisers
Executive Office Building
Washington, DC 20506
(202) 395-5084

Council on Wage and Price Stability, established in 1974 within the Executive Office of the President, the Council monitors the economy as a whole with respect to key indicators such as wages, costs, productivity, profits, and prices.

Council on Wage and Price Stability
726 Jackson Place, N.W.
Washington, DC 20506
(202) 456-6757

counseling, crisis: *see* CRISIS INTERVENTION.

counseling, employee: *see* EMPLOYEE COUNSELING.

counterproposal, offer made by a party in response to an earlier offer made by another party.

County Office Employees, National Association of ASCS: *see* LABOR ORGANIZATION, ASCS County Office Employees, National Association of.

court of appeals, also called FEDERAL COURT OF APPEALS and U.S. COURT OF APPEALS, appellate court below the U.S. Supreme Court, which hears appeals from cases tried in federal district courts. In most cases, a decision by a court of appeals is final since only a

small fraction of their decisions are ever reviewed by the U.S. Supreme Court. Before 1948 the court of appeals was called the circuit court of appeals.

cousin laboratory, a laboratory training experience for people who have no direct working relationship with each other but come from the same organization.

Couturier, Jean J. (1927-   ), professional reformer, agitator, and teacher. As the executive director of the National Civil Service League, he was the single individual most responsible for the League's promulgation of its 1970 "Model Public Personnel Administration Law," which called for the abolition of traditional civil service commissions. For an account of this abolition movement, *see* Jean J. Couturier, "The Quiet Revolution in Public Personnel Laws," *Public Personnel Management* (May-June 1976).

covered jobs, all those positions that are affected and protected by specific labor legislation.

Coxey's Army, originally a group of about 500 unemployed men who marched on Washington in 1894 in an effort to pressure the government into providing public works employment. The "army" led by a self-styled "general," Jacob S. Coxey, ended ignominiously when Coxey and a few of his followers were arrested for trespassing on White House grounds. For a history, *see* Donald L. McMurry, *Coxey's Army: A Study of the Industrial Army Movement of 1894* (Seattle, Wash.: University of Washington Press, 1929, 1968).

CPA: *see* CERTIFIED PUBLIC ACCOUNTANT.

CPI: *see* (1) CALIFORNIA PSYCHOLOGICAL INVENTORY and (2) CONSUMER PRICE INDEX.

CPI Detailed Report, U.S. Bureau of Labor Statistics' monthly publication featuring detailed data and charts on the Consumer Price Index.

CPI Detailed Report
Superintendent of Documents
Government Printing Office
Washington, DC 20402

CPM: *see* CRITICAL PATH METHOD.

craft, any occupation requiring specific skills that must be acquired by training.

craft guild: *see* GUILD.

craft union, also called HORIZONTAL UNION and TRADE UNION, labor organization that restricts its membership to skilled craft workers (such as plumbers, carpenters, etc.), in contrast to an industrial union that seeks to recruit all workers in a particular industry. The U.S. labor movement has its origins in small craft unions. For a history, *see* Lloyd Ulman, *The Rise of the National Trade Union* (Cambridge, Mass.: Harvard University Press, 1966).

craft unit, bargaining unit that consists only of workers with the same specific skill (such as electricians, plumbers, or carpenters).

Crawford Small Parts Dexterity Test, two-part, timed test of manual dexterity. Measures fine eye-hand coordination such as that used in clock repair, hearing aid repair, and in manipulation of small hand tools. TIME: 15/20 minutes. AUTHORS: John E. and Dorthea M. Crawford. PUBLISHER: Psychological Corporation (*see* TEST PUBLISHERS).

creativity test, test that stresses divergent thinking or the ability to create new or original answers; considered useful for examining the culturally disadvantaged and certain ethnic groups whose command of English is not highly developed. Such tests utilize common and familiar objects in order to sample the testee's originality, flexibility, and fluency of thinking. Tasks include suggesting improvements in familiar devices such as telephones or listing many possible uses for a broom handle. The tests are scored simply on the number of acceptable answers given by the subject. *See* John A. Hattie, "Conditions for Administering Creativity Tests," *Psychological Bulletin* (November 1977).

credentialism, an emphasis on paper manifestations, such as college degrees, instead of an actual ability to accomplish the tasks of a job. For two attacks on the value of the credentials offered by higher education, *see* John Keats, *The Sheepskin Psychosis* (Philadelphia: J. B. Lippincott, 1965); Caroline Bird, *The Case Against College* (N.Y.: David McKay Co., 1975). For how to avoid the problem, *see* H. Dudley Dewhirst, "It's Time to Put the Brakes on Credentialism," *Personnel Journal* (October 1973). For a history, *see* Randall Collins, *The Credential Society: An Historical Sociology of Education and Stratification* (New York: Academic Press, 1979).

See also RESTRICTIVE CREDENTIALISM.

credit check, reference check on a prospective employee's financial standing. Such checks are usually only conducted when fi-

nancial status may bear upon the job, as with bank tellers, for example.

credit union, not a labor union, but a cooperative savings and loan association.

credited service, employment time that an employee has for benefit purposes.

crisis bargaining, collective bargaining negotiations conducted under the pressure of a strike deadline.

crisis intervention, a formal effort to help an individual experiencing a crisis to reestablish equilibrium. A crisis is a turning point in a person's life. It can be the death of a child, spouse, or parent. It can be a heart attack. It can be anything that tests the limits of an individual's ability to cope. *See* Mike Berger, "Crisis Intervention in Personnel Administration," *Personnel Journal* (November 1969); William Getz *et al.*, *Fundamentals of Crisis Counseling: A Handbook* (Lexington, Mass.: Lexington Books, 1974); Romaine V. Edwards, *Crisis Intervention and How it Works* (Springfield, Ill.: Charles C Thomas, 1977).

criterion, plural CRITERIA, measure of job performance or other work-related behavior against which performance on a test or other predictor measure is compared.

criterion contamination, influence on criterion measures of variables or factors not relevant to the work behavior being measured. If the criterion is, for example, a set of supervisory ratings of competence in job performance and if the ratings are correlated with the length of time the supervisor has known the individual people he/she rates, then the length of acquaintance is a contaminant of the criterion measure. Similarly, if the amount of production on a machine is counted as the criterion measure and if the amount of production depends in part on the age of the machine being used, then age of machinery is a contaminant of production counts.

criterion objective: *see* PERFORMANCE OBJECTIVE.

criterion-referenced test, test by which a candidate's performance is measured according to the degree a specified criterion has been met.

criterion related validation: *see* STATISTICAL VALIDATION.

criterion relevance, judgment of the degree to which a criterion measure reflects the important aspects of job performance. Such a judgment is based on an understanding of the measurement process itself, of the job and worker requirements as revealed through careful job analysis, and of the needs of the organization.

critical-incident method, also called CRITICAL-INCIDENT TECHNIQUE, identifying, classifying and recording significant examples—critical incidents—of an employee's behavior for purposes of performance evaluation. The theory behind the critical-incidents approach holds that there are certain key acts of behavior that make the difference between success and failure. After the incidents are collected they can be ranked in order of frequency and importance and assigned numerical weights. Once scored, they can be equally as useful for employee development and counseling as for formal appraisals. For the pioneering work on the concept, *see* John C. Flanagan, "The Critical Incident Technique," *Psychological Bulletin* (July 1954); John C. Flanagan and Robert K. Burns, "The Employee Performance Record: A New Approach and Development Tool," *Harvard Business Review* (September-October 1957).

critical path method (CPM), network-analysis technique for planning and scheduling. The "critical path" is a sequence of activities that connect the beginning and end of events or program accomplishments. *See* J. D. Wiest and F. K. Levy, *A Management Guide to PERT/CPM* (Englewood Cliffs, N.J.: Prentice-Hall, 2nd ed., 1977).

critical score: *see* CUTTING SCORE.

cross-check, procedure by which the National Labor Relations Board or an appropriate state agency compares union authorization cards to an employer's payroll to determine whether a majority of the employees wish union representation. With the employer's consent, such a cross-check can bring union recognition and certification without a formal hearing and election.

cross picketing, picketing by more than one union when each claims to represent the workforce.

cross validation, process which seeks to apply the results of one validation study to another. As such, it is a check on the accuracy of the original validation study.

crude score: *see* RAW SCORE.

CSEA: *see* LABOR ORGANIZATION, Civil Service Employees Association, Inc.

CTMM: *see* CALIFORNIA TEST OF MENTAL MATURITY.

CTMM/SF: *see* CALIFORNIA SHORT FORM TEST OF MENTAL MATURITY.

cultural bias, in the context of employee selection, cultural bias refers to the indirect and incidental (as opposed to direct and deliberate) bias of individuals and instruments making selection decisions. Also, the propensity of a test to reflect favorable or unfavorable effects of certain types of cultural backgrounds. *See* Ollie A. Jensen, "Cultural Bias in Selection," *Public Personnel Review* (April 1966).

culturally disadvantaged, groups that do not have full participation in U.S. society because of low incomes, substandard housing, poor education, and other "atypical" environmental experiences.

culture-fair test, also called CULTURE-FREE TEST, a test yielding results that are not culturally biased. For an analysis, *see* R. L. Thorndike, "Concepts of Culture-Fairness," *Journal of Educational Measurement* (Summer 1971).

cumulative band chart: *see* BAND CURVE CHART.

cumulative frequency, sum of successively added frequencies (usually) of test scores.

cumulative frequency graph, graphic presentation of a cumulative frequency distribution, which has the frequencies expressed in terms of the number of cases or as a percentage of all cases.

cumulative percentage, cumulative frequency expressed as a percentage.

CUPA: *see* COLLEGE AND UNIVERSITY PERSONNEL ASSOCIATION.

Current Wage Developments, U.S. Bureau of Labor Statistics' monthly report about collective bargaining settlements and unilateral management decisions about wages and benefits.

> *Current Wage Developments*
> Superintendent of Documents
> Government Printing Office
> Washington, DC 20402

curricular validity, degree to which an examination is representative of the body of knowledge for which it is testing.

curriculum vita: *see* RESUME.

cutback, workforce reduction that results in layoffs.

cutting score, also called CRITICAL SCORE, PASSING SCORE, or PASSING POINT, test score used as an employment requirement. Those at or above such a score are eligible for selection or promotion, whereas those below the score are not.

There are many approaches to establishing the cutting score. Perhaps the most defensible is one of the job-related approaches (e.g., using data from a criterion-related validity study). A common and practical approach is the *flexible passing score*, which is established for each test on the basis of a number of factors (some of which, such as the number of positions to be filled, may not be job-related). Arbitrarily establishing a cutting score of 70 percent in an attempt to be certain all eligibles possess the traits desired for a job (the *70-percent syndrome*) is not defensible from a psychometric point of view and has resulted in the costly situation where no applicants are eligible after taking a difficult test. *See* Glenn G. McClung, *Considerations in Developing Test Passing Points* (Chicago: International Personnel Management Association, 1974).

See also MULTIPLE CUTTING SCORE.

CWA: *see* LABOR ORGANIZATION, Communications Workers of America.

cycle time: *see* JOB SCOPE.

cyclical unemployment, unemployment caused by a downward trend in the business cycle.

D

DAF: *see* DECISION-ANALYSIS FORECASTING.

Daily Labor Report, this Bureau of National Affairs, Inc., report gives Monday through Friday notification of all significant developments in the labor field. Covers congressional activities, court and NLRB decisions, arbitration, union developments, key contract negotiations, and settlements.

daily rate, basic pay earned by an employee for a standard work day.

Dale, Ernest (1917-), a leading authority on management and leadership. Major works include: *The Great Organizers* (N.Y.: McGraw-Hill, 1960); *Staff in Organization*, with L. F. Urwick (N.Y.: McGraw-Hill, 1960); *Management: Theory and Practice* (N.Y.: McGraw-Hill, 1965); *Modern Management Methods*, with C. C. Michelon (Cleveland: World Publishing, 1965).

***Danbury Hatters'* case:** *see* LAWLOR V. LOEWE.

danger-zone bonus, bonus paid to employees as an inducement to get them to work in an area that is especially hazardous.

***Darby Lumber* case:** *see* UNITED STATES V. DARBY LUMBER.

***Darlington* case:** *see* TEXTILE WORKERS V. DARLINGTON MANUFACTURING COMPANY.

DAT: *see* DIFFERENTIAL APTITUDE TESTS.

data, *datum* is a single bit of information; *data* is the plural of datum.

data bank, also called DATA BASE, information stored in a computer system so that any particular item or set of items could be extracted or organized as needed. Data bank (or data base) is also used to refer to any data-storage system.

datum: *see* DATA.

Davis–Bacon Act of 1931, also called PREVAILING WAGE LAW, federal law passed in 1931, which requires contractors on federal construction projects to pay the rates of pay and fringe benefits that prevail in their geographic areas. Prevailing rates are determined by the Secretary of Labor and must be paid on all federal contracts and subcontracts of $2,000.00 or more. For an economic analysis of the impact of the act, *see* Armand J. Thieblot, Jr., *et al.*, *The Davis–Bacon Act* (Phila.: The Wharton School of the University of Pennsylvania, 1975).

Davis, Keith (1918-), sometimes called "Mr. Human Relations" because his work marks the beginning of the modern view of human relations with its empirical approach to understanding organizational behavior. Major works include: *Human Relations in Business* (N.Y.: McGraw-Hill, 1957); *Human Relations at Work* (N.Y.: McGraw-Hill, 1962); *Business and Its Environment*, with R. L. Blomstron (N.Y.: McGraw-Hill, 1966); *Human Behavior at Work* (N.Y.: McGraw-Hill, 1977).

Davis Reading Test, this test yields two scores measuring the level and speed of reading comprehension. Used by business and industry in employee training and development and in assessment centers. TIME: 40/55 minutes. AUTHORS: F. B. and C. C. Davis. PUBLISHER: Psychological Corporation (*see* TEST PUBLISHERS).

Davis v. Passman, 60 L.Ed. 2d 846 (1979), U.S. Supreme Court case, which held that a woman discharged from employment by a U.S. congressman had the 5th Amendment right to seek to recover damages from the congressman for alleged sex discrimination.
See also CONGRESSIONAL EXEMPTION.

day wage, earnings for a set number of hours per day.

daywork, regular day shift that is paid on the basis of time rather than output.

day worker, casual, usually unskilled, worker hired by the day.

dead time, time on the job lost by a worker through no fault of his own.

dead work, mining term that refers to required work (removing debris, rocks, etc.) that does not directly produce the material being mined.

deadheading, bypassing of more senior employees in order to promote a more qualified but more junior employee. In the transportation industry, deadheading refers to (1) the movement of empty vehicles to a place where they are needed and (2) the practice of providing free transportation for the company's employees.

Dean v. Gadsden Times Publishing Corp., 412 U.S. 543 (1973), Supreme Court case, which upheld an Alabama law providing that an employee called to serve on a jury "shall be entitled to his usual compensation received from such employment less the fee or compensation he received for serving" as a juror.

death benefit, benefit provided under a pension plan that is paid to an employee's survivors or estate. Payments may be made in monthly installments or in a lump sum.

Debs, Eugene V(ictor) (1855-1926), probably the most famous labor organizer of his time and Socialist Party candidate for president of the United States five times between 1900 and 1920. For a biography, see Ray Ginger, *The Bending Cross: A Biography of Eugene Victor Debs* (New Brunswick, N.J.: Rutgers University, Press, 1949).

debugging, process of detecting, locating, and removing mistakes or imperfections from a computer program or any new system.

De Canas v. Bica, 424 U.S. 351 (1976), U.S. Supreme Court case, which upheld a California statute penalizing those who employed illegal aliens when such employment decreased the employment of citizens and other aliens.

decertification: see CERTIFICATION.

decile, division that contains one tenth of whatever is being divided.

decision-analysis forecasting (DAF), variant of the Delphi Technique developed by the U.S. Civil Service Commission to assist senior management in forecasting manpower and organizational needs. It is specifically designed for use on problems where the experience and judgments of top-level policymakers comprise the basic and often the only information.

DAF develops its forecasts by: (1) "decomposing" each manpower planning problem into its relevant factors, (2) quantifying subjective preferences and probability judgments for each problem factor and (3) combining the available data plus these quantified judgments into a table of predictions. The methodology draws largely on decision-analysis theory, using "decision trees" and some simple mathematics from probability theory.

For the complete methodology, see Bureau of Executive Manpower, U.S. Civil Service Commission, *Decision Analysis Forecasting for Executive Manpower Planning* (Wash. D.C.: U.S. Government Printing Office, June 1974).

See also DELPHI TECHNIQUE.

decisionmaking, career or occupational: see CAREER DECISIONMAKING.

decision rule, any directive established to make decisions in the face of uncertainty. For example, a payroll office might be given a decision rule to deduct one hour's pay from an employee's wages for each lateness that exceeds ten minutes but is less than one hour.

decision tree, graphic method of presenting various decisional alternatives so that the various risks, information needs and courses of action are visually available to the decisionmaker. The various decisional alternatives are displayed in the form of a tree with nodes and branches. Each branch represents an alternative course of action or decision, which leads to a node which represents an event. Thus, a decision tree shows both the different courses of action available as well as their possible outcomes. According to John F. Magee, in "Decision Trees for Decision Making," *Harvard Business Review* (July-August 1964), making a decision tree requires management to:

1. identify the points of decision and alternatives available at each point;
2. identify the points of uncertainty and the type or range of alternative outcomes at each point;
3. estimate the values needed to make the analysis, especially the probabilities of different events or results of action and

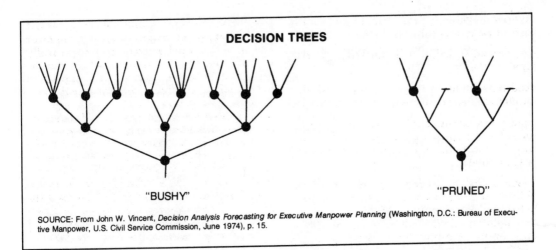

DECISION TREES

"BUSHY"

"PRUNED"

SOURCE: From John W. Vincent, *Decision Analysis Forecasting for Executive Manpower Planning* (Washington, D.C.: Bureau of Executive Manpower, U.S. Civil Service Commission, June 1974), p. 15.

the costs and gains of various events and actions; and

4. analyze the alternative values to choose a course.

decruitment, slang term for the process of recycling older middle- and top-level managers into lower-level, lower-paying positions. The concept was pioneered in Denmark, where some employers freeze promotions for managers at age 50 and start decruiting them at age 60.

deduction, any amount for any reason that is withheld from an employee's pay and credited toward a legitimate purpose such as taxes, insurance, United Fund, etc.

deferred annuity, annuity that does not start until after a specified period or until the annuitant reaches a specified age.

deferred compensation, withholding of a portion of current earnings until a later time, usually retirement, when the receiver would likely be in a lower income-tax bracket.

deferred full vesting, pension plan that provides that an employee retains rights to accrued benefits if he or she is terminated after a specified age and/or after he or she completes a specified period of service in the organization.

deferred graded vesting, pension plan that provides that an employee acquires a right to a specified percentage of accrued benefits if and when he or she meets the participation requirements stipulated by the plan.

deferred life annuity, annuity that becomes effective at a specified future date. If death occurs before the specified date, no benefits

are paid. Once the annuity has started, it continues only for the life of the insured.

deferred rating system, for most federal government positions at GS-9 and above, and for most scientific positions, vacancies are filled under a deferred rating system. There are no "standings" on one of these registers and no numerical score is assigned at time of application, since applications are not rated until specific vacancies become available. Candidates are rated and referred for appointment consideration on the basis of their relative qualifications for a particular position. The best-qualified applicants will be placed at the top of the list of eligibles and will be referred to the agency for employment consideration on the basis of their qualifications and according to the laws regarding veterans' preference and appointment. The names of all other applicants will be returned to the register for possible consideration at a later time.

deferred wage increase, negotiated pay increase that does not become effective until a specified future date.

DeFunis v. Odegaard, 416 U.S. 312 (1974), U.S. Supreme Court case, concerning a white male who was denied admission to law school at the same time minority applicants with lesser academic credentials were accepted. DeFunis challenged the school's action on the grounds that it denied him equal protection of the laws in violation of the fourteenth amendment. He was successful in local court and was admitted. On appeal, the school won a reversal in the state supreme court. Nevertheless, DeFunis remained in law school pending further action by the U.S. Supreme Court. As the nation awaited a definitive resolution of the issue of reverse discrimination, the Supreme Court sought to avoid the problem. Since DeFunis had completed all but his last quarter of law school and was not in danger of being denied his diploma no matter what was decided, a majority of the justices seized upon this fact and declared that the case was consequently "moot"—that it was beyond the court's power to render decisions on hypothetical matters of only potential constitutional substance. *See* Allan P. Sindler, *Bakke, DeFunis, and Minority Admissions: The Quest for Equal Opportunity* (New York: Longman, 1978).

See also the following entries:

REGENTS OF THE UNIVERSITY OF CALIFORNIA V. ALLEN BAKKE
REVERSE DISCRIMINATION
UNITED STEELWORKERS OF AMERICA V. WEBER, ET AL.

degrees, graduations used in the point-rating method of job evaluation to differentiate among job factors.

dehiring, generally, any means of encouraging a marginal or unsatisfactory employee to quit as an alternative to being fired. This face-saving technique allows an organization to: (1) avoid the distasteful aftermath of firing an employee, (2) avoid the implication that someone made a mistake in hiring the employee, (3) avoid the adverse effect of the public thinking that the company is not a secure place in which to be employed, and (4) protect the feelings of the employee involved. *See* Lawrence L. Steinmetz, *Managing the Marginal and Unsatisfactory Performer*, (Reading, Mass.: Addison-Wesley Publishing Company, 1969).

Dellums, C. Laurence (1900-   ), succeeded A. Philip Randolph as president of the Brotherhood of Sleeping Car Porters in 1968.

Deleware State AFL–CIO: *see* AMERICAN FEDERATION OF LABOR–CONGRESS OF INDUSTRIAL ORGANIZATIONS.

Delphi Technique, also called DELPHI EXERCISE and DELPHI METHOD, general term for any methodology that pieces together various opinions in order to arrive at a consensus on the probability of a future event. The Delphi concept involves asking various individuals or groups what their opinions are and weighing their responses by some factor that considers their relative importance or influence on the situation, their expertise, their past forecasting accuracy, etc. When all of the opinions are aggregated, a calculation can be

---

THE DELPHI TECHNIQUE: A HYPOTHETICAL EXAMPLE

The figure below presents a hypothetical decision tree designed to predict the probability of an increase in staffing for an agency that is considering a new training office. The question of the new staff seems to hinge on whether or not the organization's budget is to be cut. In the example, the group of organizational influentials consists of 20 individuals who "vote" on one of four outcomes. But, the final outcome shows that 16 of 20 voters believe the training office will be established anyway. This Delphi exercise concludes that the probability of new training being established is .8—and the organization would do well to begin plans for staffing this new office.

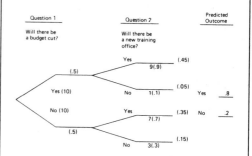

SOURCE: Adapted from John W. Vincent, *Decision Analysis Forecasting For Executive Manpower Planning* (Washington D.C.: Bureau of Executive Manpower, U.S. Civil Service Commission, June 1974).

---

obtained as to the probability of a future event. *See* Harold A. Linstone and Murray Turoff (eds.), *The Delphi Method: Techniques and Applications* (Reading, Mass.: Addison-Wesley Publishing Co., 1975).

de minimus short form of *de minimus non curat lex*; Latin for "the law does not bother with trifles."

demotion, reassignment of an employee to a job of lower status, responsibility, and pay. There are three basic kinds of demotions; (1) *voluntary demotion*, is usually the result of a reduction in force; the employee takes a job of lower status and pay rather than being laid off; (2) *involuntary demotion* results from a worker's inability to perform adequately on the job; (3) *disciplinary demotion* usually takes place after an employee has been repeatedly warned to stop some kind of misconduct or disruptive behavior. For the classic analysis of the problem, *see* F. H. Goldner, "Demotion in Industrial Management,"

American Sociological Review (October 1965).

dental plan, also called DENTAL INSURANCE, group insurance program, either contributory or noncontributory, that typically pays for some portion of the following dental services for an employee and his/her family:

1. diagnostic and preventive services (oral examinations and prophylaxis);
2. oral surgery;
3. restorative services (fillings and inlays);
4. endodontic treatment (root canal therapy);
5. periodontic treatment (treatment of gums);
6. prosthodontic services (dentures and bridgework); and
7. orthodontic services (straightening of teeth).

See Richard A. Harvey, "Designing a Corporate Dental Plan," *Compensation Review (Third Quarter 1975)*.

See also SUPPLEMENTAL MEDICAL INSURANCE.

departmental seniority, also called UNIT SENORITY, seniority based on years of service in a particular subsection of a larger organization as opposed to seniority based simply on total years of service to the larger organization, company, or governmental jurisdiction.

derivative violation: *see* UNFAIR LABOR PRACTICES (EMPLOYERS).

derived score, any test score that is obtained after some statistical treatment or manipulation of the raw score.

Derwent, Clarence (1884-1959), president of the Actor's Equity Association from 1946 to 1952. For an autobiography, *see The Derwent Story: My First Fifty Years in the Theatre in England and America* (N.Y.: H. Schuman, 1953).

descriptive average, estimate of a mean based upon incomplete data.

desk audit, also called JOB AUDIT, review of the duties and responsibilities of a position through an interview with the incumbent and/or the incumbent's supervisor made at the employee's desk or regular place of work.

detail, temporary assignment of a employee to a different position for a specified period with the assumption that the employee will return to "normal" duties at the end of the detail. Technically, a position cannot be "filled" by a detail, as the employee continues to be the incumbent of the position from which he was detailed.

Detroit Edison Company v. *National Labor Relations Board*, 59 L.Ed. 2d 333 (1979), U.S. Supreme Court case, which held that the NLRB could not order an employer to provide testing information to a union without the examinee's consent.

deviation, amount by which a score differs from a reference value such as the mean or the norm.

dexterity test, also called PSYCHOMOTOR TEST, any testing device that seeks to determine the motor/mechanical skills of an individual.

DGA: *see* LABOR ORGANIZATION, Directors Guild of America, Inc.

diagnostic test, any testing device that is primarily designed to identify the nature and/or source of an individual's disabilities.

Dickson, William J. (1904-   ), chief of the Employee Relations Research Department at the Hawthorne Works of the Western Electric Company during the famous Hawthorne experiments. As such, he collaborated with the Harvard research group led by Elton Mayo. He was co-author, with F. J. Roethlisberger, of the definitive account of the experiments, *Management and the Worker* (Cambridge, Mass.: Harvard University Press, 1939). He also wrote, again with Roethlisberger, *Counseling in An Organization*, (Cambridge, Mass.: Harvard University Press, 1966).

dicta, in its most common usage, dicta is that portion of the opinion of a judge that is not the essence of the judge's decision. In the context of arbitration, dicta becomes any opinion or recommendation an arbitrator expresses in making an award that is not necessarily essential to the resolution of the dispute. According to Anthony V. Sinicropi and Peter A. Veglahn, in "Dicta in Arbitration Awards: An Aid or Hindrance?" *Labor Law Journal* (September 1972),

> by using dicta, the arbitrator can clarify obligations of the parties in their collective bargaining relationship. Conversely, the arbitrator may upset a mutually acceptable understanding by the parties with his gratuitous advice on an issue. Dicta can either strengthen and stabilize a collective bargaining relationship or emasculate that relationship. Obviously, the parties are free to disregard the arbitrator's views as expressed in dicta.

Dictionary of Occupational Titles (DOT), the DOT is an outgrowth of the needs of the public employment service system for a comprehensive body of standardized occupational information for purposes of job placement, employment counseling and occupational career guidance. Now in its fourth edition, the DOT includes standardized and comprehensive descriptions of job duties and related information for 20,000 occupations, covers nearly all jobs in the U.S. economy, groups occupations into a systematic occupational classification structure based on interrelationships of job tasks and requirements, and is designed as a job-placement tool to facilitate matching job requirements and worker skills. *See* Employment and Training Administration, U.S. Department of Labor, *Dictionary of Occupational Titles* (Washington, D.C.: Government Printing Office, 4th ed., 1977).

See also UNITED STATES EMPLOYMENT SERVICES.

Diemer Plan, wage-incentive plan providing for normal day rates, plus an increase of 0.05 percent for each one percent of production above the standard, with a 10 percent bonus.

Die Sinkers' Conference, International: *see* LABOR ORGANIZATION.

differential, displacement: *see* DISPLACEMENT DIFFERENTIAL.

Differential Aptitude Tests (DAT), battery of aptitude tests designed for educational and vocational guidance. Provides a profile of relative strengths and weaknesses in eight abilities (verbal reasoning, numerical ability, abstract reasoning, clerical speed and accuracy, mechanical reasoning, space relations, spelling, and language usage). TIME: Approximately 3 hours. AUTHORS: G. K. Bennett, H. G. Seashore, and A. G. Wesman. PUBLISHER: Psychological Corporation (*see* TEST PUBLISHERS).

differential piece work, also DIFFERENTIAL PIECE RATE, wage program in which the money rate per piece is determined by the total number of pieces produced over a time period—usually a day.

See also TAYLOR DIFFERENTIAL PIECE-RATE PLAN.

differentials, increases in wage rates because of shift work or other conditions generally considered to be undesirable.

See also the following entries:

   NIGHT DIFFERENTIAL
   SKILL DIFFERENTIAL
   WAGE DIFFERENTIAL

differential validation, also called DIF-FERENTIAL PREDICTION, the underlying assumption of differential validation/prediction holds that different tests or test scores might predict differently for different groups. Some social groups, because of a variety of sociological factors, tend to score lower (higher) than other groups on the same test.

difficulty index, any of a variety of indexes used to indicate the difficulty of a test question. The percent of some specified group, such as students of a given age or grade, who answer an item correctly is an example of such an index.

directed interview, also NONDIRECTIVE INTERVIEW, the *directed interview* has the interviewer in full control of the interview content, typically soliciting answers to a variety of specific questions. In the *nondirective interview*, in contrast, it is more the responsibility of the interviewee to determine the subjects to be discussed.

direct labor, also INDIRECT LABOR, *direct labor* consists of work performed on a product that is a specific contribution to its completion. *Indirect labor* consists of all overhead and support activities that do not contribute directly to the completion of a product. *See* Robert V. Penfield, "A Guide to the Computation and Evaluation of Direct Labor Costs," *Personnel Journal* (June 1976).

director of personnel: *see* PERSONNEL DIRECTOR.

Directors Guild of America, Inc.: *see* LABOR ORGANIZATION.

direct relief: *see* RELIEF.

disability, also called WORK DISABILITY, according to Sar A. Levitan and Robert Taggart, *Jobs for the Disabled* (Baltimore: John Hopkins University Press, 1977), "there are essentially two interrelated dimensions of work disability: the presence or perception of physical or mental handicaps and a reduced work capacity." *See* Robert B. Nathanson, "The Disabled Employee: Separating Myth from Fact," *Harvard Business Review* (May-June 1977).

disability insurance, insurance designed to compensate individuals who lose wages because of illness or injuries.

disability retirement, retirement caused by a physical inability to perform on the job.

disabled veteran, veteran of the armed services who has a service-connected disability

Number of discouraged workers and unemployment rate, quarterly averages, 1970-76

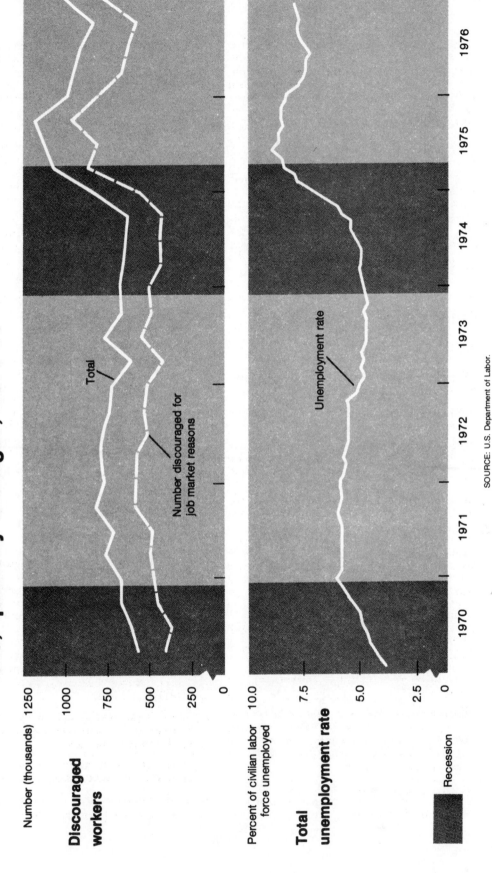

Number (thousands)

Discouraged workers

1250
1000
750
500
250
0

Total

Number discouraged for job market reasons

Percent of civilian labor force unemployed

Total unemployment rate

10.0
7.5
5.0
2.5
0

Unemployment rate

1970   1971   1972   1973   1974   1975   1976

Recession

SOURCE: U.S. Department of Labor.

and is rated 10 percent or more disabled by the Veterans Administration. Disabled veterans generally have the right to a 10-point bonus on federal government entrance examinations. Many state and local governments offer similar advantages.

See also VETERANS PREFERENCE.

disadvantaged, culturally: *see* CULTURALLY DISADVANTAGED.

disadvantaged workers, usually unemployed or underemployed and either a member of a minority group, handicapped, or over 45 years of age. They tend to have lower education rates and higher criminal-arrest rates than the rest of the population. See Lloyd Zimpel (ed.), *The Disadvantaged Worker: Readings in Developing Minority Manpower* (Reading, Mass.: Addison Wesley, 1971); James L. Koch, "Employing the Disadvantaged: Lessons from the Past Decade," *California Management Review* (Fall 1974).

disaffiliation, withdrawal of a local union from its national or international union membership or the withdrawal of a national or international union from its federation membership. When a federation or national union initiates disaffiliation, the process is more properly called suspension or expulsion.

discharge: *see* DISMISSAL.

discharge, discriminatory: *see* DISCRIMINATORY DISCHARGE.

discharge warning, formal notice to an employee that he or she will be discharged if unsatisfactory work behavior continues.

disciplinary action, any action short of dismissal taken by an employer against an employee for a violation of company policy. See Walter E. Baer, *Discipline and Discharge Under the Labor Agreement* (N.Y.: American Management Associations, 1972).

See also ADVERSE ACTION and NATIONAL LABOR RELATIONS BOARD V. J. WEINGARTEN, INC.

disciplinary demotion: *see* DEMOTION.

disciplinary fine, fine that a union may levy against a member for violating a provision of the union's bylaws. See Dell Bush Johannesen, "Disciplinary Fines as Interference with Protected Rights: Section 8(6)(1) (A)," *Labor Law Journal* (May 1973).

disciplinary layoff, suspension of an employee as punishment for violating some rule or policy.

discipline: *see* the following entries:
ADMONITION
ADVERSE ACTION
DISCIPLINARY ACTION
PREVENTIVE DISCIPLINE
PROGRESSIVE DISCIPLINE
REPRIMAND
SLIDE-RULE DISCIPLINE

discipline clause, provision of a collective bargaining agreement that stipulates the means for disciplining workers who violate management or union rules.

discount, employee: *see* EMPLOYEE DISCOUNT.

discouraged workers, also called HIDDEN UNEMPLOYED, persons who want to work but are not seeking employment because of a belief that such an effort would be fruitless. For analyses, *see* Paul O. Flaim, "Discouraged Workers and Changes in Unemployment," *Monthly Labor Review* (March 1973); Joseph L. Gastwirth, "Estimating the Number of 'Hidden Unemployed'" *Monthly Labor Review* (March 1973).

discriminant validity, evidence that a measure of a construct is indeed measuring that construct.

discrimination, in the context of employment, the failure to treat equals equally. Whether deliberate or unintentional, any action that has the effect of limiting employment and advancement opportunities because of an individual's sex, race, color, age, national origin, religion, physical handicap, or other irrelevant criteria is discrimination. Because of the EEO and civil rights legislation of recent years, individuals aggrieved by unlawful discrimination now have a variety of administrative and judicial remedies open to them. Employment discrimination has its origins in the less genteel concept of bigotry. For the standard history, *see* Gustavus Myers, *History of Bigotry in the United States*, edited and revised by Henry M. Christman (N.Y.: Capricorn Books, 1943, 1960).

See also the following entries:
AGE DISCRIMINATION
CIVIL RIGHTS ACT OF 1964
EQUAL EMPLOYMENT OPPORTUNITY
EQUAL EMPLOYMENT OPPORTUNITY ACT OF 1972
IMPACT THEORY OF DISCRIMINATION
INSTITUTIONAL DISCRIMINATION
INTERNATIONAL BROTHERHOOD OF TEAMSTERS V. UNITED STATES
MCDONNELL DOUGLAS CORP. V. GREEN
NATIONAL ORIGIN DISCRIMINATION

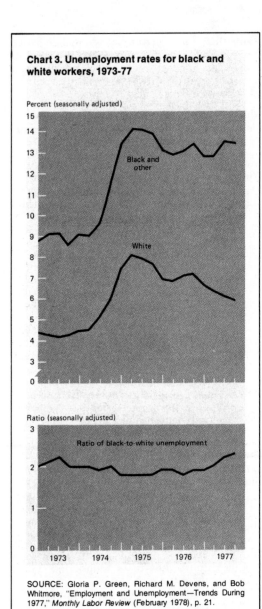

Chart 3. Unemployment rates for black and white workers, 1973-77

Percent (seasonally adjusted)

Black and other

White

Ratio (seasonally adjusted)

Ratio of black-to-white unemployment

1973   1974   1975   1976   1977

SOURCE: Gloria P. Green, Richard M. Devens, and Bob Whitmore, "Employment and Unemployment—Trends During 1977," *Monthly Labor Review* (February 1978), p. 21.

RELIGIOUS DISCRIMINATION
REVERSE DISCRIMINATION
RIGHTFUL PLACE
SEX DISCRIMINATION
SYSTEMIC DISCRIMINATION
THIRD-PARTY ALLEGATIONS OF DISCRIMINA-
TION
UNFAIR LABOR PRACTICES (EMPLOYERS)
UNFAIR LABOR PRACTICES (UNIONS)
WASHINGTON V. DAVIS

discrimination index, any of a variety of indexes used to indicate the extent to which a test item differentiates among examinees with respect to some criterion (such as the test as a whole).

discriminatory discharge, dismissal of an employee for union activity. This is an unfair labor practice.

dishonest graft: *see* HONEST GRAFT.

dismissal, also called DISCHARGE, management's removal of an employee from employment. *See* Robert W. Fisher, "When Workers Are Discharged—An Overview: A Special Report on the Handling of Dismissal Cases in U.S. Law, Contract and Custom," *Monthly Labor Review* (June 1973); Erwin S. Stanton, "The Discharged Employee and the EEO Laws," *Personnel Journal* (March 1976).
 See also the following entries:
 BISHOP V. WOOD
 BOARD OF REGENTS V. ROTH
 HINES V. ANCHOR MOTOR FREIGHT
 SAMPSON V. MURRAY
 UNFAIR LABOR PRACTICES (EMPLOYERS)

dismissal pay: *see* SEVERANCE PAY.

disparate effect, tendency of an employment screening device or criteria to limit the appointment opportunities of women and minorities at a greater rate than for nonminority males.

displaced employee, employee of the federal government who is serving or who last served under career or career-conditional appointment or an employee with competitive status who is serving or who last served with Group I or Group II tenure in an excepted position, when: (1) the employee has received a reduction-in-force notice and the employing agency determines that he or she cannot be placed on another position in his or her competitive area; (2) the employee declines to transfer within his or her function, or to accept a new assignment, to another commuting area, and the employing agency determines that he or she will not be placed in another position in his or her own commuting area; (3) the employee is receiving compensation for injuries (under subchapter 1, chapter 81, of title 5, U.S. Code); or (4) the employee is under age 60 and is a recovered disability annuitant or a disability annuitant restored to earning capacity. Federal civil service regulations require agencies to have in operation a positive program of placement assistance for their displaced employees.
 See also GROUP I TENURE/GROUP II TENURE/GROUP III TENURE.

displaced homemaker, usually a woman who

has been caring for a family and has lost her means of support through divorce, separation, death, or the disabling of a spouse and has only the briefest work experience outside the home. *See* Tish Sommers and Laurie Shields, "Displaced Homemakers: 'Forced Retirement' Leaves Many Penniless," *Civil Rights Digest* (Winter 1978).

displacement differential, compensation equal to the difference between an employee's regular pay and the rate of a temporary assignment caused by layoff or technological displacement. Such differentials are usually available only for a limited time.

Disraeli, Benjamin (1804-1881), 19th century British prime minister who inadvertently contributed to subsequent theories of test validation when he asserted that "there are three kinds of lies: lies, damned lies, and statistics."

Distillery, Rectifying, Wine and Allied Workers' International Union of America: *see* LABOR ORGANIZATION.

distractors, also called FOILS, in multiple-choice examinations, the incorrect alternatives serve the function of being, and are called, distractors or foils.

distribution, bimodal: *see* BIMODAL DISTRIBUTION.

Distributive Workers of America: *see* LABOR ORGANIZATION.

district council, a level of labor organization below the national union but above the locals. The district council is composed of local unions in a particular industry within a limited geographic area.

district court, also called FEDERAL DISTRICT COURT and U.S. DISTRICT COURT, court of original jurisdiction for most federal cases. This is the only federal court that holds trials where juries and witnesses are used. Each state has at least one district court. When equal employment opportunity problems cannot be resolved within an organization, they frequently spill over into the local, federal district court.

division of labor, also called FACTORY SYSTEM, production process that has individual workers specializing in the varying aspects of a larger task. The most famous and influential statement on the economic rationale of the factory system is found in Adam Smith's *The Wealth of Nations* (1776). Smith discusses the optimum organization of a pin factory and

finds that, while traditional pin makers could produce a few dozen pins a day, pin workers organized in a factory with each performing a limited operation could produce tens of thousands a day.

dock, deduct a part of an employee's wages as a penalty for tardiness, absenteeism, breakage, etc.

doctrine of mutuality, according to Julius Rezler and S. John Insalata, "Doctrine of Mutuality: A Driving Force in American Labor Legislation," *Labor Law Journal* (May 1967), the

> doctrine of labor mutuality basically contends that whenever a legal burden or restriction is imposed by a legislative act on a party to industrial relations, either the same burden or restriction should be imposed upon the other party or the restriction should be removed from the first party, too. The doctrine also implies that whenever a right or privilege is conferred by a legislative act on one of the parties, the same right or privilege should be conferred on the other party or be withdrawn from the first party, too.

DOL: *see* LABOR, DEPARTMENT OF.

dollar devaluation adjustments, an adjustment made to expatriate workers to compensate for the loss of purchasing power in the host country which is a direct result of a lower rate of exchange between the dollar and the host currency.

domicile, an individual's permanent legal residence. While an individual can legally have many residences, he or she can have only one domicile. Some government jurisdictions have residency requirements that require employees to be domiciled within the bounds of the jurisdiction.
See also MCCARTHY V. PHILADELPHIA CIVIL SERVICE COMMISSION.

Dorchy v. Kansas, 272 U.S. 306 (1926), U.S. Supreme Court case, which held that there is no constitutional right to strike.

DOT: *see* DICTIONARY OF OCCUPATIONAL TITLES.

Dothard v. Rawlinson, 433 U.S. 321 (1977), U.S. Supreme Court case, which upheld an Alabama regulation that prohibits the employment of women as prison guards in "contact positions" (requiring continual close physical proximity to inmates) within the state's correctional facilities.
See also BONA FIDE OCCUPATIONAL QUALIFICATION.

double-dipper, about 100,000 retired military personnel are employed by the federal government as civilian workers. Because they draw two government incomes, they are colloquially called double-dippers. The term is sometimes applied, with an intentional or unintentional lack of precision, to state and local government employees—even to elected officials—who also hold private sector jobs while occupying what are or are held to be full-time positions.

double indemnity: *see* ACCIDENTAL DEATH BENEFIT.

double time, penalty or premium rate of pay for overtime work, for holiday or Sunday work, etc., amounting to twice the employee's regular hourly wage.

dovetail seniority, the combining of two or more seniority lists (for example, when different companies merge) into a master seniority list. Each employee retains his previously earned seniority even though he may thereafter be employed by a new employer.

downgrading, reassignment of an employee to a position having a lower rate of pay and/or lesser responsibilities.

down time, periods of inactivity while waiting for the repair, setup or adjustment of equipment.

down-time pay, payments for time spent idle because of equipment failures (or routine maintenance) that are clearly beyond the responsibility of the employee.

dramaturgy, manner in which an individual acts out or theatrically stages his or her organizational role. All organization members are involved in such impression management, as Victor A. Thompson, in *Modern Organization* (N.Y.: Alfred A. Knopf, 1961), indicates:

We must try to control the information or cues imparted to others in order to protect our representations of self and to control the impressions others form about us. We are all involved, therefore, in dramaturgy.

drawing account, fixed sum advanced to sales personnel at regular time intervals (weekly or monthly) or a limited amount against which the sales person can draw as needed during a predetermined time period so long as the outstanding balance does not reach a predetermined limit. Amounts so drawn must be paid back to the company out of commission earnings during the same time period.

Drawing accounts may be guaranteed or nonguaranteed. According to William J.

Standon and Richard H. Buskirk, *Management of the Sales Force* (Homewood, Ill: Richard D. Irwin, rev. ed., 1964),

under a nonguaranteed plan the advance is strictly a loan. If a salesperson does not earn enough in commissions to pay back the advanced funds in one time period, then the balance of the debt is carried over to the next period.... A guaranteed drawing account is operated in much the same fashion, with one big exception. At the end of a stated period, if a salesman's commissions total less than his draw, the debt is canceled. It is not carried forward, he starts with a clean slate. Thus, a guaranteed draw is much like a salary. As a result, a compensation method consisting of a commission plus a guaranteed drawing account is classed as a combination plan while a commission plus a nonguaranteed draw is still considered a straight commission plan.

Drucker, Peter F. (1909-   ), the preeminent philosopher of management, the world's best-selling management author, and the man usually credited with having invented "management by objectives." Major works include: *The Concept of the Corporation* (N.Y.: John Day Co., 1946); *The New Society* (N.Y.: Harper & Row, 1950); *The Practice of Management* (N.Y.: Harper & Row, 1954); *Managing for Results* (N.Y.: Harper & Row, 1964); *The Effective Executive* (N.Y.: Harper & Row, 1967); *The Age of Discontinuity* (N.Y.: Harper & Row, 1969); *Management: Tasks, Responsibilities, Practices* (N.Y.: Harper & Row, 1974). For a biography, *see* John J. Tarrant, *Drucker: The Man Who Invented Corporate Society* (N.Y.: Warner Books, 1976). *See also* PENSION FUND SOCIALISM.

drug addiction, also DRUG ABUSE, *drug addiction* is any habitual use of a substance which leads to psychological and/or physiological dependence. *Drug abuse* consists of using drugs to one's physical, emotional and/or social detriment without being "formally" addicted. For the dimensions of the problem, *see* Pasquale A. Carone and Leonard W. Krinsky, (eds.), *Drug Abuse in Industry* (Springfield, Ill.: Charles C. Thomas Publishers, 1973); Rolf E. Rogers and John T. C. Colbert, "Drug Abuse and Organizational Response: A Review and Evaluation," *Personnel Journal* (May 1975); Ken Jennings, "The Problem of Employee Drug Use and Remedial Alternatives," *Personnel Journal* (November 1977). For how drug-abuse cases have been handled in arbitration, *see* Kenneth Jennings, "Arbitrators and Drugs," *Personnel Journal* (October

1976). For the public employer's perspective, *see* George W. Noblit, Paul H. Radtke, and James G. Ross, *Drug Use and Public Employment: A Personnel Manual* (Chicago: International Personnel Management Association, 1975).

DRWW: *see* LABOR ORGANIZATION, Distillery, Rectifying, Wine and Allied Workers' International Union of America.

dry promotion, slang term for a promotion that offers an increase in status but no monetary increase.

DSC: *see* LABOR ORGANIZATION, Die Sinkers' Conference, International.

Dual Compensation Act of 1964, (Public Law 88-448), provides that civilian employees of the federal government shall not be entitled to receive basic compensation from more than one civilian office for more than an aggregate of 40 hours of work in any one calendar week (Sunday through Saturday). The act also contains a variety of exemptions.

dual ladder, also called PARALLEL LADDER, a varient of a career ladder, provides dual or parallel career hierarchies so that both professional and managerial employees will be afforded appropriate career advancement. *See* Bertram Schoner and Thomas Harrell, "The Questionable Dual Ladder," *Personnel* (January-February 1965); Fred Goldner and R. R. Ritti, "Professionalism as Career Immobility," *American Journal of Sociology* (March 1967); Carl L. Bellas, "The Dual Track Career System within the Internal Revenue Service," *Public Personnel Management* (September-October 1972).

dual pay system, wage program that allows employees to select the more advantageous of alternative means of computing earnings. For example, transportation employees might have the option of being paid on the basis of miles traveled or on the basis of hours worked.

dual unionism, situation where two rival unions claim the right to organize workers in a particular industry or locality.

Dubinsky, David (1892-), president of the International Ladies' Garment Workers' Union from 1932 to 1966, one of the founders of the Liberal Party in New York State in 1944, and one of the founders of the Americans for Democratic Action in 1947. For an autobiography, *see* David Dubinsky and A. H. Raskin, *David Dubinsky: A Life with Labor* (N.Y.: Simon and Schuster, 1977).

due process, the due process clause of the U.S. Constitution requires that "no person shall be deprived of life, liberty, or property without due process of law." While the specific requirements of due process vary with new Supreme Court decisions, the essence of the idea is that individuals must be given adequate notice and a fair opportunity to present their side in a legal dispute and that no law or government procedure should be arbitrary or unfair. *See* Joseph Shane, "Due Process and Probationary Employees," *Public Personnel Management* (September-October 1974); Lewis R. Amis, "Due Process in Disciplinary Procedures," *Labor Law Journal* (February 1976).

dues, fees that must be periodically paid by union members in order for them to remain in good standing with their union. The dues are used to finance all of the activities of the union and its affiliates. For a survey of who pays what, *see* Charles W. Hickman, "Labor Organizations' Fees and Dues," *Monthly Labor Review* (May 1977).

See also UNFAIR LABOR PRACTICES (UNIONS).

dues checkoff: *see* CHECKOFF.

dues picket line, a common union practice before the checkoff was in widespread use was to have the union officers and their close supporters form a *dues picket line* at the factory gate on pay days in order to encourage union members to pay their dues. Any union member seeking to cross the line without paying might find himself in a situation with violent overtones.

dumping ground of management: *see* TRASHCAN HYPOTHESIS.

Dunlop, John T. (1914-), Secretary of Labor from 1975 to 1976.

Dunlop v. Bachowski, 421 U.S. 560 (1975), U.S. Supreme Court case, which held that, while a decision of the Secretary of Labor to initiate or not initiate civil action to set aside a union's election of officers is not excepted from judicial review, the reviewing court's review must be limited to determining whether the "Secretary's decision is so irrational as to be arbitrary and capricious, and the court's review may not extend to an adversary trial of a complaining union member's challenges to the factual basis for the Secretary's decision."

Dunnette, Marvin D. (1926-), industrial psychologist, one of the most prolific researchers and writers in the areas of personnel selection and organizational effectiveness. Major works include: *Psychology Applied to Business and Industry*, with W. K. Kirchner, (N.Y.: Appleton-Century-Crofts, 1965); *Personnel Selection and Placement*, (Belmont, Calif.: Wadsworth Publishing Company, 1966); *Managerial Behavior, Performance, and Effectiveness*, with J. P. Campbell, E. E. Lawler III, and K. E. Weick, Jr., (N.Y.: McGraw-Hill, 1970); *Handbook of Industrial and Organizational Psychology*, (Chicago, Illinois: Rand McNally, 1976).

Durkin, Martin P. (1900-1964), Secretary of Labor during 1953.

duty, large segment of the work done by one individual. A job is made up of one or more duties.

duty to bargain, positive obligation under various state and federal laws that employers and employees bargain with each other in good faith. Section 8 (d) of the Labor–Management Relations (Taft–Hartley) Act of 1947 holds that the duty to bargain collectively

> is the performance of the mutual obligation of the employer and the representative of the employees to meet at reasonable times and confer in good faith with respect to wages, hours, and other terms and conditions of any employment, or the negotiation of an agreement, or any question arising thereunder, and the execution of a written

contract incorporating any agreement reached if requested by either party, but such obligation does not compel either party to agree to a proposal or require the making of a concession.

For a legal analysis, *see* Archibald Cox, "The Duty to Bargain in Good Faith," *Harvard Law Review* (June 1958).

duty of fair representation, obligation of a labor union to represent all of the members in a bargaining unit fairly and without discrimination. *See* Jean T. McKelvey (ed.), *The Duty of Fair Representation* (Ithaca, N.Y.: New York State School of Industrial and Labor Relations, Cornell University, 1977).

See also ELECTRICAL WORKERS V. FOUST and UNFAIR LABOR PRACTICES (UNIONS).

DWA: *see* LABOR ORGANIZATION, Distributive Workers of America.

dyad, interpersonal encounter or relationship between two people or two groups. Dyads are frequently artificially (as opposed to spontaneously) created for sensitivity training purposes.

dynamic psychology, school of psychology that is primarily concerned with motivation.

dynamic system, any system that has its parts interrelated in such a way that a change in one part necessarily affects other parts of the system. This is in contrast to a *static system* whose parts can be affected independently of the rest of its system.

E

EAP: *see* EMPLOYEE ASSISTANCE PROGRAM.

earmark, also RED CIRCLE, terms used to designate a position for restudy when vacant to determine its proper classification before being refilled.

earnings, total remuneration of an employee or group of employees for work performed, including wages, bonuses, commissions, etc.

See also GUARANTEED EARNINGS.

Eastex, Inc.* v. *National Labor Relations Board, 57 L. Ed. 2d 428 (1978), U.S. Supreme Court case, which affirmed a National Labor Relations Board ruling that union members have the right to distribute, on their employers' property, leaflets containing articles pertaining to political issues (such as right-to-work laws and minimum wages) as well as those directly connected to the union–employer relationship.

Economic Advisers, Council of: *see* COUNCIL OF ECONOMIC ADVISERS.

economic determinism, doctrine holding that economic concerns are the primary motivating factors of human behavior.

economic man, concept that finds humans motivated *solely* by economic factors—always seeking the greatest reward at the least possible cost. Any management philosophy assuming that workers are motivated by money and can be further motivated only by more money is premised on the "economic man" concept. *See* Harvey Leibenstein, *Beyond Economic Man: A New Foundation for Microeconomics* (Cambridge, Mass.: Harvard University Press, 1976).

Economic Opportunity Act of 1964, this act, the keystone of the Johnson Administration's "war on poverty," created the Jobs Corps and other work-incentive programs. For a history, *see* Sar A. Levitan, *The Great Society's Poor Law* (Baltimore: The Johns Hopkins Press, 1969).

economic strike, strike that is undertaken for economic gain; that is, for better wages, hours, and working conditions.

See also NATIONAL LABOR RELATIONS BOARD V. MACKAY RADIO & TELEGRAPH COMPANY.

EDP: *see* ELECTRONIC DATA PROCESSING.

educable retarded person, individual who is only mildly retarded and thus employable in many simple jobs, usually requiring repetitive tasks.

education, cooperative: *see* COOPERATIVE EDUCATION.

Educational and Industrial Testing Service: *see* TEST PUBLISHERS.

Educational Testing Service (ETS), private, commercial test publisher that provides tests and related services for schools, colleges, government agencies and the professions.

Educational Testing Service
Rosedale Rd.
Princeton NJ 08541
(609) 921-9000

Education Association, National/Overseas: *see* LABOR ORGANIZATION, Education Association, National.

Edwards Personal Preference Schedule (EPPS), inventory widely used in personal counseling and personality research that is designed to measure the relative importance of 15 key needs or motives (*i.e.*, achievement, deference, order, exhibition, autonomy, affiliation, intraception, succorance, dominance, abasement, nurturance, change, endurance, heterosexuality, and aggression). Time: Approximately 45 minutes. AUTHOR: A. L. Edwards. PUBLISHER: Psychological Corporation (*see* TEST PUBLISHERS).

EEO: *see* EQUAL EMPLOYMENT OPPORTUNITY.

EEO-1, the annual report on the sex and minority status of various workforce categories that is required of all employers with 100 or more employees. The report must be filed with the Joint Reporting Committee of the Equal Employment Opportunity Commission and the Office of Federal Contract Compliance.

EEO Act of 1972: *see* EQUAL EMPLOYMENT OPPORTUNITY ACT OF 1972.

EEOC: *see* EQUAL EMPLOYMENT OPPORTUNITY COMMISSION.

EEOC Compliance Manual, publication of the Bureau of National Affairs, Inc., which provides a summary of the latest Equal Employment Opportunity Commission (EEOC) developments and the photographic text of the official operations manual that is followed by the staff of the EEOC.

EEO Counselor: *see* EQUAL EMPLOYMENT OPPORTUNITY COUNSELOR.

EEO Officer: *see* EQUAL EMPLOYMENT OPPORTUNITY OFFICER.

effective labor market, labor market from which an employer actually draws applicants, as distinct from the labor market from which an employer attempts to draw applicants.

efficiency, also EFFICIENCY RATIO, productive efficiency is generally determined by seeking the ratio of output to input, which is called the *efficiency ratio*.

$$\text{efficiency} = \frac{\text{output}}{\text{input}}$$

efficiency expert, mildly perjortive and decidedly dated term for a management or systems analyst.

efficiency rating, now dated term for performance appraisal. The Civil Service Reform Act of 1978 mandates that each federal agency will install employee "performance appraisal" systems. For an account of the old ways, *see* Mary S. Schinagl, *History of Efficiency Ratings in the Federal Government* (N.Y.: Bookman Associates, 1966).

efficiency ratio: *see* EFFICIENCY.

80-percent rule: *see* ADVERSE IMPACT.

Electrical, Radio, and Machine Workers, International Union of: *see* LABOR ORGANIZATION.

Electrical Workers, International Brotherhood of: *see* LABOR ORGANIZATION.

Electrical Workers* v. *Foust, 60 L.Ed. 2d 698 (1979), U.S. Supreme Court case, which held that an award of punitive damages for a union's breach of its duty of fair representation in processing an employee's grievance was prohibited by the Railway Labor Act.

See also DUTY OF FAIR REPRESENTATION.

electronic data processing (EDP), computer manipulation of data. The term is gradually being supplanted by "management information systems."

See also MANAGEMENT INFORMATION SYSTEM.

element, also called JOB ELEMENT, smallest

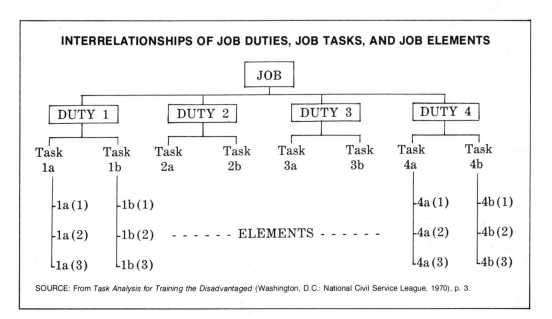

INTERRELATIONSHIPS OF JOB DUTIES, JOB TASKS, AND JOB ELEMENTS

SOURCE: From *Task Analysis for Training the Disadvantaged* (Washington, D.C.: National Civil Service League, 1970), p. 3.

unit into which a job can be divided without analyzing the physical and mental processes necessarily involved.

Elevator Constructurs, International Union of: *see* LABOR ORGANIZATION.

Elgin, Joliet & Eastern Railway **v.** *Burley*, 325 U.S. 711 (1945), U.S. Supreme Court case, which upheld the right of employees to object to a compromise settlement of a grievance committee when they had not formally authorized the committee to act for them.

eligible list, also called ELIGIBLE ROSTER and ELIGIBLE REGISTER, list of qualified applicants in rank order established from the test score results of competitive examinations.
See also RE-EMPLOYMENT LIST.

Elrod **v.** *Burns*, 427 U.S. 347 (1976), U.S. Supreme Court case, which held that the 1st Amendment, which safeguards the rights of political beliefs and association, prevents political firings of state, county, and local workers below the policymaking level.

Emergency Employment Act of 1971, federal statute that authorized federal funds for state and local government public service jobs during times of high unemployment. It was superseded by the Comprehensive Employment and Training Act of 1973. For a history, *see* Howard W. Hallman, *Emergency Employment: A Study in Federalism* (University, Ala.: University of Alabama Press, 1977).

Emerson, Harrington (1853-1931), one of the first management consultants in the U.S., known as the "high priest of efficiency" because of advocacy of eliminating "wanton, wicked waste." Major works include: *Efficiency as a Basis for Operation and Wages* (N.Y.: The Engineering Magazine Co., 1911) and *The Twelve Principles of Efficiency* (N.Y.: The Engineering Magazine Co., 1913).

emolument, any monetary gain or other advantage achieved from employment; a more comprehensive term than wager and/or salaries.

emotionally handicapped employees, also EMOTIONAL REHABILITANTS, a polite way of referring to employees who have had or are having a problem with mental illness. *Emotional rehabilitant*, a more formal label, has been defined in Charles A. Burden and Russell Faulk, "The Employment Process for Rehabilitants: Two Studies of the Hiring of Emotional Rehabilitants," *Personnel Journal* (October 1975), as "a person who has suffered an emotional illness serious enough to require hospitalization, but has since recovered and has been judged by medical and social authorities to be ready to reenter the customary, competitive work situation."

empirical, findings or conclusions derived from direct and repeated observations of a phenomenon under study.

empirical validity, validity of a test according to how well the test actually measures what it was designed to measure. Most other kinds of validity are efforts to achieve empirical validity.

employ, hire the services of an individual and/or his or her equipment.

employee, general term for all those who let themselves for hire.
See also DISPLACED EMPLOYEE and PROBATIONARY EMPLOYEE.

employee assistance program (EAP), formal program designed to assist employees with personal problems through both (1) internal counseling and aid and (2) a referral service to outside counseling resources. The thrust of such programs is to increase productivity by correcting distracting outside personal problems. *See* Richard T. Hellan and Carl R. Tisone, "Employee Assistance Programming: Personnel's Sobering Influence on the Bottom Line," *The Personnel Administrator* (May 1976).

employee benefits: *see* FRINGE BENEFITS.

employee counseling, formal efforts on the part of an organization to help its members deal with their personal and professional problems and concerns so that they will be more effective in both their personal and organizational lives. For the classic work on employee counseling, *see* William J. Dickson and F. J. Roethlisberger, *Counseling In An Organization: A Sequel to the Hawthorne Researches* (Boston: Graduate School of Business Administration, Harvard University, 1966).
See also PRE-RETIREMENT COUNSELING.

employee discount, reduction in the price of goods or services offered by an employer to employees as a benefit. For a survey of company discount policies, *see* Geneva Seybold, *Discount Privileges for Employees* (New York: The Conference Board, 1967).

employee selection: *see* PERSONNEL SELECTION.

employees, exempt: *see* EXEMPT EMPLOYEES.

Employees Retirement Income Security Act of 1974 (ERISA), popularly known as PENSION REFORM ACT OF 1974, federal statute enacted to protect "the interest of participants in employee benefit plans and their beneficiaries . . . by establishing standards of conduct, responsibility and obligations for fiduciaries of employee benefit plans, and by providing for appropriate remedies, sanctions, and ready access to the Federal courts." The basic intent of ERISA is to insure that employees will eventually gain appropriate benefits from the pension plans in which they participate. *See* Peter Henle and Raymond Schmitt, "Pension Reform: The Long Hard Road to Enactment," *Monthly Labor Review* (November 1974); Donald G. Carlson, "Responding to the Pension Reform Law," *Harvard Business Review* (November-December 1974); Bruce M. Stott, "How Will ERISA Effect Your Pension Plan?" *Personnel Journal* (June 1977).

See also LABOR-MANAGEMENT SERVICES ADMINISTRATION.

employee stock-ownership plan (ESOP), employee benefit plan that uses company stock to provide deferred compensation. For how-to-do-it, *see* Charles A. Scharf, *Guide to Employee Stock Ownership Plans: A Revolutionary Method for Increasing Corporate Profits* (Englewood Cliffs, N.J.: Prentice-Hall, 1976). For criticism, *see* Burton W. Teague, "In Review of the ESOP Fable," *The Conference Board Record* (February 1976).

employer association: *see* EMPLOYERS' ASSOCIATION.

employer paternalism: *see* PATERNALISM.

employer strike insurance: *see* MUTUAL STRIKE AID.

employer unit, any bargaining unit that holds all of the eligible employees of a single employer.

employers' association, also called EMPLOYER ASSOCIATION, voluntary organization of employers whose purpose is to deal with problems common to the group. Such associations have frequently been formed primarily to present a united front in dealing with the representatives of their respective organized workers.

employment, occupational activity, usually, but not necessarily, for pay.

See also FULL EMPLOYMENT and SEASONAL EMPLOYMENT.

Employment Act of 1946, federal statute that created the Council of Economic Advisors in the Executive Office of the President and asserted that it was the federal government's responsibility to maintain economic stability and promote full employment. For a legislative history of the act, *see* Stephen K. Bailey, *Congress Makes A Law* (N.Y.: Columbia University Press, 1950). *See also* Hugh S. Norton, *The Employment Act and the Council of Economic Advisors, 1946-1976* (Columbia: University of South Carolina Press, 1977).

employment agency, private employment agencies provide brokerage services between employers and individuals seeking work. Fees or commission are charged the employer, the worker, or both. *See* Terry L. Dennis and David P. Gustafson, "College Campuses vs. Employment Agencies as Sources of Manpower," *Personnel Journal* (August 1973); John M. Malloy, "Employment Agency Fees: An Area of Continued Litigation?" *Taxes* (February 1974); Tomas Martinez, *The Human Marketplace: An Examination of Private Employment Agencies* (New Brunswick, N.J.: Transaction Books, 1976).

Employment and Earnings, U.S. Bureau of Labor Statistics' comprehensive monthly report on employment, hours, earnings, and labor turnover by industry, area, occupation, etc.

> *Employment and Earnings*
> Superintendent of Documents
> Government Printing Office
> Washington, DC 20402

Employment and Training Administration (ETA), agency of the Department of Labor that encompasses a group of offices and services. Major units include: the U.S. Employment Service; the Office of Comprehensive Employment Development Programs which oversees both the CETA and WIN programs; the Office of National Programs (which administers employment training programs conducted directly by the federal government); the Bureau of Apprenticeship and Training; the Unemployment Insurance Service; and the Office of Policy Evaluation and Research.

> *Employment and Training Administration*
> Department of Labor
> 200 Constitution Ave., N.W.
> Washington, DC 20210
> (202) 523-8165

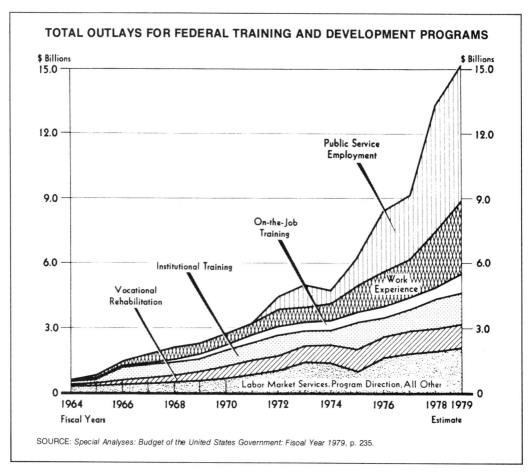

TOTAL OUTLAYS FOR FEDERAL TRAINING AND DEVELOPMENT PROGRAMS

SOURCE: *Special Analyses: Budget of the United States Government: Fiscal Year 1979, p. 235.*

Employment and Training Reporter, weekly notification-and-reference service published by the Bureau of National Affairs, Inc. Provides technical assistance on the effective utilization of the nation's human resources, including where and how to apply for employment and training funds, and how to develop successful programs. Covers the Comprehensive Employment and Training Act. Gives program guides, plus complete listings of federally funded employment and training programs and full texts of noteworthy documents.

employment contract, generally a contract is a promise or set of promises for which the law offers a remedy if the promise(s) is breached. According to John J. Villarreal, "Employment Contracts for Managers and Professionals," *Personnel Journal* (October 1974), an employment contract specifically refers to

> the agreed-upon contributions/inducements between employer and employee for the

services of each. These promises must be legally enforceable and they must be made by mature, knowledgeable and consenting individuals. . . . For each employment contract there must be agreements between the organization and the individual on goals to be accomplished, units of measurement, performance targets and organizational rewards.

employment interview: *see* INTERVIEW.

employment manager, job title sometimes given to managers who function as personnel directors.

employment parity: *see* PARITY.

employment–population ratio (E–P ratio), also called EMPLOYMENT RATIO, ratio of employment to working-age population. Some economists think that the E-P ratio is more useful for diagnosing the severity of an economic slowdown than is the unemployment rate. *See* Christopher Green, "The Employment Ratio as an Indicator of Aggregate Demand Pressure," *Monthly Labor Review* (April 1977).

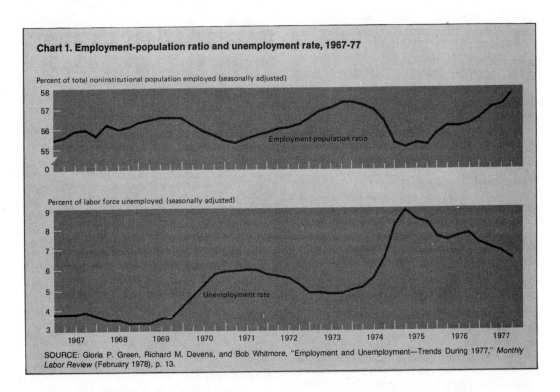

Chart 1. Employment-population ratio and unemployment rate, 1967-77

Percent of total noninstitutional population employed (seasonally adjusted)

Employment-population ratio

Percent of labor force unemployed (seasonally adjusted)

Unemployment rate

SOURCE: Gloria P. Green, Richard M. Devens, and Bob Whitmore, "Employment and Unemployment—Trends During 1977," *Monthly Labor Review* (February 1978), p. 13.

employment practice, in the context of equal employment opportunity, an employment practice is any screening device operating at any point in the employment cycle. If an employment practice is not related to job performance, it will not be able to withstand a court challenge.

employment ratio: *see* EMPLOYMENT-POPULATION RATIO.

employment relations, general term for all relationships that occur in a worker–manager context. While used synonymously with labor relations and industrial relations, it is often applied in non-union situations in order to emphasize "non-union."

employment standard, a specific requirement for employment. An employment standard can be based on a wide variety of things. For example, if assessment is based on tests, the standard might be a specific cutting score. If education is assessed, the standard might be a specific class standing, or grades of B or better in certain courses of study.

Employment Standards Administration (ESA), agency of the Department of Labor that administraters laws and regulations setting employment standards, providing workers' compensation to those injured on their jobs and requiring federal contractors to provide equal employment opportunity. Its major divisions include the Wage and Hour Division, the Office of Federal Contract Compliance, and the Office of Workers' Compensation.

employment taxes, also called PAYROLL TAXES, any of a variety of taxes levied by governments on an employer's payroll. The most common employment tax is the employer's contribution to social security known as FICA taxes (after the Federal Insurance Contribution Act). There are also FUTA taxes (after the Federal Unemployment Tax Act) and sometimes other unemployment insurance contributions required by state law. *See* Samuel S. Ress, "Payroll Taxes and Controls," *CPA Journal* (April 1977); Julian Block, "How to Save on Employment Taxes," *Administrative Management* (February 1976).

employment testing, any means of measuring the qualifications of applicants for employment in specific positions. *See* Robert M. Guion, *Personnel Testing* (N.Y.: McGraw-Hill, 1965); J. M. Thyne, *Principles of Examining* (N.Y.: John Wiley, 1974); M. T. Matteson, "Employment Testing: Where Do We Stand?" *The Personnel Administrator* (January 1975).

Emporium Capwell Co v. Western Addition Community Organization, 420 U.S. 50 (1975), U.S. Supreme Court case, which held that employees have no right to bypass union–management grievance procedures in order to protest alleged racial discrimination.

encounter group, form of group psychotherapy in which body contact and/or emotional expression are the primary forms of interaction as opposed to traditional verbal interaction. Encounter groups seek to produce experiences which force individuals to examine themselves in new and different ways, aided by others. Part of the emphasis on body movement includes attention to nonverbal communications. An individual should learn to be more conscious of his/her own nonverbal communications, to read others' signs more adequately and to practice being more adept in his/her body language. *See* A. Burton (ed.), *Encounter* (San Francisco: Jossey-Bass, 1969).

end-testing, examining individuals who have just completed a course of training on the subject in which they were trained in order to measure the individual's attainments and/or the effectiveness of the training.

enjoin, require or command. A court's injunction directs (enjoins) a person or persons to do or not do certain acts.

entrance rate, also called PROBATIONARY RATE and HIRING RATE, hourly rate of pay at which new employees are hired.

entropy, term from thermodynamics that is applicable to all physical systems and sometimes applied to social systems. It refers to the inherent tendency of all closed systems, which do not interact with their environments, to move toward a chaotic state in which there is no further potential for work. According to James G. Miller, in "Living Systems: Basic Concepts," *Behavorial Science* (July 1965), "the disorder, disorganization, lack of patterning, or randomness of organization of a system is known as its *entropy*."

Negative entropy, an arresting of the entropy process, can be acquired by an open system, according to Daniel Katz and Robert L. Kahn, in *The Social Psychology of Organizations* (N.Y.: John Wiley & Sons, 1966):

> The open system, however, by importing more energy from its environment than it expends, can store energy and can acquire negative entropy.

EPI: *see* EYSENCK PERSONALITY INVENTORY.

EPPS: *see* EDWARDS PERSONAL PREFERENCE SCHEDULE.

E-P ratio: *see* EMPLOYMENT-POPULATION RATIO.

equal employment opportunity (EEO), concept fraught with political, cultural, and emotional overtones. Generally, it applies to a set of employment procedures and practices that effectively prevent any individual from being adversely excluded from employment opportunities on the basis of race, color, sex, religion, age, national origin, or other factors that cannot lawfully be used in employment efforts. While the ideal of EEO is an employment system that is devoid of both intentional and unintentional discrimination, achieving this ideal may be a political impossibility because of the problem of definition. One man's equal opportunity may be seen by another as tainted with institutional racism or by a woman as institutional sexism. Because of this problem of definition, only the courts have been able to say if, when, and where EEO exists. For the law of EEO, *see* Barbara Lindemann Schlei and Paul Frossman, *Employment Discrimination Law* (Washington, D.C.: Bureau of National Affairs, Inc., 1976). For the history of EEO in the federal government, *see* David H. Rosenbloom, *Federal Equal Employment Opportunity: Politics and Public Personnel Administration* (N.Y.: Praeger, 1977).

See also the following entries:

DISCRIMINATION
FAIR EMPLOYMENT PRACTICE COMMITTEE
GOALS
NATIONAL ASSOCIATION FOR THE ADVANCEMENT OF COLORED PEOPLE V. FEDERAL POWER COMMISSION
REHABILITATED OFFENDER PROGRAM
RELIGIOUS DISCRIMINATION
REPRESENTATIVE BUREAUCRACY
REVERSE DISCRIMINATION
RIGHTFUL PLACE
SCHLESINGER V. BALLARD
SEX PLUS
THIRD PARTY
TITLE VII
TOKENISM
UNDERUTILIZATION
UNFAIR LABOR PRACTICES (EMPLOYERS)
UNFAIR LABOR PRACTICES (UNIONS)
UPWARD MOBILITY PROGRAM

Equal Employment Opportunity Act of 1972, also called EEO ACT OF 1972, amends Title VII of the 1964 Civil Rights Act by strengthening the authority of the Equal Employment Opportunity Commission and extending anti-discrimination provisions to

equal employment opportunity is the law

igualdad de oportunidad en el empleo es la ley

Private Industry, State, and Local Government

Title VII of the Civil Rights Act of 1964, as amended, prohibits job discrimination because of race, color, religion, sex or national origin.

Applicants to and employees of private employers, state/local governments, and public/private educational institutions are protected. Also covered are employment agencies, labor unions and apprenticeship programs. Any person who believes he or she has been discriminated against should contact immediately

The U. S. Equal Employment Opportunity Commission (EEOC)
2401 E St., N.W.
Washington, D. C. 20506

or an EEOC District Office, listed in most telephone directories under U. S. Government.

Industrias Privadas, Gobiernos Locales y Estatales

El Título VII de la Ley de Derechos Civiles de 1964, enmendado, prohibe la discriminación en el empleo por razón de raza, color, religión, sexo o nacionalidad de origen.

La ley protege a los empleados y solicitantes de empleo en empresas privadas, gobiernos estatales y locales e instituciones educacionales públicas y privadas. También abarca las agencias de empleo, sindicatos de trabajadores y programas de aprendizaje. Cualquier persona, tanto hombre como mujer, que crea que ha sido objeto de discriminación debe escribir inmediatamente a

The U. S. Equal Employment Opportunity Commission (EEOC)
2401 E St., N.W.
Washington, D. C. 20506

o a cualquier oficina regional de EEOC, las que se encuentran en las guías telefónicas locales bajo el nombre de: U. S. Government.

Federal Contract Employment

Executive Order 11246, as amended, prohibits job discrimination because of race, color, religion, sex or national origin and requires affirmative action to ensure equality of opportunity in all aspects of employment.

Section 503 of the Rehabilitation Act of 1973 prohibits job discrimination because of handicap and requires affirmative action to employ and advance in employment qualified handicapped workers.

Section 402 of the Vietnam Era Veterans' Readjustment Assistance Act of 1974 prohibits job discrimination and requires affirmative action to employ and advance in employment (1) qualified Vietnam era veterans during the first four years after their discharge and (2) qualified disabled veterans throughout their working life if they have a 30 percent or more disability.

Applicants to and employees of any company with a federal government contract or subcontract are protected. Any person who believes a contractor has violated its affirmative action obligations, including nondiscrimination, under Executive Order 11246, as amended, or under Section 503 of the Rehabilitation Act should contact immediately

The Employment Standards Administration
Office of Federal Contract Compliance
Programs (OFCCP)
Third and Constitution Ave., N.W.
Washington, D. C. 20210

or an OFCCP regional office, listed in most telephone directories under U. S. Government, Department of Labor. Complaints specifically under the veterans' law should be filed with the Veterans' Employment Service through local offices of the state employment service.

All complaints must be filed within 180 days from date of alleged violation.

Empleos En Compañías Con Contratos Federales

La Orden Ejecutiva Número 11246, enmendada, prohibe la discriminación en el empleo por razón de raza, color, religión, sexo o nacionalidad de origen y exige acción positiva para garantizar la igualdad de oportunidad en todos los aspectos del empleo.

Las Sección 503 de la Ley de Rehabilitación de 1973, prohibe la discriminación en el empleo contra personas que sufran de impedimentos físicos o mentales y exige acción positiva en el empleo y promoción de personas que sufran de impedimentos físicos o mentales, siempre que reúnan las condiciones indispensables para el desempeño del empleo.

La Sección 402 de la Ley de 1974 de Asistencia para el Reajuste de los Veteranos de la Era de Vietnam, prohibe la discriminación en el empleo y exige acción positiva en el empleo y promoción de (1) veteranos de la era de Vietnam, durante los primeros cuatro años después de haber sido separados del servicio activo, siempre que reúnan las condiciones indispensables para el desempeño del empleo (2) ciertos veteranos que tengan un 30 por ciento o más de impedimentos físicos o mentales mientras puedan trabajar, siempre que reúnan las condiciones indispensables para el desempeño del empleo.

La ley protege a los solicitantes de empleo y empleados de cualquier compañía que tenga un contrato o subcontrato con el gobierno federal. Cualquier persona que crea que uno de estos contratistas no ha cumplido con sus obligaciones de tomar acción positiva, incluyendo la de no discriminar, bajo la Orden Ejecutiva 11246, enmendada, o bajo la Sección 503 de la Ley de Rehabilitación, debe escribir inmediatamente a

The Employment Standards Administration
Office of Federal Contract Compliance
Programs (OFCCP)
Third and Constitution Ave., N.W.
Washington, D. C. 20210

o a cualquier oficina regional de OFCCP, las que se encuentran en la mayoría de las guías telefónicas bajo: U. S. Government, Department of Labor. Las reclamaciones específicamente comprendidas bajo la ley de veteranos, deben de dirigirse a Veterans' Employment Service por medio de las oficinas locales del servicio de empleo del estado.

Todas las reclamaciones deben de ser registradas dentro de los 180 días subsequentes a la fecha del supuesto acto de discriminación.

U.S. Department of Labor
Employment Standards Administration
Office of Federal Contract Compliance Programs

OFCCP-1420
(October 1976)

☆ U.S. GOVERNMENT PRINTING OFFICE: 1976 O--222-157

state and local governments and labor organizations with 15 or more employees and public and private employment agencies. *See* William Brown III, "The Equal Employment Opportunity Act of 1972—The Light at the Top of the Stairs," *Personnel Administration* (June 1972); Harry Grossman, "The Equal Employment Opportunity Act of 1972, Its Implications for the State and Local Government Manager," *Public Personnel Management* (September-October 1973).

See also HAZELWOOD SCHOOL DISTRICT V. UNITED STATES.

Equal Employment Opportunity Commission (EEOC), created by Title VII of the Civil Rights Act of 1964, the EEOC is composed of five members (one designated chair) appointed for five-year terms by the president, subject to the advice and consent of the Senate. The EEOC's mission is to end discrimination based on race, color, religion, sex, or national origin in hiring, promotion, firing,

wages, testing, training, apprenticeship, and all other conditions of employment and to promote voluntary action programs by employers, unions, and community organizations to make equal employment opportunity an actuality.

The EEOC's operations are decentralized to 5 litigation centers, 7 regional offices, and 32 district offices. The district offices receive written charges of discrimination against public and private employers, labor organizations, joint labor–management apprenticeship programs, and public and private employment agencies. EEOC members may also initiate charges alleging that a violation of Title VII has occurred. Charges of Title VII violation must be filed with the EEOC within 180 days of the alleged violation. The EEOC is responsible for notifying persons so charged within 10 days of the receipt of a new charge. Before investigation, a charge must be deferred for 60 days to a local, fair employment practices agency in states and municipalities

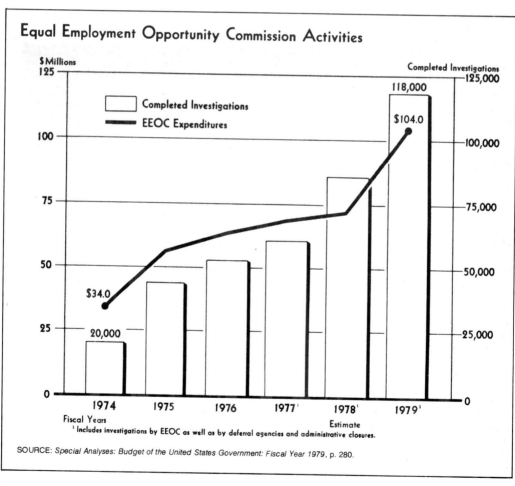

Equal Employment Opportunity Commission Activities

$ Millions

Completed Investigations

Completed Investigations

EEOC Expenditures

118,000

$104.0

$34.0

20,000

1974 1975 1976 1977[1] 1978[1] 1979[1]

Fiscal Years

Estimate

[1] Includes investigations by EEOC as well as by deferral agencies and administrative closures.

SOURCE: *Special Analyses: Budget of the United States Government: Fiscal Year 1979*, p. 280.

where an enforceable, fair employment practices law is in effect. (The deferral period is 120 days for an agency which has been operating less than one year.) After an investigation, if there is reasonable cause to believe the charge is true, the district office attempts to remedy the alleged unlawful practices through the informal methods of conciliation, conference and persuasion.

Unless an acceptable conciliation agreement has been secured, the EEOC may, after 30 days from the date the charge was filed, bring suit in an appropriate federal district court. (The U.S. Attorney General brings suit when a state government, governmental agency, or a political subdivision is involved.) If the EEOC or the Attorney General does not proceed in this manner, at the conclusion of the administrative procedures, or earlier at the request of the charging party, a "Notice of Right to Sue" is issued, which allows the charging party to proceed within 90 days in a federal district court. In appropriate cases, the EEOC may intervene in such civil action if the case is of general public interest. The investigation and conciliation of charges having an industrywide or national impact are coordinated or conducted by the EEOC's Office of Compliance Programs.

If it is concluded after a preliminary investigation that prompt judicial action is necessary to carry out the purposes of the act, the EEOC or the Attorney General, in a case involving a state government, governmental agency, or political subdivision, may bring an action for appropriate temporary or preliminary relief pending final disposition of a charge.

The EEOC encourages and assists in voluntary action by employers, unions, and employment agencies through affirmative action programs, providing the EEOC's services in developing multiplant and industrywide programs and in identifying discriminatory systems and devising ways to change them. Such programs are designed to help those organizations achieve EEO goals through nondiscriminatory recruiting, fair employee selection procedures, expanded training programs, and job upgrading. The Voluntary Compliance Division and the regional voluntary programs officers provide information, educational materials, consultation, and other assistance in the development of affirmative and other voluntary action programs; and attempt to negotiate voluntary agreements with employers to implement the programs.

The EEOC has direct liaison with state and local governments, employer and union organizations, trade associations, civil rights organizations, and other agencies and organizations concerned with employment of minority-group members and women. The EEOC engages in and contributes to the cost of research and other mutual interest projects with state and local agencies charged with the administration of fair employment practices laws. Regional offices administer the funding of mutual interest projects.

Equal Employment Opportunity Commission
2401 E St., N.W.
Washington, DC 20506
(202) 634-7040

See also 706 AGENCY.

equal employment opportunity counselor, specifically designated individual within an organization who provides an open and systematic channel through which employees may raise questions, discuss real and imagined grievances, and obtain information on their procedural rights. Counseling is the first stage in the discrimination complaint process. The counselor through interviews and inquiries attempts to informally resolve problems related to equal employment opportunity. *See* U.S. Civil Service Commission, *Equal Employment Opportunity Counseling: A Guidebook* (Washington, D.C.: Government Printing Office, October 1975).

equal employment opportunity officer, official within an organization who is designated responsibility for monitoring EEO programs and assuring that both organizational and national EEO policies are being implemented.

Equal Pay Act of 1963, basically an amendment to the Fair Labor Standards Act of 1938, the Equal Pay Act of 1963 (Public Law 88-38) prohibits pay discrimination because of sex and provides that men and women working in the same establishment under similar conditions must receive the same pay if jobs require equal (similar) skill, effort, and responsibility. *See* John E. Burns and Catherine G. Burns, "An Analysis of the Equal Pay Act," *Labor Law Journal* (February 1973).

equal pay for equal work, principle that salary rates should not be dependent upon factors unrelated to the quantity or quality of work. *See* Francine D. Blau, *Equal Pay in the Office* (Lexington, Mass.: Lexington Books, 1977); Barrie O. Pettman (ed.), *Equal Pay For Women: Progress and Problems in Seven Countries* (N.Y.: McGraw-Hill, 1977).

equated scores, scores from different tests of the same variable which are reduced by weighting in order to have a common basis for comparison.

equating, process of adjusting the raw statistics obtained from a particular sample to corresponding statistics obtained for a base group or reference population.

equipercentile equating, process that treats as equivalent those raw scores that fall at the same percentile in different samples although the raw scores themselves may be different.

equity, external/internal: *see* EXTERNAL EQUITY.

equity theory: *see* INEQUITY THEORY.

equivalent form: *see* ALTERNATE FORM.

Erdman Act of 1898, the essence of this act, which banned interstate railroads from discriminating against union-member employees, was held unconstitutional by the U.S. Supreme Court, in *Adair v. United States*, 208 U.S. 161 (1908).

ergonomics: *see* HUMAN-FACTORS ENGINEERING.

ERISA: *see* EMPLOYEES RETIREMENT INCOME SECURITY ACT OF 1974.

ESA: *see* EMPLOYMENT STANDARDS ADMINISTRATION.

escalator clause, also called COST-OF-LIVING ESCALATOR, provision of a collective bargaining agreement which allows for periodic wage adjustments in response to changes in the cost of living usually as determined by the Consumer Price Index of the Bureau of Labor Statistics. *See* Francis S. Cunningham, "The Use of Price Indexes in Escalator Contracts," *Monthly Labor Review* (August 1963); Robert H. Ferguson, *Cost-of-Living Adjustments in Union–Management Agreements* (Itaca, N.Y.: New York State School of Industrial and Labor Relations, Cornell University, 1976).

escape clause, in a maintenance-of-membership shop, a union contract may provide for a period of time during which union members may withdraw (escape) from the union without affecting their employment.

ESOP: *see* EMPLOYEE STOCK-OWNERSHIP PLAN.

Espinoza v. Farah Manufacturing Company, 414 U.S. 86 (1973), U.S. Supreme Court case, which held that an employer who refused to hire a lawfully admitted resident alien because of a longstanding policy against the employment of aliens could not be held liable under Title VII of the Civil Rights Act of 1964 if the company already employed a significant percentage of other employees who were of the same national origin but were also U.S. citizens.

esprit de corps, strong feelings of unity and common purpose on the part of a group.

estate planning, also ESTATE BUILDING, *estate planning* is concerned with the distribution of one's assets—one's estate—at death. *Estate building*, usually part of an executive compensation program, is concerned with turning portions of an executive's salary and fringe benefits into assets that will benefit his heirs after the executive's death. According to Thomas H. Patten, Jr., in *Pay: Employee Compensation and Incentive Plans* (N.Y.: The Free Press, 1977),

> an estate can be defined in the field of executive compensation as the sum and substance of the earnings and acquisitions a person has conserved for eventual transmission to others. In order to have such an estate one must take steps to create it, conserve it, and transmit it to one's heirs. To a very important extent, although it may seem flippant to put it this way, estate planning amounts to planning how to disinherit the Internal Revenue Service (but in a lawful way).

ETA: *see* EMPLOYMENT AND TRAINING ADMINISTRATION.

et al., Latin abbreviation for *et alia*: ("and others"). For example, a book may be written by Smith *et al.*, which usually means Smith and two or more other authors.

ethics, a set of moral principles or values.

There are many ethical individuals working as personnel operatives. However, their ethical standards tend to reflect their personal background rather than some abstract standards of personnel management. While professional codes of conduct have been put forth by a variety of organizations—such as the American Society for Personnel Administration (*see* CODE OF ETHICS) and the International Personnel Management Association (*see below*)—their impact has been inconsequential.

Thomas H. Patten, Jr., in "Is Personnel Administration A Profession," *Personnel Administration* (March-April 1968), has suc-

**CODE OF ETHICS
FOR THE
INTERNATIONAL PERSONNEL
MANAGEMENT ASSOCIATION**

I pledge that, according to my ability and my judgment, I will pursue these goals and keep these commitments:

I will respect and protect the dignity of individuals, honoring their right to fair consideration in all aspects of employment and to the pursuit of a rewarding career without regard to race, sex, religion, age, or national origin.

I will foster and apply management practices and merit principles which motivate employees to develop their full capability as competent, productive members of their organization.

I will endeavor to insure that full and early consideration is given to the human aspects of management plans and decisions.

I will assist employees and management in understanding and fulfilling their mutual responsibilities and obligations.

I will give freely of my knowledge and my time in the counseling and development of those pursuing a career in personnel management and will contribute to the development and dissemination of professional knowledge for the improvement of the art.

I will treat as privileged, information accepted in trust.

I will not compromise, for personal gain or accommodation, my integrity or that of my employer, but will faithfully respect and apply this Code in the conduct of my professional duties and responsibilities.

cinctly summarized the dilemma of ethical codes for personnel managers.

> In a showdown disagreement with higher management, the personnel administrator who cited his professional ethical code as a basis for a course of action (assuming he had also complied with the law) would be regarded as either a naive, high-minded idealist or simply a fool. He would also be brave to so jeopardize his mealticket and future employment status. In any event, if he were to stand firm and threaten quitting as a sanction for his convictions, the letter of resignation would probably be eagerly awaited by a disgusted management (but one well pleased to be rid of a cloud-nine character).

Charles R. Milton's book, *Ethics & Expediency in Personnel Management: A Critical History of Personnel Philosophy* (Columbia, S.C.: University of South Carolina Press, 1970), deals mainly with changing styles of personnel management and only in the most

peripheral sense with the ethic dilemmas of the personnel manager.

See also CODE OF ETHICS and STANDARDS OF CONDUCT.

Ethics in Government Act of 1978, federal statute that seeks to deal with possible conflicts of interest by former federal executive branch employees by imposing post-employment prohibitions on their activities. The restrictions in the law are concerned with former government employees' representation or attempts to influence federal agencies, not with their employment by others. What is prohibited depends on how involved a former employee was with a matter while with the government and whether he or she was one of a specified group of senior employees.

ethnic categories: *see* RACE CATEGORIES.

ethnic group, social, biological or (sometimes) political division of humankind.

ETS: *see* EDUCATIONAL TESTING SERVICE.

Etzioni, Amitai W. (1929-   ), sociologist and author of a variety of books on international relations, best known to organizational analysts for his studies of how organizations interact with the larger society and how the various parts of organizations interact, change, and survive. Major works include: *A Comparative Analysis of Complex Organizations* (Glencoe, Ill.: The Free Press, 1961); *Modern Organizations* (Englewood Cliffs, N.J.: Prentice-Hall, 1964).

eupsychian management, term originated by Abraham H. Maslow, in *Eupsychian Management: A Journal* (Homewood, Ill.: Richard D. Irwin, Inc., 1965), to describe an ideal situation with respect to workers motivation, productivity, and mental health. Relating eupsychian management to his more famous "hierarchy of needs," Maslow defines it as "the culture that would be generated by 1000 self-actualizing people on some sheltered island."

examination: *see* EMPLOYMENT TESTING.

examination, group oral: *see* GROUP ORAL INTERVIEW.

Examining Board v. Flores de Otero, 426 U.S. 572 (1976), U.S. Supreme Court case, which held that a Puerto Rican statute permitting only U.S. citizens to practice privately as civil engineers was unconstitutional and that resident aliens could not be denied the same opportunity.

Excelsior rule, the National Labor Relations Board has held that an employer must provide a list of the names and addresses of all employees eligible to vote in a forthcoming representation election. While the list is given to the NLRB, it is made available to employee organizations. The U.S. Supreme Court, in *NLRB* v. *Wyman-Gordon Co.*, 394 U.S. 759 (1969), upheld the NLRB's right to demand such a list.

excepted positions, also called EXEMPTED POSITIONS, U.S. civil service positions that have been excepted or exempted from merit system requirements. Most of the excepted positions in the U.S. Civil Service are excluded by statute and are under merit systems administered by agencies such as the Tennessee Valley Authority, the Federal Bureau of Invesgitation, U.S. Foreign Service, and the U.S. Postal Service. Excepted position has the same meaning as *unclassified position*, or *position excepted by law*, or *position excepted by executive order*, or *position excepted by civil service rule*, or *position outside the competitive service* as used in existing statutes and executive orders.

excepting language, the Attorney General of the United States has held that language relied on to establish an exception from the competitive service must be so plain and unequivocal as to admit of no doubts. When acts are silent on how appointments shall be made, the civil service laws, rules, and regulations apply.

Exchange Parts decision: *see* NATIONAL LABOR RELATIONS BOARD V. EXCHANGE PARTS.

exclusionary clause, that part of a contract that tries to restrict the legal remedies available to one side if the contract is broken.

exclusive recognition, also called EXCLUSIVE BARGAINING RIGHTS, in the private sector the only form of recognition available to a union representing a specific bargaining unit. An employer is required to negotiate in good faith, to give exclusive bargaining rights, to a union holding such recognition. In fact, a private employer may not bargain or consult with a union that does not hold exclusive recognition without committing an unfair labor practice.

As a term, exclusive recognition has had its greatest usage in the federal service. Executive Order 11491 (issued by President Nixon in 1969), which amended President Kennedy's 1962 Executive Order 10988, pro-

vided that in order to obtain exclusive recognition, a union must: (1) qualify as a bona fide union, (2) submit to the agency a roster of its officers and representatives, a copy of its constitution and bylaws, and a statement of its objectives, and (3) show that it has majority support solely by means of a secret ballot election in which it receives a majority of the votes cast. Exclusive recognition entitles the union to act for, and to negotiate agreements covering, all the employees in the unit. It guarantees the union the opportunity to be represented at discussions between management and employees concerning grievances and personnel policies.

ex-con: *see* EX-OFFENDER.

executive, any of the highest managers in an organization.
See also GROUP EXECUTIVE and PLURAL EXECUTIVE.

executive compensation, totality of the benefits paid to the members of the upper levels of the organizational hierarchy. According to William H. Cash, "Executive Compensation," *The Personnel Administrator* (September 1977),

> Executive compensation programs are generally viewed as being made up of five basic elements—base salary, short-term (annual) incentives or bonuses, long-term incentives and capital appreciation plans, fringe benefits, and perquisites.

For a bibliography, *see* Karen B. Tracy, "On Executive Compensation," *Harvard Business Review*, (January–February 1977).

executive development: *see* MANAGEMENT DEVELOPMENT.

Executive Interchange Program: *see* PRESIDENT'S EXECUTIVE INTERCHANGE PROGRAM.

executive order, any rule or regulation, issued by a chief administrative authority, that, because of precedent and existing legislative authorization, has the effect of law. Executive orders are the principal mode of administrative action on the part of the president of the United States.

Executive Order 8802, presidential executive order of June 25, 1941, which (1) required that defense contractors not discriminate against any worker because of race, creed, or national origin and (2) established a Committee on Fair Employment Practice to investigate and remedy violations.

Executive Order 10925, presidential executive order of March 6, 1961, which, for the first time, required that "affirmative action" be used to implement the policy of non-discrimination in employment by the federal government and its contractors.

Executive Order 10988, presidential executive order of January 17, 1962, which first established the right of federal employees to bargain with management over certain limited issues. Considered the "Magna Carta" of labor relations in the federal government, it was superseded by Executive Order 11491.

Executive Order 11141, presidential executive order of February 12, 1964, which prohibits employment discrimination because of age by federal government contractors.

Executive Order 11246, presidential executive order of September 24, 1965, which requires federal government contracts to contain provisions against employment discrimination because of race, color, religion, or national origin.
See also PHILADELPHIA PLAN.

Executive Order 11375, presidential executive order of October 17, 1967, which requires federal government contracts to contain provisions against employment discrimination because of sex.

Executive Order 11451: *see* PRESIDENT'S EXECUTIVE INTERCHANGE PROGRAM.

Executive Order 11478, presidential executive order of August 8, 1969, which prohibits discrimination in federal government employment because of race, color, religion, sex, or national origin.

Executive Order 11491, presidential executive order of October 29, 1969, which granted each federal employee the right to join or not join a labor organization, created the Federal Labor Relations Council (which was superseded by the Federal Labor Relations Authority) and generally expanded the scope of bargaining for federal employees. *See* Ed D. Roach and Frank W. McClain, "Executive Order 11491: Prospects and Problems," *Public Personnel Review* (July 1970).

Executive Order 11914, presidential executive order of April 28, 1976, which extends the nondiscrimination with respect to the handicapped provisions of the Vocational Rehabilitation Act of 1973 to all federal departments and agencies.

Executive Order 11935: *see* HAMPTON V. MOW SUN WONG.

Executive Order 12008: *see* PRESIDENTIAL MANAGEMENT INTERN PROGRAM.

executive recruiter: *see* HEADHUNTER.

Executive Schedule, key management and policymaking positions in the federal service are compensated under the Executive Schedule. Secretaries of cabinet departments, heads of agencies and their principal deputies, assistant secretaries, members of boards and commissions—a total of nearly 700 positions—are assigned to one of the five levels of the Executive Schedule, largely on the basis of protocol and interorganizational alignment. Virtually all the positions covered by the Executive Schedule are created by statute and carry specific statutory responsibilities and authorities.

Executive Schedule (November 1979)		
Level	Yearly Salary	Genre of Position
I	$69,630	Cabinet Secretaries
II	$60,663	Heads of Major Independent Agencies
III	$55,388	Under-Secretaries
IV	$52,750	Assistant Secretaries
V	$50,113	Heads of Major Bureaus

Executive Stock Acquisition Plan, sanctioned under Section 423 of the Internal Revenue Code, the plan allows executives who are granted options to buy company stock at a price equal to the lessor of 85 percent of the market price on the date of the option grant or 85 percent of the market price at the time the option is exercised. Executives participating in such a plan authorize payroll deductions over a pre-determined period of time, usually a year or more, that pay for all or part of the optioned stock at the end of the purchase period. James E. McKinney, "The Tax Reform Act of 1976 and Executive Stock Compensation Plan", *Personnel* (May-June 1977), discusses administration of the plan:

During the purchase period, the executive is credited with any dividends paid on the stock or the interest accrued on his payments. The executive can withdraw from the plan at any time during the purchase period, and his payments will be returned to him along with either the dividend equivalents or interest accrued. If this kind of prefinancing arrangement is utilized, options should be granted at fairly frequent intervals (at least biannually and preferably annually) and for modest amounts of stock. The use of more frequent grants is analogous to dollar-averaging stock purchases and helps avoid another problem inherent in stock options—option price. If options are granted infrequently on a one-time basis at the market price of the stock on the particular day the option was granted, the price may or may not bear a relationship to the true value of the stock.

executive supplemental compensation, type of nonproduction bonus that is based upon an estimate of an executive's contribution to the profitability of the company over a given time period.

Exemplary Rehabilitation Certificates: see UNITED STATES EMPLOYMENT SERVICE.

exempted positions: see EXCEPTED POSITIONS.

exempt employees, employees who, because of their administrative, professional or executive status, are not covered by the overtime provisions of the Fair Labor Standards Act. In consequence, their employing organizations are not legally required to pay them for overtime work. For an analysis of the problem, see Robert A. Sbarra, "Exempt Employee Overtime," *Compensation Review* (First Quarter 1976).

exemption, deduction from gross income for income tax purposes allowed for the support of one's self and dependents.

exit interview, also called SEPARATION INTERVIEW, tool to monitor employee terminations that seeks information on why the employee is leaving and what he or she liked or disliked about his or her job, working conditions, company policy, etc. Exit interviews are usually, and most desirably, conducted by the personnel department and not by the supervisor of the exiting employee. When interviews are not possible, *exit questionnaires* seek to gather the same information. See Charles Bahn, "Expanded Use of the Exit Interview, "*Personnel Journal*" (December 1965); Martin Hilb, "The Standardized Exit Interview," *Personnel Journal* (June 1978); Laura Garrison and Jacqueline Ferguson, "Separation Interviews," *Personnel Journal* (September 1977).

ex-offender, anyone who, having been convicted of a crime, served time in prison. For an analysis of the problem of employing ex-offenders, see Marvin A. Jolson, "Are Ex-

Offenders Successful Employees?" *California Management Review* (Spring 1975).

ex officio, Latin phrase ("by virtue of his office"). Many individuals hold positions on boards, commissions, councils, etc., because of an office that they temporarily occupy. For example, the mayor of a city may be an *ex officio* member of the board of trustees of a university in his city.

expectancy, probability of success on the job in terms of a specific criterion and associated with a known fact about an individual such as a test score, level of education, etc.

expectancy theory, also VALENCE, *expectancy theory* holds that individuals have cognitive "expectancies" regarding outcomes that are likely to occur as a result of what they do, and that individuals have preferences among these various outcomes. Consequently, motivation occurs on the basis of what the individual expects to occur as a result of what he chooses to do. An "expectancy" in this context refers to an employee's perceived probability that a given level of effort will result in a given outcome, such as a promotion or raise in salary. The value that an employee places on this outcome, the strength of the employee's preference for it, has been termed *valence* by Victor H. Vroom, *Work and Motivation* (N.Y.: John Wiley, 1964). Valence can be positive or negative, depending on whether an individual is attracted to or repelled by a possible outcome. See Robert J. House, H. Jack Shapiro, and Mahmoud A. Wahba, "Expectancy Theory as a Predictor of Work Behavior and Attitude: A Reevaluation of Empirical Evidence," *Decision Sciences* (July 1974).

See also PSYCHOLOGICAL CONTRACT.

expedited arbitration, because conventional arbitration is frequently so time consuming and expensive, this new streamlined process is being increasingly incorporated into union contracts in an effort to cut down the backlog of grievance cases. In 1971, in response to the concern of parties over rising costs and delays in grievance arbitration, the Labor–Management Committee of the American Arbitration Association recommended the establishment of expedited procedures, under which cases could be scheduled promptly and awards rendered no later than five days after the hearings. In return for giving up certain features of traditional labor arbitration, (such as transcripts, briefs, and extensive opinions), the parties utilizing simplified procedures can get quick decisions and realize certain cost savings. While the term expedited arbitration can be applied to any "fast" method of resolving disputes through the use of an arbitrator, it is usually characterized by on-site hearings and the minimal involvement of the hierarchies of both union and management. For details of the technique, *see* Lawrence Stessin, "Expedited Arbitration: Less Grief Over Grievances," *Harvard Business Review* (January-February 1977).

experience rating, insurance term which refers to a review of a previous year's group-claims experience in order to establish premium rates for the following year. *See* Joseph M. Becker, *Experience Rating in Unemployment Insurance: An Experiment in Competitive Socialism* (Baltimore: The Johns Hopkins University Press, 1972).

experienced unemployed, term from the U.S. Bureau of the Census that refers to "unemployed persons who have worked at any time in the past."

experimenter effect, any distortion in an experiment's findings because of the behavior or attitudes of the experimenters.
    See also HAWTHORNE EFFECT.

expert, efficiency: *see* EFFICIENCY EXPERT.

expiration date, time established by a collective bargaining agreement for the agreement to terminate.

external alignment, relationship of positions within an organization to similar positions in the near environment. In theory, the most desirable external alignment calls for compensation programs similar to those provided by other employers in the local labor market.

external equity, also INTERNAL EQUITY, a measure of the justice of an employee's wages when the compensation for his/her position is compared to the labor market as a whole within a region, profession, or industry. *Internal equity* is a measure of the justice of an employee's wages when the compensation for his/her position is compared to similar positions within the same organization. *See* Thomas A. Mahoney, "Justice and Equity: A Recurring Theme in Compensation," *Personnel* (September–October 1975).

external house organ: *see* HOUSE ORGAN.

external labor market, geographic region from which employers reasonably expect to recruit new workers.

extrinsic motivation, motivation not an inherent part of the work itself. When one works solely for the monetary rewards, one is extrinsically motivated.

Eysenck Personality Inventory (EPI), measures two independent dimensions of personality, extraversion–introversion and neuroticism–stability. Consists of 57 yes–no items with falsification scale to reflect distortion. TIME: 10/15 minutes. AUTHORS: H. J. and S.B.G. Eysenck. PUBLISHER: Educational and Industrial Testing Service (*see* TEST PUBLISHERS).

F

Fabricant, Solomon (1906-   ), labor economist, best known for his work on productivity measurement. *See* his *A Primer on Productivity* (N.Y.: Random House, 1969).

face amount, in life insurance, this is the amount, stated on the front of the policy, that is payable upon the death of the insured. The actual amount payable to the beneficiary may differ according to the policy's specific provisions, such as double indemnity, or subsequent riders.

face validity, also called FAITH VALIDITY, measure of the degree to which a test *appears* to be valid. While this is the most superficial kind of validity, it may contribute significantly to the legitimacy of the test in the eyes of the candidates (an important consideration in avoiding legal challenges). However, it can also deceive employers who may be tempted to save the time and money required for genuine validation. According to Raymond B. Cattell, "Validity and Reliability: A Proposed More Basic Set Of Concepts," *Journal of Educational Psychology* (February 1964),

> in some trival sense face or faith validity perhaps still has a role, but in diplomacy rather than psychology, as when an industrial psychologist is pressured to make tests which a chief executive will, from the depths of his ignorance commend or sanction as measuring what he conceives to be this or that trait.

facilitator, individual who serves as a catalyst, usually in a formal organization development effort, in order to improve the interactions and interpersonal relationships of a group.

FACT: *see* FLANAGAN APTITUDE CLASSIFICATION TEST.

factfinding, an impartial review of the issues in a labor dispute by a specially appointed third party, whether it be a single individual, panel, or board. The factfinder holds formal or informal hearings and submits a report to the administrative agency and/or the parties involved. The factfinder's report, usually considered advisory, may contain specific recommendations. According to Robert E. Doherty, "On Factfinding: A One-Eyed Man Lost Among the Eagles," *Public Personnel Management* (September-October 1976),

> factfinding nowadays seems to be regarded as a way station in the onward march toward the strike, unilateral management determination, or (in most instances) further haggling which eventually ends up in a settlement—a settlement which may or may not bear a relationship to the factfinder's report. The factfinder is only rarely treated with deference—and rightfully so. It takes considerable audacity to believe that after a few hours of testimony any individual whose talents are somewhat less than those of a Solomon can come to understand the issues well enough to render a report that is sufficiently clear and logical to impress both parties.

factor analysis, any of several methods of analyzing the intercorrelations among test scores or other sets of variables. *See* Wayne K. Kirchner and June A. Lucas, "Using Factor Analysis to Explore Employee Attitudes," *Personnel Journal* (June 1970); Richard L. Gorsuch, *Factor Analysis* (Phila.: W. B. Saunders, 1974); T. Gregory Morton, "Factor Analysis, Multicollinearity, and Regression Appraisal Models," *The Appraisal Journal* (October 1977).

factor evaluation system, also called FACTOR COMPARISON SYSTEM, a hybrid of traditional duties or position classification systems. With traditional duties classification, different combinations of factors are used for different positions; the factor evaluation system uses the same factors for all positions. With traditional duties classification, grade levels are ascertained by the weight and eloquence of narrative descriptions; the factor evaluation system determines grade levels by comparing positions directly to one another. The main ingredient of a factor evaluation system is, obviously, the factor—any of the various key elements individually examined in the evaluation process. Once the factors of a position have been identified, they can be ranked—the factors of one position are compared to another. Such a factor comparison can have only three outcomes. Any given factor must be higher, lower, or equal to the factor of another position. When positions are ranked by factors, all of the factors of each position are compared and an overall ranking is achieved. *See* Lawrence L. Epperson, "The Dynamics of Factor Comparison/Point Evaluation," *Public Personnel Management* (January-February 1975).

factors: *see* JOB FACTORS.

factory system: *see* DIVISION OF LABOR.

fair day's work, generally, the amount of work produced in a work day by a qualified employee of average skill exerting average effort.

Fair Employment Practice Commission (FEPC), generic term for any state or local government agency responsible for administrating/enforcing laws prohibiting employment discrimination because of race, color, sex, religion, national origin, or other factors.

Fair Employment Practice Committee, (FEPC), former federal committee. In 1941, President Franklin D. Roosevelt issued Executive Order 8802, which called for the elimination of discrimination based upon race, color, religion, or national origin within the defense production industries and the federal service. A newly created Fair Employment Practice Committee was charged with implementing the order. By almost all accounts, however, the committee was weak and even somewhat disinterested in combating discrimination in the federal service. In 1946, it met its demise through an amendment to an appropriations bill. For its history, *see* Louis C. Kesselman, *The Social Politics of FEPC* (Chapel Hill, N.C.: University of North Carolina Press, 1948); Will Maslow, "FEPC—A Case History in Parliamentary Maneuver," *University of Chicago Law Review*, Vol. 13 (June 1946).

fair employment practice laws, all government requirements designed to prohibit discrimination in the various aspects of employment.

Fair Employment Practice Service, reference service published by the Bureau of National Affairs, Inc., which covers federal and state laws dealing with equal opportunity in employment. Full texts of federal and state FEP laws, orders, and regulations, as well as federal, state, and local court opinions, and decisions of the Equal Employment Opportunity Commission.

Fair Labor Standards Act (FLSA), also called WAGES AND HOURS ACT, federal statute of 1938, which, as amended, establishes minimum-wage, overtime-pay, equal-pay, recordkeeping, and child-labor standards affecting more than 50 million full-time and part-time workers.

Basic Wage Standards. Covered non-exempt workers are entitled to a minimum wage of not less than $2.90 an hour beginning January 1, 1979, $3.10 an hour beginning January 1, 1980, $3.35 an hour beginning January 1, 1981, and overtime at not less than one and one-half times the employee's regular rate is due after 40 hours of work in the workweek. Wages required by FLSA are due on the regular pay day for the pay period covered. (Hospitals and residential care establishments may adopt, by agreement with the employees, a 14-day overtime period in lieu of the usual 7-day workweek, if the employees are paid at least time and a half their regular rate for hours worked over 8 in a day or 80 in a 14-day work period.)

Who is Covered? All employees of certain enterprises having workers engaged in interstate commerce, producing goods for interstate commerce, or handling, selling, or otherwise working on goods or materials that have been moved in or produced for such commerce by any person are covered by FLSA. A covered enterprise is the related activities performed through unified operation or common control by any person or persons for a common business purpose and is:

1. engaged in laundering or cleaning of clothing or fabrics; or
2. engaged in the business of construction or reconstruction; or
3. engaged in the operation of a hospital; an institution primarily engaged in the care of the sick, the aged, the mentally ill or defective who reside on the premises; a school for mentally or physically handicapped or gifted children; a preschool, an elementary or secondary school; or an institution of higher education (regardless of whether or not such hospital, institution or school is public or private or operated for profit or not for profit); or
4. comprised exclusively of one or more re-

tail or service establishments whose annual gross volume of sales or business done is not less than $275,000 (beginning July 1, 1978), $325,000 (beginning July 1, 1980), $362,500 (beginning January 1, 1982). (Any retail or service enterprise which has an annual gross volume of not less than $250,000 and which later ceases to be a covered enterprise as a result of increases in this dollar volume test must continue to pay its employees at least the minimum wage in effect at the time of the enterprise's removal from coverage, as well as overtime in accordance with the act.); or

5. any other type of enterprise having an annual gross volume of sales or business done of not less than $250,000.

The dollar volume standard mentioned above in (4) and (5) excludes excise taxes at the retail level which are separately stated. Any establishment which has as its only regular employees the owner thereof or members of the owner's immediate family is not considered part of any enterprise.

Federal employees are subject to the minimum-wage, overtime, child-labor, and equal-pay provisions of FLSA. Employees of state and local governments are subject to the same provisions, unless they are engaged in traditional governmental activities, in which case they are subject to the child-labor and equal-pay provisions only. The Supreme Court has indicated that such traditional governmental activities include schools, hospitals, fire prevention, police protection, sanitation, public health parks and recreation.

Employees who are not employed in a covered enterprise may still be entitled to the act's minimum-wage, overtime-pay, equal-pay, and child-labor protections if they are individually engaged in interstate commerce. These employees include:

1. communication and transportation workers;
2. employees who handle, ship, or receive goods moving in interstate commerce;
3. clerical or other workers who regularly use the mails, telephone, or telegraph for interstate communication or who keep records on interstate transactions;
4. employees who regularly cross State lines in the course of their work; and
5. employees of independent employers who perform clerical, custodial, maintenance, or other work for firms engaged in commerce or in the production of goods for commerce.

Domestic service workers such as maids, day workers, housekeepers, chauffeurs, cooks, or full-time baby sitters are covered if they (1) receive at least $100 in cash wages in a calendar year from their employer or (2) work a total of more than 8 hours a week for one or more employers.

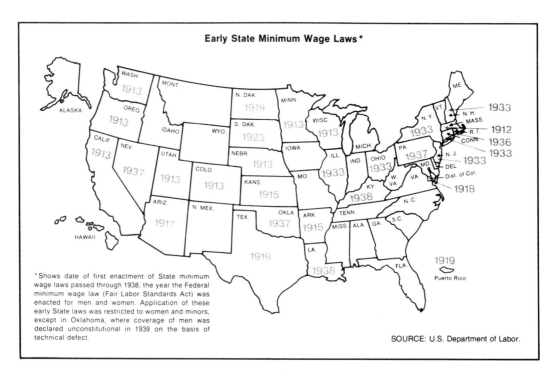

Early State Minimum Wage Laws*

*Shows date of first enactment of State minimum wage laws passed through 1938, the year the Federal minimum wage law (Fair Labor Standards Act) was enacted for men and women. Application of these early State laws was restricted to women and minors, except in Oklahoma, where coverage of men was declared unconstitutional in 1939 on the basis of technical defect.

SOURCE: U.S. Department of Labor.

Tipped Employees. Tipped employees are those who customarily and regularly receive more than $30 a month in tips. The employer may consider tips as part of wages, but such a wage credit must not exceed 50 percent of the minimum wage (beginning January 1, 1979, 45% is the maximum tip credit, and beginning January 1, 1980, 40% is the maximum tip credit).

The employer who elects to use the tip credit provision must inform the employee in advance and must be able to show that the employee receives at least the minimum wage when direct wages and the tip credit allowance are combined. Also, employees must retain all of their tips, except to the extent that they participate in a valid tip pooling or sharing arrangement.

Employer-Furnished Facilities. The reasonable cost or fair value of board, lodging, and other facilities provided by the employer may, as determined by the Wage and Hour Administrator, be considered part of wages.

Subminimum Wage Provisions. Learners, apprentices, and handicapped workers may, under certain circumstances, be paid less than the minimum wage, as well as full-time students in retail or service establishments, agriculture, or institutions of higher education. Special certificates issued by the Wage and Hour Administrator must be obtained by employers wishing to use these provisions.

Equal Pay Provisions. The equal-pay provisions of FLSA prohibit wage differentials based on sex, between men and women employed in the same establishment on jobs that require equal skills, effort, and responsibility and are performed under similar working conditions.

Exemptions from Both Minimum Wage and Overtime. Executive, administrative, and professional employees (including teachers and academic administrative personnel in elementary or secondary schools) and outside sales persons; employees of certain individually owned and operated small retail or service establishments not part of a covered enterprise; employees of certain small newspapers, switchboard operators of small telephone companies, seamen employed on foreign vessels, and employees engaged in fishing operations; farm workers employed by anyone who used no more than 500 mandays or farm labor in any calendar quarter of the preceding calendar year; casual baby sitters and persons employed as companions to the elderly or infirm.

Exemptions from Overtime Provisions Only. certain highly-paid commission employees of retail or service establishments; auto, truck, trailer, farm implement, boat, or aircraft salesworkers, or partsmen and mechanics servicing autos, trucks or farm implements, and who are employed by non-manufacturing establishments primarily engaged in selling these items to ultimate purchasers; employees of railroads and air carriers, taxi drivers, certain employees of motor carriers, seamen on U.S. vessels, and local delivery employees paid on approved trip rate plans; announcers, news editors, and chief engineers of certain nonmetropolitan broadcasting stations; domestic service workers residing in the employers' residences; employees of motion picture theaters, and farmworkers.

Child Labor Provisions. FLSA child-labor provisions are designed to protect the educational opportunities of minors and prohibit their employment in jobs and under conditions detrimental to their health or well-being. Regulations governing youth employment in nonfarm jobs differ somewhat from those pertaining to agricultural employment. In nonfarm work, the permissible kinds and hours of work, by age are:

1. *18 years or older:* any job, whether hazardous or not, for unlimited hours;
2. *16 and 17 years old:* any nonhazardous job, for unlimited hours;
3. *14 and 15 years old:* outside of school hours in various nonmanufacturing nonmining, nonhazardous jobs, under these conditions: no more than 3 hours on a school day, 18 hours in a school week, 8 hours on a nonschool day or 40 hours in a nonschool week. Also, work may not begin before 7 a.m. nor end after 7 p.m. except from June 1 through Labor Day, when evening hours are extended to 9 p.m. Under a special provision, 14 and 15 year-olds enrolled in an approved Work Experience and Career Exploration Program may be employed for up to 23 hours in school weeks and 3 hours on school days (including during school hours).

Fourteen is the minimum age for most nonfarm work. However, at any age, youths may deliver newspapers, perform in radio, television, movie or theatrical productions, work for parents in their solely owned nonfarm business (except in manufacturing or on hazardous jobs), gather evergreens, and make evergreen wreaths.

Permissible kinds and hours of work for youths employed in agriculture are:

1. *16 years and older:* any job whether hazardous or not, for unlimited hours;
2. *14 and 15 years old:* any nonhazardous

Attention Employees

Your Rights Under the Fair Labor Standards Act (Federal Wage and Hour Law)

The Act Requires . . .

Minimum Wage*

of at least:

$2.90 per hour

Beg. 1/1/80 - $3.10/hr.
Beg. 1/1/81 - $3.35/hr.

beginning January 1, 1979

This minimum wage applies to workers engaged in or producing goods for interstate commerce or employed in certain enterprises.

Overtime Pay

at least 1-1/2 times your regular rate of pay for all hours worked over 40 in one workweek.

Note: The act contains exemptions from the minimum wage and/or overtime pay requirements for certain occupations or establishments.

Equal Pay for Equal Work**

The equal pay provision prohibits sex discrimination in the payment of wages to men and women performing equal work in the same establishment. The provision does not prohibit wage differentials between employees of the same sex.

Child Labor

You must be at least 16 years old to work in most nonfarm jobs; at least 18 to work in nonfarm jobs declared hazardous by the Secretary of Labor. Youths 14 and 15 may work in various jobs outside school hours under certain conditions. Different rules apply to agricultural employment.

Enforcement:

The U.S. Government may bring civil or criminal action against employers who violate the act. In certain actions, courts may order payment of back wages. Employers may be fined up to $1,000 for each violation of the child labor provisions. The act prohibits an employer from discriminating against or discharging you if you file a complaint or participate in a proceeding under it.

State laws:

When a state law differs with the Fair Labor Standards Act, the law providing more protection or setting the higher standard applies.

Additional information:

Consult your telephone directory under U.S. Government, Department of Labor.

or write:

U.S. Department of Labor
Employment Standards Administration
Wage and Hour Division
200 Constitution Avenue, N.W.
Washington, D.C. 20210

*Certain full-time students, student learners, apprentices, and handicapped workers may be paid less than the applicable minimum but only under special Department issued certificates.

**Effective July 1, 1979, equal pay enforcement will be transferred from the Wage and Hour Division to the Equal Employment Opportunity Commission.

U.S. Department of Labor
Employment Standards Administration
Wage and Hour Division
200 Constitution Avenue, N.W.
Washington, D.C. 20210

The law requires employers to display this poster where employees can readily see it.

WH Publication 1088
Rev. January 1979

☆ U. S. GOVERNMENT PRINTING OFFICE : 1979 - 286-175

farm job outside of school hours;

3. *12 and 13 years old*: outside of school hours in nonhazardous jobs, either with parents' written consent or on the same farm as the parents;

4. *under 12 years old*: jobs on farms owned or operated by parents or, with parents' written consent, outside of school hours in nonhazardous jobs on farms not covered by minimum wage requirements.

Local minors 10 and 11 years of age may work for no more than 8 weeks between June 1 and October 15 for employers who receive approval from the Secretary of Labor. This work must be confined to hand-harvesting short season crops outside school hours under very limited and specified circumstances prescribed by the Secretary of Labor.

Minors of any age may be employed by their parents at any time in any occupation on a farm owned or operated by their parents.

Recordkeeping. Employers are required to keep records on wages, hours and other items. Most of the information is of the kind generally maintained by employers in ordinary business practice and in compliance with other laws and regulations. The records do not have to be kept in any particular form and time clocks need not be used. With respect to an employee subject to both minimum wage and overtime pay provisions, the following records must be kept:

1. personal information, including employee's name, home address, occupation, sex, and birth date (if under 19 years of age);
2. hour and day when workweek begins;
3. total hours worked each workday and each workweek;
4. total daily or weekly straight-time earnings;
5. regular hourly pay rate for any week when overtime is worked;
6. total overtime pay for the workweek;
7. deductions from or additions to wages;
8. total wages paid each pay period; and
9. date of payment and pay period covered.

Records required for exempt employees differ from those for nonexempt workers and special information is required on employees working under uncommon pay arrangements or to whom lodging or other facilities are furnished. Employers who have homeworkers must make entries in handbooks supplied by the Division.

Enforcement. The Wage and Hour Division of the U.S. Department of Labor administers and enforces FLSA with respect to private employment, state and local government employment, and federal employees of the Library of Congress, U.S. Postal Service, Postal Rate Commission, and the Tennessee Valley Authority.

The Wage and Hour Division's enforcement of FLSA is carried out by compliance officers stationed across the U.S. As the division's authorized representatives, they have the authority to conduct investigations and gather data on wages, hours, and other employment conditions or practices, in order to determine compliance with the act. Where violations are found, they also may recommend changes in employment practices, in order to bring an employer into compliance with the law.

It is a violation of FLSA to fire or in any other manner discriminate against an employee for filing a complaint or participating in a legal proceeding under the law. Willful violations may be prosecuted criminally and the violator fined up to $10,000. A second conviction may result in imprisonment. Violators of the child labor provisions are subject to a civil money penalty of up to $1,000 for each violation.

For a history of FLSA, *see* Jonathan Grossman, "Fair Labor Standards Act of 1938: Maximum Struggle for a Minimum Wage," *Monthly Labor Review* (June 1978); P. K. Elder and H. D. Miller, "The Fair Labor Standards Act: Changes of Four Decades," *Monthly Labor Review* (July 1979).

See also the following entries:

CHILD LABOR
NATIONAL LEAGUE OF CITIES V. USERY
OVERTIME
UNITED STATES V. DARBY LUMBER

fair representation: *see* DUTY OF FAIR REPRESENTATION.

fair-share agreement, arrangement whereby both the employer and the union agree that employees are not obligated to join the union, but that all employees must pay the union a prorated share of bargaining costs as a condition of employment.

faith validity: *see* FACE VALIDITY.

false negative, any incidence whereby an individual, who is in fact qualified, is excluded by a test or some other screening criteria.

false positive, any incidence whereby an individual, who is in fact unqualified, is selected because of a test or some other screening criteria.

family allowances, payments to workers, in addition to regular wages, based on the number of dependent children that a worker may have. Almost all of the major industrial countries, except the United States, have family-allowance programs financed by their governments. For an analysis, *see* George E. Rejda, "Family Allowances as a Program for Reducing Poverty," *The Journal of Risk and Insurance* (December 1970).

family-expense policy, health insurance policy that insures both the individual policyholder and his or her immediate dependents (usually spouse and children).

family T-group, work team that undertakes a T-group effort as a unit.
See also T-GROUP.

Farm Workers of America, United: *see* LABOR ORGANIZATION.

FAS: *see* FUNDAMENTAL ACHIEVEMENT SERIES.

fatigue, weariness caused by physical or mental exertion that lessens the capacity to, and the will for, work. For an analysis, *see* R. A. McFarland, "Fatigue In Industry: Understanding Fatigue in Modern Life" *Ergonomics*, Vol. 14, No. 1 (1971).

fatigue allowance, in production planning, this is that additional time added to "normal" work time to compensate for the factor of fatigue.

fatigue curve, also MONOTONY CURVE, graphic representation of productivity increases and decreases influenced by fatigue. As workers "warm up" or practice their tasks, productivity increases; thereafter fatigue sets in and productivity decreases. After lunch or coffee breaks, productivity should rise again slightly, but thereafter continuously decline until the end of the day. This pattern varies

with differing kinds of work. Fatigue curve measurements are essential in establishing realistic work standards.

A *monotony curve* is characterized by a drop in productivity in the middle of the work period, great variability in the rate of productivity, and a tendency to "end spurt"—show an increase in productivity at the end of the work period due to a feeling of relief that the work period is almost over.

The classic work on fatigue and monotony curves was done as part of the Hawthorne experiments. *See* F. J. Roethlisberger and William J. Dickson, *Management and the Worker* (Cambridge, Mass.: Harvard University Press, 1939).
See also HAWTHORNE STUDIES.

fat work, slang term for work that offers more money for no more than normal effort; also work that offers regular wages but requires a less than normal effort.

favoritism, according to John E. Fisher in "Playing Favorites in Large Organizations," *Business Horizons* (June 1977),

> one way authoritarian executives control subordinates is by permitting favorites to enjoy opportunities for highly visible accomplishments while making it difficult, if not impossible, for those who are in disfavor to do so. Then when the favorite is promoted or meritoriously cited, his sponsor can point with pride to how impressive his achievements look on paper. If a nonfavorite has the temerity to complain about the choice, he is confronted with his own predictable paucity of accomplishments. Often the latter is puzzled by his lack of accomplishments despite his application of hard work, initiative and resourcefulness. If he reflects, however, he may recall that his soundest recommendations have been turned down and his initiative curbed at every turn.

Fayol, Henri (1841-1925), French executive engineer who developed the first comprehensive theory of management. His *Administration Industrielle et Générale* (published in France in 1916), was almost ignored in the U.S. until Constance Storrs' English translation, *General and Industrial Management* (London: Pitman, 1949), appeared. Today his theoretical contributions are generally considered as significant as those of Frederick W. Taylor.

featherbedding, term, meaning an easy or superfluous job, which originated in the U.S. Army in the 1850s. Those frontier soldiers who had easy jobs at headquarters and could sleep in comfortable featherbeds were called

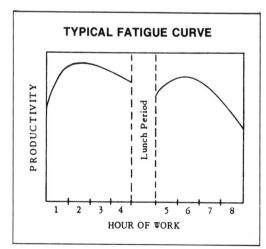

TYPICAL FATIGUE CURVE

PRODUCTIVITY

Lunch Period

1 2 3 4 5 6 7 8

HOUR OF WORK

"featherbed soldiers." So featherbedding grew to mean any job that required little or no work.

Today featherbedding connotes any labor practice that requires an employer to pay for more workers than are truly needed for a job, or to pay for work that is not performed. Featherbedding provisions in labor contracts usually have their origin in work rules that were once efficient but have become obsolete due to newer technology. Union leaders often insist on maintaining the older practices in order to protect the jobs of those whose livelihoods are threatened by the new technology.

The Labor–Management Relations (Taft–Hartley) Act of 1947 makes it an unfair labor practice "to cause or attempt to cause an employer to pay or deliver or agree to pay or deliver any money or other thing of value in the nature of an exaction, for services which are not performed." This provision has not had much effect, however, because of the legal subtleties of defining featherbedding practices. See Robert D. Leiter, *Featherbedding and Job Security* (N.Y.: Twayne Publishers, 1964); Paul A. Weinstein (ed.), *Featherbedding and Technological Change* (Boston: D.C. Heath, 1965).

See also AMERICAN NEWSPAPER PUBLISHERS ASSOCIATION V. NATIONAL LABOR RELATIONS BOARD and UNFAIR LABOR PRACTICES (UNIONS).

Federal Bureau of Apprenticeship and Training: *see* APPRENTICE.

federal court of appeals: *see* COURT OF APPEALS.

federal district court: *see* DISTRICT COURT.

Federal Employees, National Federation of: *see* LABOR ORGANIZATION.

Federal Employee's Compensation Act of 1916, federal statute administered by the U.S. Department of Labor that provides compensation for disability and death, medical care, and rehabilitation services for all civilian employees and officers of the United States who suffer injuries while in the performance of their duties.

Federal Employees Part-Time Career Employment Act of 1978, federal statute that requires federal agencies to implement employment programs for part-timers (persons working between 16 and 32 hours per week).

Federal Executive Institute, The (FEI), established by Executive Order in 1968, this is the federal government's primary in-residence training facility for executive development.

Federal Executive Institute
Route 29 North
Charlottesville, VA 22903
(804) 296-0181

Federal Job Information Centers, a nationwide network of centers that provide information on federal employment. Administered by the Office of Personnel Management, the centers are listed in telephone directories under "U.S. Government."

Federal Labor Relations Authority (FLRA), created by the Civil Service Reform Act of 1978 to oversee the creation of bargaining units, supervise elections, and otherwise deal with labor–management issues in federal agencies. The FLRA is headed by a chairman and two members, who are appointed on a bipartisan basis to staggered 5-year terms. The FLRA replaces the Federal Labor Relations Council (FLRC).

Within the FLRA, a general counsel, appointed to a 5-year term, will investigate alleged unfair labor practices and prosecute them before the FLRA. Also within the FLRA and acting as a separate body, the Federal Service Impasses Panel (FSIP) acts to resolve negotiation impasses.

Federal Labor Relations Authority
1900 E. Street, N.W.
Washington, DC 20415
(202) 632-6878

Federal Labor Relations Council (FLRC), established in 1969 by Executive Order 11491 and supplanted by the Federal Labor Relations Authority pursuant to provisions of the Civil Service Reform Act of 1978.

federal labor union, a local union affiliated directly with the AFL-CIO rather than with a national or international union.

Federal Mediation and Conciliation Service (FMCS), created by the Labor–Management Relations (Taft–Hartley) Act of 1947 as an independent agency of the federal government, FMCS helps prevent disruptions in the flow of interstate commerce caused by labor–management disputes by providing mediators to assist disputing parties in the resolution of their differences. FMCS can intervene on its own motion or by invitation of either side in a dispute. Mediators have no law enforcement authority and rely wholly on persuasive techniques. FMCS also helps provide qualified third-party neutrals as factfinders or arbitrators.

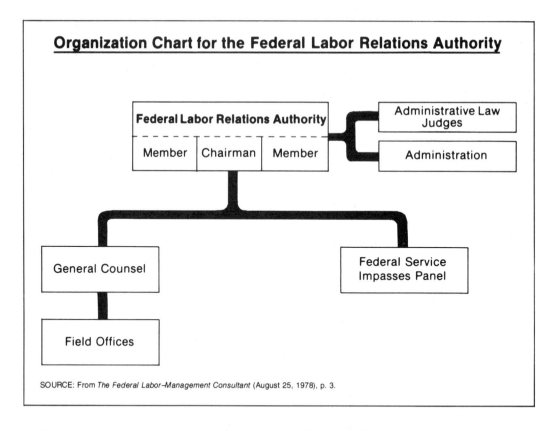

Organization Chart for the Federal Labor Relations Authority

SOURCE: From *The Federal Labor–Management Consultant* (August 25, 1978), p. 3.

The mediator's efforts are directed toward the establishment of sound and stable labor–management relations on a continuing basis. FMCS mediators assist representatives of labor and management in settling disputes about wages, hours, and other aspects of the employment relationship that arise in the course of negotiations. In this work, the mediator has a more basic function—encouraging and promoting better day-to-day relations between labor and management. He/she thereby helps to reduce the incidence of work stoppages. Issues arising in negotiations may then be faced as problems to be settled through mutual effort rather than issues in dispute.

FMCS offers its facilities in labor–management disputes in any industry affecting interstate commerce, either upon its own motion or at the request of one or more of the parties to the dispute, whenever in its judgment such dispute threatens to cause a substantial interruption of commerce. Employers and unions are required to file with FMCS a notice of every dispute affecting commerce not settled within 30 days after prior service of a notice to terminate or modify an existing contract. FMCS is required to avoid the mediation of disputes that would have only a minor effect on interstate commerce if state or other conciliation services are available to the parties. FMCS is directed to make its mediation and conciliation facilities available only as a last resort and in exceptional cases in the settlement of grievance disputes arising over the application or interpretation of existing collective bargaining agreements.

On the joint request of employers and unions, FMCS will also assist in the selection of arbitrators from a roster of private citizens who are qualified as neutrals to adjudicate matters in dispute.

FMCS has offices in 80 principal cities, with meeting facilities available for labor–management negotiations.

Federal Mediation and Conciliation Service
2100 K Street N.W.
Washington, DC 20427
(202) 655-4000

Federal Pay Comparability Act of 1970, federal statute that placed the initiative for maintaining pay comparability for federal employees with the president rather than with the Congress. *See* Raymond Jacobson, "Pay Comparability," *Civil Service Journal* (April–June 1974).

Federal Personnel Manual (FPM), publication of the Office of Personnel Management (OPM) that contains all OPM personnel regulations and instructions to federal agencies.

Federal Plant Quarantine Inspectors National Association: *see* LABOR ORGANIZATION, Quarantine Inspectors National Association, Federal Plant.

Federal Register, daily publication that is the medium for making available to the public federal agency regulations and other legal documents of the executive branch. These documents cover a wide range of government activities—environmental protection, consumer product safety, food and drug standards, occupational health and safety, and many more areas of concern to the public. Perhaps more importantly, the *Federal Register* includes *proposed* changes in regulated areas. Each proposed change published carries an invitation for any citizen or group to participate in the consideration of the proposed regulation through the submission of written data, views, or arguments, and sometimes by oral presentations.

The Office of the Federal Register conducts education workshops on how to use the *Federal Register*. "The *Federal Register*— What It Is and How to Use It" is open to the general public and federal agency personnel and is designed as an introduction for the individual who needs to use *Federal Register* publications to keep track and gain understanding of federal regulations. The *Federal Register* workshops are scheduled on a regular basis in Washington, D.C. Under certain circumstances and by special arrangement, these workshops may be scheduled in other cities. For further information on the *Federal Register* workshops, write to the Office of the Federal Register, National Archives and Records Service, Washington, DC 20408 (202) 523-5282.

Federal Salary Reform Act of 1962: *see* SALARY REFORM ACT OF 1962.

Federal Service Entrance Examination (FSEE), from 1955 through 1974, the U.S. Civil Service Commission's most basic means of selecting new college graduates for over 200 different occupational specialties. In the early 1970s, the FSEE came under increasing attack because of its adverse impact on equal employment opportunity. In 1975, it was replaced by the Professional and Administrative Careers Examination (PACE). *See* Robert Sadacca, *The Validity and Discriminatory Impact of the Federal Service Entrance*

Examination (Washington, D.C.: The Urban Institute, 1971).

See also PROFESSIONAL AND ADMINISTRATIVE CAREERS EXAMINATION.

Federal Service Impasses Panel (FSIP), located within the Federal Labor Relations Authority, the Federal Service Impasses Panel has the responsibility of aiding federal agencies and their labor organizations in settling their negotiation impasses when voluntary efforts have failed. The FSIP may authorize binding arbitration, third-party factfinding, or other appropriate measures.

Federal Service Impasses Panel
1900 E. Street, N.W.
Washington, DC 20415
(202) 632-6280

Federal Wage System, established by Public Law 92-392, this is the basic pay system for the almost half million trade, craft, and labor—blue-collar—employees of the federal government.

Rates of pay for Federal Wage System employees are maintained in line with prevailing levels of pay for comparable work within each local wage area. Within each local wage area there is a single set of wage schedules applicable to the blue-collar employees of all agencies in the area. Each nonsupervisory schedule consists of 15 grades. A single grade structure applies nationwide. Individual positions are graded on the basis of job evaluation in accordance with a uniform set of job-grading standards. There are separate leader and supervisory schedules for each area.

Uniform policies and procedures for the Federal Wage System are established by the Office of Personnel Management, but significant roles in policymaking and operation of the system are played by both agencies and employee unions.

The prevailing rate principle on which federal blue-collar pay rates are based dates from the 1860s. While there have been many changes in the determination of blue-collar pay since then, with respect to occupational and agency coverage, agency authorities, and administrative procedures, the basic principle is over 100 years old.

Federal Women's Program, established in 1967 by the U.S. Civil Service Commission to enhance the employment and the advancement of women. Executive Order 11478, signed by president Nixon on August 8, 1969, integrated the Federal Women's Program with other equal employment opportunity programs. Federal agencies must designate a

Federal Women's Program coordinator to provide advice on special concerns of women and to insure that agency affirmative action plans are designed to eliminate barriers to the full employment of women at all levels and in all occupations. For a history, *see* Helene S. Markoff, "The Federal Women's Program," *Public Administration Review* (March–April 1972).

federation, national and/or international unions joined together for common purposes. The AFL-CIO is the major U.S. union federation.

Federation of Organized Trade and Labor Unions: *see* AMERICAN FEDERATION OF LABOR.

Federation of Postal Security Police: *see* LABOR ORGANIZATION, Postal Security Police, Federation of.

feedback, information about the effect and/or results of the behavior of a person or system that is communicated back to that person or system so that human behavior or organization (mechanical) performance might be modified. For an account of how to use organization feedback, *see* David A. Nadler, *Feedback and Organization Development: Using Data-Based Methods* (Reading, Mass.: Addison-Wesley Publishing Co., 1977). For how it relates to productivity, *see* Peter G. Kirby, "Productivity Increases Through Feedback Systems," *Personnel Journal* (October 1977). For information on handling negative feedback, *see* Thomas B. Wilson, "Making Negative Feedback Work," *Personnel Journal* (December 1978).

FEI: *see* FEDERAL EXECUTIVE INSTITUTE.

FEIA: *see* LABOR ORGANIZATION, Flight Engineers' International Association.

fellow servant doctrine, common-law concept that an employer should not be held responsible for an accident to an employee if the accident resulted from the negligence of another employee.

fellowship plan, company: *see* COMPANY FELLOWSHIP PLAN.

FEPC: *see* (1) FAIR EMPLOYMENT PRACTICE COMMITTEE and (2) FAIR EMPLOYMENT PRACTICE COMMISSION.

Fibreboard Paper Products Corporation v. National Labor Relations Board, 379 U.S. 203 (1965), U.S. Supreme Court case, which held that a company was obligated to bargain over an economically motivated decision to subcontract work previously performed by union members.

Fiedler, Fred E. (1922-   ), psychologist most noted for his contingency theory of leadership effectiveness, which holds that leadership is a function both of the leader and the leadership situation. Major works include: *A Theory of Leadership Effectiveness* (N.Y.: McGraw-Hill, 1967); *Leadership and Effective Management*, with Martin Chemers (Glenview, Ill.: Scott, Foresman & Co., 1974).

field examiner, administrative agency employee who conducts certification elections and investigates charges of unfair labor practices.

field review, method of employee appraisal whereby a representative of the personnel department visits an employee's work site in order to gather the information necessary for a written evaluation.

field theory, developed by Kurt Lewin, field theory holds that an individual's behavior at any given time is the result of his/her basic personality interacting with the psychological forces of the environment. *See* Kurt Lewin, "Behavior and Development as a Function of the Total Situation," in Dorwin Cartwright (ed.), *Field Theory in Social Science* (N.Y.: Harper & Bros., 1951).

final offer arbitration, also called LAST OFFER ARBITRATION, negotiating stratagem that has an arbitrator choose from among the disputing parties' final or last offers. Peter Feuille, in *Final Offer Arbitration: Concepts, Development, Techniques* (Chicago: International Personnel Management Association, 1975), describes its intended role in the collective bargaining process:

> Since the arbitrator will not be free to compromise between the parties' positions, the parties will be induced to develop ever more reasonable positions prior to the arbitrator's decision in the hope of winning the award. And, the theory goes, these mutual attempts to win neutral approval should result in the parties being so close together that they will create their own settlement. In other words, the final offer procedure was purposefully designed to contain the seeds of its own destruction.

For a case study, *see* Gary Long and Peter Feuille, "Final Offer Arbitration: 'Sudden Death' in Eugene," *Industrial and Labor Relations Review* (January 1974).

fink, slang term for a strikebreaker—any individual who hires out to help an employer break a strike. According to H. L. Mencken, "fink" is a perversion of "pink" for "Pinkerton." The Pinkertons were employees of the Pinkerton Detective Agency who were frequently hired to harass and otherwise oppose strikes in the latter part of the 19th century. As Pinkerton's, Inc., the agency is still in business selling guard and security services.

Finley, Murray H. (1922-   ), became president of the Amalgamated Clothing Workers of America in 1972.

fire, discharge from employment. The word has such a rude connotation that it is hardly ever used for formal purposes. It seems so much more genteel and antiseptic to terminate, discharge, dismiss, sever, or lay off an employee. For two "self-help" books on firing, see John J. Tarrant, *Getting Fired: An American Ordeal* (N.Y.: Van Nostrand Reinhold Co., 1974); Auren Uris and Jack Tarrant, *How to Keep from Getting Fired* (Chicago: Henry Regnery Co., 1975). *See also* Stephen S. Kaagen, "Terminating People from Key Positions," *Personnel Journal* (February 1978).

Fire Fighters, International Association of: *see* LABOR ORGANIZATION.

Fireman and Oilers, International Brotherhood of: *see* LABOR ORGANIZATION.

FIRO B, 54-item, self-report questionnaire designed to measure interpersonal needs of inclusion, control, and affection on six scales. It obtains information on both expressed and desired behaviors in various interpersonal situations. TIME: 8–15 minutes. AUTHOR: William C. Schutz. PUBLISHER: Consulting Psychologists Press, Inc. (*see* TEST PUBLISHERS).

first-line management, level of management that is just above the workers (for example, a foreman).

FIT: *see* FLANAGAN INDUSTRIAL TEST.

Fitzgerald Act: *see* APPRENTICESHIP ACT OF 1937.

Fitzpatrick v. Bitzer, 424 U.S. 953 (1976), U.S. Supreme Court case, which ruled that the Equal Employment Opportunity Act of 1972 amendments to Title VII of the Civil Rights Act of 1964 created an exception to the immunity of states to backpay suits. The court held that this exception was authorized by the 14th Amendment's grant of power to Congress to enforce that amendment's ban on state denials of equal protection.

Fitzsimmons, Frank (Edward) (1908-   ), succeeded Jimmy Hoffa as president of the International Brotherhood of Teamsters in 1967. For details of Fitzsimmons' career, *see* Walter Sheridan, *The Fall and Rise of Jimmy Hoffa* (N.Y.: Saturday Review Press, 1972); Steven Brill, *The Teamsters* (N.Y.: Simon & Schuster, 1978).

fixed annuity, annuity that provides constant, periodic dollar payments for its entire length.

fixed-benefit retirement plan, retirement plan whose benefits consist of a fixed amount or fixed percentage.

fixed shift, work shift to which an employee is assigned indefinitely.

flagged rate, also called OVERRATE, compensation rates paid to employees whose positions warrant lower rates.

Flanagan Aptitude Classification Test (FACT), battery of 19 tests that provide specific predictions of success in 37 occupations. Each FACT test corresponds to an aptitude or job element. Multiple-choice (5 options) items that measure comprehension, expression, ingenuity, reasoning, coordination, vocabulary, alertness, etc. TIME: 10½ hours— of 3½ hours each. AUTHOR: John C. Flanagan. PUBLISHER: Science Research Associates, Inc. (*see* TEST PUBLISHERS).

For shortened version, *see* FLANAGAN INDUSTRIAL TEST.

Flanagan Industrial Test (FIT), 18 short aptitude tests designed for use in personnel selection and placement programs for a wide variety of jobs. Tests measure such items as arithmetic, coordination, electronics, ingenuity, math/reasoning, judgment/comprehension, vocabulary, memory, and planning. Shortened adaptation (for business use) of the Flanagan Aptitude Classification Test (FACT). TIME: 165/218 minutes. AUTHOR: John C. Flanagan. PUBLISHER: Science Research Associates, Inc. (*see* TEST PUBLISHERS).

flat-benefit plan, pension plan whose benefits are unrelated to earnings. Such a plan might provide a stipulated amount per month per year of service.

flat organization, also TALL ORGANIZATION, one whose structure has comparatively few levels. In contrast, a *tall organization* is one whose structure has many levels. *See* Rocco

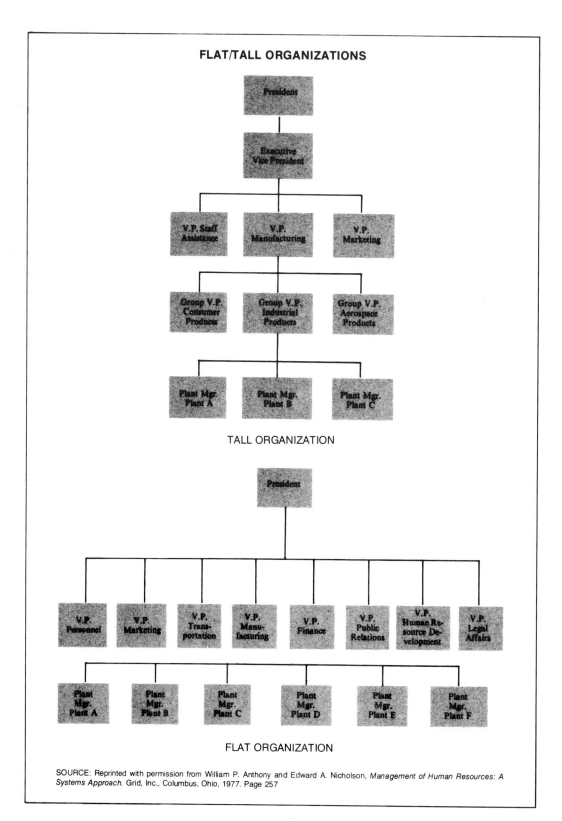

FLAT/TALL ORGANIZATIONS

TALL ORGANIZATION

FLAT ORGANIZATION

SOURCE: Reprinted with permission from William P. Anthony and Edward A. Nicholson, *Management of Human Resources: A Systems Approach*. Grid, Inc., Columbus, Ohio, 1977. Page 257

Carzo, Jr., and John N. Yanovzas, "Effects of Flat and Tall Organization Structure," *Administrative Science Quarterly* (June 1969); Edwin E. Ghiselli and Jacob P. Siegel, "Leadership and Managerial Success in Tall and Flat Organization Structures," *Personnel Psychology* (Winter 1972).

See also PYRAMID.

flat rate, also called STANDARD RATE and SINGLE RATE, pay structure offering only one rate of pay for each pay level.

Fleetwood Trailer Co. decision: *see* NA-TIONAL LABOR RELATIONS BOARD V. MACKAY RADIO & TELEGRAPH COMPANY.

flexible passing score: *see* CUTTING SCORE.

flexible working hours: *see* FLEXI-TIME.

flexi-time, flexible work schedule in which workers can, within a prescribed band of time in the morning and again in the afternoon, start and finish work at their discretion as long as they complete the total number of hours required for a given period, usually a month. That is, the workday can vary from day to day in its length as well as in the time

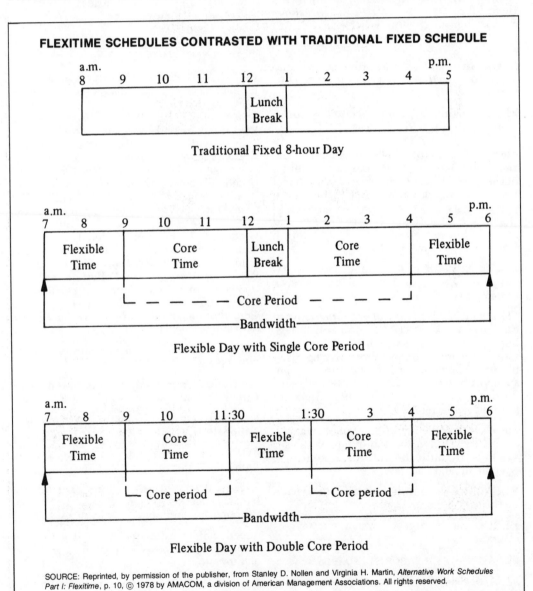

FLEXITIME SCHEDULES CONTRASTED WITH TRADITIONAL FIXED SCHEDULE

Traditional Fixed 8-hour Day

Flexible Day with Single Core Period

Flexible Day with Double Core Period

that it begins and ends. The morning and evening bands of time often are designated as "quiet time." Telephone calls and staff meetings are confined to "core time," which generally runs from midmorning to midafternoon. Time clocks or other mechanical controls for keeping track of the hours worked usually are a part of flexi-time systems.

For discussions of the concept, *see* Janice Neipert Hedges, "New Patterns for Working Time," *Monthly Labor Review* (February 1973); Alvar O. Elbing, Herman Gadon, and John R. M. Gordon, "Flexible Working Hours: It's About Time," *Harvard Business Review* (January–February 1974).

See also 4-DAY WORKWEEK.

Flight Attendants, Association of: *see* LABOR ORGANIZATION, Air Line Pilots Association.

Flight Engineers' International Association: *see* LABOR ORGANIZATION.

Flore, Edward (1877-1945), president of the Hotel and Restaurant Employee's International Alliance and Bartenders' International League of America from 1911 to his death. For a biography, *see* Jay Rubin and M. J. Obermeier, *Growth of a Union: The Life and Times of Edward Flore* (N.Y.: The Historical Union Association, Inc., 1943).

Florida AFL–CIO: *see* AMERICAN FEDERATION OF LABOR–CONGRESS OF INDUSTRIAL ORGANIZATIONS.

Florida Power & Light Co. v. Brotherhood of Electrical Workers, 417 U.S. 790 (1974), U.S. Supreme Court case, which held that supervisors who are union members may be disciplined by their unions for performing nonsupervisory tasks, so long as the supervisors do not act as management bargainers or grievance adjusters.

flowchart, graphic representation of an analysis of, or solution to, a problem that uses symbols to indicate various operations, equipment, and data flow.

FLRA: *see* FEDERAL LABOR RELATIONS AUTHORITY.

FLRC: *see* FEDERAL LABOR RELATIONS COUNCIL.

FLSA: *see* FAIR LABOR STANDARDS ACT.

FLSA decision: *see* NATIONAL LEAGUE OF CITIES V. USERY.

FMCS: *see* FEDERAL MEDIATION AND CONCILIATION SERVICE.

foils: *see* DISTRACTORS.

Foley v. Connelie, 435 U.S. 291 (1978), U.S. Supreme Court case, which upheld a New York law requiring state police to be U.S. citizens. The court reasoned that because state police exercise considerable discretion in executing the laws, a state may exclude aliens from such positions without unconstitutionally denying them equal protection of the laws.

See also the following entries:
AMBACH V. NORWICK
CITIZENSHIP, U.S.
HAMPTON V. MOW SUN WONG
SUGARMAN V. DOUGALL

Follett, Mary Parker (1868-1933), early social psychologist who anticipated, in the 1920s, many of the conclusions of the Hawthorne experiments of the 1930s and the post-World War II behavioral movement. In calling for "power with," as opposed to "power over," she anticipated the movement toward more participatory management. Her "law of the situation" is contingency management in its humble origins. Major works include: *The New State* (N.Y.: Longmans, Green, 1918); *Creative Experience* (N.Y.: Longmans, Green, 1924). For her collected papers, *see* Henry C. Metcalf and Lyndall Urwick (eds.), *Dynamic Administration: The Collected Papers of Mary Parker Follett*. For an appreciation of her contributions, *see* Elliot M. Fox, "Mary Parker Follett: The Enduring Contribution," *Public Administration Review* (November–December 1968).

Follett Educational Corporation: *see* TEST PUBLISHERS.

Food and Commercial Workers International Union, United: *see* LABOR ORGANIZATION.

Football League Players Association, National: *see* LABOR ORGANIZATION.

FOP: *see* LABOR ORGANIZATION, Police, Fraternal Order of.

force-field analysis, procedure for determining what factors, or forces, seem to be contributing to a problem.

forced choice, testing technique that requires the subject to choose from among a given set of alternatives.

forced-distribution method, performance appraisal technique that predetermines the percentage of ratees to be placed in the various performance categories.

Foreign Service pay system, actually consists of four different pay schedules that apply only to the Department of State, the Agency for International Development, the U.S. Information Agency, and ACTION:

1. *Foreign Service Officer schedule* consists of eight levels. Individual Foreign Service Officers are assigned to levels on a rank-in-person basis similar to that of the military personnel system.
2. *Foreign Service Information Officer schedule* of the U.S. Information Agency is identical in structure and operation to the Foreign Service Officer schedule.
3. *Foreign Service Reserve schedule* also consists of eight levels, and is used for temporary appointments of people who are not part of the regular Foreign Service career system.
4. *Foreign Service Staff Officer schedule* covers the administrative and support employees of the Foreign Service. It consists of 10 grades.

foreman, first-line supervisor—the first level of management responsible for securing adequate production and the managerial employee who supervises the work of nonmanagerial employees. The extent to which the foreman is responsible for the traditional functions of management varies considerably from one organization to another. For a complete analysis, *see* Thomas H. Patten, Jr., *The Foreman: Forgotten Man of Management* (N.Y.: American Management Association, 1968). For a classic account of the role of the foreman, *see* F. J. Roethlisberger, "The Foreman: Master and Victim of Double Talk," *Harvard Business Review* (Spring 1945; reprinted September–October 1965).

Present day foremen work under a fading occupational title. It has fallen victim to the U.S. Department of Labor's effort to "de-sex" the nature of work and has been retired as an officially acceptable job title by the fourth edition of the *Dictionary of Occupational Titles* (1977).

formal organization: *see* INFORMAL ORGANIZATION.

Form 171: *see* STANDARD FORM 171.

formula score, raw score on a multiple-choice test after a correction for guessing has been applied. With five-choice items, for example, the formula score is the number of correct answers minus one-fourth the number of wrong answers. This makes zero the score that would most likely be obtained by random guessing.

Formula Translating System: *see* FORTRAN.

Form W-2, also called W-2 FORM and WAGE AND TAX STATEMENT, by the end of January of each year, employers must provide each employee with at least two copies of his or her withholding statement, officially a Wage and Tax Statement or Internal Revenue Service Form W-2, showing earnings for the preceding year and various deductions. Employees must file one copy of their Form W-2 with their federal income-tax return.

FORTRAN, acronym for Formula Translating System—a computer language closely resembling algebraic notation.

Fortune, biweekly trade magazine covering all aspects of the business world. *Fortune* has long been considered the most prestigious of its kind.

Fortune
541 North Fairbanks Court
Chicago, IL 60611

Fortune 500, directory of the 500 largest U.S. industrial corporations published each year since 1955 by *Fortune*. These organizations are frequently described according to their rank in the directory, particularly in recruiting advertisements. A *Fortune* 500 company is any company on the list; a *Fortune* 100 company is one of the 100 largest. Listed below, in rank order, is the *Fortune* 100 for 1977. For the complete list and supporting statistical details, *see Fortune* (May 8, 1978).

Fortune 100 (1977)

1.General Motors	11.ITT	21.Union Carbide	31.Rockwell International
2.Exxon	12.Standard Oil	22.Goodyear Tire & Rubber	32.Caterpillar Tractor
3.Ford Motor	13.Atlantic Richfield	23.Sun	33.Union Oil (California)
4.Mobil	14.Shell Oil	24.Phillips Petroleum	34.United Technologies
5.Texaco	15.U.S. Steel	25.Dow Chemical	35.Bethlehem Steel
6.Standard Oil (California)	16.du Pont	26.Westinghouse Electric	36.Beatrice Foods
7.IBM	17.Continental Oil	27.Occidental Petroleum	37.Esmark
8.Gulf Oil	18.Western Electric	28.International Harvester	38.Kraft
9.General Electric	19.Tenneco	29.Eastman Kodak	39.Xerox
10.Chrysler	20.Procter & Gamble	30.RCA	40.General Foods

41.R.J. Reynolds Industries	56.Georgia-Pacific	71.Lockheed	86.American Brands
42.Ashland Oil	57.International Paper	72.Getty Oil	87.Consolidated Foods
43.LTV	58.Continental Group	73.Bendix	88.CPC International
44.Monsanto	59.Gulf & Western Industries	74.Weyerhaeuser	89.Raytheon
45.Amerada Hess	60.Deere	75.Sperry Rand	90.Textron
46.Firestone Tire & Rubber	61.Coca-Cola	76.TRW	91.CBS
47.Cities Service	62.Armco Steel	77.National Steel	92.Owens-Illinois
48.Marathon Oil	63.PepsiCo	78.Farmland Industries	93.American Home Products
49.Boeing	64.McDonnell Douglas	79.Signal Companies	94.Inland Steel
50.Minnesota Mining & Mfg.	65.American Can	80.Allied Chemical	95.Uniroyal
51.W.R. Grace	66.Standard Oil	81.Johnson & Johnson	96.Warner-Lambert
52.Philip Morris	67.Borden	82.Honeywell	97.Dresser Industries
53.Greyhound	68.Champion International	83.General Mills	98.NCR
54.Colgate-Palmolive	69.Litton Industries	84.Republic Steel	99.PPG Industries
55.Ralston Purina	70.Aluminum Co. of America	85.General Dynamics	100.United Brands

Forty-Plus Club, organization of unemployed executives over 40 who band together to help each other find jobs.

Foster v. Dravo Corp., 420 U.S. 92 (1975), U.S. Supreme Court case, which held that a veteran, upon being restored to his former civilian position under the Military Selective Service Act, is not entitled to full vacation benefits for the years he was in military service, if the vacation scheme was intended as a form of short-term deferred compensation for work performed and not as accruing automatically as a function of continued association with the company.

See also VETERANS REEMPLOYMENT RIGHTS.

Foster, William Z(ebulon) (1881-1961), labor organizer who became a leading figure in the American Communist Party, serving as its candidate for president of the United States in 1924, 1928, and 1932.

4-day workweek, reallocation of the standard 40-hour workweek over four days instead of five. By lengthening the workday, employees get a 3-day weekend every week with no loss of pay. This concept differs from the 4-day/32-hour workweek that some union leaders advocate. For the basic work on this subject, *see* Riva Roor (ed.), *4 Days, 40 hours and Other Forms of the Rearranged Workweek* (N.Y.: Mentor Books, 1973).

See also FLEXI-TIME.

four-fifths rule: *see* ADVERSE IMPACT.

FPM: *see* FEDERAL PERSONNEL MANUAL.

FPQI: *see* LABOR ORGANIZATION, Quarantine Inspectors National Association, Federal Plant.

Franks v. Bowman Transportation Co.: *see* RETROACTIVE SENIORITY.

Fraser, Douglas (1916-   ), became president of the United Auto Workers in 1977. For a biographical sketch, *see* Ron Chernow, "Douglas Fraser: Labor's Courtly Rebel," *Saturday Review* (March 4, 1979).

Fraternal Order of Police: *see* LABOR ORGANIZATION, Police, Fraternal Order of.

Freedom of Information Act of 1966, (Public Law 89-487, as amended by Public Law 93-502), provides for making information held by federal agencies available to the public, unless it comes within one of the specific categories of matters exempt from public disclosure. The legislative history of the act (particularly the recent amendments) makes it clear that the primary purpose was to make information maintained by the executive branch of the federal government more available to the public. At the same time, the act recognized that records that cannot be disclosed without impairing rights of privacy or important government operations must be protected from disclosure.

Virtually all agencies of the executive branch of the federal government have issued regulations to implement the Freedom of Information Act. These regulations inform the public where certain types of information may be readily obtained, how other information may be obtained on request, and what internal agency appeals are available if a member of the public is refused requested information. To locate specific agency regulations pertaining to freedom of information, consult the *Code of Federal Regulations* index under "Information Availability." For an analysis of possible conflicts between the Freedom of Information Act and the National Labor Relations Act, *see* Stephen J. Cabot, "'Freedom of Information' vs. the NLRB: Conflicts and Decisions," *Personnel Journal* (June 1977).

See also NATIONAL LABOR RELATIONS BOARD V. ROBBINS TIRE AND RUBBER CO. and

NATIONAL TECHNICAL INFORMATION SERVICE.

free-response test, technique used in psycholocial testing that places no restriction on the kind of response an individual is to make (so long as it relates to the situation presented).

free rider, derogatary term for a person working in a bargaining unit and receiving substantially all of the benefits of union representation without belonging to the union.

frequency distribution, tabulation of scores (or other data) from high to low, or low to high, showing the number of individuals who obtain each score or fall in each score interval.

frictional unemployment, unemployment that is due to the inherent time lag involved with the re-employment of labor.

friend of the court: *see* AMICUS CURIAE.

fringe benefits, also called EMPLOYEE BENEFITS, general term used to describe any of a variety of nonwage or supplemental benefits (such as pensions, insurance, vacations, paid holidays, etc.) that employees receive in addition to their regular wages. For an economic analysis, *see* Bevars Mabry, "The Economics of Fringe Benefits," *Industrial Relations* (February 1973). For discussions, *see* Ralph L. Harris, "Let's Take the 'Fringe' out of Fringe Benefits," *Personnel Journal* (February 1975); Richard C. Huseman, John D. Hatfield and Richard B. Robinson, "The MBA and Fringe Benefits," *The Personnel Administrator* (July 1978).

Fry* v. *United States, 421 U.S. 542 (1975), U.S. Supreme Court case, which held that state governments had to abide by federal wage and salary controls even though the enabling legislation did not expressly refer to the states. Such legislation was ruled constitutional because general raises to state employees, even though purely intrastate in character, could significantly affect interstate commerce, and thus could be validly regulated by Congress under the Constitution's Commerce Clause.

FSEE: *see* FEDERAL SERVICE ENTRANCE EXAMINATION.

FSIP: *see* FEDERAL SERVICE IMPASSES PANEL.

full-crew rule, safety regulation requiring a minimum number of workers for a given operation.

full employment, economic situation where all those who want to work are able to. In recent years, economists have been telling the public that "full" employment really means from 3 to 6 percent unemployment.

Full Employment and Balanced Growth Act of 1977: *see* HUMPHREY–HAWKINS ACT OF 1977.

full-time workers, also PART-TIME WORKERS, according to the Bureau of Labor Statistics, *full-time workers* are those employed at least 35 hours a week and *part-time workers* are those who work fewer hours. Workers on part-time schedules for economic reasons (such as slack work, terminating or starting a job during the week, material shortages, or inability to find full-time work) are among those counted as being on full-time status, under the assumption that they would be working full time if conditions permitted. The BLS classifies unemployed persons in full-time or part-time status by their reported preferences for full-time or part-time work. For a discussion of what the terms mean, *see* Janice Neipert Hedges and Stephen J. Gallogly, "Full and Part Time: A Review of Definitions," *Monthly Labor Review* (March 1977).

full-time-worker rate, wage rate of regular full-time employees, as distinguished from the wage rate of temporary or part-time employees performing the same job.

fully funded pension plan, pension plan whose assets are adequate to meet its obligations into the foreseeable future.

Fulton Committee, formally COMMITTEE ON THE CIVIL SERVICE, 1966-1968, British committee whose charge was to "examine the structure, recruitment and management, including training, of the Home Civil Service and to make recommendations." The committee, whose 1968 report recommended major reforms, was popularly known after its chairman, Lord Fulton. The Spring 1969 issue of *Public Administration* is devoted to summaries of the report's many volumes.

functional authority, authority inherent to a job or work assignment.

functional illiterate, individual whose reading and writing skills are so poor that he/she is incapable of functioning effectively in the most basic business, office, or factory situations. Because many functional illiterates are high school graduates, the value of such diplomas is being increasingly discounted by personnel offices.

functional job analysis, technology of work analysis that measures and describes a position's specific requirements. Functional job analysis can discard traditionally restrictive labels for positions. In their place, a variety of component descriptions are used to more accurately illustrate the specific and varied duties actually performed by an incumbent. Functional job analysis data readily lend themselves to computerized personnel management information systems. *See* Sidney A. Fine, "Functional Job Analysis: An Approach to a Technology for Manpower Planning," *Personnel Journal* (November 1974); Steven Spirn and Lanny Solomon, "A Key Element in EDP Personnel Management: Functional Job Analysis," *Personnel Journal* (November 1976).

functional leadership, concept holding that leadership emerges from the dynamics associated with the particular circumstances under which groups integrate and organize their activities, rather than from the personal characteristics or behavior of an individual. *See* Robert G. Lord, "Functional Leadership Behavior: Measurement and Relation to Social Power and Leadership Perceptions," *Administrative Science Quarterly* (March 1977).

functus officio, Latin term that can be applied to an officer who has fulfilled the duties of an office that has expired and who, in consequence, has no further formal authority. Arbitrators are said to be *functus officio* concerning a particular case after they have declared their awards on it. According to Israel Ben Scheiber, in "The Doctrine of Functus Officio with Particular Relation to Labor Arbitration," *Labor Law Journal* (October 1972),

> the need to plead the doctrine of "functus officio" cannot be regarded as a major problem or one that occurs with any significant degree of regularity. However, to an arbitrator who is asked to interpret, modify or clarify the language of his award (usually by the losing party) because of a claim that he has overlooked some fact or, in any event, not worded his opinion and/or award with sufficient clarity, a request to reopen the case and to issue a supplemental award can be a source of considerable embarrassment. This is so, in part, because to the aggrieved party, being told that an arbitrator is

"functus officio" often appears as a senseless refuge and a convenient and unsatisfactory excuse given by the arbitrator for refusing to correct or make clear something which he has written and therefore should be able to clarify to the satisfaction of the applicant.

Fundamental Achievement Series (FAS), verbal and numerical tests for educational and vocational placement of the disadvantaged individual. Can be used for assessment and placement into employment or training programs. TIME: 60 minutes. AUTHORS: G. K. Bennett and J. E. Doppelt. PUBLISHER: Psychological Corporation (*see* TEST PUBLISHERS).

funded pension plan, pension plan that provides for the periodic accumulation of money to meet the pension plan's obligations in future years.

funding method, any of the procedures by which money is accumulated to pay for pensions under a pension plan.

funeral leave, also called BEREAVEMENT LEAVE, paid time off for an employee at the time of a death in his/her immediate family. The majority of all employers offer such time off, usually three or four days. The biggest problem with administering such a benefit is defining just what constitutes a member of the "immediate" family.

furlough, period of absence from work, initiated either by the employer as a layoff or the employee as a leave of absence.

Furnco Construction Corp. v. *Waters*, 57 L.Ed. 2d 957 (1978), U.S. Supreme Court case, which held that the initial burden of proving a case of employment discrimination rests upon the complainant.

Furniture Workers of America, United: *see* LABOR ORGANIZATION.

Furuseth, Andrew (1854-1938), president of the International Seaman's Union from 1908 until his death. For a biography, *see* Hyman G. Weintraub, *Andrew Furuseth: Emancipator of the Seamen* (Berkeley, Calif.: University of California Press, 1959).

future shock, as defined in the leading work on future shock, Alvin Toffler's *Future Shock* (New York: Random House, 1970), "the distress, both physical and psychological, that arises from an overload of the human organism's physical adaptive systems and its decision making processes. Put more simply, future shock is the human response to overstimulation." Also *see* James M. Mitchell and Rolfe E. Schroeder, "Future Shock for Personnel Administration," *Public Personnel Management* (July–August 1974). For one man's antidote to the problem, *see* George S. Odiorne, "Management by Objectives: Antidote to Future Shock," *Personnel Journal* (April 1974).

futuristics, fledgling discipline that seeks to anticipate future societal developments and present alternative courses of action for the polity's consideration. Within this discipline, there is a growing literature on the future of work. For two examples, *see* Paul Dickson, *The Future of the Workplace: The Coming Revolution in Jobs* (N.Y.: Weybright and Talley, 1975); William T. Morris, *Work and Your Future: Living Poorer, Working Harder* (Reston, Va.: Reston Publishing Co., 1975).

G

gag rules, or GAG ORDERS, colloquial terms for any formal instructions from a competent authority, usually a judge, to refrain from discussing and/or advocating something. One of the most famous gag rules/orders is President Theodore Roosevelt's executive orders in 1902 and 1904, which forbade federal employees, on pain of dismissal, either as individuals or as members of organizations, to seek any pay increases or to attempt to influence legislation before Congress, except through the heads of their departments. Roosevelt's gag orders were repealed by the Lloyd–LaFollette Act of 1912, which granted public employees the right to organize unions.

gain sharing, any of a variety of wage payment methods in which the worker receives additional earnings due to increases in productivity.

GAIU: *see* LABOR ORGANIZATION, Graphic Arts International Union.

games: *see* MANAGEMENT GAMES.

gaming simulation, a model of reality with dynamic parts that can be manipulated to teach the manipulator(s) how to better cope with the represented processes in real life. *See* John G. H. Carlson and Michael J. Misshauk, *Introduction to Gaming: Management Decision Simulations* (N.Y.: John Wiley, 1972); Gilbert B. Siegel, "Gaming Simulation in the Teaching of Public Personnel Administration," *Public Personnel Management* (July–August 1977).

Gantt, Henry L(awrence) (1861-1919), contemporary and protege of Frederick W. Taylor, was a pioneer in the scientific management movement and inventor of the "Gantt Chart." For a collection of his major works, *see* Alex W. Rathe, (ed.), *Gantt on Management* (N.Y.: American Management Association, 1961). For a biography, *see* Leon

R. Alford, *Henry Lawrence Gantt: Leader in Industry* (N.Y.: Harper & Bros., 1934).

Gantt Chart, developed during World War I by Henry L. Gantt, the Gantt Chart's distinguishing feature is that work planned and work done are shown in the same space in their relation to each other and in their relation to time. Today any chart which uses straight lines to compare planned and actual progress over time could be called a Gantt Chart.

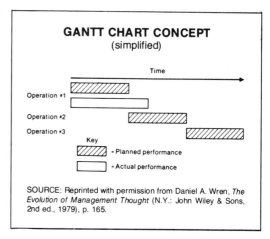

GANTT CHART CONCEPT
(simplified)

SOURCE: Reprinted with permission from Daniel A. Wren, *The Evolution of Management Thought* (N.Y.: John Wiley & Sons, 2nd ed., 1979), p. 165.

GAO: *see* GENERAL ACCOUNTING OFFICE.

Gardner-Denver **case:** *see* ALEXANDER V. GARDNER-DENVER COMPANY.

Garfield, James A(bram) (1831-1881), 20th president of the United States, was assassinated on July 2, 1881, by Charles Guiteau, an insane attorney who had worked for Garfield's election and was angry about not receiving a patronage appointment. Garfield's death gave new life to the reform movement, culminating in the passage of the Pendelton or Civil Service Act of 1883.

Garment Workers of America, United: *see* LABOR ORGANIZATION.

garnishment, any legal or equitable procedure through which earnings of any individual are required to be withheld for the payment of any debt. Most garnishments are made by court order.

The Federal Wage Garnishment Act limit's the amount of an employee's disposable earnings subject to garnishment in any one week and protects the employee from discharge because of garnishment for any one indebtedness. It does not change other matters related to garnishment, such as the right of a creditor to collect the full amount owed, and most garnishment procedures established by state laws or rules. The largest amount of total disposable earnings subject to garnishment in any workweek may not exceed the lessor of: (1) 25 percent of the disposable earnings for that week or (2) the amount by which disposable earnings for that week exceeds 30 times the federal minimum hourly wage.

No court of the United States, or any state, may make, execute, or enforce any order or process in violation of these restrictions.

The restrictions on the amount that may be garnisheed in a week do not apply to: (1) court orders for the support of any person, such as child support and alimony; (2) bankruptcy court orders under Chapter XIII of the Bankruptcy Act; and (3) Debts due for state or federal taxes. A levy against wages for a federal tax debt by the Internal Revenue Service is not restricted by this law.

The Federal Wage Garnishment Act is enforced by the Secretary of Labor, acting through the Wage and Hour Division, U.S. Department of Labor.

GATB: *see* GENERAL APTITUDE TEST BATTERY.

Gateway Coal Company **v.** *United Mine Workers*, 414 U.S. 368 (1974), U.S. Supreme Court case, which held that disputes over safety issues can be submitted to arbitration and that courts can issue injunctions against work stoppages provoked by such disputes.

GAW: *see* GUARANTEED ANNUAL WAGE.

GBBA: *see* LABOR ORGANIZATION, Glass Bottle Blowers Association of the United States and Canada.

GCIA: *see* LABOR ORGANIZATION, Granite Cutters' International Association of America, The.

Geduldig **v.** *Aiello*, 417 U.S. 484 (1974), U.S. Supreme Court case, which held that the State of California's temporary disability insurance programs, which denied benefits for pregnancy related disabilities was not in violation of the equal protection clause of the 14th Amendment.

Gellerman, Saul W. (1929-   ), industrial psychologist and an authority on the application of the behavioral sciences to management. Major works include: *Motivation and Productivity* (N.Y.: American Management Association, 1963); *The Management of Human Relations* (N.Y.: Holt, Rinehart & Winston, 1966); *Management by Motivation* (N.Y.: American Management Association, 1968).

General Accounting Office (GAO), independent agency created by the Budget and Accounting Act of 1921 to audit federal government expenditures and assist Congress with its legislative oversight responsibilities. The GAO is directed by the Comptroller General of the United States, who is appointed by the president with the advice and consent of the Senate for a term of 15 years.

General Accounting Office
441 G. Street N.W.
Washington, DC 20548
(202) 275-5540

General Aptitude Test Battery (GATB), group of tests designed by the United States Employment Service and used extensively in state employment offices. The series of 12 tests measure nine aptitude areas: intelligence, verbal aptitude, numerical aptitude, spatial aptitude, form perception, clerical perception, motor coordination, finger dexterity, and manual dexterity. Scores from the tests are combined to create measures of individual aptitudes and general intelligence. The GATB has demonstrated impressive validity. *See* Stephen E. Bennis, "Occupational Validity of the General Aptitude Test Battery," *Journal of Applied Psychology* (June 1968).

See also NONREADING APTITUDE TEST BATTERY.

General Electric Co. **v.** *Gilbert*, 429 U.S. 125 (1976), U.S. Supreme Court case, which held that excluding pregnancies from sick-leave and disability benefit programs is not "discrimination based on sex" and so is not a violation of Title VII of the Civil Rights Act of 1964. This decision led to a Title VII amendment (the Pregnancy Discrimination Act of 1978) that reversed the court's decision. *See* Steven C. Kahn, *"General Electric Co. v. Gilbert:* Retreat from Rationality?" *Employee Relations Law Journal* (Summer 1977).

See also PREGNANCY and PREGNANCY DIS-CRIMINATION ACT OF 1978.

general increase, any upward salary adjustment governing the pay of most employees.

general labor union, any labor organization that accepts as members workers in every catagory of skill.

***General Motors* decision:** *see* NATIONAL LA-BOR RELATIONS BOARD V. GENERAL MOTORS.

General Schedule (GS), basic pay system for federal white-collar employees. It is the largest of the civilian pay systems, covering approximately 1.4 million of the total of 2.8 million civilian employees.

The General Schedule, established by the Classification Act of 1949, consists of eighteen grades or "levels of work" which are described broadly. Virtually any job can be accommodated within the schedule by evaluation of its level of duties, responsibilities, and qualification requirements. As befits its title, the General Schedule exhibits great occupational diversity: messengers, typists, secretaries, engineers, administrative personnel, research scientists, as well as occupations which are neither white-collar nor blue-collar in the traditional sense (police and fire fighters, for example).

A single pay table, nationwide in its applicability, sets forth the pay rates for the General Schedule. From 1949, when the General Schedule was enacted, until 1962, pay rates were adjusted by Congress on an irregular basis, largely in response to the pressures of inflation on employees' salaries. In 1962, Congress established the principle that pay rates would be maintained on the basis of comparability with rates paid in the private sector, as these rates were arrived at through the interplay of market forces. Authority to adjust the pay rates remained with the Congress, however, and full comparability was not achieved until the passage of the Federal Pay Comparability Act of 1970, which delegated to the President authority for making annual adjustments of General Schedule pay rates under the principle of comparability.

general strike, work stoppage by a substantial portion of the total work force of a locality or country. Because general strikes have tended to be more political than pragmatic in their goals, they have historically been more popular in Europe than in the United States. General strikes have been decidedly infrequent since World War II.

general systems theory, term that describes

OCTOBER 1979 PAY TABLE
GENERAL SCHEDULE EMPLOYEES

	1	2	3	4	5	6	7	8	9	10
GS-1	$ 7,210	$ 7,450	$ 7,690	$ 7,930	$ 8,170	$ 8,410	$ 8,650	$ 8,890	$ 8,902	$ 9,126
GS-2	8,128	8,399	8,670	8,902	9,002	9,267	9,532	9,797	10,062	10,327
GS-3	8,952	9,250	9,548	9,846	10,144	10,442	10,740	11,038	11,336	11,634
GS-4	10,049	10,384	10,719	11,054	11,389	11,724	12,059	12,394	12,729	13,064
GS-5	11,243	11,618	11,993	12,368	12,743	13,118	13,493	13,868	14,243	14,618
GS-6	12,531	12,949	13,367	13,785	14,203	14,621	15,039	15,457	15,875	16,293
GS-7	13,925	14,389	14,853	15,317	15,781	16,245	16,709	17,173	17,637	18,101
GS-8	15,423	15,937	16,451	16,965	17,479	17,993	18,507	19,021	19,535	20,049
GS-9	17,035	17,603	18,171	18,739	19,307	19,875	20,443	21,011	21,579	22,147
GS-10	18,760	19,385	20,010	20,635	21,260	21,885	22,510	23,135	23,760	24,385
GS-11	20,611	21,298	21,985	22,672	23,359	24,046	24,733	25,420	26,107	26,794
GS-12	24,703	25,526	26,349	27,172	27,995	28,818	29,641	30,464	31,287	32,110
GS-13	29,375	30,354	31,333	32,312	33,291	34,270	35,249	36,228	37,207	38,186
GS-14	34,713	35,870	37,027	38,184	39,341	40,498	41,655	42,812	43,969	45,126
GS-15	40,832	42,193	43,554	44,915	46,276	47,637	48,998	*50,359	*51,720	*53,081
GS-16	47,889	49,485	*51,081	*52,677	*54,273	*55,869	*57,465	*59,061	*60,657	

*Present law establishes $50,112.50 as pay ceiling.

SOURCE: *Federal Employees Almanac 1979* (Washington, D.C.: Federal Employees' News Digest, 1979), p.8.

efforts to build theoretical models that are conceptually, as Kenneth E. Boulding, "General Systems Theory - The Skeleton of Science," *Management Science* (April 1956) puts it, "somewhere between the highly generalized constructions of pure mathematics and the specific theories of the specialized disciplines." For the work of the man who sought a unity of science by introducing this notion, *see* Ludwig von Bertalanffy, *General Systems Theory: Foundations, Development, Applications* (N.Y.: George Braziller, 1968).

See also SYSTEMS ANALYSIS and SYSTEMS APPROACH.

gentlemen's agreement, any agreement or understanding based solely on oral communications. It is usually unenforceable if one party reneges.

geographical differential, also called INTER-CITY DIFFERENTIAL, differences in wage rates for the same work in various regions or cities.

Georgia State AFL–CIO: *see* AMERICAN FEDERATION OF LABOR–CONGRESS OF INDUSTRIAL ORGANIZATIONS.

George, Leo E. (1888-1967), president of the National Federation of Post Office Clerks from 1923 until 1956. For early biography, *see* Karl Baarslag, *History of the National Federation of Post Office Clerks* (Washington, D.C.: National Federation of Post Office Clerks, 1945).

geriatrics, also GERONTOLOGY and INDUSTRIAL GERONTOLOGY, that branch of medicine concerned with the special medical problems of older people. *Gerontology* is that branch of biology which is concerned with the nature of the aging process. *Industrial gerontology* is a far more comprehensive term that summarizes all of those areas of study concerned with the employment and retirement problems of workers who are middle-aged and beyond. *See* Harold L. Sheppard (ed.), *Towards an Industrial Gerontology: An Introduction to a New Field of Applied Research and Service* (Cambridge, Mass: Schenkman Publishing Company, 1970); Arthur N. Schwartz and James A. Peterson, *Introduction to Gerontology* (New York: Holt, Rinehart and Winston, 1979).

Germer, Adolph F. (1881-1966), prominent union organizer and socialist, was one of the Congress of Industrial Organizations' most active early leaders. *See* Lorin Lee Cary, "Institutionalized Conservatism in the Early C.I.O.: Adolph Germer, A Case Study," *Labor History* (Fall 1972).

gerontology: *see* GERIATRICS.

GERR: *see* GOVERNMENT EMPLOYEE RELATIONS REPORT.

GERT, acronym for GRAPHICAL EVALUATION AND REVIEW TECHNIQUE, process that provides a framework for modeling real-world research and development projects requiring many false starts, redoings, and multiple outcomes. For a text, *see* Lawrence J. Moore and Edward R. Clayton, *GERT Modeling and Simulation: Fundamentals and Applications* (N.Y.: Petrocelli-Charter, 1976). For a specific application to personnel, *see* T. W. Bonham, Edward R. Clayton, and Lawrence J. Moore, "A GERT Model to Meet Future Organizational Manpower Needs," *Personnel Journal* (July 1975).

Gestalt therapy, psychotherapy technique pioneered by Frederic S. Perls, which emphasizes the treatment of a person as a biological and perceptual whole. "Gestalt" is a German word for a configuration, pattern, or otherwise organized whole whose parts have different qualities than the whole. According to William R. Passons, "Gestalt Therapy Interventions for Group Counseling," *Personnel and Guidance Journal* (November 1972),

> in Gestalt therapy the principal means for facilitating responsibility and integration is the enhancement of self-awareness. These changes, however, are not forced or programmed. Rather they are allowed. As Perls stated it: "This is the great thing to understand: that awareness per se—by and of itself—can be curative."
> Necessarily, then, Gestalt interventions are designed to enhance awareness of the person's "now" experience—emotionally, cognitively, and bodily. As such, many of the interventions lend themselves to group counseling.

The classic work on this subject is F. S. Perls, R. F. Hefferling and P. Goodman, *Gestalt Therapy* (N.Y.: Julian Press, 1951).

GETA: *see* GOVERNMENT EMPLOYEES TRAINING ACT OF 1958.

get the sack, be fired. At the dawn of the industrial revolution, factory workers had to use their own tools. When a worker was fired, he was given a sack in which to gather up his tools.

Gilbert case: *see* GENERAL ELECTRIC CO. V. GILBERT.

Gilbreth, Frank Bunker (1868-1924) **and Lillian Moller** (1878-1972), husband and wife team who were the pioneers of time-and-motion study.

Frank and Lillian Gilbreth's influence on the scientific management movement was rivaled only by that of Frederick W. Taylor. Frank Gilbreth became the archtypical "efficiency expert." Two of their twelve children illustrated his mania for efficiency in their memoir, *Cheaper By the Dozen*, Frank B. Gilbreth, Jr., and Ernestine Gilbreth Carey (N.Y.: Grosset & Dunlap, 1948):

> Yes, at home or on the job, Dad was always the efficiency expert. He buttoned his vest from the bottom up, instead of from the top down, because the bottom-to-top process took him only three seconds, while the top-to-bottom took seven. He even used two shaving brushes to lather his face, because he found that by so doing he could cut seventeen seconds off his shaving time. For a while he tried shaving with two razors, but he finally gave that up.
>
> "I can save forty-four seconds," he grumbled, "but I wasted two minutes this morning putting this bandage on my throat."
>
> It wasn't the slashed throat that really bothered him. It was the two minutes.

For more serious biographies, *see* Edna Yost, *Frank and Lillian Gilbreth: Partners for Life* (New Brunswick, N.J.: Rutgers University Press, 1949); Lillian Moller Gilbreth, *The Quest for the One Best Way: A Sketch of the Life of Frank Bunker Gilbreth* (Easton, PA.: Hive Publishing, 1973). For their collected works, *see* William R. Spriegel and Clark E. Myers (eds.), *The Writings of the Gilbreths* (Homewood, Ill.: Richard D. Irwin, 1953).

See also SCIENTIFIC MANAGEMENT and THERBLIG.

Ginzberg, Eli (1911-   ), political economist, and the leading authority on manpower research and employment and training policy. Major works include: *Human Resources: The Wealth of a Nation* (N.Y.: Simon and Schuster, 1958); *The American Worker in the Twentieth Century*, with Hyman Berman (The Free Press of Glencoe, 1963); *The Development of Human Resources* (N.Y.: McGraw-Hill, 1966); *Manpower Agenda for America* (N.Y.: McGraw-Hill, 1968); *Manpower Strategy for the Metropolis* (N.Y.: Columbia University Press, 1968); *The Human Economy* (N.Y.: McGraw-Hill, 1976). For biographical sketch, *see* Gloria Stevenson, "Eli Ginzberg: Pioneer in Work Force Research," *Worklife* (May 1976).

girl Friday: *see* MAN FRIDAY.

giveback, any demand by management that a union accept a reduction in their present terms of employment.

Glass Bottle Blowers Association of the United States and Canada: *see* LABOR ORGANIZATION.

Glass and Ceramic Workers of North America, United: *see* LABOR ORGANIZATION.

Glass Workers' Union of North America, American Flint: *see* LABOR ORGANIZATION.

Gleason, Thomas W. (1900-   ), became president of the International Longshoremen's Association in 1963.

GLLO: *see* LABOR ORGANIZATION, Licensed Officers' Organization, Great Lakes.

global plan, according to Kenneth E. Foster, Gerald F. Wajda, and Theordore R. Lawson, "Global Plan for Salary Administration," *Harvard Business Review* (September–October 1961), a global plan "is a survey technique by which data on salary schedules, representing all employees from similar firms, can be arranged in a form that lends itself to simple statistical measurements."

GNP: *see* GROSS NATIONAL PRODUCT.

goals, also QUOTAS and TIMETABLE, within the context of equal employment opportunity a *goal* is a realistic objective which an organization endeavors to achieve through affirmative action. A *quota*, in contrast, restricts employment or development opportunities to members of particular groups by establishing a required number or proportionate representation which managers are obligated to attain without regard to "equal" employment opportunity. To be meaningful any program of goals or quotas must be associated with a specific *timetable*—a schedule of when the goals or quotas are to be achieved. See Daniel Seligman, "How 'Equal Opportunity' turned into Employment Quotas," *Fortune* (March 1973); Neil C. Churchill and John K. Shank, "Affirmative Action and Guilt-Edged Goals," *Harvard Business Review* (March–April 1976). For a case study of how the nation's largest private employer met its government mandated goals and timetables, *see* Carol J. Loomis, "A.T. & T. in the Throes of 'Equal Employment,'" *Fortune* (January 15, 1979). *See also* David H. Rosenbloom, "The Civil Service Commission's Decision to Authorize the Use of Goals and Timetables in the Federal Equal Employment Opportunity Program," *Western Political Quarterly* (June 1973).

GOCL: *see* GORDON OCCUPATIONAL CHECK LIST.

Goesaert v. *Cleary*, 335 U.S. 464 (1948), U.S. Supreme Court case, which found state laws denying women the right to practice certain occupations to be unconstitutional under the 14th Amendment's equal protection clause.

going rate, wage rate most commonly paid to workers in a given occupation.

Goldberg, Arthur Joseph (1908-   ), appointed Secretary of Labor by President John F. Kennedy in 1961, and associate justice of the U.S. Supreme Court in 1962. In 1965, he resigned from the court to be President Lyndon B. Johnson's ambassador to the United Nations until 1968.

Goldberg v. *Kelly*, 397 U.S. 254 (1970), U.S. Supreme Court case, which held that the due process clause of the Constitution requires government agencies to provide welfare recipients with an opportunity for an evidentiary hearing before terminating their benefits.

goldbricking. A "goldbrick" was a slang term for something that had only a surface appearance of value well before it was adopted by the military to mean shirking or giving the appearance of working. The word has now come to imply industrial work slowdowns whether they be individual initiatives (or the lack of individual initiative) or group efforts (organized or otherwise).

gold-circle rate, pay rate that exceeds the maximum rate of an employee's evaluated pay level.

golden handshake, dismissing an employee while at the same time providing him/her with a large cash bonus.

goldfish-bowl bargaining: *see* SUNSHINE BARGAINING.

Gompers, Samuel (1850-1924), one of the founders of the American Federation of Labor in 1886. He was the first president of the AFL and held that post, except for one year, until his death. For his autobiography, *see Seventy Years of Life and Labor: An Autobiography,* 2 volumes (N.Y.: E. P. Dutton, 1925). Other biographies include: Bernard Mandel, *Samuel Gompers: A Biography* (Yellow Springs, Ohio: The Antioch Press, 1963);

Stuart Bruce Kaufman, *Samuel Gompers and the Origins of the American Federation of Labor: 1848-1896* (Westport, Conn.: Greenwood Press, 1973); Harold C. Livesay, *Samuel Gompers and Organized Labor in America* (Boston: Little, Brown, 1978).

good faith, in the context of equal employment opportunity, "good faith" is the absence of discriminating intent. The "good faith" of an employer is usually considered by the courts in fashioning an appropriate remedy to correct the wrongs of "unintentional" discrimination.

good-faith bargaining, Section 8(a) (5) of the National Labor Relations Act makes it illegal for an employer to refuse to bargain in good faith about wages, hours, and other conditions or employment with the representative selected by a majority of the employees in a unit appropriate for collective bargaining. A bargaining representative seeking to enforce its right concerning an employer under this section must show that it has been designated by a majority of the employees, that the unit is appropriate, and that there has been both a demand that the employer bargain and a refusal by the employer to do so.

The duty to bargain covers all matters concerning rates of pay, wages, hours of employment, or other conditions of employment. These are called "mandatory" subjects of bargaining about which the employer, as well as the employees' representative, must bargain in good faith, although the law does not require "either party to agree to a proposal or require the making of a concession." These mandatory subjects of bargaining include, but are not limited to, such matters as pensions for present and retired employees, bonuses, group insurance, grievance procedure, safety practices, seniority, procedures for discharge, layoff, recall, or discipline, and the union shop. On "nonmandatory" subjects—that is, matters that are lawful but not related to "wages, hours, and other conditions of employment"—the parties are free to bargain and to agree, but neither party may insist on bargaining on such subjects over the objection of the other party.

An employer who is required to bargain under this section must, as stated in Section 8(d), "meet at reasonable times and confer in good faith with respect to wages, hours, and other terms and conditions of employment, or the negotiation of an agreement, or any question arising thereunder, and the execution of a written contract incorporating any agreement reached if requested by either party."

An employer, therefore, will be found to have violated Section 8 (a) (5) if its conduct in bargaining, viewed in its entirety, indicates that the employer did not negotiate with a good-faith intention to reach agreement. However, the employer's good faith is not at issue where its conduct constitutes an out-and-out refusal to bargain on a mandatory subject. For example, it is a violation for an employer, regardless of good faith, to refuse to bargain about a subject it believes is not a mandatory subject of bargaining, when in fact it is.

See also the following entries:

NATIONAL LABOR RELATIONS BOARD V. IN-
SURANCE AGENTS' INTERNATIONAL UNION
NATIONAL LABOR RELATIONS BOARD V.
TRUITT MANUFACTURING
UNFAIR LABOR PRACTICES (EMPLOYERS)
UNFAIR LABOR PRACTICES (UNIONS)

goon, also GOON SQUAD, slang terms for a man or men hired to create or resist violence during a labor dispute.

gopher, while this is not formally listed as a job title on anybody's resume, many a successful manager will admit to having worked his way up from gopher—go for coffee, go for this, go for that, etc.

Gordon Occupational Check List (GOCL), test in checklist format, that includes 240 statements of job activities found in occupations with middle and lower degrees of skill and responsibility. Used in vocational counseling with noncollege-bound students. TIME: 20/25 minutes. AUTHOR: Leonard Gordon. PUBLISHER: Harcourt, Brace, Jovanovich, Inc. (*see* TEST PUBLISHERS).

Gouldner, Alvin W. (1920-   ), a leading sociologist who has made some of the most significant contributions to the field of industrial sociology. Major works include: *Patterns of Industrial Bureaucracy* (Glencoe, Ill.: The Free Press, 1954); *Wildcat Strikes*, with R.A. Peterson (Yellow Springs, Ohio: Antioch Press, 1954); *Notes on Technology and the Moral Order*, with Richard A. Peterson (Indianapolis: Bobbs-Merrill, 1962); *Enter Plato* (N.Y.: Basic Books, 1965); *The Coming Crisis of Western Sociology* (N.Y.: Basic Books, 1970).

Government Employee Relations Report (GERR) published by the Bureau of National Affairs, Inc., this is a weekly notification and reference service designed solely for the public sector. Provides comprehensive coverage of all significant developments af-fecting public employee relations on the federal, state, and local levels.

Government Employees, American Federation of: *see* LABOR ORGANIZATION.

Government Employees, National Association of: *see* LABOR ORGANIZATION.

Government Employees Training Act of 1958, federal statute (Public Law 85-507), which held that

in order to promote efficiency and economy in the operation of the Government and provide means for the development of maximum proficiency in the performance of official duties by employees thereof, to establish and maintain the highest standards of performance in the transaction of the public business, and to install and utilize effectively the best modern practices and techniques which have been developed, tested, and proved within or outside of the Government, it is necessary and desirable in the public interest that self-education, self-improvement, and self-training by such employees be supplemented and extended by Government-sponsored programs, provided for by this Act, for the training of such employees in the performance of official duties and for the development of skills, knowledge, and abilities which will best qualify them for performance of official duties.

GETA (1) was a clear-cut mandate that the federal workforce should be trained to its most effective level, (2) authorized expenditures for training, (3) provided for both centralized training by the U.S. Civil Service Commission and departmental training programs, and (4) authorized agencies to buy training from existing educational and professional institutions.

Government Inspectors and Quality Assurance Personnel, National Association of: *see* LABOR ORGANIZATION.

grade, established level or zone of difficulty. Positions of the same difficulty and responsibility tend to be placed in the same grade even though the content of the work differs greatly.

grade creep, also called GRADE ESCALATION, long-term tendency for positions to be reallocated upward. For an analysis of the problem, *see* Seymour S. Berlin, "The Manager, the Classifier, and Unwarranted Grade Escalation," *Civil Service Journal* (July–September 1964).

gradual pressure strike, concerted effort by employees to influence management by gradually reducing production until their objectives are met. *See* Michael L. Broorshire and J. Fred Holly, "Resolving Bargaining Impasses Through Gradual Pressure Strikes," *Labor Law Journal* (October 1973).

graduated wages, wages adjusted on the basis of length of service and performance.

graft, honest/dishonest: *see* HONEST GRAFT.

Grain Millers, American Federation of: *see* LABOR ORGANIZATION.

Grand Canyon management, as described by William Thomas, in "Humor for Hurdling the Mystique in Management," *Management of Personnel Quarterly* (Winter 1970),

> Few sights in the world are like the Grand Canyon. It is one of nature's most splendid scenarios. To see it from close up one can take advantage of a certain kind of tour— renting a mule and riding through the canyon itself. Mules are used on these tours instead of horses because they are surefooted and the tourist can sit relaxed, concentrating on the surroundings, secure in the knowledge that his mount will miss nary a step. That accurately describes the Grand Canyon Manager. He sits on his (mule) and watches everything going on around him. Staff people, particularly those in areas like Personnel, are frequent practitioners of Grand Canyon Management.

grandfather clause, originally a device used by some states of the Old South to disenfranchise black voters. Grandfather clauses, written into seven state constitutions during the Reconstruction era, granted the right to vote only to persons whose ancestors, "grandfathers," had voted prior to 1867. The U.S. Supreme Court ruled, in *Guinn* v. *United States*, 238 U.S. 347 (1915), that all grandfather clauses were unconstitutional because of the 15th Amendment. Today, a grandfather clause is a colloquial expression for any provision or policy that exempts a category of individuals from meeting new standards. For example, if a company were to establish a policy that all managers had to have a master's degree as of a certain date, it would probably exempt managers without such degrees who were hired prior to that date. This statement of exemption would be a grandfather clause.

Granite Cutters' International Association of America, The: *see* LABOR ORGANIZATION.

Grant's Civil Service Commission, on the last day of the legislative session of the 41st Congress in 1871, a rider was attached to an otherwise unrelated appropriations bill authorizing President Ulysses S. Grant to make rules and regulations for the civil service. The rider itself was only one sentence long and did not formally require the president to do anything. It certainly would not have passed had it been thought to be anything more than a symbolic sop to the reformers. The rider authorized the president "to prescribe such rules and regulations for the admission of persons into the civil service of the United States as will best promote the efficiency thereof, and ascertain the fitness of each candidate...." To the surprise of almost everyone, Grant proceeded to appoint a civil service commission. He authorized them to establish and implement appropriate rules and regulations. The commission required boards of examiners in each department who worked under the commission's general supervision. All things considered a viable program existed during 1872 and 1873. Several thousand persons were examined and several hundred were actually appointed. But once the Congress realized that Grant was serious about reform and intent upon cutting into their patronage powers, the program was terminated. Congress simply refused to appropriate funds for the work of the commission and the president formally abolished it in 1875.

For an exhaustive history, *see* Lionel V. Murphy, "The First Federal Civil Service Commission: 1871–1875," *Public Personnel Review* (October 1942).

grapevine, informal means by which organizational members give or receive information. According to Keith Davis, in "The Care and Cultivation of the Corporate Grapevine," *Dun's* (July 1973),

> wherever people congregate in groups, the grapevine is sure to grow. It may manifest itself in smoke rings, jungle tom-toms, taps on prison walls or just idle chitchat, but it will always be there. Indeed, the word grapevine has been part of our jargon ever since the Civil War, when telegraph lines were strung loosely from tree to tree in vine-like fashion and resulted in messages that were frequently garbled.

For a more scholarly analysis by Keith Davis, *see* "Management Communication and the Grapevine," *Harvard Business Review* (September–October 1953).

graphical evaluation and review technique: *see* GERT.

Graphic Arts International Union: *see* LABOR ORGANIZATION.

graphic rating scale, performance appraisal chart that lists traits (such as promptness, knowledge, helpfulness, etc.) with a range of performance to be indicated with each (unsatisfactory, satisfactory, etc.).

graphology: *see* HANDWRITING ANALYSIS.

graveyard shift, also called LOBSTER SHIFT, slang terms for the tour of duty of employees who work from 11 p.m. or midnight until dawn.

Great Lakes Licensed Officers' Organization: *see* LABOR ORGANIZATION, Licensed Officers' Organization, Great Lakes.

Green, William (1873-1952), succeeded Samuel Gompers as president of the American Federation of Labor in 1924 and held that office until his death. For a biography, *see* Max Danish, *William Green: A Pictorial Biography* (N.Y.: Inter-Allied Publications, 1952).

green-circle rate, also called BLUE-CIRCLE RATE, pay rate that is below the minimum rate of an employee's evaluated pay level.

green hands, slang term for inexperienced workers.

grievance, while a grievance may be any dissatisfaction felt by an employee in connection with his/her employment, the word generally refers to a formal complaint initiated by an employee, by a union, or by management concerning the interpretation or application of a collective bargaining agreement or established employment practices. For a discussion of how to avoid grievances, *see* W. B. Werther, Jr., "Reducing Grievances Through Effective Contract Administration," *Labor Law Journal* (April 1974).

grievance arbitration, also called RIGHTS ARBITRATION, arbitration concerned with disputes that arise over the interpretation/application of an existing collective bargaining agreement. The grievance arbitrator interprets the contract for the parties.

grievance committee, those union and/or management representatives who are formally designated to review grievances left unresolved by lower elements of the grievance machinery.

See also ELGIN, JOLIET & EASTERN RAILWAY V. BURLEY.

grievance machinery, totality of the methods, usually enumerated in a collective bargaining agreement, used to resolve the problems of interpretation arising during the life of an agreement. Grievance machinery is usually designed so that those closest to the dispute have the first opportunity to reach a settlement. According to Walter E. Baer, *Grievance Handling* (N.Y.: American Management Associations, 1970),

> the grievance machinery is the formal process, preliminary to any arbitration, that enables the parties to attempt to resolve their differences in a peaceful, orderly, and expeditious manner. It permits the company and the union to investigate and discuss their problems without interrupting the continued, orderly operation of the business. And, when the machinery works effectively, it can satisfactorily resolve the overwhelming majority of disputes between the parties.

grievance procedure, specific means by which grievances are channeled for their adjustment through progressively higher levels of authority in both an organization and its union. Grievance procedures, while long considered the "heart" of a labor contract, are increasingly found in non-unionized organizations as managers realize the need for a process to appeal the decisions of supervisors that employees consider unjust. For a how-to-do-it book, *see* Maurice S. Trotta, *Handling Grievances: A Guide for Management and Labor* (Washington, D.C.: Bureau of National Affairs, 1976).

See also EMPORIUM CAPWELL CO. V. WESTERN ADDITION COMMUNITY ORGANIZATION and SMITH V. ARKANSAS STATE HIGHWAY EMPLOYEES, LOCAL 1315.

grievant, one who files a formal grievance. A study of grievants and non-grievants in one company found that the grievants were more likely to be (1) better educated, (2) younger in terms of seniority, (3) more active in union matters, (4) lower paid, and (5) more likely to be absent or tardy. *See* Howard A. Sulkin and Robert W. Pranis, "Comparison of Grievants with Non-grievants in a Heavy Machinery Company," *Personnel Psychology* (Summer 1967).

Griffenhagen, Edwin O. (1886-), management engineer who became one of the pioneers in the development of position classification and job analysis. For his history of the origin of modern duties-classification systems, *see* "The Origin of Modern Occupation Classification in Personnel Administration," *Public Personnel Studies* (September 1924).

Griggs, et al. v. Duke Power Company, 401 U.S. 424 (1971), is the most significant single Supreme Court decision concerning the va-

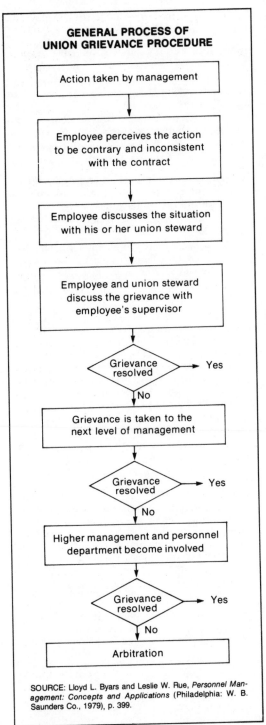

GENERAL PROCESS OF UNION GRIEVANCE PROCEDURE

Action taken by management

↓

Employee perceives the action to be contrary and inconsistent with the contract

↓

Employee discusses the situation with his or her union steward

↓

Employee and union steward discuss the grievance with employee's supervisor

↓

Grievance resolved → Yes

↓ No

Grievance is taken to the next level of management

↓

Grievance resolved → Yes

↓ No

Higher management and personnel department become involved

↓

Grievance resolved → Yes

↓ No

Arbitration

SOURCE: Lloyd L. Byars and Leslie W. Rue, *Personnel Management: Concepts and Applications* (Philadelphia: W. B. Saunders Co., 1979), p. 399.

criminatory in operation." Thus, if employment practices operating to exclude minorities "cannot be shown to be related to job performance, the practice is prohibited." The ruling dealt a blow to restrictive credentialism, stating that, while diplomas and tests are useful, the "Congress has mandated the commonsense proposition that they are not to become masters of reality." In essence, the court held that the law requires that tests used for employment purposes "must measure the person for the job and not the person in the abstract."

The *Griggs* decision applied only to the private sector until the Equal Employment Opportunity Act of 1972 extended the provisions of Title VII of the Civil Rights Act of 1964 to cover public as well as private employees. *See* Hugh Steven Wilson, "A Second Look at *Griggs* v. *Duke Power Company*: Ruminations on Job Testing, Discrimination and the Role of the Federal Courts," *Virginia Law Review* (May 1972); Alfred W. Blumrosen, "Strangers in Paradise: *Griggs* v. *Duke Power Co.* and the Concept of Employment Discrimination," *Michigan Law Review* (November 1972).

Griner, John F. (1907-   ), president of the American Federation of Government Employees (AFGE) from 1962 to 1973.

grog privileges, practice of allowing laborers to stop work during the afternoon for a drink of grog or something similar. This custom has fallen into disuse, except among higher paid executives.

Grospiron, Alvin F. (1916-   ), became president of the Oil, Chemical and Atomic Workers International Union in 1965.

gross national product (GNP), monetary value of all of the goods and services produced in a nation in a given year.

group: *see* SMALL-GROUP RESEARCH.

group annuity, any of a variety of pension plans designed by insurance companies for a group of persons to cover all of those qualified under one contract.

group cohesiveness, measure of the degree of unity and solidarity that a group possesses.

group development, loose term concerned with the various processes and circumstances that occur when individuals organize themselves into goal orientated groups. For a survey of the theory and research, *see* John M. Ivancevich and J. Timothy McMahon,

lidity of employment examinations. The court unanimously ruled that Title VII of the Civil Rights Act of 1964 "proscribes not only overt discrimination but also practices that are dis-

"Group Development, Trainer Style and Carry-over Job Satisfaction and Performance," *Academy of Management Journal* (September 1976).

group dynamics, it is generally accepted that Kurt Lewin "invented" the field of group dynamics (that is, he was responsible, either directly or indirectly, for most of the pioneering research on group dynamics). Two of Lewin's close associates, Dorwin Cartwright and Alvin Zander, went on to produce what was for many years the standard text on the subject—*Group Dynamics: Research and Theory* (N.Y.: Harper & Row, 3rd ed., 1968). They defined "group dynamics" as the field of inquiry dedicated to advancing knowledge about the nature of groups, how they develop, and their relationships to individuals, other groups, and larger institutions. *See* Kurt Lewin, "Frontiers in Group Dynamics: Concept, Method and Reality in Social Science," *Human Relations* (June 1947).

group executive, manager responsible for the work of two or more organizational divisions.

group incentive plan: *see* INCENTIVE-WAGE PLAN.

group insurance, also GROUP HEALTH INSURANCE and GROUP LIFE INSURANCE, *group insurance* refers to any insurance plan that covers individuals (and usually their dependents) by means of a single policy issued to the employer or association with which the insured individuals are affiliated. The cost of group insurance is usually significantly lower than the costs for equivalent individual policies. Group insurance policies are written in the name of the employer so that individual employees are covered only as long as they remain with the insuring employer. Sometimes group insurance policies provide that an employee can continue his/her coverage upon resignation by buying an individual policy. The most common kinds of group insurance are *group health insurance* and *group life insurance*. Many employers pay a substantial portion or all of the cost of group insurance.

group of classes, two or more closely related job classes having a common basis of duties, responsibilities, and qualification requirements but differing in some particular, (such as the nature of specialization) that is essential from the standpoint of recruitment and selection and requires that each class in the group be treated individually. Such classes have the same basic title but may be distinguished by a parenthetic. For example: Engineer (Chemical), Engineer (Electrical), etc.

group oral interview, also called GROUP ORAL EXAMINATION, measurement tool that involves a group of candidates (ideally 5–7) discussing a job-related problem. The evaluators do not actively participate in the group discussion; their role is to observe and evaluate the behavior of the participants. The value of this technique is heavily dependent on the ability of the evaluators.

Group I Tenure/Group II Tenure/Group III Tenure, federal government terms for the tenure groupings of its employees. Employees who are serving in competitive positions are grouped as follows:

>   *Group 1.* Career employees who have completed their probationary period and who are not serving in obligated positions. (An obligated position is a position to which a former employee has mandatory reemployment or restoration rights).
>   *Group II.* Career-conditional employees and career employees who have not completed probationary periods or who occupy obligated positions.
>   *Group III.* Employees serving under temporary appointments pending establishment of a register, employees serving under indefinite appointments, etc.

Employees serving under appointments to excepted positions, aliens, and attorneys are grouped according to their tenure of employment as follows:

>   *Group I.* Permanent employees whose appointments carry no restrictions or conditions.
>   *Group II.* Employees serving trial periods, those whose tenure is indefinite solely because they are occupying obligated positions and those serving under conditional appointments who have not completed the 3-year service requirement for appointment without condition or limitation.
>   *Group III.* This group includes all employees serving under appointments specifically identified as indefinite. It also includes employees serving under temporary excepted appointments limited to one year or less who have completed one year or more of current continuous employment in the excepted service.

groupthink, psychological drive for consensus, at any cost, which tends to suppress both dissent and the appraisal of alternatives in small decisionmaking groups. Groupthink, because it refers to a deterioration of mental efficiency and moral judgment due to ingroup pressures, has an invidious connotation. For the basic work on the subject, *see*

Irving L. Janis, *Victims of Groupthink: A Psychological Study of Foreign-Policy Decisions and Fiascoes* (Boston: Houghton-Mifflin Co., 1972).

GS: *see* GENERAL SCHEDULE.

GUA: *see* LABOR ORGANIZATION, Guards Union of America, International.

guaranteed annual wage (GAW), any of a variety of plans whereby an employer agrees to provide employees with a predetermined minimum (1) number of hours of work or (2) salary each year.

guaranteed base rate: *see* GUARANTEED RATE.

guaranteed earnings, provision in some union contracts that employees will be paid (guaranteed) a specified minimum wage, even when production must cease because of a machinery breakdown or some other cause beyond the control of the employee.

guaranteed rate, also called GUARANTEED BASE RATE, minimum wage guaranteed to an employee working under an incentive pay program.

guaranteed workweek, provision in some union contracts that an employee will be paid a full week's wages even when there is not enough actual work available to otherwise warrant a full week's pay.

Guards and Watchmen, International Union of: *see* LABOR ORGANIZATION.

Guards Union of America, International: *see* LABOR ORGANIZATION.

Guest, Robert H. (1916-   ), known for his pioneering studies of life on the assembly line and of job design. Major works include: *The Man on the Assembly Line*, with Charles R. Walker (Cambridge, Mass.: Harvard University Press, 1952); *Organizational Change: The Effect of Successful Leadership* (Homewood, Ill.: Dorsey Press, 1962).

guest worker, European term for foreign workers allowed to enter and work in a country for a temporary period.

guide chart, tool used by a factor-ranking system of job evaluation, which contains a narrative description and point value for each degree of each factor.

guideline method, job evaluation technique that determines the value of a position in an organization not by an analysis of the posi-

tion's content, but by what the labor market says it is worth.

guidelines, also called GUIDEPOSTS, (1) general standards, usually expressed as a percentage, by which the federal government measures wage and price increases to determine if they are consistent with the national economic interest or (2) published outlines for action or suggested courses of conduct that many federal agencies issue for the guidance of their clients.

guideposts: *see* GUIDELINES.

guild, also called CRAFT GUILD, in medieval Western Europe, an association for mutual aid and/or for the furtherance of religious and business interests. Merchant guilds date from the 11th century. Although there was a craft-guild movement in ancient Rome, the modern union movement usually traces its lineage to the craft guilds of the Middle Ages, which paralleled the merchant guilds of the time. Craft guilds were associations of individual workers who sought to regulate production, establish standards, and fix prices. These craft guilds gave us the now familiar rankings for their classes of membership—apprentice, journeyman, and master.

Guild Socialism, political movement that advocated workers' control of industry by means of a system of national guilds. This movement had its greatest popularity in England just before and just after World War I.

Guilford–Zimmerman Temperament Survey (GZTS), personality inventory developed to provide a single comprehensive inventory of the following traits: general activity, restraint, ascendence, sociability, masculinity, emotional stability, objectivity, friendliness, thoughtfulness, personal relations. TIME: Approximately 45 minutes. AUTHOR: J. P. Guilford and Wayne S. Zimmerman. PUBLISHER: Sheridan Psychological Services, Inc. (*see* TEST PUBLISHERS).

Guinan, Matthew (1910-   ), became president of the Transport Workers Union of America in 1966.

Gulick, Luther (1892-   ), highly honored reformer, researcher, and practitioner of public administration, best known to management generalists for having invented POSDCORB (*see entry*). Major works include: *Papers on the Science of Administration*, edited with Lyndall Urwick (N.Y.: Institute of Public Administration, 1937); *Administrative Reflections from World War*

II (University of Alabama Press, 1948); *The Metropolitan Problem and American Ideas* (N.Y.: Knopf, 1962).

gypsy, slang term for an independent operator of a truck, taxi, etc., who owns his/her own vehicle.

GZTS: *see* GUILFORD–ZIMMERMAN TEMPERAMENT SURVEY.

H

Hagglund, Joel Emmanuel: *see* HILL, JOE.

Hall v. Cole, 412 U.S. 1 (1973), U.S. Supreme Court case, which held that union members who successfully challenge a union action in court can be awarded attorneys' fees if it could be shown that litigant's victory benefited the entire union.

Hall Occupational Orientation Inventory (HOOI), 345-item, free-choice test used to assess the attractiveness or relative importance to the individual of various occupational attributes or factors. The 23 scales measured include such items as: creativity/independence, risk, belongingness, security, aspiration, esteem, people-orientation, concerns about money, environment, co-workers, time, extremism, and defensiveness. TIME: 40/60 minutes. AUTHOR: L. G. Hall. PUBLISHER: Follett Educational Corporation (*see* TEST PUBLISHERS).

Hall, Paul (1914-　　), president of the Seafarers International Union of North America.

halo effect, bias in ratings arising from the tendency of a rater to be influenced in his/her rating of specific traits by his general impression of the person being rated. The concept was "discovered" by Edward L. Thorndike in "A Constant Error in Psychological Ratings," *Journal of Applied Psychology*, Vol. 4 (March 1920).

Halsey Plan, Frederick A. Halsey's "premium plan" was first presented to the American Society of Mechanical Engineers in 1891. Halsey proposed that workers be allowed to use their individual past performance as a standard, with the value of any increased output divided between the employee and the employer.

Hammer v. Dagenhart, 247 U.S. 251 (1918), U.S. Supreme Court case, which held unconstitutional a federal statute barring goods made by child labor from interstate commerce. The court would not concede that the federal government could regulate child labor in interstate commerce until 1941, when it upheld the Fair Labor Standards Act of 1938 that put restrictions on the use of child labor. The landmark case was *United States v. Darby Lumber Company*, 312 U.S. 100 (1941).

Hampton v. Mow Sun Wong, 426 U.S. 88 (1976), U.S. Supreme Court case, which held that a U.S. Civil Service Commission regulation excluding resident aliens from the federal competitive service had been adopted in violation of the due process clause of the 5th Amendment. Because the court expressly decided only the validity of the regulations promulgated by the Civil Service Commission and reserved comment on the appropriateness of a citizenship requirement instituted by the president, on September 2, 1976, President Ford issued Executive Order 11935, which provides that only U.S. citizens and nationals may hold permanent positions in the federal competitive service except when necessary to promote the efficiency of the service. For a legal analysis, *see* Eric C. Scoones, "Procedural Due Process and the Exercise of Delegated Power: The Federal Civil Service Employment Restriction on Aliens," *The Georgetown Law Journal* (October 1977).
See also SUGARMAN V. DOUGALL.

handicapped employees, emotionally: *see* EMOTIONALLY HANDICAPPED EMPLOYEES.

handicapped individual, also QUALIFIED HANDICAPPED INDIVIDUAL, according to the Vocational Rehabilitation Act of 1973 (as amended), federal contractors and subcontractors are required to take affirmative action to seek out qualified handicapped individuals for employment. A *handicapped individual* is any person who (1) has a physical or mental impairment which substantially limits one or more of such person's major life activities, (2) has a record of such an impairment, or (3) is regarded as having such an impairment. A *qualified handicapped individual*, with respect to employment, is one who with reasonable accommodation can perform the essential functions of a job in question. *See* Robert B. Nathanson, "The Disabled Employee: Separating Myth from Fact," *Harvard Business Review* (May–June 1977); Sar A. Levitan and Robert Taggart, "Employment Problems of Disabled Persons *Monthly Labor Review* (March 1977); Gopal C. Pati, "Countdown on Hiring the Handicapped," *Personnel Journal* (March 1978).

See also the following entries:

ARCHITECTURAL BARRIERS
NATIONAL REHABILITATION ASSOCIATION
READING ASSISTANT
REASONABLE ACCOMMODATION
REHABILITATED OFFENDER PROGRAM
SHELTERED WORKSHOP
VOCATIONAL REHABILITATION ACT OF 1973
WAGNER-O'DAY ACT
WORK-ACTIVITIES CENTERS
WORK-READY

hands-on test, performance test that uses the actual tools of the job.

handwriting analysis, scientific name GRAPHOLOGY, psychological tool sometimes used to evaluate the personality and character of employment applicants. A handwriting analyst is a graphologist; the science is graphology. *See* Jitendra M. Sharma and Harsh Vardhan, "Graphology: What Handwriting Can Tell You About an Applicant," *Personnel* (March–April 1975).

Hanna Mining Co. v. District 2, Marine Engineers, 382 U.S. 181 (1965), U.S. Supreme Court case, which held that while supervisory personnel are not employees for purposes of the National Labor Relations Act, the act does not preempt state labor laws affecting supervisors.

Harcourt, Brace, Jovanovich, Inc.: *see* TEST PUBLISHERS.

hard-core unemployed, those individuals who, because of racial discrimination, an impoverished background, or the lack of appropriate education, have never been able to hold a job for a substantial length of time. *See* Leonard Nadler, "Helping the Hard-Core Adjust to the World of Work," *Harvard Business Review* (March–April 1970); Keith C. Weir, "Hard Core Training and Employment," *Personnel Journal* (May 1971); Daniel M. Seifer, "Continuing Hard Problems: The 'Hard-

Core' and Racial Discrimination," *Public Personnel Management* (May–June 1974).

hardship allowance, additional money paid to an employee who accepts an assignment that offers difficult living conditions, physical hardships, unattractive climate, and/or a lack of the usual amenities found in the United States.

hardware, formally, the mechanical, magnetic, electrical, and electronic devices or components of a computer. Informally, any piece of computer or automatic-data-processing equipment.

See also SOFTWARE.

Hardy, George (1911-   ), president of the Service Employees International Union.

Harvard Business Review (HBR), journal for professional managers, published bimonthly by the faculty of the Harvard University Graduate School of Business Administration. The editors modestly state that, in selecting articles for publication, they "try to pick those that are timeless rather than just timely." The *Harvard Business Review* is almost universally considered the foremost business journal in the United States.

Harvard Business Review
Editorial Address:
Harvard Business Review
Boston, MA 02163

Subscriptions:
Harvard Business Review
Subscription Service Department
P.O. Box 9730
Greenwich, CT 06835

Harvard Business School (HBS), the most prestigious of the prestigious "B" schools. Robert Townsend, in *Up the Organization* (N.Y.: Knopf, 1970), suggests that you "don't hire Harvard Business School graduates. This worthy enterprise confesses that it trains its students for only three posts—executive vice-president, president, and board chairman. The faculty does not blush when HBS is called the West Point of capitalism." For the "inside" story about the education of the managerial elite in the U.S., *see* Peter Cohn, *The Gospel According to the Harvard Business School* (Garden City, N.Y.: Doubleday & Co., 1973).

Harvard Fatigue Laboratory (HFL), research organization that existed within the Harvard Business School from 1927 to 1947. According to Steven M. Horvath and Elizabeth C. Horvath, in *The Harvard Fatigue Laboratory: Its History and Contributions* (Englewood Cliffs, New Jersey: Prentice-Hall, Inc., 1973), its highly influential research efforts tended to focus on the notion that "group psychology, social problems and the physiology of fatigue of normal man must be studied, not only as individual factors in determining physical and mental health, but more especially to determine their interrelatedness and the effect upon work."

Hatch Act, collective popular name for two federal statutes. The Hatch Act of 1939, 53 Stat. 410 (1939), restricted the political activities of almost all federal employees, whether in the competitive service or not. The impetus for this legislation came primarily from a decrease in the proportion of federal employees who were in the competitive service. This was a direct result of the creation of several New Deal agencies that were placed outside the merit system. Senator Carl Hatch, a Democrat from New Mexico, had worked for several years to have legislation enacted that would prevent federal employees from being active in political conventions. He feared that their involvement and direction by politicians could lead to the development of a giant national political machine.

A second Hatch Act in 1940, 54 Stat. 640 (1940), extended these restrictions to positions in state employment having federal financing. Penalties for violation of the Hatch Act by federal employees have been softened considerably over time. Originally, removal was mandatory, but, by 1962, the minimum punishment was suspension for 30 days.

It has never been possible to define completely the political activities prohibited by the Hatch Act. However, the following are among the major limitations:

1. serving as a delegate or alternate to a political party convention;
2. soliciting or handling political contributions;
3. being an officer or organizer of a political club;
4. engaging in electioneering;
5. with some exceptions, being a candidate for elective political office; and
6. leading or speaking to partisan political meetings or rallies.

The constitutionality of these regulations was first upheld by the Supreme Court in *United Public Workers* v. *Mitchell*, 330 U.S. 75 (1947) and reaffirmed in *Civil Service Commission* v. *National Association of Letter Carriers*, 413 U.S. 548 (1973). Repeal of the Hatch Act (or relaxation of some of its provisions) has been high on the legislative

agenda of unions, especially since union legal challenges to the act have been unsuccessful. *See* Philip L. Martin, "The Hatch Act: The Current Movement for Reform," *Public Personnel Management* (May–June 1974); Henry Rose, "A Critical Look at the Hatch Act," *Harvard Law Review* (January 1962).

See also UNITED STATES CIVIL SERVICE COMMISSION V. NATIONAL ASSOCIATION OF LETTER CARRIERS.

hatchet man, according to Qass Aquarius, *The Corporate Prince: A Handbook of Administrative Tactics* (N.Y.: Van Nostrand Reinhold Co., 1971),

> when dirty work must be done, the wise administrator tries to keep his hands clean. Perhaps he may have a subordinate, a hatchet man, to do his dirty work for him, thereby avoiding the displeasure of those who do not approve of the actions. For this reason many administrators prefer to have their subordinates do their firing for them. Sometimes a board of directors deliberately brings in a president as a hatchet man to clean house, prune the corporate tree of its deadwood, thereby incurring great displeasure among people within the organization. After all the bloodletting has taken place, the board can find other work for the hatchet man and a new man can be brought in who immediately bestows benefits upon a grateful, relieved organization.

Hatters, Cap and Millinery Workers International Union, United: *see* LABOR ORGANIZATION.

HAU *see* LABOR ORGANIZATION, Hebrew Actors Union, Inc., under Actors and Artistes of America, Associated.

Hawaii State Federation of Labor: *see* AMERICAN FEDERATION OF LABOR–CONGRESS OF INDUSTRIAL ORGANIZATIONS.

Hawkins v. *Bleakly*, 243 U.S. 210 (1917), U.S. Supreme Court case, which upheld the constitutionality of state workmen's compensation laws.

Hawthorne Effect, Elton Mayo and his associates, while conducting their now famous Hawthorne Studies, discovered that the researchers' concern for and attention to the workers led to increases in production. Any production increase due to known presence of benign observers can be attributed to a "Hawthorne Effect." For Mayo's account, *see* Elton Mayo, *The Human Prolems of an Industrial Civilization* (N.Y.: Viking Press, 1933, 1960).

Hawthorne Studies, also called HAWTHORNE EXPERIMENTS, conducted at the Hawthorne Works of the Western Electric Company near Chicago, are probably the most important single management study yet reported. Beginning in the late 1920s, a research team led by Elton Mayo of the Harvard Business School started a decade-long series of experiments aimed at determining the relationship between work environment and productivity. The experimenters, because they were initially unable to explain the results of their findings, literally stumbled upon what today seems so obvious—that factories and other work situations are first of all social situations. The Hawthorne Studies are generally considered to the genesis of the human relations school of management thought. The definitive account of the experiments is given in F. J. Roethlisberger and William J. Dickson's *Management and the Worker* (Cambridge, Mass.: Harvard University Press, 1939).

Work group behavior, output restriction, supervisory training, personnel research, interviewing methodology, employee counseling, socio-technical systems theory, small group incentive plans, and organizational theory became prime concerns of management, because, in one way or another, they were brought to the fore or elucidated by the Hawthorne Studies. For a re-examination of the studies a generation later, *see* Henry A. Landsberger, *Hawthorne Revisited* (Ithaca, N.Y.: Cornell University Press, 1958).

Hay, Edward N. (1891-1958), editor and publisher of the *Personnel Journal* from 1947 to 1958 who pioneered the development of modern testing and job evaluation techniques. Major works include: *Manual of Job Evaluation: Procedures of Job Analysis And Appraisal*, with Eugene J. Benge and Samuel L. H. Burk (N.Y.: Harper & Bros., 1941); *Psychological Aids in the Selection of Workers*, with G. W. Wadsworth, Jr. D. W. Cook and C. L. Shartle (N.Y.: American Management Association, 1641).
See also HAY SYSTEM.

Hay Guide Chart-Profile Method: *see* HAY SYSTEM.

Haymarket Riot, the 19th century's most famous confrontation between police and labor demonstrators. On May 3, 1886, police killed four strikers at the McCormick Harvesting Machine Company in Chicago. In response, labor leaders called a protest meeting for the night of May 4, 1886, in Chicago's Haymarket Square. Police arrived toward the end of the meeting and ordered the crowd to disperse. Suddenly, a bomb exploded among the approximately 180 police. Sixty-six were wounded; seven would die. The uninjured police opened fire on the crowd. Estimates of the killed vary from several to ten; of the wounded from 50 to 200. The identity of the bomb thrower was never determined. In the midst of an hysterical atmosphere, eight labor leaders were tried and convicted of murder on the grounds that they had conspired with or aided an unknown murderer. Four were hanged on November 11, 1887. One committed suicide, and the other three remained in prison until pardoned by Illinois Governor John P. Altgeld in 1893. For histories, *see* Frank Harris, *Bomb: The Haymarket Riot* (Chicago: University of Chicago Press, 1963); Wendy Snyder, *Haymarket* (Cambridge, Mass.: M. I. T. Press, 1970).

Hay System, Edward N. Hay developed one of the best known job evaluation methods. Essentially a modification of the factor-comparison technique, Hay's Guide Chart-Profile Method is based on three factors: know-how, problemsolving and accountability. Many organizations have adopted variations of the Hay System for job evaluation. For an analysis, *see* Charles W. G. Van Horn, "The Hay Guide Chart-Profile Method," *Handbook of Wage and Salary Administration*, Milton L. Rock (ed.), (N.Y.: McGraw-Hill, 1972).

Haywood, William Dudley (1869-1928), nicknamed BIG BILL HAYWOOD, a founder of the Industrial Workers of the World and one of the most violent and radical of the early labor leaders. For a biography, *see* Joseph R. Conlin, *Big Bill Haywood and the Radical Union Movement* (Syracuse: Syracuse University Press, 1969).

hazard pay, compensation paid to an employee above regular wages for work that is potentially dangerous to his/her health.

Hazelwood School District* v. *United States, 433 U.S. 299 (1977), U.S. Supreme Court case, which held that a public employer did not violate Title VII of the Civil Rights Act of 1964 if, from March 24, 1972 (when Title VII ecame effective for public employers), all of its employment decisions were made in a "non-discriminatory way," even if it had "formerly maintained an all-white workforce by purposefully excluding Negroes."

HBR: *see* HARVARD BUSINESS REVIEW.

HBS: *see* HARVARD BUSINESS SCHOOL.

HCMW: *see* LABOR ORGANIZATION, Hatters, Cap and Millinery Workers International Union, United.

headhunter, also called CORPORATE HEADHUNTER and PEOPLE PLUCKER, slang terms for executive recruiter. For an account of the business, *see* Allan J. Cox, *Confessions of a Corporate Headhunter* (N.Y.: Trident Press, 1973). What should you do if a headhunter calls? According to Herbert E. Meyer, "The Headhunters Come Upon Golden Days, *Fortune* (October 1978),

> for those who have always wondered what is the proper response to this kind of telephone call, headhunters have a stock piece of advice: get up and close your office door. The purpose of the call is first, to verify that you are who the headhunter thinks you are, and second, to arrange a meeting if you are at all interested in considering a change of jobs. Not surprisingly, headhunters say that most people they call are willing, if not eager, to meet them.

health benefits, total health service and health insurance programs that an organization provides for its employees.

health insurance, group: *see* GROUP INSURANCE.

Health Maintenance Organization (HMO), according to Robert Gumbiner, "Selection of a Health Maintenance Organization," *Personnel Journal* (August 1978), a HMO is

> a nonprofit organization which maintains clinics and hospitals and supplies physicians, health care specialists and medication at little or no additional cost. It differs from indemnity insurance in that for a monthly fee, total health and medical care are provided. That is, indemnity insurance pays only in case of illness or accident, but an HMO allows a person to see a doctor for preventive care, and without extra charges. (Since an HMO commits itself to paying all medical expenses, it is in its own interest to keep people healthy.) Thus its subscribers are sometimes able to avoid serious illness.

Also see Jeffery Cohelan, "HMO's—How They Can Keep the Lid on Escalating Health Care Costs," *Pension World* (March 1978).

Health Maintenance Organization Act of 1973, federal statute that sets standards of qualifications for an HMO and mandates that employers of 25 or more who currently offer a medical benefit plan offer the additional option of joining a qualified HMO, if one exists in the area.

hearing, legal or quasi-legal proceeding, in which arguments, witnesses, or evidence are heard by a judical officer or administrative body.

hearing examiner/officer: *see* ADMINISTRATIVE LAW JUDGE.

HEARS: *see* HIGHER EDUCATION ADMINISTRATION REFERRAL SERVICE.

Hebrew Actors Union, Inc.: *see* LABOR ORGANIZATION, under Actors and Artistes of America, Associated.

Heinz **case:** *see* H.J. HEINZ CO. V. NATIONAL LABOR RELATIONS BOARD.

helping interview, interview that consists of a genuine dialogue between the interviewer and the interviewee; the interviewer is an empathic listener rather than a mere technician recording information. *See* Alfred Benjamin, *The Helping Interview* (Boston: Houghton Mifflin, 2nd ed., 1974).

Helvering **v.** *Davis,* 301 U.S. 619 (1937), U.S. Supreme Court case, which held constitutional the Social Security Act of 1935.

Herzberg, Frederick (1923-   ), a major influence on the conceptualization of job design, especially job enrichment. His motivation–hygiene or two-factor theory of motivation is the point of departure and a common reference point for analyses of the subject. Major works include: *The Motivation To Work*, with Bernard Mausner and Barbara Snyderman (N.Y.: John Wiley & Sons, 1959); *Work And The Nature of Man* (Cleveland: World Publishers, 1966); and *The Managerial Choice* (Homewood, Ill.: Dow Jones-Irwin, 1976).

See also JOB ENRICHMENT and MOTIVATION–HYGIENE THEORY.

heuristic, short-cut process of reasoning that searches for a satisfactory, rather than an optimal, solution to a very large, complex and/or poorly defined problem. *See* Charles L. Hinkle and Alfred A. Kuehn "Heuristic Models: Mapping the Maze for Management," *California Management Review* (Fall 1967).

HFIA: *see* LABOR ORGANIZATION, Asbestos Workers, International Association of Heat and Frost Insulators and.

HFL: *see* HARVARD FATIGUE LABORATORY.

Hicklin **v.** *Orbeck,* 57 L. Ed. 2d 397 (1978), U.S. Supreme Court case, which held unconstitutional an Alaska law granting employment preferences to Alaskan residents. The law violated the constitutional requirement that states grant all U.S. citizens the same "privileges and immunities" granted to its own citizens.

hidden agenda, unannounced or unconscious goals, personal needs, expectations, and strategies that each individual brings with his/her participation in a group. Parallel to the group's open agenda are the private or hidden agendas of each of its members.

hidden unemployed: *see* DISCOURAGED WORKERS.

hierarchy, any ordering of persons, things, or ideas by rank or level. *See* Arnold S. Tannenbaum, *Hierarchy in Organizations* (San Francisco: Jossey-Bass, 1974).

Higher Education Administration Referral Service (HEARS), nonprofit organization that helps institutions locate qualified individuals for non-academic administrative vacancies. HEARS is co-sponsored by 19 major higher-education associations.

> HEARS
> Suite 510
> One Dupont Circle
> Washington, DC 20036
> (202) 857-0710

Hill, Joe (1879-1915), born JOEL EMMANUEL HAGGLUND, emigrated from Sweden to America in 1902 and became active as a union organizer. After joining the radical Industrial Workers of the World (IWW), he began writing "folk" songs dealing with union themes. In 1915, he was executed in Utah after being convicted on circumstantial evidence for the murder of a grocer and his son. His death made him a martyr to the union cause. One of his last requests was to be buried in another state, because "I don't want to be found dead in Utah." For accounts of his life and legend, *see* Vernon H. Jensen, "The Legend of Joe Hill," *Industrial and Labor Relations Review* (April 1951); Gibbs M. Smith, *Joe Hill* (Salt Lake City: University of Utah Press, 1969).

Hillman, Sydney (1887-1946), president of the Amalgamated Clothing Workers from its creation in 1913 to his death. A close political advisor of President Franklin D. Roosevelt, Hillman was the Sydney in FDR's famous order to "clear it with Sydney." For a biography, *see* Matthew Josephson, *Sidney Hillman: Statesman of American Labor* (Garden City, N.Y.: Doubleday, 1952).

Hines v. Anchor Motor Freight, 424, U.S. 554 (1976), U.S. Supreme Court case, which held that, if a union member can prove that he was erroneously discharged and that his union's representation tainted the decision of the arbitration committee which upheld the discharge, then he is entitled to take legal action against both the employer and the union.

hire: *see* EMPLOY.

hiring, preferential: *see* PREFERENTIAL HIRING.

hiring hall, also called UNION HIRING HALL and CENTRAL HIRING HALL, employment office usually run by the union to coordinate the referral of its members to jobs. Sometimes hiring halls are operated jointly with management and/or state government assistance. Hiring halls are especially important for casual or seasonal trades (such as construction and maritime work). For an analysis of the hiring-hall process, *see* Stuart B. Philpott, "The Union Hiring Hall as a Labor Market: A Sociological Analysis, *British Journal of Industrial Relations* (March 1965). For a history, *see* Philip Ross, "Origin of the Hiring Hall in Construction," *Industrial Relations* (October 1972).

hiring rate: *see* ACCESSION RATE and ENTRANCE RATE.

Hispanic Employment Program: *see* SPANISH SPEAKING PROGRAM.

histogram, bar graph of a frequency distribution.

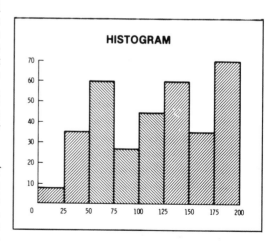

hit the bricks, slang phrase for going out on strike.

H. J. Heinz Co. v. *National Labor Relations Board*, 311 U.S. 514 (1941), U.S. Supreme Court case, which held that a company had to sign a collective bargaining agreement, even when wages, hours and other terms and conditions of employment were not in dispute.

HMO: *see* HEALTH MAINTENANCE ORGANIZATION.

Hobbs Act: *see* ANTI-RACKETEERING ACT OF 1934.

Hockey League Players Association, National: *see* LABOR ORGANIZATION.

Hodgson, James D. (1915-   ), Secretary of Labor from 1970 to 1973.

Hoffa, Jimmy, full name JAMES RIDDLE HOFFA (1913-1975), president of the International Brotherhood of Teamsters from 1957 to 1971 who was convicted of jury tampering and other charges in 1964. After exhausting appeals, he entered federal prison in 1967 to begin serving a 13-year term. His sentence was commuted by President Richard M. Nixon on condition that he not participate in union affairs until 1980. In 1975, Hoffa "disappeared" and is presumed dead. For an autobiography, *see The Trials of Jimmy Hoffa:* (Chicago: H. Regnery Co., 1970); For a biography, *see* Walter Sheridan, *The Fall and Rise of Jimmy Hoffa* (N.Y.: Saturday Review Press, 1972). *See also* Steven Brill, *The Teamsters* (N.Y.: Simon and Schuster, 1978)

Holden v. *Hardy*, 169 U.S. 336 (1898), U.S. Supreme Court case, which held that a state, in exercising its police power to protect the public health, had the right to legislate hours of work.

holiday pay, premium rate, usually provided for in union contracts, paid for work performed on holidays.

Hollerith cards, punched cards used by computers, which were first developed by Herman Hollerith of the U.S. Bureau of the Census in 1889.

Homans, George C. (1910-   ), industrial sociologist, best known for his early application of "systems" to organizational analysis. Major works include: *An Introduction to Pareto: His Sociology*, with C. P. Curtis, Jr., (N.Y.: Knopf, 1934); *The Fatigue of Workers: Its Relation to Industrial Production*, (N.Y.: Reinhold Publishing Company, 1941); *The Human Group* (N.Y.: Harcourt Brace Jovano-

vich, 1950); *Sentiments and Activities*, (N.Y.: The Free Press, 1962); *Nature of Social Science*, (N.Y.: Harcourt Brace Jovanovich, 1967); *Social Behavior: Its Elementary Forms* (N.Y.: Harcourt Brace Jovanovish, rev. ed., 1974).

homeostasis, maintenance of equilibrium among bodily and systemic processes. The normal functioning of the body or system is dependent upon maintaining such internal stability. For an introduction to the concept, *see* L. L. Langley, *Homeostatis* (N.Y.: Reinhold Publishing, 1965).

Homestead Strike, in July 1892, the members of the Amalgamated Association of Iron, Steel and Tin Workers struck the Homestead (Pennsylvania) plant of the Carnegie Steel Company (forerunner of the United States Steel Corporation). The company thereupon hired 300 Pinkerton detectives to enable it to import strikebreakers. The strikers met the Pinkertons as they were arriving. After a 12-hour "battle," the Pinkertons, with three dead and dozens wounded, literally ran up a white flag, laid down their arms, and were allowed to go back to Pittsburgh. A week later, 8,000 state militia opened the plant to strikebreakers. By November 1892, the union was smashed—2,000 strikebreakers were at work and only 800 of the 4,000 who had gone out on strike were rehired. Unionism in the steel industry suffered a setback that would last for decades. For the history of the strike, *see* R. I. Finch, "Unionism in the Iron and Steel Industry," *Political Science Quarterly*, Vol. 24 (1909); Arthur C. Burgoyne, *Homestead* (N.Y.: Augustus M. Kelley, 1893; reprinted 1969).

hometown plan, voluntary affirmative action plan for the construction crafts and trades developed by a local construction industry, usually in cooperation with the U.S. Department of Labor.

honcho, slang word for a boss or any person in charge of a work detail. U.S. soldiers first adopted the term from the Japanese word *hancho* ("group leader").

honest graft also DISHONEST GRAFT, the classic distinction between the two genre of graft was made by George Washington Plunkitt, a politico associated with New York's Tammany Hall early in this century. *Dishonest graft*, as the name implies involves bribery, blackmailing, extortion and other obviously illegal activities. As for *honest graft*, let Plunkitt speak:

Just let me explain by examples. My party's in power in the city, and it's goin' to undertake a lot of public improvements. Well, I'm tipped off, say, that they're going to lay out a new park at a certain place.

I see my opportunity and I take it, I go to that place and I buy up all the land I can in the neighborhood. Then the board of this or that makes its plan public, and there is a rush to get my land, which nobody cared particular for before.

Ain't it perfectly honest to charge a good price and make a profit on my investment and foresight? Of course, it is. Well, that's honest graft.

For more of Plunkitt's wisdom, *see* William Riordon, *Plunkitt of Tammany Hall* (N.Y.: E. P. Dutton & Co., 1963).

honeymoon period, that period of time immediately following a major agreement between management and labor when both sides may seek to de-emphasize the normal difficulties inherent in their relationships.

HOOI: *see* HALL OCCUPATIONAL ORIENTATION INVENTORY.

hooking, also ROPING, slang term for convincing a worker to spy on fellow union members, usually by means of bribery or blackmail.

horizontal communication: *see* COMMUNICATION.

horizontal loading: *see* JOB LOADING.

horizontal occupational mobility: *see* OCCUPATIONAL MOBILITY.

horizontal promotion, advancement for an employee within his/her basic job category. For example, a promotion from Window Washer I to Window Washer II or from Junior Accountant to Intermediate Accountant.

horizontal union: *see* CRAFT UNION.

horizontal work group, work group that contains individuals whose positions are essentially the same in terms of rank, prestige, and level of skill.

Horseshoers of the United States and Canada, International Union of Journeymen: *see* LABOR ORGANIZATION.

hospitalization, group insurance program that pays employees for all or part of their hospital, nursing, surgical, and other related medical expenses due to injury or illness to them or their dependents.

hot-cargo provisions, contract clauses that allow workers to refuse to work on or handle "unfair goods" or "hot cargo"—products coming from a factory where there is a labor dispute. The Labor–Management Reporting and Disclosure (Landrum–Griffin) Act of 1959 outlawed such provisions (except for those affecting suppliers or subcontractors in construction work and jobbers in the garment industry). For a legal analysis, *see* Paul A. Brinker, "Hot Cargo Cases Since 1958," *Labor Law Journal* (September 1971).

See also UNFAIR LABOR PRACTICES (UNIONS).

Hotel and Restaurant Employees and Bartenders International Union: *see* LABOR ORGANIZATION.

Houghton Mifflin Company: *see* TEST PUBLISHERS.

hourly-rate workers, employees whose weekly pay is determined solely by the actual number of hours worked during a week.

house account, also called NO-COMMISSION ACCOUNT, account serviced by branch or home office executives. Usually no credit is given nor commissions paid when sales are made to such accounts.

housekeeping agency: *see* AUXILIARY AGENCY.

House of Labor, informal term for the AFL–CIO. *See* AMERICAN FEDERATION OF LABOR–CONGRESS OF INDUSTRIAL ORGANIZATIONS.

house organ also INTERNAL HOUSE ORGAN and EXTERNAL HOUSE ORGAN, any publication—magazine, newspaper, newsletter, etc.—produced by an organization to keep its employees informed about the activities of the organization and its employees. *Internal house organs* are directed primarily to an organization's employees; *external house organs* find a wider distribution as part of the organization's public relations program. *See* Jim Mann, "Is Your House Organ A Vital Organ?" *Personnel Journal* (September 1977).

housework, domestic chores that one performs or has performed in one's domicile. *See* Ann Oakley, *The Sociology of Housework* (N.Y.: Pantheon, 1975).

housing allowance, special compensation, consisting of a flat rate or a salary percentage, for the purpose of subsidizing the living expenses of an employee, usually paid only to employees sent overseas.

Howard Johnson Co., Inc. v. Detroit Local Joint Executive Board, Hotel and Restaurant Employees, 417 U.S. 249 (1974), U.S. Supreme Court case, which held that one company, upon purchasing another, was not required to arbitrate the extent of its obligations to the purchased company's union under the so-called "successorship" doctrine announced in the case of *John Wiley & Sons v. Livingston*, 376 U.S. 543 (1964). In the *Wiley* case, the court held that a successor employer may be compelled, under certain circumstances, to arbitrate the question of his obligations toward the employees covered by his predecessor's labor contract. *See* Evan J. Spelfogel, "A Corporate Seccessor's Obligation to Honor His Predecessor's Labor Contract: The Howard Johnson Case" *Labor Law Journal* (May 1974).

See also JOHN WILEY & SONS V. LIVINGSTON.

HREU: *see* LABOR ORGANIZATION, Hotel and Restaurant Employees and Bartenders International Union.

HRM: *see* HUMAN RESOURCES MANAGEMENT.

H.R. 10 Plan: *see* KEOGH PLAN.

Hudgens v. National Labor Relations Board, 424 U.S. 507 (1976), U.S. Supreme Court case, which held that pickets did not have a 1st Amendment right to enter a shopping center (private property) for the purpose of advertising a strike against their employer.

human capital, a concept that views employees as assets in the same sense as financial capital. It presupposes that an investment in human potential will yield significant returns for the organization. *See* Theodore W. Schultz, *Investment in Human Capital* (N.Y.: The Free Press, 1971); Thomas K. Connellan, "Management as a Capital Investment," *Human Resource Management* (Summer 1972).

human-factors engineering, also called ERGONOMICS, design for human use. The objective of human factors engineering, usually called ergonomics in Europe, is to increase the effective use of physical objects and facilities by people at work, while at the same time attending to concerns such as health, safety, job satisfaction, etc. These objectives are sought by the systematic application of relevant information about human behavior to the design of the things (usually machines) that people use and to the environments in which they work. The leading text is Ernest J. McCormick, *Human Factors Engineering* (N.Y.: McGraw-Hill 3rd ed., 1970). *Also see* Roy J. Shepard, *Men at Work: Applications of Ergonomics to Performance and Design* (Springfield, Ill.: Charles C Thomas, 1974).

human relations, discipline concerned with the application of the behavioral sciences to the analysis and understanding of human behavior in organizations.

Personnel operations still tend to live in the shadow of the old-style human-relations approach to management that emphasized sympathetic attitudes on the part of managers. Its critics contended that the human-relations approach (most popular during the late 1940s and 1950s) was little more than a gimmick—that there was sincere interest in the workers only to the extent that they could be manipulated for management's ends. The goal was to adjust the worker—the same old interchangeable part of the scientific management movement—so that he or she would be content in the industrial situation, not to change the situation so that the workers would find more contentment in his or her work.

Today, human relations is in a more mature period. Like the caterpillar that turned into the butterfly, it simply evolved into something much more desirable. By expropriating advances in the behavioral sciences as its own, it grew into its current definition. For texts, *see* Keith Davis, *Human Behavior at Work: Human Relations and Organizational Behavior* (N.Y.: McGraw-Hill, 1972); Aubrey C. Sanford, *Human Relations: Theory and Practice* (Columbus, Ohio: Charles E. Merrill, 1973).

Human Relations, monthly journal founded on the belief that social scientists in all fields should work toward integration in their attempts to understand the complexities of human problems. Articles tend to be theoretical analyses of human interactions in the workplace, as well as society in general.

Editorial Address:
Coordinating Editor
Human Relations
University of Pennsylvania
Wharton School
Management and Behavioral Science Center
Philadelphia, PA 19174

Subscriptions:
Plenum Publishing Corp.
227 West 17th St.
New York, NY 10011

Human Relations, Mr.: *see* DAVIS, KEITH.

human resource accounting, concept that views the employees of an organization as capital assets similar to plant and equipment. While the concept is intuitively attractive, calculating the value, replacement cost, and depreciation of human assets poses significant problems. Consequently, it is viewed with considerable skepticism by managers and accountants. For the methodology, *see* Eric G. Flamholtz, "Human Resources Ac-

counting: Measuring Positional Replacement Costs," *Human Resource Management* (Spring 1973); Robert Wright, "Managing Man as a Capital Asset," *Personnel Journal* (April 1970). For a text, *see* Edwin H. Caplan and Stephen Landekich, *Human Resource Accounting: Past, Present and Future* (N.Y.: National Association of Accountants, 1974).

Human Resource Management, previously titled MANAGEMENT OF PERSONNEL QUARTERLY, quarterly whose articles deal with a variety of topics related to personnel practices and human resource management. Most articles are written by academics and tend to be either theoretical analyses and/or reports of research.

Human Resource Management
Graduate School of Business Administration
University of Michigan
Ann Arbor, MI 48109

Human Resource Planning, quarterly journal of the Human Resource Planning Society, which is devoted to the advancement of the practice, technology, and theory of planning for human resources.

Human Resource Planning
P.O. Box 2553
Grand Central Station
New York, NY 10017

Human Resource Planning Society, nonprofit organization devoted to the advancement of the practice, technology, and theory of planning for human resources. Its quarterly journal is *Human Resource Planning*.

Human Resource Planning Society
P.O. Box 2553
Grand Central Station
New York, NY 10017

human resources, also called MANPOWER, general term for all of the employees in an organization or the workers in a society. It is gradually replacing the more sexist "manpower."

Human Resources Abstracts, formerly POVERTY AND HUMAN RESOURCES ABSTRACTS, quarterly publication that contains abstracts of current literature on human, social, and manpower problems and solutions ranging from slum rehabilitation and job development training to compensatory education, minority group problems, and rural poverty.

Human Resources Abstracts
Sage Publications, Inc.
275 South Beverly Drive
Beverly Hills, CA 90212

human resources administration, increasingly

Model for Measurement of Human Resource Replacement Costs

SOURCE: Eric G. Flamholtz, "Human Resources Accounting: Measuring Positional Replacement Costs," *Human Resource Management* (Spring 1973), p. 11.

popular euphemism for the management of social welfare programs. Many jurisdictions that had Departments of Welfare have replaced them with Departments of Human Resources.

human resources management (HRM), although often used synonomously with personnel management, HRM transcends traditional personnel concerns, taking the most expansive view of the personnel department's mandate. Instead of viewing the personnel function as simply that collection of desparate duties necessary to recruit, pay, and discharge employees, a HRM approach assumes that personnel's appropriate mission is the maximum utilization of its organization's human resources. Recent textbooks are beginning to reflect this larger vision of the personnel function. *See* Andrew F. Sikula, *Personnel Administration and Human Resources Management* (N.Y.: John Wiley, 1976); William P. Anthony and Edward A. Nicholson, *Management of Human Resources: A Systems Approach to Personnel Management* (Columbus, Ohio: Grid, Inc., 1977); Lawrence A. Klatt, Robert G. Murdick and Fred E. Schuster, *Human Resources Management: A Behavioral Systems Approach* (Homewood, Ill.: Richard D. Irwin, 1978); Richard B. Peterson and Lane Tracy, *Systematic Management of Human Re-*

sources (Reading, Mass.: Addison-Wesley, 1979).

human resources planning, also called MANPOWER PLANNING, there is no universally accepted definition of what human resources planning (or its more sexist equivalent, "manpower planning") is or consensus on what activities should be associated with it. Organizations claiming that they do such planning appear to use a wide variety of methods to approach their own unique problems.

Historically, management planning was most associated with the Johnson Administration's Great Society Programs of the 1960s. It was and remains an integral part of numerous government programs whose objective was to affect the labor market in order to improve the employment status and welfare of individuals. All such programs have a macro focus—they deal with the aggregate labor force of the country (all employed and unemployed individuals). At roughly the same time of the new management initiatives of the Johnson Administration, parallel thinking on human resources planning began to emerge at the firm and organizational level. Both situations involve projecting and managing the supply and demand of human resources, only at different levels. Both are concerned with future demand aspects; that

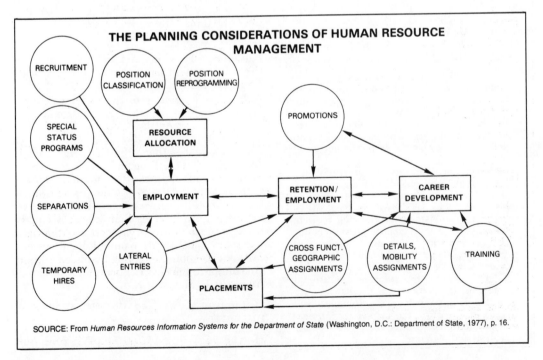

THE PLANNING CONSIDERATIONS OF HUMAN RESOURCE MANAGEMENT

SOURCE: From *Human Resources Information Systems for the Department of State* (Washington, D.C.: Department of State, 1977), p. 16.

is, what will be the requirements for the future work force. At the macro level, this means projecting what skills will be in demand to service the economy. At the micro level, this entails projecting specific requirements for the work force of the organization, or what quantities and qualities of personnel will be needed to carry out organizational objectives. Both levels are concerned with future supply aspects. At the macro level this means that projections must be made on what the national work force will consist of in terms of future skills, both surpluses and deficits. For the micro level, the organization must forecast what its future force work will consist of as well as evaluating its competitive position in order to decide what quantities and qualities of personnel it can encourage to enter the organization as replacements.

Some of the better works on human resources planning include: D. J. Bell, *Planning Corporate Manpower* (London: Longman Group, 1974); Elmer H. Burack and James H. Walker, *Manpower Planning and Programming* (Boston: Allyn and Bacon, 1972); Edward B. Jakubauskas and Neil A. Palomba, *Manpower Economics* (Reading, Mass.: Addison-Wesley, 1973); and Ray A. Killian, *Human Resource Management* (N.Y.: American Management Association, 1976).

human resources planning models, also called MANPOWER PLANNING MODELS, according to Richard C. Grinold and Kneale T. Marshall, *Manpower Planning Models* (N.Y.: Elsevier North-Holland, 1977), personnel planning models use systems analysis to

(a) *Forecast* the future manpower requirements that will be satisfied by the current inventory of personnel; forecast the future manpower budget commitments represented by the current stock of personnel. (b) *Analyze* the impact of proposed changes in policy, such as changes in promotion or retirement rules, changes in salary and benefits, changes in transfers into and out of the organization, and changes in the organization's rate of growth. (c) *Test* the rationale of historical policy for consistency, and establish the relations among operating rules of thumb. (d) *Explore* regions of possible policy changes and allow a planner to experiment with and perhaps discover new policies. (e) *Understand* the basic flow process, and thus aid in assessing the relative operational problems. (f) *Design* systems that balance the flows of manpower, requirements, and costs. (g) *Structure* the manpower information system in a manner suitable for policy analysis and planning.

human resources requirements analysis, also called MANPOWER REQUIREMENTS ANALYSIS, analysis and projection of (a) the personnel movements and (b) the numbers and kinds of vacancies to be expected during each stage of management's workforce plan. According to the Office of Personnel Management, the essential steps in manpower requirements analysis are:

- *First*, to estimate what portion of the workforce present at the start of the planning period, or hired during the period, will leave their positions during the period.
- *Second*, to estimate how many of these position leavers will move to other positions in the workforce during the period and how many will leave the service entirely.
- *Third*, to estimate the positions to be occupied by in-service movers at the end of the planning period.
- *Fourth*, by comparison of this retained workforce with the workforce specified in management's workforce plan, to identify the numbers and kinds of positions to be filled during the planning period.

human resources utilization, also called MANPOWER UTILIZATION, general terms for the selection, development and placement of human resources within an economic or organizational system in order to use these resources in the most efficient manner. *See* Edward B. Jakubauskas and Neil A. Palomba, *Manpower Economics* (Reading, Mass.: Addison-Wesley, 1973); Edward J. Giblin and Oscar A. Ornati, "Optimizing the Utilization of Human Resources," *Organizational Dynamics* (Autumn 1976).

Humphrey–Hawkins Act of 1977, formally the FULL EMPLOYMENT AND BALANCED GROWTH ACT OF 1977, federal statute that asserts it is the policy of the federal government to reduce overall unemployment to a rate of four percent by 1983, while reducing inflation to a rate of three percent. The act explicitly states that it is the "right of all Americans able, willing and seeking to work" to have "full opportunities for useful paid employment." However, the discussion of the act in the *Congressional Record* of December 6, 1977, states that "there is clearly no right to sue for legal protection of the right to a job." The popular name of the act comes from its co-sponsors, former Senator Hubert H. Humphrey (D-Minn.) and Representative Augustus F. Hawkins (D-Calif.)

Hutcheson case: *see* UNITED STATES V. HUTCHESON, ET AL.

Hutcheson, William L. (1874-1953), president

of the Brotherhood of Carpenters from 1915 to 1953. For a biography, *see* Maxwell C. Raddock, *Portrait of An American Labor Leader: William L. Hutcheson* (N.Y.: American Institute of Social Science, Inc., 1955).

hypothesis, testable assertion, statement, or proposition about the relationship between two variables that are in some way related to each other. For example, a personnel manager might hypothesize that a specific kind of job performance can be predicted from a particular kind of knowledge about an applicant (such as scores on tests or grades in school). Hypotheses of this kind are proven—one way or another—by validation studies.

I

IAFF: *see* LABOR ORGANIZATION, Fire Fighters, International Association of.

IAG: *see* INTERAGENCY ADVISORY GROUP.

IAPB: *see* INTERNATIONAL ASSOCIATION OF PROFESSIONAL BUREAUCRATS.

IAPES: *see* INTERNATIONAL ASSOCIATION OF PERSONNEL IN EMPLOYMENT SECURITY.

IAPW: *see* INTERNATIONAL ASSOCIATION OF PERSONNEL WOMEN.

IAS: *see* LABOR ORGANIZATION, Siderographers, International Association of.

IATC: *see* LABOR ORGANIZATION, Tool Craftsmen, International Association of.

IATSE: *see* LABOR ORGANIZATION, Theatrical Stage Employees and Moving Picture Machine Operators of the United States and Canada, International Alliance of.

IBEW: *see* LABOR ORGANIZATION, Electrical Workers, International Brotherhood of.

IBFO: *see* LABOR ORGANIZATION, Firemen and Oilers, International Brotherhood of.

IBT: *see* LABOR ORGANIZATION, Teamsters, Chauffeurs, Warehousemen and Helpers of America, International Brotherhood of.

IBT-LWIU: *see* LABOR ORGANIZATION, Laundry, Dry Cleaning and Dye House Workers International Union, *under* Teamsters, Chauffeurs, Warehousemen and Helpers of America, International Brotherhood of.

ICMA: *see* INTERNATIONAL CITY MANAGEMENT ASSOCIATION.

ICMA Retirement Corporation, nonprofit, tax-exempt organization providing a deferred compensation retirement plan for the mobile employees of state and local government. The Retirement Corporation was organized because of the inability of state and local governments to provide retirement security for those types of public servants whose careers require a periodic change in employment from one government or agency to another. State and local governments and agencies may also use the plan as a supplement to existing employee benefit programs.

The plan was developed by the International City Management Association, which underwrote the Retirement Corporation. In recognition of the plan's importance, most of the major public interest and professional associations related to state and local government have become sponsors of the plan.

ICSC: *see* INTERNATIONAL CIVIL SERVICE COMMISSION.

ICW: *see* LABOR ORGANIZATION, Chemical Workers Union, International.

Idaho Public Employees Association: *see* LABOR ORGANIZATION.

IDAHO-SEA: *see* LABOR ORGANIZATION, Idaho State Employees Association.

Idaho State AFL–CIO: *see* AMERICAN FEDERATION OF LABOR–CONGRESS OF INDUSTRIAL ORGANIZATIONS.

idle time, time for which employees are paid but not able to work because of mechanical malfunctions or other factors not within their control.

IDP: *see* INDIVIDUAL DEVELOPMENT PLAN.

ILA: *see* LABOR ORGANIZATION, Longshoremen's Association, International.

ILA-MMP: *see* LABOR ORGANIZATION, Masters, Mates and Pilots, International Organization of, *under* Longshoremen's Association, International.

ILGWU: *see* LABOR ORGANIZATION, Ladies' Garment Workers' Union, International.

illegal aliens, also called UNDOCUMENTED WORKERS, individuals from other countries

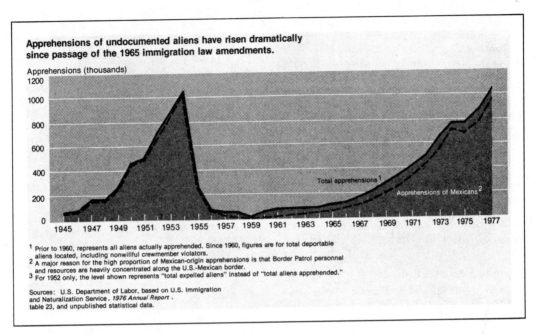

Apprehensions of undocumented aliens have risen dramatically since passage of the 1965 immigration law amendments.

Apprehensions (thousands)

Total apprehensions[1]

Apprehensions of Mexicans[2]

[1] Prior to 1960, represents all aliens actually apprehended. Since 1960, figures are for total deportable aliens located, including nonwillful crewmember violators.
[2] A major reason for the high proportion of Mexican-origin apprehensions is that Border Patrol personnel and resources are heavily concentrated along the U.S.-Mexican border.
[3] For 1952 only, the level shown represents "total expelled aliens" instead of "total aliens apprehended."

Sources: U.S. Department of Labor, based on U.S. Immigration and Naturalization Service, *1976 Annual Report*, table 23, and unpublished statistical data.

who are living/working in the United States unlawfully. The U.S. Department of Labor prefers to refer to these individuals as "undocumented workers." *See* Jose A. Rivera, "Aliens Under the Law: A Legal Perspective," *Employee Relations Law Journal* (Summer 1977).

See also DE CANAS V. BICA.

illegal bargaining items, any proposal made during the collective bargaining process that is expressly forbidden by law. For example, a union shop in a "right-to-work" state.

illegal strike, strike that violates existing law. While most public sector strikes are illegal, so are strikes that violate a contract, that are not properly authorized by the union membership, and that violate a court injunction.

Illinois State AFL–CIO: *see* AMERICAN FEDERATION OF LABOR–CONGRESS OF INDUSTRIAL ORGANIZATIONS.

Illinois State Employees Association: *see* LABOR ORGANIZATION.

ILL-SEA: *see* LABOR ORGANIZATION, Illinois State Employees Association.

ILO: *see* INTERNATIONAL LABOR ORGANIZATION.

ILWU: *see* LABOR ORGANIZATION, Longshoremen's and Warehousemen's Union, International.

IMAGE: *see* LABOR ORGANIZATION, Minnesota Association of Government Employees, Independent.

IMAW: *see* LABOR ORGANIZATION, Molders' and Allied Workers' Union, International.

immediate full vesting, pension plan that entitles an employee to all of the retirement income—both his/her contributions as well as those of his/her company—accrued during his/her time of participation in the plan.

impact theory of discrimination, concept that asserts it is the consequences of employment practices that are relevant, not their intent. Even though an intent is benign, its consequences could foster systemic discrimination.

impasse, a condition that exists during labor–management negotiations when either party feels that no further progress can be made toward reaching a settlement. Impasses are resolved either by strikes or the helpful intervention of neutral third parties. *See* Karl A. Van Asselt, "Impasse Resolution," *Public Administration Review* (March–April 1972).

IMU: *see* LABOR ORGANIZATION, Mailers Union, International.

in-basket exercise, training technique and type of test frequently used in management assessment centers to simulate managerial problems by presenting the subject with an array of written materials (the kinds of items that might accumulate in an "in-basket") so that responses to the various items and problems can be evaluated. *See* F. M. Lopez, Jr., *Evaluating Executive Decision Making—The In-Basket Technique* (N.Y.: American Management Association, 1966); Cabot L. Jaffeee, *Problems in Supervision: An In-Basket Training Exercise* (Reading, Mass.: Addison-Wesley Publishing Co., 1968).

incentive, reward, whether monetary or psychic, that motivates and/or compensates an employee for performance above standard.

incentive awards, also called INCENTIVE SCHEME, formal plan or program designed to motivate individual or group efforts to improve the economy and efficiency of organizational operations. There are essentially two kinds of awards—monetary and honorary.

incentive contract, that portion or clause of a collective bargaining agreement that establishes the terms and conditions of an incentive-wage system.

incentive pay, wage system that rewards a worker for productivity above an established standard.

incentive plan, individual/group: *see* INCENTIVE-WAGE PLAN.

incentive rate, special wage rate for production above a previously fixed standard of performance.

incentive scheme: *see* INCENTIVE AWARD.

incentive-wage plan, also GROUP INCENTIVE PLAN, wage program that has wages rise with increases in productivity. Individual incentive plans are based on the performance of the individual employee while *group incentive plans* are based on the performance of the total work group. For a survey of the relevant research in both the U.S. and the U.K., *see* R. Marriott, *Incentive Payment Systems: A Review of Research and Opinion* (London: Staples, 4th ed., 1971). For a how-to-do-it approach, *see* H. K. Von Kaas, *Making Incentives Work* (N.Y.: American Management Association, 1971). For a critique of their faults, *see* Arch Patton, "Why Incentive Plans Fail," *Harvard Business Review* (May–June 1972).

incidental learning, also called LATENT LEARNING, learning that takes place without formal instruction, intent to learn, or ascertainable motive. The information obtained tends to lie dormant until an occasion for its use arises.

income, indirect: *see* INDIRECT WAGES.

incomes policy, general term for the totality of the federal government's influence upon wages, prices and profits.

incompetence, demonstrated failure of an employee to meet minimum standards of job performance. For the classic analysis of why such people manage to hang in there despite their poor performance, *see* William J. Goode, "The Protection of the Inept," *American Sociological Review* (February 1967).

increment, also called STEP INCREASE, established salary increase between steps of a given salary grade, marking a steady progression from the minimum of the grade to the maximum.

incumbent, person presently serving in a position.

indemnify, act of compensating insured individuals for their losses.

indemnity, insurance contract to reimburse an individual or organization for possible losses of a particular type.

Independent Minnesota Association of Government Employees: *see* LABOR ORGANIZATION, Minnesota Association of Government Employees, Independent.

independent union, union that is not affiliated with the AFL–CIO. The United Auto Workers, the United Mine Workers, and the Teamsters are three of the largest independent unions.

Independent Union of Plant Protection Employees: *see* LABOR ORGANIZATION, Protection Employees, Independent Union of Plant.

Independent Unions, Congress of: *see* LABOR ORGANIZATION.

Independent Watchmen's Association: *see* LABOR ORGANIZATION, Watchmen's Association, Independent.

index of agreement, index, usually expressed as a percentage, showing the extent to which examiners agree on a candidate's scores.

index number, measure of relative value compared with a base figure for the same series. In a time series in index form, the base period usually is set equal to 100, and data for other periods are expressed as percentages of the value in the base period. Most indexes published by government agencies are presently expressed in terms of a 1967 = 100 base.

Index numbers possess a number of advantages over the raw data from which they are derived. First, they facilitate analysis by their simplicity. Second, they are a more useful basis for comparison of changes in data originally expressed in dissimilar units. Third, they permit comparisons over time with some common starting point—the index base period.

Indiana State AFL–CIO: *see* AMERICAN FEDERATION OF LABOR–CONGRESS OF INDUSTRIAL ORGANIZATIONS.

Indiana State Employees Association: *see* LABOR ORGANIZATION.

indirect compensation/income: *see* INDIRECT WAGES.

indirect labor: *see* DIRECT LABOR.

indirect labor costs, loose term for the wages of nonproduction employees.

indirect validity: *see* SYNTHETIC VALIDITY.

indirect wages, also called INDIRECT INCOME and INDIRECT COMPENSATION, nonfinancial benefits employees receive from their work situations—favorable organizational environment, nontaxable benefits, perquisites, and the authority, power, and/or status that may come with their jobs.

individual agreement, also called INDIVIDUAL CONTRACT, formal agreement between a single employee and his/her employer that determines the employee's conditions and terms of employment.

individual bargaining, negotiations between a single employee and his/her employer. Before the advent of modern collective bargaining, individual bargaining prevailed, and the employee was usually bargaining from a position of slight strength.

individual-contract pension trust, pension plan that creates a trust to buy and hold title to employees' individual insurance and/or annuity contracts. The employer makes payments to the trust, which then pays the insurance premiums on its various contracts.

individual development plan (IDP), periodically prepared schedule of developmental experiences, including both work assignments and formal training, designed to meet particular developmental objectives needed to improve current performance and/or to prepare the individual for positions of greater responsibility.

Individual Retirement Account (IRA), the Pension Reform Act of 1974 allows individuals who are not covered by corporate or other pension plans to set up retirement programs—individual retirement accounts—into which they can put aside cash that builds up tax free until retirement. Funds can be invested in savings accounts, mutual funds, annuities, government bonds, etc. Qualified individuals can presently contribute up to 15 percent of their earned income in any one year, not to exceed $1,500. Individuals *may* start withdrawing funds at age 59½ and *must* begin withdrawals by age 70½. Funds are taxed in the year they are withdrawn. *See* James E. Smith, "Individual Retirement Plans: An Expansion of Tax-Favored Retirement Plan Opportunities," *Taxes* (July 1975); L. L. Unthank and Harry M. Behrendt, *What You Should Know About Individual Retirement Accounts* (Homewood, Ill.: Dow Jones-Irwin, 1978).

individual test, testing device designed to be administered (usually by a specially trained person) to only one subject at a time.

IND-SEA: *see* LABOR ORGANIZATION, Indiana State Employees Association.

industrial accident insurance: *see* WORKMEN'S COMPENSATION.

Industrial and Labor Relations Review, scholarly quarterly containing theoretical articles and research reports in the areas of labor–management relations; labor organizations; labor law; politics, government, and industrial relations; international and comparative industrial relations; labor market; income security, insurance, and benefits; labor conditions; manpower; personnel; management; organization; and work performance and satisfaction.

> *Industrial and Labor Relations Review*
> The New York State School of
> Industrial and Labor Relations
> Cornell University
> Ithaca, NY 14853

industrial and organizational psychology: *see* INDUSTRIAL PSYCHOLOGY.

industrial democracy, also PARTICIPATIVE MANAGEMENT, any of a variety of efforts designed to encourage employees to participate in an organization's decisionmaking processes by identifying problems and suggesting solutions to them in a formal manner. While the terms "industrial democracy" and "participative management" tend to be used almost interchangeably, there is a distinction.

Industrial democracy was used as far back as 1897 by Beatrice and Sidney Webb to describe democratic practices within the trade union movement. The term's modern usage to cover innumerable types of joint or cooperative management programs dates from World War I. Then it connoted a scheme to avoid labor-management disputes which might adversely affect war production. Today industrial democracy connotes joint action by management and worker's representatives. *Participative management*, in contrast, connotes cooperative programs that are unilaterally implemented from on high. Nevertheless, both terms seem to be rapidly losing their distinctive connotations. The most comprehensive survey of the state of industrial democracy throughout the world is David Jenkins, *Job Power: Blue and White Collar Democracy* (Garden City, N.Y.: Doubleday, 1973). For a bibliography, *see* Ronald L. Weiher, "Sources on Industrial Democracy," *Harvard Business Review* (September–October 1975). For a review of practices in Sweden, Great Britain and the United States, *see* Nancy Foy and Herman Gadon, "Worker Participation: Contrasts in Three Countries," *Harvard Business Review* (May–June 1976). For more on participative management, *see* William P. Anthony, *Participative Management* (Reading, Mass.: Addison-Wesley, 1978).

See also SCANLON PLAN and WORKERS' COUNCILS.

industrial engineering, defined by the American Institute of Industrial Engineers as being

> concerned with the design, improvement, and installation of integrated systems of men, materials and equipment; drawing upon specialized knowledge and skill in the mathematical, physical, and social sciences together with the principles and methods of engineering analysis and design, to specify, predict, and evaluate the results to be obtained from such systems.

A basic reference is: H. B. Maynard (ed.), *Industrial Engineering Handbook* (N.Y.: McGraw-Hill, 3rd ed., 1971).

industrial gerontology: *see* GERIATRICS.

industrial hygiene, that branch of preventive medicine devoted to protecting the health of industrial workers.

Industrial Management, a bimonthly that publishes both theoretical and practical articles/reports covering those areas of management and social science relevant to industry.

Industrial Management
Industrial Management Society
570 Northwest Highway
Des Plaines, IL 60016

industrial medicine, that branch of medicine that is concerned with protecting workers from hazards in the workplace and with dealing with health problems/emergencies that may occur during working hours.

industrial paternalism: *see* PATERNALISM.

industrial psychiatry: *see* OCCUPATIONAL PSYCHIATRY.

industrial psychology, also called OCCUPATIONAL PSYCHOLOGY, INDUSTRIAL AND ORGANIZATIONAL PSYCHOLOGY/, and I/O PSYCHOLOGY, industrial or occupational psychology has traditionally been concerned with those aspects of human behavior related to work organizations; its focus has been on the basic relations in organizations between (1) employees and their co-workers, (2) employees and machines, and (3) employees and the organization. Because the term industrial psychology holds a restrictive connotation, the field is increasingly referred to as industrial and organizational psychology or I/O Psychology. For the most comprehensive summary of the state-of-the-art, *see* Marvin D. Dunnette (ed.), *Handbook of Industrial and Organizational Psychology* (Chicago: Rand McNally, 1976).

Industrial Psychology, Inc.: *see* TEST PUBLISHERS.

industrial relations, generally used to refer to all matters of mutual concern to employers and employees and their representatives. In a more technical sense, its use should be limited to labor–management relationships in private sector manufacturing organizations.

Industrial Relations, this thrice-yearly journal publishes scholarly articles and symposia on all aspects of the employment relationship, with special attention given to pertinent developments in the fields of labor economics, sociology, psychology, political science and law.

Industrial Relations
Institute of Industrial Relations
University of California
Berkeley, CA 94720

industrial relations common law: *see* COMMON LAW OF THE SHOP.

Industrial Relations Law Journal, a quarterly dedicated to scholarly analysis and comments on issues and developments in the field of industrial relations. Published by the students of the School of Law of the University of California, Berkeley, this is the only "law review" devoted exclusively to industrial relations.

Industrial Relations Law Journal
Boalt Hall, Room 1
School of Law
University of California
Berkeley, CA 94720

industrial relations research: *see* PERSONNEL RESEARCH.

Industrial Relations Research Association (IRRA), private organization of 4,500 members formed in 1947 to encourage and disseminate research on industrial relations.

IRRA
7226 Social Science Building
University of Wisconsin
Madison, WI 53706
(608) 262-2762

industrial revolution, a very general term that refers to a society's change from an agrarian to an industrial economy. The Industrial Revolution of the Western world is considered to have begun in England in the 18th century. For the case that it actually began much earlier, *see* Jean Gimpel, *The Industrial Revolution of the Middle Ages* (N.Y.: Holt, Rinehart and Winston, 1976).

industrial sociology: *see* OCCUPATIONAL SOCIOLOGY.

Industrial Test, Flanagan: *see* FLANAGAN INDUSTRIAL TEST.

Industrial Trade Unions, National Organization of: *see* LABOR ORGANIZATION.

Industrial Training, International: *see* JOURNAL OF EUROPEAN INDUSTRIAL TRAINING.

industrial union, also called VERTICAL UNION, union whose members work in the same industry and encompass a whole range of skilled and unskilled occupations. *See* Harold W. Aurand, *From the Molly Maguires to the United Mine Workers: The Social Ecology of an Industrial Union, 1869-1897* (Phila.: Temple University Press, 1971).

Industrial Union of Marine and Shipbuilding Workers of America: *see* LABOR ORGANIZATION, Marine and Shipbuilding Workers of America, Industrial Union of.

Industrial Workers of America, International Union Allied *see* LABOR ORGANIZATION.

Industrial Workers of the World (IWW) nicknamed WOBBLIES, radical U.S. union whose main goal was to replace capitalism with a worker's democracy. It had its greatest strength before World War I, but most of its waning membership joined the American Communist Party after it was organized in 1919. For histories, *see* Melvyn Dubofsky, *We Shall Be All: A History of the Industrial Workers of the World* (Westminster, Md.: Quadrangle Books, 1969); Patrick Renshaw, *Wobblies: The Story of Syndicalism in the United States* (Garden City, N.Y.: Doubleday, 1967).

Industrial Workers Union, National: *see* LABOR ORGANIZATION.

industry-wide bargaining, collective bargaining that results in a single master agreement negotiated by all of the major employers in an industry and one or more unions who represent workers throughout the industry.

inequity theory, also EQUITY THEORY, most fully developed by J. Stacy Adams (he premised his work upon Leon Festinger's theory of cognitive dissonance), who holds that inequity exists for Worker A whenever his/her perceived job inputs and outcomes are inconsistent with Worker B's job inputs and outcomes. Inequity would exist if a person perceived that he/she was working much harder than another person who received the same pay. Adams suggests that the presence of inequity creates tension within Person A to reduce the inequity by, for example, increasing (or decreasing) one's efforts if it is perceived to be low (or high) relative to others' work effort. *See* J. Stacy Adams, "Toward an Understanding of Inequity," *Journal of Abnormal and Social Psychology* (November 1963); Paul S. Goodman and Abraham Friedman, "An Examination of Adam's Theory of Inequity," *Administrative Science Quarterly* (December 1971).
See also COGNITIVE DISSONANCE.

informal organization, also FORMAL ORGANIZATION, within each formally structured organization there exists an informal organization consisting of spontaneously developed relationships and patterns of interaction between employees. According to Chester I. Barnard's classic statement on the subject, "Informal Organizations and Their Relation to Formal Organizations," Chapter IX from his *The Functions of the Executive* (Cambridge, Mass.: Harvard University Press, 1938),

> informal organization, although comprising the processes of society which are unconscious as contrasted with those of formal organization which are conscious, has two important classes of effects: (a) it establishes certain attitudes, understandings, customs, habits, institutions; and (b) it creates the condition under which formal organization may arise.

initiation fees, payments required by unions of all new members and/or of employees who having once left the union wish to return. Initiation fees serve several purposes: (1) they are a source of revenue, (2) they force the new member to pay for the advantages secured by those who built the union, and (3) they (when the fees are high enough) can be used as a device to restrict membership.

injunction, also called LABOR INJUNCTION, court order forbidding specific individuals or groups from performing acts the court considers injurious to property or other rights of an employer or community. There are two basic types of injunctions: (1) *temporary restraining order*, which is issued for a limited time prior to a formal hearing and (2) *permanent injunction*, which is issued after a full formal hearing. Once an injunction is in effect, the court has contempt power to enforce its rulings through fines and/or imprisonment. For an analysis, *see* Richard D. Sibbernsen, "New Developments in the Labor Injunction," *Labor Law Journal* (October 1977).

See also MUNIZ V. HOFFMAN.

ink-blot test: *see* RORSCHACH TEST.

Inland Boatmen's Union of the Pacific: *see* LABOR ORGANIZATION, *under* Seafarer's International Union of North America.

Inland Steel Co. v. National Labor Relations Board, decision by the U.S. Court of Appeals, 7th Circuit (1948), which held that a company was required to bargain with its union over retirement and pension matters. The decision was indirectly upheld by the U.S. Supreme Court when it denied certiorari in the case, 336 U.S. 960 (1949).

input, raw material of any process.

in-service training, term used mainly in the public sector to refer to job-related instruction and educational experiences made available to employees. In-service training programs are usually offered during normal working hours. However, some programs, especially those offering college credit, are available to the employee only on his/her own time.

Institute of Personnel Management (IPM), professional personnel management organization in Great Britain. Its monthly magazine, *Personnel Management*, is concerned with the practical aspects of the personnel manager's job. Its quarterly journal, *Personnel Review*, reports on developments in the theory and practice of personnel management. Institute membership is open to those engaged in or concerned with personnel management who can fulfill certain professional requirements specified by the Institute. In 1978, IPM had over 19,500 members.

> Institute of Personnel Management
> Central House
> Upper Woburn Place
> London WCIH OHX

Institute for Social Research (ISR), established at the University of Michigan in 1946, the ISR conducts research on a broad range of subjects within its four constituent research centers: (1) *Survey Research Center*—concerned primarily with the study of large populations, organizations, and special segments of society, and generally utilizes interview surveys; (2) *Research Center for Group Dynamics*—concerned with the development of the basic science of behavior in groups, seeking to explain the nature of the social forces which affect group behavior, the relations among members, and the activities of the group as a whole; (3) *Center for Research on Utilization of Scientific Knowledge*—studies the processes required for the full use of research findings and new knowledge; and (4) *Center for Political Studies*—investigates political behavior, focusing on national politics in many countries, and maintains a rich collection of election data.

> Institute for Social Research
> The University of Michigan
> P.O. Box 1248
> Ann Arbor, MI 48106
> (313) 764-8354

institutional discrimination, practices contrary to EEO policies that occur even though there was no intent to discriminate. Institutional discrimination exists whenever a practice or procedure has the effect of treating one group of employees differently from another.

instrumented laboratory, laboratory training experience that uses feedback from measurements taken during laboratory sessions of the behavior and feelings of the group and/or its component individuals.

insurance, also INSURANCE PREMIUM, contractual arrangement that has a customer pay a specified sum, the insurance premium, in return for which the insurer will pay compensation if specific events occur (*e.g.*, death for life insurance, fire for fire insurance, hospitalization for health insurance, etc.). The insurance premiums are calculated so that their total return to the insurance company is sufficient to cover all policyholder claims plus administrative costs and profit.
See also the following entries:

DENTAL INSURANCE
DISABILITY INSURANCE
GROUP INSURANCE
PLAN TERMINATION INSURANCE

Insurance Agents' decision: *see* NATIONAL LABOR RELATIONS BOARD V. INSURANCE AGENTS' INTERNATIONAL UNION.

insurance premium: *see* INSURANCE.

Insurance Workers International Union: *see* LABOR ORGANIZATION.

insured, person who buys insurance on property or the person whose life is insured.

insurer, person, company, or governmental agency that provides insurance.

intangible rewards, satisfactions of no monetary value that an individual gains from a job.

integrative bargaining: *see* PRODUCTIVITY BARGAINING.

intelligence, there is no agreement on any single definition of intelligence, save that it is a hypothetical construct. Generally, it refers to an individual's ability to cope with his/her environment and deal with mental abstractions. The military, as well as some other organizations, use the word "intelligence" in its original Latin sense—as information.

intelligence quotient (IQ), measure of an individual's general intellectual capability. IQ tests have come under severe criticism because of their declining relevancy as a measurement tool for individuals past the age of adolescence and because of their inherent cultural bias, which has tended to discriminate against minorities. For an analysis of the politics of IQ's, *see* Brigitte Berger, "A New Interpretation of the I.Q. Controversy," *The Public Interest* (Winter 1978).

IQ Classifications

The following table illustrates a traditional classification of IQ's and indicates the percentage of persons in a normal population who would fall into each classification.

Classification	IQ	Percentage of Population
Gifted	140 and above	1
Very Superior	130-139	2.5
Superior	120-129	8
Above Average	110-119	16
Average	90-109	45
Below Average	80-89	16
Dull or Borderline	70-79	8
Moron	60-69	2.5
Imbecile, idiot	59 and under	1

---

intelligence test, any of a variety of standardized tests that seek to measure a range of mental abilities and social skills. For an annual listing of standardized intelligence tests and their uses, *see* Oscar K. Buros (ed.), *The Mental Measurements Yearbook* (Highland Park, N.J.: Gryphon Press, Annually).

Intelligence Test, Cattell Culture Fair: *see* CATTELL CULTURE FAIR INTELLIGENCE TEST.

Interagency Advisory Group (IAG), the Office of Personnel Management's key link for the purposes of communication, consultation, and coordination with the rest of the federal personnel community. Its members are the top personnel officials from the departments and agencies of the federal government.

Interagency Committee on Handicapped Employees: *see* VOCATIONAL REHABILITATION ACT OF 1973.

intercity differential: *see* GEOGRAPHICAL DIFFERENTIAL.

interdisciplinary team: *see* TASK GROUP.

interest, community of: *see* COMMUNITY OF INTEREST.

interest arbitration, arbitration of a dispute arising during the course of contract negotiations where the arbitrator must decide what will or will not be contained in the agreement. *See* Ronald W. Haughton, "Some Successful Uses of 'Interest' Arbitration," *Monthly Labor Review* (September 1973); Betty Southard Murphy, "Interest Arbitration," *Public Personnel Management* (September–October 1977).

interest inventory, questionnaire designed to measure the intensity of interest that an individual has in various objects and activities. Interest inventories are widely used in vocational guidance. *See* Donald G. Zytowski, *Contemporary Approaches to Interest Measurement* (Minneapolis: University of Minnesota Press, 1973).
See also SELF-DIRECTED SEARCH and STRONG-CAMPBELL INTEREST INVENTORY.

interest test, battery of questions designed to determine the interest patterns of an individual, particularly with regard to vocational choice.

interexaminer reliability: *see* INTERRATER RELIABILITY.

interface, point of contact, the boundary between organizations, people, jobs and/or systems. For analyses, *see* Frank T. Paine, "The Interface Problem," *The Personnel Administrator* (January–February 1965); Daniel A. Wren, "Interface and Interorganizational Coordination," *Academy of Management Journal* (March 1967).

interference, an unfair labor practice. Section 8 (a) (1) of the Labor–Management Relations (Taft–Hartley) Act of 1947 makes it unlawful for an employer "to interfere with, restrain, or coerce employees" who are exercising their right to organize and bargain collectively.

Intergovernmental Personnel Act of 1970 (IPA); (Public Law 91-648), federal statute designed to strengthen the personnel resources of state and local governments by making available to them a wide range of assistance. The act contains a declaration of policy that (1) the quality of public service at all levels can be improved through personnel systems that are consistent with merit principles, and (2) it is in the national interest for federal assistance to be directed toward strengthening state and local personnel systems in line with merit principles.
Specifically, IPA:

1. authorizes the U.S. Civil Service Commission (now the Office of Personnel Management) to make grants to help meet the costs of strengthening personnel management capabilities of state and local governments in such areas as recruitment, selection, and pay administration, and for research and demonstration projects;

2. authorizes grants to help states and localities develop and carry out training programs for employees, particularly in such core management areas as financial management, automatic data processing and personnel management;
3. authorizes awards for Government Service Fellowship grants to support graduate-level study by employees selected by state and local governments;
4. authorizes a wide range of technical assistance in personnel management to be made available to state and local governments on a reimbursable, nonreimbursable, or partly reimbursable basis;
5. provides for the temporary assignment of personnel between federal agencies and state and local governments or institutions of higher education;
6. allows employees of state and local governments to benefit from training courses conducted for federal employees by federal agencies;
7. fosters cooperative recruitment and examining efforts; and
8. makes the Office of Personnel Management the sole federal agency responsible for prescribing and maintaining merit system standards required under federal grant programs.

interim agreement, collective bargaining agreement designed to avoid a strike and/or to maintain the current conditions of employment while the settlement of a dispute or the signing of a final comprehensive contract is pending.

intern: *see* INTERNSHIP.

internal alignment, relationship among positions in an organization in terms of rank and pay. In theory, the most desirable internal alignment calls for similar treatment of like positions, with the differences in treatment in direct proportion to differences in the difficulty, responsibilities, and qualifications needed for a position.

internal consistency reliability, measure of the reliability of a test based on the extent to which items in the test measure the same traits.

internal equity: *see* EXTERNAL EQUITY.

internal house organ: *see* HOUSE ORGAN.

International Alliance of Theatrical Stage Employees and Moving Picture Machine Operators of the United States and Canada: *see* LABOR ORGANIZATION, Theatrical Stage Employees and Moving Picture Machine Operators of the United States and Canada, International Alliance of.

International Association of Bridge and Structural Iron Workers: *see* LABOR ORGANIZATION, Iron Workers, International Association of Bridge and Structural.

International Association of Fire Fighters: *see* LABOR ORGANIZATION, Fire Fighters, International Association of.

International Association of Personnel in Employment Security (IAPES), organization founded in 1913 for individuals working in job placement and unemployment compensation in the public sector. It now claims over 29,000 members.

IAPES
Box 173
Frankfort, KY 40601
(502) 223-4459

International Association of Personnel Women (IAPW), A professional association of women personnel workers in business, government, and education established to expand and improve the professionalism of women working in personnel management.

IAPW
P.O. Box 3057
Grand Central Station
New York, NY 10017
(212) 734-8160

International Association of Professional Bureaucrats (IAPB), founded and headed by James H. Boren (a former college professor, congressional staffer, and State Department official), IAPB is an organization dedicated to bureaucratic reform and maintaining the status quo. Its motto is: "When in charge, ponder. When in trouble, delegate. When in doubt, mumble." In addition to conducting seminars on fingertapping and eloquent mumbling, IAPB sponsors a number of annual awards banquets at which the organization's highest award, "The Order of the Bird," has been presented to leading bureaucrats in the governmental, corporate, and academic fields. The U.S. Postal Service was presented The Order of the Bird in recognition of its orderly postponement patterns in delivering special delivery mail. *See* James H. Boren, *When In Doubt, Mumble: A Bureaucrat's Handbook* (N.Y.: Van Nostrand Reinhold, 1972); James H. Boren, *Have Your Way With Bureaucrats* (Radnor, Penn.: Chilton Books Co., 1975).

IAPB
National Press Building
Washington, DC 20004
(202) 347-2490

International Association of Siderographers: *see* LABOR ORGANIZATION, Siderographers, International Association of.

International Association of Tool Craftsmen: *see* LABOR ORGANIZATION, Tool Craftsmen, International Association of.

International Brotherhood of Electrical Workers: *see* LABOR ORGANIZATION, Electrical Workers, International Brotherhood of.

International Brotherhood of Firemen and Oilers: *see* LABOR ORGANIZATION, Firemen and Oilers, International Brotherhood of.

International Brotherhood of Painters and Allied Trades of the United States and Canada: *see* LABOR ORGANIZATION, Painters and Allied Trades of the United States and Canada, International Brotherhood of.

International Brotherhood of Pottery and Allied Workers: *see* LABOR ORGANIZATION, Pottery and Allied Workers, International Brotherhood of, *under* Seafarer's International Union of North America.

International Brotherhood of Teamsters, Chauffeurs, Warehousemen and Helpers of America: *see* LABOR ORGANIZATION, Teamsters, Chauffeurs, Warehousemen, and Helpers of America, International Brotherhood of.

International Brotherhood of Teamsters v. *United States*, 431 U.S. 324 (1977), U.S. Supreme Court case, which held that a seniority system is not unlawful merely because it perpetuates an employer's pervious discriminatory policies. The majority found that Title VII protects "bona-fide" seniority systems—those designed without discriminatory intent—even though they lock in the effects of illegal employment discrimination. The congressional judgment, the court said, was that Title VII should not "destroy or water down the vested seniority rights of employees simply because their employer had engaged in discrimination prior to the passage of the Act." For an analysis, *see* Stephen L. Swanson, "The Effect of the Supreme Court's Seniority Decisions," *Personnel Journal* (December 1977).

See also RETROACTIVE SENIORITY.

International Chemical Workers Union: *see* LABOR ORGANIZATION, Chemical Workers Union, International.

International City Management Association (ICMA), professional organization for appointed chief executives in cities, counties, towns, and other local governments. Its primary goals include strengthening the quality of urban government through professional management and developing and disseminating new concepts and approaches to management through a wide range of information services, training programs, and publications.

As an educational and professional association, ICMA is interested in the dissemination and application of knowledge for better urban management. To further these ends, ICMA utilizes a comprehensive research, data collection, and information dissemination program to facilitate reference and research by local government officials, university professors and students, researchers, and others concerned with urban affairs. Among ICMA publications are: Winston W. Crouch (ed.), *Local Government Personnel Administration* (1976), *The Municipal Year Book, The County Year Book*, and its monthly magazine, *Public Management*.

ICMA
1140 Connecticut Ave., N.W
Washington, DC 20036
(202) 293-2200

international civil service, term that does not refer to any particular government entity, but to any bureaucratic organization that is by legal mandate composed of differing citizenships and nationalities. Examples include the United Nations Secretariat, the International Labour Organization, and the Commission of the European Communities. Sometimes the term is used to collectively refer to the employees of all international bureaucracies. For a symposium, *see* Sidney Mailick (ed.), "Toward an International Civil Service," *Public Administration Review* (May–June 1970). For the standard work on the legal aspects of the subject, *see* M. B. Akehurst, *The Law Governing Employment in International Organizations* (Cambridge, England: Cambridge University Press, 1967).

International Civil Service Commission (ICSC), 15-member commission created by the United Nations in 1974 to make recommendations concerning the personnel policies of the various United Nations secretariats. For a history and analysis, *see* John P. Renninger, "Staffing International Organizations: The Role of the International Civil Service Commission," *Public Administration Review* (July–August 1977).

International Die Sinkers' Conference: *see* LABOR ORGANIZATION, Die Sinkers' Conference, International.

International Federation of Professional and Technical Engineers: *see* LABOR ORGANIZATION, Technical Engineers, International Federation of Professional and.

International Guards Union of America: *see* LABOR ORGANIZATION, Guards Union of America, International.

International Jewelry Workers' Union: *see* LABOR ORGANIZATION, Jewelry Workers' Union, International.

International Journal of Group Psychotherapy, official quarterly of the American Group Psychotherapy Association. Devoted to reporting and interpreting research and practice in group psychotherapy in various settings in the United States and in other countries, it reflects the types of group psychotherapy now employed, and helps stimulate the study of validation of practice and results. It also serves as a forum of ideas and experiences, with a view toward clarifying and enlarging the scope of group psychotherapy techniques.

International Journal of Group Psychotherapy
American Group Psychotherapy Association, Inc.
1995 Broadway—14th Floor
New York, NY 10023

International Labor Organization (ILO), specialized agency associated with the United Nations, created by the Treaty of Versailles in 1919 as a part of the League of Nations. The United States joined this autonomous intergovernmental agency in 1934 and is currently one of 132-member countries that finance ILO operations. Governments, workers, and employers share in making the decisions and shaping its policies. This tripartite representation gives the ILO its balance and much of its strength and makes it distinct from all other international agencies.

The purpose of the ILO is to improve labor conditions, raise living standards, and promote economic and social stability as the foundation for lasting peace throughout the world. The standards developed by the annual ILO Conference are guides for countries to follow and form an international labor code that covers such questions as employment, freedom of association, hours of work, migration for employment, protection of women and young workers, prevention of industrial accidents, workmen's compensation, other labor problems, conditions of seamen, and social security. The only obligation on any country is to consider these standards; no country is obligated to adopt, accept, or ratify them. For a history, *see* Antony Alcock, *History of the International Labor Organization* (N.Y.: Octagon Books, 1972).

International Labor Organization
International Labor Office:
Geneva, Switzerland

Washington Branch
1750 New York Ave., N.W.
Washington, DC 20006
(202) 634-6335

International Labour Office: *see* INTERNATIONAL LABOUR REVIEW and YEARBOOK OF LABOUR STATISTICS.

International Labour Review, this monthly has published original research, comparative studies, and articles of interest to the international labor community since 1897.

International Labour Review
International Labour Office
CH—1211 Geneva 22
SWITZERLAND

International Ladies' Garment Workers' Union: *see* LABOR ORGANIZATION, Ladies' Garment Workers' Union, International.

International Leather Goods, Plastic and Novelty Workers' Union: *see* LABOR ORGANIZATION, Leather Goods, Plastic and Novelty Workers' Union, International.

International Longshoremen's and Warehousemen's Union: *see* LABOR ORGANIZATION, Longshoremen's and Warehousemen's Union, International.

International Longshoremen's Association: *see* LABOR ORGANIZATION, Longshoremen's Association, International.

International Mailers Union: *see* LABOR ORGANIZATION, Mailers Union, International.

International Molders' and Allied Workers' Union: *see* LABOR ORGANIZATION, Molders' and Allied Workers' Union, International.

International Organization of Masters, Mates and Pilots: *see* LABOR ORGANIZATION, *under* Longshoremen's Association, International.

International Personnel Management Association (IPMA), established in January 1973 through the consolidation of the Public Personnel Association (successor to the Civil Service Assembly of the United States and Canada) and the Society for Personnel Administration, IPMA is a nonprofit membership organization for agencies and persons in the public personnel field. Its members are located in federal, state, provincial and local governments throughout the United States, Canada, and elsewhere around the world. Among IPMA'S continuing purposes are the improvement of personnel administration, promoting merit principles of employment, and assisting persons and agencies engaged in personnel work.

IPMA is divided into national sections (for example, the U.S. section is "International Personnel Management Association-United States"), geographic regions, and local chapters.

IPMA
1850 K Street, N.W.
Washington, DC 20006
(202) 833-5860

International Plate Printers', Die Stampers' and Engravers' Union of North America: *see* LABOR ORGANIZATION, Plate Printers', Die Stampers' and Engravers' Union of North America, International.

International Printing and Graphic Communications Union: *see* LABOR ORGANIZATION, Printing and Graphic Communications Union, International.

international representative, title sometimes used by agents of international unions.

International Typographical Union: *see* LABOR ORGANIZATION, Typographical Union, International.

international union, also called NATIONAL UNION, parent union composed of affiliated unions known as "locals." Many international unions in the United States are "international" solely because of their affiliates in Canada. The international or national union is supported by a per capita tax on each of its locals' members.

International Union Allied Industrial Workers of America: *see* LABOR ORGANIZATION, Industrial Workers of America, International Union Allied.

International Union of Bricklayers and Allied Craftsmen: *see* LABOR ORGANIZATION, Bricklayers and Allied Craftsmen, International Union of.

International Union of Dolls, Toys, Playthings, Novelties and Allied Products of the United States and Canada: *see* LABOR ORGANIZATION, Toys, Playthings, Novelties and

Allied Products of the United States and Canada, International Union of Dolls.

International Union of Electrical, Radio, and Machine Workers: see LABOR ORGANIZATION, Electrical, Radio, and Machine Workers, International Union of.

International Union of Elevator Constructors: see LABOR ORGANIZATION, Elevator Constructors, International Union of.

International Union of Guards and Watchmen: see LABOR ORGANIZATION, Guards and Watchmen, International Union of.

International Union of Journeymen Horseshoers of the United States and Canada: see LABOR ORGANIZATION, Horseshoers of the United States and Canada, International Union of Journeymen.

International Union of Operating Engineers: see LABOR ORGANIZATION, operating Engineers, International Union of.

International Union of Petroleum and Industrial Workers: see LABOR ORGANIZATION, under Seafarer's International Union of North America.

International Union of Tool, Die and Mold Makers: see LABOR ORGANIZATION, Tool, Die and Mold Makers, International Union of.

International Union of Wood, Wire, and Metal Lathers: see LABOR ORGANIZATION, Lathers, International Union of Wood, Wire and Metal.

International Union, United Automobile, Aerospace and Agricultural Implement Workers of America: see LABOR ORGANIZATION, Automobile, Aerospace and Agricultural Implement Workers of America, International Union, United.

International Union, United Plant Guard Workers of America: see LABOR ORGANIZATION, Plant Guard Workers of America, International Union, United.

International Woodworkers of America: see LABOR ORGANIZATION, Woodworkers of America, International.

internship, any of a variety of formal training programs for new employees or students that allows them to learn on-the-job by working closely with professionals in their field. Almost all professional educational programs at universities require or allow their students to undertake internships of one kind or another.

See Daniel S. Golmmen and Francis B. Atkinson, "The Business Intern—New Source of Employees," *Management World* (January 1978); Thomas P. Murphy, *Government Management Internships and Executive Development* (Lexington, MA.: Lexington Books, 1973).

interpersonal competence, measure of an individual's ability to work well in a variety of situations. To have interpersonal competence while occupying any given position, one would have to be proficient in meeting all of a position's role demands. See David Moment and Abraham Zaleznik, *Role Development and Interpersonal Competence* (Boston: Harvard University Graduate School of Business Administration, 1963); Chris Argyris and Roger Harrison, *Interpersonal Competence and Organizational Effectiveness* (Homewood, Ill.: Richard D. Irwin, 1962).

interpolation, process of estimating intermediate values between two known values.

interrater reliability, also called INTER-EXAMINER RELIABILITY, extent to which examiners give the same score to like performing candidates. See J. M. Greenwood and W. J. McNamara, "Interrater Reliability in Situational Tests," *Journal of Applied Psychology* (April 1967).

interval, distance of time or space between two units.

intervention, one of the most basic techniques of organization development. According to Chris Argyris, *Intervention Theory and Method: A Behavioral Science View* (Reading, Mass.: Addison-Wesley, 1970),

> to intervene is to enter into an ongoing system of relationship, to come between or among persons, groups, or objects for the purpose of helping them. There is an important implicit assumption in the definition that should be made explicit: the system exists independently of the intervenor. There are many reasons one might wish to intervene. These reasons may range from helping the clients make their own decisions about the kind of help they need to coercing the clients to do what the intervenor wishes them to do. Examples of the latter are ...executives who invite interventionists into their system to manipulate subordinates for them; trade union leaders who for years have resisted systematic research in their own bureaucratic functioning at the highest levels because they fear that valid information might lead to entrenched interests— especially at the top—being unfrozen.

interview, also called EMPLOYMENT INTERVIEW and SELECTION INTERVIEW, conversation between two or more persons for a particular purpose. The purpose of an employment or selection interview is evaluation. According to Richard A. Fear, *The Evaluation Interview* (N.Y.: McGraw-Hill, rev. 2nd ed., 1978), "the interview is designed to perform three basic functions; (1) to determine the relevance of the applicant's experience and training to the demands of a specific job, (2) to appraise his personality, motivation, and character, and (3) to evaluate his intellectual functioning." For texts, *see* J. D. Drake, *Interviewing for Managers* (N.Y.: AMACOM, 1972); R. L. Gordon, *Interviewing* (Homewood, Ill.: Richard D. Irwin, rev. ed., 1975); Felix M. Lopez, *Personnel Interviewing* (N.Y.: McGraw-Hill, 2nd ed., 1975).

Interviewers who ask questions that are not job related could inadvertently violate EEO provisions. *See* Robert D. Gatewood and James Ledvinka, "Selection Interviewing and EEO: Mandate for Objectivity," *The Personnel Administrator* (May 1976); James G. Goodale, "Tailoring the Selection Interview to the Job," *Personnel Journal* (February 1976).

See also the following entries:
  COMPLIMENTARY INTERVIEW
  DIRECTED INTERVIEW
  EXIT INTERVIEW
  GROUP ORAL INTERVIEW
  HELPING INTERVIEW
  PATTERNED INTERVIEW
  SCREENING INTERVIEW
  STRESS INTERVIEW

interview schedule, formal list of questions that an interviewer puts to an interviewee.

intrinsic reward, also called PSYCHIC INCOME, reward contained in the job itself such as personal satisfaction, a sense of achievement, and the prestige of office. *See* William E. Reif, "Intrinsic Versus Extrinsic Rewards: Resolving The Controversy," *Human Resource Management* (Summer 1975).
  See also TITLES.

inventory, questionnaire designed to obtain non-intellectual information about a subject. Inventories are often used to gain information on an individual's personality traits, interests, attitude, etc. *See* Robert C. Droege and John Hawk, "Development of a U.S. Employment Service Interest Inventory," *Journal of Employment Counseling* (June 1977).

inventory, interest: *see* INTEREST INVENTORY.

inverse seniority, concept that allows workers with the greatest seniority to elect temporary layoff so the most recently hired, (who would normally be subject to layoff) can continue working. The key to making the concept practical is the provision that senior workers who are laid off receive supplementary compensation in excess of state unemployment compensation and have the right to return to their previous jobs. *See* R. T. Lund, D. C. Bumstead, and S. Friedman, "Inverse Seniority: Timely Answer to the Layoff Dilemma?" *Harvard Business Review* (September–October 1975); S. Friedman, D. C. Bumstead, and R. T. Lund, "Inverse Seniority as an Aid to Disadvantaged Groups," *Monthly Labor Review* (May 1976).

involuntary demotion: *see* DEMOTION.

I/O psychology *see* INDUSTRIAL PSYCHOLOGY.

Iowa Federation of Labor: *see* AMERICAN FEDERATION OF LABOR–CONGRESS OF INDUSTRIAL ORGANIZATIONS.

IPA: *see* INTERGOVERNMENTAL PERSONNEL ACT OF 1970.

IPGCU: *see* LABOR ORGANIZATION, Printing and Graphic Communications Union, International.

IPM: *see* INSTITUTE OF PERSONNEL MANAGEMENT.

IPMA: *see* INTERNATIONAL PERSONNEL MANAGEMENT ASSOCIATION.

IQ: *see* INTELLIGENCE QUOTIENT.

IRA: *see* INDIVIDUAL RETIREMENT ACCOUNT.

iron-clad oath, also IRON-CLAD CONTRACT, a pre-World War I anti-union tactic that had employees take an oath and/or sign a contract agreeing not to join or encourage the formation of a union. Such practices were made illegal by the Norris–LaGuardia Act of 1932.

iron law of oligarchy, according to Robert Michels' "iron law of oligarchy," in *Political Parties* (Glencoe, Ill.: The Free Press, 1915, 1949), organizations are by their nature oligarchic because majorities within an organization are not capable of ruling themselves:

> Organization implies the tendency to oligarchy. In every organization, whether it be a political party, a professional union, or any other association of the kind, the aristocratic tendency manifests itself very clearly. The

mechanism of the organization, while conferring a solidity of structure, induces serious changes in the organized mass, completely inverting the respective position of the leaders and the led. As a result of organization, every party or professional union becomes divided into a minority of directors and a majority of directed.

iron law of wages, also called SUBSISTENCE THEORY OF WAGES, concept, variously stated as a law or theory, which holds that in the long run workers will be paid merely the wages that they require for bare survival. It is premised upon the notion that as wages rise, workers have larger families. This increases the labor force and, in turn, drives down wages. The ensuing poverty causes family sizes to decline and, in turn, drives wages higher. Then the cycle begins again. While various writers popularized these notions in the last century, they are most fully stated in David Ricardo's *Principles of Political Economy and Taxation* (N.Y.: E. P. Dutton & Co., 1817, 1962).

Iron Workers, International Association of Bridge and Structural: *see* LABOR ORGANIZATION.

IRRA: *see* INDUSTRIAL RELATIONS RESEARCH ASSOCIATION.

ISR: *see* INSTITUTE FOR SOCIAL RESEARCH.

IT: *see* LABOR ORGANIZATION, Industrial Trade Unions, National Organization of.

Italian Actors Union: *see* LABOR ORGANIZATION, under Actors and Artistes of America, Associated.

item, smallest unit of an employment test; a test question.
See also RECALL ITEM and RECOGNITION ITEM.

item analysis, statistical description of how a particular question functioned when used in a particular test. An item analysis provides information about the difficulty of the question for the sample on which it is based, the relative attractiveness of the options, and how well the question discriminated among the examinees with respect to a chosen criterion. The criterion most frequently used is the total score on the test of which the item is a part. However, the criterion may be the score on a subtest, or some other test or, in general, on any appropriate measure that ranks the examinee from high to low.

item validity, extent to which a test item measures what it is supposed to measure.

itinerant worker, employee who finds work by traveling from one employer or community to another.

ITU: *see* LABOR ORGANIZATION, Typographical Union, International.

IUBAC: *see* LABOR ORGANIZATION, Bricklayers and Allied Craftsmen, International Union of.

IUE: *see* LABOR ORGANIZATION, Electrical, Radio, and Machine Workers, International Union of.

IUEC: *see* LABOR ORGANIZATION, Elevator Constructors, International Union of.

IUMSW: *see* LABOR ORGANIZATION, Marine and Shipbuilding Workers of America, Industrial Union of.

IUOE: *see* LABOR ORGANIZATION, Operating Engineers, International Union of.

IWA: *see* LABOR ORGANIZATION, Woodworkers of America, International.

IWIU: *see* LABOR ORGANIZATION, Insurance Workers International Union.

IWW: *see* INDUSTRIAL WORKERS OF THE WORLD.

J

Jackson, Andrew (1767-1845), president of the United States from 1829-1837 who has been blamed for inventing the spoils system. Prior to Jackson, the federal service was a stable, long-tenured corps of officials decidedly elitist in character and remarkably barren of corruption. Jackson, for the most part, continued with this tradition in practice, turning out of office about as many appointees as had Jefferson. In his most famous statement on the character of public office, Jackson asserted that the duties of public office are "so plain and simple that men of intelligence may readily qualify themselves for their performance; and I cannot but believe that more is lost by the long continuance of men in office than is generally to be gained by their experience." Jackson was claiming that all men, especially the newly enfranchised who did so much to elect him, should have an equal opportunity for public office. In playing to his plebian constituency, Jackson put the patrician civil service on notice that they had no natural monopoly on public office. His rhetoric on the nature of the public service was to be far more influential than his administrative example. While Jackson's personal indulgence in spoils were more limited than popularly thought, he did establish the intellectual and political rationale for the unmitigated spoils system that was to follow.

The classic work on Jackson's patronage policies is Erik M. Eriksson, "The Federal Civil Service Under President Jackson," *Mississippi Valley Historical Review* (March 1927); For later studies, *see* Sidney H. Aronson, *Status and Kinship in the Higher Civil Service* (Cambridge, Mass.: Harvard University Press, 1964); Leonard D. White, *The Jacksonians* (N.Y.: Macmillan, 1954).

jargon: *see* BUZZWORDS.

jargonaphasia, physiological disorder manifested by the intermingling of correct words with unintelligible speech. Many writers of organization memoranda and government regulations seem to suffer from this ailment.

jawboning, any presidential pressure on labor, management, or both to make their behavior more compatible with the national interest. The jawbone in jawboning refers to the biblical "jawbone of an ass" with which Samson "slew a thousand men." According to Theodore C. Sorenson, in *Kennedy* (N.Y.: Harper & Row, 1965), the term was first used by Walter Heller (then Chairman of the Council of Economic Advisors) in reference to President Kennedy's efforts to impose his economic guidelines on price-setting and collective bargaining. While President Kennedy never used the term itself, his successor, President Johnson admittedly used jawboning extensively because it neatly complimented both his policies and personality. Subsequent presidents have tried to avoid the term but stuck with the practice.

Jewelry Workers' Union, International: *see* LABOR ORGANIZATION.

J. I. Case Co.* v. *National Labor Relations Board, 321 U.S. 332 (1944), U.S. Supreme Court case, which held that individual contracts—no matter what the circumstances that justify their execution or what their terms—cannot be used to defeat or delay any procedures or rights under the National Labor Relations Act.

Jimerson, Earl W. (1889-1957), president of the Amalgamated Meat Cutters and Butcher Workmen of North America who helped his union grow from 5,000 members in 1921 to 350,000 at the time of his death. For biographical information, *see* David Brody, *The Butcher Workmen: A Study of Unionization* (Cambridge, Mass.: Harvard University Press, 1964).

job, one of three common usages: (1) colloquial term for one's position or occupation, (2) group of positions that are identical with respect to their major duties and responsibilities, (3) discrete unit of work within an occupational specialty. Historically, jobs were restricted to manual labor. Samuel Johnson's *English Dictionary* (1755) defines a job as "petty, piddling work; a piece of chance work." Anyone not dwelling in the lowest strata of employment had a position, a profession, a calling, or (at the very least) an occupation. However, our language strives ever toward egalitarianism and now even an executive at the highest level would quite properly refer to his position as a job.

job, bridge: *see* BRIDGE JOB.

job, covered: *see* COVERED JOB.

job action, according to William and Mary Morris, in their *Morris Dictionary of Word and Phrase Origins* (N.Y.: Harper & Row, 1977), job action

> has to be the most asinine linguistic invention of the 1960s. The expression literally interpreted means exactly the opposite of what it describes. It's truly something out of *Alice in Wonderland* or, more ominously, out of George Orwell's *1984.* Clarence Barnhart's admirable *Barnhart Dictionary of New English* gives the earliest appearance of job action as 1968 and defines it as "a protest by workers without undertaking a general strike, such as a slowdown or a work-to-rules action." But the term now is used to describe complete work stoppages. The only explanation we have ever heard for the use of this euphemism is that in many areas, what we laughingly refer to as "public servants" are specifically forbidden to strike when it is against the public interest. So they call it a job action and strike anyway.

job analysis, determination of a position's specific tasks and of the knowledges, skills and abilities that an incumbent should possess. This information can then be used in making recruitment and selection decisions, creating selection devices, developing compensation systems, approving training needs, etc. *See* Clement J. Berwitz, *The Job Analysis Approach to Affirmative Action* (New York: John Wiley, 1975); Eugene Rouleau and Burton F. Krain, "Using Job Analysis to Design Selection Procedures," *Public Personnel Management* (September–October 1975).

job analysis, functional: *see* FUNCTIONAL JOB ANALYSIS.

job audit: *see* DESK AUDIT.

job bank, tool first developed in the late 1960s by the U.S. Employment Service so that its local offices could provide applicants with greater access to job openings and employers with a greater choice of workers from which to choose. The job bank itself is a computer. Each day the computer is fed information on new job openings and on jobs just filled. Its daily printout provides up-to-the-minute information for all jobseekers, greater exposure of employers' needs, and a faster referral of job applicants.

job ceiling, maximum number of employees authorized at a given time.

job classification evaluation method, method by which jobs are grouped into classes based on the job's level of difficulty.
See also POSITION CLASSIFICATION.

job coding, numbering system used to categorize jobs according to their job families or other areas of similarity. For example, all positions in a clerical series might be given numbers from 200 to 299 or all management positions might be numbered from 500 to 599. Higher numbers usually indicate higher skill levels within a series.

job content, duties and responsibilities of a specific position.

Job Corps, federal program, presently authorized by the Comprehensive Employment and Training Act of 1973, which provides leadership and overall direction and guidance for the administration of a nationwide training program offering comprehensive development for disadvantaged youth through centers with the unique feature of residential facilities for all or most enrollees. Its purpose is to prepare these youth for the responsibilities of citizenship and to increase their employability by providing them with education, vocational training, and useful work experience in rural, urban, or inner-city centers.

Enrollees may spend a maximum of two years in the Job Corps. However, a period of enrollment, from six months to a year, is usually sufficient to provide adequate training and education to improve employability to a substantial degree.

Job Corps recruiting is accomplished primarily through state employment services. In certain areas, private organizations are the principal source of referrals. State employment services and private, nonprofit organizations provide assistance to enrollees in locating jobs after completion of training.

For the early history, *see* Christopher Weeks, *Job Corps: Dollars and Dropouts*

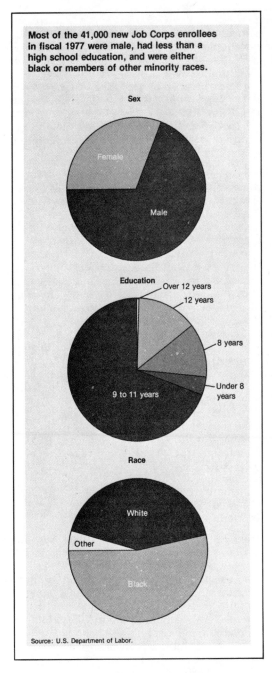

Most of the 41,000 new Job Corps enrollees in fiscal 1977 were male, had less than a high school education, and were either black or members of other minority races.

Sex

Female

Male

Education
Over 12 years
12 years
8 years
Under 8 years
9 to 11 years

Race

White

Other

Black

Source: U.S. Department of Labor.

requirements of a job. The term is frequently used interchangeably with job description.

job depth, measure of the relative freedom that the incumbent of a position has in the performance of his assigned duties.

job description, also called POSITION GUIDE, summary of the duties and responsibilities of a job. According to Robert Townsend, in *Up the Organization* (N.Y.: Knopf, 1970),

> at best, a job description freezes the job as the writer understood it at a particular instant in the past. At worst, they're prepared by personnel people who can't write and don't understand the jobs.

For how-to-do-it treatments, *see* W. J. Walsch, "Writing Job Descriptions: How and Why," *Supervisory Management* (February 1972); R. I. Henderson, "Job Descriptions—Critical Documents, Versatile Tools," *Supervisory Management* (December 1975). *See also* SPECIFICATION.

job design, also called JOB REDESIGN, one of the central concerns of industrial society. In addition to providing all of our goods and services, work provides our social identities and is the single most significant determinant of our physical and emotional health. Organizing work in a manner consistent with societal goals has been the basic task of management since prehistory. This task is made more difficult today by the ever-increasing educational levels and expectations of employees. During the first phase of industrialization, workers were content to be human interchangeable parts of machines (it was more desirable than the alternative of subsistance agriculture). But the modern day archetypical industrial citizens are highly educated individuals who exhibit little resemblance to their illiterate forebearers. The scientific management movement, which grew up as an adjunct of industrial engineering, concerned itself solely with the physical considerations of work; it was human engineering. The research findings of medicine and the behavioral sciences of the last half century have thoroughly demonstrated that the social and psychological basis of work is as significant to long-term productivity and efficiency as are the traditional physiological factors. A modern job design purview seeks to address the totality of these concerns. *See* Harold M. F. Rush, *Job Deisgn for Motivation* (N.Y.: The Conference Board, 1971); Louis E. Davis and James C. Taylor (eds.), *The Design of Jobs* (Santa Monica, Calif.: Goodyear Publishing Co., 2nd ed., 1979); Sar

(Boston: Little, Brown & Co., 1967); Sar A. Levitan, "Job Corps Experience with Manpower Training," *Monthly Labor Review* (October 1975).

job cycle, amount of time required for an employee to perform a discrete unit of work.

job definition, formal statement of the task

A. Levitan and William B. Johnston, "Job Redesign, Reform, Enrichment—Exploring the Limitations," *Monthly Labor Review* (July 1973); Richard W. Woodman and John J. Sherwood, "A Comprehensive Look at Job Design," *Personnel Journal* (August 1977).

job dilution, dividing a relativity sophisticated job into parts that can be performed by less skilled labor.

job element: *see* ELEMENT.

job enlargement: *see* JOB ENRICHMENT.

job enrichment, also JOB ENLARGEMENT, the term *job enrichment* is often confused or used interchangeably with *job enlargement*. However, enlarging a job—adding additional but similar duties—does not substantively change and by no means enriches it. For example, an assembly-line worker performing two menial tasks is not going to have his/her attitudes affected in any significant way if he/she is allowed to perform additional menial tasks. Job enrichment can only occur when motivational factors are designed into the work. Job enlargement is nothing more than horizontal loading—similar tasks laid along side one another. But job enrichment comes only with vertical loading—building into lower level jobs the very factors that make work at the higher levels of the organization more satisfying, more responsible, even more fun. Two such factors would be personal responsibility for discrete units of work and the ability to set one's own pace within an overall schedule.

The most influential individual in the movement towards more enriched jobs has been Frederick Herzberg. For summaries of his work, *see* "One More Time: How Do You Motivate Employees?" *Harvard Business Review* (January–February 1968); "The Wise Old Turk," *Harvard Business Review* (September–October 1974). *Also see* Robert N. Ford, "Job Enrichment Lessons from AT&T," *Harvard Business Review* (January–February 1973); J. Richard Hackman *et al.*, "A New Strategy for Job Enrichment," *California Management Review* (Summer 1975); Roy W. Walters and Associates, *Job Enrichment for Results* (Reading, Mass.: Addison-Wesley, 1975).

job evaluation, process that seeks to determine the relative worth of a position. It implies a formal comparison of the duties and responsibilities of various positions in order to ascertain the worth, rank, or classification of one position relative to all others in an or-

ganization. While job content is obviously the primary factor in evaluation, market conditions must also be considered. *See* Bryan Livy, *Job Evaluation: A Critical Review* (N.Y.: John Wiley, 1975); Philip M. Oliver, "Modernizing A State Job Evaluation and Pay Plan," *Public Personnel Management* (May–June 1976); Thomas H. Patten, Jr., "Job Evaluation and Job Enlargement: A Collision Course?" *Human Resource Management* (Winter 1977).

See also WHOLE-JOB RANKING.

Job Evaluation and Pay Review Task Force, created by the Job Evaluation Policy Act of 1970 (Public Law 91-216), which asserted that it was the sense of the Congress that there be a coordinated position classification system for all civilian positions and authorized the Civil Service Commission to establish a temporary planning unit that would submit a report within two years. The unit became known as the Job Evaluation and Pay Review Task Force. Its final report, released in January 1972, is popularly known as the *Oliver Report* after the task force director, Philip M. Oliver. The report found the federal government's classification and ranking systems to be obsolete and recommended a new job evaluation system. The new system was field tested and revised and became the Civil Service Commission's factor evaluation system. For the report, *see Report of the Job Evaluation and Pay Review Task Force to the United States Civil Service Commission* (Committee on Post Office and Civil Service, Subcommittee on Employee Benefits, 92d Cong., 2d Sess., House Committee Print No. 16., January 12, 1972).

Job Evaluation Policy Act of 1970: *see* JOB EVALUATION AND PAY REVIEW TASK FORCE.

job factors, also called FACTORS, while there are an infinite number of specific factors that pertain to differing jobs, the factors themselves can usually be categorized within the following groupings:

    I. *Job Requirements*—the knowledges, skills, and abilities needed to perform the duties of a specific job.

    II. *Difficulty of Work*—the complexity or intricacy of the work and the associated mental demands of the job.

    III. *Responsibility*—the freedom of action required by a job and the impact of the work performed upon the organizational mission.

    IV. *Personal Relationships*—the importance of interpersonal relationships to the success of mission accomplishment.

V. *Other Factors*—Specific job-oriented elements which should be considered in the evaluation process. For example, physical demands, working conditions, accountability, number of workers directed.

job family, group or series of jobs in the same general occupational area, such as accounting or engineering.

job freeze, formal halt to an organization's discretionary hiring and promoting. Such an action is inherently temporary.

job grading; *see* POSITION RANKING.

job hopper, person who frequently changes jobs.

job loading, also HORIZONTAL LOADING and VERTICAL LOADING, to load a job is to assign to it a greater variety of duties and responsibilities. It is *horizontal loading* when the newly assigned tasks are at the same level of interest and responsibility as the job's original tasks. It is *vertical loading* when the newly assigned tasks allow for increased responsibility, recognition, and personal achievement. The horizontal/vertical terminology comes from Frederick Herzberg, "One More Time: How Do You Motivate Employees?" *Harvard Business Review* (January–February 1968).

See also JOB ENRICHMENT.

job placement, assigning an individual to a job.

job posting, system that allows and encourages employees to apply for other jobs in their organization. According to Dave R. Dahl and Patrick R. Pinto, in "Job Posting: An Industry Survey," *Personnel Journal* (January 1977),

> it is also a complicated system for employee self-development, which embraces internal recruitment, counseling regarding realistic job expectations, encouragement of training and development experiences, and support for the personal risk that any change incurs.

job preview: *see* WORK PREVIEW.

job pricing, determining the dollar value that a particular job is worth.

job ranking, also called RANKING, most rudimentary method of job evaluation, which simply ranks jobs in order of their importance to an organization.

job redesign: *see* JOB DESIGN.

job-relatedness, degree to which an applicant appraisal procedure's knowledges, skills, abilities, and other qualification requirements have been determined to be necessary for successful job performance through a careful job analysis.

job restructuring, also called WORK RESTRUCTURING, element of job analysis that involves the identification of jobs within the context of the system of which they are a part and the analysis and rearrangement of their tasks to achieve a desired purpose. Although the term is relatively new, the concept is familiar. Employers frequently find it necessary to rearrange or adjust the contents (tasks performed) of jobs within a system because of economic conditions, technological changes, and the inability to fill vacant positions among other reasons. Because the interdependencies and relationships among jobs in a system cannot be ignored, job restructuring should be thought of not as changing one job but, rather, as rearranging the contents of jobs within a system. *See* Manpower Administration, U.S. Department of Labor, *A Handbook for Job Restructuring* (Washington, D.C.: U.S. Government Printing Office, 1970); Leonard A. Schlesinger and Richard E. Walton, "The Process of Work Restructuring, and Its Impact on Collective Bargaining," *Monthly Labor Review* (April 1977).

job rotation, transferring a worker from one assignment to another in order to minimize boredom and/or enhance skills. *See* Martin J. Gannon, Brian A. Poole, and Robert E. Prangley, "Involuntary Job Rotation and Worker Behavior," *Personnel Journal* (June 1972).

job sample: *see* WORK SAMPLE.

job sampling: *see* WORK SAMPLING.

job satisfaction, according to Edwin A. Locke, "job satisfaction is the pleasurable emotional state resulting from the appraisal of one's job as achieving or facilitating one's job values." For an exhaustive analysis, *see* Edwin A. Locke, "The Nature and Causes of Job Satisfaction," in Marvin D. Dunnette (ed.), *Handbook of Industrial and Organizational Psychology* (Chicago: Rand McNally, 1976).

job scope, also CYCLE TIME, relative complexity of a particular task. This is usually reflected by the *cycle time*—the time it takes to complete the task.

job security, presence of safeguards that protect an employee from capricious assign-

No. 652. Satisfied Workers as Percent of Total Workers: 1962 to 1977

[Survey questions asked were variants of "How satisfied are you with your job (or your work)?" Figures for "satisfied" combined responses such as "very satisfied," "somewhat satisfied," and "fairly satisfied"]

WORKER CHARACTERISTIC	1962	1964	1972	1973	1974	1975	1976	1977
Male	84	92	86	86	87	90	87	87
Female	81	(NA)	86	89	89	87	87	90
White	84	92	87	87	89	89	88	88
Black and other	[1] 76	[1] 88	78	85	83	85	79	85
21-29 years	74	[2] 87	76	80	81	82	84	83
30-39 years	82	[3] 93	88	87	84	88	91	88
40-49 years	84	92	89	88	91	92	89	86
50 years and over	88	94	92	93	94	93	93	95
Education: Grade school	83	94	86	86	86	87	83	88
High school	81	90	86	85	90	91	88	88
Some college	86	89	83	86	87	90	88	86
College degree	90	94	85	93	86	85	87	88
Graduate work	84	93	95	98	93	87	92	92

NA   Not available.   [1] Black only.   [2] 21–30 years.   [3] 31–40 years.

SOURCE: Bureau of the Census, *Statistical Abstract of the United States* (Washington, D.C.: Government Printing Office, 1978), p. 402.

ments, demotion, or discharge. *See* Edward Yemin, "Job Security: Influence of ILO Standards and Recent Trends," *International Labour Review* (January–February 1976).

job-sharing, concept that has two persons— each working part-time—sharing the same job. For a discussion, *see* Barney Olmsted, "Job-Sharing—A New Way to Work," *Personnel Journal* (February 1977).
See also WORKSHARING.

job specification: *see* SPECIFICATION.

job spoiler: *see* RATEBUSTER.

Job Tests Program, comprehensive battery of aptitude tests, personality/attitude questionnaires and biographical/experience questionnaires for use in selection for a wide variety of business and industry jobs (*i.e.*, clerical, mechanical, sales, technical, and supervisory/management areas). Tests in the battery include Factored Aptitude Series (J. E. King and H. B. Osborn, Jr.); Employee Attitude Series (R. B. Cattell, J. E. King and A. K. Schuettler); Application-Interview Series (J. E. King). TIME: Varies. PUBLISHER: Industrial Psychology Inc. (*see* TEST PUBLISHERS).

job upgrading, reclassifying a position from a lower to a higher classification.

job vacancy, also called JOB-VACANCY RATE, an available job for which an organization is actively seeking to recruit a worker. The *job-vacancy rate* is the ratio of the number of job vacancies to the sum of actual employ-

ment plus job vacancies. *See* Daniel Creamer, *Measuring Job Vacancies* (N.Y.: National Industrial Conference Board, 1967).

Johari Window, model, frequently used in laboratory training, for examining the mirror image of one's self. The window, developed

JOHARI WINDOW

	KNOWN TO SELF	NOT KNOWN TO SELF
KNOWN TO OTHERS	PUBLIC SELF (1)	BLIND SELF (2)
NOT KNOWN TO OTHERS	PRIVATE SELF (3)	UNKNOWN AREA (4)

by Joseph Luft and Harry Ingham (Joe + Harry = Johari), consists of the following four quadrants:

1. The first quadrant, the *public self*, contains knowledge that is known to both the subject and others.
2. The second quadrant, the *blind self*, contains knowledge that is known to others and unknown to the subject.
3. The third quadrant, the *private self*, con-

tains all of those things that a subject keeps secret.

4. The fourth quadrant, the *unknown area*, contains information that neither the subject nor others know.

The Johari Window model is usually used as a visual aid for explaining the concepts of interpersonal feedback and disclosure. *See* Joseph Luft, *Group Processes: An Introduction to Group Dynamics* (Palo Alto, Calif.: National Press Books, 1963).

John Wiley & Sons v. Livingston, 376 U.S. 543 (1964), U.S. Supreme Court case, which held that a successor employer may be compelled, under certain circumstances, to arbitrate the question of his obligations toward the employees covered by his predecessor's labor contract.

See also HOWARD JOHNSON CO., INC. V. DETROIT LOCAL JOINT EXECUTIVE BOARD, HOTEL AND RESTAURANT EMPLOYEES.

Johnson v. Railway Express, 421 U.S. 454 (1975), U.S. Supreme Court case, which held that the timely filing of an employment discrimination charge with the Equal Employment Opportunity Commission, pursuant to Title VII of the Civil Rights Act of 1964, does not toll the running of the limitation period applicable to an action.

joint bargaining, two or more unions united to negotiate with a single employer.

joint council, labor–management committee established to resolve disputes arising during the life of a contract.

joint training, training program that brings management and union officials together in a learning situation focusing on some aspect of labor relations.

Jones, Mother (1830-1930), formally MARY HARRIS JONES, first became an organizer for the United Mine Workers of America in her sixties and thereafter became famous as a colorful agitator for union causes. For her autobiography, *see* Mary Parton (ed.), *The Autobiography of Mother Jones* (Chicago: Charles H. Kerr & Co., 1925; reprint edition, ARNO Press, 1969). For a biography, *see* Dale Fetherling, *Mother Jones, the Miners' Angel: A Portrait* (Carbondale, Ill.: Southern Illinois University Press, 1974).

Jones and Laughlin decision: *see* NATIONAL LABOR RELATION BOARD V. JONES AND LAUGHLIN STEEL CORP.

Journal of Applied Behavioral Science, quarterly directed at those interested in inducing social/organizational changes by means of the behavioral sciences.

Journal of Applied Behavioral Science
NTL Institute for Applied Behavioral Science
P.O. Box 9155
Rosslyn Station
Arlington, VA 22209

Journal of European Industrial Training, bimonthly that emphasizes the practical application of training and development activities. While the *Journal* has contributors from both the business and academic worlds, it does not publish formal research papers. In 1977, *Industrial Training International* and the *Journal of European Training* merged to form the present *Journal of European Industrial Training*.

Journal of European Industrial Training
200 Keighley Road
Bradford, West Yorkshire
England, BD9 4JQ

Journal of European Training: *see* JOURNAL OF EUROPEAN INDUSTRIAL TRAINING.

Journal of Human Resources, quarterly that provides a forum for analysis of the role of education and training in enhancing production skills, employment opportunities, and income, as well as of manpower, health, and welfare policies as they relate to the labor market and to economic and social development. It gives priority to studies having empirical content.

Journal of Human Resources
Editorial Office:
Social Science Building
1180 Observatory Drive
Madison, WI 53706

Subscriptions and Advertising Office:
Journals Department
P.O. Box 1379
The University of Wisconsin Press
Madison, WI 53701

journeyman, also called JOURNEY WORKER, originally one of the three grades of workers recognized by the medieval guilds—masters, journeymen, and apprentices. The journeyman had completed apprenticeship training and was considered a fully skilled worker who was eligible to be hired by a master and receive specified wages. A master was a journeyman who was enterprising enough to "open his own store" and hire others as journeymen and apprentices.

Today, a *journey worker* (the de-sexed designation) is any worker who has completed a specified training program as an apprentice in learning a trade or craft or who can provide evidence of having spent a number of years qualifying for his/her trade or craft.

journeyman pay, also called JOURNEYMAN RATE and UNION SCALE, minimum wages paid to all journeymen/journey workers in a given community. Craft unions tend to refer to this minimum rate of pay as union scale.

Joy Silk Mills* v. *National Labor Relations Board, 185 F. 2d 732, decision of the U.S. Court of Appeals, which held that a company would have to bargain with a union that lost a representation election if it could be shown that the union's loss of strength was due to the employer's coercive activities. The decision was indirectly upheld by the U.S. Supreme Court when it denied certiorari in the case, 341 U.S. 914 (1951). For an analysis, *see* William A. Krupman, "The Joy Silk Rule—The Courts Weave A New Fabric," *Labor Law Journal* (October 1968).

judicial review, power of the U.S. Supreme Court to declare actions by the president or the Congress to be invalid or unconstitutional. It was first asserted by the Supreme Court in *Marbury* v. *Madison*, 1 Cranch 137 (1803).

jurisdiction, union's exclusive right to represent particular workers within specified industrial, occupational, or geographical boundaries.

jurisdictional dispute, disagreement between two unions over which should control a particular job or activity.
See also UNITED STATES V. HUTCHESON.

jurisdictional strike, strike that results when two unions have a dispute over whose members should perform a particular task and one or the other strikes in order to gain its way. For example, both electricians and carpenters may claim the right to do the same task at a construction site. Because the employer is caught in the middle, the Labor–Management Relations (Taft–Hartly) Act of 1947 makes jurisdictional strikes illegal.
See also STRIKE and UNFAIR LABOR PRACTICES (UNIONS).

jury-duty pay, the practice of giving employees leave with pay if they are called to jury duty. Many organizations reduce such pay by the amount the employee is paid by the court for his jury service.
See also DEAN V. GADSDEN TIMES PUBLISHING CORP.

JWU: *see* LABOR ORGANIZATION, Jewelry Workers' Union, International.

K

Kahn, Alfred E. (1917-   ), became chairman of the Council of Wage and Price Stability in 1978.

Kahn, Robert L. (1918-   ), psychologist and a leading authority on organizational behavior. Major works include: *The Dynamics of Interviewing*, with Charles F. Cannell (N.Y.: John Wiley, 1957); *Organizational Stress: Studies in Role Conflict and Ambiguity*, with others (N.Y.: Wiley, 1964); *The Social Psychology of Organizations*, with Daniel Katz (N.Y.: John Wiley, 2nd ed., 1978).

Kaiser Aluminum & Chemical Corp. v. *Weber, et al.: see* UNITED STEELWORKERS OF AMERICA V. WEBER, ET AL.

Kansas State Federation of Labor: *see* AMERICAN FEDERATION OF LABOR–CONGRESS OF INDUSTRIAL ORGANIZATIONS.

Katz, Daniel (1903-   ), psychologist and a leading authority on organizational behavior. Major works include: *Bureaucratic Encounters: A Pilot Study in the Evaluation of Government Services* (Ann Arbor, Mich.: Institute for Social Research, University of Michigan, 1975); *The Social Psychology of Organizations*, with Robert L. Kahn (N.Y.: John Wiley, 2nd ed., 1978).

Kelley v. *Johnson*, 425 U.S. 238 (1976), U.S. Supreme Court case, which upheld a municipal regulation limiting the hair length of police.

Kentucky State AFL–CIO: *see* AMERICAN FEDERATION OF LABOR–CONGRESS OF INDUSTRIAL ORGANIZATIONS.

Keogh Plan also called H.R. 10 PLAN, the Self-Employed Individuals Tax Retirement Act of 1962 encourages the establishment of voluntary pension plans by self-employed individuals. The act allows individuals to have tax advantages similar to those allowed for corporate pension plans. Congressman Eugene J. Keogh was the prime sponsor of the Act. H.R. 10 was the number assigned to the bill prior to its passage.

key class, occupations or positions for which data are gathered from other employers (via a salary survey) in order to serve as a basis for establishing wage rates.

Keyishian v. *Board of Regents*, 385 U.S. 589 (1967), U.S. Supreme Court case, which held that laws "which make Communist Party membership, as such, prima facie evidence of disqualification for employment in the public school system are overbroad and therefore unconstitutional."

KGIS: *see* KUDER GENERAL INTEREST SURVEY.

Kheel, Theodore W. (1914-   ), New York lawyer and one of the nation's most visible labor mediators. For a profile, *see* Richard Karp, "The Many Worlds of Theodore Kheel," *New York* (January 8, 1979).

kickback, employers or third parties who extort money from employees or contractors by threatening to sever or have severed the employment relationship are soliciting kickbacks. Most kickbacks are obviously unethical if not illegal. The Anti-Kickback Act of 1934 (or the Copeland Act, as amended) prohibits kickbacks by federal contractors and subcontractors.

kicked upstairs, slang term for the removal of an individual from a position where his or her performance is not thought satisfactory by promoting him or her to a higher position in the organization.

kick-in-the-ass motivation: *see* KITA.

Kingsley, J. Donald (1908-   ), formerly Director-General of the United Nations' International Refugee Organization, co-author of the first full scale text on public personnel administration, and creator of the concept "representative bureaucracy." Major works include: *Public Personnel Administration*, with William E. Mosher (N.Y.: Harper & Bros., 1936); *Representative Bureaucracy: An Interpretation of the British Civil Service* (Yellow Springs, Ohio: Antioch Press, 1944).

Kirkland, Lane (1922-   ), became president of the AFL–CIO in 1979.

Kirkland v. New York State Department of Correctional Services, federal court of appeals case, 520 F. 2d 420 (2d Cir. 1975), cert. denied, 429 U.S. 974 (1976), dealt with the permissible range of remedies for illegal employment discrimination. While approving portions of a lower court ruling ordering New York State to develop an unbiased, job-related test for hiring correctional officials and instituting temporary hiring and promotion quotas until such a test could be developed, the appeals court overturned the portion of the order requiring a "permanent" quota to be followed until members of minority groups reached a specified proportion of correctional sergeants. *See* Roscoe W. Wisner, "The Kirkland Case—Its Implications for Personnel Selection," *Public Personnel Management* (July–August 1975).

KITA, mnemonic device used by Frederick Herzberg to refer to "kick-in-the-ass" attempts at worker motivation. Variants of KITA include "negative physical KITA" (literally using physical force); "negative psychological KITA" (hurting someone with a psychic blow); and "positive KITA" (offering rewards for performance). Herzberg states that KITA cannot create motivation; its only ability is to create movement. *See* Frederick Herzberg, "One More Time: How Do You Motivate Employees?" *Harvard Business Review* (January–February 1968).

Knights of Labor, first significant national labor organization in the United States, founded in 1869 as the Noble and Holy Order of the Knights of Labor. It was originally a secret society (to protect its members from employer reprisals), but its sundry rituals gained it the opposition of the Catholic Church. It lifted its veil of secrecy in 1881, removed the religious connotations from its rituals, saw the Catholic Church withdraw its condemnation, and grew to over 100,000 members within three years. It reached its peak of influence in 1886 when it claimed a national membership of 700,000. Then, a long series of strike failures caused member-

ship to fall away as rapidly as it had grown. By the late 1880s, the Knights were increasingly overshadowed by the American Federation of Labor. Though weakened by loss of membership, the Knights of Labor persisted until 1917 when its formal organization was disbanded.

Because the Knights of Labor was a mass organization accepting all workers, it proved difficult for such a diverse group to agree upon particular courses of action, and so it tended to concentrate on broad political issues and social reform. Skilled workers found that they had little in common with the unskilled masses, nor with a leadership preaching social gospel instead of bread-and-butter issues.

Knights of St. Crispin, union of shoemakers formed in 1867, which grew to about 50,000 members and 600 chapters before it disappeared after the panic of 1873.

knocked off, slang term for being fired. But, be careful how you use it! It is also used as an underworld term for murder.

knock off work, it is thought that the phrase "knocking off" has its origins in the slave galleys of old. So that the oarsmen would row with the proper timing, an overseer would beat rhythmically on a block or drum. When it was time to stop, a special knock would indicate that the oarsmen could knock off or stop their work.

knowledge, understanding of facts or principles relating to a particular subject or subject area.

knowledge worker, Peter F. Drucker's term, in *The New Society: The Anatomy of Industrial Order* (N.Y.: Harper Torchbooks, 1949, 1962), for the largest and most rapidly growing group in the working population of the developed countries, especially the United States:

> It is a group of "workers" though it will never identify itself with the "proletariat," and will always consider itself "middle-class" if not "part of management." And it is an independent group because it owns the one essential resource of production: knowledge. . . . It is this group whose emergence makes ours a "new" society. Never before has any society had the means to educate large numbers of its citizens, nor the opportunities for them to make their education productive. Our society however, cannot get enough educated people, nor can it really effectively utilize any other resource but the educated man who works with his knowl-

edge rather than with his animal strength or his manual skill.

Also see Edward Mandt, "Managing the Knowledge Worker of the Future," *Personnel Journal* (March 1978).

KOIS: *see* KUDER OCCUPATIONAL INTEREST SURVEY.

Kreps, Juanita M. (1921-   ), Secretary of Commerce from 1977 to 1979.

Kroll, Fred J. (1935-   ), became president of the Brotherhood of Railway and Airline Clerks in 1976.

Kuder General Interest Survey (KGIS), vocational interest inventory with 10 occupational scales (*i.e.*, outdoor, mechanical, scientific, artistic, musical, clerical, social services). Revision of Kuder Preference Record-Vocational. TIME: 45/60 minutes. AUTHOR: G. F. Kuder. PUBLISHER: Science Research Associates, Inc. (*see* TEST PUBLISHERS).

Kuder Occupational Interest Survey (KOIS) 100-triad interest inventory. Test subject picks most and least preferred occupational activity from three alternatives. This measures how an individual's preferences are like those typical of people in the various occupations and fields of study. TIME: 30/40 minutes. AUTHOR: G. F. Kuder. PUBLISHER: Science Research Associates, Inc. (*see* TEST PUBLISHERS).

Kuder Preference Record, self-report inventory designed to disclose relative interest in 38 broadly defined vocational interest areas (*i.e.*, outdoor, mechanical, clerical, artistic, musical, scientific, etc.) TIME: Untimed. AUTHOR: G. F. Kuder. PUBLISHER: Science Research Associates, Inc. (*see* TEST PUBLISHERS).

Kuder–Richardson Formulas, variety of formulas for estimating test reliability.

L

labor, collective term for an organization's workforce exclusive of management.

See also the following entries:

CASUAL LABOR
CHILD LABOR
CONTRACT LABOR
DIRECT LABOR
DIVISION OF LABOR
SKILLED LABOR

Labor, Department of (DOL), U.S. federal agency whose purpose is to foster, promote, and develop the welfare of the wage earners of the United States, to improve their working conditions, and to advance their opportunities for profitable employment. In carrying out this mission, DOL administers more than 130 federal labor laws guaranteeing workers' rights to safe and healthful working conditions, a minimum hourly wage and overtime pay, freedom from employment discrimination, unemployment insurance, and workers' compensation. DOL also protects workers' pension rights; sponsors job training programs; helps workers find jobs; works to strengthen free collective bargaining; and keeps track of changes in employment, prices, and other national economic measurements.

Department of Labor
200 Constitution Ave. N.W.
Washington, DC 20210
(202) 523-8165

Labor Affairs, Bureau of International: *see* BUREAU OF INTERNATIONAL LABOR AFFAIRS.

labor agreement, formal results achieved by collective bargaining.

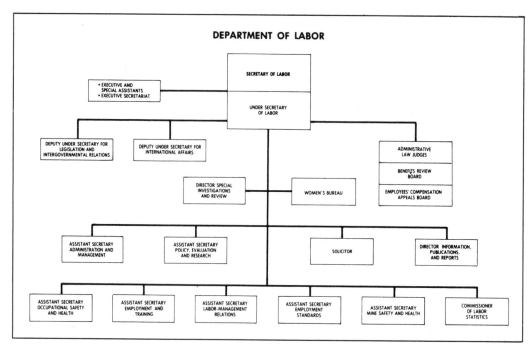

Labor Arbitration Reports, published by the Bureau of National Affairs, Inc., this weekly report is the standard authority on awards and recommended settlements by arbitrators, emergency boards, factfinding bodies, permanent referees and umpires. Reports on company and union positions, dissenting opinions.

laboratory education also called LABORATORY METHOD, method of learning about human behavior through experiencing group activities. According to Clayton P. Alderfer, in "Understanding Laboratory Education: An Overview," *Monthly Labor Review* (December 1970):

> the various forms of laboratory education include a number of common elements such as acceptance of experience-based learning technology, recognition of the role of emotions in human relationships, and utilization of the small group (10 to 12 persons) as a central component in training designs.
>
> The learning laboratory usually takes place on a "cultural island." Participants are taken away from their normal day-to-day activities to a setting where the learning experiences occur. Frequently this new setting is naturally beautiful, but at the very least it is different and thereby provides the participant with both safety from former distractions and a setting that does not necessarily reinforce his usual ways of behaving. A second component of the laboratory involves the use of unstructured or semistructured learning tools. The staff usually attempts to design a set of experiences that serve to heighten certain aspects of human behavior and emotions. Participants learn by becoming actively involved in these activities and by developing skills which allow them to observe both themselves and others during these experiences. A person is asked to engage himself in the unfolding events and later to step back and try to see the patterns in his own and others' behavior. Much of the sense of excitement and high level of emotionality comes from the participant's becoming involved. Experiential learning is based on the assumption that experience precedes intellectual understanding.

laboratory training, also SENSITIVITY TRAINING and T-GROUP, generic term for those educational/training experiences that are designed (1) to increase an individual's sensitivity to his/her own motives and behavior, (2) to increase sensitivity to the behavior of others and, (3) to ascertain those elements of interpersonal interactions that either facilitate or impede a group's effectiveness. While laboratory training and *sensitivity training* tend to be used interchangeably, sensitivity

training is the subordinate term (being the most common method of laboratory training) and the popular name given to almost all experience-based learning exercises. The basic vehicle for the sensitivity training experience is the *T-Group* (T for Training). According to Chris Argyris in "T-Groups for Organizational Effectiveness," *Harvard Business Review* (March–April 1964), the T-Group experience is

> designed to provide maximum possible opportunity for the individuals to expose their behavior, give and receive feedbacks, experiment with new behavior, and develop everlasting awareness and acceptance of self and others. The T-group, when effective, also provides individuals with the opportunity to learn the nature of effective group functioning. They are able to learn how to develop a group that achieves specific goals with minimum possible human cost.

See Robert T. Golembiewski and Arthur Blumberg (eds.), *Sensitivity Training and the Laboratory Approach* (Itasca, Ill.: Peacock, 3rd ed., 1977); Henry Clay Smith, *Sensitivity Training: The Scientific Understanding of Individuals* (N.Y.: McGraw-Hill, 1973; C. L. Cooper and I. L. Mangham, *T-Groups: A Survey of Research* (N.Y.: Wiley, 1971); Dee G. Appley and Alvin E. Winder, *T-Groups and Therapy Groups in A Changing Society* (San Francisco: Jossey-Bass, 1973).

See also the following entries:

INSTRUMENTED LABORATORY
NATIONAL TRAINING LABORATORIES INSTITUTE FOR APPLIED BEHAVIORAL SCIENCE
ROLE
TRAINERLESS LABORATORY

Labor Board v. *Fruit Packers*, 377 U.S. 58 (1964), U.S. Supreme Court case that upheld picketing at independent retail stores by workers urging consumers not to buy items produced by their employer.

labor cost, that part of the cost of a product or service that is attributable to wages.

labor costs, also UNIT LABOR COST, total expenses an employer must meet in order to retain the services of employees. The *unit labor cost* is the expense for labor divided by the number of units of output produced.

labor costs, indirect: *see* INDIRECT LABOR COSTS.

labor court, some European countries have a permanent court of industrial arbitration available to settle labor disputes. *See* Joseph J. Shutkin, "One Nation Indivisible—A Plea for a U.S. Court of Labor Relations," *Labor Law Journal* (February 1969).

Labor Day, in 1894, the U.S. Congress mandated that the first Monday after the first Tuesday in September would be a federal holiday honoring the nation's workers.

labor dispute, according to Section 2(9) of the National Labor Relations Act, as amended, the term "labor dispute" includes

> any controversy concerning terms, tenure or conditions of employment, or concerning the association or representation of persons in negotiating, fixing, maintaining, changing, or seeking to arrange terms or conditions of employment.

See also LAUF V. E. G. SHINNER AND COMPANY and LINN V. UNITED PLANT GUARD WORKERS.

labor economics, the subfield of economics concerned with wages and the supply/allocation of manpower. *See* F. Ray Marshall, Allan M. Cartter, and Allan G. King, *Labor Economics: Wages, Employment, and Trade Unionism* (Homewood, Ill.: Richard D. Irwin, 1976); Gordon F. Bloom and Herbert R. Northrup, *Economics of Labor Relations* (Homewood, Ill.: Richard D. Irwin, 1977). For a how-to-do-it approach, *see* George S. Odiorne, "How to Become your Company's Labor Economist," *Management of Personnel Quarterly* (Spring 1968).

Laborers' International Union of North America: *see* LABOR ORGANIZATION.

labor force, also CIVILIAN LABOR FORCE and TOTAL LABOR FORCE, according to the Bureau of Labor Statistics the *civilian labor force* consists of all employed or unemployed persons in the civilian non-institutional population; the *total labor force* includes military personnel. Persons not in the labor force are those not classified as employed or unemployed; this group includes persons retired, those engaged in their own housework, those not working while attending school, those unable to work because of long-term illness, those discouraged from seeking work because of personal or job market factors and those who are voluntarily idle. The non-institutional population comprises all persons 16 years and older who are not inmates of penal or mental institutions, sanitariums, or homes for the aged, infirm, or needy. *See* Howard N. Fullerton, Jr., and Paul O. Flaim, "New Labor Force Projections to 1990," *Monthly Labor Review* (December 1976).

labor-force participation, rate at which a given group (women, blacks, handicapped, etc.) is represented (either nationally, regionally, or locally) in the labor force.

labor grade, one of a series of steps in a wage-rate structure established by a process of job evaluation or collective bargaining.

Labor History, quarterly, scholarly journal that publishes original research in U.S. labor history, studies of specific unions and of the impact labor problems have upon ethnic and minority groups, theory of labor history, biographical portraits of important trade union figures, comparative studies and analyses of foreign labor movements that shed light on U.S. labor developments, studies of radical groups or of radical history related to U.S. labor history.

> *Labor History*
> Bobst Library, Tamiment Institute
> New York University
> 70 Washington Square South
> New York, NY 10012

labor injunction: *see* INJUNCTION and BOYS MARKET V. RETAIL CLERKS' LOCAL 770.

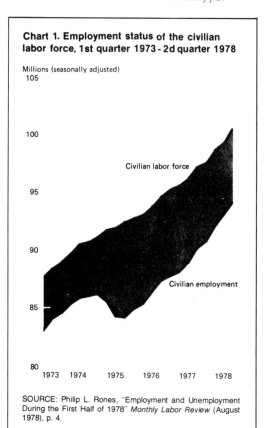

Chart 1. Employment status of the civilian labor force, 1st quarter 1973 - 2d quarter 1978

Millions (seasonally adjusted)

Civilian labor force

Civilian employment

SOURCE: Philip L. Rones, "Employment and Unemployment During the First Half of 1978" *Monthly Labor Review* (August 1978), p. 4.

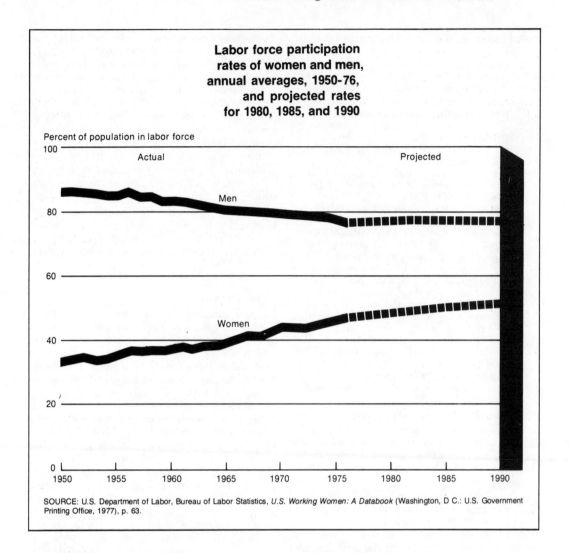

Labor force participation rates of women and men, annual averages, 1950-76, and projected rates for 1980, 1985, and 1990

Percent of population in labor force

Actual

Projected

Men

Women

SOURCE: U.S. Department of Labor, Bureau of Labor Statistics, *U.S. Working Women: A Databook* (Washington, D C.: U.S. Government Printing Office, 1977), p. 63.

labor intensive, any production process requiring a large proportion of human effort relative to capital investment.

labor law, body of law applied to concerns of employment, wages, conditions of work, unions, labor–management relations, etc. *See* Ronald A. Wykstra and Eleanour V. Stevens, *Labor Law and Public Policy* (N.Y.: Odyssey Press, 1970); Benjamin J. Taylor and Fred Witney, *Labor Relations Law* (Englewood Cliffs, N.J.: Prentice-Hall, 2nd ed., 1971); A. Howard Myers and David Twomey, *Labor Law and Legislation* (Cincinnati: Southwestern Publishing Co., 1975).

Labor Law Journal, monthly, devoted to legislative, administrative, and judicial developments pertaining to legal problems in the labor field.

Labor Law Journal
Commerce Clearing House, Inc.
4025 W. Peterson Ave.
Chicago, IL 60646

labor lobby, those elements of organized labor that seek to influence legislation affecting labor's interests.

labor–management relations, general term referring to the formal and informal dealings and agreements between employees or employee organizations and managers.

Labor–Management Relations Act of 1947 (LMRA), also called TAFT–HARTLEY ACT, federal statute that modified what the Congress thought was pro-union bias of the National Labor Relations (Wagner) Act of 1935. Essentially a series of amendments to the National Labor Relations Act, Taft–Hartley provided:

1. that "National Emergency Strikes" could be put off for an 80 day cooling-off period during which the president might make recommendations to Congress for legislation that might cope with the dispute;
2. a list of unfair labor practices by unions, which balanced the list of unfair labor practices by employers delineated in the Wagner Act;
3. that the "closed shop" was illegal (this provision allowed states to pass "right-to-work" laws);
4. that supervisory employees be excluded from coverage under the act;
5. that suits against unions for contract violations were allowable (judgements enforceable only against union assets);
6. that a party seeking to cancel an existing collective bargaining agreement is required to give 60 days' notice;
7. that employers have the right to seek a representation election if a union claimed recognition as a bargaining agent;
8. that the National Labor Relations Board was reorganized and enlarged from 3 to 5 members; and
9. that the Federal Mediation and Conciliation Service be created to mediate labor disputes.

The Taft–Hartley Act was passed over the veto of President Truman.

See also NATIONAL LABOR RELATIONS BOARD V. WOOSTER DIVISION OF BORG-WARNER CORP. and UNFAIR LABOR PRACTICES (UNIONS).

Labor–Management Reporting and Disclosure Act of 1959, also called LANDRUM–GRIFFIN ACT, federal statute enacted in response to findings of corruption in the management of some unions. The purpose of the act is to provide for

the reporting and disclosure of certain financial transactions and administrative practices of labor organizations and employers, to prevent abuses in the administration of trusteeships by labor organizations, to provide standards with respect to the election of officers of labor organizations and for other purposes.

Congress determined that certain basic rights should be assured to members of labor unions, and these are listed in Title I of the act as a Bill of Rights. Existing rights and remedies of union members under other federal or state laws, before any court or tribunal, or under the constitution and bylaws of their unions are not limited by the provisions of Title I. Executive Order 11491 made these rights applicable to members of unions

representing employees of the executive branch of the federal government.

Titles II through VI of the act deal primarily with the following: reporting by unions, by union officers and employees, by employers, by labor relations consultants, and by surety companies; union trusteeships; union safeguards. The Secretary of Labor has varying administrative and enforcement responsibilities under these titles. In addition, Titles II through VI contain a number of criminal provisions which involve enforcement responsibilities of the U.S. Department of Justice. Title VII contains amendments to the Labor–Management Relations Act of 1947.

See also the following entries:

AMERICAN FEDERATION OF MUSICIANS V. WITTSTEIN
LABOR–MANAGEMENT RELATIONS ACT OF 1947
TRUSTEESHIP

Labor–Management Services Administration (LMSA), agency of the U.S. Department of Labor that provides a framework within which workers and employers can resolve their differences together. It helps both labor and management through special studies of collective bargaining problems and research on labor–management policy development. Unions are required to make annual reports to it and comply with standards for union elections under the Labor–Management Reporting and Disclosure Act of 1959. Under the Employee Retirement Income Security Act of 1974, the agency administers reporting and disclosure, fiduciary, and minimum standards that protect the benefits and rights of pension and welfare plan participants and beneficiaries. LMSA also administers the veterans' reemployment rights provisions of the Veterans' Readjustment Assistance Act of 1974 and similar earlier laws.

LMSA
Department of Labor
200 Constitution Ave., N.W.
Washington, DC 20210
(202) 523-8165

labor market, according to Everett Johnson Burtt, Jr., in *Labor Markets, Unions, and Government Policies* (N.Y.: St. Martin's Press, 1963), a labor market

consists of those forces of demand and supply that establish a single price and the quantity sold of a particular labor service. Most labor markets can be defined spatially as local in character: the supply of machinists in Springfield, Vermont, for example, does not influence the price of machinists in Cleveland, Ohio. National markets can, however, be said to exist for some occupa-

---

BILL OF RIGHTS OF MEMBERS OF LABOR ORGANIZATIONS

Sec. 101. (a)(1) Equal Rights.—Every member of a labor organization shall have equal rights and privileges within such organization to nominate candidates, to vote in elections or referendums of the labor organization, to attend membership meetings and to participate in the deliberations and voting upon the business of such meetings, subject to reasonable rules and regulations in such organization's constitution and bylaws.

(2) *Freedom of Speech and Assembly.*—Every member of any labor organization shall have the right to meet and assemble freely with other members; and to express any views, arguments, or opinions; and to express at meetings of the labor organization his views, upon candidates in an election of the labor organization or upon any business properly before the meeting, subject to the organization's established and reasonable rules pertaining to the conduct of meetings: *Provided*, That nothing herein shall be construed to impair the right of a labor organization to adopt and enforce reasonable rules as to the responsibility of every member toward the organization as an institution and to his refraining from conduct that would interfere with its performance of its legal or contractual obligations.

(3) *Dues, Initiation Fees, and Assessments.*—Except in the case of a federation of national or international labor organizations, the rates of dues and initiation fees payable by members of any labor organization in effect on the date of enactment of this Act shall not be increased, and no general or special assessment shall be levied upon such members, except—

(A) in the case of a local organization, (i) by majority vote by secret ballot of the members in good standing voting at a general or special membership meeting, after reasonable notice of the intention to vote upon such question, or (ii) by majority vote of the members in good standing voting in a membership referendum conducted by secret ballot; or

(B) in the case of a labor organization, other than a local labor organization or a federation of national or international labor organizations, (i) by majority vote of the delegates voting at a regular convention, or at a special convention of such labor organization held upon not less than thirty days' written notice to the principal office of each local or constituent labor organization entitled to such notice, or (ii) by majority vote of the members in good standing of such labor organization voting in a membership referendum conducted by secret ballot, or (iii) by majority vote of the members of the executive board of similar governing body of such labor organization, pursuant to express authority contained in the constitution and bylaws of such labor organization: *Provided*, That such action on the part of the executive board or similar governing body shall be effective only until the next regular convention of such labor organization.

(4) *Protection of the Right to Sue.*—No labor organization shall limit the right of any member thereof to institute an action in any court, or in a proceding before any administrative agency, irrespective of whether or not the labor organization or its officers are named as defendants or respondents in such action or proceeding, or the right of any member of a labor organization to appear as a witness in any judicial, administrative, or legislative proceeding, or to petition any legislature or to communicate with any legislator: *Provided*, That any such member may be required to exhaust reasonable hearing procedures (but not to exceed a four-month lapse of time) within such organization, before instituting legal or administrative proceedings against such organizations or any officer thereof: *And provided further*, That no interested employer or employer association shall directly or indirectly finance, encourage, or participate in, except as a party, any such action, proceeding, appearance, or petition.

(5) *Safeguards Against Improper Disciplinary Action.*—No member of any labor organization may be fined, suspended, expelled, or otherwise disciplined except for nonpayment of dues by such organization or by any officer thereof unless such member has been (A) served with written specific charges; (B) given a reasonable time to prepare his defense; (C) afforded a full and fair hearing.

(b) Any provision of the constitution and bylaws of any labor organization which is inconsistent with the provisions of this section shall be of no force or effect.

---

tions, such as transistor engineers, airplane pilots, or certain types of government administrators. The factors determining the geographical size of a labor market depend upon the concentration demand in certain centers and upon the degree of mobility of labor supplies.

See Paul D. Montagna, *Occupations and Society: Toward A Sociology of the Labor Market* (N.Y.: John Wiley & Sons, 1977).

See also the following entries:

EFFECTIVE LABOR MARKET
EXTERNAL LABOR MARKET
SPLIT LABOR MARKET

labor mobility, degree of ease with which workers can change jobs and occupations.

labor monopoly, dominance over the supply of labor by a union or group of unions.

labor movement, inclusive term for the progressive history of U.S. unionism. Sometimes it is used in a broader sense to emcompass the fate of the "workers." For histories, *see* Leon Litwack, *The American Labor Movement* (Englewood Cliffs, N.J.: Prentice-Hall, 1962); Joel Seidman, "The Labor Movement Today: A Diagnosis," *Monthly Labor Review* (February 1965).

labor organization, as defined by Section 2(5) of the National Labor Relations act (as amended), a labor organization

> means any organization of any kind, or any agency or employee representation committee or plan, in which employees participate and which exists for the purpose, in whole or part, of dealing with employers concerning grievances, labor disputes, wages, rates of pay, hours of employment, or conditions of work.

See Thomas A. Kochan, "How American Workers View Labor Unions," *Monthly Labor Review* (April 1979).

The following listing of labor organizations was drawn from the U.S. Department of Labor's *Directory of National Unions and Employee Associations, 1975* (Washington, D.C.: Government Printing Office, 1977) and updated from a variety of other sources:

Actors and Artistes of America, Associated (AFL-CIO)
1500 Broadway
New York, NY 10036
Phone: (212) 869-0358
Membership: 76,000. *Branches:* 9.

- **Actors' Equity Association**
1500 Broadway
New York, NY 10036
Phone: (212) 869-8530
Membership: 27,000. *Local Unions:* 0.
- **American Federation of Television and Radio Artists**
1350 Avenue of the Americas, 2nd Floor
New York, NY 10019
Phone: (212) 265-7700
Membership: 26,917. *Local Unions:* 32.
- **American Guild of Musical Artists**
1841 Broadway
New York, NY 10023
Phone: (212) 265-3687
Membership: 4,000. *Local Unions:* 0.
- **American Guild of Variety Artists**
1540 Broadway
New York, NY 10036
Phone: (212) 765-0800
Membership: 5,000. *Local Unions:* 5.
- **Hebrew Actors Union, Inc.**
31 East 7th Street
New York, NY 10003
Phone: (212) 674-1923
Membership: 190. *Local Unions:* 0.
- **Italian Actors Union**
1674 Broadway
New York, NY 10019
Phone: (212) 582-6170
Membership: 75. *Local Unions:* 0.
- **Screen Actors Guild**
7750 Sunset Boulevard
Hollywood, CA 90046
Phone: (213) 876-3030
Membership: 29,797. *Local Unions:* 0.

- **Screen Extras Guild**
3629 Chauenga Boulevard
West Hollywood, CA 90029
Phone: (213) 851-4301
Membership: 3,000. *Local Unions:* 2.

Aeronautical Examiners, National Association of (Ind.)
2178 18th Avenue
San Francisco, CA 94116
Phone: (415) 869-2474
Membership: 400. *Local Union:* 5.

Aeronautical Production Controllers, National Association of (Ind.)
743 Red Mill Road
Norfolk, VA 23502
Phone: (804) 461-3451
Membership: 725. *Local Unions:* 4.

Air Line Dispatchers Association (AFL-CIO): merged with the Transport Workers Union, effective March 15, 1977.

Air Line Pilots Association (AFL-CIO)
Pilot Division
1625 Massachusetts Avenue, N.W.
Washington, DC 20036
Phone: (202) 797-4000
Membership: 27,707. *Local Unions:* 105.

- **Association of Flight Attendants**
1625 Massachusetts Avenue, N.W.
Washington, DC 20036
Phone: (202) 797-4075
Membership: 15,000. *Local Unions:* 61.
- **Air Line Employees Association**
5600 South Central Avenue
Chicago, IL 60638
Phone: (312) 767-3333
Membership: 10,000. *Local Unions:* 70.
- **Union of Professional Airmen**
1625 Massachusetts Avenue, N.W.
Washington, DC 20036
Phone: (202) 797-4280
Membership: 220. *Local Unions:* 10.

Air Traffic Specialists, Inc., National Association of (Ind.): affiliated with the Professional Air Traffic Controllers of the Marine Engineers Beneficial Association (AFL-CIO) on July 20, 1976.

Alabama State Employees Association (Ind.)
110 North Jackson Street
Montgomery, AL 36104
Phone: (205) 834-6965
Membership: 12,500. *Chapters:* 88.

Alaska Public Employees Association (Ind.)
130 Seward Street, Suite 508
Juneau, AK 99801
Phone: (907) 586-2334
Membership: 8,500. *Affiliates:* 20.

Allied Workers International Union, United (Ind.)
5506 Calumet Avenue, Box 723
Hammond, IN 46320
Phone: (219) 932-9400
Membership: 200. *Local Unions:* 2.

Aluminum Workers International Union (AFL-CIO)
Paul Brown Building
818 Olive Street, Suite 338
St. Louis, MO 63101
Phone: (314) 621-7292

Membership: 32,000. *Local Unions:* 91.

Arizona Public Employees Association (Ind.)
1820 West Washington
Phoenix, AZ 85007
Phone: (602) 252-6501
Membership: 12,000. *Affiliates:* 27.

Asbestos Workers, International Association of Heat and Frost Insulators and (AFL-CIO)
505 Machinists Building
1300 Connecticut Avenue N.W.
Washington, DC 20036
Phone: (202) 785-2388
Membership: 18,255. *Local Unions:* 119.

ASCS County Office Employees, National Association of (Ind.)
P. O. Box 242
Gettysburg, PA 17325
Phone: (717) 334-4216
Membership: 9,400. *Local Unions:* 46.

Atlantic Independent Union (Ind.)
3207 U Centre Square E
1500 Market Street
Philadelphia, PA 19101
Phone: (215) 564-3790
Membership: 3,255. *Local Unions:* 7.

Automobile, Aerospace and Agricultural Implement Workers of America; International Union, United (Ind.)
8000 East Jefferson Avenue
Detroit, MI 48214
Phone: (313) 926-5000
Membership: 1,544,859. *Local Unions:* 1,580.

Bakery and Confectionery Workers' International Union of America (AFL-CIO)
1828 L Street, N.W., Suite 900
Washington, DC 20036
Phone: (202) 466-2500
Membership: 134,158. *Local Unions:* 195.

Baseball Players of America, Association of Professional
12062 Valley View Street, Suite 211
Garden Grove, CA 92645
Phone: (714) 892-9900
Membership: 48,665. *Local Unions:* 0.

Brick and Clay Workers of America, The United (AFL-CIO)
P. O. Box 809
150 E. Mound Street, Suite 308
Columbus, OH 43216
Phone: (614) 464-2593
Membership: 15,000. *Locals:* 255.

Bricklayers and Allied Craftsmen, International Union of (AFL-CIO)
815 15th Street, N.W.
Washington, DC 20005
Phone: (202) 783-3788
Membership: 147,715. *Local Unions:* 758.

Broadcast Employees and Technicians, National Association of (AFL-CIO)
7101 Wisconsin Avenue, Suite 1303
Bethesda, MD 20012

Phone: (301) 657-8420
Membership: 6,600. *Local Unions:* 47.

California State Employees' Association (Ind.)
1108 O Street
Sacramento, CA 95814
Phone: (916) 444-8134
Membership: 106,000. *Affiliates:* 191.

Carpenters and Joiners of America, United Brotherhood of (AFL-CIO)
101 Constitution Avenue, N.W.
Washington, DC 20001
Phone: (202) 546-6206
Membership: 820,000. *Local Unions:* 2,301.

Cement, Lime and Gypsum Workers International Union, United (AFL-CIO)
7830 West Lawrence Avenue
Chicago, IL 60656
Phone: (312) 774-2217
Membership: 37,500. *Local Unions:* 327.

Chemical Workers Union, International (AFL-CIO)
1655 West Market Street
Akron, OH 44313
Phone: (216) 867-2444
Membership: 85,215. *Local Unions:* 450.

Christian Labor Association of the United States of America (Ind.)
9820 Gordon Street, Box 65
Zeeland, MI 49464
Phone: (616) 772-9153

Civil Service Employees Association, Inc. (New York State Ind.)
33 Elk Street
Albany, NY 122207
Phone: (518) 434-0191
Membership: 207,000. *Chapters:* 900.

Classified School Employees, American Association of (Ind.)
1585 Liberty Street S.E.
P. O. Box 3011
Salem, OR 97302
Phone: (503) 588-0121
Membership: 89,000. *Affiliates:* 5.

Clothing and Textile Workers Union, Amalgamated (AFL-CIO)
15 Union Square
New York, NY 10003
Phone: (212) 255-7800
Membership: 517,000. *Local Unions:* 1,535.

Colorado Association of Public Employees (Ind.)
1390 Logan Street, Room 200
Denver, CO 80203
Phone: (303) 832-1001
Membership: 11,200. *Affiliates:* 52.

Communications Workers of America (AFL-CIO)
1925 K Street, N.W.
Washington, DC 20006
Phone: (202) 785-6700
Membership: 498,743. *Local Unions:* 874.

Composers & Lyricists Guild of America (Ind.)
6565 Sunset Boulevard
Los Angeles, CA 90028
Phone: (213) 462-6068
Membership: 363. *Local Unions:* 1.

Connecticut Employees Union (Ind.)
72 Court Street
Middletown, CT 06457
Phone: (203) 344-0311
Membership: 3,200. *Affiliates:* 56.

Connecticut State Employees Association (Ind.)
760 Capitol Avenue
Hartford, CT 06106
Phone: (203) 525-6614
Membership: 27,400. *Affiliates:* 204.

Coopers' International Union of North America (AFL-CIO)
183 Mall Office Center
400 Sherburn Lane
Louisville, KY 40207
Phone: (502) 897-3274
Membership: 1,700. *Local Unions:* 36.

Die Sinkers' Conference, International (Ind.)
One Erieview Plaza
Cleveland, OH 44114
Phone: (216) 522-1050
Membership: 3,690. *Local Unions:* 29.

Directors Guild of America, Inc. (Ind.)
7950 Sunset Boulevard
Hollywood, CA 90046
Phone: (213) 656-1220
Membership: 4,154. *Local Unions:* 0.

Distillery, Rectifying, Wine and Allied Workers' International Union of America (AFL-CIO)
66 Grand Avenue
Englewood, NJ 07631
Phone: (201) 569-9212
Membership: 31,000. *Local Unions:* 88.

Distributive Workers of America (Ind.)
13 Astor Place
New York, NY 10003
Phone: (212) 673-5120
Membership: 50,000. *Local Unions:* 40.

Education Association, National (Ind.)
1201 16th Street, N.W.
Washington, DC 20036
Phone: (202) 833-4000
Membership: 1,470,212. *Affiliates:* 9,815.

● Overseas Education Association, Inc.
1201 16th Street, N.W., Room 210
Washington, DC 20036
Phone: (202) 833-4276
Membership: 3,067. *Affiliates:* 70.

Electrical, Radio, and Machine Workers, International Union of (AFL-CIO)
1126 16th Street N.W.
Washington, DC 20036
Phone: (202) 296-1200
Membership: 298,231. *Local Unions:* 633.

Electrical, Radio, and Machine Workers of America, United (Ind.)

11 East 51st Street
New York, NY 10022
Phone: (212) 753-1960
Membership: 163,000. *Local Unions:* 180.

Electrical Workers, International Brotherhood of (AFL-CIO)
1125 15th Street, N.W.
Washington, DC 20005
Phone: (202) 833-7000
Membership: 991,228. *Local Unions:* 1,583.

Elevator Constructors, International Union of (AFL-CIO)
Suite 332, Clarke Building
5565 Sterrett Place
Columbia, MD 21044
Phone: (301) 997-9000
Membership: 18,902. *Local Unions:* 109.

Farm Workers of America, United (AFL-CIO)
P. O. Box 62
Keene, CA 93531
Phone: (805) 822-5571
Membership: 12,000. *Local Unions:* 16.

Federal Employees, National Federation of (Ind.)
1016 16th Street, N.W.
Washington, DC 20036
Phone: (202) 862-4400
Membership: 100,000. *Local Unions:* 1,700.

Fire Fighters, International Association of (AFL-CIO)
1750 New York Avenue N.W.
Washington, DC 20006
Phone: (202) 872-8484
Membership: 171,674. *Local Unions:* 1,798.

Firemen and Oilers, International Brotherhood of (AFL-CIO)
VFM Building, 5th Floor
200 Maryland Avenue N.E.
Washington, DC 20002
Phone: (202) 547-7540
Membership: 40,000.

Flight Engineers' International Association (AFL-CIO)
905 16th Street N.W.
Washington, DC 20006
Phone: (202) 347-4511
Membership: 4,291. *Local Unions:* 17.

Food and Commercial Workers International Union, United (AFL-CIO)
Suffridge Building
1775 K Street, N.W.
Washington, DC 20006
Phone: (202) 223-3111
Membership: 1,159,500. *Local Unions:* 254.

Football League Players Association, National (Ind.)
1300 Connecticut Avenue N.W.
Washington, DC 20006
Phone: (202) 833-3335
Membership: 1,350. *Clubs:* 28.

Furniture Workers of America, United (AFL-CIO)

700 Broadway, 4th Floor
New York, NY 10003
Phone: (202) 533-1900
Membership: 29,967. *Local Unions:* 106.

Garment Workers of America, United (AFL-CIO)
200 Park Avenue, South
Suite 1610-1614
New York, NY 10003
Phone: (212) 677-0573
Membership: 25,000. *Local Unions:* 166.

Glass Bottle Blowers Association of the United States and Canada (AFL-CIO)
608 E. Baltimore Pike
Media, PA 19063
Phone: (215) 565-5051
Membership: 80,162. *Local Unions:* 244.

Glass and Ceramic Workers of North America, United (AFL-CIO)
556 East Town Street
Columbus, OH 43215
Phone: (614) 221-4465
Membership: 38,500. *Local Unions:* 197.

Glass Workers' Union of North America, American Flint (AFL-CIO)
1440 South Byrne Road
Toledo, OH 43614
Phone: (419) 385-6687
Membership: 35,000. *Local Unions:* 260.

Government Employees, American Federation of (AFL-CIO)
1325 Massachusetts Avenue N.W.
Washington, DC 20005
Phone: (202) 737-8700
Membership: 300,000. *Local Unions:* 1,500.

Government Employees, National Association of (Ind.)
285 Dorchester Avenue
Boston, MA 02127
Phone: (617) 268-5002
Membership: 150,000. *Local Unions:* 500.

Government Inspectors and Quality Assurance Personnel, National Association of (Ind.)
P. O. Box 13277
Chesapeake, VA 23325
Phone: (804) 444-8851
Membership: 703. *Local Unions:* 9.

Grain Millers, American Federation of (AFL-CIO)
4949 Olson Memorial Highway
Minneapolis, MN 55422
Phone: (612) 545-0211
Membership: 35,000. *Local Unions:* 204.

Granite Cutters' International Association of America, The (AFL-CIO)
18 Federal Avenue
Quincy, MA 02169
Phone: (617) 472-0209
Membership: 3,200. *Local Unions:* 17.

Graphic Arts International Union (AFL-CIO)
1900 L Street N.W.
Washington, DC 20036

Phone: (202) 872-7900
Membership: 100,000. *Local Unions:* 281.

Guards Union of America, International (Ind.)
1444 Gardiner Lane
Louisville, KY 40213
Phone: (303) 934-7360
Membership: 3,250. *Local Unions:* 50.

Guards and Watchmen, International Union of (Ind.)
452 Harrison Street, Room 213
San Francisco, CA 94105
Phone: (415) 895-9905
Membership: 3,500. *Local Unions:* 1.

Hatters, Cap and Millinery Workers International Union, United (AFL-CIO)
105 Madison Avenue
New York, NY 10016
Phone: (212) 683-5200
Membership: 14,000. *Local Unions:* 54.

Hockey League Players Association, National (Ind.)
Suite 1905, 80 Richmond Street W.
Toronto, Ontario, Canada
Phone: (416) 868-6574
Membership: 396. *Clubs:* 18.

Horseshoers of the United States and Canada, International Union of Journeymen (AFL-CIO)
P. O. Box 504
Pleasanton, CA 94566
Phone: (415) 846-2756
Membership: 370. *Local Unions:* 25.

Hotel and Restaurant Employees and Bartenders International Union (AFL-CIO)
120 East 4th Street
Cincinnati, OH 45202
Phone: (513) 621-0300
Membership: 451,989. *Local Unions:* 386.

Idaho Public Employees Association (Ind.)
430 North 9th Street
Boise, ID 83702
Phone: (208) 336-2841
Membership: 4,200. *Chapters:* 24.

Illinois State Employees Association (Ind.)
2800 South Walnut Street
Springfield, IL 62704
Phone: (217) 525-1944
Membership: 13,000. *Chapters:* 55.

Independent Unions, Congress of (Ind.)
303 Ridge Street
Alton, IL 62002
Phone: (618) 462-2447
Membership: 25,000. *Local Unions:* 10.

Indiana State Employees Association (Ind.)
632 Illinois Bldg.,
17 West Market Street
Indianapolis, IN 46204
Phone: (317) 632-7254
Membership: 3,500. *Local Chapters:* 38.

Industrial Trade Unions; National Organization of (Ind.)
148-06 Hillside Avenue
Jamaica, NY 11435

Phone: (212) 291-3434
Membership: 5,142. *Local Unions:* 10.

Industrial Workers of America, International Union Allied (AFL-CIO)
3520 West Oklahoma Avenue
Milwaukee, WI 53215
Phone: (414) 645-9500
Membership: 96,817. *Local Unions:* 440.

Industrial Workers Union, National (Ind.)
514 N. Main Street
P. O. Box 1893
Lima, OH 45802
Phone: (419) 223-8555
Membership: 759. *Local Unions:* 11.

Insurance Workers International Union (AFL-CIO)
1017 12th Street N.W.
Washington, DC 20005
Phone: (202) 783-1127
Membership: 21,896. *Local Unions:* 250.

Iron Workers, International Association of Bridge and Structural (AFL-CIO)
1750 New York Avenue N.W., Suite 400
Washington, DC 20006
Phone: (202) 872-1566
Membership: 181,647. *Local Unions:* 322.

Jewelry Workers' Union, International (AFL-CIO)
8 West 40th Street, Room 501
New York, NY 10018
Phone: (212) 244-8793
Membership: 10,000. *Local Unions:* 30.

Laborers' International Union of North America (AFL-CIO)
905 16th Street, N.W.
Washington, DC 20006
Phone: (202) 737-8320
Membership: 650,000. *Local Unions:* 850.

Lace Operatives of America, Amalgamated (Ind.)
4013 Glendale Street
Philadelphia, PA 19124
Phone: (215) 743-9358
Membership: 1,500. *Local Unions:* 9.

Ladies' Garment Workers' Union, International (AFL-CIO)
1710 Broadway
New York, NY 10019
Phone: (212) 265-7000
Membership: 348,380. *Local Unions:* 454.

Lathers, International Union of Wood, Wire and Metal (AFL-CIO)
815 16th Street, N.W.
Washington, DC 20006
Phone: (202) 628-0400
Membership: 14,428. *Local Unions:* 252.

Laundry and Dry Cleaning International Union (AFL-CIO)
Carlton House, Suite 435
550 Grant Street
Pittsburgh, PA 15219
Phone: (412) 471-4829
Membership: 19,543. *Local Unions:* 32.

Leather Goods, Plastic and Novelty Workers' Union, International (AFL-CIO)
265 West 14th Street, 14th Floor
New York, NY 10011
Phone: (212) 675-9240
Membership: 40,000. *Local Unions:* 97.

Leather Workers International Union of America (AFL-CIO)
11 Peabody Square
Peabody, MA 01960
Phone: (617) 531-5605
Membership: 3,000. *Local Unions:* 15.

Letter Carriers of the United States of America, National Association of (AFL-CIO)
100 Indiana Avenue, N.W.
Washington, DC 20001
Phone: (202) 393-4695
Membership: 232,000. *Local Unions:* 5,600.

Licensed Officers' Organization, Great Lakes (Ind.)
P. O. Box 387
Ludington, MI 49431
Phone: (616) 843-9543
Membership: 42. *Local Unions:* 0.

Licensed Practical Nurses, National Federation of (Ind.)
250 West 57th Street
New York, NY 10019
Phone: (212) 246-6629
Membership: 25,997. *Local Associations:* 38.

Locomotive Engineers, Brotherhood of (Ind.)
1112 Brotherhood of Locomotive Engineers Building
Cleveland, OH 44114
Phone: (216) 241-2630
Membership: 39,245. *Local Unions:* 779.

Log Scalers Association, Pacific (Ind.)
1675 Sixteenth Street
North Bend, OR 97459
Phone: (503) 759-4372
Membership: 290. *Local Unions:* 3.

Longshoremen's Association, International (AFL-CIO)
17 Battery Place, Room 1530
New York, NY 10004
Phone: (212) 425-1200
Membership: 76,579. *Local Unions:* 367.

• Masters, Mates and Pilots, International Organization of (ILA-Marine Division)
39 Broadway
New York, NY 10006
Phone: (212) 425-3860
Membership: 5,874. *Local Unions:* 4.

Longshoremen's and Warehousemen's Union, International (Ind.)
1188 Franklin Street
San Francisco, CA 94109
Phone: (415) 775-0533
Membership: 55,000. *Local Unions:* 76.

Machine Printers and Engravers Association of the United States (Ind.)
690 Warren Avenue
E. Providence, RI 02914

Phone: (401) 438-5849
Membership: 1,150. *Local Unions:* 14.

Mailers Union, International (Ind.)
7888 S. Turkeycreek Road
Morrison, CO 80465
Phone: (303) 697-8210
Membership: 3,500. *Local Unions:* 75.

Maine State Employees Association (Ind.)
65 State Street
Augusta, ME 04330
Phone: (207) 622-3151
Membership: 8,917. *Chapters:* 45.

Maintenance of Way Employees, Brotherhood of (AFL-CIO)
12050 Woodward Avenue
Detroit, MI 48203
Phone: (313) 868-0490
Membership: 119,184. *Local Unions:* 1,040.

Marine Engineers' Beneficial Association, National (AFL-CIO)
444 North Capitol Street, Room 800
Washington, DC 20001
Phone: (202) 347-8585
Membership: 9,150. *Districts:* 2.

● Professional Air Traffic Controllers Organization
2100 M Street N.W. 0706
Washington, DC 20037
Phone: (202) 638-6500
Membership: 12,535. *Local Unions:* 402.

Marine and Shipbuilding Workers of America, Industrial Union of (AFL-CIO)
1126 16th Street N.W.
Washington, DC 20036
Phone: (202) 223-0902
Membership: 25,000. *Local Unions:* 36.

Maritime Union of America, National (AFL-CIO)
346 West 17th Street
New York, NY 10011
Phone: (212) 924-3900
Membership: 35,000. *Local Unions:* 0.

Maryland Classified Employees Association, Inc. (Ind.)
2113 North Charles Street
Baltimore, MD 21218
Phone: (301) 685-7154
Membership: 29,000. *Chapters:* 216.

Massachusetts State Employees Association (Ind.); merged with National Association of Government Employees, effective January 1977.

Meat Cutters and Butcher Workmen of North America, Amalgamated (AFL-CIO): merged with the Retail Clerks International Union on June 7, 1979 to form the United Food and Commercial Workers International Union.

Mechanics Educational Society of America (AFL-CIO)
1421 First National Building
Detroit, MI 48226
Phone: (313) 965-6990
Membership: 25,000. *Local Unions:* 29.

Metal Polishers, Buffers, Platers and Allied Workers International Union (AFL-CIO)
5578 Montgomery Road
Cincinnati, OH 45212
Phone: (513) 531-2500
Membership: 10,000. *Local Unions:* 60.

Michigan State Employees Association (Ind.)
Box 1154
Lansing, MI 48904
Phone: (517) 372-9104
Membership: 18,500. *Chapters:* 158.

Mine Workers of America, United (Ind.)
900 15th Street N.W.
Washington, DC 20005
Phone: (202) 638-0530
Membership: 220,000. *Local Unions:* 850.

Minnesota Association of Government Employees, Independent (Ind.)
P. O. Box 3215
St. Paul, MN 55165
Phone: (612) 291-1049
Membership: 460. *Chapters:* 4.

Molders' and Allied Workers' Union, International (AFL-CIO)
1225 East McMillan Street
Cincinnati, OH 45206
Phone: (513) 221-1525
Membership: 75,000. *Local Unions:* 247.

Montana Public Employees Association (Ind.)
P. O. Box 1184
Helena, MT 59601
Phone: (406) 442-4600
Membership: 3,800. *Affiliates:* 9.

Musicians, American Federation of (AFL-CIO)
1500 Broadway
New York, NY 10036
Phone: (212) 869-1330
Membership: 330,000. *Local Unions:* 620.

National Labor Relations Board Professional Association (Ind.)
1717 Pennsylvania Avenue N.W.
Washington, DC 20006
Phone: (202) 254-9312
Membership: 125. *Local Unions:* 0.

National Labor Relations Board Union (Ind.)
Room 23, Federal Office Building
575 No. Penn Street
Indianapolis, IN 46204
Phone: (317) 269-7384
Membership: 1,150. *Local Unions:* 33.

Nebraska Association of Public Employees (Ind.)
521 South 14th Street, Suite 310
Lincoln, NE 68508
Phone: (402) 432-5381
Membership: 1,100. *Chapters:* 12.

New Hampshire State Employees Association (Ind.)
157 Manchester Street
Concord, NH 03301
Phone: (603) 271-3411
Membership: 4,177. *Affiliates:* 52.

New Jersey State Employees Association (Ind.)
15 W. State Street
Trenton, NJ 08606
Phone: (609) 394-8099
Membership: 8,000. *Chapters:* 11.

Newspaper Guild, The (AFL-CIO)
1125 15th Street N.W.
Washington, DC 20005
Phone: (202) 296-2990
Membership: 32,207. *Local Unions:* 84.

Newspaper and Mail Deliverers' Union of New York and Vicinity (Ind.)
41-18 27th Street
Long Island City, NY 11101
Phone: (212) 786-9565
Membership: 3,500. *Local Unions:* 0.

North American Soccer League Association (Ind.)
1300 Connecticut Avenue N.W.
Washington, DC 20036
Phone: (202) 833-3335
Membership: 375. *Teams:* 24.

North Carolina State Employees Association (Ind.)
P. O. Drawer 27727
Raleigh, NC 27602
Phone: (919) 833-6436
Membership: 25,000. *Affiliates:* 20.

North Carolina State Government Employees Association (Ind.)
3535 South Wilmington Street, Suite 103
Raleigh, NC 27603
Phone: (919) 772-1113
Membership: 9,900. *Affiliates:* 22.

North Dakota State Employees Association (Ind.)
P. O. Box 1764
Bismark, ND 58501
Phone: (701) 223-1964
Membership: 3,000. *Affiliates:* 28.

Nurses' Association, American (Ind.)
2420 Pershing Road
Kansas City, MO 64108
Phone: (816) 474-5720
Membership: 196,499. *Affiliates:* 53.

Office and Professional Employees International Union (AFL-CIO)
265 W. 14th Street, Suite 610
New York, NY 10011
Phone: (212) 675-3210
Membership: 89,468. *Local Unions:* 245.

Ohio Civil Service Employees Association, Inc. (Ind.)
88 East Broad Street, Suite 300
Columbus, OH 43215
Phone: (614) 221-2409
Membership: 33,000. *Affiliates:* 150.

Oil, Chemical and Atomic Workers International Union (AFL-CIO)
P. O. Box 2812
1636 Champa Street
Denver, CO 80201

Phone: (303) 893-0811
Membership: 177,433. *Local Unions:* 617.

Operating Engineers, International Union of (AFL-CIO)
1125 17th Street N.W.
Washington, DC 20036
Phone: (202) 347-8560
Membership: 415–395. *Local Unions:* 255.

Oregon State Employees Association (Ind.)
1127-25th Street S.E.
Salem, OR 97301
Phone: (503) 581-1505
Membership: 15,337. *Chapters:* 83.

Packinghouse and Industrial Workers, National Brotherhood of (Ind.)
500 Adams Street
Kansas City, KS 66105
Phone: (913) 371-9076
Membership: 2,000. *Local Unions:* 13.

Painters and Allied Trades of the United States and Canada, International Brotherhood of (AFL-CIO)
United Unions Bldg., 1750 New York Ave. N.W.
Washington, DC 20006
Phone: (202) 872-1444
Membership: 211,373. *Local Unions:* 904.

Paperworkers International Union, United (AFL-CIO)
163-03 Horace Harding Expressway
Flushing, NY 11365
Phone: (212) 762-6000
Membership: 300,684. *Local Unions:* 1,322.

Patent Office Professional Association (Ind.)
Patent Office
Washington, DC 20231
Phone: (703) 557-2975
Membership: 650. *Local Unions:* 1.

Pattern Makers' League of North America (AFL-CIO)
1000 Connecticut Avenue N.W., Suite 204
Washington, DC 20036
Phone: (202) 296-3790
Membership: 10,912. *Local Unions:* 81.

Physicians National Housestaff Association (Ind.)
1625 L Street N.W.
Washington, DC 20036
Phone: (202) 452-0081
Membership: 5,000. *Local Unions:* 80.

Planner-Estimators and Progressmen, National Association of (Ind.)
3705 Forsyth Court
Chesapeake, VA 23321
Phone: (804) 444-7761
Membership: 1,200. *Local Unions:* 16.

Plant Guard Workers of America, International Union, United (Ind.)
25510 Kelly Road
Roseville, MI 48066
Phone: (313) 772-7250
Membership: 34,000. *Local Unions:* 150.

Plasterers' and Cement Masons' Interna-

tional Association of the United States and Canada, Operative (AFL-CIO)
1125 17th Street N.W.
Washington, DC 20036
Phone: (202) 393-6569
Membership: 65,000. *Local Unions:* 450.

Plate Printers', Die Stampers' and Engravers' Union of North America, International (AFL-CIO)
228 South Swarthmore Avenue
Ridley Park, PA 19078
Phone: (215) 521-2495
Membership: 400. *Local Unions:* 10.

Plumbing and Pipe Fitting Industry of the United States and Canada, United Association of Journeymen and Apprentices of the (AFL-CIO)
901 Massachusetts Avenue N.W.
Washington, DC 20001
Phone: (202) 628-5823
Membership: 228,000. *Local Unions:* 542.

Police, Fraternal Order of (Ind.)
G-3136 W. Pasadena Avenue
Flint, MI 48504
Phone: (313) 732-6330
Membership: 147,000. *Affiliates:* 1,036.

Postal and Federal Employees, National Alliance of (Ind.)
1644 11th Street N.W.
Washington, DC 20001
Phone: (202) 332-4313
Membership: 20,000. *Local Unions:* 137.

Postal Security Police, Federation of (Ind.)
40-18 Bell Blvd.
Bayside, NY 11361
Phone: (212) 631-0914

Postal Supervisors, National Association of (Ind.)
P. O. Box 23456
L'Enfant Plaza Station
Washington, DC 20024
Phone: (202) 484-6070
Membership: 35,000. *Local Unions:* 450.

Postal Workers Union, American (AFL-CIO)
817 14th Street N.W.
Washington, DC 20005
Phone: (202) 638-2304
Membership: 249,000. *Local Unions:* 4,900.

Postmasters of the United States, National League of (Ind.)
P. O. Box 23753
Washington, DC 20024
Phone: (703) 892-2940
Membership: 25,000. *Local Unions:* 50.

Pottery and Allied Workers, International Brotherhood of (AFL-CIO): affiliated with Seafarer's International Union, effective June 21, 1976.

Printing and Graphic Communications Union, International (AFL-CIO)
1730 Rhode Island Avenue N.W.
Washington, DC 20036
Phone: (202) 293-2185

Membership: 128,714. *Local Unions:* 785.

Protection Employees, Independent Union of Plant (Ind.)
122 Pickard Drive
Mattydale, NY 13211
Phone: (617) 233-3529
Membership: 320. *Local Unions:* 14.

Pulp and Paper Workers, Association of Western (Ind.)
1430 Southwest Clay
Portland, OR 97201
Phone: (503) 228-7486
Membership: 20,781. *Local Unions:* 58.

Quarantine Inspectors National Association, Federal Plant (Ind.)
P. O. Box 592136
Miami, FL 31559
Phone: (305) 522-1567
Membership: 362. *Local Unions:* 30.

Radio Association, American (AFL-CIO)
270 Madison Avenue, Room 207
New York, NY 10016
Phone: (212) 689-5754
Membership: 618. *Local Unions:* 0.

Railroad Signalmen; Brotherhood of (AFL-CIO)
601 West Golf Road
Mt. Prospect, IL 60056
Phone: (312) 439-3732
Membership: 12,000. *Local Unions:* 205.

Railroad Yardmasters of America (AFL-CIO)
1411 Peterson Avenue, Room 202
Park Ridge, IL 60068
Phone: (312) 696-2510
Membership: 5,121. *Local Unions:* 75.

Railway, Airline and Steamship Clerks, Freight Handlers, Express and Station Employees; Brotherhood of (AFL-CIO)
O'Hare International Transportation Center
6300 River Road
Rosemont, IL 60018
Phone: (312) 692-7711
Membership: 235,000. *Local Unions:* 980.

Railway and Airway Supervisors Association, The American (AFL-CIO)
4250 West Montrose Avenue
Chicago, IL 60641
Phone: (312) 282-9424
Membership: 6,250. *Local Unions:* 53.

Railway Carmen of the United States and Canada, Brotherhood (AFL-CIO)
Carmen's Bldg, 4929 Main Street
Kansas City, MO 64112
Phone: (816) 561-1112
Membership: 95,954. *Local Unions:* 661.

Retail Clerks International Union (AFL-CIO): merged with the Amalgamated Meat Cutters and Butcher Workmen of North America on June 7, 1979 to form the United Food and Commercial Workers International Union.

Retail, Wholesale and Department Store Union (AFL-CIO)
101 West 31st Street
New York, NY 10001
Phone: (212) 947-9303
Membership: 180,000. *Local Unions:* 315.

Retail Workers Union, United (Ind.)
9865 West Roosevelt Road
Westchester, IL 60153
Phone: (312) 681-1000
Membership: 22,000. *Local Unions:* 4.

Roofers, Damp and Waterproof Workers Association, United Slate, Tile and Composition (AFL-CIO)
1125 17th Street N.W.
Washington, DC 20036
Phone: (202) 638-3228
Membership: 28,000. *Local Unions:* 205.

Rubber, Cork, Linoleum and Plastic Workers of America, United (AFL-CIO)
URWA Building
87 South High Street
Akron, OH 44308
Phone: (216) 376-6181
Membership: 190,523. *Local Unions:* 565.

Rural Letter Carriers' Association, National (Ind.)
1750 Pennsylvania Avenue, N.W.
Washington, DC 20006
Phone: (202) 393-5840
Membership: 60,000. *County Units:* 1,200.

School Administrators, American Federation of (AFL-CIO)
110 East 42nd Street
New York, NY 10017
Phone: (212) 697-5111
Membership: 8,000. *Local Unions:* 32.

Seafarers' International Union of North America (AFL-CIO)
675 Fourth Avenue
Brooklyn, NY 11232
Phone: (212) 499-6600
Membership: 80,000. *Affiliates:* 27.
- Atlantic, Gulf, Lakes and Inland Waters District
  675 Fourth Avenue
  Brooklyn, NY 11232
  Phone: (212) 499-6600
  Membership: 25,000.
- Inland Boatmen's Union of the Pacific
  1501 Norton Building
  Seattle, WA 98104
  Phone: (206) 622-9736
  Membership: 4,000.
- International Union of Petroleum and Industrial Workers
  335 California Avenue
  Bakersfield, CA 93304
  Phone: (805) 327-1614
  Membership: 2,500. *Local Unions:* 17.
- Marine Cooks and Stewards' Union
  350 Fremont Street
  San Francisco, CA 94105
  Phone: (415) 543-5855
  Membership: 1,895. *Branches:* 5.
- Pacific Coast Marine Firemen, Oilers, Watertenders and Wipers Association
  240 Second Street
  San Francisco, CA 94105
  Phone: (415) 362-4592
- Pottery and Allied Workers, International Brotherhood of
  P. O. Box 988

East Liverpool, OH 43920
Phone: (216) 386-5653
Membership: 17,051. *Local Unions:* 112.
- Sailors' Union of the Pacific
  450 Harrison Street
  San Francisco, CA 94105
  Phone: (415) 362-8363
  Membership: 3,340. *Port Branches:* 6.

Service Employees' International Union (AFL-CIO)
2020 K Street N.W.
Washington, DC 20006
Phone: (202) 452-8750
Membership: 550,000. *Local Unions:* 360.

Sheet Metal Workers' International Association (AFL-CIO)
United Unions Building, New York Avenue N.W.
Washington, DC 20006
Phone: (202) 296-5880
Membership: 160,860. *Local Unions:* 436.

Shoe and Allied Craftsmen, Brotherhood of (Ind.)
838 Main Street
Brockton, MA 02401
Phone: (617) 587-2606
Membership: 1,250. *Local Unions:* 17.

Shoe Workers of America, United (AFL-CIO)
120 Boylston Street, Suite 222
Boston, MA 02116
Phone: (617) 523-6121
Membership: 35,000. *Local Unions:* 125.

Shoe Workers' Union, Boot and (AFL-CIO): merged with the Retail Clerks International Union, effective September 1, 1977.

Siderographers, International Association of (AFL-CIO)
1134 Boulevard
New Milford, NJ 07646
Phone: (201) 836-9158
Membership: 18. *Local Unions:* 3.

Sleeping Car Porters, Brotherhood of (AFL-CIO)
1716–18 7th Street
Oakland, CA 94607
Phone: (415) 893-0894
Membership: 1,300. *Local Unions:* 20.

Southern Labor Union (Ind.)
Alberta Avenue & 2nd Street
Oneida, TN 37841
Phone: (615) 569-8335
Membership: 2,200. *Local Unions:* 54.

State, County, and Municipal Employees, American Federation of (AFL-CIO)
1625 L Street N.W.
Washington, DC 20036
Phone: (202) 452-4800
Membership: 648,160. *Local Unions:* 2,570.

Steelworkers of America, United (AFL-CIO)
Five Gateway Center
Pittsburgh, PA 15222
Phone: (412) 562-2306
Membership: 1,300,000. *Local Unions:* 5,300.

Stove, Furnace and Allied Appliance Workers' International Union of North America (AFL-CIO)
2929 South Jefferson Avenue
St. Louis, MO 63118
Phone: (314) 664-3736
Membership: 9,500. *Local Unions:* 45.

Teachers, American Federation of (AFL-CIO)
11 Dupont Circle N.W.
Washington, DC 20036
Phone: (202) 797-4400
Membership: 444,000. *Local Unions:* 1,938.

Teamsters, Chauffeurs, Warehousemen and Helpers of America, International Brotherhood of (Ind.)
25 Louisiana Avenue N.W.
Washington, DC 20001
Phone: (202) 624-6800
Membership: 1,973,272. *Local Unions:* 805.

• Laundry, Dry Cleaning and Dye House Workers' International Union
360 North Michigan Avenue
Chicago, IL 60601
Phone: (312) 726-9416
Membership: 33,284. *Local Unions:* 54.

Technical Engineers, International Federation of Professional and (AFL-CIO)
1126 16th Street N.W., Suite 200
Washington, DC 20036
Phone: (202) 223-1811
Membership: 19,500. *Local Unions:* 78.

Technicians, Association of Civilian (Ind.)
348 A Hungerford Court
Rockville, MD 20850
Phone: (301) 762-5656
Membership: 5,500. *Local Unions:* 52.

Telegraph Workers, United (AFL-CIO)
701 Gude Drive
Rockville, MD 20850
Phone: (301) 762-4444
Membership: 13,588. *Local Unions:* 90.

Textile Workers of America, United (AFL-CIO)
420 Common Street
Lawrence, MA 01842
Phone: (617) 686-2901
Membership: 47,344. *Local Unions:* 275.

Textile Workers Union of America (AFL-CIO): merged into Clothing and Textile Workers Union, effective June 3, 1976.

Theatrical Stage Employees and Moving Picture Machine Operators of the United States and Canada, International Alliance of (AFL-CIO)
1515 Broadway, Suite 601
New York, NY 10036
Phone: (212) 730-1770
Membership: 61,471. *Local Unions:* 870.

Tile, Marble and Terrazzo Finishers and Shopmen International Union (AFL-CIO)
801 N. Pitt Street, Suite 116

Alexandria, VA 22314
Phone: (703) 549-3050
Membership: 8,000. *Local Unions:* 107.

Tobacco Workers International Union (AFL-CIO)
1522 K Street N.W., Suite 616
Washington, DC 20005
Phone: (202) 659-1366
Membership: 34,627. *Local Unions:* 63.

Tool Craftsmen, International Association of (Ind.)
3243 37th Avenue
Rock Island, IL 61201
Phone: (309) 788-9776
Membership: 496. *Local Unions:* 11.

Tool, Die and Mold Makers, International Union of (Ind.)
71 Cherry Street
Rahway, NJ 07065
Phone: (201) 388-3323
Membership: 501. *Local Unions:* 4.

Toys, Playthings, Novelties and Allied Products of the United States and Canada, International Union of Dolls (AFL-CIO)
147–149 East 26th Street
New York, NY 10010
Phone: (212) 889-1212
Membership: 31,000. *Local Unions:* 23.

Trademark Society Inc. (Ind.)
P. O. Box 2062
EADS Station
Arlington, VA 22202
Phone: (703) 557-3273
Membership: 48. *Local Unions:* 0.

Train Dispatchers Association, America (AFL-CIO)
1401 S. Harlem Avenue
Berwyn, IL 60402
Phone: (312) 795-5656
Membership: 3,229. *Local Unions:* 79.

Transit Union, Amalgamated (AFL-CIO)
5025 Wisconsin Avenue N.W.
Washington, DC 20016
Phone: (202) 537-1645
Membership: 140,000. *Local Unions:* 350.

Transport Workers Union of America (AFL-CIO)
1980 Broadway
New York, NY 10023
Phone: (212) 873-6000
Membership: 150,000. *Local Unions:* 105.

Transportation Union, United (AFL-CIO)
14600 Detroit Avenue
Cleveland, OH 44107
Phone: (216) 228-9400
Membership: 238,000. *Local Unions:* 1,211.

Treasury Employees Union, National (Ind.)
1730 K Street N.W.
Washington, DC 20006
Phone: (202) 785-4411
Membership: 50,000. *Local Unions:* 130.

Typographical Union, International (AFL-CIO)
P. O. Box 157
Colorado Springs, CO 80901
Phone: (303) 636-2341
Membership: 111,362. *Local Unions:* 636.

University Professors; American Association of (Ind.)
1 Dupont Circle, Suite 500
Washington, DC 20036
Phone: (202) 466-8050
Membership: 72,265. *Chapters:* 1,360.

Upholsterers' International Union of North America (AFL-CIO)
25 North Fourth Street
Philadelphia, PA 19106
Phone: (215) 923-5700
Membership: 59,000. *Local Unions:* 170.

Utah Public Employees Association (Ind.)
438 South 6th East
Salt Lake City, UT 84102
Phone: (801) 328-4995
Membership: 10,039. *Districts:* 51.

Utility Workers of New England, Inc., Brotherhood of (Ind.)
212 Union Street
Providence, RI 02903
Phone: (401) 751-6829
Membership: 4,500. *Local Unions:* 19.

Utility Workers Union of America (AFL-CIO)
815 16th Street N.W., Suite 605
Washington, DC 20006
Phone: (202) 347-8105
Membership: 60,000. *Local Unions:* 250.

Vermont State Employees Association, Inc. (Ind.)
79 Main Street
Montpelier, VT 05602
Phone: (802) 223-5247
Membership: 3,700. *Chapters:* 17.

Warehouse Industrial International Union (Ind.)
222 17 Northern Boulevard
Bayside, NY 11361
Phone: (212) 776-5437
Membership: 50. *Local Unions:* 0.

Washington Public Employees Association (Ind.)
124 West 10th Street
Olympia, WA 98501
Phone: (206) 943-1121
Membership: 4,000. *Chapters:* 36.

Watch Workers Union, American (Ind.)
617 West Orange Street
Lancaster, PA 17603
Phone: (717) 397-1339
Membership: 735. *Local Unions:* 2.

Watchmen's Association, Independent (Ind.)
11 Broadway
New York, NY 10004
Phone: (212) 943-5880
Membership: 10,000. *Local Unions:* 14.

Western States Service Station Employees Union (Ind.)
703 Market Street
San Francisco, CA 94103
Phone: (213) 342-2610
Membership: 426. *Local Unions:* 14.

Woodworkers of America, International (AFL-CIO)
1622 North Lombard Street
Portland, OR 97217
Phone: (503) 285-5281
Membership: 107,966. *Local Unions:* 231.

Writers Guild of America
● Writers Guild of America, East, Inc. (Ind.)
22 W. 48th Street
New York, NY 10036
Phone: (212) 575-5060
Membership: 1,600.
● Writers Guild of America West, Inc. (Ind.)
8955 Beverly Blvd.
Los Angeles, CA 90048
Phone: (213) 550-1000
Membership: 3,204.

Wyoming State Employees Association (Ind.)
408 West 23rd Street
Cheyenne, WY 82001
Phone: (307) 635-5633
Membership: 2,850. *Affiliates:* 27.

labor organizer: *see* ORGANIZER.

labor piracy, attracting employees away from one organization and into another by offering better wages and other benefits.

labor pool, set of trained workers from which prospective employees are recruited.

labor racketeer, broad term that applies to a union leader who uses his/her office as a base for unethical and illegal activities. For a history, *see* John Hutchinson, *The Imperfect Union: A History of Corruption in American Trade Unions* (N.Y.: E. P. Dutton & Co., 1972).

See also ANTI-RACKETEERING ACT OF 1934 and UNFAIR LABOR PRACTICES (UNIONS).

labor relations, totality of the interactions between an organization's management and organized labor. For texts, *see* Arthur A. Sloane and Fred Witney, *Labor Relations* (Englewood Cliffs, N.J.: Prentice-Hall, 3rd ed., 1977); Murray B. Nesbitt, *Labor Relations in the Federal Government Service* (Washington, D.C.: Bureau of National Affairs, Inc., 1976).

labor reserve, general term that refers to potential members of the workforce. Historically the concept has been applied to the least skilled and the least able. For a modern definition, *see* Christopher G. Gellner, "Enlarging the Concept of a Labor Reserve," *Monthly Labor Review* (April 1975).

labor-saving equipment, any device that re-

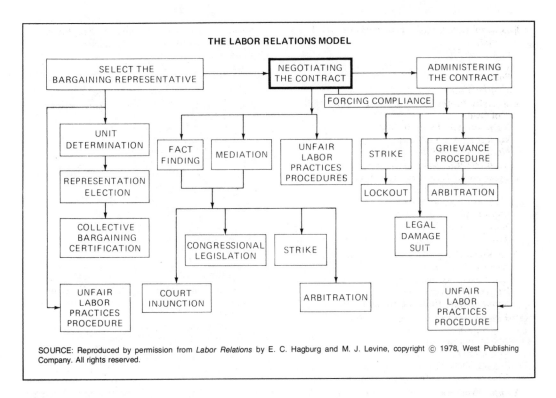

THE LABOR RELATIONS MODEL

duces an organization's need for human labor.

labor slowdown: *see* SLOWDOWN.

labor spy: *see* COMPANY SPY.

Labor Statistics, Bureau of: *see* BUREAU OF LABOR STATISTICS.

labor studies, formal academic degree concentrations or certificate programs concerned with the various aspects of labor relations. *See* Lois S. Gray, "Academic Degrees for Labor Studies—A New Goal for Unions," *Monthly Labor Review* (1977).

Labor Studies Journal, journal published three times a year by the University and College Labor Education Association, which offers articles and reviews on all aspects of labor studies.

> *Labor Studies Journal*
> **Subscription Address:**
> Transaction Periodicals Consortium
> Rutgers University
> Box L
> New Brunswick, NJ 08903
> **Editorial Address:**
> George Meany Center for Labor Studies
> 10,000 New Hampshire Ave.
> Silver Springs, MD 20903

labor theory of value, notion that the value of

a product is dependent or determined by the amount (or value) of the labor needed to produce it. Karl Marx used this concept (developed earlier by Adam Smith and David Ricardo) to denounce capitalists who exploited the working class by selling products at higher prices than the cost of the labor that went into them.

Lace Operatives of America, Amalgamated: *see* LABOR ORGANIZATION.

Ladies' Garment Workers' Union, International: *see* LABOR ORGANIZATION.

laissez-faire, "hands off" style of leadership that emphasizes loose supervision.

Lake, Mother: *see* BARRY, LEONORA.

lame duck, in U.S. politics, any officeholder who is serving out the remainder of a fixed term after declining to run, or being defeated, for reelection. Since he/she will soon be leaving, his/her authority is considered impaired or "lame." The term is used in an organizational sense to refer to anyone whose leaving has been announced whether for retirement, promotion, transfer, etc.

Landrum–Griffin Act: *see* LABOR–MANAGEMENT REPORTING AND DISCLOSURE ACT OF 1959.

last offer arbitration: *see* FINAL OFFER ARBITRATION.

latent learning: *see* INCIDENTAL LEARNING.

lateral entry, appointment of an individual from outside of the organization to a position above the bottom level of a generally recognized career ladder.

lateral transfer: *see* TRANSFER.

Lathers, International Union of Wood, Wire and Metal: *see* LABOR ORGANIZATION.

Lauf **v.** *E. G. Shinner and Company*, 303 U.S. 323 (1938), U.S. Supreme Court case, which held that organizational picketing was a "labor dispute" within the meaning of the Norris–LaGuardia Act of 1932. This meant the employer could not seek an injunction in a federal court to stop the picketing.

Laundry and Dry Cleaning International Union: *see* LABOR ORGANIZATION.

Laundry, Dry Cleaning and Dye House Workers' International Union: *see* LABOR ORGANIZATION, Teamsters, Chauffeurs, Warehousemen and Helpers of America, International Brotherhood of.

law: *see* ACT.

Lawler, Edward E., III (1938–   ), psychologist who has written widely in the areas of organizational behavior and a leading authority on the relationship between pay and organizational effectiveness. Major works include: *Managerial Attitudes and Performance*, with L. W. Porter (Homewood, Illinois: Richard D. Irwin, 1968); *Managerial Behavior, Performance and Effectiveness*, with J. P. Campbell, M. D. Dunnette, and K. E. Weick, Jr. (N.Y.: McGraw-Hill, 1970); *Pay and Organizational Effectiveness: A Psychological View* (N.Y.: McGraw-Hill, 1971); *Motivation in Work Organizations* (Monterey, California: Brooks/Cole Publishing Company, 1973); *Behavior in Organizations*, with L. W. Porter and J. R. Hackman (N.Y.: McGraw-Hill, 1975).

Lawlor **v.** *Loewe*, also called DANBURY HATTERS' CASE, 235 U.S. 522 (1915), U.S. Supreme Court case, which held that the hatter's union which was seeking to organize a factory in Danbury, Connecticut, was in violation of the Sherman Anti-Trust Act of 1890 when it successfully organized a boycott against the company. The court ruled against the union because its boycott had the assistance of other affiliates of the American Federation of Labor and the Sherman Act prohibited "any combination whatever to secure action which essentially obstructs the free flow of commerce between the states, or restricts in that regard, the liberty of a trader to engage in business." The uproar over this decision led to the passage of the Clayton Act of 1914, which disallowed the application of the Sherman Act to combinations of labor.

Law of Effect, fundamental concept in learning theory that holds that, other things being equal, an animal will learn those habits leading to satisfaction and will not learn (or learn only slowly) those habits causing annoyance. It was first formulated by Edward L. Thorndike, in *Education: A First Book* (N.Y.: MacMillan, 1920), as follows:

> the greater the satisfyingness of the state of affairs which accompanies or follows a given response to a certain situation, the more likely that response is to be made to that situation in the future. Conversely, the greater the discomfort or annoyingness of the state of affairs which comes with or after a response to a situation, the more likely that response is not to be made to that situation in the future.

Law of the Situation, Mary Parker Follett's notion, in Henry C. Metcalf and Lyndall Urwick, ed's., *Dynamic Administration The Collected Papers of Mary Parker Follett* (N.Y.: Harper & Bros., 1940), that

> one person should not give orders to another person, but both should agree to take their orders from the situation. If orders are simply part of the situation, the question of someone giving and someone receiving does not come up.

Law of Triviality, C. Northcote Parkinson's discovery that "the time spent on any item of the agenda will be in inverse proportion to the sum involved." Parkinson attempted to head off his critics by asserting

> the statement that this law has never been investigated is not entirely accurate. Some work has actually been done in this field, but the investigators pursued a line of inquiry that led them nowhere. They assumed that the greatest significance should attach to the order in which items of the agenda are taken. They assumed, further, that most of the available time will be spent on items one to seven and that the latter items will be allowed automatically to pass. The result is well known.... We realize now that position on the agenda is a minor consideration.

For more, *see* C. Northcote Parkinson, *Parkinson's Law and other Studies in Administration* (Boston: Houghton Mifflin Co., 1957).

For a methodological analysis, *see* Ross Curnow, "An Empirical Examination of the Parkinsonian Law of Triviality," *Public Personnel Review* (January 1971).

layoff, temporary or indefinite separation from employment, without prejudice or loss of seniority, resulting from slack work, a shortage of materials, decline in product demand, or other factors over which the worker has no control. The Bureau of Labor Statistics compiles monthly layoff rates by industry. For an account of how a General Electric division sought to do it "nicely," *see* Ken Leinweber, "Showing Them the Door," *Personnel* (July–August 1976).

The "last hired–first fired" policy of layoffs has come under increasing criticism because of the disparate impact that it has had upon minorities. For analyses of layoffs dealing with this problem, *see* William R. Walter and Anthony J. Obadal, "Layoffs: The Judicial View," *Personnel Administrator* (May 1975); James Ledvinka, "EEO, Seniority, and Layoffs," *Personnel* (January–February 1976).

See also the following entries:

DISCIPLINARY LAYOFF
RECALL
RE-EMPLOYMENT LIST
RETENTION STANDING

LDC: *see* LABOR ORGANIZATION, Laundry and Dry Cleaning International Union.

leadership, exercise of authority, whether formal or informal, in directing and coordinating the work of others. The literature on the concept of leadership is immense. The best one volume summary is Ralph M. Stogdill, *Handbook of Leadership: A Survey of Theory and Research* (N.Y.: The Free Press, 1974). The best quote on the problems of leadership comes from Harry S. Truman, who said while discoursing on his job as president of the United States: "I sit here all day trying to persuade people to do the things they ought to have sense enough to do without my persuading them."

See also CHARISMATIC LEADERSHIP and FUNCTIONAL LEADERSHIP.

leadership effectiveness, contingency model of: *see* CONTINGENCY MODEL OF LEADERSHIP EFFECTIVENESS.

leadership style, patterns of a leader's interactions with his/her subordinates.

learning, generally, any behavior change occurring because of interaction with the environment. *See* Lee Hess and Len Sperry, "The Psychology of the Trainee as Learner," *Personnel Journal* (September 1973).

See also INCIDENTAL LEARNING and PROGRAMMED LEARNING.

learning curve, in industry the concept holds

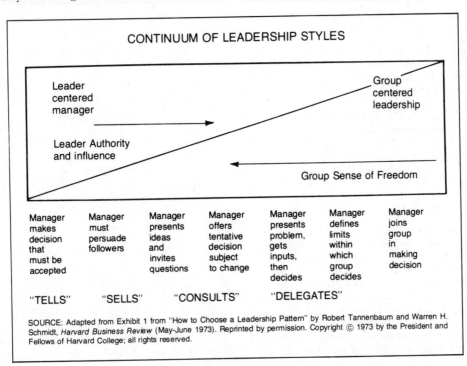

CONTINUUM OF LEADERSHIP STYLES

Leader centered manager

Group centered leadership

Leader Authority and influence

Group Sense of Freedom

| Manager makes decision that must be accepted | Manager must persuade followers | Manager presents ideas and invites questions | Manager offers tentative decision subject to change | Manager presents problem, gets inputs, then decides | Manager defines limits within which group decides | Manager joins group in making decision |

"TELLS"   "SELLS"   "CONSULTS"   "DELEGATES"

SOURCE: Adapted from Exhibit 1 from "How to Choose a Leadership Pattern" by Robert Tannenbaum and Warren H. Schmidt, *Harvard Business Review* (May–June 1973). Reprinted by permission. Copyright © 1973 by the President and Fellows of Harvard College; all rights reserved.

that when workers repeatedly perform a task, the amount of labor required per unit of output decreases according to a constant pattern. Generally speaking, with traditional, mass-production processes, each time output doubles, the new average of effort per unit should decline by a certain percentage, and so on for each successive doubling of output. Of course, as production processes become more dependent upon machines, the learning curve becomes less and less significant. *See* Raymond B. Jordan, *How To Use The Learning Curve* (Boston: Materials Management Institute, 1965). For a critique of its limitations, *see* William J. Abernathy and Kenneth Wayne, "Limits of the Learning Curve," *Harvard Business Review* (September–October 1974)

The learning curve as a concept in training describes a learning process in which increases of performance are large at the beginning but become smaller with continued practice. Learning of any new thing eventually levels off as mastery is attained, at which point the curve becomes horizontal. For further details, *see* Bernard M. Bass and James A. Vaughn, *Training in Industry: The Management of Learning* (Belmont, Calif.: Wadsworth Publishing Co., 1966). *See also* Winfred B. Hirschmann, "Profit from the Learning Curve," *Harvard Business Review* (January–February 1964).

learning plateau, that flat part of a learning curve that indicates there has been little or no additional learning.

Leather Goods, Plastic and Novelty Workers' Union, International: *see* LABOR ORGANIZATION.

Leather Workers International Union of America: *see* LABOR ORGANIZATION.

leave, birth: *see* BIRTH LEAVE.

leave of absence: *see* FURLOUGH and LEAVE WITHOUT PAY.

leave without pay, a temporary nonpay status and short-term absence from duty, granted upon the employee's request. The permissive nature of leave without pay distinguishes it from absence without leave. A *leave of absence* is the same as leave without pay except for duration. A leave of absence implies a more substantial amount of time away from one's position.

L. Ed., abbreviation for *Lawyer's Edition* of the U.S. Supreme Court Reports.

leptokurtic, frequency distribution or curve that is more peaked, as opposed to flat-topped, than a normal curve.

Letter Carriers **decision:** *see* UNITED STATES CIVIL SERVICE COMMISSION V. NATIONAL ASSOCIATION OF LETTER CARRIERS.

Letter Carriers of the United States of America, National Association of: *see* LABOR ORGANIZATION.

Letter Carriers **v.** *Austin:* *see* OLD DOMINION BRANCH NO. 496, NATIONAL ASSOCIATION OF LETTER CARRIERS V. AUSTIN.

level annual premium funding method, after the pension costs for a new employee are actuarially determined, pension contributions or premiums are paid into a fund (or to an insurance company) in equal installments during the employee's remaining working life so that upon retirement the pension benefit is fully funded.

Levinson, Harry (1922-), psychologist and a leading authority on organizational mental health and work motivation. Major works include: *Men, Management and Mental Health*, with C. R. Price, H. J. Munden & C. M. Solley (Cambridge, Mass.: Harvard University Press, 1962); *Emotional Health in the World of Work* (N.Y.: Harper & Row, 1964); *Organizational Diagnosis* (Cambridge, Mass.: Harvard University Press, 1972); *The Exceptional Executive: A Psychological Conception* (Cambridge, Mass.: Harvard University Press, 1968); *Executive Stress* (N.Y.: Harper & Row, 1970); *The Great Jackass Fallacy* (Boston: Harvard Graduate School of Business Administration, 1973).

Lewin, Kurt (1890-1947), popularly noted for his assertion that "there is nothing so practical as a good theory," was the most influential experimental psychologist of the twentieth century. His research originated the modern concepts of group dynamics, action research, field theory, and sensitivity training. Major works include: *Principles of Topological Psychology* (N.Y.: McGraw-Hill, 1936); *Resolving Social Conflicts: Selected Papers on Group Dynamics* (N.Y.: Harper & Row, 1948); *Field Theory In Social Science: Selected Theoretical Papers*, edited by Dorwin Cartwright (London: Tavistock, 1963). For a biography, *see* Alfred J. Marrow, *The Practical Theorist: The Life and Work of Kurt Lewin* (N.Y.: Basic Books, 1969).

Lewis, John L. (1880-1969), president of the United Mine Workers of America from 1920 to 1960, a founder and first president of the Congress of Industrial Organizations (CIO), and probably the most controversial, most hated, and most revered labor leader of his time. For biographies, *see* Saul Alinsky, *John L. Lewis: An Unauthorized Biography* (N.Y.: G. P. Putnam's Sons, 1949); Melvyn Dubofsky and Warren Van Tine, *John L. Lewis: A Biography* (N.Y.: Quadrangle, 1977).

LGPN: *see* LABOR ORGANIZATION, Leather Workers International Union of America.

Licensed Officers' Organization, Great Lakes: *see* LABOR ORGANIZATION.

Licensed Practical Nurses, National Federation of: *see* LABOR ORGANIZATION.

licensing: *see* OCCUPATIONAL LICENSING.

lie detector, also called POLYGRAPH, also VOICE STRESS ANALYZER, and PSYCHOLOGICAL STRESS ANALYZER, an instrument for recording physiological phenomena such as blood pressure, pulse rate, and the respiration rate of individuals as they answer questions put to them by an operator. The technique is based on the assumption that when an individual experiences apprehension, fear, or emotional excitement, his/her respiration rate, blood pressure, etc., will sharply increase. These physiological data are then interpreted by an operator who makes judgements on whether or not a subject is lying. Only one thing is certain about polygraph tests; they are not 100 percent accurate. Lie detectors have been used in police investigations since the 1920s, and have been increasingly used for employee screening since World War II. However the authority of employers to use polygraph tests in personnel investigations has been challenged. Many state and local legislative actions have placed legal limitations on the public and private employers' use of lie detectors. Thirteen states prohibit the use of polygraphs as a condition of employment or continued employment. In addition, labor arbitrators often refuse to admit test results as evidence of "just cause" for discharge and have upheld a worker's right to refuse to take such a test. According to David T. Lykken, in "Psychology and The Lie Detector Industry," *American Psychologist* (October 1974), "the general use of lie detectors in employee screening cannot be justified, however, and psychologists have a professional responsibility to oppose this growing practice." For other analyses, *see* Burke M. Smith, "The Polygraph," *Scientific American* (January

1967); Mary Ann Coghill, *The Lie Detector In Employment* (Ithaca, N.Y.: New York State School of Industrial and Labor Relations, Cornell University, rev. ed., 1973); John A. Beit and Peter B. Holden, "Polygraph Usage Among Major U.S. Corporations," *Personnel Journal* (February 1978).

The *voice stress analyzer* or *psychological stress analyzer* is a lie detector that can be used without the subject knowing that he/she is being tested. By simply analyzing the stress in the subject's voice it purports to tell whether or not the truth is being told. As such devices have only been available since the mid 1970s, their use should still be considered experimental.

life cycle theory of leadership, theory put forth by Paul Hersey and Kenneth R. Blanchard, which suggests that the appropriate leadership style for a particular situation should be primarily dependent upon the task maturity level of the follower(s). Maturity is defined as a function of task relevant education and experience, achievement motivation, and willingness and ability to accept responsibility. Leadership is seen as a combination of two types of behavior: "Task Behavior" (Directive), ranging from low to high, and "Relationships Behavior" (Supportive), ranging from low to high. If a follower is assessed to be extremely "immature," the theory suggests that high task-low relationships is

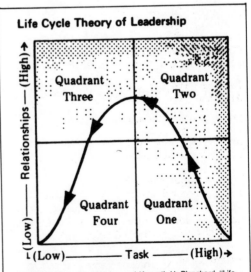

SOURCE: From Paul Hersey and Kenneth H. Blanchard, "Life Cycle Theory of Leadership." Reproduced by special permission from the May 1969 TRAINING AND DEVELOPMENT JOURNAL. Copyright 1969 by the American Society for Training and Development, Inc.

the appropriate leadership style. As the follower matures the theory suggests that the leader's behavior should move from high task-low relationships (Quadrant I), to high task-high relationships (Quadrant II), to high relationship-low task Quadrant III), to low task-low relationships (Quadrant IV).

life insurance, insurance that provides for the payment of a specific amount to a designated beneficiary in the event of the death of the insured.

See also the following entries:

GROUP LIFE INSURANCE
SPLIT-DOLLAR LIFE INSURANCE
TERM LIFE INSURANCE
VARIABLE LIFE INSURANCE

Likert, Rensis (1903-   ), one of the pioneers of organizational survey research and director of the Institute of Social Research at the University of Michigan from 1948 to 1970. He is perhaps best known for his linking-pin theory and his concepts of Systems 1, 2, 3, and 4. Major works include: *New Patterns of Management* (N.Y.: McGraw-Hill, 1961); *The Human Organization: Its Management and Value* (N.Y.: McGraw-Hill, 1967); *New Ways of Managing Conflict*, with Jane Gibson Likert (N.Y.: McGraw-Hill, 1976).

Likert Scale, also called LIKERT-TYPE SCALE, one of the most widely used scales in social research. Named after Rensis Likert, who first presented it in "A Technique for the Measurement of Attitudes," *Archives of Psychology* (No. 140, 1932), the scale presents a subject with a statement to which the subject expresses his/her reaction or opinion by selecting one of five (or more) possible responses.

Typical Questions on a Likert Scale

1. The sick-leave policies of this company are not liberal enough.
   (a) strongly agree
   (b) agree
   (c) no opinion
   (d) disagree
   (e) strongly disagree

2. My supervisor is a good leader.
   (a) strongly agree
   (b) agree
   (c) uncertain
   (d) disagree
   (e) strongly disagree

Lincoln Incentive Plan, combination profit sharing and piecework incentive system developed in 1934 by J. F. Lincoln of the Lincoln Electric Company of Cleveland.

Lincoln Mills **case:** *see* TEXTILE WORKERS V. LINCOLN MILLS.

line of authority: *see* SCALAR CHAIN.

line organization, those segments of a larger organization that perform the major functions of the organization and have the most direct responsibilities for achieving organizational goals.

line–staff conflict, according to Charles Coleman and Joseph Rich, "Line, Staff and the Systems Perspective," *Human Resources Management* (Fall 1973),

> one of the pillars of traditional organization theory is the concept that line officers possess command authority in core areas of the organization and that staff officers provide them with specialized assistance. However, empirical studies have shown time and again that the traditional line-staff idea leads to large amounts of conflict.

See Melville Dalton, "Conflict Between Staff and Line Managerial Officers," *American Sociological Review* (June 1950); Philip J. Browne and Robert T. Golembiewski, "The Line–Staff Concept Revisited: An Empirical Study of Organizational Images," *Academy of Management Journal* (September 1974).

linking pin, concept developed by Rensis Likert in his *New Patterns of Management* (New York: McGraw-Hill, 1961). A "linking pin" is anyone who belongs to two groups within the same organization, usually as a superior in one and as a subordinate in the other. *See* George Graen *et al.*, "Effects of Linking-Pin Quality on the Quality of Working Life of Lower Participants," *Administrative Science Quarterly* (September 1977).

Linn **v.** *United Plant Guard Workers*, 383 U.S. 53 (1966), U.S. Supreme Court case, which held that the National Labor Relations Act does not bar libel actions brought by either party to a labor dispute who alleges the circulation of false and defamatory statements during a union organizing campaign as long as the complainant pleads and proves that the statements were made with malice and injured him/her.

listening, one of the oldest and most useful of personnel management techniques. According to John A. Wilson, *The Culture of Ancient Egypt* (Chicago: University of Chicago Press, 1951), the ancient Egyptians advised their leaders to

> be calm as thou listenest to what the petitioner has to say. Do not rebuff him before he has swept out his body or before he has

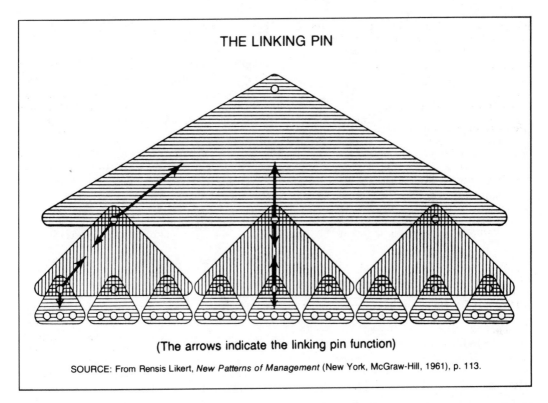

THE LINKING PIN

(The arrows indicate the linking pin function)

SOURCE: From Rensis Likert, *New Patterns of Management* (New York, McGraw-Hill, 1961), p. 113.

said that for which he came.... It is not [necessary] that everything about which he has petitioned should come to pass, [for] a good hearing is soothing to the heart.

Some things haven't changed much in 4000 years! For a modern pep talk on how to be a good listener, *see* Thomas G. Banville, *How to Listen—How to be Heard* (Chicago: Nelson-Hall, 1978).

list of eligibles: *see* ELIGIBLE LIST.

Little, Frank H. (1879-1917), one of the most radical leaders of the Industrial Workers of the World (IWW). He became a major IWW martyr when, after agitating against U.S. involvement in World War I and being branded a traitor by the press, he was murdered in Montana by six men who were never identified. *See* Arnon Gutfeld, "The Murder of Frank Little," *Labor History* (Spring 1969).

Little Steel: *see* BIG STEEL.

LIUNA: *see* LABOR ORGANIZATION, Laborers' International Union of North America.

living wage, also STARVATION WAGES, although one might suspect that *starvation wages* would be necessarily of limited duration, many a union leader will assert that the workers have been putting up with them far too long. A *living wage*, in contrast, wards off starvation and even provides for some of the comforts of life. However, the ultimate goal of the union must be a "decent living wage," which affords a standard of luxury that can hardly be imagined by those on starvation wages.

Lloyd–LaFollette Act of 1912, federal statute that guarantees civilian employees of the federal government the right to petition Congress, either individually or through their organizations. The act was the only statutory basis for the organization of federal employees until the Civil Service Reform Act of 1978. In addition, it provided the first statutory procedural safeguards for federal employees facing removal. It provides that "no person in the classified civil service of the United States shall be removed or suspended without pay therefrom except for such cause as will promote the efficiency of such service and for reasons given in writing."

LMRA: *see* LABOR–MANAGEMENT RELATIONS ACT OF 1947.

LMSA: *see* LABOR–MANAGEMENT SERVICES ADMINISTRATION.

loading, job/horizontal/vertical: *see* JOB LOADING.

lobster shift: *see* GRAVEYARD SHIFT.

local: *see* COSMOPOLITAN–LOCAL CONSTRUCT.

local independent union, local union not affiliated with a national or international union.

local industrial union, local union consisting of workers in a variety of occupations in an industry.

Local 174, Teamsters v. Lucas Flour Co., 369 U.S. 95 (1962), U.S. Supreme Court case, which held that a strike to settle a dispute which a collective bargaining agreement provides shall be settled by compulsory arbitration is a violation of the agreement.

local union, regional organization of union members who are part of a national or international union. A local union is chartered by the national or international union with which it is affiliated.

Lochner v. New York, 198 U.S. 45 (1905), U.S. Supreme Court case, which declared unconstitutional a New York law which sought to regulate the hours of employment.

lockout, employer's version of a strike—the closing of a business in order to pressure the employees and/or the union to accept the employer's offered terms of employment. This early weapon against the union movement lost much of its effect when locked-out employees became eligible for unemployment compensation. Almost all union contracts with a no-strike clause contain a similar ban against lockouts. For an analysis, *see* Willard A. Lewis "The 'Lockout as Corollary of Strike' Controversy Reexamined," *Labor Law Journal* (November 1972).

See also AMERICAN SHIPBUILDING CO. V. NATIONAL LABOR RELATIONS BOARD and TEXTILE WORKERS V. DARLINGTON MANUFACTURING COMPANY.

Locomotive Engineers, Brotherhood of: *see* LABOR ORGANIZATION.

lodge, organizational unit of some labor unions, equivalent to a local union.

Lodge 76, International Association of Machinists v. Wisconsin Employment Relations Commission, 427 U.S. 132 (1976), U.S. Supreme Court case, which held that a state cannot interfere with a union's power to collectively refuse overtime during contract negotiations or to engage in other partial strike activities unregulated by federal labor laws.

Log Scalers Association, Pacific: *see* LABOR ORGANIZATION.

longevity pay, also called LONGEVITY RATE, salary additions based on length of service. Contracts or pay plans frequently state specific time periods to qualify for such upward wage adjustments.

longitudinal survey, study of a group of subjects that follows them through time. *See* Herbert S. Parnes, "Longitudinal Surveys: Prospects and Problems," *Monthly Labor Review* (February 1972).

Longshoremen's and Warehousemen's Union, International: *see* LABOR ORGANIZATION.

Longshoremen's Association, International: *see* LABOR ORGANIZATION.

Lordstown strike, three-week wildcat strike at the General Motors automobile assembly plant at Lordstown, Ohio, in April 1972. One of the most technically sophisticated plants of its kind in the world, the plant could produce about 100 Chevrolet Vega cars per hour. In 1971, assembly-line workers began to purposely disrupt production, while claiming that management was seeking to "speedup" the assembly line. This problem festered and led to the strike. While the strike gained no economic benefits for the workers, it did focus national attention on the problems of job monotony and worker alienation. For accounts, *see* Barbara Garson, "Luddites in Lordstown," *Harpers* (June 1972); Stanley Aronwitz, *False Promise: The Shaping of American Working Class Consciousness* (N.Y.: McGraw-Hill, 1973).

Lordstown syndrome, workers perception that they are required to perform dehumanized and monotonous work. Among the dysfunctional aspects of this syndrome are high absenteeism, low productivity, sabotage, and wildcat strikes. While the term has its origins in the 1972 strike at the General Motors plant in Lordstown, Ohio, the phenomenon itself is more widespread. For a discussion, *see* "The Spreading Lordstown Syndrome," *Business Week* (March 4, 1972).

Lorenz curve, most commonly used in macroeconomics to show the unequal distribution of national income, the Lorenz curve can be applied to wage and salary structures to demonstrate the spread of wages from the lowest paid employee to the highest paid. A curve is constructed by plotting the cumulative percentage of employees against the cumulative percentage of wages and salaries. This curve is compared to a 45° line and the area between the two computed as a value L. The greater the L value, the greater the inequality of wages. See T. M. Husband and A. P. Schofield, "The Use of the Lorenz Curve and the Pareto Distribution in Internal Pay Structuring: A Research Note," *The Journal of Management Studies* (October 1976).

Los Angeles Department of Water and Power v. Manhart: see CITY OF LOS ANGELES, DEPARTMENT OF WATER & POWER V. MANHART.

Louisiana AFL–CIO: see AMERICAN FEDERATION OF LABOR–CONGRESS OF INDUSTRIAL ORGANIZATIONS.

love, also called OFFICE ROMANCE, when individuals working in the same organization discover that they have an emotional and/or physical attraction for each other, that may be very nice for them but a potential problem for their organization's management. For general advice on handling this kind of situation, see Auren Uris, *The Blue Book of Broadminded Business Behavior* (N.Y.: Thomas Y. Crowell, Co., 1977). For a scholarly analysis, see Robert E. Quinn, "Coping with Cupid: The Formation, Impact, and Management of Romantic Relationships in Organizations," *Administrative Science Quarterly* (March 1977).
See also SEXUAL HARASSMENT.

low man on the totem pole, refers to the lowest person in any organizational hierarchy. The phrase is credited to Fred Allen, who, while writing an introduction to a book by H. Allen Smith, said, "If Smith were an Indian, he would be low man on any totem pole." Smith then used the phrase as the title of his next book, *Low Man on A Totem Pole* (Garden City, N.Y.: Doubleday Doran and Co., 1941).

loyalty, also LOYALTY OATH, loyalty is allegiance. A *loyalty oath* is an affirmation of allegiance. Many public employers may legitimately require their employees to swear or affirm their allegiance to the Constitution of the United States and of a particular state. See Paul E. Donnelly, "The Pervasive Effect of McCarthyism on Recent Loyalty Oath Cases," *St. Louis University Law Journal* (Spring 1972).
See also COLE V. RICHARDSON and CONNELL V. HIGGINBOTHAM.

LPN: see LABOR ORGANIZATION, Licensed Practical Nurses, National Federation of.

Luddite, the original "Luddities,"—they first appeared in Nottingham, England, in 1811 —were organized bands of handicraftsmen who, masked and operating at night, sought to destroy the new textile machinery that was displacing them. Their name is thought to have come from Ned Ludd, a village idiot who gained local notoriety in 1779 by destroying some stocking frames belonging to his employer. While Ned Ludd has the same historical stature as Robin Hood (that is, more likely to be mythical than real), his namesakes today would include anyone who seeks to destroy machinery in order to protect a job. For a history, see Malcolm I. Thomis, *The Luddites: Machine-Breaking in Regency England* (N.Y.: Schocken Books, 1972).

Ludlow Massacre, because of a strike called by the United Mine Workers, (UMW) against various Colorado coal companies in 1913, "guards" employed by the companies attacked a tent city where strikers were living and otherwise harrassed the UMW. Martial law was thereupon imposed by the governor. Then, in April 1914, the state militia sought to clear out the strikers from their tent city in Ludlow. The soldiers killed three people while clearing the camp and then burned it. The next day, the bodies of two women and eleven children were discovered in the remains. The miners called the incident "The Ludlow Massacre." Thoughts of revenge became reality when the miners armed themselves and literally attacked both the state militia and the company guards. After a week of the most ferocious warfare in U.S. labor history, federal troops were sent in to restore order. In the end the UMW lost, it formally called off the strike in December 1914. The most comprehensive account of the whole affair is George S. McGovern and Leonard F. Guttridge, *The Great Coalfield War* (Boston: Houghton Mifflin Co., 1972). This is a "rewrite" of Senator McGovern's 1953 Northwestern University Ph. D. dissertation. But, be assured, it has been thoroughly rewritten and reads like a "real" book.

LWU: see LABOR ORGANIZATION, Leather Workers International Union of America.

Lyons, John H. (1919-   ), succeeded his father as president of the International Association of Bridge, Structural and Ornamental Iron Workers in 1961.

M

Machiavelli, Niccolò (1469-1527), most famous management analyst of the Italian Renaissance, is often credited with having established the moral foundations of modern personnel management. In *Discorsi sopra la prima deca di Tito Livio* ("Discourses on the First Decade of Tito Livy") he offers his advice to all staff specialists:

> If you tender your advice with modesty, and the opposition prevents its adoption, and, owing to someone else's advice being adopted, disaster follows, you will acquire very great glory. And, though you cannot rejoice in the glory that comes from disasters which befall your country or your prince, it at any rate counts for something.

For a modern appreciation, *see* Anthony Jay, *Management and Machiavelli: An Inquiry into the Politics of Corporate Life* (N.Y.: Holt, Rinehart, and Winston, 1967).

Machine Printers and Engravers Association of the United States: *see* LABOR ORGANIZATION.

MacKay Rule: *see* NATIONAL LABOR RELATIONS BOARD V. MACKAY RADIO & TELEGRAPH COMPANY.

***Magnavox* decision:** *see* NATIONAL LABOR RELATIONS BOARD V. MAGNAVOX.

Mahon, William D. (1861-1949), president of the Amalgamated Association of Street, Electric Railway and Motor Coach Employees of America from 1893 to 1946. For biographical information, *see* Emerson P. Schmidt, *Industrial Relations in Urban Transportation* (Minneapolis: University of Minnesota Press, 1937).

Maier, Norman R. F. (1900-1977), psychologist best known for his research in industrial psychology, human relations, and executive development. Major works include: *Principles of Human Relations* (N.Y. John Wiley, 1952); *The Appraisal Interview* (N.Y.: John Wiley, 1958); *Psychology in Industrial Or-*

ganizations (Boston: Houghton Mifflin, 4th ed., 1973).

Mailers Union, International: *see* LABOR ORGANIZATION.

Maine AFL–CIO: *see* AMERICAN FEDERATION OF LABOR–CONGRESS OF INDUSTRIAL ORGANIZATIONS.

MAINE-SEA: *see* LABOR ORGANIZATION, Maine State Employees Association.

Maine State Employees Association: *see* LABOR ORGANIZATION.

maintenance-of-membership shop, union security provision found in some collective bargaining agreements, holds that employees who are members of the union at the time the agreement is negotiated, or who voluntarily join the union subsequently, must maintain their membership for the duration of the agreement as a condition of employment.

Maintenance of Way Employes, Brotherhood of: *see* LABOR ORGANIZATION.

major-medical insurance, medical insurance that offers protection against catastrophic medical expenses occurred by a major accident or illness.

make-up pay, allowances paid to piece workers to make-up the difference between actual piece work earnings and guaranteed rates (or statutory minimum wages).

make whole, legal remedy that provides for an injured party to be placed, as near as may be possible, in the situation he or she would have occupied if the wrong had not been committed. The concept was first put forth by the U.S. Supreme Court in the 1867 case of *Wicker* v. *Hoppock*. In 1975, the Court held, in the case of *Albermarle Paper Company* v. *Moody* (422 U.S. 405), that Title VII of the Civil Rights Act of 1964 (as amended) intended a "make whole" remedy for unlawful discrimination.

See also RETROACTIVE SENIORITY and RIGHTFUL PLACE.

make-work, any effort to reduce or limit labor output so that more labor must be employed.

Malek Manual, guidebook concerning the operations of the federal personnel system that was prepared for Fred Malek, the manager of the White House Personnel Office during the early part of the Nixon Administration. Its Machiavellian character (it asserted that "There is no merit in the merit system") gave it tremendous notoriety. For a dispassionate analysis, *see* Frank J. Thompson and Raymond G. Davis, "The Malek Manual Revisited," *The Bureaucrat* (Summer 1977). For Malek Manual excerpts, *see* Frank J. Thompson (ed.), *Classics of Public Personnel Policy* (Oak Park, Ill.: Moore Publishing Company, 1979).

Maloney, William E. (1884-1964), president of the International Union of Operating Engineers from 1940 to 1958, when the union grew from 58,000 to 294,000. For biographical information, *see* Garth L. Mangum, *The Operating Engineers: The Economic History of a Trade Union* (Cambridge, Mass.: Harvard University Press, 1964).

management, can refer to both (1) the people responsible for running an organization and (2) the running process itself—the utilizing of numerous resources to accomplish an organizational goal. For general histories, *see* Claude S. George, Jr., *The History of Management Thought* (Englewood Cliffs, N.Y.: Prentice-Hall, 1972); Daniel A. Wren, *The Evolution of Management Thought* (N.Y.: John Wiley & Sons, 2nd ed., 1979).

See also the following entries:

CAREER MANAGEMENT
CONTINGENCY MANAGEMENT
EUPSYCHIAN MANAGEMENT
FIRST-LINE MANAGEMENT
GRAND CANYON MANAGEMENT
INDUSTRIAL DEMOCRACY
MUSHROOM MANAGEMENT
PRINCIPLES OF MANAGEMENT
PROJECT MANAGEMENT
REACTION MANAGEMENT
SANDWICH MANAGEMENT
SCIENTIFIC MANAGEMENT
SYSTEMS MANAGEMENT

management audit, any comprehensive examination of the administrative operations and organizational arrangements of a company or government agency which uses generally accepted standards of practice for the purposes of evaluation. The pioneering work on this is Jackson Martindell, *The Scientific Appraisal of Management* (N.Y.: Harper and Row, 1950). *Also see* William P. Leonard, *The Management Audit* (Englewood Cliffs, N.J.: Prentice-Hall, 1962).

management by exception, management control process that has a subordinate report to an organizational superior only exceptional or unusual events that might call for decision-making on the part of the superior. In this way, a manager may avoid unnecessary detail that only confirms that all is going according to plan. This concept originated with Frederick Taylor. For an update, *see* Lester R. Bittel, *Management by Exception* (N.Y.: McGraw-Hill, 1964).

management by objectives (MBO), approach to managing whose hallmark is a mutual—by both organizational subordinate and superior—setting of measurable goals to be accomplished by an individual or team over a set period of time. According to George S. Odiorne, in *Management by Objectives* (New York: Pitman Publishing Company, 1965), "The superior and subordinate managers of an organization jointly define its common goals, define each individual's major areas of responsibility in terms of the results expected of him and use these measures as guides for operating the unit and assessing the contribution of each of the members." The phrase and concept of MBO was first popularized by Peter F. Drucker, in his *The Practice of Management* (N.Y.: Harper & Row, 1954).

One of the major uses of MBO is for formal performance appraisals. For an assertion that this use is dysfunctional, *see* Harry Levinson, "Management by Whose Objectives?" *Harvard Business Review* (July–August 1970).

For analysis of MBO in the public sector, *see* Dale D. McConkey, *MBO for Nonprofit Organizations* (N.Y.: AMACOM, 1975); George L. Morrisey, *Management by Objectives and Results in the Public Sector* (Reading, Mass.: Addison-Wesley Publishing Co., 1976). In addition, there is a symposium on MBO in *Public Administration Review* (January–February 1976).

management clause: *see* MANAGEMENT RIGHTS CLAUSE.

management development, also called EXECUTIVE DEVELOPMENT, any conscious effort on the part of an organization to provide a manager with skills that he might need for future duties, such as rotational assignments or formal educational experiences, constitutes management development. The semantic difference between training workers and developing managers is significant. A manager is trained so that he can be of greater organizational value not only in his present but in his future assignments as well. In such a context the development investment made by the organization in a junior manager may only pay off when and if that individual grows into a bureau or division chief. For an analysis, *see* Edgar H. Schein, "Management Development: Full Spectrum Training," *Training and Development Journal* (March 1975); Raymond Pomerleau, "The State of Management Development in the Federal Service," *Public Personnel Management* (January–February 1974).

management games, also called BUSINESS GAMES, any of a variety of simulation exercises used in management development and education. *See* Joel M. Kibbee, Clifford J. Craft, and Burt Nanus, *Management Games: A New Technique for Executive Development* (N.Y.: Van Nostrand Reinhold, 1961); Robert G. Graham and Clifford F. Gray, *Business Games Handbook* (N.Y.: American Management Association, 1969); David W. Zukerman and Robert E. Horn, *The Guide to Simulations/Games for Education and Training* (Lexington, Mass.: Information Resources, 1973). For a view of all of modern business as a game, *see* John McDonald, *The Games of Business* (Garden City, N.Y.: Doubleday, 1975). For an analysis of the players, *see* Michael Maccoby, *The Gamesman: The New Corporate Leaders* (N.Y.: Simon & Schuster, 1976).

management information system (MIS), any formal process in an organization that provides managers with facts that they need for decisionmaking. Modern management information systems are almost invariably dependent upon computers. For the theory behind a modern MIS, *see* Jaglit Singh, *Great Ideas in Information Theory, Language and Cybernetics* (N.Y.: Dover Publications, 1966). For what can go wrong, *see* Russell L. Ackoff, "Management Misinformation Systems," *Management Science* (December 1967).

Management of Personnel Quarterly: *see* HUMAN RESOURCE MANAGEMENT.

management   prerogatives: *see* MANAGEMENT RIGHTS.

management rights, also called MANAGEMENT PREROGATIVES and RESERVED RIGHTS, those rights reserved to management that manage-

ment feels are intrinsic to its ability to manage and, consequently, not subject to collective bargaining. According to Paul Prasow and Edward Peters, "New Perspectives on Management's Reserved Rights," *Labor Law Journal* (January 1967),

> management's authority is supreme in all matters except those it has expressly conceded in the collective agreement, or in those areas where its authority is restricted by law. Put another way, management does not look to the collective agreement to ascertain its rights; it looks to the agreement to find out which and how much of its rights and powers it has conceded outright or agreed to share with the union.

For further analyses of management rights, *see* George Bennett, "Management Rights in the Public Sector," *Labor Law Journal* (Sept. 1977); Bruno Stein, "Management Rights and Productivity," *The Arbitration Journal* (December 1977).

management rights clause, also called MANAGEMENT CLAUSE, that portion of a collective bargaining agreement that defines the scope of management rights, functions, and responsibilities—essentially all those activities which management can undertake without the consent of the union. A typical management rights clause might read: "It is the intention hereof that all of the rights, powers, prerogatives, authorities that the company had prior to the signing of this agreement are retained by the company except those, and only to the extent that they are specifically abridged, delegated, granted, or modified by the agreement." *See* Richard F. Groner and Leon E. Lunden, "Management Rights Provisions in Major Agreements," *Monthly Labor Review* (February 1966).

management science, also called OPERATIONS RESEARCH, approach to management dating from World War II that seeks to apply the scientific method to managerial problems. Because of its emphasis on mathematical techniques, management, science as a term is frequently used interchangeably with operations research. Management science should not be confused with Frederick W. Taylor's Scientific Management Movement. For an elementary introduction, *see* Stafford Beer, *Management Science: The Business Use of Operations Research* (N.Y.: Doubleday and Co., 1968). For a governmental perspective, *see* Michael J. White, *Management Science in Federal Agencies: The Adoption and Diffusion of a Socio-Technical Innovation* (Lexington, Mass.: Lexington Books, 1975).

"**Management Theory Jungle**," title of an article by Harold Koontz that appeared in the *Journal of the Academy of Management* (December 1961), wherein Koontz sought to classify the major schools of management theory into six groupings: (1) the management process school, (2) the empirical school, (3) the human behavior school, (4) the social system school, (5) the decision theory school and (6) the mathematical school. Koontz noted that the terminology and principles of the various schools of management thought have resulted in a "semantics jungle."

management trainee, administrative job title loosely assigned to a wide variety of entry-level positions that are usually reserved for new college graduates. *See* Hal Anderson, "Selecting Management Trainees," *Personnel Journal* (November 1976).

manager, project: *see* PROJECT MANAGER.

managerial grid, the basis of Robert R. Blake and Jane S. Mouton's widely implemented organization development program. By using a graphic gridiron format, which has an X axis locating various degrees of orientation toward production and a Y axis locating various degrees of orientation toward people, individuals scoring this "managerial grid" can place themselves at one of 81 available positions that register their relative orientations toward people or production. Grid scores can then be used as the point of departure for a discussion of individual and organizational growth needs. *See* Robert R. Blake and Jane S. Mouton, *The Managerial Grid* (Houston: Gulf Publishing, 1964).

managerial obsolescence: *see* OCCUPATIONAL OBSOLESCENCE.

managerial philosophy, all organizations are guided by a philosophy of management. It

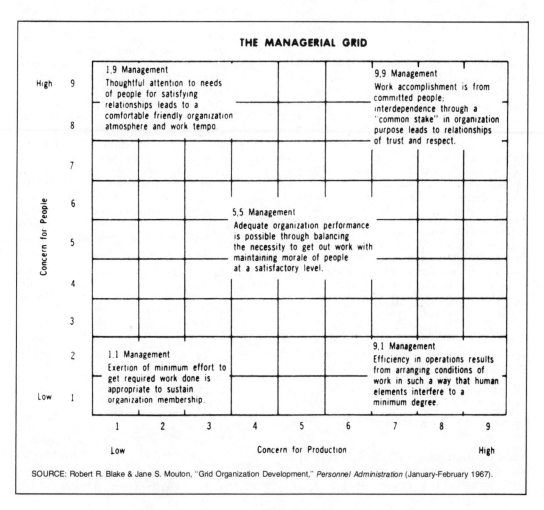

THE MANAGERIAL GRID

1,9 Management
Thoughtful attention to needs of people for satisfying relationships leads to a comfortable friendly organization atmosphere and work tempo.

9,9 Management
Work accomplishment is from committed people; interdependence through a "common stake" in organization purpose leads to relationships of trust and respect.

5,5 Management
Adequate organization performance is possible through balancing the necessity to get out work with maintaining morale of people at a satisfactory level.

1,1 Management
Exertion of minimum effort to get required work done is appropriate to sustain organization membership.

9,1 Management
Efficiency in operations results from arranging conditions of work in such a way that human elements interfere to a minimum degree.

Concern for People — High 9, 8, 7, 6, 5, 4, 3, 2, Low 1

Concern for Production — Low 1 2 3 4 5 6 7 8 9 High

SOURCE: Robert R. Blake & Jane S. Mouton, "Grid Organization Development," *Personnel Administration* (January-February 1967).

need not be formally expressed. Indeed, many managers would deny that they have one. But it's always there, somewhere—whether stated or unstated, conscious or unconscious, intentional or unintentional. It is this philosophy that facilitates management's decisionmaking process. Of course, different managerial philosophies have evolved in reflection of differing organizational environments and work situations. For example, a managerial philosophy appropriate for a military combat unit would hardly be suitable for a medical research team seeking to find a cure for cancer. The sincerity and rigor of an employee's motivation toward his or her duties is a direct reflection of the host organization's managerial philosophy.

managerial psychology, generally, all those concepts of human behavior in organizations that are relevant to managerial problems. A standard text is Harold J. Leavitt, *Managerial Psychology: An Introduction to Individuals, Pairs, and Groups in Organizations* (Chicago: University of Chicago Press, 3rd ed., 1972).

managerial revolution, refers to James Burnham's concept that as the control of the large corporations passes from the hands of the owners into the hands of professional administrators, the society's new governing class will not be the possessors of wealth but of technical administrative expertise. *See* James Burnham, *The Managerial Revolution* (N.Y.: The John Day Co., 1941). For a history of this new managerial class, *see* Alfred D. Chandler, Jr., *The Visible Hand: The Managerial Revolution in American Business* (Cambridge, Mass.: Harvard University Press, 1977).

mandamus, also called WRIT OF MANDAMUS, court order that compels the performance of an act.

mandatory bargaining items, those collective bargaining items that each party must bargain over if introduced by the other party.

man-day, amount of work that can be accomplished in a single normal day of work.

man Friday or GIRL FRIDAY, in Daniel Defoe's 1719 novel, *Robinson Crusoe*, the hero, a castaway on a desolate island, was fortunate to find a black man who developed into a hardworking helper. He was named Friday because that was the day of the week when Crusoe rescued him from acquaintances who thought he was good enough to eat. Over time, a man Friday or girl Friday became synonymous with a general and cheerful helper.

Manhart decision: *see* CITY OF LOS ANGELES, DEPARTMENT OF WATER & POWER V. MANHART.

manit, contraction for man-minute.

man–machine systems, according to W. T. Singleton, in his *Man-Machine Systems* (Baltimore: Penguin Books, 1974), man-machine systems have

> to do with the design of work, on the assumption that work nowadays is never done by men, nor is it done by machine, it is always done by man-machine systems. The man-machine system has proved enormously successful because men and machines are so different, each compensates for the weaknesses of the other. There are therefore, problems of deciding what men should do and what machines should do in the pursuit of any objective. That is what the man-machine allocation function is about.

manning table, also called PERSONNEL INVENTORY, listing of all of the employees in an organization by job and personal characteristics, which serves as a basic reference for planning and other purposes.

manpower: *see* HUMAN RESOURCES.

Manpower Development and Training Act of 1962 (MDTA), federal statute that authorized the U.S. Department of Labor to identify the skills and capability needs of the economy and to initiate and find appropriate training programs. It was superseded by the Comprehensive Employment and Training Act of 1973. *See* Garth L. Mangum, *MDTA: Foundation of Federal Manpower Policy* (Baltimore: Johns Hopkins Press, 1968).

manpower planning: *see* HUMAN RESOURCES PLANNING.

manpower planning models: *see* HUMAN RESOURCES PLANNING MODELS.

manpower requirements analysis: *see* HUMAN RESOURCES REQUIREMENTS ANALYSIS.

manpower utilization: *see* HUMAN RESOURCES UTILIZATION.

marginal analysis, any technique that seeks to determine the point at which the cost of something (for example, an additional employee or machine) will be worth while or pay for itself.

marginal productivity theory of wages, theory

holding the wages of workers will be determined by the value of the productivity of the marginal worker; additional workers will not be hired if the value of the added production is less than the wages that must be paid them. Consequently, wages will tend to equal the value of the product contributed by the last (the marginal) worker hired. The theory, first formulated by John Bates Clark in 1899, has been severely criticized for being premised upon business circumstances that tend to be uncommon in real life. For the original source, *see* John Bates Clark, *The Distribution of Wealth* (N.Y.: Macmillan, 1899). For analysis, *see* J. R. Hicks, *The Theory of Wages* (London: Macmillan, 2nd ed., 1963).

Marine and Shipbuilding Workers of America, Industrial Union of: *see* LABOR ORGANIZATION.

Marine Cooks and Stewards' Union: *see* LABOR ORGANIZATION, *under* Seafarers' International Union of North America.

Marine Engineers' Beneficial Association, National *see* LABOR ORGANIZATION.

Maritime Union of America, National: *see* LABOR ORGANIZATION.

Marshall, F. Ray (1928-), labor economist, appointed Secretary of Labor by President Jimmy Carter in 1977. Major works include: *The Negro Worker* (N.Y.: Random House, 1967); *Cooperatives and Rural Poverty in the South*, with Lamond Godwin (Baltimore: Johns Hopkins Press, 1971); *Labor Economics: Wages, Employment and Trade Unionism*, with Allan Murray Cartter (Homewood, Ill.: R. D. Irwin, rev. ed., 1972); *Human Resources and Labor Markets*, with Sar A. Levitan and Garth L. Mangum (N.Y.: Harper & Row, 1972).

Marshall* v. *Barlow's, Inc., 56 L. Ed. 2d 305 (1978), U.S. Supreme Court case, which interpreted the 4th Amendment's prohibition on unreasonable searches to impose a warrant requirement on Occupational Safety and Health Administration inspections. The court ruled that such warrants do not require evidence establishing probable cause that a violation has occurred on the premises. Rather, a judge can issue an OSHA warrant upon a showing that the inspection follows a reasonable administrative or legislative plan for enforcing the Occupational Safety and Health Act.

martinet, strict disciplinarian. The word comes from an inspector general in the army of France's Louis XIV, Jean Martinet, who was so despised for his spit-and-polish discipline that he was "accidentally" killed by his own soldiers while leading an assault in 1672.

Maryland Classified Employees Association, Inc.: *see* LABOR ORGANIZATION.

Maryland State and District of Columbia AFL–CIO: *see* AMERICAN FEDERATION OF LABOR–CONGRESS OF INDUSTRIAL ORGANIZATIONS.

Maryland* v. *Wirtz: *see* NATIONAL LEAGUE OF CITIES V. USERY.

Maslow, Abraham H. (1908-1970), psychologist best known for his theory of human motivation, which was premised upon a "needs hierarchy" within which an individual moved up or down as the needs of each level were satisfied or threatened. Major works include: *Motivation and Personality* (N.Y.: Harper & Row, 1954; 2nd ed., 1970); *Eupsychian Management* (Homewood, Ill.: Richard D. Irwin, 1965). For a biography, *see* Frank G. Goble, *The Third Force: The Psychology of Abraham Maslow* (N.Y.: Grossman Publishers, 1970).

See also SELF-ACTUALIZATION.

Massachusetts Board of Retirement* v. *Murgia, 427 U.S. 307 (1976), U.S. Supreme Court case, which held that a state statute requiring uniformed state police to retire at age 50 was not a violation of equal protection. The court ruled that the state had met its burden of showing some rational relationship between the statute and the purpose of maintaining the physical condition of its police.

Massachusetts State Employees Association: *see* LABOR ORGANIZATION.

Massachusetts State Labor Council: *see* AMERICAN FEDERATION OF LABOR–CONGRESS OF INDUSTRIAL ORGANIZATIONS.

mass picketing, when a union wants to indicate broad support for a strike it sometimes assembles a "mass" of strikers to picket a place of business in order to discourage nonstrikers from entering the premises.

MASS-SEA: *see* LABOR ORGANIZATION, Massachusetts State Employees Association.

master, skilled worker in a trade who is qualified to train apprentices.

See also JOURNEYMAN.

master agreement, also called MASTER CON-

TRACT, collective bargaining contract that serves as a model for an entire industry or segment of that industry. While the master agreement serves to standardize the economic benefits of all of the employees covered by it, it is often supplemented by a local contract which deals with the varying circumstances of the various local unions.

Masters, Mates and Pilots, International Organization of: *see* LABOR ORGANIZATION, *under* Longshoremen's Association, International.

mastery, perfect performance on a test.

Mastro Plastics Corp. v. National Labor Relations Board, 350 U.S. 270 (1956), U.S. Supreme Court case, which held that in the absence of contractual or statutory provision to the contrary, an employer's unfair labor practices provide adequate ground for an orderly strike. In such circumstances, the striking employees "do not lose their status and are entitled to reinstatement with back pay, even if replacements for them have been made."

MAT: *see* (1) MILLER ANALOGIES TEST and (2) MULTIPLE APTITUDE TESTS.

matching item, test item that asks which one of a group of words, pictures, etc., matches up with those of another group.

maternity leave, formally approved absence from work for childbirth and its aftermath.
See also the following entries:
  BIRTH LEAVE
  CLEVELAND BOARD OF EDUCATION V. LA-
    FLEUR
  MONELL V. DEPT. OF SOCIAL SERVICES, NEW
    YORK CITY
  NASHVILLE GAS CO. V. SATTY
  PREGNANCY DISCRIMINATION ACT OF 1978

Mathews v. Eldridge, 424 U.S. 319 (1976), U.S. Supreme Court case, which held that while due process requires pre-termination hearings for recipients of welfare benefits, it does not require such hearings for those who receive disability benefits.

matrix diamond, basic structural form of matrix organizations; this is in contrast to the pyramid—the basic structural form of traditional organizations.

matrix manager, any manager who shares formal authority over a subordinate with another manager.

matrix organization, any organization using a multiple command system whereby an employee might be accountable to one superior for overall performance as well as to one or more leaders of particular projects. "Matrix" is a generic term that is used to refer to various organizational structures. For an exhaustive analysis, *see* Stanley M. Davis and Paul R. Lawrence, *Matrix* (Reading, Mass.: Addison-Wesley Publishing Co., 1977). For a critique, *see* Kenneth Knight, "Matrix Organization: A Review," *Journal of Management Studies* (May 1976).
See also PROJECT MANAGEMENT and TASK FORCE.

maturity curve also called CAREER CURVE and SALARY CURVE, technique for determining the salaries of professional and technical employees that relates the employee's education and experience to on-the-job performance. For example, after it is determined what the average compensation for a professional employee is for each of various categories of experience, the individual employee is assigned a salary based upon whether he or she is considered average, below average, or above average in performance. *See* H. C. Rickard, "Maturity Curve Surveys," *Handbook of Wage and Salary Administration*, M. L. Rock, ed. (N.Y.: McGraw-Hill, 1972); Robert L. McCornack, "A New Method for Fitting Salary Curves," *Personnel Journal* (October 1967).

May Day, in 1889, the International Socialist Congress fixed May 1 as the day to publicize the eight-hour day because the American Federation of Labor planned a major demonstration on May 1, 1890. Since then May Day has become a major holiday in socialist countries. In 1955, President Eisenhower proclaimed May 1 as "Loyalty Day."

Mayo, Elton (1880-1949), principle organizer and researcher of the famous Hawthorne experiments and considered the founder of the human-relations approach in industry. Major works include: *The Human Problems of An Industrial Civilization* (N.Y.: The Viking Press, 1933); *The Social Problems of An Industrial Civilization* (N.Y.: The Viking Press, 1945). For a biography, *see* Lyndall F. Urwick, *The Life and Work of Elton Mayo* (London: Urwick, Orr & Partners, Ltd., 1960).

MBA also MPA, Master of Business Administration and Master of Public Administration, respectively. These are the leading managerial degrees for practitioners in both the private and public sectors. While such degrees are obviously helpful, it has long been established that there is no direct relationship between scholastic performance and success

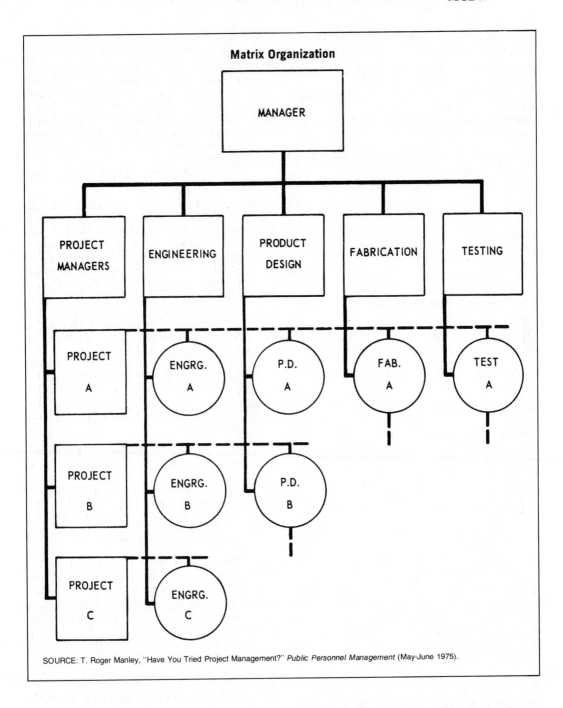

Matrix Organization

MANAGER

PROJECT MANAGERS

ENGINEERING

PRODUCT DESIGN

FABRICATION

TESTING

PROJECT A

ENGRG. A

P.D. A

FAB. A

TEST A

PROJECT B

ENGRG. B

P.D. B

PROJECT C

ENGRG. C

SOURCE: T. Roger Manley, "Have You Tried Project Management?" *Public Personnel Management* (May-June 1975).

in management. For an analysis of this seeming contradiction, *see* J. Sterling Livingston, "Myth of the Well-Educated Manager," *Harvard Business Review* (January–February 1971). *See also* Philip T. Crotty, "The Value of MBA and Executive Development Programs," *Training and Development Journal* (May 1972).

MBO: *see* MANAGEMENT BY OBJECTIVES.

McBride, Lloyd (1916-   ), became president of the United Steelworkers of America in 1977.

MCBW: *see* LABOR ORGANIZATION, Meat Cutters and Butcher Workmen of North America, Amalgamated.

McCann Associates, Inc.: *see* TEST PUB-LISHERS.

***McCarthy* v. *Philadelphia Civil Service Commission*,** 424 U.S. 645 (1976), U.S. Supreme Court case, which upheld an ordinance requiring that city employees live within city limits.

McClellan Committee, in the late 1950s, Senator John L. McClellan of Arkansas chaired the Senate Committee on Improper Activities in Labor–Management Relations. The committee's findings of violence and corruption spurred the passage of the Labor–Management Reporting and Disclosure (Landrum–Griffin) Act of 1959. For accounts of the committee's work by its chairman and legal counsel, *see* John L. McClellan, *Crime Without Punishment* (N.Y.: Duell, Sloan and Pearce, 1962); Robert F. Kennedy, *The Enemy Within* (N.Y.: Harper & Row, 1960).

McClelland, David C. (1917-   ), psychologist widely considered the foremost authority on achievement motivation. The body of McClelland's work asserts that achievement motivation can be developed within individuals, provided that the environment in which they live and work is supportive. Major works include: *The Achievement Motive*, with J. W. Atkinson, R. A. Clark, and E. A. Lowell (N.Y.: Appleton-Century-Crofts, 1953); *The Achieving Society* (Princeton, N.J.: Van Nostrand, 1961); *Motivating Economic Achievement*, with D. G. Winter (N.Y.: The Free Press, 1969).

McClennan, William H. (1934-   ), elected president of the International Association of Fire Fighters in 1968.

McDonald, David John (1902-1979), president of the United Steelworkers of America from 1953 to 1965 when he was defeated for reelection by I. W. Abel. For an account of his last election contest, *see* John A. Orr, "The Steelworker Election of 1965," *Labor Law Journal* (February 1969). For McDonald's autobiography, *see Union Man* (N.Y.: E. P. Dutton, 1969).

***McDonald* v. *Sante Fe Trail Transportation Co.*,** 424 U.S. 952 (1976), U.S. Supreme Court case, which held an employer could not impose racially discriminatory discipline on employees guilty of the same offense.

***McDonnell Douglas Corporation* v. *Green*,** 411 U.S. 792 (1973), U.S. Supreme Court case, which held that an employee could es-tablish a prima facie case of discrimination by initially showing (1) that he or she was a member of a racial minority; (2) that he or she applied and was qualified in an opening for which the employer sought applicants; (3) that despite qualifications he or she was rejected; (4) that after rejection the position remained open and the employer continued to seek applicants.

McGregor, Douglas M. (1906-1964), organizational humanist and managerial philosopher who is best known for his conceptualization of Theory X and Theory Y. Major works include: *The Human Side of Enterprise* (N.Y.: McGraw-Hill, 1960); *The Professional Manager* (N.Y.: McGraw-Hill, 1967). For an evaluation of McGregor's impact and contribution, *see* Warren G. Bennis, "Chairman Mac in Perspective," *Harvard Business Review* (September–October 1972).

MCT: *see* MINNESOTA CLERICAL TEST.

MD-CEA: *see* LABOR ORGANIZATION, Maryland Classified Employees Association.

MDTA: *see* MANPOWER DEVELOPMENT AND TRAINING ACT OF 1962.

mean, simple average of a set of measurements, obtained by summing the measurements and dividing by the number of them.

mean deviation: *see* AVERAGE DEVIATION.

Meany, George (1894-   ), labor leader who started out as a plumber in a Bronx local and was president of the AFL-CIO from its creation in 1955 to 1979. For a biography, *see* Joseph C. Goulden, *Meany* (N.Y.: Atheneum, 1972).

measure of dispersion, also called MEASURE OF VARIABILITY, any statistical measure showing the extent to which individual test scores are concentrated about or spread out from a measure of central tendency.

measured day work, also called MEASURED DAY RATE, an incentive wage plan that is premised upon a guaranteed base wage rate that is based upon previous job performance. *See* Andrew J. Waring, "The Case for the Measured Day Rate Plan," *Personnel Journal* (October 1961).

Meat Cutters and Butcher Workmen of North America, Amalgamated: *see* LABOR ORGANIZATION.

MEBA: *see* LABOR ORGANIZATION, Marine Engineers' Beneficial Association, National.

MEBA-PATCO: *see* LABOR ORGANIZATION, Professional Air Traffic Controllers Organization, under Marine Engineers' Beneficial Association, National.

mechanical aptitude tests, tests designed to measure how well an individual can learn to perform tasks that involve the understanding and manipulation of mechanical devices. Classified in two subgroups—mechanical reasoning and spatial relations.

Mechanical Comprehension Test, Bennett: *see* BENNETT MECHANICAL COMPREHENSION TEST.

Mechanics Educational Society of America: *see* LABOR ORGANIZATION.

mechanistic system, organization‐form, proven to be most appropriate under stable conditions, which is characterized by: (1) a high‐degree of task differentiation and specialization with a precise delineation of rights and

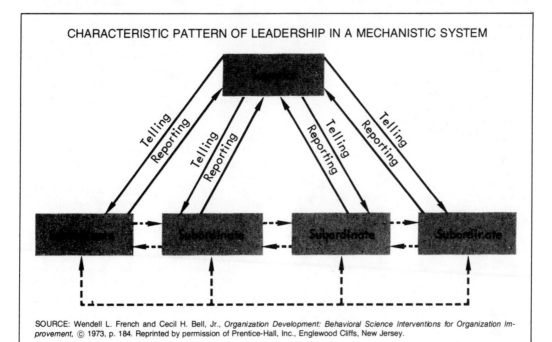

CHARACTERISTIC PATTERN OF LEADERSHIP IN A MECHANISTIC SYSTEM

SOURCE: Wendell L. French and Cecil H. Bell, Jr., *Organization Development: Behavioral Science Interventions for Organization Improvement*, © 1973, p. 184. Reprinted by permission of Prentice-Hall, Inc., Englewood Cliffs, New Jersey.

MECHANISTIC AND ORGANIC ORGANIZATIONS COMPARED

Mechanistic		Organic
High: many and sharp differentiation	**Specialization**	*Low:* no hard boundaries relative few different jobs
High: methods spelled out	**Standardization**	*Low:* individuals decide own methods
Means	**Orientation of Members**	Goals
By superiority	**Conflict Resolution**	Interaction
Hierarchy based on contractural relations	**Authority, Control and Communication**	Wide net based on common commitment
At top of organization	**Locus of Superior Competence**	Wherever there is skill and competence
Direction, orders	**Communication Content**	Advice, information
To organization position	**Loyalty Prestige**	To project and groups personal contribution

SOURCE: Reprinted from Jerome B. McKinney and Lawrence C. Howard, *Instructor's Manual* for *Public Administration: Balancing Power and Accountability* (Oak Park, Ill.: Moore Publishing, 1979), p. 19. Copyright © 1979 Moore Publishing Company, Inc.

responsibilities; (2) a high degree of reliance on the traditional hierarchical structure; (3) a tendency for the top of the hierarchy to control all incoming and outgoing communications; (4) an emphasis on vertical interactions between superiors and subordinates; (5) a demand for loyalty to the organization and to superiors; and (6) a greater importance placed on internal (local) knowledge, skill, and experience, in contrast to more general (cosmopolitan) knowledge, experience, and skill. The classic analysis of mechanistic systems is to be found in Tom Burns and G. M. Stalker, *The Management of Innovation* (Chicago: Quadrangle Books, 1961).

See also ORGANIC SYSTEM.

mechanization: *see* AUTOMATION.

median, middle score in a distribution, the 50th percentile, the point that divides the group into two equal parts. Half of a group of scores fall below the median and half above it.

mediation, also CONCILIATION, any attempt by an impartial third party to help settle disputes between labor and management. A mediator has no power but that of persuasion. The mediator's suggestions are advisory in nature and may be rejected by both parties. Mediation and conciliation tend to be used interchangeably to denote the entrance of an impartial third party into a labor dispute. However, there is a distinction. *Conciliation* is the less active term. It technically refers simply to efforts to bring the parties together so that they may resolve their problems themselves. *Mediation*, in contrast, is a more active term. It implies that an active effort will be made to help the parties reach agreement by clarifying issues, asking questions, and making specific proposals. However, the usage of the two terms has been so blurred that the only place where it is absolutely necessary to distinguish between them is in a dictionary. For a text, *see* William E. Simkin, *Mediation and the Dynamics of Collective Bargaining* (Washington, D.C.: Bureau of National Affairs, 1971). For a legal analyses, *see* Lon L. Fuller, "Mediation—Its Forms and Functions," *Southern California Law Review* (Winter 1971). For a public sector perspective, *see* Paul D. Staudohar, "Some Implications of Mediation for Resolution of Bargaining Impasses in Public Employment," *Public Personnel Management* (July–August 1973). For a bibliography, *see* Edward Levin and Daniel V. DeSantis, *Mediation: An Annotated Bibliography* (Ithaca, N.Y.: New York State School of Industrial and Labor Relations, Cornell University, 1978).

See also PREVENTIVE MEDIATION.

Mediation Service, abbreviated way of referring to the Federal Mediation and Conciliation Service or state agencies performing a similar function.

mediator, individual who acts as an impartial third party in order to help resolve labor–management disputes. Appointed by an administrative agency or by the parties involved, the mediator's role is to help the parties reach an agreement short of a strike. See Arthur S. Meyer, "Function of the Mediator in Collective Bargaining," *Industrial and Labor Relations Review* (January 1960).

medical insurance, supplemental: *see* SUPPLEMENTAL MEDICAL INSURANCE.

Medicare, the National Health Insurance Program for the elderly and the disabled. The two parts of Medicare—hospital insurance and medical insurance—help protect people 65 and over from the high costs of health care. Also eligible for Medicare are disabled people under 65 who have been entitled to social security disability benefits for 24 or more consecutive months (including adults who are receiving benefits because they have been disabled since childhood). Insured workers and their dependents who need dialysis treatment or a kidney transplant because of permanent kidney failure also have Medicare protection. For a history of how the medicare bill passed, *see* Max J. Skidmore, *Medicare and the American Rhetoric of Reconciliation* (University: University of Alabama Press, 1970).

Mee, John F. (1908-   ), industrial psychologist known for his advocacy that motivation be considered a management function. He edited the first practical handbook on the modern personnel function, *Personnel Handbook*, (N.Y.: Ronald Press Company, 1951).

meet-and-confer discussions, technique, used mostly in the public sector, of determining conditions of employment whereby the representatives of the employer and the employee organization hold periodic discussions to seek agreement on matters within the scope of representation. Any written agreement is in the form of a nonbinding memorandum of understanding. This technique is often used where formal collective bargaining is not authorized.

menial, originally a household servant. For centuries, it has been used as a term of disparagement and contempt to describe work of degrading drudgery. According to Albert L. Porter, "Repugnance for 'Menial Jobs'," *Management of Personnel Quarterly* (Winter 1971),

> a man's sense of well-being and meaningfulness in work is not so much a matter of external circumstances—the kind of job he has—as it is of his deepdown belief that he is a worthy human being. If he lacks that, any job can seem dissatisfying and "menial." Executives may suffer from this (or related behaviors) as much as assembly-line workers.

mentally handicapped employees, also called MENTALLY RETARDED EMPLOYEES, individuals with less than normal intellectual abilities. On standard tests, an intelligence quotient of 70 is usually thought to be the upper borderline for those who are classified as retarded. Until comparatively recently, the retarded had only the most limited opportunities in the open job market. But more enlightened attitudes towards dealing with retarded individuals and an employment climate influenced by the concept of equal employment opportunity for all are rapidly improving the employment prospects for the mentally handicapped/retarded. Mental deficiency and vocational deficiency are not synonymous. According to Donn E. Prolin, *Vocational Preparation of Retarded Citizens* (Columbus, Ohio: Charles E. Merrill, 1976), "one of the greatest problems that persons with mental retardation encounter is the continual underestimation of their potentials by the general public and professional workers." *Also see* Howard F. Rudd, "Supervising the Mentally Handicapped: The Procedures, the Rewards," *Supervisory Management* (December 1976); The National Association for Retarded Citizens, "Mentally Retarded Persons in the Open Job Market," *Personnel Journal* (May 1977).

mentally ill employees: *see* EMOTIONALLY HANDICAPPED EMPLOYEES.

mentally retarded employees: *see* MENTALLY HANDICAPPED EMPLOYEES.

mentor, wise counselor. The word comes from Homer's *The Odyssey*. When Odysseus set off for the war at Troy, he left his house and wife in the care of a friend named Mentor. When things got rough at home for Odysseus' family, Athene, the goddess of wisdom, assumed the shape of Mentor and provided Telemachus, the son of Odysseus, with some very helpful advice about how to deal with the problems of his most unusual adolescence. For an analysis of the importance of mentoring in organizational careers, *see* Eileen C. Shapiro, Florence P. Haseltine, and Mary P. Rowe, "Moving Up: Role Models, Mentors and the 'Patron System'," *Sloan Management Review* (Spring 1978). For a case study, *see* Barbara Kellerman, "Mentoring in Political Life: The Case of Willy Brandt," *American Political Science Review* (June 1978).

merchant guild: *see* GUILD.

Merit Employment Assessment Services, Inc.: *see* TEST PUBLISHERS.

merit increase, raise in pay based upon a favorable review of an employee's performance. This is the way most organization's seek to relate quality of performance to financial rewards. *See* A. Mikalachki, "There Is No Merit in Merit Pay!" *The Business Quarterly* (Spring 1976); Ernest C. Miller, "Top- and Middle-Management Compensation—Part 2: Incentive Bonus and Merit Increase Plans," *Compensation Review* (Fourth Quarter 1976); Douglas L. Fleuter, "A Different Approach to Merit Increases," *Personnel Journal* (April 1979).

merit pay system, also called MERIT PAY PROGRAM, set of procedures designed to reward employees with salary increases reflective of their on-the-job performance. According to Myles H. Goldberg, "Another Look at Merit Pay Programs," *Compensation Review* (Third Quarter 1977),

> Many merit pay programs are built around the concept of a fixed pool of merit increase dollars. This pool is derived usually by applying a percentage merit increase factor to the salaries of currently employed staff. Administrative guidelines define the average merit increase (usually as a percentage of salary) and restrict the increase to an amount within a set range. Typically, satisfactory or acceptable performance merits an average pay increase, better-than-acceptable performance merits a larger increase, and less-than-acceptable performance merits a lower increase.

merit principle, the concept that members of an organization are selected and promoted based on achievements measured in a standard way through open competition.

merit promotion, selection to a higher grade made solely on the basis of job-related qualifications without regard to factors such as race, color, religion, national origin, sex, age, political belief, marital status, or physical handicap.

merit raise: *see* MERIT INCREASE.

merit system, a public sector concept of staffing, which implies that no test of party membership is involved in the selection, promotion, or retention of government employees and that a constant effort is made to select the best qualified individuals available for appointment and advancement. For a classic analysis of why it ain't necessarily so, *see* E. S. Savas and Sigmund G. Ginsburg, "The Civil Service: A Meritless System?" *The Public Interest* (Summer 1973).

merit system principles, the Civil Service Reform Act of 1978 put into law the nine basic merit principles that should govern all personnel practices in the federal government and defined prohibited practices. The principles and prohibitions are:

**Personnel Practices
and Actions in the
Federal Government Require:**

- Recruitment from all segments of society, and selection and advancement on the basis of ability, knowledge, and skills, under fair and open competition.
- Fair and equitable treatment in all personnel management matters, without regard to politics, race, color, religion, national origin, sex, marital status, age, or handicapping condition, and with proper regard for individual privacy and consitutional rights.
- Equal pay for work of equal value, considering both national and local rates paid by private employers, with incentives and recognition for excellent performance.
- High standards of integrity, conduct, and concern for the public interest.
- Efficient and effective use of the Federal work force.
- Retention of employees who perform well, correcting the performance of those whose work is inadequate, and separation of those who cannot or will not meet required standards.
- Improved performance through effective education and training.
- Protection of employees from arbitrary action, personal favoritism, or political coercion.
- Protection of employees against reprisal for lawful disclosures of information.

**Officials and Employees Who Are
Authorized to Take Personnel
Actions Are Prohibited From:**

- Discriminating against any employee or applicant.

- Soliciting or considering any recommendation on a person who requests or is being considered for a personnel action unless the material is an evaluation of the person's work performance, ability, aptitude, or general qualifications, or character, loyalty, and suitability.
- Using official authority to coerce political actions, to require political contributions, or to retaliate for refusal to do these things.
- Willfully deceiving or obstructing an individual as to his or her right to compete for Federal employment.
- Influencing anyone to withdraw from competition, whether to improve or worsen the prospects of any applicant.
- Granting any special preferential treatment or advantage not authorized by law to a job applicant or employee.
- Appointing, employing, promoting, or advancing relatives in their agencies.
- Taking or failing to take a personnel action as a reprisal against employees who exercise their appeal rights; refuse to engage in political activity; or lawfully disclose violations of law, rule, or regulation, or mismanagement, gross waste of funds, abuse of authority, or a substantial and specific danger to public health or safety.
- Taking or failing to take any other personnel action violating a law, rule, or regulation directly related to merit system principles.

Merit Systems Protection Board (MSPB), independent federal government agency created by the Civil Service Reform Act of 1978 and designed to safeguard both the merit system and individual employees against abuses and unfair personnel actions. The MSPB is headed by three board members, appointed on a bipartisan basis to 7-year nonrenewable terms. The MSPB will hear and decide employee appeals and order corrective and disciplinary actions against an employee or agency when appropriate. It will also oversee the merit system and report annually to Congress on how the system is functioning.

Within the MSPB will be an independent special counsel, appointed by the president for a 5-year term. The special counsel will have the power to investigate charges of prohibited personnel practices (including reprisals against whistleblowers), to ask MSPB to stop personnel actions in cases involving prohibited personnel practices, and to bring disciplinary charges before the MSPB against those who violate merit system law.

Merit Systems Protection Board
1717 H. Street, N.W.
Washington, DC 20415
(202) 254-3063

meritocracy, word coined by Michael Young, in his *The Rise of the Meritocracy, 1870-2033* (London: Thames & Hudson, 1958; Penguin Books, 1961). Referred to a governing class that was both intelligent and energetic, yet sowed the seeds of its own destruction because of its obsession with test scores and paper qualifications that eventually forced those deemed to have lessor IQs to revolt. A favorite slogan of the revolutionaries was "Beauty is achievable by all." Today meritocracy is often used to refer to any elitist system of government or education. The grisly connotation of the word's original use has been effectively forgotten.

Merrick differential piece rate, also called MERRICK MULTIPLE PIECE RATE, incentive wage plan that establishes three different piece rates on the basis of performance—one for beginners, one for average workers, and one for superior workers.

MESA: *see* LABOR ORGANIZATION, Mechanics Educational Society of America.

Metal Polishers, Buffers, Platers and Allied Workers International Union: *see* LABOR ORGANIZATION.

Metcalf, Henry C. (1867-1942), a leading advocate of a "humanized industrialism" and co-author of one of the earliest and most influential texts on personnel administration. Major works include: *Personnel Administration: Its Principles and Practices*, with Ordway Tead (N.Y.: McGraw-Hill, 1920); *Scientific Foundations of Business Administration* (Baltimore: The Williams & Wilkins Co., 1926); *Dynamic Administration: The Collected Papers of Mary Parker Follett*, edited with Lyndall Urwick (N.Y.: Harper & Bros., 1942).

MGD data: *see* MINORITY GROUPS DESIGNATOR DATA.

Michigan Business Review: *see* UNIVERSITY OF MICHIGAN BUSINESS REVIEW.

Michigan State AFL–CIO: *see* AMERICAN FEDERATION OF LABOR–CONGRESS OF INDUSTRIAL ORGANIZATIONS.

Michigan State Employees Association: *see* LABOR ORGANIZATION.

MICH-SEA: *see* LABOR ORGANIZATION, Michigan State Employees Association.

Mickey Mouse, pejorative term for many aspects of personnel administration. When Walt Disney's famous mouse made it "big" in the 1930s, he appeared in a variety of cartoon shorts that had him building something that would later fall apart (such as a house or boat) or generally going to a great deal of trouble for little result. So Mickey Mouse gradually gave his name to anything requiring considerable effort for slight result, including many of the Mickey Mouse requirements of personnel. The term is also applied to policies or regulations felt to be needless, silly, or mildly offensive.

mid-career change: *see* CAREER CHANGE.

mid-career crisis, also MID-LIFE CRISIS, terms used to refer to a period in a person's life, usually during his/her 30s, which is marked by feelings of (1) personal frustration and (2) professional failure. Such feelings may or may not have a basis in fact. For general accounts of mid-life crises, *see* Gail Sheehy, *Passages: Predictable Crises of Adult Life* (N.Y.: E. P. Dutton, 1976); Roger Gould, *Transformations* (N.Y.: Simon and Schuster, 1978). For analyses of the problem of mid-career crises, *see* Harry Levinson, "On Being a Middle-Aged Manager," *Harvard Business Review* (July–August, 1969); Robert T. Golembiewski, "Mid-Life Transition and Mid-Career Crisis: A Special Case For Individual Development," *Public Administration Review* (May–June, 1978).
See also STRESS.

middle management, vague delineation of organizational authority and leadership that lies below top management and above first-level supervisors. *See* Emmanuel Kay, *The Crises in Middle-Management* (N.Y.: American Management Association, 1974); Steven H. Appelbaum, "The Middle Manager: An Examination of Aspirations and Pessimism," *The Personnel Administrator* (January 1977). For a thorough examination of the roles of mid-level managers in the public sector, *see* Jerome B. McKinney and Lawrence C. Howard, *Public Administration: Balancing Power and Accountability* (Oak Park, Ill.: Moore Publishing Company, 1979).

mid-level managers: *see* MIDDLE MANAGEMENT.

mid-life crisis: *see* MID-CAREER CRISIS.

midnight shift, tour of duty that usually runs from midnight to 8 am.

migratory worker, individual whose principal income is earned from temporary employment (typically in agriculture) and who, in order to find work, moves several times a year through as many states. For accounts of the life of migrant workers, *see* Robert Coles, *Uprooted Children: The Early Life of Migrant Farm Workers* (N.Y.: Harper & Row, 1971); Carey McWilliams, *Ill Fares the Land: Migrants and Migratory Labor in the United States* (N.Y.: Barnes & Noble, 1967).

mileage allowance, specific amount an employee is reimbursed for each mile that his personal automobile is used on company business. For how to determine a mileage allowance rate, *see* Joseph A. Capolarello, "Employee Mileage Allowances: Too High or Too Low?" *Personnel Journal* (February 1975).

military leave, lengthy leave of absence for service in the armed forces of the United States or a short-term leave of absence for service in the military reserves.

military service, as a general rule, military service for civil service retirement purposes is creditable provided it was active service, was terminated under honorable conditions, and was performed before separation from a civilian position under the retirement system. The federal government defines military service for retirement purposes as "service in the Army, Navy, Air Force, Marine Corps, and Coast Guard, including the service academies, and, after June 30, 1960, in the Regular Corps or Reserve Corps of the Public Health Service, and, after June 30, 1961, as a commissioned officer of the Coast and Geodetic Survey."

Miller Analogies Test (MAT), 100 verbal analogies designed to measure scholastic aptitude at the graduate school level and to aid in the selection of individuals for personnel positions. Primarily a measure of verbal ability that covers a broad range of knowledge. TIME 50/55 minutes. AUTHOR: W. S. Miller. PUBLISHER: Psychological Corporation (*see* TEST PUBLISHERS).

Miller, Arnold (1922-   ), president of the United Mine Workers of America from 1972 to 1979.

Miller v. Wilson, 236 U.S. 373 (1915), U.S. Supreme Court case, which held that a state law limiting the employment of women to eight hours a day was constitutional.

Mine Safety and Health Administration (MSHA), agency of the Department of Labor created by the Federal Mine Safety and Health Amendments Act of 1977 to bring all mines in the United States under a single safety and health program.

Mine Safety and Health Administration
4015 Wilson Blvd.
Arlington, VA 22203
(703) 235-1452

Mine Workers of America, United: *see* LABOR ORGANIZATION.

minimum wage, smallest hourly rate that may be paid to a worker. While many "minimum wages" are established by union contracts and organizational pay policies, "the" minimum wage usually refers to the federal minimum wage law—the Fair Labor Standards Act (FLSA). The minimum wage at any given time is established by Congress via FLSA amendments. The Secretary of Labor

FLSA Minimum Wage Standards, 1938-81

Legislation	Hourly Rate	Effective Date
Act of 1938	$ .25	Oct. 24, 1938
	.30	Oct. 24, 1939
	.40	Oct. 24, 1945
Amendments of:		
1949	.75	Jan. 25, 1950
1955	1.00	Mar. 1, 1956
1961	1.15	Sept. 3, 1961
	1.25	Sept. 3, 1963
1966	1.40	Feb. 1, 1967
	1.60	Feb. 1, 1968
1974	2.00	May 1, 1974
	2.10	Jan. 1, 1975
	2.30	Jan. 1, 1976
1977	2.65	Jan. 1, 1978
	2.90	Jan. 1, 1979
	3.10	Jan. 1, 1980
	3.35	Jan. 1, 1981

regulates some exceptions to the minimum wage. Persons with impaired earning or production capacity because of age, physical or mental deficiencies, or injury may be paid as low as 50 percent of the wage paid to a nonhandicapped worker for the same type, quality and quantity of work. Full-time students may be employed at 85 percent of the minimum wage under certain conditions. For an analysis of how youth unemployment, particularly black youth, would be reduced if a lower minimum wage was available for teenagers, *see* "Would the 'Teenwage' Cut Unemployment?" *Business Week* (September 19, 1977). *Also see* Peyton Elder, "The 1977 Amendments to the Federal Minimum Wage Law," *Monthly Labor Review* (January 1978); Sar A. Levitan and R. S. Belous, "The Minimum Wage Today: How Well Does It Work?" *Monthly Labor Review* (July 1979).

See also NATIONAL LEAGUE OF CITIES V. USERY and WEST COAST HOTEL V. PARRISH.

mini-shift, tour of duty for a permanent part-time employee. For an analysis of its utility, *see* William B. Werther, Jr., "Mini-Shifts: An Alternative to Overtime," *Personnel Journal* (March 1976).

Minnesota AFL–CIO: *see* AMERICAN FEDERATION OF LABOR–CONGRESS OF INDUSTRIAL ORGANIZATIONS.

Minnesota Association of Government Employees, Independent: *see* LABOR ORGANIZATION.

Minnesota Clerical Test (MCT), test of clerical ability that measures perception of detail and perceptual speed. The two test parts (numbers and names) list identical and nonidentical pairs for the subject to detect unlike pairs. TIME: 15/20 minutes. AUTHORS: D. C. Andrew, D. G. Paterson, and H. P. Longstaff. PUBLISHER: Psychological Corporation (*see* TEST PUBLISHERS).

Minnesota Multiphasic Personality Inventory (MMPI), 566-item, paper-and-pencil inventory that measures degrees of hypochondriasis, depression, hysteria, psychopathic deviation, masculinity-femininity, paranoia, psychasthenia, schizophrenia, hypomania, and social introversion. Originally designed to reveal pathological tendencies, this test is now widely used by business and industry in personnel selection and counseling procedures. However, proper interpretation of test results requires considerable psychological sophistication. TIME: Untimed. AUTHORS: S. R. Hathaway, J. C. McKinley. PUBLISHER: Psychological Corporation (*see* TEST PUBLISHERS).

Minnesota Rate of Manipulation Test, two-part test that measures arm–hand dexterity. The test requires an individual to place 58 round blocks into a board with matching slots, turn the blocks out, and again place them in the holes. Person is scored on total time required to complete the task. TIME: 30/40 minutes. AUTHOR: Minnesota Employment Stabilization Research Institute. PUBLISHER: American Guidance Services, Inc. (*see* TEST PUBLISHERS).

Minnesota Spatial Relations Test, test that measures both manual dexterity and spatial perceptions. It consists of four form boards with 58 cut-out geometric shapes to be placed in appropriate cut-out slots. TIME: 20 minutes. AUTHOR: Minnesota Employment Stabilization Research Institute. PUBLISHER: American Guidance Services, Inc. (*see* TEST PUBLISHERS).

Minnesota Vocational Interest Inventory (MVII), consists of 158 forced-choice items that provide 21 occupational and 9 area scales of interest patterns. Designed for men (age 15 and over) contemplating occupations at the semiskilled and skilled levels (*i.e.,* baker, printer, carpenter/painter, truck driver, sales and office clerk, electronics, etc.). TIME: 45/50 minutes. AUTHORS: K. E. Clark and David P. Campbell. PUBLISHER: Psychological Corporation (*see* TEST PUBLISHERS).

minority groups designator data, also called MGD DATA, data base or system which provides statistical employment information by race or national origin. In theory, such data should only be used in studies and analyses that evaluate an organization's equal employment opportunity programs.

MIS: *see* MANAGEMENT INFORMATION SYSTEM.

mission agency, any government department or agency whose legislation gives it responsibility for promotion of some cause or operation of some system as its primary reason for existence (mission) and which is appropriated funds for the conduct of this mission.

Mississippi AFL–CIO: *see* AMERICAN FEDERATION OF LABOR–CONGRESS OF INDUSTRIAL ORGANIZATIONS.

Missouri State Labor Council: *see* AMERICAN FEDERATION OF LABOR–CONGRESS OF INDUSTRIAL ORGANIZATIONS.

Mitbestimmungsrecht: *see* CODETERMINATION.

Mitchell, James P. (1900-1964), Secretary of Labor from 1953 to 1961.

Mitchell, John (1870-1919), president of the United Mine Workers from 1898 to 1907 when membership grew from 33,000 to 260,000. For a biography, *see* Elsie Gluck, *John Mitchell, Miner* (N.Y.: John Day Co., 1929; reprinted AMS Press, 1971).

MLR: *see* MONTHLY LABOR REVIEW.

MMPI: *see* MINNESOTA MULTIPHASIC PERSONALITY INVENTORY.

mobility: *see* OCCUPATIONAL MOBILITY.

mobility assignment, term generally used for the sharing of talent between the federal government and states, local governments, and institutions of higher education, as authorized by Title IV of the Intergovernmental Personnel Act of 1970, Public Law 91-648.

Title IV is designed to: (1) improve the delivery of government services at all levels of government by bringing the specialized knowledge and experience of skilled people to bear on problems that are of mutual concern to state or local jurisdictions and the federal government; (2) strengthen intergovernmental understanding, broaden perspective and increase capacity of personnel resources; and (3) help preserve the rights and benefits of employees so they will be better able to accept temporary assignments.

The ground rules for IPA Mobility Assignments are as follows:

1. Assignments can be made to or from federal agencies and states, local governments, and private and public colleges and universities for any period up to two years. They must be with the consent of the employee and for work of mutual benefit to the jurisdictions involved.
2. Employees can be assigned on a "detail" or leave without pay basis. If on detail, the employee is considered to continue on active duty with the organization from which detailed. If on leave, the employee goes on the rolls of the receiving organization.
3. No person-for-person exchange is required, although this can and does happen.
4. Federal employee salary, job rights, and benefits are protected, and travel and moving expenses are authorized.
5. For state, local and university employees, Title IV permits federal agencies to pay the employer's share of certain fringe benefits where this is appropriate, but job rights and continuation of benefit coverage remain the responsibility of the state or local employer.
6. Program officials of participating governments arrange assignments. Costs of the assignment, including salary, may be shared or borne entirely by either jurisdiction. This is subject to negotiation.

For further information contact the Intergovernmental Personnel Programs Division of the Office of Personnel Management.

mode, score or value that occurs most frequently in a distribution.

model agreement, collective bargaining agreement developed by a national or international union to serve as a standard for its locals.

modified union shop, variation of the union shop that exempts certain classes of employees from joining the union. Such exemptions might include employees who were employed before a certain date, seasonal workers, work study students, etc.

Molders' and Allied Workers' Union, International: *see* LABOR ORGANIZATION.

mole: *see* SANDHOG.

Molly Maguires, originally members of an Irish secret society—the Ancient Order of Hibernians (founded in 1843), to prevent the eviction of tenant farmers by process-servers of the English landlords—the Molly Maguires got their name because of their tendency to disguise themselves as women while engaging in their terrorist activities. After the U.S. Civil War, they established themselves as secret worker societies in the coal fields of Pennsylvania and West Virginia. Their terror tactics ceased and their organization disappeared in 1876 when 10 of their leaders were executed and 14 others jailed. For a history, *see* Wayne G. Broehl, Jr., *The Molly Maguires* (Cambridge, Mass: Harvard University Press, 1964). *See also* Sidney Lens, *The Labor Wars: From the Molly Maguires to the Sitdowns* (Garden City, N.Y.: Doubleday, 1973).

Monell v. Dept. of Social Services, New York City, 56 L. Ed. 2d 611 (1978), U.S. Supreme Court case, which held that cities and municipalities may be held liable when their official policies (in this case a mandatory maternity leave policy) or customs violate a person's constitutional rights.

money purchase benefit, pension that is entirely dependent on contributions made to an individual's account.

monotony curve: *see* FATIGUE CURVE.

Montana Public Employees Association: *see* LABOR ORGANIZATION.

MONT-PEA: *see* LABOR ORGANIZATION, Montana Public Employees Association.

Montana State AFL–CIO: *see* AMERICAN FEDERATION OF LABOR–CONGRESS OF INDUSTRIAL ORGANIZATIONS.

Monte Carlo techniques, operations research processes premised upon the laws of probability.

Monthly Labor Review (MLR), major publication of the U.S. Bureau of Labor Statistics. Articles deal with labor relations, trends in the labor force, new laws and court decisions effecting workers, etc. Lists the major labor agreements expiring each month and gives monthly current labor statistics on employment, unemployment, wages and prices, and productivity.

Monthly Labor Review
Editorial Address:
Bureau of Labor Statistics
U.S. Department of Labor
Washington, D.C. 20212
Subscriptions:
Superintendent of Documents
Government Printing Office
Washington, D.C. 20402

Mooney, Tom (1882-1942), full name THOMAS JOSEPH MOONEY, socialist and radical unionist sentenced to hang because of a bombing that killed ten people in a San Francisco parade in 1916. Because it later became obvious that he was convicted on false testimony, his case became a *cause celèbre* of the union movement. The governor of California commuted his death sentence to life imprisonment in 1918; a later governor pardoned him in 1939. For accounts of his troubles, *see* Richard H. Frost, *The Mooney Case* (Stanford, Calif.: Stanford University Press, 1968); Curt Gentry, *Frame-Up: The Incredible Case of Tom Mooney and Warren Billings* (N.Y.: Norton, 1967).

moonlighting, in the 19th century, moonlighting referred to any illicit nighttime activity. In the mid 1950s, it gained currency as a slang term for a second job. Employee moonlighting may impede primary job productivity and otherwise cause problems when there are questions about sick leave claims, absenteeism, tardiness, overtime scheduling, and potential conflicts of interest. Many employers—because of union contracts, civil service regulations, or company policy—formally restrict moonlighting by their employees. Typically, such restrictions require advance approval and stipulate that moonlighting be done outside of regularly scheduled work periods. According to the Bureau of Labor Statistics of the U.S. Department of Labor, 4.7 percent of all employed persons hold two or more jobs. Men employed in the protective services (primarily police and fire) and as teachers (except college) had the highest rates of moonlighting—10.4 percent and 16.3 percent respectively. For a complete analysis, *see* Kopp Michelotti, "Multiple Jobholding in May 1975," *Monthly Labor Review* (November 1975).

Moore, Ely (1798-1861), first president of the New York General Trades' Union in 1833 who later served in the U.S. Congress. For a biography, *see* Walter E. Hugins, "Ely Moore: The Case History of a Jacksonian Labor Leader," *Political Science Quarterly* (March 1950).

morale, collective attitude of the workforce toward their work environment and a crude measure of the organizational climate. Peter F. Drucker insists that the only true test of morale is performance. As such, morale is one of the most significant indicators of organizational health. "What physical health is to a physical organization, morale is to a cooperative system," said Fritz J. Roethlisberger, in *Management and Morale* (Cambridge, Mass.: Harvard University Press, 1941). *Also see* Louis C. Schroeter, *Organizational Elan* (N.Y.: American Management Association, 1970).

more-favorable-terms clause: *see* MOST-FAVORED-NATION CLAUSE.

Mosher, Frederick C. (1913-   ), a major voice in public administration who wrote the standard historical analysis of the civil serv-

No. 661. Persons With Two or More Jobs: 1970 to 1977

[In thousands of persons 16 years old and over, except percent. As of May]

YEAR AND INDUSTRY OF PRIMARY JOB	Persons with 2 or more jobs	Multiple job holding rate [1]	SECONDARY JOB IN—		YEAR AND INDUSTRY OF PRIMARY JOB	Persons with 2 or more jobs	Multiple job holding rate [1]	SECONDARY JOB IN—	
			Agriculture	Nonagriculture				Agriculture	Nonagriculture
1970, total	4,048	5.2	738	3,310	**1976, total**	3,948	4.5	674	3,273
Nonagriculture	3,772	5.1	667	3,105	Nonagriculture	3,749	4.5	620	3,129
1975, total	3,918	4.7	705	3,213	**1977, total**	4,558	5.0	755	3,803
Nonagriculture	3,665	4.6	637	3,028	Nonagriculture	4,333	5.0	697	3,637

[1] Percent of all employed in specified group.

SOURCE: Bureau of the Census, *Statistical Abstract of the United States* (Washington, D.C.: Government Printing Office, 1978), p. 406.

ice in the United States, *Democracy and the Public Service* (N.Y.: Oxford University Press, 1968). Other works include: *Governmental Reorganizations: Cases and Commentary* (Indianapolis, Indiana: Bobbs-Merrill, 1967); *Programming Systems and Foreign Affairs Leadership* (N.Y.: Oxford University Press, 1970); *American Public Administration: Past, Present, and Future* (University, Alabama, University of Alabama Press, 1975).

Mosher, William E. (1877-1945), founder and first president (1940-1941) of the American Society for Public Administraion. Co-author, with J. Donald Kingsley, of the first public personnel text, *Public Personnel Administration* (N.Y.: Harper Bros., 1936).

most-favored-nation clause, also called MORE-FAVORABLE-TERMS CLAUSE, that portion of a collective bargaining agreement where a union agrees not to sign contracts with any other employers under more favorable terms.

Mother Lake: *see* BARRY, LEONORA.

motion study, according to Benjamin W. Niebel, *Motion and Time Study* (Homewood, Ill.: Richard D. Irwin, 6th ed., 1976), motion study

> may be defined as the study of the body motions used in performing an operation, with the thought of improving the operation by eliminating unnecessary motions and simplifying necessary motions, and then establishing the most favorable motion sequence for maximum efficiency.

See also TIME STUDY.

motivation, also WORK MOTIVATION, an emotional stimulus that causes a person to act. *Work motivation* is an amalgam of all of the factors in one's working environment that foster (positively or negatively) productive efforts. Classic analyses of worker motivation include: A. H. Maslow, *Motivation and Personality* (N.Y.: Harper & Row, 1954); F. Herzberg, B. Mausner, and B. Snyderman, *The Motivation to Work* (N.Y.: John Wiley, 1959); V. H. Vroom, *Work and Motivation* (N.Y.: John Wiley, 1964). *See also* Kae H. Chung, *Motivational Theories and Practices* (Columbus, Ohio: Grid, Inc., 1977).

See also the following entries:

EXTRINSIC MOTIVATION
REINFORCEMENT
SELF-ACTUALIZATION
STROKING

Motivation–Hygiene Theory, also called TWO-FACTOR THEORY, put forth in a land-

mark study by Frederick Herzberg, Bernard Mausner, and Barbara Snyderman, in *The Motivation to Work* (N.Y.: John Wiley & Sons, 1959). It was one of the first extensive empirical demonstrations of the primacy of internal worker motivation. Five factors were isolated as determiners of job satisfaction: achievement, recognition, work itself, responsibility and advancement. Similarly, the factors associated with job dissatisfaction were realized: company policy and administration, supervision, salary, interpersonal relations, and working conditions. The satisfying factors were all related to job content, the dissatisfying factors to the environmental context of the job. The factors that were associated with job satisfaction were quite separate from those factors associated with job dissatisfaction. According to Herzberg, in "The Motivation-Hygiene Concept and the Problems of Manpower," *Personnel Administration* (January–February 1964):

> Since separate factors needed to be considered depending on whether job satisfaction or job dissatisfaction was involved, it followed that these two feelings were not the obverse of each other. The opposite of job satisfaction would not be job dissatisfaction but rather NO job satisfaction; and similarly the opposite of job dissatisfaction is NO job dissatisfaction—not job satisfaction.

Because the environmental context of jobs, such as working conditions, interpersonal relations, and salary, served primarily as preventatives, they were termed hygiene factors, as an analogy to the medical use of hygiene meaning preventative and environmental. The job-content factors such as achievement, advancement, and responsibility were termed motivators because these are the things that motivate people to superior performance. Again according to Herzberg, in *Work and the Nature of Man* (Cleveland: World Publishers, 1966):

> The principal result of the analysis of this data was to suggest that the hygiene or maintenance events led to job dissatisfaction because of a need to avoid unpleasantness; the motivator events led to job satisfaction because of a need for growth or self-actualization. At the psychological level, the two dimensions of job attitudes reflected a two-dimensional need structure: one need system for the avoidance of unpleasantness and a parallel need system for personal growth.

Since its original presentation, a considerable number of empirical investigations by a wide variety of researchers has tended to confirm the Motivation–Hygiene Theory. Its chief fault seems to be its rejection of the view that pay is a unique incentive capable, in differing circumstances, of being a hygiene as well as a motivator factor. But the theory's main holding—that worker motivation is essentially internal—remains largely unchallenged.

See also HERZBERG, FREDERICK.

Motor Coach Employees v. Lockridge: see AMALGAMATED ASSOCIATION OF STREET, ELECTRIC RAILWAY, AND MOTOR COACH EMPLOYEES OF AMERICA V. LOCKRIDGE.

Mountain Timber Company v. Washington, 343 U.S. 238 (1917), U.S. Supreme Court case, which held constitutional state workmen's compensation laws.

Mouton, Jane S.: see BLAKE, ROBERT R. AND JANE S. MOUTON.

MPA: see MBA.

MPBP: see LABOR ORGANIZATION, Metal Polishers, Buffers, Platers and Allied Workers International Union.

MPEA: see LABOR ORGANIZATION, Machine Printers and Engravers Association of the United States.

Ms. title of courtesy for a woman, which is used without regard to her marital status. On January 26, 1977, the U.S. Civil Service Commission announced that it would revise all of its personnel forms—including job application forms—to make "Ms." available for those who prefer it. As present stocks are depleted and the forms are reprinted, the change will be incorporated in all forms that require a title. The commission also instructed all federal agencies under its jurisdiction to incorporate "Ms." in addition to "Miss," "Mrs.," and "Mr." on their internal personnel forms.

MSHA: see MINE SAFETY AND HEALTH ADMINISTRATION.

MSPB: see MERIT SYSTEMS PROTECTION BOARD.

Mt. Clemens case: see ANDERSON V. MT. CLEMENTS POTTERY.

Mt. Healthy Board of Education v. Doyle, 429 U.S. 274 (1977), U.S. Supreme Court case, which held that the first amendment does not demand that a discharged employee be placed "in a better position as a result of the exercise of constitutionally protected activity than he would have occupied had he

done nothing." An employer should not be inhibited from evaluating an employee's performance and "reaching a decision not to rehire on the basis of that record, simply because the protected conduct makes the employer more certain of the correctness of its decision." See William H. DuRoss, III, "Toward Rationality in Discriminatory Cases: The Impact of *Mt. Healthy Board of Education v. Doyle* Upon the NLRA," *The Georgetown Law Journal* (April 1978).

Muller v. Oregon, 208 U.S. 412 (1908), U.S. Supreme Court case, which held constitutional an Oregon law that limited the employment of women to ten hours a day as a health measure.

multicraft union, craft union that encompasses several different skilled occupations.

multiemployer bargaining, collective bargaining involving more than one company, usually in the same industry. For a summary of public sector experiences, see Richard Pegnetter, *Multiemployer Bargaining in the Public Sector: Purposes and Experiences* (Chicago: International Personnel Management Association, 1975).

Multiple Aptitude Tests (MAT), battery of nine tests used for vocational guidance. Measures word meaning, paragraph meaning, language usage, routine clerical facility, arithmetic reasoning, arithmetic computation, applied science and mechanical and spatial relations. TIME: 175/220 minutes (3 sessions). AUTHORS: David Segel and Evelyn Raskin. PUBLISHER: California Test Bureau/McGraw-Hill (see TEST PUBLISHERS).

multiple-choice test, test consisting entirely of multiple-choice items, which require the examinee to choose the best or correct answer from several that are given as options.

multiple cutting score, assignment of a cutting score to each of several tests (or other standards) and the requirement that an applicant achieve a passing score on each of them to be hired or eligible for hire.

multiple regression analysis: see REGRESSION ANALYSIS.

multiple time plan, wage incentive plan that provides for higher base rates as progressively higher levels of production are reached.

Muniz v. Hoffman, 422 U.S. 454 (1975), U.S. Supreme Court case, which held that a union did not have a statutory or constitutional right to a jury trial on charges of criminal contempt stemming from its violation of an injunction issued under the authority of the National Labor Relations Act.

Munsterberg, Hugo (1863-1916), German psychologist who spent his later years at Harvard and earned the title of "father" of industrial or applied psychology by proposing the use of psychology for practical purposes. His major book is *Psychology and Industrial Efficiency* (Boston: Houghton Mifflin, 1913). For a sympathic biography, *see* Margaret Munsterberg, *Hugo Munsterberg: His Life and Work* (N.Y.: Appleton-Century-Crofts, 1922).

***Murgia* decision:** *see* MASSACHUSETTS BOARD OF RETIREMENT V. MURGIA.

Murphy's Law, *Public Administration Review* (July 1976) published the following Murphy's Laws:

1. Anything that can go wrong will go wrong.
2. Anything that can go wrong will—at the worst possible time.
3. Nothing is as easy as it seems.
4. If there is a possibility of several things going wrong, the one that will go wrong is the one that will do the most damage.
5. Everything takes longer than it should.
6. Left to themselves, things will go from bad to worse.
7. Nature always sides with the hidden flaw.
8. If everything seems to be going well, you have obviously overlooked something.

Murphy seems related to that famous literary wit, Anonymous. Only one thing seems certain—Murphy's laws were not written by Murphy, but by another person with the same name.

Murray, Philip (1886-1952), first president of the United Steelworkers of American and president of the Congress of Industrial Organizations (CIO) from 1940 until his death.

mushroom management, all that mushrooms need in order to grow is to be left undisturbed in the dark and fed fertilizer frequently. Mushroom managers keep subordinates in the dark and feed them lots of manure. Unfortunately, this technique works better on real mushrooms than it does on subordinates—they cease to

grow at all. *Source:* William Thomas, "Humor for Hurdling the Mystique in Management," *Management of Personnel Quarterly* (Winter 1970).

Musicians, American Federation of: *see* LABOR ORGANIZATION.

Muste, A. J. (1885-1967), in full ABRAHAM JOHANNES MUSTE, labor leader until the late 1930s when he turned his major efforts toward Christian pacifism. For a biography, *see* Nat Hentoff, *Peace Agitator: The Story of A. J. Muste* (N.Y.: MacMillan, 1963).

Mutual Aid Pact: *see* MUTUAL STRIKE AID.

mutuality: *see* DOCTRINE OF MUTUALITY.

mutual rating: *see* PEER RATING.

mutual strike aid, also called EMPLOYER STRIKE INSURANCE, also MUTUAL AID PACT, formal strike insurance program that has employers in a particular industry share the financial burden of a strike. Companies operating normally return a portion of their additional earnings to the company whose employees are on strike. Some mutual strike aid programs operate by assessing their member companies on an annual basis. *Mutual Aid Pact* is the strike insurance program of the airline industry. *See* John S. Hirsch, Jr., "Strike Insurance and Collective Bargaining," *Industrial and Labor Relations Review* (April 1969). For a legal analysis, *see* Frank M. Tuerkheimer, "Strike Insurance: An Analysis of the Legality of Inter-Employer Economic Aid Under Present Federal Legislation," *New York University Law Review* (January 1963).

MVII: *see* MINNESOTA VOCATIONAL INTEREST INVENTORY.

Myers, M. Scott (1922-   ), industrial psychologist and leading authority on job design and motivation. Major works include: *Every Employee a Manager: More Meaningful Work Through Job Enrichment* (N.Y.: McGraw-Hill, 1970); "Overcoming Union Opposition to Job Enrichment," *Harvard Business Review* (May–June 1971); *Managing with Unions* (Reading, Mass.: Addison-Wesley, 1978).

N

N, mathematical symbol commonly used to represent the number of cases in a distribution, study, etc. The symbol of the number of cases in a subgroup of *N* is *n*.

NAACP v. Federal Power Commission: see NATIONAL ASSOCIATION FOR THE ADVANCEMENT OF COLORED PEOPLE V. FEDERAL POWER COMMISSION.

NAATS: see LABOR ORGANIZATION, Air Traffic Specialists, National Association of.

NAB: see NATIONAL ALLIANCE OF BUSINESSMEN.

NABET: see LABOR ORGANIZATION, Broadcast Employees and Technicians, National Association of.

NAGE: see LABOR ORGANIZATION, Government Employees, National Association of.

NAGI: see LABOR ORGANIZATION, Government Inspectors, National Association of.

Nagler, Isidore, (1895-1959), one of the pioneering labor organizers and leaders of the garment industry.

NALC: see LABOR ORGANIZATION, Letter Carriers of the United States of America, National Association of.

NALC decision: see UNITED STATES CIVIL SERVICE COMMISSION V. NATIONAL ASSOCIATION OF LETTER CARRIERS.

NAM: see NATIONAL ASSOCIATION OF MANUFACTURERS.

NAPA: see NATIONAL ACADEMY OF PUBLIC ADMINISTRATION.

NAPEP: see LABOR ORGANIZATION, Planners, Estimators, and Progressmen, National Association of.

NAPFE: see LABOR ORGANIZATION, Postal and Federal Employees, National Alliance of.

NAPS: see LABOR ORGANIZATION, Postal Supervisors, National Association of.

Nashville Gas Co. v. Satty, 434 U.S. 136 (1977), U.S. Supreme Court case, which held that pregnant women, forced to take maternity leave, cannot be denied their previously accumulated seniority rights when they return to work.

NASS: see NATIONAL ASSOCIATION OF SUGGESTION SYSTEMS.

NATB: see NONREADING APTITUDE TEST BATTERY.

National Academy of Arbitrators, founded in 1947 "to establish and foster high standards and competence among those engaged in the arbitration of labor–management disputes on a professional basis; to adopt canons of ethics to govern the conduct of arbitrators; to promote the study and understanding of the arbitration of labor–management disputes." The Academy is not an agency for the selection or appointment of arbitrators. It does invite and sponsor activities designed to improve general understanding of the nature of arbitration and its use as a means of settling labor disputes.

Membership in the National Academy of Arbitrators is conferred by vote of the Board of Governors upon recommendation of the Membership Committee.

In considering applications for membership, the Academy applies the following standards: (1) the applicant should be of good moral character, as demonstrated by adherence to sound ethical standards in professional activities; (2) the applicant should have substantial and current experience as an impartial arbitrator of labor–management disputes, so as to reflect general acceptability by the parties; and (3) as an alternative to (2), the applicant with limited but current experience in arbitration should have attained general recognition through scholarly publication or other activities as an impartial authority on labor–management relations. Membership will not be conferred upon applicants who serve partisan interests as advocates or consultants for Labor or Management in labor–management relations or who are associated with or are members of a firm which performs such advocate or consultant work. The Academy had about 500 members in 1978.

National Academy of Arbitrators
4335 Cathedral Ave., N.W.
Washington, DC 20016
(202) 362-8316

National Academy of Public Administration (NAPA), organization of more than 200 distinguished practitioners and scholars in public administration, supported by a small staff and dedicated to improving the role of public management in a democratic society. The Academy was founded in 1967 to serve as a source of advice and counsel to government and public officials on problems of public administration; to help improve the policies, processes, and institutions of public administration through early identification of important problems and significant trends; to evaluate program performance and assess administrative progress; and to increase public understanding of public administration and its critical role in a democratic society.

National Academy of Public Administration
1225 Connecticut Avenue, N.W.
Washington, DC 20036
(202) 659-9165

See also AMERICAN SOCIETY FOR PUBLIC ADMINISTRATION.

National Alliance of Businessmen (NAB), business group formed to work in partnership with the federal government in order to find permanent jobs for the hard core unemployed.

National Alliance of Businessmen
1730 K Street, N.W.
Washington, DC 20506
(202) 254-1707

National Alliance of Postal and Federal Employees: *see* LABOR ORGANIZATION, Postal and Federal Employees, National Alliance of.

National Association for the Advancement of Colored People v. *Federal Power Commission*, 425 U.S. 663 (1976), U.S. Supreme Court case, which held that the Federal Power Commission is authorized to consider the consequences of discriminatory employment practices on the part of its regulatees only insofar as such consequences are di-

rectly related to its establishment of just and reasonable rates in the public interest. To the extent that illegal, duplicative, or unnecessary labor costs are demonstrably the product of a regulatee's discriminatory employment practices and can be or have been demonstrably quantified by judicial decree or the final action of an administrative agency the Federal Power Commission should disallow them.

National Association of Aeronautical Examiners: *see* LABOR ORGANIZATION, Aeronautical Examiners, National Association of.

National Association of Aeronautical Production Controllers: *see* LABOR ORGANIZATION, Aeronautical Production Controllers, National Association of.

National Association of Air Traffic Specialists, Inc.: *see* LABOR ORGANIZATION, Air Traffic Specialists, Inc., National Association of.

National Association of ASCS County Office Employees: *see* LABOR ORGANIZATION, ASCS County Office Employees, National Association of.

National Association of Broadcast Employees and Technicians: *see* LABOR ORGANIZATION, Broadcast Employees and Technicians, National Association of.

National Association of Government Employees: *see* LABOR ORGANIZATION, Government Employees, National Association of.

National Association of Government Inspectors and Quality Assurance Personnel: *see* LABOR ORGANIZATION, Government Inspectors and Quality Assurance Personnel, National Association of.

National Association of Letter Carriers of the United States of America: *see* LABOR ORGANIZATION, Letter Carriers of the United States of America, National Association of.

National Association of Manufacturers (NAM), largest non-trade employer's association in the United States. NAM's purpose is to unite the manufacturers of the country in order to promote public progress and general prosperity. While NAM supports the abstract rights of labor, its specific policies tend to be thought of (by organized labor at least) as being anti-labor.

National Association of Manufacturers
1776 F Street
Washington, DC 20006
(202) 331-3700

National Association of Planners, Estimators, and Progressmen: *see* LABOR ORGANIZATION, Planners, Estimators, and Progressmen, National Association of.

National Association of Postal Supervisors: *see* LABOR ORGANIZATION, Postal Supervisors, National Association of.

National Brotherhood of Packinghouse and Industrial Workers: *see* LABOR ORGANIZATION, Packinghouse and Industrial Workers, National Brotherhood of.

National Association of Sheltered Workshops and Homebound Programs: *see* ASSOCIATION OF REHABILITATION FACILITIES.

National Association of Suggestion Systems (NASS), non-profit organization founded in 1942 to promote and develop suggestions systems in industry and government. NASS seeks to develop new technology and disseminate information about suggestion systems to its more than 1,000 members and to all others interested in suggestion systems.

National Association of Suggestion Systems
435 North Michigan Ave.
Chicago, IL 60671
(312) 644-0075

National Center for Productivity and Quality of Working Life, federal agency that existed from 1975 to 1978. In 1970, the National Commission on Productivity was formed to focus public attention on the importance of productivity and to enlist the cooperation of labor, management, government, and the public in a sustained effort to improve the economy's performance. In 1975, Public Law 94-136 created the National Center for Productivity and Quality of Working Life as an independent agency with no regulatory authority to work with Congress and federal agencies to develop a national policy for greater productivity, improved worker morale and work quality. The new National Center thereupon assumed much of the work and the staff of the expired National Commission. After publishing a variety of reports, the National Center expired on September 30, 1978.

National Civil Service League (NCSL), a good-government lobby formed in 1881 by patrician reformers concerned with the debilitating and corrupting effects of patronage and the "spoils system" on the efficiency and moral stature of government. The Pendleton Act, drawn up by the League and sponsored by a League member, Senator George Pendleton of Ohio, introduced merit principles into federal employment.

The League continues its reform efforts. Its Model Public Personnel Administration Law of 1970, which advocates replacing civil service commissions with personnel directors appointed by the chief executive, has been adopted in whole or in part by hundreds of governmental jurisdictions.

National Civil Service League
5530 Wisconsin Ave., N.W.
Washington, DC 20015
(301) 654-6884

See also COUTURIER, JEAN J. and PENDLETON ACT OF 1883.

National Commission for Industrial Peace, presidential advisory commission established in 1961 as the President's Advisory Committee on Labor–Management Policy. It became the National Commission for Industrial Peace in 1973 and was abolished by Executive Order 11823 of December 12, 1974.

National Commission on Productivity: *see* NATIONAL CENTER FOR PRODUCTIVITY AND QUALITY OF WORKING LIFE.

National Commission on State Workmen's Compensation Laws: *see* WORKMEN'S COMPENSATION.

national consultation rights, generally a union of federal government employees may be accorded national consultation rights if it holds exclusive recognition for either 10 percent or more, or 5,000 or more, of the employees of an agency. According to Section 7213 of the Civil Service Reform Act of 1978:

> When a labor organization holds national consultation rights, the agency must give the labor organization notice of proposed new substantive personnel policies and proposed changes in established personnel policies and an opportunity to comment on such proposals. The labor organization has a right to suggest changes in personnel policies and to have those suggestions carefully considered. The labor organization also has a right to consult, in person at reasonable times, upon request, with appropriate officials on personnel policy matters and a right to submit its views in writing on personnel policy matters at any time. National consultation rights do not include the right to negotiate. Further, the agency is not required to consult with a labor organization on any matter which would be outside the scope of negotiations if the labor organization held national exclusive recognition in that agency.

National consultation rights were first granted to federal employees under Executive Order 11491 of October 29, 1969.

National Education Association: *see* LABOR

ORGANIZATION, Education Association, National.

National Employ the Handicapped Week, also called NETH WEEK, the first full week in October, which has been set aside by the U.S. Congress to emphasize the employment of the handicapped.

National Federation of Federal Employees: *see* LABOR ORGANIZATION, Federal Employees, National Federation of.

National Federation of Licensed Practical Nurses: *see* LABOR ORGANIZATION, Licensed Practical Nurses, National Federation of.

National Football League Players Association: *see* LABOR ORGANIZATION, Football League Players Association, National.

National Hockey League Players Association: *see* LABOR ORGANIZATION, Hockey League Players Association, National.

National Industrial Recovery Act of 1933 (NIRA), federal statute that guaranteed employees "the right to organize and bargain collectively through representatives of their own choosing . . . free from the interference, restraint or coercion of employers." The act, which created the National Recovery Administration (NRA) to administer its provisions, was designed to establish self-government of industry through codes of fair competition which tended to eliminate competitive practices. Companies adopting their industries' codes of fair practice were entitled to display the "Blue Eagle," a flag or poster indicating compliance. The Supreme Court declared the act to be unconstitutional in 1935, but the Wagner Act of that year provided employees with even stronger collective bargaining guarantees.

National Industrial Workers Union: *see* LABOR ORGANIZATION, Industrial Workers Union, National.

National Institute for Occupational Safety and Health (NIOSH), established within the Department of Health, Education, and Welfare under the provisions of the Occupational Safety and Health Act of 1970 (P.L. 91-596). Administratively, NIOSH is located within HEW's Health Services and Mental Health Administration. As the federal agency responsible for formulating new or improved occupational safety and health standards, NIOSH not only carries out HEW's responsibilities under the Occupational Safety and Health Act, but also the health program of the Federal Coal Mine Health and Safety Act of 1969 (P.L. 91-173). NIOSH is the principal federal agency engaged in research, education and training in a national effort to eliminate on-the-job hazards to the health and safety of U.S. working men and women.

Under the Occupational Safety and Health Act, NIOSH has the responsibility for conducting research designed to produce recommendations for new occupational safety and health standards. These recommendations are transmitted to the Department of Labor which has the responsibility for the final setting, promulgation and enforcement of the standards.

In the case of the Federal Coal Mine Health and Safety Act, NIOSH transmits recommended health standards to the Department of the Interior, which has the enforcement responsibilities under that law.

National Institute for Occupational Safety and Health
5600 Fishers Lane
Rockville, MD 20852
(301) 443-2404

National Labor Relations Act of 1935 (NLRA), also called WAGNER–CONNERY ACT and WAGNER ACT, the nation's principal labor relations law applying to all interstate commerce except railroad and airline operations (which are governed by the Railway Labor Act). The NLRA seeks to protect the rights of employees and employers, to encourage collective bargaining, and to eliminate certain practices on the part of labor and management that are harmful to the general welfare. It states and defines the rights of employees to organize and to bargain collectively with their employers through representatives of their own choosing. To ensure that employees can freely choose their own representatives for the purpose of collective bargaining, the act establishes a procedure by which they can exercise their choice at a secret ballot election conducted by the National Labor Relations Board. Further, to protect the rights of employees and employers, and to prevent labor disputes that would adversely affect the rights of the public, Congress has defined certain practices of employers and unions as unfair labor practices. The NLRA is administered and enforced principally by the National Labor Relations Board, which was created by the act.

In common usage, the National Labor Relations Act refers not to the act of 1935, but to the act as amended by the Labor–Management Relations (Taft–Hartley) Act of 1947 and the Labor–Management Reporting and Disclosure (Landrum–Griffin) Act of 1959.

See also the following entries:

HANNA MINING CO. V. DISTRICT 2, MARINE ENGINEERS

LINN V. UNITED PLANT GUARD WORKERS

NATIONAL LABOR RELATIONS BOARD V. JONES AND LAUGHLIN STEEL CORP.

UNFAIR LABOR PRACTICES (EMPLOYERS)

UNFAIR LABOR PRACTICES (UNIONS)

National Labor Relations Board (NLRB), federal agency that administers the nation's laws relating to labor relations. The NLRB is vested with the power to safeguard employees' rights to organize, to determine through elections whether workers want unions as their bargaining representatives, and to prevent and remedy unfair labor practices (*see also* AMERICAN FEDERATION OF LABOR V. NATIONAL LABOR RELATIONS BOARD).

The NLRB is an independent agency created by the National Labor Relations Act of 1935 (Wagner Act), as amended in 1947 (Taft–Hartley Act) and 1959 (Landrum–Griffin Act). The act affirms the right of employees to self-organization and to bargain collectively through representatives of their own choosing or to refrain from such activities. The act prohibits certain unfair labor practices by employers and labor organizations or their agents and authorizes the NLRB to designate appropriate units for collective bargaining and to conduct secret ballot elections to determine whether employees desire representation by a labor organization. The Postal Reorganization Act of 1971 conferred jurisdiction upon the NLRB over unfair labor practice charges and representation elections affecting U.S. Postal Service employees. Jurisdiction over all privately operated health care institutions was conferred on the NLRB by an amendment to the act in 1974.

The NLRB has two principal functions— preventing and remedying unfair labor practices by employers and labor organizations or their agents, and conducting secret ballot elections among employees in appropriate collective bargaining units to determine whether or not they desire to be represented by a labor organization. The NLRB also conducts secret ballot elections among employees who have been covered by a union-shop agreement to determine whether or not they wish to revoke their union's authority to make such agreements; in jurisdictional disputes, decides and determines which competing group of workers is entitled to perform the work involved; and conducts secret ballot elections among employees concerning employers' final settlement offers in national emergency labor disputes.

The NLRB's general counsel has final authority in unfair labor practice cases to investigate charges, issue complaints, and prosecute such complaints before the board. The general counsel, on behalf of the board, prosecutes injunction proceedings; handles courts of appeals proceedings to enforce or review NLRB orders; participates in miscellaneous court litigation; and obtains compliance with NLRB orders and court judgments. The general counsel is responsible for the processing by field personnel of the several types of employee elections referred to above.

Under general supervision of the general counsel, 32 regional directors and their staffs process representation, unfair labor practice, and jurisdictional dispute cases. (Some regions have subregional or resident offices.) They issue complaints in unfair labor practice cases; seek settlement of unfair labor practice charges; obtain compliance with Board orders and court judgments; and petition district courts for injunctions to prevent or remedy unfair labor practices. The regional directors also direct hearings in representation cases; conduct elections pursuant to agreement or the decisionmaking authority delegated to them by the NLRB, or pursuant to NLRB directions; and issue certifications of representatives when unions win or certify the results when unions lose employee elections. They process petitions for bargaining unit clarification, for amendment of certification, and for rescission of a labor organization's authority to make a union-shop agreement. They also conduct national emergency employee referendums.

The NLRB can act only when it is formally requested to do so. Individuals, employers, or unions may initiate cases by filing charges of unfair labor practices or petitions for employee representation elections with the NLRB field offices serving the area where the case arises.

In the event a regional director declines to proceed on a representation petition, the party filing the petition may appeal to the NLRB. Where a regional director declines to proceed on an unfair labor practice charge, the filing party may appeal to the general counsel. Administrative law judges conduct hearings in unfair labor practice cases, make findings, and recommend remedies for violations found. Their decisions are reviewable by the NLRB if exceptions to the decision are filed.

NLRB Field Offices

Albany, NY 12207
New Federal Bldg.
(518) 472-2215

Albuquerque, NM 87110
5000 Marble Ave. NE
(505) 766-2508

Anchorage, AK 99501
632 W. 6th Ave.
(907) 265-5271

Atlanta, GA 30308
730 Peachtree St. NE
(404) 881-4760

Baltimore, MD 21201
Federal Bldg.
(301) 962-2822

Birmingham, AL 35203
City Federal Bldg.
(205) 254-1492

Boston, MA 02110
99 High St.
(617) 223-3300

Brooklyn, NY 11241
16 Court St.
(212) 330-7550

Buffalo, NY 14202
Federal Bldg.
(716) 842-3100

Chicago, IL 60604
219 S. Dearborn St.
(312) 353-7570

Cincinnati, OH 45202
Federal Office Bldg.
(513) 684-3686

Cleveland, OH 44199
Federal Office Bldg.
(216) 522-3715

Coral Gables, FL 33146
1570 Madruga Ave.
(305) 350-5391

Denver, CO 80202
U.S. Custom House
(303) 837-3551

Detroit, MI 48226
Federal Bldg.
(313) 226-3200

El Paso, TX 79902
4100 Rio Bravos St.
(915) 543-7737

Fort Worth, TX 76102
Federal Office Bldg.
(817) 334-2921

Hato Rey, PR 00918
U.S. Courthouse
(809) 763-6363

Honolulu, HI 96813
677 Ala Moana
(808) 546-5100

Houston, TX 77002
500 Dallas Ave.
(713) 226-4296

Indianapolis, IN 46204
Federal Office Bldg.
(317) 269-7430

Jacksonville, FL 32202
Federal Bldg.
(904) 791-3768

Kansas City, KS 66101
4th at State
(816) 374-4518

Little Rock, AR 72201
1 Union Plaza
(501) 378-6311

Las Vegas, NV 89101
300 Las Vegas Blvd. S.
(702) 385-6416

Los Angeles, CA 90024 Region 31
Federal Bldg.
(213) 824-7351

Los Angeles, CA 90014 Region 21
849 Broadway
(213) 688-5200

Memphis, TN 38103
Federal Bldg.
(901) 521-3161

Milwaukee, WI 53203
744 N. 4th St.
(414) 224-3861

Minneapolis, MN 55401
Federal Bldg.
(612) 725-2611

Nashville, TN 37203
Federal Bldg.
(615) 749-5921

Newark, NJ 07102
Federal Bldg.
(201) 645-2100

New Orleans, LA 70113
1001 Howard Ave.
(504) 589-6361

New York, NY 10007
Federal Bldg.
(212) 264-0300

Oakland, CA 94607
492 9th St.
(415) 556-4806

Peoria, IL 61602
Savings Center Tower
(309) 671-7080

Philadelphia, PA 19106
Federal Bldg.
(215) 597-7601

Phoenix, AZ 85014
6107 N. 7th St.
(602) 261-3717

Pittsburgh, PA 15219
601 Grant St.
(412) 644-2977

Portland, OR 97205
610 SW. Broadway
(503) 221-3085

St. Louis, MO 63101
210 N. 12th Blvd.
(314) 425-4167

San Antonio, TX 78206
Federal Office Bldg.
(512) 225-5511

San Francisco, CA 94102
Federal Bldg.
(415) 556-3197

Seattle, WA 98174
Federal Bldg.
(206) 442-4532

Tampa, FL 33602
Federal Office Bldg.
(813) 228-2641

Tulsa, OK 74135
6128 E. 38th St.
(918) 664-1420

Washington, DC 20037
2120 L St. NW
(202) 254-7612

Winston-Salem, NC 27101
Federal Bldg.
(919) 761-3201

National Labor Relations Board
1717 Pennsylvania Ave. N.W.
Washington, DC 20570
(202) 655-4000

See also the following entries:

MASTRO PLASTICS CORP. V. NATIONAL LABOR
RELATIONS BOARD

NEWPORT NEWS SHIPBUILDING AND DRY
DOCK CO. V. SCHAUFFLER

PORTER CO. V. NATIONAL LABOR RELATIONS
BOARD

SEARS, ROEBUCK, & CO. V. SAN DIEGO COUNTY
DISTRICT COUNCIL OF CARPENTERS

National Labor Relations Board Professional Association: *see* LABOR ORGANIZATION.

National Labor Relations Board Union: *see* LABOR ORGANIZATION.

National Labor Relation Board v. Allis-Chalmers, 388 U.S. 175 (1967), U.S. Supreme Court case, which held that a union could fine its members for breaking a lawful strike and could obtain a judgment in court in order to enforce payment of the fine.

National Labor Relations Board v. Babcock and Wilcox, 351 U.S. 105 (1956), U.S. Supreme Court case, which held that non-employee union organizers may have access to an employer's grounds for organizational purposes only if there is no other practical means of access to the employees.

National Labor Relations Board v. Boeing, 412 U.S. 67 (1973), U.S. Supreme Court case, which held that the validity of a fine imposed by a union upon a member does not depend upon the fine being reasonable in amount.

National Labor Relations Board* v. *Burns International Security Services, 406 U.S. 272 (1972), U.S. Supreme Court case, which ruled that a successor employer who does not change the nature of the acquired business and hires most of its employees represented by a certified union is duty-bound to recognize and bargain with the union, but is not obligated to honor his predecessor's labor contract unless he has agreed to do so. *See* Robert E. Wachs, "Successorship: The Consequences of Burns," *Labor Law Journal* (April 1973).

National Labor Relations Board* v. *Exchange Parts, 375 U.S. 405 (1964), U.S. Supreme Court case, which held that the conferral of employee benefits while a representation election is pending, for the purpose of inducing employees to vote against the union, interferes with the right to organize guaranteed by the National Labor Relations Act.

National Labor Relations Board* v. *Fansteel Metallurgical Corp.: *see* SIT-DOWN STRIKE.

National Labor Relations Board* v. *General Motors, 373 U.S. 734 (1963), U.S. Supreme Court case, which held that the agency shop is not an unfair labor practice.

National Labor Relations Board* v. *Gissel Packing Co.: *see* AUTHORIZATION CARD.

National Labor Relations Board* v. *Granite State Joint Board, Textile Workers, 409 U.S. 213 (1972), U.S. Supreme Court case, which held that a union could not collect fines imposed upon employees who had returned to work after resigning their membership during a strike. Since at the time there were no valid restraints on their freedom of resignation, the employees' action was an exercise of their statutory rights. "When a member lawfully resigns from the union, its power over him ends," said Justice Douglas in delivering the court's opinion.

National Labor Relations Board* v. *Insurance Agents' International Union, 361 U.S. 477 (1960), U.S. Supreme Court case, which held that a union does not fail to bargain in good faith by sponsoring on-the-job conduct designed to interfere with the employer's business and place economic pressure on him at the same time that it is negotiating a contract.

National Labor Relations Board* v. *Iron Workers: *see* PRE-HIRE AGREEMENT.

National Labor Relations Board* v. *Jones and Laughlin Steel Corp., 301 U.S. 1 (1937), U.S. Supreme Court case, that upheld the National Labor Relations Act (Wagner Act) of 1935, which gave labor the right to organize and bargain collectively. The NLRB, created by the act to enforce its provisions, ordered the Jones and Laughlin Steel Corporation to reinstate some employees it had discharged because of their union activities. The corporation responded by challenging both the authority of the NLRB to issue such an order and the legality of the act itself. The court ruled that

> Employees have as clear a right to organize and select their representatives for lawful purposes as the respondent to organize its business and select its own officers and agents. Discrimination and coercion to prevent the free exercise of the right of employees to self-organization and representation is a proper subject for condemnation by competent legislative authority.

National Labor Relations Board* v. *J. Weingarten, Inc., 420 U.S. 251 (1975), U.S. Supreme Court case, which held that an employee under company investigation for misconduct has a right to the presence of a union representative while being interrogated by a company investigator.

National Labor Relations Board* v. *Local 103, International Association of Bridge, Structural, and Ornamental Iron Workers: *see* PRE-HIRE AGREEMENT.

National Labor Relations Board* v. *MacKay Radio & Telegraph Company, 304 U.S. 33 (1938), U.S. Supreme Court case, which held that an employer could hire permanent replacements for workers on strike for economic reasons. The court expanded the *MacKay* rule in the *Fleetwood Trailer Co.* decision, 389 U.S. 375, (1967), when it held that if a striker has been replaced and no suitable employment is available, the status of a striker as an employee continues until he has obtained "other regular and substantially equivalent employment. Until then, the striker remains on a preferred hiring list, unless there is a "legitimate and substantial business justification" for not hiring him at all."

National Labor Relations Board* v. *Magnavox, 415 U.S. 322 (1974), U.S. Supreme Court case, which held that a union cannot waive the distribution rights of employees who seek to distribute literature in support of the bargaining unit.

National Labor Relations Board* v. *Robbins Tire and Rubber Co., 57 L. Ed. 2d 159 (1978),

U.S. Supreme Court case, which held that witness' statements in pending unfair labor practice cases are exempt from disclosure under the Freedom of Information Act.

National Labor Relations Board v. Truitt Manufacturing, 351 U.S. 149 (1956), U.S. Supreme Court case, which held that a refusal by an employer to attempt to substantiate a claim of inability to pay increased wages may support a finding of a failure to bargain in good faith.

National Labor Relations Board v. Wooster Division of Borg-Warner Corp., 356 U.S. 342 (1958), U.S. Supreme Court case, which held there were three categories of bargaining proposals under the Labor–Management Relations (Taft–Hartley) Act of 1947—illegal subjects, mandatory subjects, and voluntary subjects.

National Labor Relations Board v. Wyman-Gordon Co.: *see* EXCELSIOR RULE.

National Labor Union, union of local unions and reform groups that fostered an active political program. Born in 1866, it collapsed in 1872.

National League of Cities (NLC), formerly AMERICAN MUNICIPAL ASSOCIATION, known until 1964 as the American Municipal Association, NLC was founded in 1924 by and for reform-minded state municipal leagues. Membership in NLC was opened to individual cities in 1947, and NLC now has more than 700 direct member cities. The 27 U.S. cities with populations greater than 500,000 are all NLC direct members, as are 87 percent of all cities with more than 100,000 residents. NLC is an advocate for municipal interests before Congress, the executive branch, and the federal agencies and in state capitals across the nation where other matters of importance to cities are decided.

National League of Cities
1620 Eye Street, N.W.
Washington, DC 20006
(202) 293-7310

National League of Cities v. Usery, 426 U.S. 833 (1976), U.S. Supreme Court case, which held that the doctrine of federalism as expressed in the Tenth Amendment invalidates the 1974 amendments to the Fair Labor Standards Act (FLSA) extending minimum-wage and overtime provisions to state and local employees performing traditional governmental functions. This decision reversed the Court's decision in *Maryland v. Wirtz*,

392 U.S. 183 (1968), which approved the extension of the FLSA to certain state-operated hospitals, institutions, and schools.

National League of Postmasters of the United States: *see* LABOR ORGANIZATION, Postmasters of the United States, National League of.

National Marine Engineers' Beneficial Association: *see* LABOR ORGANIZATION, Marine Engineers Beneficial Association, National.

National Maritime Union of America: *see* LABOR ORGANIZATION, Maritime Union of America, National.

National Mediation Board, federal agency that provides the railroad and airline industries with specific mechanisms for the adjustment of labor–management disputes; that is, the facilitation of agreements through collective bargaining, investigation of questions of representation, and the arbitration and establishment of procedures for emergency disputes. First created by the Railway Labor Act of 1934, today the board's major responsibilities are: (1) the mediation of disputes over wages, hours, and working conditions which arise between rail and air carriers and organizations representing their employees, and (2) the investigation of representation disputes and certification of employee organizations as representatives of crafts or classes of carrier employees.

Disputes growing out of grievances or out of interpretation or application of agreements concerning rates of pay, rules, or working conditions in the railroad industry are referable to the National Railroad Adjustment Board. In the airline industry no national airline adjustment board has been established for settlement of grievances. Over the years the employee organizations and air carriers with established bargaining relationships have agreed to grievance procedures with final jurisdiction resting with a system board of adjustment. The National Mediation Board is frequently called upon to name a neutral referee to serve on a system board when the parties are deadlocked and cannot agree on such an appointment themselves.

The board is charged with mediating disputes between carriers and labor organizations relating to initial contract negotiations or subsequent changes in rates of pay, rules, and working conditions. When the parties fail to reach accord in direct bargaining either party may request the board's services or the board may on its own motion invoke its services. Thereafter, negotiations continue until the board determines that its efforts to mediate have been unsuccessful, at which time it seeks to induce the parties to submit the dispute to arbitration. If either party refuses to arbitrate, the board issues a notice stating that the parties have failed to resolve their dispute through mediation. This notice commences a 30-day cooling off period after which resort to self-help is normally available to either or both parties.

If a dispute arises among a carrier's employees as to who is to be the representative of such employees, it is the board's duty to investigate such dispute and to determine by secret ballot election or other appropriate means whether or not and to whom a representation certification should be issued. In the course of making this determination, the board must determine the craft or class in which the employees seeking representation properly belong.

Additional duties of the board are: the interpretation of agreements made under its mediatory auspices; the appointment of neutral referees when requested by the National Railroad Adjustment Board, the appointment of neutrals to sit on System Boards and Special Boards of Adjustments; and finally, the duty of notifying the president when the parties have failed to reach agreement through the board's mediation efforts and the labor dispute, in the judgment of the board, threatens substantially to interrupt interstate commerce to a degree such as to deprive any section of the country of essential transportation service. In these cases, the president may, at his discretion, appoint an emergency board to investigate and report to him on the dispute.

National Mediation Board
1425 K Street, N.W.
Washington, DC 20572
(202) 523-5920

National Organization of Industrial Trade Unions: *see* LABOR ORGANIZATION, Industrial Trade Unions, National Organization of.

national origin discrimination, Title VII of the Civil Rights Act of 1964 prohibits disparate treatment whether overt or covert, of any individual or group of individuals because of their national origin except when such treatment is necessary because of a bona fide occupational qualification; for example it might be lawful to require native fluency in Spanish for a position as a translator. The Equal Employment Opportunity Commission

(EEOC) gives as examples of national origin discrimination,

the use of tests in the English language where the individual tested came from circumstances where English was not that person's first language or mother tongue, and where English language skill is not a requirement of the work to be performed; denial of equal opportunity to persons married to or associated with persons of a specific national origin; denial of equal opportunity because of membership in lawful organizations identified with or seeking to promote the interests of national groups; denial of equal opportunity because of attendance at schools or churches commonly utilized by persons of a given national origin; denial of equal opportunity because their name or that of their spouse reflects a certain national origin, and denial of equal opportunity to persons who as a class of persons tend to fall outside national norms for height and weight where such height and weight specifications are not necessary for the performance of the work involved.

Some states have laws prohibiting the employment of noncitizens in varying circumstances. According to the EEOC, "where such laws have the purpose or effect of discriminating on the basis of national origin, they are in direct conflict with and are, therefore, superseded by Title VII of the Civil Rights Act of 1964, as amended."

National Panel of Arbitrators: *see* AMERICAN ARBITRATION ASSOCIATION.

National Railroad Adjustment Board, federal agency created by the Railway Labor Act of 1934. The National Railroad Adjustment Board has the responsibility of deciding disputes growing out of grievances or out of interpretation or application of agreements concerning rates of pay, rules, or working conditions in the railroad industry.

National Railroad Adjustment Board
220 South State Street
Chicago, IL 60604
(312) 427-8383

National Recovery Administration: *see* NATIONAL INDUSTRIAL RECOVERY ACT OF 1933.

National Rehabilitation Association (NRA), founded in 1925, a private, nonprofit organization of 30,000 people whose purpose is to advance the rehabilitation of all handicapped persons.

National Rehabilitation Association
1522 K Street, N.W.
Washington, DC 20005
(202) 659-2430

National Right to Work Committee, also NA-
TIONAL RIGHT TO WORK LEGAL DEFENSE
FOUNDATION, INC., the *National Right to Work
Committee* advocates legislation to prohibit all
forms of forced union membership. The *National Right to Work Legal Defense Foundation, Inc.* seeks to establish legal precedents
protecting workers against compulsory unionism.

> *National Right to Work Committee*
> 8316 Arlington Blvd.
> Fairfax, VA 22038
> (703) 573-8550

National Rural Letter Carriers' Association:
see LABOR ORGANIZATION, Rural Letter Carriers' Association, National.

National Safety Council, nongovernmental,
nonprofit, public service organization dedicated to reducing the number and severity of
all kinds of accidents by gathering and distributing information about the causes of accidents and ways to prevent them.

> *National Safety Council*
> 444 North Michigan Avenue
> Chicago, IL 60611
> (312) 527-4800

National Technical Information Service
(NTIS), established in 1970 to simplify and
improve public access to Department of Commerce publications and to data files and scientific and technical reports sponsored by federal
agencies. It is the central point in the United
States for the public sale of government-
funded research and development reports and
other analyses prepared by federal agencies,
their contractors, or grantees.

> *National Technical Information Service*
> 5285 Port Royal Road
> Springfield, VA 22161
> (703) 537-4660

**National Training Laboratories Institute for
Applied Behavioral Science** (NTL), also
called NTL INSTITUTE, founded as the National Training Laboratories in 1947 in Bethel, Maine. The early years at Bethel were devoted to the development of human relations
laboratories. It was during this period that
NTL proved the effectiveness of the new
concept of the T Group ("T" for training).
NTL's concept of the T Group—in which individuals, working in small groups, develop
new insights into self and others—is still an
important element in NTL programs and has
been widely imitated. During the 1950s and
1960s, major areas for experimentation and
development were expanded to include
group dynamics, organization development

and community development. During the
1960s and early 1970s, the development of
individual potential in personal growth programs became an added thrust, as did innovation in working with large systems. In the
late 1970s, NTL helps men and women recognize and develop their potential in response to the array of alternatives in life-
styles, careers and patterns of interaction
available to them. It works toward keeping
change from becoming chaos by promoting
flexibility and innovation and by providing
help in planning for individuals, organizations and large systems.

Today, NTL Institute is internationally
recognized as a focal agency for experience-
based learning programs. It is also known as
the institution which has had most to do with
developing the new profession of laboratory
education, with exploring new means of relating, with new approaches to social change,
and with new methods of managing organizations. Interest in laboratory education has
grown rapidly, and NTL defines as one of
its roles helping to maintain professional
standards in a field now popularized and
often misunderstood.

> *National Training Laboratories Institute*
> **Mailing Address:**
> P.O. Box 9155
> Rosslyn Station
> Arlington, VA 22209
>
> **Address:**
> 1501 Wilson Blvd.
> Arlington, VA 22209
> (703) 527-1500

National Treasury Employees Union: *see*
LABOR ORGANIZATION, Treasury Employees
Union, National.

national union, union composed of a variety
of widely dispersed affiliated local unions.
The Bureau of Labor Statistics defines a national union as one with agreements with different employers in more than one state. *See
also* INTERNATIONAL UNION.

*National Woodwork Manufactures Associa-
tion v. National Labor Relations Board*, 386
U.S. 612 (1967), U.S. Supreme Court case,
which held that when a boycott is used as a
shield to preserve customary jobs, rather than
as a sword to gather new ones, it does not violate the National Labor Relations Act's pro-
scription against secondary boycotts, Section
8(6)(4)(B).

native ability, actual ability. A test score is
usually interpreted to mean that an individual's native ability lies somewhere in a range

(plus or minus 50 points, for example) surrounding the score.

NBPW: *see* LABOR ORGANIZATION, Packinghouse and Industrial Workers, National Brotherhood of.

NC-SEA: *see* LABOR ORGANIZATION, North Carolina State Employees Association.

NC-SGEA: *see* LABOR ORGANIZATION, North Carolina State Government Employees Association.

NCSL: *see* NATIONAL CIVIL SERVICE LEAGUE.

NEA: *see* LABOR ORGANIZATION, Education Association, National.

NEA-OEA: *see* LABOR ORGANIZATION, Overseas Education Association, under Education Association, National.

NEB-APE: *see* LABOR ORGANIZATION, Nebraska Association of Public Employees.

Nebraska Association of Public Employees: *see* LABOR ORGANIZATION.

Nebraska State AFL–CIO: *see* AMERICAN FEDERATION OF LABOR–CONGRESS OF INDUSTRIAL ORGANIZATIONS.

needs analysis, any of a variety of approaches that seek to establish the requirements of a particular situation in order to determine what, if any, program activity should be initiated.

needs hierarchy, in the July 1943 issue of *Psychological Review*, Abraham H. Maslow published his now classic, "A Theory of Human Motivation," in which he put forth his hierarchical conception of human needs. Maslow asserted that humans had five sets of goals or basic needs arranged in a hierarchy of prepotency: physiological needs, safety needs, love or affiliation needs, esteem needs

and the need for self-actualization—the desire "to become everything that one is capable of becoming." Once lower needs are satisfied, they cease to be motivators of behavior. Conversely, higher needs cannot motivate until lower needs are satisfied. It is commonly recognized that there are some inescapable incongruities in Maslow's needs hierarchy. Some lower needs in some people, such as security, love and status, never seem to be satiated. However, this does not take away from the importance of the desire for higher level needs as a motivational force in others. *See* Abraham Maslow, *Motivation and Personality* (N.Y.: Harper & Row, 1954, 2nd ed., 1970).

See also SELF-ACTUALIZATION.

negative entropy: *see* ENTROPY.

negatively skewed: *see* SKEWNESS.

negative reinforcement: *see* REINFORCEMENT.

negative strike: *see* POSITIVE STRIKE.

negative stroking: *see* STROKING.

negative transfer: *see* TRANSFER OF LEARNING.

negotiating committee, continuous: *see* CONTINUOUS NEGOTIATING COMMITTEE.

negotiation, process by which representatives of labor and management bargain, directly discuss proposals and counterproposals, in order to establish the conditions of work— wages, hours, benefits, the machinery for handling grievances, etc. For general theories on the negotiating process, *see* Gerald I. Nierenberg, *The Art of Negotiating: Psychological Strategies for Gaining Advantageous Bargains* (N.Y.: Hawthorn Books, 1968); Otomar J. Bartos, *Process and Outcome of Negotiations* (N.Y.: Columbia University Press, 1974); Jeffrey Z. Rubin and Bert R. Brown, *The Social Psychology of Bargaining and Negotiation* (N.Y.: Academic Press, 1975). For a specific application to labor relations, *see* Richard E. Walton and Robert B. McKersie, *A Behavioral Theory of Labor Negotiations* (N.Y.: McGraw-Hill, 1965).

negotiation, career: *see* CAREER NEGOTIATION.

negotiations, collective: *see* COLLECTIVE NEGOTIATIONS.

Negotiations & Contracts, Collective Bar-

MASLOW'S HIERARCHY OF NEEDS

SELF-ACTUALIZATION

EGO NEEDS

AFFILIATION NEEDS

SAFETY NEEDS

PHYSIOLOGICAL NEEDS

gaining: see COLLECTIVE BARGAINING NEGOTIATIONS & CONTRACTS.

neoclassical organization theory: *see* ORGANIZATION THEORY.

nepotism, any practice by which officeholders award positions to members of their immediate family. It is derived from the Latin *nepos,* meaning nephew or grandson. The rulers of the medieval church were often thought to give special preference to their nephews in distributing churchly offices. At that time, "nephew" became a euphemism for their illegitimate sons.

nervous breakdown, catch-all expression for mental illness that does not refer to any particular disorder. Individuals in high pressure jobs who can no longer cope with the associated mental strains are frequently said to have had nervous breakdowns, but the actual clinical reason for their incapacity could be any of a large variety of mental and/or physical maladies.

See also OCCUPATIONAL NEUROSIS and STRESS.

Nestor, Agnes (1880-1948), a leader of the International Glove Workers Union and Women's Trade Union League. For an autobiography, *see Women's Labor Leader: Autobiography of Agnes Nestor* (Rockford, Ill.: Bellevue Books Pub. Co., 1954).

NETH Week: *see* NATIONAL EMPLOY THE HANDICAPPED WEEK.

net pay: *see* TAKE-HOME PAY.

network, pattern of "interrelated and interconnected individuals, groups and/or organizations that form a system of communication." *See* Jeffalyn Johnson, "Networking: A Management Tool," *The Bureaucrat* (Winter 1977).

neutral, any third party who is actively engaged in labor–management negotiations in order to facilitate a settlement.

Nevada State AFL–CIO: *see* AMERICAN FEDERATION OF LABOR–CONGRESS OF INDUSTRIAL ORGANIZATIONS.

new girls' network: *see* OLD BOYS' NETWORK.

New Hampshire State Employees Association: *see* LABOR ORGANIZATION.

New Hampshire State Labor Council: *see* AMERICAN FEDERATION OF LABOR–CONGRESS OF INDUSTRIAL ORGANIZATIONS.

new hire, individual who has just joined an organization as an employee.

See also PROBATIONARY EMPLOYEE.

New Jersey State AFL–CIO: *see* AMERICAN FEDERATION OF LABOR–CONGRESS OF INDUSTRIAL ORGANIZATIONS.

New Jersey State Employees Association: *see* LABOR ORGANIZATION.

New Mexico State AFL–CIO: *see* AMERICAN FEDERATION OF LABOR–CONGRESS OF INDUSTRIAL ORGANIZATIONS.

Newport News Shipbuilding and Dry Dock Co. **v.** *Schauffler,* 303 U.S. 54 (1938), U.S. Supreme Court case, which held that a company was subject to the authority of the National Labor Relations Board even if its participation in interstate commerce was limited to receiving goods from other states.

Newspaper and Mail Deliverers' Union of New York and Vicinity: *see* LABOR ORGANIZATION.

Newspaper Guild, The: *see* LABOR ORGANIZATION.

New York State AFL–CIO: *see* AMERICAN FEDERATION OF LABOR–CONGRESS OF INDUSTRIAL ORGANIZATIONS.

New York Telephone Co. **v.** *New York State Department of Labor,* 59 L. Ed. 2d 553 (1979), U.S. Supreme Court case, which held that the payment of unemployment compensation to strikers was not in conflict with the policy of free collective bargaining established by the National Labor Relations Act.

New York Times **v.** *Sullivan,* 376 U.S. 254 (1964), U.S. Supreme Court case, which held that a state cannot, under the 1st and 14th Amendments, award damages to a public official for defamatory falsehood relating to his official conduct unless he proves "actual malice"—that the statement was made with knowledge of its falsity or with reckless disregard of whether it was true or false.

NFFE: *see* LABOR ORGANIZATION, Federal Employees, National Federation of.

NFLPA: *see* LABOR ORGANIZATION, Football League Players Association, National.

NHLPA: *see* LABOR ORGANIZATION, Hockey League Players Association, National.

NH-SEA: *see* LABOR ORGANIZATION, New Hampshire State Employees Association.

nibbling, also called PIECE RATE NIBBLING,

practice of cutting the piece rates paid to employees upon an increase in their output.

night premium, also called NIGHT DIFFERENTIAL, addition to regular wage rates that is paid to employees who work on shifts other than the regular day shift.

NIOSH: *see* NATIONAL INSTITUTE FOR OCCUPATIONAL SAFETY AND HEALTH.

NIRA: *see* NATIONAL INDUSTRIAL RECOVERY ACT OF 1933.

NIW: *see* LABOR ORGANIZATION, Industrial Workers Union, National.

NJ-SEA: *see* LABOR ORGANIZATION, New Jersey State Employees Association.

NLC: *see* NATIONAL LEAGUE OF CITIES.

NLC v. *Usery: see* NATIONAL LEAGUE OF CITIES V. USERY.

NLP: *see* LABOR ORGANIZATION, Postmasters of the United States, National League of.

NLRA: *see* NATIONAL LABOR RELATIONS ACT OF 1935.

NLRB: *see* NATIONAL LABOR RELATIONS BOARD.

NLRBP: *see* LABOR ORGANIZATION, National Labor Relations Board Professional Association.

NLRBU: *see* LABOR ORGANIZATION, National Labor Relations Board Union.

NMD: *see* LABOR ORGANIZATION, Newspaper and Mail Deliverers' Union of New York and Vicinity.

NMU: *see* LABOR ORGANIZATION, Maritime Union of America, National.

noble, slang term for an armed guard hired by industry to escort strikebreakers or otherwise harass the budding union movement.

no-commission account: *see* HOUSE ACCOUNT.

Noise Regulation Reporter, bi-weekly notification and reference service published by the Bureau of National Affairs, Inc., which covers all significant legislative and administrative efforts to control noise. Includes information on regulations and programs under the Noise Control Act of 1972, the Occupational Safety and Health Act, the Noise Pollution Abatement Act, the Federal Aviation Act, and state statutes.

Nolde Brothers, Inc. v. *Local No. 358, Bakery Workers* 430 U.S. 243 (1977), U.S. Supreme Court case, which held that a "party to a collective-bargaining contract may be required to arbitrate a contractual dispute over severance pay pursuant to the arbitration clause of that agreement even though the dispute, although governed by the contract, arises after its termination."

noncompetitive appointment, government employment obtained without competing with others, in the sense that it is done without regard to civil service registers. Includes reinstatements, transfers, reassignments, demotions, and some promotions.

noncontributory pension plan, pension program that has the employer paying the entire cost.

nondirective interview: *see* DIRECTED INTERVIEW.

nonproduction bonus, also called CHRISTMAS BONUS and YEAR-END BONUS, payments to workers that are, in effect, gratuities upon which employees cannot regularly depend. Richard P. Helwig, in "The Christmas Bonus: A Gift or a Give-Away?" *Personnel Journal* (November 1973), warns that

> it is an unfair labor practice if an employer refuses to bargain as to wages, hours of employment, or other conditions of employment. The factual question to be determined is whether a Christmas gift constitutes a condition of employment such as compensation for service, as distinguished from a mere discretionary gift? If so, the discontinuance of such a program is a bargainable matter and must be discussed with the union prior to taking such action.

Nonreading Aptitude Test Battery (NATB), form of the General Aptitude Test Battery designed by the United States Employment Service for individuals so disadvantaged that testing premised upon literacy would be inappropriate. *See* Patricia Marshall, "Tests Without Reading," *Manpower* (May 1971).

nonsuability clause, that portion of a labor contract where a company agrees that it will not sue a labor union because of a wildcat strike, provided that the union lives up to its obligation to stop the strike.

nonverbal communication, any means of projecting opinion, attitudes and desires through the use of body postures, movements, expressions, gestures, eye contact, use of space and time, or other means of expressing such ideas short of written and/or verbal communications. For the classic work, *see* Edward T. Hall, *The Silent Language* (Garden City, N.Y.: Doubleday, 1959). For a text, *see* Mark L. Knapp, *Nonverbal Communication In Human Interaction* (N.Y.: Holt, Rinehart and Winston, Inc., 1972).

norm, standard or criteria against which an individual's test score or production rate can be compared and evaluated.

normal distribution, frequency distribution that follows the pattern of the normal "bell shaped" curve, characterized by symmetry about the mean and a standard relationship between width and height of the curve.

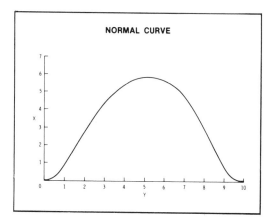

NORMAL CURVE

normal time: *see* ALLOWED TIME.

normative, those findings or conclusions that are premised upon morally established norms of right or wrong.

normative standard, standard of performance obtained by examining the relative performance of a group or sample of candidates.

norm-referenced test, any test that describes a candidate's performance in terms of its relation to the performance of other candidates.

norms, in psychological testing, norms are tables of scores from a large number of people who have taken a particular test. For an analysis of norm referenced test scores, *see* H. B. Lyman, *Test Scores and What They Mean* (Englewood Cliffs, N.J.: Prentice-Hall, 2nd ed., 1971).

Norris–LaGuardia Act of 1932, federal statute that generally removed the power of the federal courts to prevent coercive activities by unions if such actions did not involve fraud or violence. The act was significant because it finally allowed unions to exert effective economic pressures against employees. It

also declared yellow-dog contracts to be unenforceable. Many states have "Little Norris–LaGuardia" acts that cover industries not engaged in interstate commerce.
See also YELLOW-DOG CONTRACT.

North American Soccer League Association: *see* LABOR ORGANIZATION.

North Carolina State AFL–CIO: *see* AMERICAN FEDERATION OF LABOR–CONGRESS OF INDUSTRIAL ORGANIZATIONS.

North Carolina State Employees Association: *see* LABOR ORGANIZATION.

North Dakota AFL–CIO: *see* AMERICAN FEDERATION OF LABOR–CONGRESS OF INDUSTRIAL ORGANIZATIONS.

North Dakota State Employees Association: *see* LABOR ORGANIZATION.

no-show jobs, government positions for which the incumbent collects a salary but is not required to report to work. While no-show jobs are by their nature illegal, they are not uncommon. In 1975, when a New York State assemblyman was tried in Albany County Court for authorizing no-show jobs on his legislative payroll, he claimed discriminatory prosecution and asked that his case be dismissed because the practice was so commonplace. The judge concurred and the case was dismissed. *See* Albany, N.Y., *Times-Union*, September 23–28, 1975.

no-solicitation rule, employer's rule that prohibits solicitation of employees for any purpose during working hours.

notary public, semi-public official who can administer oaths, certify the validity of documents, and perform a variety of formal witnessing duties.

NRA: *see* (1) NATIONAL INDUSTRIAL RECOVERY ACT OF 1933 or (2) NATIONAL REHABILITATION ASSOCIATION.

NTEU: *see* LABOR ORGANIZATION, Treasury Employees Union, National.

NTIS: *see* NATIONAL TECHNICAL INFORMATION SERVICE.

NTL: *see* NATIONAL TRAINING LABORATORIES FOR APPLIED BEHAVIORAL SCIENCE.

null hypothesis, hypothesis used in statistics that asserts there is no difference between two populations that cannot be explained by chance.

Nurses' Association, American: *see* LABOR ORGANIZATION.

O

OASDI: *see* OLD AGE, SURVIVORS, AND DISABILITY INSURANCE.

objective test, any examining device whose scoring is not dependent upon the discretion of the examiners.

objectivity, an applicant appraisal procedure is objective if it elicits observable responses that can be recorded and reported in a precise, specified way. Objectivity seeks to remove personal opinion by reducing the impact of individual judgement.

obligatory arbitration, arbitration requested by one party in a situation where the other party is obligated (for example, by a contract provision) to accept it.

obsolescence: *see* OCCUPATIONAL OBSOLESCENCE.

OCAW: *see* LABOR ORGANIZATION, Oil, Chemical and Atomic Workers International Union.

occupation, relatively continuous pattern of activity that (1) provides a livelihood for an individual and (2) serves to define an individual's general social status.

occupational career, according to Walter L. Slocum, in "Occupational Careers in Organizations: A Sociological Perspective," *Personnel and Guidance Journal* (May 1965), "an occupational career, ideally, consists of entry into a position at the lowest rung of a career ladder, followed by an orderly sequence of promotions to positions at successively higher status levels and finally to retirement."

occupational certification, also called CERTIFICATION, practice that permits practitioners in a particular occupation to claim minimum levels of competence. While certification enables some practitioners to claim a competency which others cannot, this type of regulation does not prevent uncertified people from supplying the same services as certified people.
See also OCCUPATIONAL LICENSING.

Occupational Check List, Gordon: *see* GORDON OCCUPATIONAL CHECK LIST.

occupational decisionmaking: *see* CAREER DECISIONMAKING.

occupational disease: *see* OCCUPATIONAL ILLNESS.

occupational grouping, grouping of classes within the same broad occupational category, such as engineering, nursing, accounting, etc.

occupational hazard, any danger directly associated with one's work. *See* Nicholas A. Ashford, *Crisis in the Workplace: Occupational Disease and Injury–A Report to the Ford Foundation* (Cambridge, Mass.: The MIT Press, 1976).

occupational health, all the activities related to protecting and maintaining the health and safety of employees. *See* Joseph A. Page and Mary-Win O'Brien, *Bitter Wages: Ralph Nader's Study Group Report on Disease and Injury on the Job* (N.Y.: Grossman, 1973); John Mendeloff, *Regulating Safety: An Economic and Political Analysis of Occupational Safety and Health Policy* (Cambridge, Mass.: The MIT Press, 1979).

occupational illness, also called OCCUPATIONAL DISEASE, any abnormal condition or disorder, other than one resulting from an occupational injury, caused by exposure to environmental factors associated with employment. It includes acute and chronic illnesses or diseases which may be caused by inhalation, absorption, ingestion, or direct contact.

occupational injury, any injury (such as a cut, fracture, sprain, amputation, etc.), that results from a work accident or from exposure involving a single incident in the work environment (*see graph p. 235*).

No. 679. Employed Persons, by Major Occupation Group and Sex: 1960 to 1978

[In thousands of persons 16 years old and over. Annual averages of monthly figures, except as indicated. Beginning 1973, not strictly comparable with prior years due to reclassification of census occupations. For details, see text, p. 396. See *Historical Statistics, Colonial Times to 1970*, series D 182–232, for related but not comparable data]

OCCUPATION GROUP AND SEX	1960	1965	1970	1973	1974	1975	1976	1977	1978, Jan.–Apr.
Total	**65,778**	**71,088**	**78,627**	**84,409**	**85,936**	**84,783**	**87,485**	**90,546**	**91,846**
White-collar workers	28,522	31,852	37,997	40,386	41,738	42,227	43,700	45,187	46,673
Percent of total	43.4	44.8	48.3	47.8	48.6	49.8	50.0	49.9	50.8
Professional and technical	7,469	8,872	11,140	11,777	12,338	12,748	13,329	13,692	14,252
Managers and administrators [1]	7,067	7,340	8,289	8,644	8,941	8,891	9,315	9,662	10,026
Salesworkers	4,224	4,499	4,854	5,415	5,417	5,460	5,497	5,728	5,795
Clerical workers	9,762	11,141	13,714	14,548	15,043	15,128	15,558	16,106	16,600
Blue-collar workers	24,057	26,247	27,791	29,869	29,776	27,962	28,958	30,211	30,095
Craft and kindred workers	8,554	9,216	10,158	11,288	11,477	10,972	11,278	11,881	11,853
Operatives, exc. transport	11,950	13,345	13,909	10,972	10,627	9,637	10,085	10,354	10,539
Transport equip. operatives				3,297	3,292	3,219	3,271	3,476	3,487
Nonfarm laborers	3,553	3,686	3,724	4,312	4,380	4,134	4,325	4,500	4,217
Service workers	8,923	8,936	9,712	11,128	11,373	11,657	12,005	12,392	12,608
Farmworkers	5,176	4,053	3,126	3,027	3,048	2,936	2,822	2,756	2,469
Male	**43,904**	**46,340**	**48,960**	**51,963**	**52,519**	**51,230**	**52,391**	**53,861**	**53,904**
White-collar workers	16,423	17,746	20,054	20,705	21,155	21,134	21,552	22,008	22,438
Percent of total	37.4	38.3	41.0	38.9	40.3	41.3	41.1	40.9	41.6
Professional and technical	4,766	5,596	6,842	7,066	7,346	7,481	7,726	7,856	8,114
Managers and administrators [1]	5,968	6,230	6,968	7,054	7,291	7,162	7,373	7,511	7,719
Salesworkers	2,544	2,641	2,763	3,175	3,152	3,137	3,140	3,250	3,191
Clerical workers	3,145	3,279	3,481	3,409	3,366	3,355	3,313	3,391	3,415
Blue-collar workers	20,420	22,107	23,020	24,625	24,581	23,220	23,852	24,856	24,625
Craft and kindred workers	8,332	8,947	9,826	10,826	10,966	10,472	10,733	11,282	11,209
Operatives, exc. transport	8,617	9,581	9,605	6,653	6,464	5,934	6,135	6,258	6,383
Transport equip. operatives				3,134	3,126	3,037	3,062	3,238	3,232
Nonfarm laborers	3,471	3,579	3,589	4,012	4,026	3,777	3,922	4,079	3,801
Service workers	2,844	3,194	3,285	4,120	4,218	4,400	4,622	4,715	4,758
Farmworkers	4,219	3,295	2,601	2,513	2,564	2,476	2,365	2,282	2,082
Female	**21,874**	**24,748**	**29,667**	**32,446**	**33,417**	**33,553**	**35,095**	**36,685**	**37,942**
White-collar workers	12,099	14,106	17,943	19,681	20,583	21,092	22,148	23,179	24,235
Percent of total	55.3	57.0	60.5	60.6	61.6	62.9	63.2	63.2	63.9
Professional and technical	2,703	3,276	4,298	4,711	4,992	5,267	5,603	5,836	6,138
Managers and administrators [1]	1,099	1,110	1,321	1,590	1,650	1,729	1,942	2,151	2,308
Salesworkers	1,680	1,858	2,091	2,240	2,265	2,324	2,357	2,478	2,605
Clerical workers	6,617	7,862	10,233	11,140	11,676	11,772	12,245	12,715	13,185
Blue-collar workers	3,637	4,140	4,771	5,244	5,195	4,742	5,106	5,355	5,470
Craft and kindred workers	222	269	332	463	511	500	545	599	644
Operatives, exc. transport	3,333	3,764	4,303	4,319	4,164	3,703*	3,950	4,096	4,156
Transport equip. operatives				163	167	182	208	238	255
Nonfarm laborers	82	107	136	299	354	357	403	422	415
Service workers	5,179	5,742	6,427	7,008	7,156	7,258	7,383	7,677	7,850
Farmworkers	957	758	525	514	484	460	458	473	387

[1] Excludes farm.

SOURCE: Bureau of the Census, *Statistical Abstract of the United States* (Washington, D.C.: Government Printing Office, 1978), p. 418.

INJURY AND ILLNESS INCIDENCE RATES BY INDUSTRY DIVISION, UNITED STATES, 1975

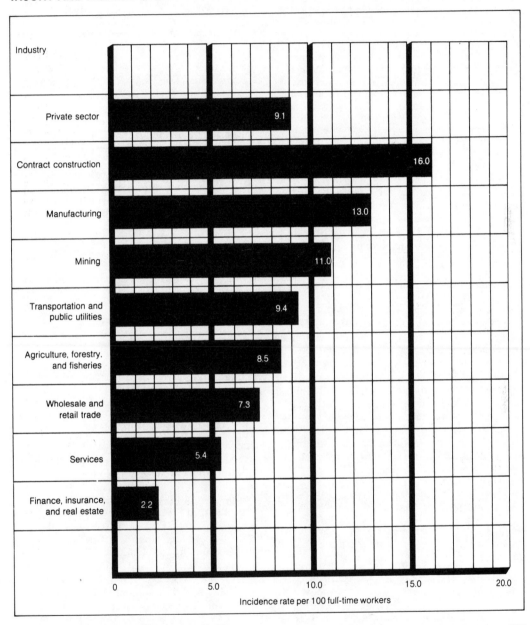

SOURCE: U.S. Department of Labor, Bureau of Labor Statistics, *Occupational Injuries and Illnesses in the United States by Industry, 1975* (Washington, D.C.: Government Printing Office, 1978), p. 12.

occupational licensing, also called LICENS-
ING, according to Clifford Elliott and Vincent
H. Smith, "Occupational Licensing: An Em-
pirical Approach," *University of Michigan
Business Review* (July 1978), occupational
licensing

> requires that all non-licensed persons cease
> to practice and be excluded from future par-
> ticipation in the licensed occupation. The
> additional benefit provided to the commu-
> nity from licensing occupations is to protect
> the community from the spillover costs that
> might result if individual consumers choose
> low quality services. A classic example of
> this possibility is to be found in medicine. A
> man with a contagious disease who hires the
> services of a low-cost quack and consequent-
> ly fails to be cured, may impose the disease
> on people who might not have caught it if he
> had been forced to utilize the services of a
> more competent person.

Also see Alex Maurizi, "Occupational Licensing and the Public Interest," *Journal of Political Economy* (March–April 1974); Barbara
F. Esser, Daniel H. Kruger, and Benjamin
Shimberg, *Occupational Licensing: Practices
and Politics* (Washington, D.C.: Public Affairs Press, 1973).
See also OCCUPATIONAL CERTIFICATION.

occupational mobility, also HORIZONTAL and
VERTICAL OCCUPATIONAL MOBILITY, *Occupational mobility* refers to the movement of
individuals from one occupation to another. A
change from one occupation to another of
similiar occupational status is an example of
horizontal occupational mobility. A change
of occupational status levels within the same
occupation is an example of *vertical occupational mobility. See* Dixie Sommers and Alan
Eck, "Occupational Mobility in the American
Labor Force," *Monthly Labor Review* (January 1977); Harrison C. White, *Chains of Opportunity: System Models of Mobility in Organizations* (Cambridge, Mass.: Harvard
University Press, 1970).

occupational neurosis, development of in-
capacitating physical symptoms that make it
impossible to continue one's work.

occupational obsolescence, concept usually
associated with professional employees who
lack currency with their discipline. For
example, an engineer who has served as an
administrator for a significant number of
years may, in consequence, be unable to
function in his/her engineering speciality because the "state of the art" has moved too far.
For thorough analyses of the concept and the
problem, *see* H. G. Kaufman, *Obsolescence*

and Professional Career Development (New
York: AMACOM, 1974); Samuel S. Dubin,
"Obsolescence or Lifelong Education: A
Choice for the Professional," *American Psychologist* (May 1972); Clayton Reeser, "Managerial Obsolescence—An Organization Dilemma," *Personnel Journal* (January 1977).

Occupational Orientation Inventory, Hall:
see HALL OCCUPATIONAL ORIENTATION
INVENTORY.

Occupational Outlook Handbook, the Bureau of Labor Statistics' biennial survey of
employment trends that contains descriptive
information and employment prospects for
hundreds of occupational categories. The
1978–79 edition reports that an estimated
335,000 professionals were working in the
area of personnel and labor relations in 1976
and projects that approximately 23,000 new
positions for personnel and labor relations
professionals will become available annually
to 1985.

Occupational Outlook Quarterly, the U.S.
Bureau of Labor Statistics' magazine designed to help high school students and
guidance counselors assess career opportunities.

> *Occupational Outlook Quarterly*
> Superintendent of Documents
> Government Printing Office
> Washington, DC 20402

occupational parity: *see* PARITY.

**Occupational Preference Survey, Califor-
nia:** *see* CALIFORNIA OCCUPATIONAL PREF-
ERENCE SURVEY.

occupational prestige, also called OCCUPA-
TIONAL STATUS, ascribed status associated
with an individual's employment. Opinion
surveys typically find physicians, college professors, psychologists, bankers, and architects
at the top of a hierarchy of occupational prestige, while unskilled farm workers and gar-
bage collectors compete for the lowest rankings. According to Donald J. Treiman, in
*Occupational Prestige in Comparative
Perspective* (N.Y.: Academic Press, 1977),

> people in all walks of life share un-
> derstandings about occupations—how much
> skill they require, how physically demand-
> ing they are, whether they are considered
> men's work or women's work, and so
> on—but particularly about their prestige.
> Every adult member of society ordinarily is
> able to locate occupations on a hierarchy of
> prestige. These perceptions form part of the
> *conscience collective.* This permits one to

rank oneself and others with respect to the social honor derived from occupational status.

See also Andre L. Delebec and James Vigen, "Prestige Ratings of Business and Other Occupations," *Personnel Journal* (February 1970).

occupational psychiatry, also called INDUSTRIAL PSYCHIATRY, any of the professional activities of psychiatry conducted at the workplace of the clients. *See* W. E. Powles and W. D. Ross, "Industrial and Occupational Psychiatry," in S. Arieti (ed.), *American Handbook of Psychiatry* (N.Y.: Basic Books, 1966).

occupational psychology: *see* INDUSTRIAL PSYCHOLOGY.

occupational registration, simple requirement that persons active in a particular occupation file their names with an appropriate authority. As such regulations place no restrictions upon the persons engaged in the particular occupation, registration is no indication of competence.

Occupational Safety and Health Act of 1970, also called WILLIAMS–STEIGER ACT, federal government's basic legislation for providing for the health and safety of employees on the job. The act created the Occupational Safety and Health Review Commission, the Occupational and Health Administration, and the National Institute for Occupational Safety and Health. *See* George C. Guenther, "The Significance of the Occupational Safety and Health Act to the Worker in the United States," *International Labor Review* (January 1972).

See also WORKMEN'S COMPENSATION.

Occupational Safety and Health Administration (OSHA), established by the Occupational Safety and Health Act of 1970, OSHA develops and promulgates occupational safety and health standards, develops and issues regulations, conducts investigations and inspections to determine the status of compliance with safety and health standards and regulations, and issues citations and proposes penalties for noncompliance with safety and health standards and regulations. The Assistant Secretary for Occupational Safety and Health has responsibility for occupational safety and health activities. OSHA has ten regional offices. *See* Albert L. Nichols and Richard Zeckhauser, "Government Comes to the Workplace: An Assessment of OSHA," *The Public Interest* (Fall 1977).

OSHA
U.S. Department of Labor
Washington, DC 20210

See also MARSHALL V. BARLOW'S, INC. and MINE SAFETY AND HEALTH ADMINISTRATION.

Occupational Safety & Health Reporter, weekly notification and reference service published by the Bureau of National Affairs, Inc. Covers significant legislative, administrative, judicial, and industrial developments under the Occupational Safety and Health Act. Includes information on standards, legislation, regulations, enforcement, research, advisory committee recommendations, union activities, and state programs.

See also BUREAU OF NATIONAL AFFAIRS, INC.

Occupational Safety and Health Review Commission (OSHRC), independent adjudicatory agency established by the Occupational Safety and Health Act of 1970 to adjudicate enforcement actions initiated under the act when they are contested by employers, employees, or representatives of employees.

Within OSHRC there are two levels of adjudication. All cases which require a hearing are assigned to a OSHRC judge who will decide the case. Each such decision is subject to discretionary review by the three OSHRC members upon the motion of any one of the three. However, approximately 90 percent of the decisions of the judges become final orders without any change whatsoever.

The Occupational Safety and Health Act covers virtually every employer in the country. It requires employers to furnish their employees with employment and a place of employment free from recognized hazards that are causing or are likely to cause death or serious physical harm to employees and to comply with occupational safety and health standards promulgated under the act.

The Secretary of Labor has promulgated a substantial number of occupational safety and health standards, which, pursuant to the act, have the force and effect of law. He has also initiated a regular program of inspections in order to check upon compliance. A case for adjudication by OSHRC arises when a citation is issued against an employer as the result of such an inspection and it is contested within 15 working days thereafter.

When a case is docketed, it is assigned for hearing to a OSHRC judge. The hearing will ordinarily be held in or near the community where the alleged violation occurred. At the

job safety and health protection

The Occupational Safety and Health Act of 1970 provides job safety and health protection for workers through the promotion of safe and healthful working conditions throughout the Nation. Requirements of the Act include the following:

Employers: Each employer shall furnish to each of his employees employment and a place of employment free from recognized hazards that are causing or are likely to cause death or serious harm to his employees; and shall comply with occupational safety and health standards issued under the Act.

Employees: Each employee shall comply with all occupational safety and health standards, rules, regulations and orders issued under the Act that apply to his own actions and conduct on the job.

The Occupational Safety and Health Administration (OSHA) of the Department of Labor has the primary responsibility for administering the Act. OSHA issues occupational safety and health standards, and its Compliance Safety and Health Officers conduct jobsite inspections to ensure compliance with the Act.

Inspection: The Act requires that a representative of the employer and a representative authorized by the employees be given an opportunity to accompany the OSHA inspector for the purpose of aiding the inspection.

Where there is no authorized employee representative, the OSHA Compliance Officer must consult with a reasonable number of employees concerning safety and health conditions in the workplace.

Complaint: Employees or their representatives have the right to file a complaint with the nearest OSHA office requesting an inspection if they believe unsafe or unhealthful conditions exist in their workplace. OSHA will withhold, on request, names of employees complaining.

The Act provides that employees may not be discharged or discriminated against in any way for filing safety and health complaints or otherwise exercising their rights under the Act.

An employee who believes he has been discriminated against may file a complaint with the nearest OSHA office within 30 days of the alleged discrimination.

Citation: If upon inspection OSHA believes an employer has violated the Act, a citation alleging such violations will be issued to the employer. Each citation will specify a time period within which the alleged violation must be corrected.

The OSHA citation must be prominently displayed at or near the place of alleged violation for three days, or until it is corrected, whichever is later, to warn employees of dangers that may exist there.

Proposed Penalty: The Act provides for mandatory penalties against employers of up to $1,000 for each serious violation and for optional penalties of up to $1,000 for each nonserious violation. Penalties of up to $1,000 per day may be proposed for failure to correct violations within the proposed time period. Also, any employer who willfully or repeatedly violates the Act may be assessed penalties of up to $10,000 for each such violation.

Criminal penalties are also provided for in the Act. Any willful violation resulting in death of an employee, upon conviction, is punishable by a fine of not more than $10,000 or by imprisonment for not more that six months, or by both. Conviction of an employer after a first conviction doubles these maximum penalties.

Voluntary Activity: While providing penalties for violations, the Act also encourages efforts by labor and management, before an OSHA inspection, to reduce injuries and illnesses arising out of employment.

The Department of Labor encourages employers and employees to reduce workplace hazards voluntarily and to develop and improve safety and health programs in all workplaces and industries.

Such cooperative action would initially focus on the identification and elimination of hazards that could cause death, injury, or illness to employees and supervisors. There are many public and private organizations that can provide information and assistance in this effort, if requested.

More Information: Additional information and copies of the Act, specific OSHA safety and health standards, and other applicable regulations may be obtained from your employer or from the nearest OSHA Regional Office in the following locations:

Atlanta, Georgia
Boston, Massachusetts
Chicago, Illinois
Dallas, Texas
Denver, Colorado
Kansas City, Missouri
New York, New York
Philadelphia, Pennsylvania
San Francisco, California
Seattle, Washington

Telephone numbers for these offices, and additional Area Office locations, are listed in the telephone directory under the United States Department of Labor in the United States Government listing.

Washington, D.C.
1977
OSHA 2203

Ray Marshall
Ray Marshall
Secretary of Labor

U. S. Department of Labor
Occupational Safety and Health Administration

hearing, the Secretary of Labor will have the burden of proving his case.

After the hearing, the judge must issue a report, based on findings of fact, affirming, modifying, or vacating the secretary's citation or proposed penalty, or directing other appropriate relief. His report will become a final order of OSHRC 30 days thereafter unless, within such period, any OSHRC member directs that such report shall be reviewed by OSHRC itself. When that occurs, the OSHRC members will thereafter issue their own decision on the case.

Once a case is decided, any person adversely affected or aggrieved thereby, may obtain a review of such a decision in a United States court of appeals.

> OSHRC
> 1825 K Street N.W.
> Washington, DC 20006
> (202) 634-7943

occupational socialization, process by which an individual absorbs and adopts the values, norms, and behavior of the occupational role models with whom he/she interacts. Occupational socialization is complete when an individual internalizes the values and norms of the occupational group. *See* Wilbert E. Moore, "Occupational Socialization," in David A. Goslin (ed.), *Handbook of Socialization Theory and Research* (Chicago: Rand McNally & Co., 1969).

occupational sociology, also called INDUSTRIAL SOCIOLOGY and SOCIOLOGY OF WORK, subspecialty of sociology concerned with examining the social structures and institutions which a society develops to facilitate its work. For texts, *see* Walter S. Neff, *Work and Human Behavior* (Chicago: Aldine Publishing Company, 1968); Lee Taylor, *Occupational Sociology* (N.Y.: Oxford University Press, 1968); Elliott A. Krause, *The Sociology of Occupations* (Boston: Little, Brown, 1971).

occupational status: *see* OCCUPATIONAL PRESTIGE.

occupational survey, an organization's study of all positions in a given class, series of classes, or occupational group in whatever departments or divisions they may be located.

occupational therapy, health profession providing services to people whose lives have been disrupted by physical injury or illness, developmental problems, the aging process and social or psychological difficulties.

OD: *see* ORGANIZATION DEVELOPMENT.

Odiorne, George S. (1920-   ), one of the foremost authorities on MBO. Major works include: *Management by Objectives—A System of Managerial Leadership* (N.Y.: Pitman, 1965); *Management Decisions by Objectives* (Englewood Cliffs, N.Y.: Prentice-Hall 1969); *Personnel Policy: Issues and Practices* (Columbus, Ohio: Charles E. Merrill, 1963); *Training by Objectives* (N.Y.: Macmillan, 1970); *Personnel Administration by Objectives* (Homewood, Ill.: Richard D. Irwin, 1971).

OFCCP: *see* OFFICE OF FEDERAL CONTRACT COMPLIANCE PROGRAMS.

office: *see* OPEN OFFICE and TURKEY FARM.

Office and Professional Employees International Union: *see* LABOR ORGANIZATION.

Office of Federal Contract Compliance Programs (OFCCP), agency within the Department of Labor delegated the responsibility for ensuring that there is no employment discrimination by government contractors because of race, religion, color, sex, or national origin, and to ensure affirmative action efforts in employing Vietnam Era veterans and handicapped workers. *See* Frank Erwin, "The New OFCCP Guidelines: What Happened?" *The Personnel Administrator* (February 1977).

> OFCCP
> 200 Constitution Ave., N.W.
> Washington, DC 20210
> (202) 523-8165

Office of Personnel Management (OPM), the central personnel agency of the federal government, created by the Civil Service Reform Act of 1978. OPM took over many of the responsibilities of the U.S. Civil Service Commission, including central examining and employment operations, personnel investigations, personnel program evaluation, executive development, and training. OPM administers the retirement and insurance programs for federal employees and exercises management leadership in labor relations and affirmative action. As the central personnel agency, OPM develops policies governing civilian employment in executive branch agencies and in certain agencies of the legislative and judicial branches. Subject to its standards and review, OPM delegates certain personnel powers to agency heads.

> *Office of Personnel Management*
> 1900 E. Street, N.W.
> Washington, DC 20415
> (202) 632-6101

OFFICE OF PERSONNEL MANAGEMENT

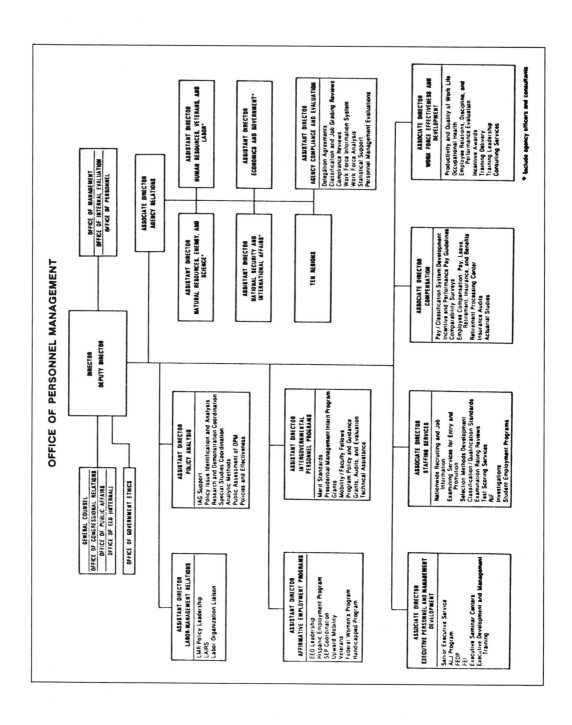

OFFICE OF MANAGEMENT
OFFICE OF INTERNAL EVALUATION
OFFICE OF PERSONNEL

DIRECTOR
DEPUTY DIRECTOR

GENERAL COUNSEL
OFFICE OF CONGRESSIONAL RELATIONS
OFFICE OF PUBLIC AFFAIRS
OFFICE OF EEO (INTERNAL)

OFFICE OF GOVERNMENT ETHICS

ASSOCIATE DIRECTOR
AGENCY RELATIONS

ASSISTANT DIRECTOR
HUMAN RESOURCES, VETERANS, AND LABOR*

ASSISTANT DIRECTOR
ECONOMICS AND GOVERNMENT*

ASSISTANT DIRECTOR
AGENCY COMPLIANCE AND EVALUATION
Delegation Agreements
Classification and Job Grading Reviews
Compliance Reviews
Work Force Information System
Work Force Analysis
Statistical Support
Personnel Management Evaluations

ASSISTANT DIRECTOR
NATURAL RESOURCES, ENERGY, AND SCIENCE*

ASSISTANT DIRECTOR
NATIONAL SECURITY AND INTERNATIONAL AFFAIRS*

TEN REGIONS

ASSOCIATE DIRECTOR
WORK FORCE EFFECTIVENESS AND DEVELOPMENT
Productivity and Quality of Work Life
Occupational Health
Employee Relations, Discipline, and Performance Evaluation
Incentive Awards
Training Delivery
Training Leadership
Consulting Services

ASSOCIATE DIRECTOR
COMPENSATION
Pay/Classification System Development
Incentive and Performance Pay Guidelines
Comparability Surveys
Employee Compensation: Pay, Leave, Retirement, Insurance, and Benefits
Retirement Processing Center
Insurance Audits
Actuarial Studies

ASSISTANT DIRECTOR
LABOR-MANAGEMENT RELATIONS
LMR Policy Leadership
LAIRS
Labor Organization Liaison

ASSISTANT DIRECTOR
POLICY ANALYSIS
IAG Support
Policy Issue Identification and Analysis
Research and Demonstration Coordination
Special Studies Coordination
Analytic Methods
Public Assessment of OPM
Policies and Effectiveness

ASSISTANT DIRECTOR
AFFIRMATIVE EMPLOYMENT PROGRAMS
EEO Leadership
Hispanic Employment Program
SEP Coordination
Upward Mobility
Veterans
Federal Women's Program
Handicapped Program

ASSISTANT DIRECTOR
INTERGOVERNMENTAL PERSONNEL PROGRAMS
Merit Standards
Presidential Management Intern Program
Grants
Mobility/Faculty Fellows
Program Policy and Guidance
Grants, Audits, and Evaluation
Technical Assistance

ASSOCIATE DIRECTOR
EXECUTIVE PERSONNEL AND MANAGEMENT DEVELOPMENT
Senior Executive Service
ALJ Program
FEDP
FEI
Executive Seminar Centers
Executive Development and Management Training

ASSOCIATE DIRECTOR
STAFFING SERVICES
Nationwide Recruiting and Job Information
Examining Services for Entry and Promotion
Selection Methods Development
Classification/Qualification Standards
Examination Rating Reviews
Test Scoring Services
RiF
Investigations
Student Employment Programs

* Include agency officers and consultants

240

Federal Contract Compliance Activities

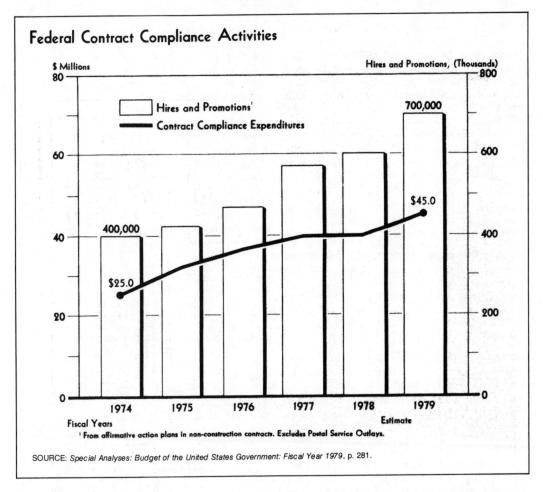

$ Millions

Hires and Promotions, (Thousands)

- ☐ Hires and Promotions'
- ▬ Contract Compliance Expenditures

700,000

$45.0

400,000

$25.0

1974   1975   1976   1977   1978   1979

Fiscal Years   Estimate

' From affirmative action plans in non-construction contracts. Excludes Postal Service Outlays.

SOURCE: *Special Analyses: Budget of the United States Government: Fiscal Year 1979*, p. 281.

office romance: *see* LOVE.

office title, job title that differs from the classified title assigned to a job and is used to describe a particular position for other than payroll, budget, or official purposes. For example, a Head Clerk position might have an "office" title of Office Supervisor.

off-line, computer system whose operation's are not under the control of a central processing unit, or a computer system that does not process information as it is received, but stores and processes it at a later time.

ogive, a cumulative frequency graph.

Ohio Bureau of Employment Services* v. *Hodory, 431 U.S. 471 (1977), U.S. Supreme Court case, which ruled that a "State can withhold jobless benefits from workers laid off as a result of a strike against their employer even when they are not involved in the strike because it occurs at another location."

Ohio Civil Service Employees Association, Inc.: *see* LABOR ORGANIZATION.

OHIO-CSEA: *see* LABOR ORGANIZATION, Ohio Civil Service Employees Association, Inc.

Ohio State AFL–CIO: *see* AMERICAN FEDERATION OF LABOR–CONGRESS OF INDUSTRIAL ORGANIZATIONS.

Ohio Vocational Interest Survey (OVIS), interest inventory used in vocational guidance and counseling. Consists of 280 items that yield a profile of interests in 24 occupational scales (*i.e.*, teaching, art, management, sales, medical, manual labor, nursing, clerical work, etc.). TIME: 60/90 minutes. AUTHORS: A. G. D'Costa, J. G. Odgers, D. W. Winefordner, P. B. Koons, Jr., PUBLISHER: Harcourt, Brace, Jovanovich, Inc. (*see* TEST PUBLISHERS).

Oil, Chemical and Atomic Workers International Union: *see* LABOR ORGANIZATION.

Oil Workers v. **Mobile Oil Co.**, 426 U.S. 407 (1976), U.S. Supreme Court case, which considered the express authorization in the National Labor Relations Act for states to enact "right-to-work" laws forbidding union shops. Texas, a right-to-work state, tried to apply its statute to oil-tanker workers who were hired and often based in Texas. Because the workers spent the bulk of their working time on the high seas, however, the court decided that Texas law should not govern these workers and upheld a union-shop clause in their contract.

Oklahoma State AFL–CIO: *see* AMERICAN FEDERATION OF LABOR–CONGRESS OF INDUSTRIAL ORGANIZATIONS.

Old Age, Survivors, and Disability Insurance (OASDI), federal program, created by the Social Security Act, which taxes both workers and employers to pay benefits to retired and disabled people, their dependents, widows, widowers, and children of deceased workers. *See also* SOCIAL SECURITY.

old boys' network also NEW GIRLS' NETWORK, colloquial way of referring to the fact that men who went to school together or belong to the same clubs tend to help each other in the business world as the occasion arises. Many a career was advanced because a college roommate was in a critical position 20 years later. In an effort to develop similar ties for similar advantages, some women have been purposely trying to create a "new girls' network" by sponsoring appropriate social events. As Sarah Weddington, President Carter's "women's advisor," told one such group, "where you are tomorrow may well depend upon whom you meet tonight." *See* Stephen L. Slavin, "The Old Boy Network at Six Big Banks," *Business and Society Review* (Fall 1977).

Old Dominion Branch No. 496, National Association of Letter Carriers v. **Austin**, 418 U.S. 264 (1974), U.S. Supreme Court case, which held use of the epithet "scab," which was literally and factually true and in common parlance in labor disputes, was protected under federal law.

oligarchy: *see* IRON LAW OF OLIGARCHY.

Oliver Report: *see* JOB EVALUATION AND PAY REVIEW TASK FORCE.

OLMAT: *see* OTIS–LENNON MENTAL ABILITY TEST.

ombudsman, also ORGANIZATION OMBUDSMAN, official whose job is to investigate the complaints of the citizenry concerning public services. Originally a Swedish word meaning "representative of the King," ombudsmen are now found in many countries at a variety of jurisdictional levels. For a comprehensive discussion, *see* Stanely V. Anderson (ed.), *Ombudsmen for American Government?* (Englewood Cliffs, N.J.: Prentice-Hall, 1968).

An *organization ombudsman* is a high-level staff officer who receives complaints and grievances about his organization directly from the employees. Such an officer mainly serves as an open channel of communication between employees and top management. *See* Isidore Silver, "The Corporate Ombudsman," *Harvard Business Review* (May–June 1967).

on-line, computer system whose operations are under the control of a central processing unit or a computer system in which information is processed as received.

on-the-job training, any training that takes place during regular working hours and for which normal wages are paid. *See* Earl R. Gomersall and M. Scott Myers, "Breakthrough in On-the-Job Training," *Harvard Business Review* (July–August 1966); Martin M. Broadwell, "It Pays to Increase Your Support of On-the-Job Training," *Training* (October 1977); Delbert W. Fisher, "Educational Psychology Involved in On-the-Job Training," *Personnel Journal* (October 1977). *See also* UNDERSTUDY.

OPCM: *see* LABOR ORGANIZATION, Plasterers' and Cement Masons' International Association of the United States and Canada, Operative.

OPEIU: *see* LABOR ORGANIZATION, Office and Professional Employees International Union.

open-book test, test that allows candidates to consult textbooks or other relevant material while the examination is in progress.

open-end agreement, collective bargaining agreement providing for a contract that will remain in effect until one of the parties wants to reopen negotiations.

open office, completely open room without walls, doors, or dividers; room with partitions and potted plants where walls once were; room with partitioned cubicles that curve and connect; and/or an office laid out according to how information flows from one person to the next.

open shop, any work organization that is not unionized. The term also applies to organizations that have unions but do not have union membership as a condition of employment. Historically, an "open shop" was one that tended to discriminate against unions.

open system, any organism or organization that interacts with its environment.

open union, union willing to admit any qualified person to its membership upon payment of initiation fees.

Operating Engineers, International Union of: *see* LABOR ORGANIZATION.

operational validity, the three basic elements of operational validity are test administration, interpretation, and application. According to William C. Byham and Stephen Temlock, in "Operational Validity—A New Concept in Personnel Testing," *Personnel Journal* (September 1972), "operational validity includes everything that happens with and to a test after test research has been completed. Operational validity can never make invalid tests predictive; it can only assure maximum prediction within the limits of the tests used." According to Dennis M. Groner, in "A Note on 'Operational' Validity," *Personnel Journal* (March 1977), "in the strictest sense of the word, operational validity is not validity at all, but a source of error which reduces the correlation between a predictor and a criterion."

operations research: *see* MANAGEMENT SCIENCE.

Operative Plasterers' and Cement Masons' International Association of the United States and Canada: *see* LABOR ORGANIZATION, Plasterers' and Cement Masons' International Association of the United States and Canada, Operative.

OPM: *see* OFFICE OF PERSONNEL MANAGEMENT.

oral board, committee formed for the purpose of interviewing candidates for employment, promotion, or evaluation.

oral examination, group: *see* GROUP ORAL INTERVIEW.

oral interview, group: *see* GROUP ORAL INTERVIEW.

oral test, any test that has an examiner ask a candidate a set of questions, as opposed to a paper-and-pencil test.

Oregon AFL–CIO: *see* AMERICAN FEDERATION OF LABOR–CONGRESS OF INDUSTRIAL ORGANIZATIONS.

Oregon State Employees Association: *see* LABOR ORGANIZATION.

ORE–SEA: *see* LABOR ORGANIZATION, Oregon State Employees Association.

organic system, that organization form that

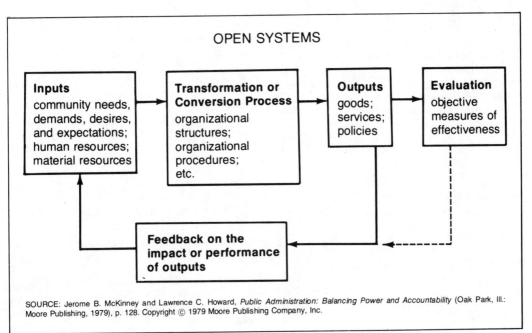

OPEN SYSTEMS

Inputs
community needs, demands, desires, and expectations; human resources; material resources

Transformation or Conversion Process
organizational structures; organizational procedures; etc.

Outputs
goods; services; policies

Evaluation
objective measures of effectiveness

Feedback on the impact or performance of outputs

SOURCE: Jerome B. McKinney and Lawrence C. Howard, *Public Administration: Balancing Power and Accountability* (Oak Park, Ill.: Moore Publishing, 1979), p. 128. Copyright © 1979 Moore Publishing Company, Inc.

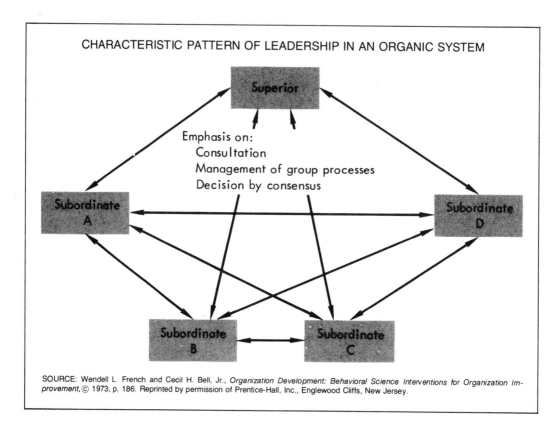

CHARACTERISTIC PATTERN OF LEADERSHIP IN AN ORGANIC SYSTEM

Superior

Emphasis on:
Consultation
Management of group processes
Decision by consensus

Subordinate A

Subordinate D

Subordinate B

Subordinate C

SOURCE: Wendell L. French and Cecil H. Bell, Jr., *Organization Development: Behavioral Science Interventions for Organization Improvement,* © 1973, p. 186. Reprinted by permission of Prentice-Hall, Inc., Englewood Cliffs, New Jersey.

has proved to be most appropriate under changing conditions. It is characterized by: (1) constant reassessment of tasks, assignments, and the use of organizational expertise; (2) authority, control, and communication are frequently *ad hoc* depending upon specific commitments and tasks; (3) communications and interactions between members are both very open and extensive; (4) leadership stressing consultation and group decisional processes; and (5) greater commitment to the organization's tasks and goals than to traditional hierarchical loyalty. The classic analysis of organic systems is to be found in Tom Burns and G. M. Stalker, *The Management of Innovation* (Chicago: Quadrangle Books, 1961).

See also MECHANISTIC SYSTEM.

organization, any structure and process of allocating jobs so that common objectives may be achieved. *See* James G. March and Herbert A. Simon, *Organizations* (N.Y.: John Wiley, 1958); James G. March (ed.), *Handbook of Organizations* (Chicago: Rand McNally, 1965); Harold J. Leavitt, William R. Dill, and Henry B. Eyring, *The Organizational World* (N.Y.: Harcourt Brace Jovanovich, 1973).

organization, flat/tall: *see* FLAT ORGANIZATION.

organization, formal/informal: *see* INFORMAL ORGANIZATION.

Organization Behavior & Human Performance, published bimonthly (beginning each year in February), this journal of fundamental research and theory in applied psychology seeks papers describing original empirical research and theoretical developments in all areas of human performance theory and organizational psychology. Preference is given to those articles contributing to the development of theories relevant to human performance or organizational behavior.

*Organizational Behavior &
    Human Performance*
Academic Press, Inc.
111 Fifth Avenue
New York, NY 10003

organizational conflict: *see* CONFLICT RESOLUTION.

Organizational Dynamics, quarterly publication of the American Management Associations that is a review of organizational behavior for professional managers.

Organizational Dynamics
AMACOM
135 West 50th Street
New York, NY 10020

organizational humanism, movement to create more humane work environments.

organizational iceberg, concept that the formal or overt aspects of an organization are just the proverbial tip of the iceberg. The greater part of the organization—the feelings, attitudes, and values of its members, for example—remain covert or hidden from obvious view. In short, the formal organization is visible, while the informal is hidden and waiting to sink any ship that ignores it.

organizational identification, according to Douglas T. Hall, Benjamin Schneider, and Harold T. Nygren, in "Personal Factors in Organizational Identification," *Administrative Science Quarterly* (June 1970), organization identification "is the process by which the goals of the organization and those of the individual become increasingly integrated or congruent."

organizational mirror, according to Jack K. Fordyce and Raymond Weil, in *Managing with People* (Reading, Mass.: Addison-Wesley, 1971),

> an organization mirror is a particular kind of meeting that allows an organizational unit to collect feedback from a number of key organizations to which it relates (*e.g.*, customers, suppliers, users of services within the larger organization). The meeting closes with a list of specific tasks for improvement of operations, products, or services.

organizational picketing, picketing an employer in order to encourage union membership. The Landrum–Griffin Act severely limited such picketing.

organizational pyramids: *see* PYRAMIDS.

organization chart, graphic description of the structure of an organization, usually in the form of a diagram.

organization climate, as a concept that can both explain and describe, organization climate studies seek (1) to show why things are as good or as bad as they are in a particular organization and/or (2) to characterize an organization's overall ambience. For a comprehensive introduction to the concept, *see* Fritz Steele and Stephen Jenks, *The Feel of the Work Place: Understanding and Improving Organization Climate* (Reading, Mass.: Addison-Wesley Publishing Co., 1977). For how to evaluate the climate in your organization, *see* William R. LaFollette, "How Is the Climate in Your Organization," *Personnel Journal* (July 1975).

organization development (OD), premised upon the notion that any organization wishing to survive must periodically divest itself of those parts or characteristics that contribute to its malaise, OD is a process for increasing an organization's effectiveness. As a process it has no value bias, yet it is usually associated with the idea that maximum effectiveness is to be found by integrating an individual's desire for personal growth with organizational goals. Wendell L. French and Cecil H. Bell, Jr., in *Organization Development: Behavioral Science Interventions for Organization Improvement* (Englewood Cliffs, N.J.: Prentice-Hall, 1973), provide a formal definition:

> organization development is a long-range effort to improve an organization's problem-solving and renewal processes, particularly through a more effective and collaborative management of organization culture—with special emphasis on the culture of formal work teams—with the assistance of a change agent, or catalyst, and the use of the theory and technology of applied behavioral science, including action research.

Other major texts include: Warren Bennis, *Organization Development: Its Nature, Origin, and Prospects* (Reading, Mass.: Addison-Wesley, 1969); Chris Argyris, *Management and Organizational Development: The Path From XA to YB* (N.Y.: McGraw-Hill, 1971); Edgar F. Huse, *Organization Development and Change* (St. Paul, Minn.: West Publishing, 1975).

See also the following entries:
ARGYRIS, CHRIS
BENNIS, WARREN
BLAKE, ROBERT R. AND JANE S. MOUTON
CONFRONTATION MEETING
NATIONAL TRAINING LABORATORIES INSTITUTE FOR APPLIED BEHAVIORAL SCIENCE
PROCESS CONSULTATION
SMALL-GROUP RESEARCH
TEAM BUILDING

organization man, now generic term to describe any individual within an organization who accepts the values of the organization and finds harmony in conforming to its policies. The term was popularized by William H. Whyte, Jr., in his best selling book, *The Organization Man* (New York: Simon & Schuster, 1956). Whyte wrote that these individuals were "the ones of our middle class who have left home, spiritually as well as physically, to take the vows of organization life, and it is they who are the mind and soul of our great self-perpetuating institutions." For the organization man's replacement, *see* Robert Stephen Silverman and D. A. Heming, "Exit The Organization Man: Enter the Professional Person," *Personnel Journal* (March 1975).

organization ombudsman: *see* OMBUDSMAN.

organization theory, also CLASSICAL ORGANIZATION THEORY and NEOCLASSICAL ORGANIZATION THEORY, theory that seeks to explain how groups and individuals behave in varying organizational structures and circumstances.

Classical organization theory, as its name implies, was the first theory of its kind, is considered traditional, and will continue to be the base upon which subsequent theories are built. The development of any theory must be viewed in the context of its time. The beliefs of early management theorists about how organizations worked or should work was a direct reflection of the social values of their times. And the times were harsh. Individual workers were not viewed as individuals, but as the interchangeable parts in an industrial machine whose parts were made of flesh when it was impractical to make them of steel. Consequently, the first theories of organizations were concerned with the anatomy, with the structure, of formal organizations. This is the hallmark of classical organization theory—a concern for organizational structure that is premised upon the assumed rational behavior of its human parts.

There is no firm definition as to just what "neoclassical" means in *neoclassical organization theory,* but the general connotation is that of a theoretical perspective that revises and/or is critical of traditional (classical) organization theory because it does not pay enough attention to the needs and interactions of organizational members. The watershed between classical and neoclassical organization theory is World War II. The major writers of the classical school (Taylor, Fayol, Weber, Gulick, etc.) did their most significant work before World War II. The major neoclassical writers (Simon, March, Selznick, Parsons, etc.) gained their reputations as organization theorists by attacking the classical writers after the war.

For the historical evolution of organization theory, *see* William G. Scott, "Organization Theory: An Overview And An Appraisal," *Academy of Management Journal* (April 1961); Charles Perrow, "The Short and Glo-

rious History of Organizational Theory," *Organizational Dynamics* (Summer 1973); Jay M. Shafritz and Philip H. Whitbeck, *Classics of Organization Theory* (Oak Park, Illinois: Moore Publishing Company, 1978).

See also REALPOLITIK.

organized labor, collective term for members of labor unions. *See* Sanford Cohen, *Labor in the United States* (Columbus, Ohio: Charles E. Merrill, 5th ed., 1979).

organizer, also called LABOR ORGANIZER and UNION ORGANIZER, individual, employed by a union, who acts to encourage employees of a particular plant or organization to join the union that the organizer represents. *See* Stephen I. Scholossberg and Frederick E. Sherman, *Organizing and the Law: A Handbook for Union Organizers* (Washington, D.C.: Bureau of National Affairs, Inc., rev. ed., 1972).

See also the following entries:

BETH ISRAEL HOSPITAL V. NATIONAL LABOR RELATIONS BOARD

NATIONAL LABOR RELATIONS BOARD V. BABCOCK AND WILCOX

PANDOL & SONS V. AGRICULTURAL LABOR RELATIONS BOARD

organizing: *see* CENTRAL HARDWARE CO. V. NATIONAL LABOR RELATIONS BOARD and PANDOL & SONS V. AGRICULTURAL LABOR RELATIONS BOARD.

orientation, formal introduction and guided adjustment of new employees to their new job, new co-workers, and new working environment. *See* Murray Lubliner, "Employee Orientation," *Personnel Journal* (April 1978).

orientation checklist, a listing in an orderly and logical sequence of all of the items about which a new employee should be informed or must do as part of the orientation process.

Oscar Mayer & Co. v. Evans, 60 L. Ed. 2d 609 (1979), U.S. Supreme Court case, which held an employee must exhaust state remedies for age discrimination before bringing federal action under the Age Discrimination in Employment Act.

OSHA: *see* OCCUPATIONAL SAFETY AND HEALTH ADMINISTRATION.

OSHRC: *see* OCCUPATIONAL SAFETY AND HEALTH REVIEW COMMISSION.

Otis–Lennon Mental Ability Test (OLMAT), test battery widely used for industrial personnel screening to measure general reasoning ability or scholastic aptitude by sampling a broad range of cognitive abilities. Most commonly used in the placement of individuals in lower level jobs—clerks, office machine operators, and assembly-line workers, etc. TIME: 30/45 minutes. AUTHORS: Arthur S. Otis and Roger T. Lennon. PUBLISHER: Psychological Corporation (see TEST PUBLISHERS).

outlaw strike: *see* WILDCAT STRIKE.

out-of-title work, also called OUT-OF-CLASS EXPERIENCE, duties performed by an incumbent of a position that are not appropriate to the class to which the position has been assigned.

outplacement, according to John Scherba, in "Outplacement: An Established Personnel Function," *The Personnel Administrator* (July 1978),

> outplacement is the extension of services to a terminated employee to: 1) minimize the impact of termination, 2) reduce the time necessary to secure a new position, 3) improve the person's job search skills and 4) ultimately bring about the best possible match between the person and available jobs.

Also useful is J. D. Erdlen, "Guidelines for Retaining an Outplacement Consultant," *The Personnel Administrator* (January 1978).

See also DEHIRING.

output, end result of any process.

output curve: *see* WORK CURVE.

overachievement, also UNDERACHIEVEMENT, psychological concepts that describe a discrepancy between predicted and actual achievement/performance. Individuals whose performance exceeds or goes below expectations are described as overachievers or underachievers. See Robert L. Thorndike, *The Concepts of Over and Underachievements* (N.Y.: Columbia University Press, 1963).

overhead agency: *see* AUXILIARY AGENCY.

overrate: *see* FLAGGED RATE.

Overseas Education Association, Inc.: *see* LABOR ORGANIZATION, under Education Association, National.

overseas premium, payment that serves to induce an employee to accept a foreign assignment. It is usually paid each year that the employee is overseas and can either be a fixed dollar amount or a percentage of salary. Overseas premiums are designed to reimburse an employee for the cost of living in a foreign country in excess of what it would

normally cost to live in the United States. *See* Cecil G. Howard, "Overseas Compensation Policies of U.S. Multinationals," *The Personnel Administrator* (November 1975).

overtime, work performed in excess of the basic workday/workweek as defined by law, collective bargaining, or company policy. For an economic analysis, *see* Ronald G. Ehrenberg, *Fringe Benefits and Overtime Behavior: Theoretical and Econometric Analysis* (Lexington, Mass.: D.C. Heath, 1971).

See also BAY RIDGE COMPANY V. AARON and LODGE 76, INTERNATIONAL ASSOCIATION OF MACHINISTS V. WISCONSIN EMPLOYMENT RELATIONS COMMISSION.

overtime computations, for employees covered by the Fair Labor Standards Act, overtime must be paid at a rate of at least 1½ times the employee's regular pay rate for each hour worked in a workweek in excess of the maximum allowable in a given type of employment. Generally, the regular rate includes all payments made by the employer to or on behalf of the employee (excluding certain statutory exceptions). The following examples are based on a maximum 40-hour workweek:

1. **Hourly rate** (regular pay rate for an employee paid by the hour). If more than 40 hours are worked, at least 1½ times the regular rate for each hour over 40 is due. *Example:* An employee paid $3.80 an hour works 44 hours in a workweek. The employee is entitled to at least 1½ times $3.80, or $5.70, for each hour over 40. Pay for the week would be $152 for the first 40 hours, plus $22.80 for the four hours of overtime—a total of $174.80.

2. **Piece rate.** The regular rate of pay for an employee paid on a piecework basis is obtained by dividing the total weekly earnings by the total number of hours worked in the same week. The employee is entitled to an additional ½ of this regular rate for each hour over 40, besides the full piecework earnings. *Example:* An employee paid on a piecework basis works 45 hours in a week and earns $162. The regular pay rate for that week is $162 divided by 45, or $3.60 an hour. In addition to the straight time pay, the employee is entitled to $1.80 (half the regular rate) for each hour over 40. Another way to compensate pieceworkers for overtime, if agreed to before the work is performed, is to pay 1½ times the piece rate for each piece produced during overtime hours. The piece rate must be the one actually paid during non-overtime hours and must be enough to yield at least the minimum wage per hour.

3. **Salaries.** The regular rate for an employee paid a salary for a regular or specified number of hours a week is obtained by dividing the salary by the number of hours. If, under the employment agreement, a salary sufficient to meet the minimum wage requirement in every workweek is paid as straight time for whatever number of hours are worked in a workweek, the regular rate is obtained by dividing the salary by the number of hours worked each week. To illustrate, suppose an employee's hours of work vary each week and the agreement with the employer is that the employee will be paid $200 a week for whatever number of hours of work are required. Under this pay agreement, the regular rate will vary in overtime weeks. If the employee works 50 hours, the regular rate is $4 ($200 divided by 50 hours). In addition to the sal-ary, ½ the regular rate, or $2 is due for each of the 10 overtime hours, for a total of $220 for the week. If the employee works 54 hours, the regular rate will be $3.70 ($200 divided by 54). In that case, an additional $1.85 is due for each of the 14 overtime hours, for a total of $225.90 for the week.

In no case may the regular rate be less than the minimum wage required by the Act. If a salary is paid on other than a weekly basis, the weekly pay must be determined in order to compute the regular rate and overtime. If the salary is for a half month, it must be multiplied by 24 and the product divided by 52 weeks to get the weekly equivalent. A monthly salary should be multiplied by 12 and the product divided by 52.

OVIS: *see* OHIO VOCATIONAL INTEREST SURVEY.

P

PACE: *see* PROFESSIONAL AND ADMINIS-
TRATIVE CAREERS EXAMINATION.

**Pacific Coast Marine Firemen, Oilers, Water-
tenders and Wipers Association:** *see* LABOR
ORGANIZATION, under Seafarers' International Union of North America.

Pacific Log Scalers Association: *see* LABOR
ORGANIZATION, Log Scalers Association, Pacific.

package settlement, term that describes the
total money value (usually quoted as cents
per hour) of an increase in wages and benefits achieved through collective bargaining.
For example, a new contract might give employees an increase of 50¢ an hour. However,
when the value of increased medical and
pension benefits are included, the "package
settlement" might come to 74¢ an hour. *See*
John G. Kilgour, "'Wrapping the Package' of
Labor Agreement Costs," *Personnel Journal*
(June 1977).

**Packinghouse and Industrial Workers, Na-
tional Brotherhood of:** *see* LABOR ORGANI-
ZATION.

pact, an agreement.

**Painters and Allied Trades of the United
States and Canada, International Brotherhood
of:** *see* LABOR ORGANIZATION.

PAIR, acronym for "personnel and industrial
relations."

***Pandol & Sons* v. *Agricultural Labor Rela-
tions Board***, 429 U.S. 802 (1976), U.S. Supreme Court case, which upheld state regulations permitting union organizers access to
private property for the purpose of organizing
California's farmworkers.

paper locals, local unions created as vehicles
for unethical or illegal actions.

Paperworkers International Union, United:
see LABOR ORGANIZATION.

PAQ: *see* POSITION ANALYSIS QUESTION-
NAIRE.

PAR: *see* PUBLIC ADMINISTRATION REVIEW.

paralegal: *see* PARAPROFESSIONAL.

parallel forms, two or more forms of a test
that are assembled as closely as possible to
the same statistical and content specifications
so that they will provide the same kind of
measurement at different administrations.

parallel ladder: *see* DUAL LADDER.

paramedic: *see* PARAPROFESSIONAL.

paraprofessional, any individual with less
than standard professional credentials who
assists a fully credentilized professional with
the more routine aspects of his/her professional work. For example, paralegals assist
lawyers and paramedics assist medical doctors. *See* Robert Cohen, *"New Careers"
Grows Older: A Perspective on the Paraprofessional Experience, 1965–1975* (Baltimore:
The Johns Hopkins University Press, 1976).

parity, also EMPLOYMENT PARITY, OCCUPA-
TIONAL PARITY, and WAGE PARITY, long term
goal of all affirmative action efforts, which
will exist after all categories of an organization's employees are proportionately representative of the population in the organization's geographic region. *Employment parity*
exists when the proportion of protected
groups in the external labor market is equivalent to their proportion in an organization's
total work force without regard to job classifications. *Occupational parity* exists when the
proportion of an organization's protected
group employees in all job classifications is
equivalent to their respective availability in
the external labor market.
  Wage parity requires that the salary level
of one occupational classification be the same
as for another. The most common example of
wage parity is the linkage between the

249

salaries of police and firefighters. Over two thirds of all cities in the United States have parity policies for their police and firefighters. But according to David Lewin, in "Wage Parity and the Supply of Police and Firemen," *Industrial Relations* (February 1973),

> parity contributes to the problem of attracting and retaining qualified personnel in police ranks; it also inflates wages in the fire services beyond the level necessary to secure adequate staffing, thus imposing a heavy burden on local taxpayers. Furthermore, parity implies that police and fire occupations are similar in nonpay characteristics when, in fact, policemen and firemen not only perform substantially different functions, but also have different promotional opportunities. Thus, from the perspective of the external labor market and from considerations of internal equity, wage parity is a deficient policy and should no longer guide the wage setting process for the protective services.

For a legal analysis of the police/fire parity issue, *see* Hoyt N. Wheeler, Richard Berger, and Stephen McGarry, "Parity: An Evaluation of Recent Court and Board Decisions," *Labor Law Journal* (March 1978).

Parkinson's Law, C. Northcote Parkinson's famous law that "work expands so as to fill the time available for its completion" first appeared in his *Parkinson's Law and Other Studies in Administration* (Boston: Houghton Mifflin Co., 1957). With mathematical precision, he "discovered" that any public administrative department will invariably increase its staff an average of 5.75 percent per year. In anticipation of suggestions that he advise what might be done about this problem, he asserted that "it is not the business of the botanist to eradicate the weeds. Enough for him if he can tell us just how fast they grow."

Parsons, Albert R(oss) (1848-1887), anarchist and radical labor leader who was convicted (with seven others) of the murder of seven policemen during the Haymarket "riot" of 1886. For a biography, *see* Alan Calmer, *Labor Agitator: The Story of Albert R. Parsons* (N.Y.: International Publishers, 1937).

participative management: *see* INDUSTRIAL DEMOCRACY.

part-time workers: *see* FULL-TIME WORKERS.

PAS: *see* PUBLIC ADMINISTRATION SERVICE.

passing point: *see* CUTTING SCORE.

passing score: *see* CUTTING SCORE.

passing the buck: *see* BUCKOLOGY.

passionate leave: *see* COMPASSIONATE LEAVE.

pass rate, proportion of candidates who pass an examination.

past practice, manner in which a similar issue was resolved before the occasion of a present grievance.

PAT: *see* LABOR ORGANIZATION, Painters and Allied Trades, International Brotherhood of.

PATCO: *see* LABOR ORGANIZATION, Professional Air Traffic Controllers Organization, under Marine Engineers' Beneficial Association, National.

Patent Office Professional Association: *see* LABOR ORGANIZATION.

paternalism, also called INDUSTRIAL PATERNALISM and EMPLOYER PATERNALISM, in the United States, the word is a derogatory reference to an organization's "fatherly" efforts to better the lot of its employees. Historically, the U.S. labor movement has considered paternalistic efforts to be a false and demeaning charity which inhibited the growth of union membership. In other societies where there are well established paternalistic traditions, the derogatory connotations of the word may be absent. Japan is undoubtedly the most paternalistic of all the major industrial societies. For a history and analysis of the concept, *see* John W. Bennett, "Paternalism," David L. Sills (ed.), *International Encyclopedia of the Social Sciences* (N.Y.: Macmillan Co. & The Free Press, 1968)

path-goal theory of leadership, a leadership style that has the leader indicate to his or her followers the "path" by which to accomplish their individual and organizational goals, then help to make that "path" as easy to follow as possible. According to Robert J. House, in "A Path-Goal Theory of Leader Effectiveness," *Administrative Science Quarterly* (September 1971),

> The motivational function of the leader consists of increasing personal pay-offs to subordinates for work-goal attainment, and making the path to these pay-offs easier to travel by clarifying it, reducing roadblocks and pitfalls, and increasing the opportunities for personal satisfaction in route.

Also see, Robert J. House and T. R. Mitchell, "Path-Goal Theory of Leadership," *Journal of Contemporary Business* (Autumn 1974).

patronage, the power of elected officials to make partisan appointments to office or to confer contracts, honors, or other benefits to their political supporters. For the most comprehensive survey of U.S. patronage practices, *see* Martin and Susan Tolchin, *To the Victor: Political Patronage from the Clubhouse to the White House* (N.Y.: Random House, 1971).

See also ELROD V. BURNS.

patronage jokes, the definitive statement on the disillusioning aspects of political patronage is credited to President William Howard Taft, who was moved to conclude that whenever he made a patronage appointment, he created "nine enemies and one ingrate." Actually, this quip is generally attributed to all sophisticated dispensers of patronage from Thomas Jefferson to Louis XIV. U.S. presidents have produced only two memorable patronage jokes (other than many of the appointees themselves). In addition to President Taft's remark, there is the story that Abraham Lincoln, while lying prostrate in the White House with an attack of smallpox, said to his attendants: "Tell all the office-seekers to come in at once, for now I have something I can give to all of them."

pattern bargaining, collective bargaining in which key contract terms agreed to by one bargaining unit are copied by other companies in the same industry during subsequent negotiations.

See also UNITED MINE WORKERS V. PENNINGTON.

patterned interview, also UNPATTERNED INTERVIEW, interview that seeks to ask the same questions of all applicants. An *unpatterned interview* does not seek such uniformity.

Pattern Makers' League of North America: *see* LABOR ORGANIZATION.

pay: *see* the following entries:

BASIC RATE OF PAY
CALL-BACK PAY
CALL-IN PAY
COMPENSATION
DOWN-TIME PAY
HAZARD PAY
HOLIDAY PAY
INCENTIVE PAY
JOURNEYMAN PAY
JURY-DUTY PAY
LONGEVITY PAY
MAKE-UP PAY
RETROACTIVE PAY
SEVERANCE PAY

STRIKE PAY
TAKE-HOME PAY
VACATION PAY
WELL PAY
WORK PREMIUM

pay-as-you-go plan, pension plan that has employers paying pension benefits to retired employees out of current income.

Pay Board, 15-member tripartite board consisting of business, labor, and public representatives whose function was to set and administer wage and salary policies. The Pay Board, authorized by the Economic Stabilization Act of 1970 and established by Executive Order 11627 on October 28, 1971, officially functioned under the Economic Stablization Program of the Executive Office of the President. It was abolished by Executive Order 11695 on January 11, 1973.

pay criteria: *see* WAGE CRITERIA.

pay for performance, concept of paying an employee on the basis of job performance—all bonuses, raises, promotions, etc., would be directly related to the measurable results of the employee's efforts. *See* Thomas H. Patten, Jr., "Pay for Performance or Placation?" *The Personnel Administrator* (September 1977); Paula Cowan, "How Blue Cross Put Pay-for-Performance to Work," *Personnel Journal* (May 1978).

pay grade, also called PAY LEVEL, an increment that makes up a pay structure. Each represents a range of pay or a standard rate of pay for a specific class of jobs.

pay increase, any permanent raise in an employee's basic salary or wage level. *See* Linda A. Krefting and Thomas A. Mahoney, "Determining the Size of a Meaningful Pay Increase," *Industrial Relations* (February 1977)

pay level: *see* PAY GRADE.

payments in kind, noncash payments for services rendered.

pay plan, while a position classification plan essentially arranges positions in classes on the basis of their similarities, a pay plan establishes rates of pay for each class of positions. Consequently, if a position is improperly classified, the corresponding salary can not be in accord with the principle of "equal pay for equal work." *See* Donald E. Hoag and Robert J. Trudel, *How to Prepare a Sound Pay Plan* (Chicago: International Personnel Management Association, 1976).

pay range, also called SALARY RANGE and WAGE RANGE, most positions in formal organizations are assigned to a pay, salary or wage range, which indicates minimum, intermediate, and maximum pay rates usually in the form of pay steps.

payroll, listing of all the wages and/or salaries earned by employees within an organization for a specific time period (usually weekly, bimonthly, or monthly).

payroll taxes: *see* EMPLOYMENT TAXES.

pay satisfaction, according to Edward E. Lawler, III, in *Pay and Organizational Effectiveness: A Psychological View* (N.Y.: Mc-Graw-Hill, 1971), pay satisfaction, "is basically determined by the difference between pay and the person's belief about what his pay should be." If employees find themselves assuming substantially similar duties and responsibilities as co-workers, who, because of seniority or education, have higher paying classifications, they are going to be dissatisfied with their pay. It is very difficult to convince employees that their pay is determined fairly if they have before them on a daily basis other more highly paid employees, who serve not as role models that one should strive to emulate, but rather as glaring examples of the inequities of the pay program.

pay secrecy, policy of keeping confidential the compensation levels of various catagories of employees, most usually those in managerial positions. For analyses, *see* Mary G. Miner, "Pay Policies: Secret or Open? And Why?" *Personnel Journal* (February 1974); Jay R. Schuster and Jerome A. Colletti, "Pay Secrecy: Who Is For and Against It?" *Academy of Management Journal* (March 1973); Thomas A. Mahoney and William Weitzer, "Secrecy and Managerial Compensation," *Industrial Relations* (May 1978).

pay step, each of the various increments that make up a pay range.

pay survey: *see* WAGE SURVEY.

pay system, dual: *see* DUAL PAY SYSTEM.

pay system, Foreign Service: *see* FOREIGN SERVICE PAY SYSTEM.

PBGC: *see* PENSION BENEFIT GUARANTY CORPORATION.

P-C: *see* PROCESS CONSULTATION.

peaked out, negative way of referring to an employee who has reached the maximum step in his salary range or has already made his or her maximum contributions to the organization.

pecking order, ever since social psychologists discovered that chickens have a pecking order—the strongest or most aggressive fowl get to eat, or to peck, first—the term has been used to describe the comparative ranks that humans hold in their social organizations. No aspect of our society is immune from the pecking order's fowl antics. According to Lyndon Johnson's former press secretary, George E. Reedy, in *The Twilight of the Presidency* (Cleveland: World Publishing, 1970),

> the inner life of the White House is essentially the life of the barnyard, as set forth so graphically in the study of the pecking order among chickens which every freshman sociology student must read. It is a question of who has the right to peck whom and who must submit to being pecked. There are only two important differences. The first is that the pecking order is determined by the individual strength and forcefulness of each chicken, whereas in the White House it depends upon the relationship to the barnyard keeper. The second is that no one outside the barnyard glorifies the chickens and expects them to order the affairs of mankind. They are destined for the frying pan and that is that.

peer rating, also called MUTUAL RATING, performance evaluation technique that calls for each employee to evaluate all of the other employees in his/her work unit.

Pendleton Act of 1883, this "Act to Regulate and Improve the Civil Service of the United States" introduced the merit concept into federal employment and created the U.S. Civil Service Commission.

See also the following entries:
CIVIL SERVICE REFORM ACT OF 1978
GRANT'S CIVIL SERVICE COMMISSION
NATIONAL CIVIL SERVICE LEAGUE

penetration rate, also PENETRATION RATIO, in the context of equal employment opportunity, the *penetration rate* for an organization is the proportion of its workforce belonging to a particular minority group. The *penetration ratio* is the ratio of an organization's penetration rate to the penetration rate for its geographic region (usually the standard metropolitan statistical area or SMSA). The rate and ratio are derived as follows:

$$\text{Penetration Rate} = \frac{\text{Total Minority Employment}}{\text{Total Employment}}$$

The Determinants of Pay Satisfaction

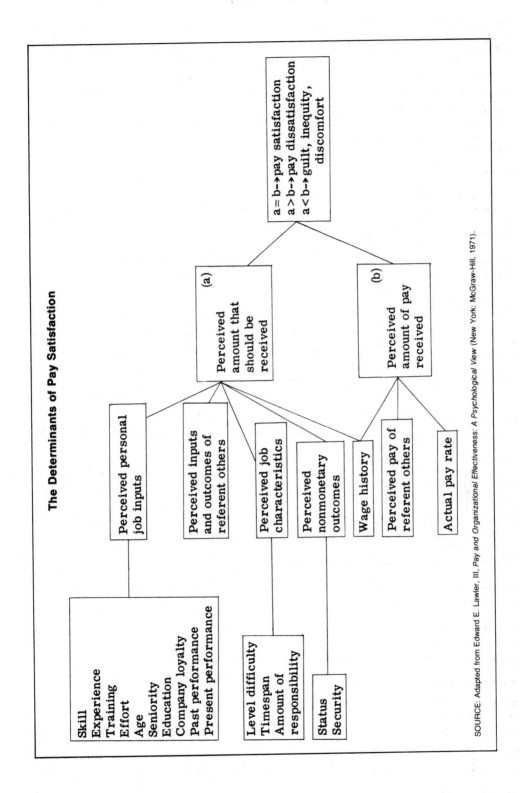

SOURCE: Adapted from Edward E. Lawler, III, *Pay and Organizational Effectiveness: A Psychological View* (New York: McGraw-Hill, 1971).

$$\text{Penetration Ratio} = \frac{\text{Penetration Rate for an Organization}}{\text{Penetration Rate for the SMSA}}$$

See also REPRESENTATIVE BUREAUCRACY.

Pennington decision: *see* UNITED MINE WORKERS V. PENNINGTON.

Pennsylvania AFL-CIO: *see* AMERICAN FEDERATION OF LABOR–CONGRESS OF INDUSTRIAL ORGANIZATIONS.

pension, periodic payments to an individual who retires from employment (or simply from a particular organization) because of age, disability, or the completion of a specific period of service. Such payments usually continue for the rest of the recipient's life and sometime extend to legal survivors.

While pensions have a long history as royal beneficences, the populace did not always view such royal largess as deserving. Samuel Johnson, in his 1755 *English Dictionary*, defined pension by stating, "in England it is generally understood to mean pay given to a state hireling for treason to his country." While early industrial pension plans were informal and based upon oral agreements, the first formal pension plan in the United States was the 1875 program of the American Express Company. In the public sector, the first civilian pension plans appeared just before World War I for some of the larger municipal police and fire departments. Federal civilian employees had to wait for the Retirement Act of 1920 before they were eligible for any retirement benefits. For a history and analysis of pension programs, *see* William C. Greenough and Francis P. King, *Pension Plans and Public Policy* (N.Y.: Columbia University Press, 1976). *See also* William D. Hall and David L. Landsittel, *A New Look at Accounting for Pension Costs* (Homewood, Ill.: Richard D. Irwin, 1977); Everett T. Allen, Jr., Joseph J. Melone, and Jerry S. Rosenbloom, *Pension Planning* (Homewood, Ill.: Richard D. Irwin, 3rd ed., 1976).

See also the following entries:

CITY OF LOS ANGELES, DEPARTMENT OF WATER & POWER V. MANHART
PORTABILITY
VARIABLE ANNUITY
VESTING

Pension Benefit Guaranty Corporation (PBGC), federal agency that guarantees basic pension benefits in covered private plans if they terminate with insufficient assets. Title IV of the Employee Retirement Income Security Act of 1974 (ERISA) established the corporation to guarantee payment of insured benefits if covered plans terminate without sufficient assets to pay such benefits. The PBGC, a self-financing, wholly-owned government corporation is governed by a Board of Directors consisting of the Secretaries of Labor, Commerce and the Treasury. The Secretary of Labor is chairman of the board and is responsible for administering the PBGC in accordance with policies established by the board. A seven-member Advisory Committee, composed of two labor, two business, and three public members appointed by the President, advises the PBGC on various matters.

Title IV of ERISA provides for mandatory coverage of most private defined benefit plans. These are those plans that provide a benefit, the amount of which can be determined from a formula in the plan, for example, based on factors such as age, years of

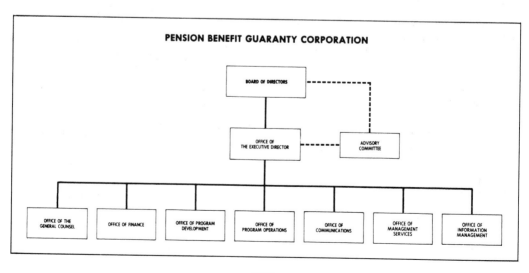

service, average or highest salary, etc. In 1978, approximately 33 million participants, in about 90,000 plans, were covered. All covered pension plans are required to pay prescribed premium rates to PBGC.

Pension Benefit Guaranty Corporation
2020 K Street N.W.
Washington, DC 20006
(202) 254-4817

pension fund socialism, Peter F. Drucker's term for the phenomenon that is turning traditional thinking about the "inherent" and historical separation of capital and labor upside down—namely, that the "workers" of the United States are rapidly and literally becoming the owners of the nation's industry through their pension fund investments in diverse common stocks. According to Drucker, by 1985 pension funds "will own at least 50—if not 60—percent of equity capital." For Drucker's complete analysis, *see* his *The Unseen Revolution: How Pension Fund Socialism Came to America* (N.Y.: Harper & Row, 1976).

pension plan, contributory: *see* CONTRIBUTORY PENSION PLAN.

pension plan, fully funded: *see* FULLY FUNDED PENSION PLAN.

pension plan, funded: *see* FUNDED PENSION PLAN.

Pension Reform Act of 1974: *see* EMPLOYEES RETIREMENT INCOME SECURITY ACT OF 1974.

Pension Reporter: see BNA PENSION REPORTER.

Pension World, monthly trade magazine whose articles are aimed at practitioners in the field of pension and benefit administration.

Pension World
Communications Channels, Inc.
461 Eighth Avenue
New York, NY 10001

peonage, forced labor. The 13th Amendment prohibits such involuntary servitude.

people plucker: *see* HEADHUNTER.

per capita tax, tax on each head and the regular payment made on the basis of membership by a local union to its national organization.

percentile, that point or score in a distribution below which falls the percent of cases indicated by the given percentile. Thus the 15th percentile denotes the score or point below which 15 percent of the scores fall.

percentile band, interval between percentiles, corresponding to score limits one standard error of measurement above and below an obtained score. The chances are approximately 2 out of 3 that the true score of an examinee with a particular obtained score is within these score limits.

percentile rank, percent of scores in a distribution equal to or lower than a particular obtained score.

per diem, Latin for "by the day." Temporary employees may be paid a "per-diem" rate or a travel expense program may reimburse employees using a flat "per-diem" amount.

performance, demonstration of a skill or competence.

performance appraisal, also called PERFORMANCE EVALUATION and PERFORMANCE REPORTING, title usually given to the formal method by which an organization documents

---

The Ultimate Performance Appraisal Scale

Check One

1. Individual is inept *within* tolerable organizational standards. ____

2. Individual is inept *beyond* tolerable organizational standards. ____

3. Individual is *hopelessly inept.* ____

4. Individual is a *classic case* of *dysfunctional ineptness.* ____

5. Individual is so *totally* and *completely inept* that even the *ineptitude* is marred by *ineptness.* ____

---

the work performance of its employees. Performance appraisals are designed to serve a variety of functions, such as:

1. changing or modifying dysfunctional work behavior;
2. communicating to employees managerial perceptions of the quality and quantity of their work;
3. assessing future potential of an employee in order to recommend appropriate training or developmental assignments;

4. assessing whether the present duties of an employee's position have an appropriate compensation level; and
5. providing a documented record for disciplinary and separation actions.

For a classic analysis of the problems of performance appraisal, *see* Douglas McGregor, "An Uneasy Look at Performance Appraisal," *Harvard Business Review* (May–June 1957; reprinted May–June 1975). For a legal analysis, *see* William H. Holley and Hubert S. Feild, "Performance Appraisal and the Law," *Labor Law Journal* (July 1975). For an overview, *see* Alan H. Locher and Kenneth S. Teel, "Performance Appraisal—A Survey of Current Practices," *Personnel Journal* (May 1977).

See also SELF-APPRAISAL.

performance evaluation: *see* PERFORMANCE APPRAISAL.

performance incentive: *see* INCENTIVE.

performance objective, also called CRITERION OBJECTIVE, statement specifying exactly what behavior is to be exhibited, the conditions under which behavior will be accomplished, and the minimum standard of acceptable performance.

performance reporting: *see* PERFORMANCE APPRAISAL.

performance standards: *see* STANDARDS OF PERFORMANCE.

performance test, examination that has candidates perform a sample of the actual work that would be found on the job. *See* Roscoe W. Wisner, "Construction and Use of Performance Tests," J. J. Donovan (ed.), *Recruitment and Selection in the Public Service* (Chicago: Public Personnel Association, 1968).

peripheral employees, according to Martin J. Gannon, "The Management of Peripheral Employees," *Personnel Journal* (September 1975), peripheral employees are those that

are not totally committed to the organization and, in fact, view their work, not as a career, but as a job which can be easily discarded. Included in this segment of the labor force would be part-time employees, temporary employees, working students, moonlighters and women who decide to take a job only for a short period of time.

See also Dean Morse, *The Peripheral Worker* (N.Y.: Columbia University Press, 1969).

Perkins, Frances (1882-1965), Secretary of Labor from 1933 to 1945 and the first woman to hold a cabinet post in the U.S. government. For a biography, *see* George Martin, *Madam Secretary: Frances Perkins* (Boston: Houghton Mifflin, 1976).

perks: *see* PERQUISITES.

permanent arbitrator, arbitrator who hears all disputes during the life of a contract or other stipulated term.

permanent injunction: *see* INJUNCTION.

perquisites, also called PERKS, the special benefits, frequently tax exempt, made available only to the top executives of an organization. There are two basic kinds of executive perquisites: (1) those with "take-home" value (such as company cars, club memberships, etc.) and (2) those that have no "take-home" value, but serve mainly to confer status (such as the proverbial executive washroom, office size and decor, etc.). Historically, the U.S. Internal Revenue Service has striven to restrict the tax exempt status of executives perquisites. According to Robert C. Coffin, in "Developing A Program of Executives Benefits and Perquisites," *The Personnel Administrator* (February 1977),

the possibilities of executive benefits are numerous. Some are clearly tax advantaged. Some are tax advantaged under certain circumstances—conceivably they could be tax advantaged for some executives and not for others. Some executive benefits, though valuable, have no tax advantage—their value is the same as the equivalent in direct pay. Remember, however, that the legal niceties are not always observed by small companies not heavily subject to public, stockholder or IRS scrutiny, that certain perquisites are easily hidden even by large, exposed corporations and that in some cases (expense accounts, for example), the tax aspect is a private matter between the beneficiary of the perquisite and IRS.

Perry* v. *Sinderman, 408 U.S. 593 (1972), U.S. Supreme Court case, which held that while a teacher's subjective "expectancy" of tenure is not protected by procedural due process, an allegation that a school had a *de facto* tenure policy entitles one to an opportunity of proving the legitimacy of a claim to job tenure. Such proof would obligate a school to hold a requested hearing when the teacher could both be informed of the grounds for nonretention and challenge the sufficiency of those grounds.

persona, term developed by Carl Jung that refers to the personality or facade that each individual shows to the world. The persona is distinguished from our inner being, because it is adopted and put on like a mask to meet the demands of social life. Persona is the word for the masks that actors wore in ancient Greece.

personal, having to do with a human being's thoughts, possessions, feelings and things.

personal financial planning, some corporations provide investment counseling or personal financial planning for their executives as a fringe benefit. For how to do it, *see* James E. Cheeks, *How To Compensate Executives* (Homewood, Ill.: Dow-Jones Irwin, 1974).

personality inventory, also called SELF-REPORT INVENTORY, questionnaire concerned with personal characteristics and behavior that an individual answers about himself/herself. Then, the individual's self-report is compared to norms based upon the responses given to the same questionnaire by a large representative group.

See also the following entries:

BERNREUTER PERSONALITY INVENTORY
EYSENCK PERSONALITY INVENTORY
MINNESOTA MULTIPHASIC PERSONALITY INVENTORY
PERSONALITY RESEARCH FORM.

personal-rank system: *see* RANK-IN-MAN SYSTEM.

Personality Research Form (PRF), self-report personality inventory. Available in Standard Edition (300 items, 15 scores) and Long Edition (440 items, 22 scores). TIME: varies. AUTHOR: D. N. Jackson. PUBLISHER: Research Psychologists Press, Inc. (*see* TEST PUBLISHERS).

personality test, test designed to measure any of the non-intellectual aspects of an individual's psychological disposition. It seeks information on a person's motivations and attitudes as opposed to his or her abilities.

personal space, the area that individuals actively maintain around themselves, into which others cannot intrude without arousing discomfort. *See* Leslie Alec Hayduk, "Personal Space: An Evaluative and Orienting Overview," *Psychological Bulletin* (January 1978).

personal time, that time an employee uses to tend to personal needs. This time is usually separate from lunch and rest breaks and is sometimes written into union contracts.

personnel, collective term for all of the employees of an organization. The word is of military origin—the two basic components of a traditional army being materiel and personnel. Personnel is also commonly used to refer to the personnel management function or the organizational unit responsible for administering personnel programs. *See* Cyril Curtis Ling, *The Management of Personnel Relations: History and Origins* (Homewood, Ill.: Richard D. Irwin, 1965).

Personnel, bimonthly magazine of the American Management Associations, which contains articles by scholars and practitioners on every phase of human resource management and personnel administration.

Personnel
Editorial Address:
American Management Associations
135 West 50th Street
New York, NY 10020

Subscriptions:
Subscription Services
Box 319
Saranac Lake, NY 12983

personnel administration, also PERSONNEL MANAGEMENT, that aspect of management concerned with the recruitment, selection, development, utilization, and compensation of the members of an organization. While the terms *personnel administration* and *personnel management* tend to be used interchangeably, there is a distinction. The former is mainly concerned with the technical aspects of maintaining a full complement of employees within an organization, while the latter concerns itself as well with the larger problems of the viability of an organization's human resources. For analyses of how personnel administration has been evolving into personnel management, *see* Edward J. Giblin, "The Evolution of Personnel," *Human Resource Management* (Fall 1978); Lawrence A. Wangler, "The Intensification of the Personnel Role," *Personnel Journal* (February 1979).

See also STAFFING and PUBLIC PERSONNEL MANAGEMENT.

Personnel Administrator, The, published nine times a year (in January, February, April, May, June, August, September, October, and November), this is the official publication of the American Society for Personnel Administration. Its major purpose is to further the professional aims of the ASPA and the human resources management profession. Articles cover all aspects of personnel management, human resources development, and industrial relations.

The Personnel Administrator
American Society for Personnel
   Administration
19 Church Street
Berea, OH 44017

Personnel Administrator of Massachusetts v. Feeney, 60 L.Ed. 2d 870 (1979), U.S. Supreme Court case, which held that a state law operating to the advantage of males by giving veterans lifetime preference for state employment was not in violation of the equal protection clause of the 14th Amendment. The court found that a veterans preference law's disproportionate impact on women did not prove intentional bias.
See also VETERANS PREFERENCE.

Personnel and Guidance Journal, The, official journal of the American Personnel and Guidance Association, which publishes articles of common interest to counselors and personnel workers in schools, colleges, community agencies and government. Articles deal with current professional and scientific issues, new techniques or innovative practices and programs, APGA as an association and its role in society, critical integrations of published research, and research reports of unusual significance to practitioners. Published ten times a year, monthly from September through June.

The Personnel and Guidance Journal
American Personnel and Guidance
   Association
1607 New Hampshire Avenue, N.W.
Washington, DC 20009

personnel audit, evaluation of one or more aspects of the personnel function. *See* Eugene Schmuckler, "The Personnel Audit: Management's Forgotten Tool," *Personnel Journal* (November 1973); Paul Sheibar, "Personnel Practices Review: A Personnel Audit Activity," *Personnel Journal* (March 1974).

personnel director, manager responsible for all of an organization's personnel programs. In larger corporations, the personnel director is frequently a vice-president for personnel. *See* Herbert E. Myers, "Personnel Directors Are the New Corporate Heroes," *Fortune* (February 1976).

personnel examiner, job title for an individual who is a professional staff member of that unit of a personnel department which is concerned with selection.

personnel files: *see* PERSONNEL RECORDS.

personnel function, service to line management. Fred K. Foulkes and Henry M. Morgan, in "Organizing and Staffing the Personnel Function," *Harvard Business Review* (May–June 1977), warn that "personnel must, however, guard against becoming a servant to, as opposed to a service to, the line organization."
See also TRASHCAN HYPOTHESIS.

personnel game, the way some personnel directors, personnel officers, personnel technicians, personnel examiners, and vice presidents for personnel refer to their occupation.

personnel generalist, personnelist who, instead of concentrating in one subspeciality, is minimally competent in a variety of personnel management subspecialities.

personnel inventory: *see* MANNING TABLE.

personnelist, also called PERSONNEL MANAGER, one who is professionally engaged in the practice of personnel management. *See* George Ritzer and Harrison M. Trice, *An Occupation in Conflict: A Study of the Personnel Manager* (Ithaca, N.Y.: New York State School of Industrial and Labor Relations, Cornell University, 1969); Tony J. Watson, *The Personnel Managers: A Study in the Sociology of Work and Employment* (London: Routledge and Kegan Paul, 1977).

personnel jacket, file folder containing all personnel data on, and personnel actions pertaining to, an employee.

Personnel Journal, monthly that publishes articles on all aspects of industrial relations, human relations, and personnel management.

Personnel Journal
1131 Olympic Blvd.
Santa Monica, CA 90404

personnel journals, see separate entries for the following:

Academy of Management Journal
Academy of Management Review
Administrative Management
Administrative Science Quarterly
Arbitration Journal
Business History Review
Business and Society Review
California Management Review
Civil Service Journal
Columbia Journal of World Business
Compensation Review
Fortune
Havard Business Review
Human Relations
Human Resources Abstracts
Human Resource Management
Human Resources Planning

Table 6-1: Major Activities of the Corporate Personnel Unit
(668 Companies)

Activity	All Corporate Staffs	Corporate Unit Is Only Unit	Personnel Units also at Intermediate Level	Personnel Units also at Intermediate and Plant Levels	Personnel Units also at Group Intermediate and Plant Levels
	100%	100%	100%	100%	100%
Compensation	67	61	74	78	78
Equal employment opportunity	66	58	71	80	74
Benefits	64	49	72	77	74
Recruitement, selection, employment	64	69	64	64	52
Contract negotiations	59	25	46	61	57
Training and development	58	54	66	63	48
Compensation of managers	57	42	67	73	74
Labor relations	54	35	66	75	65
Recruitment of managers	53	42	59	66	70
Compensation of senior management	49	30	59	71	78
Managerial training	48	38	57	57	56
Occupational safety and health	47	38	52	56	48
General administration	45	58	43	35	30
Communication	44	36	48	52	52
Planning and research	44	35	48	56	56
Monitoring compliance re OSHA	42	31	43	53	44
Organization development	41	27	51	56	74
Manpower forecasting and planning	40	31	46	53	44
Compensation, hourly and nonsupervisory	39	40	41	37	35
Medical programs	36	28	38	44	44
Employee publications	36	26	45	44	48
Organization structure	36	23	44	54	44
Recruitment, selection, employment-hourly	32	28	31	27	35
Safety	31	26	32	36	30
Employee services	30	28	36	35	9
Grievance handling	28	29	33	20	22
Sales compensation	28	21	34	22	26
Employee attitude surveys	26	18	30	35	35
Training, hourly	25	32	29	15	22
Industrial hygiene	24	18	22	32	22
Sales recruitment	23	20	29	23	26
Human resource accounting	23	18	25	33	26
Training of the disadvantaged	19	20	25	17	9
Recreation	19	21	19	20	0
Sales training	19	17	22	16	17
Human productivity analysis	18	14	22	21	26
Food service	16	15	18	16	9

SOURCE: Allen R. Janger, *The Personnel Function: Changing Objectives and Organization* (N.Y.: The Conference Board, Inc., 1977), p. 63.

Industrial and Labor Relations Review
Industrial Management
Industrial Relations
Industrial Relations Law Journal
International Journal of Group Psychotherapy
Journal of Applied Behavioral Science
Journal of European Industrial Training
Journal of Human Resources
Labor History
Labor Law Journal
Labor Studies Journal
Michigan Business Review
Monthly Labor Review
Organizational Behavior and Human Performance
Organizational Dynamics
Pension World
Personnel

Personnel Administrator
Personnel and Guidance Journal
Personnel Journal
Personnel Literature
Personnel Management
Personnel Management Abstracts
Personnel Psychology
Psychological Review
Public Administration Review
Public Personnel Management
Public Productivity Review
Sloan Management Review
Supervisory Management
Training
Training and Development Journal

Personnel Literature, monthly bibliography compiled by the library of the U.S. Office of Personnel Management.

Personnel Literature
Superintendent of Documents
Government Printing Office
Washington, DC 20402

personnel management: *see* PERSONNEL ADMINISTRATION.

Personnel Management (PM), this monthly is the official journal of The Institute of Personnel Management of Great Britain and publishes articles by scholars and practitioners on all aspects of personnel management and industrial relations.

Personnel Management
Business Publications, Ltd.
117 Waterloo Road
London, ENGLAND SE1 8UL

Personnel Management Abstracts (PMA), this quarterly abstracts major articles in personnel management magazines, journals, and books that relate to the management of people and organizational behavior.

Personnel Management Abstracts
Office of Publications
Graduate School of Business Administration
University of Michigan
Ann Arbor, MI 48104

personnel management evaluation, formal effort to determine the effectiveness of any or all of an organization's personnel management program. *See* Michael E. Gordon, "Three Ways to Effectively Evaluate Personnel Programs," *Personnel Journal* (July 1972); Donald J. Peterson and Robert L. Malone, "The Personnel Effectiveness Grid (PEG): A New Tool for Estimating Personnel Department Effectiveness," *Human Resource Management* (Winter 1975).

personnel manager: *see* PERSONNELIST.

personnel manual, written record of an organization's personnel policies and procedures. *See* William B. Cobaugh, "When It's Time to Rewrite Your Personnel Manual," *Personnel Journal* (December 1978).
See also FEDERAL PERSONNEL MANUAL.

personnel officer, common job title for the individual responsible for administering the personnel program of an organizational unit.

personnel planning, process that (1) forecasts future supply and demand for various categories of personnel, (2) determines net shortages or excesses, and (3) develops plans for remedying or balancing these forecasted situations.
See also HUMAN RESOURCES PLANNING.

personnel practices, prohibited: *see* MERIT SYSTEM PRINCIPLES.

personnel psychology, that branch of psychology "concerned with individual differences in behavior and job performance and with measuring and predicting such differences," according to Wayne F. Cascio, in *Applied Psychology in Personnel Management* (Reston, VA.: Reston Publishing Company, 1978).

Personnel Psychology, quarterly aimed at operating personnel officials, personnel technicians and industrial psychologists. The articles in each issue are confined to reports on personnel management research and reviews of books relating to industrial psychology, human resource management, personnel practices, and organizational behavior.

Personnel Psychology
P.O. Box 6965
College Station
Durham, NC 27708

personnel ratio, number of full-time employees of a personnel department (usually exclusive of clerical support) per 100 employees of the total organization. *See* Thomas L. Wood, "The Personnel Staff: What Is a Reasonable Size?" *Personnel Journal* (March 1967).

personnel records, also called PERSONNEL FILES, all recorded information about employees kept by an employer, usually in the form of, and under the name, "personnel files." *See* Mordechai Mironi, "The Confidentiality of Personnel Records: A Legal and Ethical View," *Labor Law Journal (May 1974).*

personnel research, also called INDUSTRIAL RELATIONS RESEARCH, systematic inquiry into any or all of those problems, policies, programs, and procedures growing out of the employee-employer relationship. For a summary of the origins and importance of personnel management research, *see* Thomas H. Patten, Jr., "Personnel Research: Status Key," *Management of Personnel Quarterly* (Fall 1965). *See also* John R. Hinrichs, "Characteristics of the Personnel Research Function," *Personnel Journal* (August 1969).

Personnel Review: see INSTITUTE OF PERSONNEL MANAGEMENT.

personnel runaround, what happens to job applicants who apply for positions for which individuals have been preselected.
See also REALPOLITIK.

personnel selection, also called SELECTION and EMPLOYEE SELECTION, the object of a personnel/employee selection program is to

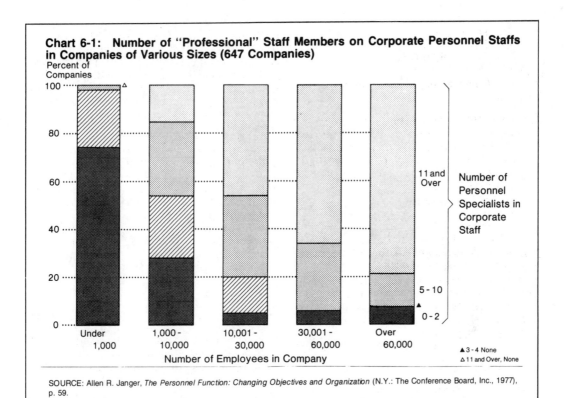

Chart 6-1:   Number of "Professional" Staff Members on Corporate Personnel Staffs in Companies of Various Sizes (647 Companies)

Percent of Companies

SOURCE: Allen R. Janger, *The Personnel Function: Changing Objectives and Organization* (N.Y.: The Conference Board, Inc., 1977), p. 59.

choose for employment those applicants who best meet an organization's needs in particular jobs. *See* Mary Green Miner and John B. Miner, *Employee Selection Within the Law* (Washington, D.C.: The Bureau of National Affairs, Inc., 1978). *See* chart p. 283.

personnel technician, job title for an individual who is a professional staff member of a specialized unit (recruitment, classification and pay, examinations, etc.) of a personnel department.

Personnel Tests for Industry (PTI), short, low-level intelligence battery used for screening of industrial personnel applicants (*i.e.,* laborer, maintenance and service worker, messenger). Battery includes a 5-minute Verbal Test, a 20-minute Numerical Test, and a 15-minute Oral Direction Test. Tests may be used together or separately. TIME: 5-40 minutes. AUTHOR: Charles R. Langmuir. PUBLISHER: Psychological Corporation (*see* TEST PUBLISHERS).

personnel textbooks, personnel textbooks abound. Listed below is a representative sample:

Dale J. Beach, *Personnel: The Management of People at Work* (N.Y.: Macmillan,

3rd ed., 1975); Richard W. Beatty and Craig Eric Schneier, *Personnel Administration: An Experiential/Skill-Building Approach* (Reading, Mass.: Addison-Wesley, 1977); Elmer H. Burack and Robert D. Smith, *Personnel Management: A Human Resource Systems Approach* (St. Paul, Minn.: West Publishing, 1977); Lloyd L. Byars and Leslie W. Roe, *Personnel Management: Concepts and Applications* (Philadelphia: W. B. Saunders Co., 1979); Herbert J. Chruden and Arthur W. Sherman, Jr., *Personnel Management* (Cincinnati: South-Western Publishing, 4th ed., 1972); Gary Dessler, *Personnel Management: Modern Concepts and Techniques* (Reston, VA.: Reston Publishing Co., 1978); Wendell L. French, *The Personnel Management Process* (Boston: Houghton Mifflin, 4th ed., 1978); William F. Glueck, *Personnel: A Diagnostic Approach* (Dallas, Texas: Business Publications, rev. ed., 1978); Michael J. Jucius, *Personnel Management* (Homewood, Ill.: Richard D. Irwin, 9th ed., 1979); Robert L. Mathis and John H. Jackson, *Personnel: Contemporary Perspectives and Applications* (St. Paul, Minn.: West Publishing, 2nd ed., 1979); Leon C. Megginson, *Personnel and Human Resources Administration* (Homewood, Ill.: Richard D. Irwin, 3rd ed., 1977); John B. Miner and Mary Green Miner, *Personnel and Industrial Relations: A Managerial Approach* (N.Y.: Macmillan,

3rd ed., 1977); Mitchel S. Novit, *Essentials of Personnel Management* (Englewood Cliffs, N.J.: Prentice-Hall, 1979); George S. Odiorne, *Personnel Administration by Objectives* (Homewood, Ill.: Richard D. Irwin, 1971); Thomas H. Patten, Jr. (ed.), *Classics of Personnel Management* (Oak Park, Ill.: Moore Publishing Co., 1979); Paul Pigors and Charles A. Myers, *Personnel Administration: A Point of View and a Method* (N.Y.: McGraw-Hill, 1973); Stephen P. Robbins, *Personnel: The Management of Human Resources* (Englewood Cliffs, N.J.: Prentice-Hall, 1978); George Strauss and Leonard R. Sayles, *Personnel: The Human Problems of Management* (Englewood Cliffs, N.J.: Prentice-Hall, 3rd ed., 1972); Joseph P. Yaney, *Personnel Management: Reaching Organizational and Human Goals* (Columbus, Ohio: Charles E. Merrill, 1975); Dale Yoder, *Personnel Management and Industrial Relations* (Englewood Cliffs, N.J.: Prentice-Hall, 6th ed., 1970).

PERT, acronym for "Program Evaluation and Review Technique," a planning and control process that requires identifying the accomplishments of programs and the time and resources needed to go from one accomplishment to the next. A PERT diagram would show the sequence and interrelationships of activities from the beginning of a project to the end. *See* J. D. Wiest and F. K. Levy, *A Management Guide to PERT/CPM* (Englewood Cliffs, N.J.: Prentice-Hall, 2nd ed., 1977).

Peter Principle, promulgated by Laurence J. Peter, in his worldwide best seller, *The Peter Principle: Why Things Always Go Wrong*, with Raymond Hull (N.Y.: William Morrow, 1969), the "principle" held that "in a hierarchy every employee tends to rise to his level of incompetence." Corollaries of the Peter Principle hold that "in time, every post tends to be occupied by an employee who is incompetent to carry out its duties." In answer to the logical question of who then does the work that has to be done, Peter asserts that "work is accomplished by those employees who have not yet reached their level of incompetence."

See also REALPOLITIK.

Petrillo, James Caesar (1892-   ), president of the American Federation of Musicians from 1940 to 1958. For a biography, *see* Robert D. Leiter, *The Musicians and Petrillo* (N.Y.: Bookman Associates, 1953).

PGW: *see* LABOR ORGANIZATION, Plant Guard Workers of America, International Union, United.

phantom-stock plan, incentive plan that grants an executive a theoretical number of shares of stock—phantom stock. Since the executive is told that he or she will be paid a cash bonus at some later date that is equal to the then value of the theoretical or phantom shares, there should exist within the executive a great desire to see the value of the company's stock appreciate.

phantom unemployment, jobless citizens who, for a variety of reasons, fall between the statistical cracks and are never officially counted among the unemployed. They have the double misfortune of being both unemployed and "invisible" to their government. For an analysis, *see* Alan Mark Mendelson, "Phantom Unemployment: What Government Figures Don't Tell," *Washington Journalism Review* (April–May 1978).

phased testing, also called PROGRESS TESTING, testing of those in a training program after specific phases of the program.

phatic language, any language used to create an atmosphere of sociability rather than to convey information. For example, a manager might observe that "It's nice weather today" or ask an employee "How are you?" before being critical of some aspect of the employee's work. The initial phatic language is an attempt to make the employee more receptive to the ensuing criticism.

Phelps Dodge Corp. v. National Labor Relations Board, 313 U.S. 177 (1946), U.S. Supreme Court case, which held that an employer subject to the National Labor Relations Act cannot refuse to hire individuals solely because of their affiliation with a union.

phenomenology, frame of reference with which to view organizational phenomena. To a phenomenologist, an organization exists on two planes—in reality and in the mind of the person perceiving its actions. Phenomenology is the integrated study of reality as well as its perceptions. According to Howard E. McCurdy, in "Fiction, Phenomenology, and Public Administration," *Public Administration Review* (January–February 1973), "Under phenomenology, concepts as 'hierarchy' and 'patterned behavior' are not seen as objects; rather they are concepts created intuitively and supported by fictions in order to help us conceptualize and eventually manipulate reality." For a broad introduction to the concept, *see* Pierre Thevenaz, *What*

PERT DIAGRAM FOR PUBLICATION OF A DIRECTORY

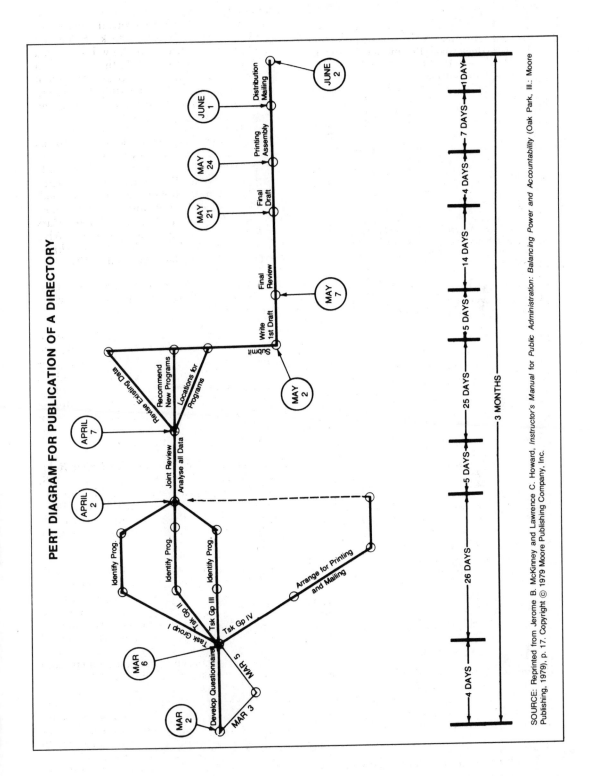

SOURCE: Reprinted from Jerome B. McKinney and Lawrence C. Howard, *Instructor's Manual for Public Administration: Balancing Power and Accountability* (Oak Park, Ill.: Moore Publishing, 1979), p. 17. Copyright © 1979 Moore Publishing Company, Inc.

Is Phenomenology? (Chicago: Quadrangle Books, 1962).

Philadelphia Plan, equal opportunity compliance program that requires bidders on all federal and federally-assisted construction projects exceeding $500,000 to submit affirmative action plans setting specific goals for the utilization of minority employees. The plan went into effect on July 18, 1969 in the Philadelphia area and affected six of the higher-paying trades in construction—iron work, plumbing and pipefitting, steamfitting, sheetmetal work, electrical work, and elevator construction work.

The plan was issued under Executive Order 11246 of 1965, which charges the Secretary of Labor with responsibility for administering the government's policy requiring equal employment opportunity in federal contracts and federally-assisted construction work.

Phillips Curve, graphic presentation of the theory put forth in 1958 by the British economist, A. W. Phillips, holding that there is a measurable, direct relationship between unemployment and inflation. In short, as unemployment declines, wages and prices can be expected to rise. For an analysis, *see* N. J. Simler and A. Tella, "Labor Reserve and The Phillips Curve," *Review of Economics and Statistics* (February 1968).

Phillips v. Martin Marietta: *see* SEX PLUS.

philosophy: *see* MANAGERIAL PHILOSOPHY.

physical examination, medical review to determine if an applicant is able to perform the duties of a position.

Physicians National Housestaff Association: *see* LABOR ORGANIZATION.

Pickering **v. Board of Education** 391 U.S. 563 (1968), U.S. Supreme Court case, which held that when public employees' rights to freedom of speech are in question, the special duties and obligations of public employees cannot be ignored; the proper test is whether the government's interest in limiting public employees' "opportunities to contribute to public debate is . . . significantly greater than its interest in limiting a similar contribution by any member of the general public." The court identified six elements which would generally enable the state to legitimately abridge a public employee's freedom of expression:

1. The need for maintaining discipline and harmony in the workforce.
2. The need for confidentiality.
3. The possibility that an employee's position is such that his or her statements might be hard to counter due to his or her presumed greater access to factual information.
4. The situation in which an employee's statements impede the proper performance of work.
5. The instance where the statements are so without foundation that the individual's basic capability to perform his or her duties comes into question.
6. The jeopardizing of a close and personal loyalty and confidence.

In addition to the above factors, it has been held that the nature of the remarks or expression, degree of disruption, and likelihood that the public will be prone to accepting the statements of an employee because of his or her position must be weighed. In general, however, only expressions on matters of public concern, as opposed to those primarily of interest to co-workers, are subject to constitutional protection.

picketing, occurs when one or more persons are present at an employer's business in order (1) to publicize a labor dispute, (2) to influence others (both employees and customers) to withhold their services or business, and/or (3) to demonstrate a union's desire to represent the employees of the business being picketed.

The U.S. Supreme Court held, in the case of *Thornhill* v. *Alabama*, 310 U.S. 88 (1940), that the dissemination of information concerning the facts of a labor dispute was within the rights guaranteed by the 1st Amendment. However picketing may be lawfully enjoined if it is not peaceful, for an unlawful purpose, or in violation of some specific state or federal law.

See also the following entries:
AMERICAN STEEL FOUNDRIES V. TRI-CITY CENTRAL TRADES COUNCIL
ANTI-STRIKEBREAKER ACT OF 1936
CHAIN PICKETING
COMMON SITUS PICKETING
CROSS PICKETING
HUDGENS V. NATIONAL LABOR RELATIONS BOARD
LABOR BOARD V. FRUIT PACKERS
LAUF V. E.G. SHINNER AND COMPANY
MASS PICKETING
ORGANIZATIONAL PICKETING
RECOGNITION PICKETING
SEARS ROEBUCK & CO. V. SAN DIEGO COUNTY DISTRICT COUNCIL OF CARPENTERS
SENN V. TILE LAYERS' PROTECTIVE UNION
TEAMSTERS, LOCAL 695 V. VOGT
UNFAIR LABOR PRACTICES (UNIONS)
UNITED STATES V. HUTCHESON

picket line, dues: *see* DUES PICKET LINE.

piece rate, also called PIECE-WORK RATE, incentive wage program in which a predetermined amount is paid to an employee for each unit of output.

    See also DIFFERENTIAL PIECE RATE.

piece rate nibbling: *see* NIBBLING.

piece work, differential: *see* DIFFERENTIAL PIECE WORK.

piece-work rate: *see* PIECE RATE.

Pillard, Charles H. (1918-   ), became president of the International Brotherhood of Electrical Workers in 1968.

pilot study, method of testing and validating a survey research instrument by administering it to a small sample of the subject population. According to Sigmund Nosow, in "The Use of the Pilot Study in Behavioral Research," *Personnel Journal* (September 1974), "there is a significant latent use for the pilot study, in a sense somewhat related to feasibility, and that is the creation of a climate of acceptance for such research. For organizations which have not used such research, it is very possible that the acceptance function may be the most important one for a pilot study."

pilot testing, experimental testing of a newly devised test in order to discover any problems before it is put into operational use.

pink-collar jobs, those jobs in which noncollege women form the bulk of the labor force, in which the pay is usually low in comparison to men of the same or lower educational levels, in which unionization is nil or weak, and where "equal-pay-for-equal-work" provisions are of little effect because women tend to compete only with other women are pink-collar jobs. *Pink-collar workers* include nurses, elementary school teachers, typists, telephone operators, secretaries, hairdressers, waiters and waitresses, private household workers, etc. *See* Louise Kapp Howe, *Pink Collar Workers* (New York: G. P. Putnam's Sons, 1977)

***Pittsburgh Press Co.* v. *The Pittsburgh Commission on Human Relations*,** 413 U.S. 376 (1973), U.S. Supreme Court case, which held that a municipal order forbidding newspapers to segregate job announcements according to sex when gender is not a required qualification did not violate the constitutional freedom of the press.

placement, acceptance by an employer or hiring authority of a candidate for a position as a direct result of the efforts of an employment agency or central personnel office. *See* Ronald C. Pilenzo, "Placement by Objectives," *Personnel Journal* (September 1973).

Planners, Estimators, and Progressmen, National Association of: *see* LABOR ORGANIZATION.

planning, career: *see* CAREER PLANNING.

plan termination insurance, pension insurance available through the Pension Benefit Guarantee Corporation, which provides that in the event of the financial collapse of a private pension fund wherein the pension fund assests are not sufficient to meet its obligations, the interests of vested employees will be protected. *See* Powell Niland, "Reforming Private Pension Plan Administration," *Business Horizons* (February 1976).

Plant Guard Workers of America, International Union, United: *see* LABOR ORGANIZATION.

Plasterers' and Cement Masons' International Association of the United States and Canada, Operative: *see* LABOR ORGANIZATION.

Plate Printers', Die Stampers' and Engravers Union of North America, International: *see* LABOR ORGANIZATION.

platykurtic, frequency distribution or curve that is more flat-topped, as opposed to peaked, than a normal curve.

PLSA: *see* LABOR ORGANIZATION, Pacific Log Scalers Association.

Plumbing and Pipe Fitting Industry of the United States and Canada, United Association of Journeymen and Apprentices of the: *see* LABOR ORGANIZATION.

plural executive, concept that has a committee assuming the normal responsibilities of an executive. For an account of this in action, *see* William H. Mylander, "Management by Executive Committee," *Harvard Business Review* (May–June 1955).

PM: *see* PERSONNEL MANAGEMENT (journal).

PMA: *see* PERSONNEL MANAGEMENT ABSTRACTS.

PML: *see* LABOR ORGANIZATION, Pattern Makers' League of North America.

pneunoconiosis: *see* BLACK LUNG DISEASE.

PNHA: *see* LABOR ORGANIZATION, Physicians National Housestaff Association.

point system, also called POINT METHOD, most widely used method of job evaluation, in which the relative worth of the jobs being evaluated is determined by totaling the number of points assigned to the various factors applicable to each of the jobs.
See also BEDAUX POINT SYSTEM.

Police, Fraternal Order of: *see* LABOR ORGANIZATION.

Policy and Practice Series: *see* BNA POLICY AND PRACTICE SERIES.

polygraph: *see* LIE DETECTOR.

POPA: *see* LABOR ORGANIZATION, Patent Office Professional Association.

population, also called SET and UNIVERSE, population, set or universe is composed of all of the cases in a class of things under statistical examination.
See also CANDIDATE POPULATION.

pork chopper, disrespectful term for a union official, who in the opinion of the workers he represents, is mainly concerned with his own pay and perquisites.

pork chops, slang term for the benefits that union workers expect from a strike.

portability, characteristic of a pension plan that allows participating employees to have the monetary value of accrued pension benefits transfered to a succeeding pension plan should they leave their present organization. According to Susan Meredith Phillips and Linda Pickthorne Fletcher, "The Future of the Portable Pension Concept," *Industrial and Labor Relations Review* (January 1977), "the portable pension concept has been offered as a solution to the problem of providing a secure retirement income to a mobile labor force."

portal-to-portal pay, wages paid while traveling from a plant, factory, or mine's entrance to the employee's specific work station and vice versa.

Portal-to-Portal Pay Act of 1947, federal statute that established a cutoff date for back claims of portal-to-portal pay (May 14, 1947) except where a written contract or established custom was already in effect.

Porter Co. **v.** *National Labor Relations Board*, 397 U.S. 99 (1970), U.S. Supreme Court case, which held that the National Labor Relations Board did not have the power to compel a company or union to agree to a substantive provision of a collective bargaining agreement.

POSDCORB, mnemonic device invented by Luther Gulick in 1937 to call attention to the various functional elements of the work of a chief executive. POSDCORB stands for the following activities:

Planning, that is working out in broad outline the things that need to be done and the methods for doing them to accomplish the purpose set for the enterprise;

Organizing, that is the establishment of the formal structure of authority through which work subdivisions are arranged, defined and co-ordinated for the defined objective;

Staffing, that is the whole personnel function of bringing in and training the staff and maintaining favorable conditions of work;

Directing, that is the continuous task of making decisions and embodying them in specific and general orders and instructions and serving as the leader of the enterprise;

Co-ordinating, that is the all important duty of interrelating the various parts of the work;

Reporting, that is keeping those to whom the executive is responsible informed as to what is going on, which thus includes keeping himself and his subordinates informed through records, research and inspection;

Budgeting, with all that goes with budgeting in the form of fiscal planning, accounting and control.

Source: Luther Gulick, "Notes on the Theory of Organization," in Luther Gulick and L. Urwick (eds.), *Papers on the Science of Administration* (N.Y.: Institute of Public Administration, 1937). For a re-examination, *see* David S. Brown, "POSDCORB Revisited and Revised," *Personnel Administration* (May–June 1966).

position, group of duties and responsibilities requiring the full or part-time employment of one individual. A position may, at any given time, be occupied or vacant.

position, benchmark: *see* BENCHMARK POSITION.

Position Analysis Questionnaire (PAQ), job analysis questionnaire that is a tool for quantitatively describing the various aspects of a job. It was developed and copyrighted by the Purdue University Research Foundation and is available from the Purdue University Book Store, 360 West State Street, West Lafayette,

IN 47906. *See* Ernest J. McCormick, Angelo S. DeNisi and James B. Shaw, "Uses of Position Analysis Questionnaires in Personnel Administration," *The Personnel Administrator* (July 1978).

position ceiling: *see* JOB CEILING.

position classification, process of using formal job descriptions to organize all jobs in a given organization into classes on the basis of duties and responsibilities for the purpose of delineating authority, establishing chains of command, and providing equitable salary scales. The principles and practices of position classification that are generally used in the public service are throwbacks to the heyday of the scientific management movement. They were conceived at a point in time—the second two decades of this century—when this school of management thought held sway, and they have never really adapted to modern currents of management thought. While position classifications tend to be required of public personnel programs, their allegiance to notions of the past occasions their frequent denunciation as unreasonable constraints on top management, sappers of employee morale, and for being little more than polite fictions in substance. For a "how-to-do-it" text, *see* Harold Suskin (ed.), *Job Evaluation and Pay Administration in the Public Sector* (Chicago: International Personnel Management Association, 1977). For a critical analysis, *see* Jay M. Shafritz, *Position Classification: A Behavioral Analysis for the Public Service* (N.Y.: Praeger, 1973).

See also SERIES OF CLASSES and SPECIFICATION.

position classification principles, basic principles of position classification that constitute the foundation of most position classification systems in government were promulgated by the 1919 Congressional Joint Commission on Reclassification of Salaries. The commission's 1920 Report recommended that:

1). positions and not individuals should be classified;
2). the duties and responsibilities pertaining to a position constitute the outstanding characteristics that distinguish it from, or mark its similarity to, other positions;
3). qualifications in respect to education, experience, knowledge, and skill necessary for the performance of certain duties are determined by the nature of those duties (Therefore, the qualifications for a position are an important factor in the determination of the classification of a position.);

4). the individual characteristics of an employee occupying a position should have no bearing on the classification of the position; and
5). persons holding positions in the same class should be considered equally qualified for any other position in that class.

For the total report, *see Report of the Congressional Joint Commission on Reclassification of Salaries* (H. Doc. 686, 66th Cong. 2nd Sess., March 12, 1920).

position description, formal statement of the duties and responsibilities assigned to a position.

position excepted by law/executive order/ civil service rule: *see* EXCEPTED POSITION.

position guide: *see* JOB DESCRIPTION.

position management, term used to describe the key management actions involved in the process of organizing work to accomplish the missions of federal departments and agencies. It involves, essentially, the determination of the needs for positions, the determination of required skills and knowledges, and the organization, grouping, and assignment of duties and responsibilities among positions. There are no absolute rules for managers to follow in the complex and evolving art of position management; however, there are basic *system* requirements for position management in government agencies, which are designed to assure that work structures and organizational designs are systematically being assessed for improvement, that positions are correctly classified, and that the allocation of positions and deployment of people reflect the best that is known about managing human resources.

position ranking, also called JOB GRADING, method of comparing jobs on a "whole job" basis in order to rank such jobs in a hierarchy from highest to lowest.

positively skewed: *see* SKEWNESS.

positive recruitment, aggressive action designed to encourage qualified individuals to apply for positions, as opposed to just waiting for the right person to "knock on the door."

positive reinforcement: *see* REINFORCEMENT.

positive strike, also NEGATIVE STRIKE, a *positive strike* is one whose purpose is to gain new benefits. A *negative strike* is one whose purpose is to prevent the loss of present benefits.

positive stroking: *see* STROKING.

WORK PLAN FOR UPDATE OF A TRADITIONAL POSITION CLASSIFICATION AND COMPENSATION PLAN

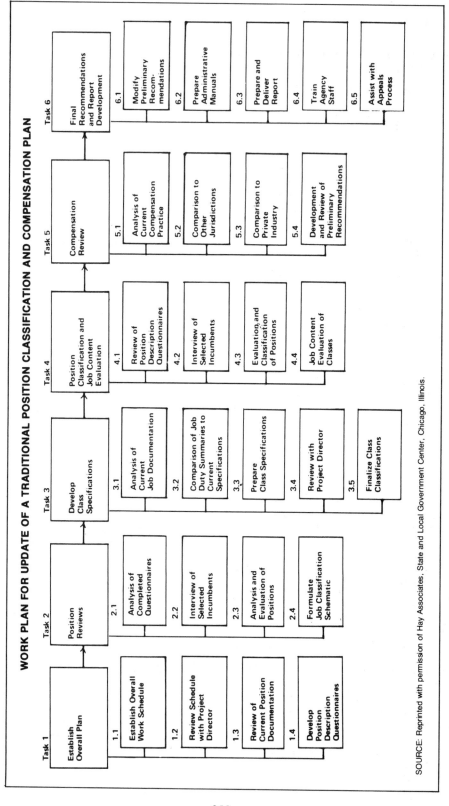

Task 1
Establish Overall Plan

1.1 Establish Overall Work Schedule

1.2 Review Schedule with Project Director

1.3 Review of Current Position Documentation

1.4 Develop Position Description Questionnaires

Task 2
Position Reviews

2.1 Analysis of Completed Questionnaires

2.2 Interview of Selected Incumbents

2.3 Analysis and Evaluation of Positions

2.4 Formulate Job Classification Schematic

Task 3
Develop Class Specifications

3.1 Analysis of Current Job Documentation

3.2 Comparison of Job Duty Summaries to Current Specifications

3.3 Prepare Class Specifications

3.4 Review with Project Director

3.5 Finalize Class Classifications

Task 4
Position Classification and Job Content Evaluation

4.1 Review of Position Description Questionnaires

4.2 Interview of Selected Incumbents

4.3 Evaluation and Classification of Positions

4.4 Job Content Evaluation of Classes

Task 5
Compensation Review

5.1 Analysis of Current Compensation Practice

5.2 Comparison to Other Jurisdictions

5.3 Comparison to Private Industry

5.4 Development and Review of Preliminary Recommendations

Task 6
Final Recommendations and Report Development

6.1 Modify Preliminary Recommendations

6.2 Prepare Administrative Manuals

6.3 Prepare and Deliver Report

6.4 Train Agency Staff

6.5 Assist with Appeals Process

SOURCE: Reprinted with permission of Hay Associates, State and Local Government Center, Chicago, Illinois.

positive transfer: *see* TRANSFER OF LEARNING.

Postal and Federal Employees, National Alliance of: *see* LABOR ORGANIZATION.

Postal Reorganization Act of 1970, federal statute that converted the Post Office Department into an independent establishment—within the executive branch of the government, but free from direct political pressures—to own and operate the nation's postal system known as the United States Postal Service. The act also provided for collective bargaining by postal workers—the first instance of true collective bargaining in the federal service.

Postal Security Police, Federation of: *see* LABOR ORGANIZATION.

Postal Supervisors, National Association of: *see* LABOR ORGANIZATION.

Postal Workers Union, American: *see* LABOR ORGANIZATION.

postbureaucratic organizations, in 1952, Dwight Waldo, in the *American Political Science Review,* prophesied a future society in which "bureaucracy in the Weberian sense would have been replaced by more democratic, more flexible, though more complex, forms of large-scale organization." Waldo called such a society "postbureaucratic." However, it remained for Warren G. Bennis, in the 1960s, to make the term particularly his own with a series of articles and books predicting the "end of bureaucracy." In its place, "there will be adaptive, rapidly changing *temporary systems.* These will be task forces composed of groups of relative strangers with diverse professional backgrounds and skills organized around problems to be solved. The groups will be arranged in an organic, rather than mechanical, model, meaning that they will evolve in response to a problem rather than to preset, programmed expectations. People will be evaluated not vertically according to rank and status, but flexibly according to competence. Organizational charts will consist of project groups rather than stratified functional groups." Warren G. Bennis and Philip E. Slater, *The Temporary Society* (N.Y.: Harper & Row, 1968). *Also see* Warren G. Bennis, *Changing Organizations* (N.Y.: McGraw-Hill, 1966). For a reader in organizational futures, *see* Jong S. Jun and William B. Storm, eds., *Tomorrow's Organizations: Challenges and Strategies* (Glenview, Ill.: Scott, Foresman and Co., 1973)

post-entry training, activities designed to upgrade the capabilities of an employee once he has joined an organization. Everything from executive development seminars constructed to improve the decisionmaking skills of top management to an orientation program which has as its objective acquainting new employees with the purposes and structure of the organization may be identified as post-entry training.

post-industrial society, term coined by Daniel Bell to describe the new social structures evolving in modern societies in the second half of the twentieth century. Bell holds that the "axial principle" of post-industrial society is the centrality of theoretical knowledge as the source of innovation and of policy formation for the society. Hallmarks of post-industrial society include a change from a goods-producing to a service economy, the pre-eminence of a professional and technical class, and the creation of a new "intellectual" technology. For the definitive work to date, *see* Daniel Bell, *The Coming of Post-Industrial Society: A Venture in Social Forecasting* (N.Y.: Basic Books, 1973). *Also see* John Schmidman, *Unions in Postindustrial Society* (University Park, Penn.: The Pennsylvania State University Press, 1979).

Postmasters of the United States, National League of: *see* LABOR ORGANIZATION.

post-test, test given at the end of a training program to determine if the training objectives have been met.

Potofsky, Jacob S. (1895–1979), president of the Amalgamated Clothing Workers of America from 1946 to 1972.

Pottery and Allied Workers, International Brotherhood of: *see* LABOR ORGANIZATION.

Poverty and Human Resources Abstracts: *see* HUMAN RESOURCES ABSTRACTS.

power of attorney, document authorizing one person to act as attorney for, or in the place of, the person signing the document.

power test, test intended to measure level of performance unaffected by speed of response—there is either no time limit or a very generous one.

Powderly, Terence Vincent (1849-1924), grand worthy foreman of the Knights of Labor (1879–1893), three-term mayor of Scranton, Pennsylvania, U.S. Commissioner General of Immigration (1897–1902), and chief of the Division of Information in the Bureau of Immigration (1907-1921). For an autobiography, *see* Harry J. Carman, Henry David, and Paul N. Guthrie (eds.), *The Path I Trod: The Autobiography of Terence V. Powderly* (N.Y.: Columbia University Press, 1940).

PPDSE: *see* LABOR ORGANIZATION, Plate Printers', Die Stampers' and Engravers' Union of North America, International.

PPE: *see* LABOR ORGANIZATION, Protection Employees, Independent Union of Plant.

PPF: *see* LABOR ORGANIZATION, Plumbing and Pipe Fitting Industry of the United States and Canada, United Association of Journeymen and Apprentices of the.

PPM: *see* PUBLIC PERSONNEL MANAGEMENT (journal).

practice effect, the influence of previous experience with a test on a later administration of the same test or a similar test—usually an increase in score on the second testing that can be attributed to increased familiarity with the directions, kinds of questions, or content of particular questions. Practice effect is greatest when the interval between testings is small, when the materials in the two tests are very similar, and when the initial test taking represents a relatively novel experience for the subjects.

prediction, differential: *see* DIFFERENTIAL VALIDATION.

predictive efficiency, measure of accuracy of a test or other predictive device in terms of the proportion of its predictions that have been shown to be correct.

predictive validity, obtained by giving a test to a group of subjects and then comparing the test results with the job performance of those tested. Predictive validity is the type of validity most strongly advocated by the EEOC, because predictively valid tests are excellent indicators of future performance.

predictor, any test or other employment procedure used to assess applicant characteristics and from which predictions of future performance may be made.

preferential hiring, union security agreement under which an employer, in hiring new workers, will give preference to union members.

preferential shop, work unit where the employer must give union members preference in hiring.

pregnancy, according to Equal Employment Opportunity Commission guidelines,

a written or unwritten employment policy or practice which excludes from employment applicants or employees because of pregnancy is in prima facie violation of Title VII (of the Civil Rights Act of 1964).

Disabilities caused or contributed to by pregnancy, miscarriage, abortion, childbirth, and recovery therefrom are, for all job-related purposes, temporary disabilities and should be treated as such under any health or temporary disability insurance or sick leave plan available in connection with employment. Written and unwritten employment policies and practices involving matters such as the commencement and duration of leave, the availability of extensions, and the accrual of seniority and other benefits and privileges, reinstatement and payment under any health or temporary disability insurance or sick leave plan, formal or informal, shall be applied to disability due to pregnancy or childbirth on the same terms and conditions as they are applied to other temporary disabilities. Where the termination of an employee who is temporarily disabled is caused by an employment policy under which insufficient or no leave is available, such a termination violates the Act if it has a disparate impact on employees of one sex and is not justified by business necessity.

See also the following entries:

GEDULDIG V. AIELLO
GENERAL ELECTRIC CO. V. GILBERT
MATERNITY LEAVE
NASHVILLE GAS CO. V. SATTY
SEX DISCRIMINATION
TITLE VII

Pregnancy Discrimination Act of 1978, an amendment to Title VII of the Civil Rights Act of 1964, which holds that discrimination on the basis of pregnancy, childbirth or related medical conditions constitutes unlawful sex discrimination. The amendment was enacted in response to the Supreme Court's ruling in *General Electric Co.* v. *Gilbert*, 429 U.S. 125 (1976) that an employer's exclusion of pregnancy related disabilities from its comprehensive disability plan did not violate Title VII. The amendment asserts that:

1. A written or unwritten employment policy or practice which excludes from employment opportunities applicants or employees because of pregnancy, childbirth or related medical conditions is in prima facie violation of Title VII.

2. Disabilities caused or contributed to by pregnancy, childbirth, or related medical conditions, for all job-related purposes, shall be treated the same as disabilities caused or

contributed to by other medical conditions, under any health or disability insurance or sick leave plan available in connection with employment. Written or unwritten employment policies and practices involving matters such as the commencement and duration of leave, the availability of extensions, the accrual of seniority and other benefits and privileges, reinstatement, and payment under any health or disability insurance or sick leave plan, formal or informal, shall be applied to disability due to pregnancy, childbirth, or related medical conditions on the same terms and conditions as they are applied to other disabilities. Health insurance benefits for abortion, except where the life of the mother would be endangered if the fetus were carried to term or where medical complications have arisen from an abortion, are not required to be paid by an employer; nothing herein, however, precludes an employer from providing abortion benefits or otherwise affects bargaining agreements in regard to abortion.

3. Where the termination of an employee who is temporarily disabled is caused by an employment policy under which insufficient or no leave is available, such a termination violates the Act if it has a disparate impact on employees of one sex and is not justified by business necessity.

pre-hire agreement, in the U.S. Supreme Court case of *National Labor Relations Board* v. *Iron Workers*, 54 L. Ed. 2d 586 (1978), the court accepted the NLRB's claim that, although the Taft–Hartley amendments to the National Labor Relations Act authorizes "pre-hire" agreements in construction (under which a union is not required to establish its majority status before bargaining with an employer), employers are nevertheless free to renounce the agreements at any time. Under the NLRB's ruling as affirmed by the Supreme Court, a pre-hire agreement is valid until an employer chooses to renounce it, at which time a union is limited to 30 days of recognitional picketing before it must either stop picketing or face an election to determine whether it represents a majority of the employees.

premium pay: *see* WORK PREMIUM.

prepaid legal services, employee benefit that has the employee and/or employer contribute to a fund that pays for legal services in the same way the medical insurance pays for hospitalization. *See* Guvenc G. Alpander and Jordon I. Kobritz, "Prepaid Legal Services: An Emerging Fringe Benefit," *Industrial and Labor Relations Review* (January 1978).

pre-retirement counseling, efforts on the part of an organization to give to those of its employees who will be eligible to retire information about all of the options that retirement entails. *See* Don F. Pellicano, "Overview of Corporate Pre-Retirement Counseling," *Personnel Journal* (May 1977).

See also RETIREMENT COUNSELING.

preselection, process by which a person is informally selected for a position prior to the normal competitive selection procedures. The ensuing selection process is necessarily a sham.

President's Advisory Commission on Labor–Management Policy: *see* NATIONAL COMMISSION FOR INDUSTRIAL PEACE.

Presidential Management Intern Program, established August 25, 1977, by Executive Order 12008, the Presidential Management Intern Program provides a special means of entry into the federal service for recipients of graduate degrees in general management with a public sector focus. Each year, up to 250 interns receive two-year appointments to developmental positions throughout the executive branch of the federal government. These internships differ from most entry-level positions in their emphasis on career development. Through rotational assignments, on-the-job training, seminars, discussion groups, career counseling, and other activities, interns are exposed to a variety of management areas and issues. At the successful completion of the two-year term, the interns are eligible for conversion to regular civil service appointments without further competition.

Presidential Management Intern Program
Office of Presidential Management
Internships
1900 E. Street, N.W.
Washington, DC 20415

President's Executive Interchange Program, federal government program, established in 1969 by Executive Order 11451, which arranges for managers from the public and private sector to work in a different sector for a year or more. *See* Herman L. Weiss, "Why Business and Government Exchange Executives," *Harvard Business Review* (July–August 1974).

President's Executive Interchange Program
1900 E. Street, N.W.
Washington, DC 20415
(202) 632-6834

pressure bargaining: *see* PRODUCTIVITY BARGAINING.

pre-test, test given before training in order to measure existing levels of proficiency. Such levels should later be compared to end-test scores in order to evaluate the quality of the training program as well as the attainments of the individuals being trained. Also a test designed for the purpose of validating new items and obtaining statistics for them before they are used in a final form.

prevailing wage, average pay for a specific job in a given geographical region. Because wages in the private sector are determined to a large extent by market forces, the prevailing wage concept is used more extensively in the public sector where wage "comparability" is frequently mandated by law. For an analysis, *see* David Lewin, "The Prevailing-Wage Principle and Public Wage Decisions," *Public Personnel Management* (November–December 1974).

Prevailing Wage Law: *see* DAVIS-BACON ACT OF 1931.

preventive discipline, premised on the notion that knowledge of disciplinary policies tends to inhibit infractions, preventive discipline seeks to heighten employees' awareness of organizational rules and policies.

preventive mediation, in order to avoid last minute crisis bargaining, the negotiating parties sometimes seek preventive mediation— the use of a mediator before an impasse has been reached.

PRF: *see* PERSONALITY RESEARCH FORM.

primary boycott, concerted effort by a union to withdraw and to induce others to withdraw from economic relationships with an offending employer. While the mere withholding of patronage is not unlawful, all contracts, combinations and conspiracies to do so are.

principles of classification: *see* POSITION CLASSIFICATION PRINCIPLES.

principles of management, fundamental truths or working hypotheses that serve as guidelines to management thinking and action. The first complete statement of the principles of management was produced by Henri Fayol in 1916. *See* his *General and Industrial Management*, trans. by Constance Storrs (London: Pitman, 1949). For a modern treatment, *see* George R. Terry, *Principles of Management* (Homewood, Ill.: Richard D. Irwin, 7th ed., 1977).
See also the following entries:

POSDCORB
PROVERBS OF ADMINISTRATION
SPAN OF CONTROL

Printing and Graphic Communications Union, International: *see* LABOR ORGANIZATION.

Prisoner Rehabilitation Act of 1965, federal statute that permits selected federal prisoners to work in the community while still in an inmate status.

Privacy Act of 1974, (Public Law 93-579), federal statute that reasserts the fundamental right to privacy as derived from the Constitution of the United States and provides a series of basic safeguards for the individual to prevent the misuse of personal information by the federal government.

The act provides for making known to the public the existence and characteristics of all personal information systems kept by every federal agency. It permits an individual to have access to records containing personal information on that individual and allows the individual to control the transfer of that information to other federal agencies for non-routine uses. The act also requires all federal agencies to keep accurate accountings of transfers of personal records to other agencies and outsiders, and to make the accountings available to the individual. It further provides for civil remedies for the individual whose records are kept or used in contravention of the requirements of the act.

Virtually all agencies of the federal government have issued regulations implementing the Privacy Act. These regulations generally inform the public how to determine if a system of records contains information on themselves, how to gain access to such records, how to request amendment of such records, and the method of internal appeal of an adverse agency determination on such a request. The Office of the Federal Register publishes an annual compilation, which includes descriptions of all the systems of records maintained by each agency of the federal government, the categories of individuals about whom each record system is maintained, and the agency rules and procedures whereby an individual may obtain further information. The most recent compilation, entitled Privacy Act Issuances, 1976 Compilation, is divided into five volumes, and is available at many public libraries or from the Superintendent of Documents. For an examination of the adequacy of privacy legislation, ... rivacy Protection and Personnel Administration: Are New Laws Needed?" *The Personnel Administrator* (April 1979).

private sector organization, all of those industries or activities considered to be within the domain of free enterprise.

See also THIRD SECTOR.

DISTINCTIONS BETWEEN THE PUBLIC AND PRIVATE SECTORS

Public	**Private**

1. MAJOR PURPOSE

Public	Private
A. Provides nonprofit goods and services	**A.** Sells goods and services for a profit.
B. Individual agencies survive based upon continuing legislative authorization.	**B.** Survival depends upon both profits and growth.
C. Decisions reflect client or constituent preferences.	**C.** Decisions are governed partly, at least by market factors (consumer demands).

2. CONSTRAINTS

Public	Private
A. Legal constraints permeate the entire administrative process.	**A.** Laws provide the outside limits of business activity. There is a large body of regulation, but compliance is secondary to profit-making.
B. Administrators are sensitive to the political climate in which their agencies must operate. Solutions reached through compromise are standard.	**B.** The market is the major constraining force and format. As long as customers are willing to buy, producers will endeavor to provide the quantity yielding the maximum profit.

3. FINANCIAL BASE

Public	Private
A. Resources obtained through the ability to borrow and to tax.	**A.** Resources obtained from return on investments
B. The budget process is fragmented and politicized.	**B.** Financial planning is integrated and related to income.

4. MANAGING PERSONNEL

Public	Private
A. The public service comprises persons selected through merit systems or by political appointment. The effort is to build a career service. Much of recruitment and the monitoring of promotions is handled by an independent regulatory commission.	**A.** The private workforce is generally selected on the basis of qualifications for a needed task, although nepotism is also common. There is usually little assurance of tenure. The promotion or separation of personnel is free of external rules and procedures.
B. The idea prevails that government is staffed by less efficient personnel, although supporting evidence for this view is limited.	**B.** The idea prevails that business operates with efficiency and free from the influence of politics. What might be called waste in government is often hidden under labels of research and development.

5. MEASURES OF EFFECTIVENESS

Public	Private
A. The legitimacy of the acts performed is a primary measure of effectiveness. Also concerns with building consensus and reducing conflict rank ahead of assessment of the costs of providing a public good. The criteria for effectiveness are likely to be subjective.	**A.** Effectiveness is gauged by such measures as the ratio of net sales to working capital, profit per dollar of sales, and net return on capital. The social costs associated with making a profit are seldom assessed.

SOURCE: Reprinted from Jerome B. McKinney and Lawrence C. Howard, *Public Administration: Balancing Power and Accountability* (Oak Park, Ill.: Moore Publishing, 1979), p. 43. Copyright © 1979 Moore Publishing Company, Inc.

probability, chance of an occurrence—the likelihood that an event will occur, expressed as a number from 0 to 1.

probationary employee, also PROBATIONARY PERIOD, new employees are frequently considered probationary until they satisfactorily complete a period of on-the-job trial—the *probationary period*. During this time they have no seniority rights and may be discharged without cause, so long as such a discharge does not violate laws concerning union membership and equal employment opportunity.

See also SAMPSON V. MURRAY.

probationary rate: *see* ENTRANCE RATE.

procedural rights, various protections that all citizens have against arbitrary actions by public officials.

process consultation (P-C), the standard work on process consultation, Edgar H. Schein's *Process Consultation: Its Role in Organization Development* (Reading, Mass.: Addison-Wesley Publishing Co., 1969), defines it as "a set of activities on the part of the consultant which help the client to perceive, understand, and act upon process events which occur in the client's environment."

According to Schein, P-C makes the following seven assumptions:

1. Managers often do not know what is wrong and need special help in diagnosing what their problems actually are.
2. Managers often do not know what kinds of help consultants can give to them; they need to be helped to know what kind of help to seek.
3. Most managers have a constructive intent to improve things but need help in identifying what to improve and how to improve it.
4. Most organizations can be more effective if they learn to diagnose their own strengths and weaknesses. No organizational form is perfect; hence every form of organization will have some weaknesses for which compensatory mechanisms need to be found.
5. A consultant could probably not, without exhaustive and time-consuming study, learn enough about the culture of the organization to suggest reliable new courses of action. Therefore, he must work jointly with members of the organization who do know the culture intimately from having lived within it.
6. The client must learn to see the problem for himself, to share in the diagnosis, and to be actively involved in generating a remedy. One of the process consultant's

roles is to provide new and challenging alternatives for the client to consider. Decision-making about these alternatives must, however, remain in the hands of the client.
7. It is of prime importance that the process consultant be expert in how to diagnose and how to establish effective helping relationships with clients. Effective P-C involves the passing on of both these skills.

prodigy, any individual who demonstrates phenomenal ability in an activity at an unusually early age. The 30-year-old president of a major corporation would either be a management prodigy or the inheritor of a controlling interest in the corporation.

Producer Prices and Price Indexes, U.S. Bureau of Labor Statistics' comprehensive monthly report on price movements of both farm and industrial commodities, by industry and stage of processing.

> *Producer Prices and Price Indexes*
> Superintendent of Documents
> Government Printing Office
> Washington, DC 20402

production bonus, regularly scheduled additional payments to workers for exceeding production quotas.

production workers, those employees directly concerned with the manufacturing or operational processess of an organization, as opposed to supervisory and clerical employees.

productivity, measured relationship between the quantity (and quality) of results produced and the quantity of resources required for production. Productivity is, in essence, a measure of the work efficiency of an individual, a work unit, or a whole organization. *See* Solomon Fabricant, *A Primer on Productivity* (N.Y.: Random House, 1969); Marc Holzer (ed.), *Productivity in Public Organizations* (Port Washington, N.Y.: Kennikat Press, 1976); Allan S. Udler, "Productivity Measurement of Administrative Services," *Personnel Journal* (December 1978).

productivity bargaining, there are two basic approaches to productivity bargaining—integrative bargaining and pressure bargaining. The latter is the stuff of confrontation and is best illustrated by the adversary model of labor relations—the most commonly adopted model in the United States. Its dysfunctional consequences—strikes and hostility—are well known. The other approach—integrative bargaining—is, in essence, participative management. It is premised upon the notions that a decrease in hostility is mutually advantageous and that management does not have a natural monopoly on brains. The crucial aspect of integrative bargaining is its joint procedures in defining problems, searching for alternatives, and selecting solutions.

The two productivity bargaining strategies are not mutually exclusive. Each side develops what it believes to be the best mix of both approaches for any given situation. While the end of labor–management conflict is far from at hand, mixed strategies are a step in the right direction. Since financial resources are finite and imagination is frequently infinite, a mixed approach to productivity bargaining holds out more hope for radical changes in job design and organization environment than for radical changes in salaries.

The best survey of productivity bargaining tactics in the private sector is R. B. McKersie and L. C. Hunter, *Pay, Productivity and Collective Bargaining* (London: The Macmillan Press, Ltd., 1973). For a public sector analysis, *see* Raymond D. Horton, "Productivity and Productivity Bargaining in Government: A Critical Analysis," *Public Administration Review* (July–August 1976).

profession, occupation requiring specialized knowledge that can only be gained after intensive preparation. Professional occupations tend to possess three features: (1) a body of erudite knowledge which is applied to the service of society; (2) a standard of success measured by accomplishments in serving the needs of society rather than purely serving personal gain; and (3) a system of control over the professional practice which regulates the education of its new members and maintains both a code of ethics and appropriate sanctions. The primary characteristic that differentiates it from a vocation is its theoretical commitment to rendering a public service. *See* Kenneth S. Lynn (ed.), *The Professions in America* (Boston: Houghton Mifflin, 1965); Edgar H. Schein, *Professional Education* (N.Y.: McGraw-Hill, 1972); Judith V. May, *Professionals and Clients: A Constitutional Struggle* (Beverly Hills, Calif.: Sage Publications, 1976).

Professional Airmen, Union of: *see* LABOR ORGANIZATION, under Air Line Pilots Association.

Professional Air Traffic Controllers Organization: *see* LABOR ORGANIZATION, under Marine Engineers' Beneficial Association, National.

The Little Red Hen: A Productivity Fable

Once upon a time there was a little red hen who scratched about the barnyard until she uncovered some grains of wheat. She turned to other workers on the farm and said: "If we plant this wheat, we'll have bread to eat. Who will help me plant it?"

"We never did that before," said the horse, who was the supervisor.

"I'm too busy," said the duck.

"I'd need complete training," said the pig.

"It's not in my job description," said the goose.

"Well, I'll do it myself," said the little red hen. And she did. The wheat grew tall and ripened into grain. "Who will help me reap the wheat?" asked the little red hen.

"Let's check the regulations first," said the horse.

"I'd lose my seniority," said the duck.

"I'm on my lunch break," said the goose.

"Out of my classification," said the pig.

"Then I will," said the little red hen, and she did.

At last it came time to bake the bread.

"Who will help me bake the bread?" asked the little red hen.

"That would be overtime for me," said the horse.

"I've got to run some errands," said the duck.

"I've never learned how," said the pig.

"If I'm to be the only helper, that's unfair," said the goose.

"Then I will," said the little red hen.

She baked five loaves and was ready to turn them in to the farmer when the other workers stepped up. They wanted to be sure the farmer knew it was a group project.

"It needs to be cleared by someone else," said the horse.

"I'm calling the shop steward," said the duck.

"I demand equal rights," yelled the goose.

"We'd better file a copy," said the pig.

But the little red hen turned in the loaves by herself. When it came time for the farmer to reward the effort, he gave one loaf to each worker.

"But I earned all the bread myself!" said the little red hen.

"I know," said the farmer, "but it takes too much paperwork to justify giving you all the bread. It's much easier to distribute it equally, and that way the others won't complain."

So the little red hen shared the bread, but her co-workers and the farmer wondered why she never baked any more.

SOURCE: *Federal News Clip Sheet* (June 1979).

Professional and Administrative Careers Examination (PACE), the principal means of entry into the federal government for liberal arts graduates, although it is open to all majors and applicants with equivalent experience. Each year, 10,000–12,000 hires are made through this route for more than 100 different positions and career fields. These are primarily administrative, technical, and professional positions offering developmental opportunities that lead trainees entering at grades GS-5 and 7 to target jobs at GS-9, 11, 12 and beyond. Applications of candidates who receive passing scores are placed in the inventory in score order and referred for positions as their scores are reached. Those whose college records show outstanding academic achievement receive supplementary credit. PACE replaced the Federal Service Entrance Examination (FSEE) in 1975. *See also* FEDERAL SERVICE ENTRANCE EXAMINATION.

professionalism, conducting one's self in a manner that characterizes a particular occupation. For example, a professional fireman is a full-time fireman who is thoroughly skilled in his trade. Nevertheless, a fireman is not a "professional" in the traditional sense.

professionalization, process by which occupations acquire professional status. For example, U.S. police departments are becoming more professional as increasing numbers of their members gain advanced degrees and take their ethical responsibilities more seriously. This process of professionalization will be complete only when the overwhelming majority of police officers meet the same high standards of the present minority. *See* M. S. Larson, *The Rise of Professionalism: A Sociological Analysis* (Berkeley, Calif.: University of California Press, 1977).

proficiency test, device to measure the skill or knowledge that a person has acquired in an occupation.

profit sharing, in 1889, profit sharing was defined at the International Congress on Profit Sharing as "an agreement freely entered into, by which the employees receive a share fixed in advance, of the profits." The Council of Profit-Sharing Industries of America has defined a profit sharing plan as "any procedure under which an employer pays to all employees in addition to good rates of regular pay, special current or deferred sums based not only upon individual or group performances but on the business as a whole."

Profit sharing plans fall into three basic categories

1). *immediate*—profits paid as soon as they are determined;
2). *deferred*—profits are credited to individual employee accounts and paid out according to specific withdrawal provisions; and
3). *combined*—any combination of the above.

For the history of profit sharing, *see* Lyle W. Cooper, "Profit Sharing," *Encyclopedia of the Social Sciences* (N.Y.: MacMillian, 1934). For a survey on current thinking, *see Guide to Modern Profit Sharing* (Chicago: Profit Sharing Council of America, 1973).

program, major organizational endeavor, mission oriented, that fulfills statutory or executive requirements and is defined in terms of the principal actions required to achieve a significant end objective.

program, also PROGRAMMER and PROGRAMMING, in computer terminology, a set of instructions telling the computer what to do. A *programmer* is a person who writes a computer program. As the programmer does his or her job, he or she can be said to be *programming* the computer.

Program Evaluation and Review Technique: *see* PERT.

program management: *see* PROJECT MANAGEMENT.

programmed instruction: *see* PROGRAMMED LEARNING.

programmed learning, also called PROGRAMMED INSTRUCTION, technique that has learning materials presented in a predetermined order, with provisions that permit the learner to proceed at his/her own pace and gain immediate feedback on his/her answers. Programmed learning usually requires the use of a teaching machine or programmed text. The rationale for and methodology of programmed learning is generally credited to B. F. Skinner. *See* J. G. Holland and B. F. Skinner, *The Analysis of Behavior: A Program for Self-Instruction* (N.Y.: McGraw-Hill, 1961). For a report of the efficacy of programmed instruction, *see* J. W. Buckley, "Programmed Instruction in Industry," *California Management Review* (Winter 1967).

programmer: *see* PROGRAM.

programming: *see* PROGRAM.

progressive discipline, concept predicated on the notion that employees are both aware of the behavior expected of them and subject to disciplinary action to the extent that they violate the norms of the organization. A policy of progressive discipline would then invoke penalties appropriate to the specific infraction and its circumstances.

progress testing: *see* PHASED TESTING.

prohibited personnel practices: *see* MERIT SYSTEM PRINCIPLES.

projective test, also called PROJECTIVE TECHNIQUE, any method which seeks to discover an individual's attitudes, motivations, and characteristic traits through responses to unstructured stimuli such as ambiguous pictures or inkblots. *See* D. L. Grant, W. Katkovsky, and D. W. Bray, "Contributions of Projective Techniques to Assessment of Management Potential," *Journal of Applied Psychology* (June 1967).

See also RORSCHACH TEST and THEMATIC APPERCEPTION TEST.

project manager, manager whose task is to achieve a temporary organizational goal using as his/her primary tool the talents of diverse specialists from the larger organization. The authority and responsibility of a project manager varies enormously with differing projects and organizations. *See* Paul O. Gaddis, "The Project Manager," *Harvard Business Review* (June 1959).

project management, also called PROGRAM MANAGEMENT, a project is an organizational unit created to achieve a specific goal. While a project may last from a few months to a few years, it has no further future. Indeed, a primary measure of its success is its dissolution. The project staff necessarily consists of a mix of skills from the larger organization. The success of project management is most dependent upon the unambiguous nature of the project's goal and the larger organization's willingness to delegate sufficient authority and resources to the project manager. Project or program management is an integral part of matrix organizations. *See* Charles C. Martin, *Project Management: How to Make it Work* (N.Y.: AMACOM, 1976); Arthur G. Butler, "Project Management: A Study in Organizational Conflict," *Academy of Management Journal* (March 1973). For a comparative focus, *see* Per Jonason, "Project Management, Swedish Style," *Harvard Business Review* (November–December 1971).

See also MATRIX ORGANIZATION and TASK FORCE.

proletariat, in ancient Rome, the word referred to those members of society who were so poor that they could contribute nothing to the state but their offspring. In the 19th century, Karl Marx used it to refer to the working class in general. Because of the word's political taint, it should not be used to refer simply to workers, but only to the "oppressed" workers.

promotion, process of advancing employees to positions that usually carry more responsibilities and greater salaries. For analyses of what it takes to get promoted, *see* Sexton Adams and Don Fyffe, *The Corporate Promotables* (Houston: Gulf Publishing Co., 1969); Vinay Kothari, "Promotional Criteria—Three Views," *Personnel Journal* (August 1976). For what to do when you can't get promoted, *see* Edward Roseman, *Confronting Unpromotability: How To Manage A Stalled Career* (New York, AMACOM, 1977).

See also the following entries:
CAREER PROMOTION
COMPETITIVE PROMOTION
HORIZONTAL PROMOTION
MERIT PROMOTION

promotion plan, a federal government promotion plan covers a group of positions, such as all regional positions below GS-12, or all regional supervisory positions, or all central office positions at GS-5 and below. The plan describes the methods to be followed in locating, evaluating, and selecting employees for promotion. It also explains what records will be kept, how information will be given to employees about the promotion program, etc.

protected classes/groups: *see* AFFIRMATIVE ACTION GROUPS.

Protection Employees, Independent Union of Plant: *see* LABOR ORGANIZATION.

Protestant ethic, also called WORK ETHIC, Max Weber's term from his 1904-05 book, *The Protestant Ethic and the Spirit of Capitalism*, which refers to his theory that modern capitalism has its origins in the Calvinistic concern for moral obligation and economic success. While some dispute Weber's historical analysis, any society whose members have a strong drive for work and the accumulation of wealth is colloquially said to have a "Protestant" or work ethic. For a history of the U.S. work ethic, *see* Daniel T. Rodgers, *The Work Ethic in Industrial America: 1850-1920* (Chicago: University of Chicago Press, 1978). For a present day analysis, *see* M. Scott Myers and Susan S. Myers, "Toward Understanding the Changing Work Ethic," *California Management Review* (Spring 1974).

proverbs of administration, a significant landmark in the history of administrative theory was Herbert A. Simon's refutation of the principles approach that dominated administrative thinking until after World War II. Simon asserted, in "The Proverbs of Administration," *Public Administration Review* (Winter 1946), that the principles of administration, like proverbs, almost always occur in mutually contradictory pairs:

> Most of the propositions that make up the body of administrative theory today share, unfortunately, this defect of proverbs. For almost every principle one can find an equally plausible and acceptable contradictory principle. Although the two principles of the pair will lead to exactly opposite organizational recommendations, there is nothing in the theory to indicate which is the proper one to apply.

provisional appointment, usually government employment without competitive examination because there is no appropriate eligible list available. Most jurisdictions have a 3, 6, or 12 month limitation on provisional appointments.

pseudo-effectiveness, according to Chris Argyris, in *Integrating the Individual and the Organization* (N.Y.: John Wiley & Sons, 1964), organizational pseudo-effectiveness is "a state in which no discomfort is reported but which, upon diagnosis, ineffectivenesss is found." Since the underlying ineffectiveness is not evident, the true costs of continuing in such a state remain hidden by compensatory mechanisms. Eventually, such compensatory mechanisms will require so much energy that they will influence the organization negatively and call attention to the underlying problem.

psychiatry, industrial/occupational: *see* OCCUPATIONAL PSYCHIATRY.

psychic income: *see* INTRINSIC REWARD.

psychobabble, indiscriminate use of psychological concepts and terms as an affected style of speech. R. D. Rosen, in *Psychobabble* (N.Y.: Atheneum, 1977), says that psychobabblers

> free-float in an all-purpose linguistic atmosphere, a set of repetitive verbal formalities that kills off the very spontaneity, candor, and understanding it pretends to promote.

It's an idiom that reduces psychological insight to a collection of standardized observations, that provides a frozen lexicon to deal with an infinite variety of problems. *Uptight,* for instance, is a word used to describe an individual experiencing anything from mild uneasiness to a clinical depression.... One is no longer fearful; one is *paranoid....* Increasingly, people describe their moody acquaintances as *manic-depressives,* and almost anyone you don't like is *psychotic* or at the very least *schizzed-out.*

psychological contract, Edgar H. Schein, in his *Organizational Psychology* (Englewood Cliffs, N.J.: Prentice-Hall, 2nd ed., 1970) asserts that the

> notion of a psychological contract implies that the individual has a variety of expectations of the organization and that the organization has a variety of expectations of him. These expectations not only cover how much work is to be performed for how much pay, but also involve the whole pattern of rights, privileges, and obligations between worker and organization. For example, the worker may expect the company not to fire him after he has worked there for a certain number of years and the company may expect that the worker will not run down the company's public image or give away company secrets to competitors. Expectations such as these are not written into any formal agreement between employee and organization, yet they operate powerfully as determinants of behavior.

For a discussion of this concept in the context of employment, *see* Emanuel C. Salemi and John B. Monohan, "The Psychological Contract of Employment: Do Recruiters and Students Agree?" *Personnel Journal* (December 1970); Michael H. Dunahee and Lawrence A. Wangler, "The Psychological Contract: A Conceptual Structure for Management/Employee Relations," *Personnel Journal* (July 1974).
See also EXPECTANCY THEORY.

Psychological Corporation, The: *see* TEST PUBLISHERS.

psychological examination: *see* PSYCHOLOGICAL TEST.

Psychological Inventory, California: *see* CALIFORNIA PSYCHOLOGICAL INVENTORY.

Psychological Review, bimonthly that publishes articles making theoretical contributions to any area of scientific psychology. Preference is given to papers that advance theory rather than review it.

> *Psychological Review*
> American Psychological Association, Inc.

1200 Seventeenth Street, N.W.
Washington, DC 20036

psychological stress analyzer: *see* LIE DE-
TECTOR.

psychological test, a general term for any effort (usually a standardized test) that is designed to measure the abilities or personality
traits of individuals or groups. *See* A. Anas-
tasi, *Psychological Testing* (N.Y.: Macmillan,
4th ed., 1976).

psychology, generally, the scientific study of
human and animal behavior. According to
Bergen Evans and Cornelia Evans, *A Dictionary of Contemporary American Usage*
(N.Y.: Random House, 1957),

> in an age which James Joyce has described
> as "jung and easily freudened," *psychology*
> is a word thrown about knowingly by about
> everyone capable of articulating a four-
> syllabled word, though not necessarily of
> spelling it. Basically it means the science of
> mind, of mental states or processes, the sci-
> ence of human nature.

See also the following entries:

DYNAMIC PSYCHOLOGY
INDUSTRIAL PSYCHOLOGY
PERSONNEL PSYCHOLOGY
VOCATIONAL PSYCHOLOGY

psychometrician, psychologist who deals
with mental tests and their associated statistical procedures.

psychometrics, that branch of psychology that
deals with mental tests and their associated
statistical procedures. *See* Judson Gooding,
"Psychometrics: The Use and Misuse of
Psychological Tests in Executive Employment," *Across The Board* (November 1976).

psychometry, mental measurements and/
or testing.

psychomotor test: *see* DEXTERITY TEST.

PTI: *see* PERSONNEL TESTS FOR INDUSTRY.

Public Administration Fellows, jointly sponsored by the National Association of Schools
of Public Affairs and Administration and the
U.S. Office of Personnel Management, this
program is designed to enhance understanding of the public policy process and the relationship between theory and practice in government by providing policy-level positions
in the executive branch of the federal government to college and university faculty
teaching in the field of public administration
and other supportive public policy areas.
Public Administration Fellows are placed in
federal agencies that best suit each Fellow's

qualifications and the agency's needs. Compensation, determined for each Fellow according to experience and educational background, generally ranges from GS-12 to
GS-15. Appointments are usually for a period
of one year, generally beginning in early September, and are located in the Washington,
D.C., metropolitan area. For further information, write:

> *Public Administration Fellows Program*
> NASPAA
> 1225 Connecticut Ave., N.W., Suite 300
> Washington, DC 20036

Public Administration Review (PAR), leading
professional journal on all aspects of managing public and nonprofit institutions.

> *Public Administration Review*
> American Society for Public
>   Administration
> 1225 Connecticut Ave., N.W.
> Washington, DC 20036

Public Administration Service (PAS), established in 1933 as a private, self-supporting,
not-for-profit institution dedicated to improving the quality and effectiveness of governmental operations. PAS performs a wide
variety of consulting and research work in
serving the special needs of governments and
other public service institutions. Its services
are provided on a cost–reimbursement basis
and range from technical studies of central
management problems to analyses of public
policy issues.

> *Public Administration Service*
> 1313 East 60th Street
> Chicago, Illinois 60637
> (312) 947-2000
>
> 1776 Massachusetts Ave., N.W.
> Washington, DC 20036
> (202) 833-2505

public bureaucracy: *see* BUREAUCRACY.

public employee, any person who works for a
governmental agency. Civilian public employment in the United States totaled 15.2
million in Fiscal Year 1976 (*see* table "Civilian Government Employment—1948-1976").

public employee relations, labor-management relations in the public sector. For texts,
see Hugh D. Jascourt (ed.), *Government
Labor Relations* (Oak Park, Ill.: Moore Publishing Co., 1979); Marvin J. Levine and
Eugene C. Hagburg, *Public Sector Labor Relations* (St. Paul, Minn.: West Publishing,
1979). *See* table p. 281.

Public Employees' Fair Employment Act:
see TAYLOR LAW.

CIVILIAN GOVERNMENT EMPLOYMENT — 1948-1976 (thousands)

Fiscal Year	Federal Exec. Branch	State & Local Government	All Government Units
1948	2,044	3,776	5,820
1949	2,075	3,906	5,981
1950	1,934	4,078	6,012
1951	2,456	4,031	6,487
1952	2,574	4,134	6,708
1953	2,532	4,282	6,814
1954	2,382	4,552	6,934
1955	2,371	4,728	7.099
1956	2,372	5,064	7,436
1957	2,391	5,380	7,771
1958	2,355	5,630	7,985
1959	2,355	5,806	8,161
1960	2,371	6,073	8,444
1961	2,407	6,295	8,702
1962	2,485	6,533	9,018
1963	2,490	6,834	9,324
1964	2,469	7,236	9,705
1965	2,496	7,683	10,179
1966	2,664	8,259	10,923
1967	2,877	8,730	11,607
1968	2,951	9,141	12,092
1969	2,980	9,496	12,476
1970	2,944	9,869	12,813
1971	2,883	10,257	13,140
1972	2,823	10,640	13,463
1973	2,775	11,065	13,840
1974	2,847	11,463	14,310
1975	2,848	12,025	14,873
1976	2,832	12,410	15,242

SOURCE: Adapted from *Special Analysis: Budget of the United States for the Fiscal Year 1978.*

Public Personnel Association: *see* INTERNATIONAL PERSONNEL MANAGEMENT ASSOCIATION.

public personnel management, personnel management in government. The essential difference between personnel management in the private sector and personnel management in the public sector can be summed up in one word—politics. The public personnel process is a political process; except in the most sophisticated jurisdictions, management processes are decidedly subordinate to political considerations. For texts, see N. Joseph Cayer, *Public Personnel Administration in the United States* (N.Y.: St. Martin's Press, 1975); O. Glenn Stahl, *Public Personnel Administration* (N.Y.: Harper & Row, 7th ed., 1976); Jay M. Shafritz, Walter L. Balk, Albert C. Hyde, and David H. Rosenbloom, *Personnel Management in Government: Politics and Process* (N.Y.: Marcel Dekker, 1978); Frank J. Thompson (ed.), *Classics of Public Personnel Policy* (Oak Park, Ill.: Moore Publishing Company, 1979). *See* charts pp. 282, 283.

Public Personnel Management (PPM), bimonthly journal of the International Personnel Management Association, which offers articles dealing with all aspects of personnel management in government.

Public Personnel Management
Suite 870
1850 K Street, N.W.
Washington, DC 20006

Public Productivity Review, quarterly devoted to all of the concerns of productivity enhancement in the public sector.

Public Productivity Review
Center for Productive Public
Management
John Jay College of Criminal Justice
City University of New York
445 West 59th Street
New York, NY 10019

public sector organization, any agency or institution funded, directly or indirectly, by public taxation.

See also THIRD SECTOR.

STATE COLLECTIVE BARGAINING LAWS

Coverage	States
1. All-inclusive laws	Florida,[a] Hawaii, Iowa, Massachusetts, Minnesota, Montana,[b] New Hampshire, New Jersey, New York,[a] and Oregon
2. "All" employees, separate laws	Alaska, California, Connecticut, Delaware, Kansas, Maine, Nebraska, North Dakota, Pennsylvania, Rhode Island, South Dakota, Vermont, and Wisconsin
3. *Some employees covered:*	
Teachers	Indiana and Maryland
Police and fire	Kentucky, Oklahoma, and Texas
Fire	Alabama,[c] Georgia,[c] and Wyoming
All but state civil service	Michigan and Washington
Local employees and teachers	Nevada
Fire and teachers	Idaho
Local employees and police	Missouri
4. No laws	Arizona, Arkansas, Colorado, Illinois,[d] Louisiana, Mississippi, New Mexico,[d] North Carolina, Ohio, South Carolina, Tennessee, Utah, Virginia, and West Virginia
5. *Employees covered by separate laws (even if other employees covered by other laws):*	
Teachers	Alaska, California, Connecticut, Delaware, Indiana, Idaho, Kansas, Maryland, Nebraska, North Dakota, Oklahoma, Rhode Island, Vermont, and Washington
Police and fire	Kentucky, Oklahoma, Pennsylvania, Rhode Island, South Dakota, and Texas
Fire	Alabama, Georgia, Idaho, Wyoming
State service	California, Connecticut, Maine, Rhode Island, Vermont, and Wisconsin

[a]Allow local governments to have own systems if in conformity with state laws.
[b]Except separate law for nurses.
[c]Law operative only upon enactment of local ordinances.
[d]State service under nonstatutory system.

SOURCE: Hugh D. Jascourt, *Government Labor Relations: Trends and Information for the Future* (Oak Park, Illinois: Moore Publishing, 1979), p. 10. Copyright © 1979 Moore Publishing Company, Inc.

Puerto Rico Federation of Labor (AFL-CIO): *see* AMERICAN FEDERATION OF LABOR–CONGRESS OF INDUSTRIAL ORGANIZATIONS.

Pulp and Paper Workers, Association of Western: *see* LABOR ORGANIZATION.

Purdue Pegboard Test, two-part, timed test designed to measure two types of activity, one requiring gross movements of hands, fingers, and arms, and the other involving tip-of-the-finger dexterity needed in small assembly work. TIME: 10/20 minutes. AUTHOR: Purdue Research Foundation. PUBLISHER: Science Research Association, Inc. (*see* TEST PUBLISHERS).

public works, generic term for government sponsored construction projects. *See* Ellis Armstrong (ed.), *History of Public Works in the United States: 1776-1976* (Chicago: American Public Works Association, 1976).

pyramid, also called ORGANIZATIONAL PYRAMID, colloquial term for an organization's hierarchy. According to Vance Packard, *The Pyramid Climbers* (N.Y.: McGraw-Hill, 1962),

> The number of ledges—or steps—in a company's hierarchy varies of course with the company's size and philosophy of organization. Some like tall, slender pyramids, with only a few people under each leader; others prefer short, squat pyramids. Occasionally, one literally sees these modern pyramids in brick and mortar, where the home office occupies a skyscraper with the suites of the highest officers at the pinnacle.

This is equally true for government. For example, in the U.S. State Department, the highest officials occupy the seventh and highest floor of their building. Policy is frequently said to come—not from any particular official—but simply from the "seventh floor."

See also FLAT ORGANIZATION.

Organization of a Central Personnel Office to Serve a City of 4000 Employees

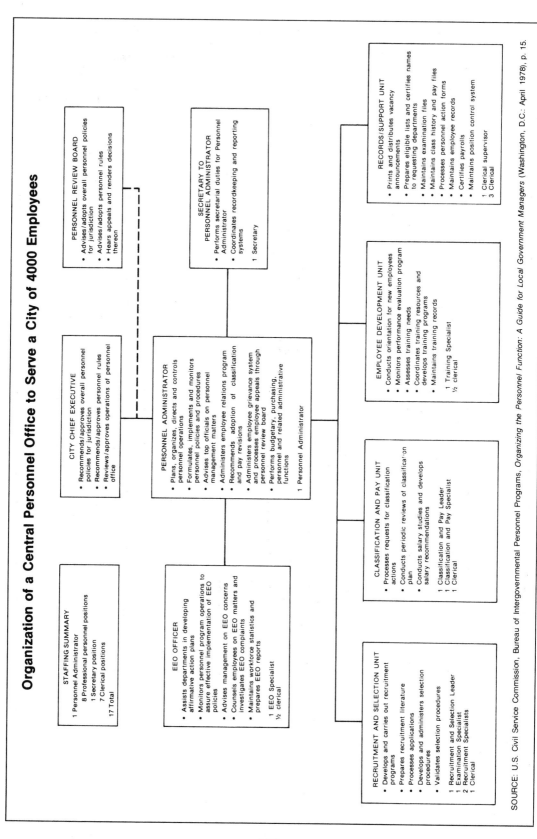

SOURCE: U.S. Civil Service Commission, Bureau of Intergovernmental Personnel Programs, *Organizing the Personnel Function: A Guide for Local Government Managers* (Washington, D.C.: April 1978), p. 15.

STEPS IN THE EMPLOYMENT PROCESS

Merit		Patronage

Merit

1. ANNOUNCEMENT

Patronage

Formally printed and posted statement of openings

Informal communication of the possibility of a job, usually sent out through campaign workers

2. APPLICATION

Applicant obtains qualifications and complete job interest card

Aspirant tells elected officials of his desire for public employment

If a vacancy occurs

3. EXAMINATION

Professions record of graduation or certification submitted.

Written test or the completion of a background resume required

Competence for doing the job checked either formally or informally

4. EVALUATION

Score assigned by civil service examiners and name placed on register in order

Clearance given by relevant political leader and informal order established

5. REFERRAL TO AGENCY REQUESTING APPLICATIONS

Top three names on register sent to agency

Names of persons highly recommended sent to agency

6. REFERENCE CHECK

References complete formal evaluation forms

References contacted by phone

7. SELECTION

Interviews

Interviews

Name goes back to civil service register

YES **NO**

Sponsor informed of non placement

8. YOU ARE HIRED

Selection and Induction

Selection and Induction

9. BEGIN WORK

SOURCE: Reprinted from Jerome B. McKinney and Lawrence C. Howard, *Public Administration: Balancing Power and Accountability* (Oak Park, Ill.: Moore Publishing, 1979), p. 287. Copyright © 1979 Moore Publishing Company, Inc.

Q

qualified handicapped individual: *see* HANDICAPPED INDIVIDUAL.

qualifying test, examination used to simply qualify or disqualify individuals for employment or promotion in contrast to tests that rank order individuals in terms of their scores.

Quality B School, when recruiting notices say that they are looking for someone who has an MBA from a "Quality B School", they are usually referring to the graduate programs in business from any of the following universities: Harvard, Stanford, Chicago, Penn (Wharton), Michigan, MIT (Sloan), Carnegie-Mellon, Northwestern, Dartmouth (Tuck), Columbia, UCLA, and New York University. However, quality, which is ignorant of ascribed status, is also to be found in hundreds of other schools of management, if only in smaller concentrations.

quality of working life, area of concern that addresses the problem of creating more humane working environments. For a summary of the "state of the art," *see* Louis E. Davis & Albert B. Cherns (eds.), *The Quality of Working Life* (N.Y.: The Free Press, 1975) volumes I and II. For an analysis of cooperative union-management projects, *see:* Edward E. Lawer III and John A. Drexler, Jr., "Dynamics of Establishing Cooperative Quality-of-Worklife Projects," *Monthly Labor Review* (March 1978).

See also NATIONAL CENTER FOR PRODUCTIVITY AND QUALITY OF WORKING LIFE.

Quarantine Inspectors National Association, Federal Plant: *see* LABOR ORGANIZATION.

quartile, one of three points that divide the test scores in a distribution into four equal groups.

questionnaire, set of questions to be answered by a subject. *See* J. L. Stone, "The Use of an Applicant Service Questionnaire," *Public Personnel Management* (March–April 1974); Donald P. Warwick and Charles A. Lininger, *The Sample Survey* (N.Y.: McGraw-Hill, 1975).

questionnaire, exit: *see* EXIT INTERVIEW.

quickie strike, spontaneous or unannounced strike of short duration.

Quill, Mike (1905-1966), full name MICHAEL JOSEPH QUILL, one of the founders of the Transport Workers Union of America and president of that union from 1936 until his death. For a biography, *see* L. H. Whittemore, *The Man Who Ran the Subways: The Story of Mike Quill* (N.Y.: Holt, Rinehart, and Winston, 1968).

quit, volunteered resignation. According to Ken Jennings, in "When A Quit Is Not a Quit," *Personnel Journal* (December 1971), a quit can be considered a discharge for the purposes of arbitral review if "intent to resign is not evidenced." Arbitrators have reasoned "that if this treatment of quit as discharge were not applied, management could escape from the 'just cause' provisions of the labor contract by insisting that an undesirable employee's quit (voluntary or coerced) was not subject to the grievance procedure."

quota: *see* GOAL.

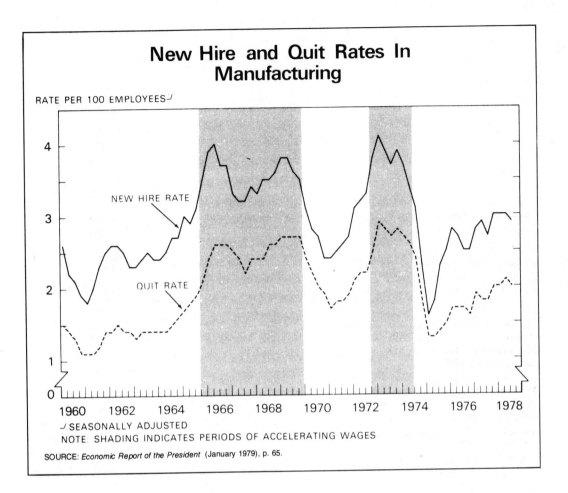

New Hire and Quit Rates In Manufacturing

RATE PER 100 EMPLOYEES⌐

NEW HIRE RATE

QUIT RATE

⌐ SEASONALLY ADJUSTED
NOTE: SHADING INDICATES PERIODS OF ACCELERATING WAGES

SOURCE: *Economic Report of the President* (January 1979), p. 65.

R

r: *see* CORRELATION COEFFICIENT.

race, a United Nations publication, *Race and Science* (N.Y.: UNESCO, 1961), has found that

> the term 'race' designates a group or population characterized by some concentrations, relative as to requency and distribution, of hereditary particles (genes) or physical characters, which appear, fluctuate, and often disappear in the course of time by reason of geographic and/or cultural isolation. The varying manifestations of these traits in different populations are perceived in different ways by each group. What is perceived is largely preconceived, so that each group arbitrarily tends to misinterpret the variability which occurs as a fundamental difference which separates that group from all others.

A more expansive definition is provided by G. E. Simpson and J. M. Yinger in *Racial and Cultural Minorities* (N.Y.: Harper & Row, 3rd ed., 1965). They find that there are really three basic approaches to race: (1) the "mystical" or "political" approach "has been the stock in trade in the chicanery of rabble rousers, fanatics, demagogues, adventurers, and charlatans (rational or psychopathic)", (2) the "administrative conception of race" has government actions based on certain "racial" categories established by legislative act or bureaucratic practice; (3) and the biological approach based on crude observations of obvious physical differences.

race categories, also ETHNIC CATEGORIES, the race/ethnic categories that the Equal Employment Opportunity Commission insists be used for EEO reporting purposes follow:

> *White, not of Hispanic Origin.* Persons having origins in any of the original peoples of Europe, North Africa, or the Middle East.
> *Black, not of Hispanic Origin.* Persons having origins in any of the black racial groups of Africa.
> *Hispanic.* Persons of Mexican, Puerto Rican, Cuban, Central or South American or other Spanish culture or origin, regardless of race.
> *American Indian or Alaskan Native.* Persons having origins in any of the original peoples of North America and who maintain cultural identification through tribal affiliation or community recognition.
> *Asian or Pacific Islander.* Persons having origins in any of the original peoples of the Far East, Southeast Asia, the Indian subcontinent, or the Pacific Islands. This area includes, for example, China, Japan, Korea, the Philippine Islands, and Samoa.

race differential: *see* SEX DIFFERENTIAL.

racist, any person or organization that consciously or unconsciously practices racial discrimination.

racketeering, labor: *see* LABOR RACKETEER.

Radio Association, American: *see* LABOR ORGANIZATION.

radius clause, provision used in some training program agreements that requires an employee not to seek other employment for a specified time over a specified geographic area, so that the investment made in the employee's training cannot be used to benefit a competitor.

raiding, generally, efforts by one organization to gain members of a competing organization for their own. As a tactic, raiding is used by both management and labor.

Railroad Retirement Act, the Railroad Retirement Act of 1934 was declared unconstitutional by the U.S. Supreme Court in *Railroad Retirement Board* v. *Alton Railroad Company*, 295 U.S. 330 (1935). The Railroad Retirement Act of 1935, as amended, provides for a federal retirement program for employees in the railroad industry and their families.

Railroad Retirement Board (RRB), federal agency that administers retirement–survivor

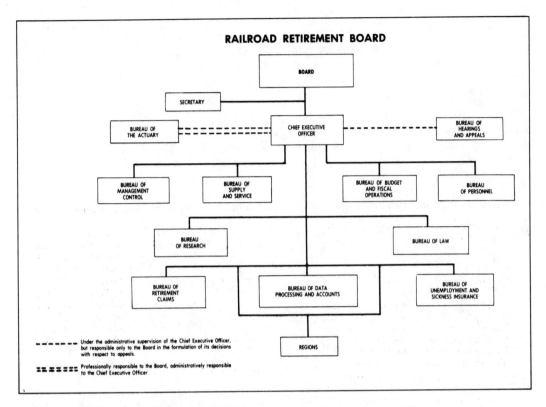

RAILROAD RETIREMENT BOARD

and unemployment–sickness benefit programs provided by federal laws for the nation's railroad workers and their families. Under the Railroad Retirement Act, annuities are paid by the RRB to rail employees with at least 10 years of service who retire because of age or disability and to their eligible wives. When other requirements are met, annuities are also provided to the surviving widows and children or parents of deceased employees. These retirement–survivor benefit programs are closely coordinated with social security benefit programs and include Medicare health insurance coverage. Under the Railroad Unemployment Insurance Act, biweekly benefits are payable by the RRB to workers with qualifying railroad earnings who become unemployed or sick. About 100 field offices are maintained across the country.

The RRB is composed of three members appointed by the president by and with the advice of the Senate—one upon recommendations of representatives of employees, one upon recommendations of carriers, and one, the chairman, as a public member.

Railroad Retirement Board
844 Rush Street
Chicago, IL 60611
(312) 751-4500

Washington Liaison Office
Room 444
425 Thirteen Street N.W.
Washington, DC 20004
(202) 382-4791

Railroad Retirement Board v. *Alton Railroad Co.: see* RAILROAD RETIREMENT ACT.

Railroad Signalmen, Brotherhood of: *see* LABOR ORGANIZATION.

Railroad Unemployment Insurance Act of 1938, federal statute that created a national system to provide railroad employees with unemployment and sickness benefits.

Railroad Yardmasters of America: *see* LABOR ORGANIZATION.

Railway and Airway Supervisors Association, The American: *see* LABOR ORGANIZATION.

Railway, Airline and Steamship Clerks, Freight Handlers, Express and Station Employees, Brotherhood of: *see* LABOR ORGANIZATION.

Railway Carmen of the United States and Canada, Brotherhood: *see* LABOR ORGANIZATION.

Railway Labor Act of 1926, federal statute, amended in 1934 to include airlines, that protects the collective bargaining rights of employees and established the National Railroad Adjustment Board to arbitrate grievances that arise from labor–management contracts.

R & D, abbreviation for research and development.

Randolph, A(sa) Philip (1889-1979), one of the founders and first president of the Brotherhood of Sleeping Car Porters; one of the most significant voices in the labor and civil rights movements.

Randolph, Woodruff (1892-1966), president of the International Typographical Union from 1944 to 1958. For biographical information, see Seymour M. Lipset, *et al., Union Democracy: The Internal Politics of the International Typographical Union* (Glencoe, Ill.: The Free Press, 1956).

random sample, sample of members of a population drawn in such a way that every member of the population has an equal chance of being included in the sample.

range, difference between the lowest and highest scores obtained on a test by some group.

rank, place in a hierarchical ordering of positions.

rank and file, colloquial expression referring to the masses. When used in an organizational context, it refers to those members of the organization who are not part of management. The term is frequently used to describe those members of a union having no status as officers or shop stewards. Rank and file was originally a military term referring to the enlisted men who had to line up in ranks, side by side, and files, one behind the other. Officers, being gentlemen, were spared such indignities.

ranking: see JOB RANKING.

ranking test, examination used to rank individuals according to their scores so that those with the higher scores have an advantage in gaining employment or promotion.

rank-in-man system, also called PERSONAL-RANK SYSTEM, method of establishing pay primarily on the basis of an employee's qualifications without consideration given to the specific duties and responsibilities that would be performed by the employee. Such personal rank systems tend to be restricted to the military, the U.S. Foreign Service, and

other similar officer corps systems. *See* Harold H. Leich, "Rank in Man or Job? Both!" *Public Administration Review* (Spring 1960).

rank performance rating, method of performance appraisal that requires superiors to rank order employees according to their merit.

rapport, generally, a spirit of harmony, accord, and mutual confidence between individuals.

RASA: *see* LABOR ORGANIZATION, Railway and Airway Supervisors Association, The American.

rate, beginner's: *see* BEGINNER'S RATE.

rate, incentive: *see* INCENTIVE RATE.

rate, trainee: *see* BEGINNER'S RATE.

ratebuster, also called JOB SPOILER, general term for any employee whose production level far exceeds the norms established by the majority of the work force. Ratebusters usually face considerable peer pressure to conform to average production levels, and sometimes this pressure can be physical. A *job spoiler* is a British ratebuster. For a study of the personality traits of ratebusters, *see* Melville Dalton, "The Industrial 'Ratebuster': A Characterization," *Applied Anthropology* (Winter 1948).

ratification, formal confirmation by the union membership of a contract that has been signed on their behalf by union representatives.

rating, efficiency: *see* EFFICIENCY RATING.

rating, rank-performance: *see* RANK-PERFORMANCE RATING.

rating chart, graphic: *see* GRAPHIC RATING CHART.

rating system, deferred: *see* DEFERRED RATING SYSTEM.

ratio, efficiency: *see* EFFICIENCY.

ratio delay, work sampling technique that uses a large number of observations taken at random intervals in order to determine the parts of the work day (expressed in minutes or hours) during which an employee is working productively or is engaged in activities other than productive work. See L.H.C. Tippett, "The Ratio-Delay Technique," *Time and Motion Study* (May 1953).

rational validity, involves the use of a detailed job analysis to determine the knowledges, skills, and abilities that are necessary for effective performance in a particular job. Measurement instruments are then designed to measure such factors. For example, if a job requirement is the ability to type errorless copy at 50 words a minute, a test can be designed to measure that ability.

rat race, slang phrase for the relentless pursuit of success. The "race" is usually engaged in and won by workaholics who can't think of anything better to do anyway. Vermin lovers consider the phrase a gross libel of a species that would be innocent save for the bubonic plague.
See also WORKAHOLIC.

raw score, also called CRUDE SCORE, number of items correct, when there is no correction for guessing, or the formula score, when a correction for guessing has been applied.

RCIA: *see* LABOR ORGANIZATION, Retail Clerks International Association.

RCLA: *see* LABOR ORGANIZATION, Rural Letter Carriers' Association, National.

RDWW: *see* LABOR ORGANIZATION, Roofers, Damp and Waterproof Workers Association, United Slate, Tile and Composition.

reaction management, management posture that is limited to responding to immediate problems and pressures.

reading assistant, reader for a blind employee. Public Law 87-614 of 1962 authorizes the employment of readers for blind federal employees. These reading assistants serve without compensation from the government, but they can be paid by the blind employees, nonprofit organizations, or state offices of vocational rehabilitation. They may also serve on a volunteer basis.

Reading Test, Davis: *see* DAVIS READING TEST.

Reagan, Ronald (1911-   ), governor of California from 1966 to 1974 and president of the Screen Actors Guild (1947–1952; 1959–1960).

reallocate: *see* ALLOCATE.

reallocation, also called RECLASSIFICATION, change in the position classification of an existing position resulting from significant changes in assigned duties and responsibilities.

Realpolitik, originally a German word meaning "realist politics." Applied to politics—whether of the organizational or societal variety—that are premised upon material or practical factors rather than theoretical or ethical considerations. According to John E. Fisher, in "Playing Favorites in Large Organizations," *Business Horizons* (June 1977),

> the realpolitiks of business offices may be overlooked by students of business administration who are surfeited in the literature of management techniques. Yet the literature actually reveals far less about how organizations operate internally than can be learned from studying office patronage and politics. Pre-occupation with management techniques may be misleading to callow youth just coming from the halls of academe into the occupational armies of business. Unsophisticated tyros are led to believe that their technical qualifications will be highly regarded and will play a significant role in their advancement. And so it may, in some instances. In organizations dominated by authoritarians, however, office patronage and politics hold the key to what is to be accomplished and what is forbidden. Office patronage provides a means for people of indifferent ability who have acquired power to be secure in its exercise.

real time, computer term that describes an information processing speed sufficient to control an ongoing process.

real wages, wages after they have been adjusted for changes in the level of prices. The buying power of wages, the "real" wages, are computed by dividing the dollar amount by an index measuring changes in prices (such as the Consumer Price Index).

reasonable accommodation, once a handicapped employee is hired, an employer is required to take reasonable steps to accommodate the individual's disability unless such steps would cause the employer undue hardship. Examples of "reasonable accommodations" include providing a reader for a blind employee, an interpreter for a deaf person requiring telephone contacts, or adequate workspace for an employee confined to a wheelchair. *See* Janet Asher and Jules Asher, "How To Accommodate Workers in Wheelchairs," *Job Safety and Health* (October 1976); Leslie Milk, "What Is Reasonable Accommodation?" *Civil Service Journal* (October–December 1978)

reassignment, transfer of an employee while serving continuously within the same organization, from one position to another without promotion or demotion.

Rebnick v. *McBride*, 277 U.S. 350 (1928), U.S. Supreme Court case, which held that the activities of employment offices were subject to state regulation.

recall, rehiring employees from a layoff. In a recall, union contracts usually require that the union be given both notice of the recall and the names of the employees to be recalled. This enables the union to determine if employees were being called back in the order required by the agreement. *See* Bureau of Labor Statistics, U.S. Department of Labor, *Major Collective Bargaining Agreements: Layoff, Recall, and Worksharing Procedures* (Washington, D.C.: U.S. Government Printing Office, Bulletin 1425-13, 1972).

recall item, test question that requires the examinee to supply the correct answer from memory, in contrast to a recognition item where the examinee need only identify the correct answer.

reclassification: *see* REALLOCATION.

reclassify: *see* CLASSIFY.

recognition, employer's acceptance of a union as the bargaining agent for all of the employees in a particular bargaining unit.
See also EXCLUSIVE RECOGNITION.

recognition item, test question that calls for the examinee to recognize or select the correct answer from among two or more alternatives.

recognition picketing, picketing to encourage an employer to recognize a particular union as the bargaining agent for his or her employees. Recognition picketing is usually an unfair labor practice.
See also PRE-HIRE AGREEMENT.

recognition strike, work stoppage that seeks to force an employer to formally recognize and deal with a union.

record copy, copy of a document that is regarded by an organization as the most important or the key official copy.

recruitment, total process by which an organization gathers individuals to occupy its various positions. *See* Robert M. Guion, "Recruiting, Selection, and Job Placement," in Marvin D. Dunnette (ed.), *Handbook of Industrial and Organization Psychology* (Chicago: Rand McNally, 1976); Erwin S. Stanton, *Successful Personnel Recruiting and Selection within EEO/Affirmative Action Guidelines* (N.Y.: AMACON, 1977).

See also POSITIVE RECRUITMENT.

red circle (position classification): *see* EARMARK.

red-circle rate, also called RINGED RATE, rate of pay that is higher than the established rate for a particular job.

red rash, job action by firefighters who, because they cannot legally strike, call in sick. When police suffer from this affliction, it is called the "blue flu."
See also BLUE FLU and STRIKE.

red tape, this despised symbol of excessive formality and attention to routine has its origins in the red ribbon with which clerks bound up official documents in the last century. The ribbon has disappeared, but the practices it represents linger on.
Herbert Kaufman's *Red Tape: Its Origins, Uses, and Abuses* (Washington, D.C.: The Brookings Institution, 1977), finds that the term "is applied to a bewildering variety of organizational practices and features." After all, "one person's 'red tape' may be another's treasured procedural safeguard." Kaufman concludes that "red tape turns out to be at the core of our institutions rather than an excrescence on them."

reduction in force: *see* RIF.

re-employed annuitant, employee who, having retired with a pension from an organization, is again employed by that same organization. Most of the re-employed annuitants working for the federal government (about 3,000 in 1975) are subject to a law that has their salary reduced by the amount of the annuity.

re-employment list, also called RE-EMPLOYMENT ELIGIBILITY LIST, most merit systems and union contracts require that, in the event of lay-offs, employees will be ranked on a re-employment list in order of their seniority. Usually, re-employment lists must be exhausted before new hires can be considered.
See also the following entries:
  LAYOFF
  RECALL
  RIF

reference checking, verifying information provided by a job applicant. *See* Edward L. Levine, "Legal Aspects of Reference Checking for Personnel Selection," *The Personnel Administrator* (November 1977); John D. Rice, "Privacy Legislation: Its Effect on Pre-employment Reference Checking," *The*

Personnel Administrator (February 1978); Edward L. Levine and Stephone M. Rudolph, *Reference Checking for Personnel Selection: The State of the Art* (Berea, Ohio: American Society for Personnel Administration, 1978).

reference group, also called SOCIAL REFERENCE GROUP, social group with which an individual identifies to the extent that his/her personal values are derived from the group's norms and attitudes. *See* Herbert H. Hyman and Eleanor Singer (eds.), *Readings in Reference Group Theory and Research* (N.Y.: The Free Press, 1968).

Regents of the University of California v. Allan Bakke, 438 U.S. 265 (1978), U.S. Supreme Court case, which upheld a white applicant's claim of reverse discrimination because he was denied admission to the University of California Medical School at Davis when 16 out of the school's 100 class spaces were set aside for minority applicants. The court ruled that Bakke must be admitted to the Davis Medical School as soon as possible, but that the university had the right to take race into account in its admissions criteria. The imprecise nature of taking race into account as one factor among many has created considerable speculation about the potential impact this case may have on voluntary affirmative action programs concerning employment. *See* Allan P. Sindler, *Bakke, Defunis, and Minority Admissions: The Quest for Equal Opportunity* (N.Y.: Longman, 1978); Joel Dreyfuss and Charles Lawrence III, *The Bakke Case: The Politics of Inequality* (New York: Harcourt, Brace, Jovanovich, 1979); J. Harvie Wilkinson III, *From Brown to Bakke: The Supreme Court and School Integration 1954–1978* (New York: Oxford University Press, 1979).

   See also the following entries:

   DEFUNIS V. ODEGAARD
   REVERSE DISCRIMINATION
   UNITED STEEL WORKERS OF AMERICA V. WEBER, ET AL.

regional bargaining, collective bargaining between a union and the representatives of an industry in a given region.

register of eligibles: *see* ELIGIBLE LIST.

registration: *see* OCCUPATIONAL REGISTRATION.

regression analysis, also MULTIPLE REGRESSION ANALYSIS, method for describing the nature of the relationship between two variables, so that the value of one can be predicted if the value of the other is known. *Multiple regression analysis* involves more than two variables.

rehabilitants, emotional: *see* EMOTIONALLY HANDICAPPED EMPLOYEES.

Rehabilitated Offender Program, federal government's program to assure fair federal employment opportunity for qualified applicants convicted of a crime who are subsequently declared rehabilitated offenders. The federal government seeks to carefully and selectively hire rehabilitated offenders for jobs where they are needed and for which they are qualifed by experience, education, and training, as determined by normal competitive examining procedures. Rehabilitated offenders who are mentally retarded or otherwise severely handicapped are appointed under the same procedures used for other such handicapped persons, with appointing officials taking into account their record, conduct, and rehabilitative efforts. In both competitive and excepted appointments, the hiring agency makes the final decision on whether an applicant would be the right person for a particular opening.

reinforcement, also POSITIVE REINFORCEMENT and NEGATIVE REINFORCEMENT, inducement to perform in a particular manner. *Positive reinforcement* occurs when an individual receives a desired reward that is contingent upon some prescribed behavior. *Negative reinforcement* occurs when an individual works to avoid an undesirable reward. *See* B. F. Skinner, *Contingencies of Reinforcement: A Theoretical Analysis* (N.Y.: Appleton-Century-Crofts, 1969); Harry Wiard, "Why Manage Behavior? A Case for Positive Reinforcement," *Human Resource Management* (Summer 1972); Jerry A. Wallinand and Ronald D. Johnson, "The Positive Reinforcement Approach to Controlling Employee Absenteeism," *Personnel Journal* (August 1976).

reinstatement, restoration of an employee to his/her previous position without any loss of seniority or other benefits. In a governmental context, reinstatement is the noncompetitive reentrance into the competitive service of a person who acquired eligibility for such action as a result of previous service. Reinstatement is a privilege accorded in recognition of and on the basis of former service and is not a "right" to which one is entitled.

relevance: *see* CRITERION RELEVANCE.

reliability, dependability of a testing device,

as reflected in the consistency of its scores when repeated measurements are made of the same group. When a test is said to have a high degree of reliability, it means that an individual tested today and tested again at a later time with the same test and under the same conditions will get approximately the same score. In short, a test is reliable if it gives a dependable measure of whatever it seeks to measure.

See also INTERNAL CONSISTENCY RELIABILITY and INTERRATER RELIABILITY.

reliability coefficient, numerical index of reliability that is obtained by correlating scores on two forms of a test, from statistical data on individual test items, or by correlating scores on different administrations of the same test. A reliability coefficient can be a perfect 1.00 or a perfectly unreliable −1.00. A reliability of .90 or greater is generally considered adequate for a test used as a personnel selection device.

relief, also WORK RELIEF, terms usually refer to the public assistance program available during the depression of the 1930s. *Relief* or *direct relief* referred to straight welfare payments. *Work relief* referred to any of the numerous public works projects initiated specifically to provide jobs for the unemployed.

religious discrimination, any act that manifests unfavorable or inequitable treatment toward employees or prospective employees because of their religious convictions. Because of section 703(a) (1) of the Civil Rights Act of 1964, an individual's religious beliefs or practices cannot be given any consideration in making employment decisions. The argument that a religious practice may place an undue hardship upon an employer—for example, where such practices require special religious holidays and hence absence from work—has been upheld by the courts. However, because of the sensitive nature of discharging or refusing to hire an individual on religious grounds, the burden of proof to show that such a hardship exists is placed upon the employer.

relocation allowance, payment by an employer of all or part of the cost of moving one's self and one's household to a distant place of employment. See Peter J. Di-Domenico, Jr., "Relocation Benefits for New Hires," *The Personnel Administrator* (February 1978).

remuneration: *see* COMPENSATION.

reopener clause, also WAGE REOPENER CLAUSE, provision in a collective bargaining agreement stating the circumstances under which portions of the agreement, usually concerning wages, can be renegotiated before the agreement's normal expiration date. Typically such clauses provides for renegotiation at the end of a specified time period (such as one year) or when the Consumer Price Index increases by an established amount.

reporting pay: *see* CALL-IN PAY.

Report of the Job Evaluation and Pay Review Task Force to the United States Civil Service Commission: see JOB EVALUATION AND PAY REVIEW TASK FORCE.

representation election: see AUTHORIZATION ELECTION.

representative bureaucracy, concept originated by J. Donald Kingsley, in *Representative Bureaucracy* (Yellow Springs, Ohio: Antioch Press, 1944), which asserts that all social groups have a right to participation in their governing institutions. In recent years, the concept has developed a normative overlay—that all social groups should occupy bureaucratic positions in direct proportion to their numbers in the general population. For defenses of this normative position, see Samuel Krislov, *Representative Bureaucracy* (Englewood Cliffs, N.J.: Prentice-Hall, 1974); Harry Kranz, *The Participatory Bureaucracy: Women and Minorities in a More Representative Public Service* (Lexington, Mass.: Lexington-Books, 1976).

representative sample, sample that corresponds to or matches the population of which it is a sample with respect to characteristics important for the purposes under investigation. For example, a representative national sample of secondary school students should probably contain students from each state, from large and small schools, and from public and independent schools in approximately the same proportions as these exist in the nation as a whole.

reprimand, formal censure for some job related behavior. A reprimand is less severe than an adverse action; more forceful than an admonition.

Research Center for Group Dynamics: *see* INSTITUTE FOR SOCIAL RESEARCH.

Research Psychologists Press, Inc.: *see* TEST PUBLISHERS.

reserved rights: *see* MANAGEMENT RIGHTS.

residency requirement: *see* the following entries:

DOMICILE
HICKLIN V. ORBECK
MCCARTHY V. PHILADELPHIA CIVIL SERVICE
  COMMISSION

residual unemployment, no matter how many jobs are available, there will always be some people out of work because of illness, indolence, movement from one job or community to another, etc. The total number of these individuals is a measure of residual unemployment.

resignation, employee's formal notice that his or her relationship with the employing organization is being terminated.

resignation, volunteered: *see* QUIT.

response rate, in survey research, the percentage of those given questionnaires who complete and return them.

rest period, recuperative pause during working hours.

restraining order, temporary: *see* INJUNCTION.

restriction of output, reduced productivity on the part of a worker or workforce because of informal group norms, personal grievances, or sloth. For the classic study of this phoenomena, *see* Stanley B. Mathewson, *Restriction of Output Among Unorganized Workers* (Carbondale: Southern Illinois University Press, 1931, 1969). *Also see* Harry Cohen, "Dimensions of Restriction of Output," *Personnel Journal* (December 1971).

restrictive credentialism, general term for any selection policy adversely affecting disadvantaged groups because they lack the formal qualifications for positions that, in the opinion of those adversely affected, do not truly need such formal qualifications.

resume, also CURRICULUM VITA, brief account of one's education and experience that job applicants typically prepare for prospective employers to review. In the academic world, a resume is more pompously called a *curriculum vita*. For a how-to-do-it book, *see* Adele B. Lewis, *How To Write Better Resumes* (Woodbury, N.Y.: Barron's Educational Series, 1977).

Retail Clerks International Union: *see* LABOR ORGANIZATION.

Retail/Services Labor Report, weekly report published by the Bureau of National Affairs, Inc., for management and unions in the retail/services field. Covers personnel administration, legislative developments, equal employment opportunity, union organizing, collective bargaining, contract settlements, equal pay, job safety, and hours and earnings. Provides full texts of important court and labor board rulings.

See also BUREAU OF NATIONAL AFFAIRS, INC.

Retail, Wholesale and Department Store Union: *see* LABOR ORGANIZATION.

Retail Workers Union, United: *see* LABOR ORGANIZATION.

retention period, stated period of time during which personnel records are to be retained.

retention register, federal government's record of employees occupying positions in a competitive level. Employees on the register are arranged by tenure groups and subgroups and according to their relative retention standing within the subgroups.

retention standing, precise rank among employees competing for a position in the event of a reduction-in-force or layoff. It is determined by tenure groups and subgroups and by length of creditable service.

retirement, voluntary or involuntary termination of employment because of age, disability, illness or personal choice. *See* James W. Walker and Harriet L. Lazer, *The End of Mandatory Retirement: Implication's for Management* (N.Y.: John Wiley, 1978); Thomas S. Litras, "The Battle over Retirement Policies and Practices," *Personnel Journal* (February 1979).

See also the following entries:

DISABILITY RETIREMENT
MASSACHUSETTS BOARD OF RETIREMENT V.
  MURGIA
PRE-RETIREMENT COUNSELING
RE-EMPLOYED ANNUITANT
SURVIVORS BENEFITS

Retirement Account, Individual: *see* INDIVIDUAL RETIREMENT ACCOUNT.

retirement age, a 1978 amendment to the Age Discrimination in Employment Act raised the minimum mandatory retirement age to 70 years for workers in private companies and state and local governments. It banned forced retirement at any age for federal workers. Tenured college teachers are exempt from coverage until July 1, 1982; business executives with private annual pensions over $27,000 are also exempt from the higher retirement age. In cases where mandatory retirement is part of a collective bargaining agreement in effect on Sept. 1, 1977, the new age will not apply until Jan 1, 1980, or the expiration of the contract, whichever comes first.

See also VANCE V. BRADLEY.

retirement counseling, systematic efforts by an organization to help its employees who are retiring to adjust to their new situation. For how to establish a retirement counseling program, *see* Douglas M. Bartlett, "Retirement Counseling: Make Sure Employees Aren't Dropouts," *Personnel* (November–December 1974); Don Pellicano, "Retirement Counseling," *Personnel Journal* (July 1973).

See also PRE-RETIREMENT COUNSELING.

retirement plan, fixed-benefit: *see* FIXED-BENEFIT RETIREMENT PLAN.

retroactive pay, wages for work performed during an earlier time at a lower rate. Retroactive pay would make up the difference between the new and old rates of pay.

retroactive seniority, seniority status that is retroactively awarded back to the date that a woman or minority group member was proven to have been discriminatorily refused employment. The U.S. Supreme Court has interpreted the "make whole" provision of Title VII of the Civil Rights Act of 1964 to include the award of retroactive seniority to proven discriminatees; however, retroactive seniority cannot be awarded further back than 1964—the date of the act.

See FRANKS V. BOWMAN TRANSPORTATION CO. and INTERNATIONAL BROTHERHOOD OF TEAMSTERS V. UNITED STATES.

Reuther, Walter P. (1907-1970), president of the United Automobile Workers from 1946 until his death. For biographies, *see* Frank Cormier and William J. Eaton, *Reuther* (Englewood Cliffs, N. J.: Prentice-Hall, 1970); Jean Gould and Lorena Hickok, *Walter Reuther: Labor's Rugged Individualist* (N. Y.: Dodd, Mead, 1972).

reverse collective bargaining, occurs when economic conditions force collective bargaining agreements to be renegotiated so that employees end up with a less favorable wage package. *See* Peter Henle, "Reverse Collective Bargaining? A Look at Some Union Concession Situations," *Industrial and Labor Relations Review* (April 1973).

reverse discrimination, although generally understood to mean preferential treatment for women and minorities, as opposed to white males, the practice has no legal standing. Indeed, Section 703 (j) of Title VII of the Civil Rights Act of 1964 holds that nothing in the title shall be interpreted to require any employer to "grant preferential treatment to any individual or group on the basis of race, color, religion, sex or national origin." Yet, affirmative action programs necessarily put some otherwise innocent white males at a disadvantage that they would not have otherwise had. The whole matter may have been summed up by George Orwell in his 1945 novella, *Animal Farm,* when he observed that "All animals are equal, but some animals are more equal than others." For an analysis of the problem, *see* Gopal C. Pati, "Reverse Discrimination: What Can Managers Do?" *Personnel Journal* (July 1977). For a political analysis, *see* Nathan Glazer, *Affirmative Discrimination* (N.Y.: Basic Books, 1975). For a defense, *see* Boris Bittker, *The Case for Black Reparations* (N.Y.: Random House, 1973). For a philosophic approach, *see* Barry R. Gross, *Discrimination in Reverse: Is Turnabout Fair Play?* (N.Y.: New York University Press, 1978).

See also the following entries:
DEFUNIS V. ODEGAARD
REGENTS OF THE UNIVERSITY OF CALIFORNIA V. ALLAN BAKKE
UNITED STEELWORKERS OF AMERICA V. WEBER, ET AL.

Revised Minnesota Paper Form Board Test, paper-and-pencil instrument consisting of 64 multiple-choice items that measure mechanical aptitude. Each item consists of a figure cut into two or more parts. The individual must determine how the pieces would fit together into a complete figure, then choose the drawing that correctly shows the arrangement. Valid instrument for measuring the ability to visualize and manipulate objects in space. TIME: 20/25 minutes. AUTHORS: Rensis Likert and W. H. Quasha. PUBLISHER: Psychological Corporation (*see* TEST PUBLISHERS).

Rhode Island AFL–CIO: *see* AMERICAN FEDERATION OF LABOR–CONGRESS OF INDUSTRIAL ORGANIZATIONS.

RIF, acronym for "reduction in force"—the phrase the federal government uses when it eliminates specific job categories in specific organizations. While an employee who has been "riffed" has not been fired, he or she is nevertheless still without a job. This acronym has become so common that it is often used as a verb and seems to be spreading well beyond the federal bureaucracy. *See* Robert Rudary and J. Garrett Ralls, Jr., "Manpower Planning for Reduction-in-Force," *University of Michigan Business Review* (November 1978).

See also the following entries:
LAYOFF
RECALL
RE-EMPLOYMENT LIST
REINSTATEMENT
RETENTION REGISTER
RETENTION STANDING

rightful place, judicial doctrine that an individual who has been discriminated against should be restored to the job—to his or her "rightful place"—as if there had been no discrimination and given appropriate seniority, merit increases, and promotions.

rights arbitration: *see* GRIEVANCE ARBITRATION.

right-to-work laws, state laws that make it illegal for collective bargaining agreements to contain maintenance of membership, preferential hiring, union shop, or any other clauses calling for compulsory union membership. A typical "right-to-work" law might read: "No person may be denied employment and employers may not be denied the right to employ any person because of that person's membership or nonmembership in any labor organization."

It was the Labor–Management Relations (Taft–Hartley) Act of 1947 that authorized right-to-work laws, when it provided in section 14(b) that "nothing in this Act shall be construed as authorizing the execution or application of agreements requiring membership in a labor organization as a condition of employment in any State or Territory in which such execution or application is prohibited by State or Territorial law."

The law does not prohibit the union or closed shop; it simply gives each state the option of doing so. Twenty states have done so: Alabama, Arizona, Arkansas, Florida, Georgia, Iowa, Kansas, Louisiana, Mississippi, Nebraska, Nevada, North Carolina, North Dakota, South Carolina, South Dakota, Tennessee, Texas, Utah, Virginia, and Wyoming.

See also NATIONAL RIGHT TO WORK COMMITTEE.

ringed rate: *see* RED-CIRCLE RATE.

rival unionism, competition between two or more unions for the same prospective members.

robber barons, label applied to the big business titans of the United States toward the end of the 19th century. Now it is an invidious term for corporate leadership in general. For the historical account, *see* Matthew Josephson, *The Robber Barons: The Great American Capitalists, 1861–1901* (N.Y.: Harcourt, Brace & Co., 1934).

***Robbins* decision:** *see* NATIONAL LABOR RELATIONS BOARD V. ROBBINS TIRE AND RUBBER CO.

Robertson, David Brown (1876-1961), president of the Brotherhood of Locomotive Firemen and Enginemen from 1922 to 1953.

Robins, Margaret Dreier (1868-1945), a leader of the Women's Trade Union League and president of the International Federation of Working Women from 1921 to 1923. For a biography, *see* Mary Dreier, *Margaret Dreier Robins: Her Life, Letters and Work* (N.Y.: Island Press Cooperative, 1950).

Robinsion* v. *Lorrilard Corp.: *see* BUSINESS NECESSITY.

robot, general term for any machine that does the work that a person would otherwise have to do. The word comes from *robotnik,* the Czech word for slave.

Rockefeller Public Service Awards Program, awards that honor significant achievement in public service. The program, which is sponsored by John D. Rockefeller III and administered by the Woodrow Wilson School of Public and International Affairs of Princeton University, grants five awards of $10,000 each year to individuals who have made outstanding contributions toward the resolution of critical problems facing the nation. Nominees must be U.S. citizens and cannot hold elective office, be candidates for office at the time of the nomination or receipt of the awards, or be sitting judges. Awards are intended primarily for individuals, but collaborations by two or more individuals who may have worked as a team may be nominated. The awards program does not recognize committees or organizations.

Rockefeller Public Service Awards
Woodrow Wilson School
Princeton University
Princeton, NJ 08540

Roethlisberger, Fritz J. (1898-1974), with Elton Mayo, one of the founders of the human relations movement in industry. As one of the prime researchers of the Hawthorne experiments, he co-authored the definitive report on them—*Management and the Worker*, with William J. Dickson (Cambridge, Mass.: Harvard University Press, 1939). Other major works include: *Management and Morale* (Cambridge, Mass: Harvard University Press, 1941); *Man-in-Organization* (Cambridge, Mass.: Harvard University Press, 1968); *The Elusive Phenomena: An Autobiographical Account of My Work in the Field of Organizational Behavior at the Harvard Business School*, edited by George F. F. Lombard (Cambridge: Harvard University Press, 1977). *Also see* George F. F. Lombard (ed.), *The Contributions of F. J. Roethlisberger to Management Theory and Practice* (Cambridge, Mass: Harvard University Graduate School of Business, 1976).

Rogers Act of 1924, federal statute that created a merit-based career system for the Foreign Service of the U.S. Department of State.

role, also ROLE PLAYING, in social psychology, the term "role" is used to describe the behavior expected of an individual occupying a particular position. Just as an actor acts out his role on the stage, a personnel manager, for example, performs his role in real life. Role playing is a very common training technique and is based on the assumption that the process of acting out a role will enable an individual to gain insights concerning the behavior of others that cannot be realized by reading a book or listening to a lecture. *See* R. J. Corsini, M. Shaw, and R. Blake, *Role-playing in Business and Industry* (N.Y.: Free Press, 1961); Norman R. F. Maier, Allen Solem, and Ayesha A. Maier, *The Role-Play Technique: A Handbook for Management and Leadership Practice* (La Jolla, Calif.: University Associates, 1975); Frank Sherwood, "The Role Concept in Administration," *Public Personnel Review* (January 1964).
See also STRUCTURED ROLE PLAYING.

role conception: *see* ROLE PERCEPTION.

role conflict, when an individual is called upon to perform mutually exclusive acts by parties having legitimate "holds" on him/her, role conflict may be said to exist. For example, a rising young manager may not make it to the "big" meeting if he must at that moment rush his child to the hospital for an emergency appendectomy. When such conflicts arise, most individuals invoke a hierarchy of role obligation that gives some roles precedence over others. To most fathers, their child's life would be more important

than a business meeting—no matter how "big." Real life is not always so unambiguous, however, and role conflict is a common dilemma in the world of work. *See* J. R. Rizzo, R. J. House, and S. I. Lirtzman, "Role Conflict and Ambiguity in Complex Organizations," *Administrative Science Quarterly* (June 1970); R. H. Miles and W. D. Perreault, Jr., "Organizational Role Conflict: Its Antecedents and Consequences," *Organizational Behavior and Human Performance* (October 1976).

role perception, also called ROLE CONCEPTION, an individual's role perception or role conception delineates the position that the individual occupies in his/her organization and establishes for the individual the minimum and maximum ranges of permissible behavior in "acting" out his/her organizational role. For empirical studies, *see* Andrew D. Szilagyi, "An Empirical Test of Causal Inference between Role Perceptions, Satisfaction with Work, Performance and Organizational Level," *Personnel Psychology* (Autumn 1977); Randell S. Schuler, "The Effects of Role Perceptions on Employee Satisfaction and Performance Moderated by Employee Ability," *Organizational Behavior and Human Performance* (February 1977).

role playing: *see* ROLE and STRUCTURED ROLE PLAYING.

romance: *see* LOVE.

Roney, Frank (1841-1925), West Coast labor organizer in the late 1900s. For an autobiography, *see* Ira B. Cross, editor, *Frank Roney: Irish Rebel and Labor Leader* (Berkeley, Calif.: University of California Press, 1931).

Roofers, Damp and Waterproof Workers Association, United Slate, Tile and Composition: *see* LABOR ORGANIZATION.

roping: *see* HOOKING.

Rorschach test, also called INK-BLOT TEST, projective test in which the responses to standard ink blots are interpreted to gain clues to the subject's personality. Developed by the Swiss psychiatrist, Hermann Rorschach (1884-1922), the Rorschach test is no longer considered to be a valid tool for predicting vocational success.
See also PROJECTIVE TEST and THEMATIC APPERCEPTION TEST.

roster of eligibles: *see* ELIGIBLE LIST.

rotating shift, work schedule designed to give

employees an equal share of both day and night work.

Roth **decision:** *see* BOARD OF REGENTS V. ROTH.

Rowan Plan, incentive wage plan that gives a worker a standard rate for completing a job within an established time, plus a premium determined on the basis of the percentage of time saved.

RRB: *see* RAILROAD RETIREMENT BOARD.

Rubber, Cork, Linoleum and Plastic Workers of America, United: *see* LABOR ORGANIZATION.

Rucker Plan, employee incentive plan developed in the 1950s by Allen W. Rucker of the Eddy-Rucker-Nickels consulting firm. According to R. C. Scott, in "Rucker Plan of Group Incentives," Carl Heyel (ed.), *The Encyclopedia of Management* (N.Y.: Van Nostrand Reinhold Co., 2nd ed., 1973), the plan

> uses day-to-day employee participation and broad coverage to develop cost reductions and improve profits. It is backed by a precise measurement of productivity gains in money terms (not physical units). It recognizes and reinforces those gains with an equitable, automatic method of sharing them between the participants (added pay) and the company (added margin).

rule-making authority, powers exercised by administrative agencies that have the force of law.

rule of three, also RULE OF ONE and RULE OF THE LIST, practice of certifying to an appointing authority the top three names on an eligible list. The rule of three is intended to give the appointing official an opportunity to weigh intangible factors, such as personality, before making a formal offer of appointment. The *rule of one* has only the single highest ranking person on the eligible list certified. The *rule of the list* gives the appointing authority the opportunity to choose from the entire list of eligibles.

runaway shop, term used by unionists to describe a company or company subdivision that moves to another state or area to avoid a union or state labor laws.

run-off election, when no single union receives a majority in a representation election, a second election—the run-off election—is held and participants choose between the two unions that got the most votes in the first election.

Rural Letter Carriers' Association, National: *see* LABOR ORGANIZATION.

RWDSU: *see* LABOR ORGANIZATION, Retail, Wholesale and Department Store Union.

RWU: *see* LABOR ORGANIZATION, Retail Workers Union, United.

RYA: *see* LABOR ORGANIZATION, Railroad Yardmasters of America.

S

sabbath: *see* TRANS WORLD AIRLINES V. HARDISON.

sabbatical, lengthy paid leave for professional, intellectual or emotional refurbishment. It was an ancient Hebrew tradition to allow fields to lie fallow every seventh year. The words sabbath and sabbatical both come from the Hebrew word *shabath*, meaning to rest. In modern times, a sabbatical has been a period of paid leave and rejuvenation for teachers at colleges and universities, but it has recently gained a broader meaning. *See* Angelos A. Tsaklanganos, "Sabbaticals for Executives," *Personnel Journal* (May 1973).

sabotage, deliberate destruction of property or the slowing down of work in order to damage a business. During a 1910 railway strike in France, strikers destroyed some of the wooden shoes or *sabots* that held the rails in place. Sabotage soon came into English, but it wasn't until World War II that the word gained widespread popularity as a description of the efforts of secret agents to hinder an enemy's industrial/military capabilities.

There is also the story of the French wool finishers who, in the 1820s rioted to protest the use of machinery that might supplant them. They were said to have used their wooden shoes or *sabots* to kick the machines to pieces. While this may have been the first instance of sabotage, the use of the word in English dates from the 1910 railway strike.

sack: *see* GET THE SACK.

safety, also SAFETY DEPARTMENT, an organization's total effort to prevent and eliminate the causes of accidents. Some organizations have a safety department responsible for administering the various aspects of the safety program. For a text, *see* John V. Grimaldi and Rollin H. Simonds, *Safety Management* (Homewood, Ill: Richard D. Irwin, Inc., 1975). For how to staff a safety department, *see* Robert E. McClay, "Professionalizing the Safety Function," *Personnel Journal* (February 1977).

See also the following entries:
> GATEWAY COAL CO. V. UNITED MINE WORKERS
> MINE SAFETY AND HEALTH ADMINISTRATION
> NATIONAL SAFETY COUNCIL
> OCCUPATIONAL SAFETY AND HEALTH ADMINISTRATION
> TRIANGLE SHIRTWAIST FACTORY FIRE

Sailors' Union of the Pacific: *see* LABOR ORGANIZATION, under Seafarers' International Union of North America.

salary: *see* WAGES.

salary, straight: *see* STRAIGHT SALARY.

salary compression, also called WAGE COMPRESSION, according to M. Sami Kassem, in "The Salary Compression Problem," *Personnel Journal* (April 1971), salary/wage compression is "the shrinking difference of pay being given newcomers as opposed to the amount paid to the experienced regulars."

salary curve: *see* MATURITY CURVE.

salary range: *see* PAY RANGE.

Salary Reform Act of 1962, (Public Law 87-793) federal statute that provided "federal salary rates shall be comparable with private enterprise salary rates for the same levels of work."

salary review, formal examination of an employee's rate of pay in terms of his or her recent performance, changes in the cost of living and other factors.

salary structures, according to Robert E. Sibson, in "New Practices and Ideas in Compensation Administration," *Compensation Review* (Third Quarter 1974), salary structures were originally

> largely conceived as boxes within which salaries must be paid. Increasingly, though, companies are viewing their salary struc-

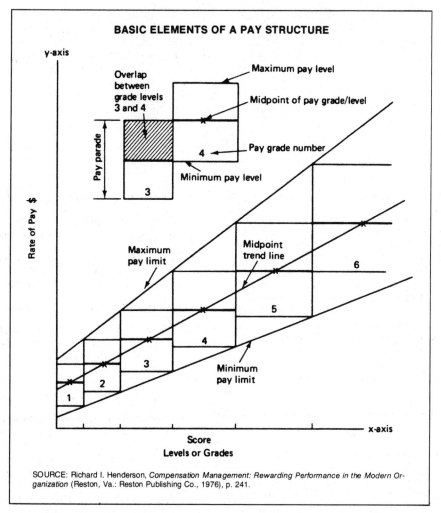

BASIC ELEMENTS OF A PAY STRUCTURE

y-axis

Overlap between grade levels 3 and 4

Maximum pay level

Midpoint of pay grade/level

Pay grade number

Minimum pay level

Pay parade

Rate of Pay $

Maximum pay limit

Midpoint trend line

Minimum pay limit

Score
Levels or Grades

x-axis

SOURCE: Richard I. Henderson, *Compensation Management: Rewarding Performance in the Modern Organization* (Reston, Va.: Reston Publishing Co., 1976), p. 241.

tures essentially as a uniform accounting system, intended primarily as an information source, rather than a control mechanism. Furthermore, the use of salary structures is changing in very fundamental ways. For instance, the use of the bottom part of the salary range in management positions is seldom used in many companies today, because paying managers at the bottom part of the range suggests that they are trainees or not qualified to do the work.

salary survey: *see* WAGE SURVEY.

salary survey, community: *see* COMMUNITY WAGE SURVEY.

sales commission: *see* COMMISSION EARNINGS.

SAM: *see* SOCIETY FOR THE ADVANCEMENT OF MANAGEMENT.

SAM Advanced Management Journal, quar-

terly offering articles on all phases of management and career development.

SAM Advanced Management Journal
Society for Advancement of Management
135 West 50th Street
New York, NY 10020

sample, any deliberately chosen portion of a larger population that is representative of that population as a whole.

See also BIASED SAMPLE, RANDOM SAMPLE, and REPRESENTATIVE SAMPLE.

sampling error, error caused by generalizing the behavior of a population from a sample of that population that is not representative of the population as a whole.

sampling population, entire set or universe from which a sample is drawn.

Sampson v. Murray, 415 U.S. 61 (1974), U.S. Supreme Court case, which held that the federal courts did not have the authority to issue a temporary restraining order (pending an administrative appeal to the U.S. Civil Service Commission) on behalf of a probationary federal government employee who had been discharged. A federal court's authority to review agency action does not come into play until it may be authoritatively said that the administrative decision to discharge an employee does, in fact, fail to conform to the applicable regulations. Until administrative action has become final, no court is in a position to say that such action did or did not conform to the regulations.

sandhogs, slang term for a worker who works underground digging subways, tunnels, etc.

sandwich management. This technique is one that is adopted most innocently. In fact, it has been perpetrated for years as managers have been encouraged to manipulate people rather than level with them. A typical statement by a sandwich manager goes something like this. "Fred, you've been doing a splendid job in many respects since you came aboard. On the other hand, there have been times when your work was so late, it caused problems for the whole department. You will have to get on the ball, son, or else we might have to transfer you to a job you can handle for sure. But I am sure we can count on you to do the right thing. Your past history indicates you have great potential." Upon analyzing that statement closely you can see a loss of "bread," neatly sandwiched between two slices of baloney. *Source* William Thomas, "Humor for Hurdling the Mystique in Management," *Management of Personnel Quarterly* (Winter 1970).

satisfactory-performance increase, annual incremental salary step increase awarded for satisfactory performance within a single salary grade.

satisficing, also called BOUNDED RATIONALITY, term coined by Herbert A. Simon, in *Administrative Behavior* (N.Y.: Macmillan 1947), while explaining his concept of *bounded rationality*. Simon asserts that it is impossible to ever know "all" of the facts that bear upon any given decision. Because truly rational research on any problem can never be completed, humans put "bounds" on their rationality and make decisions, not on the basis of optimal information, but on the basis of satisfactory information. Humans tend to make their decisions by satisficing—choosing a course of action that meets one's minimum standards for satisfaction.

scab, also called BLACKLEG, generally, an employee who continues to work for an organization while it is being struck by co-workers. Since the 1500s, scab has been used as a term for a rascal or scoundrel. Early in the 1800s, Americans started using it to refer to workers who refused to support organized efforts on behalf of their trade. A scab should be distinguished from a fink or strikebreaker who is brought into an organization only after a strike begins. Samuel Gompers, the first president of the American Federation of Labor, said that "a 'scab' is to his trade what a traitor is to his country. He is the first to take advantage of any benefit secured by united action, and never contributes anything toward its achievement." *Blackleg* is the British word for scab.

See also OLD DOMINION BRANCH NO. 496, NATIONAL ASSOCIATION OF LETTER CARRIERS V. AUSTIN and STRIKEBREAKER.

scalar chain, also LINE OF AUTHORITY, according to Henri Fayol, *General and Industrial Management,* trans. by Constance Storrs (London: Pitman Publishing, Ltd., 1949),

> the scalar chain is the chain of superiors ranging from the ultimate authority to the lowest ranks. The *line of authority* is the route followed—via every link in the chain—by all communications which start from or go to the ultimate authority. This path is dictated both by the need for some transmission and by the principle of unity of command, but it is not always the swiftest. It is even at times disastrously lengthy in large concerns, notably in governmental ones.

scaled score, score on a test when the raw score obtained has been converted to a number or position on a standard reference scale. Test scores reported to examinees and users of tests are usually scaled scores. The purpose of converting scores to a scale is to make reported scores as independent as possible of the particular form of a test an examinee has taken and of the composition of the candidate group at a particular administration. For example, the College Board Achievement tests are all reported on a scale of 200 to 800. A score of 600 on a College Board Achievement test is intended to indicate the same level of ability from year to year.

Scanlon Plan, employee incentive plan developed in the 1930s by Joseph N. Scanlon (then an officer of the United Steelworkers of America), which seeks to enhance productivity and organizational harmony through bonus and suggestion systems. The suggestion system demanded by a "true" Scanlon Plan is so sophisticated that it is more properly considered a form of participatory management. For details, *see* Frederick G. Lesieur, *The Scanlon Plan: A Frontier in Labor–Management Cooperation* (N.Y.: and Cambridge: John Wiley and the Technology Press of MIT, 1958); Frederick G. Lesieur and Elbridge Pluckett, "The Scanlon Plan Has Proved Itself," *Harvard Business Review* (October 1969); Brian E. Moore and Timothy L. Ross, *The Scanlon Way to Improved Productivity: A Practical Guide* (N.Y.: John Wiley & Sons, 1978).

SCAT: *see* COOPERATIVE SCHOOL AND COLLEGE ABILITY TEST.

scatter diagram, display of the relationship between variables using dots on a graph.

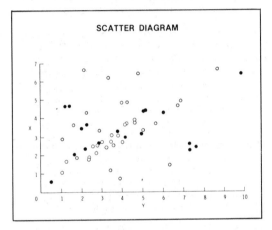

SCATTER DIAGRAM

Schedule A, category used by the Office of Personnel Management (OPM) for those excepted federal positions for which it is not practicable to hold any examinations and which are not of a confidential or policy determining nature. Included here are teachers in dependent school systems overseas, faculty members of the service academies, narcotics agents for undercover work, certain part-time positions at isolated localities, positions on vessels operated by the Military Sealift Command, and many purely seasonal positions not of a continuing nature. In addition, because the OPM is forbidden by law to examine for attorneys, they have also been placed in Schedule A. There are about 75,000 positions in this schedule (This number increases during the summer months to include temporary seasonal personnel).

Schedule B, category used by the Office of Personnel Management for those excepted

federal positions for which competitive examinations are impracticable, but for which the person must pass a *noncompetitive* examination. Included here are positions assigned to Navy or Air Force Communications Intelligence activities and national bank examiners in the Treasury Department. Only about 3,000 positions are covered by Schedule B.

Schedule C, category used by the Office of Personnel Management (OPM) for the excepted positions which are policy-determining or which involve a close personal relationship between the incumbent and the agency head or his/her key officials. It contains key positions that should be filled by the administration in power with persons who will fully support its political aims and policies as well as the positions of secretaries, special assistants, and other members of the immediate staffs of key officials. There are about 1,200 positions in Schedule C.

No examination is required for appointment to Schedule C jobs. Departments and agencies may recommend to OPM that a position be placed in Schedule C if they feel the duties assigned are either policy-determining or require the incumbent to serve in a confidential relationship to a key official. If OPM considers the duties of the position are actually policy-determining in nature or if they establish a confidential relationship to a key official, it places the position in Schedule C. If not, OPM rejects the recommendation. Each job is considered on an individual basis.

Schein, Edgar H. (1928-   ), psychologist who has written some of the most influential work on organizational psychology, organization development, and career management. Major works include: *Personnel and Organizational Change Through Group Methods: The Laboratory Approach*, with Warren Bennis (N.Y.: John Wiley, 1965); *Process Consultation: Its Role in Organization Development* (Reading, Mass.: Addison-Wesley, 1969); *Organizational Psychology* (Englewood Cliffs, N.J.: 2nd ed., Prentice-Hall, 1970); *Professional Education: Some New Directions* (N.Y.: McGraw-Hill, 1972); *Career Dynamics: Matching Individual and Organizational Needs* (Reading, Mass.: Addison-Wesley, 1978).

***Schlesinger* v. *Ballard*,** 419 U.S. 498 (1975), U.S. Supreme Court case, which held that women could be judged by a more lenient standard than men in measuring their performance in the military services because their promotional opportunities were fewer.

schmoozing, collective term for all of the social interactions engaged in by employees that are seemingly unrelated to their organization's productivity.

scholarship plan, company: *see* COMPANY FELLOWSHIP PLAN.

School Administrators, American Federation of: *see* LABOR ORGANIZATION.

Schwellenbach, Lewis B. (1894-1948), Secretary of Labor from 1945 to 1948.

Science Research Associates, Inc.: *see* TEST PUBLISHERS.

scientific management, systematic approach to managing that seeks the "one best way" of accomplishing any given task by discovering the fastest, most efficient, and least fatiguing production methods. The job of the scientific manager, once the "one best way" was found, was to impose this procedure upon the workforce. Frederick W. Taylor is considered to be the "father" of scientific management. *See* his *Principles of Scientific Management* (N.Y.: Harper & Bros., 1911).

See also the following entries:
GILBRETH, FRANK BUNKER AND LILLIAN MOLLER
MOTION STUDY
TIME STUDY

SCII: *see* STRONG–CAMPBELL INTEREST INVENTORY.

scope of bargaining, those issues over which management and labor negotiate during the collective bargaining process. *See* Joan Weitzman, *The Scope of Bargaining in Public Employment* (N.Y.: Praeger, 1975); Robert M. Tobias, "The Scope of Bargaining in the Federal Sector: Collective Bargaining or Collective Consultation," *The George Washington Law Review* (May 1976).

score, crude/raw: *see* RAW SCORE.

score, formula: *see* FORMULA SCORE.

score, scaled: *see* SCALED SCORE.

score, standard: *see* STANDARD SCORE.

Scott, Walter Dill (1869-1955), psychologist who was one of the pioneers of modern personnel management and industrial psychology. He is generally credited with having convinced the U.S. Army to use psychological techniques for the classification and as-

signment of men during World War I. For a biography, *see* Edmund C. Lynch, *Walter Dill Scott: Pioneer in Personnel Management* (Austin, Texas: Bureau of Business Research, The University of Texas at Austin, 1968).

Scott, William G. (1926-), a leading authority on organizational theory and behavior. Major works include: *Human Relations in Management* (Homewood, Ill: Richard D. Irwin, 1962); *The Management of Conflict: Appeal Systems in Organizations* (Homewood, Ill.: Richard D. Irwin, 1965); *Organizational Concepts and Analysis* (Belmont, Calif: Dickenson, 1969); *Organization Theory: A Structural and Behavioral Analysis* (Homewood, Ill.: Richard D. Irwin, rev. ed., 1972).

SCP: *see* LABOR ORGANIZATION, Sleeping Car Porters, Brotherhood of.

Screen Actors Guild: *see* LABOR ORGANIZATION, under Actors and Artistes of America, Associated.

Screen Extras Guild: *see* LABOR ORGANIZATION, under Actors and Artistes of America, Associated.

screening interview, initial interview for a job that serves to determine which applicants are to be given further consideration. *See* Jack Bucalo, "The Balanced Approach to Successful Screening Interviews," *Personnel Journal* (August 1978); Larry F. Moore and J. Cameron Craik, "Video Tape and the Screening Interview," *Personnel Journal* (March 1972).

scrip, temporary document entitling the bearer to something of value. This token money was once commonly used to pay workers in lieu of cash. As the scrip could only be redeemed at a company store with inflated prices, some states passed laws making it illegal to pay employees with anything but legal tender.

SDS: *see* SELF–DIRECTED SEARCH.

Seafarers' International Union of North America: *see* LABOR ORGANIZATION.

Sears, Roebuck, & Co. v. San Diego County District Council of Carpenters, 56 L. Ed. 2d 209 (1978), U.S. Supreme Court case, which ruled that courts may apply state trespass law to cases involving picketing that might either be protected or prohibited by the National Labor Relations Act. This holding carved out an exception for the traditional rule of federal preemption by permitting the application of state law in situations where an employer has no right to seek relief from the National Labor Relations Board if the union does not present the case to the NLRB.

seasonal adjustments, statistical modifications made to compensate for fluctuations in a time series which recur more or less regularly each year. The cause of these movements may be climatic (farm income, for example, is highest in the fall) or institutional (retail sales reach a peak just before Christmas). These seasonal movements are often so strong that they distort the underlying changes in economic data and tend to obscure trends that might be developing.

seasonal employment, also SEASONAL UNEMPLOYMENT, work that is available only during certain times of the year, such as (1) jobs picking or canning fruit in the fall, (2) jobs playing Santa Claus in a shopping mall, and (3) jobs as lifeguards at summer resorts. *Seasonal unemployment* is unemployment occasioned by the seasonal variations of particular industries. Jobs affected by the weather as in construction and agriculture are particularly susceptible to seasonal unemployment.

secondary boycott, concerted effort by a union engaged in a dispute with an employer to seek another union to boycott a fourth party (usually their employers) who, in response to such pressure, might put like pressure on the original offending employer. Secondary boycotts are forbidden by the Labor–Management Relations (Taft–Hartley) Act of 1947. For a legal analysis, *see* Ralph M. Dereshinsky, *The NLRB and Secondary Boycotts* (Philadelphia: University of Pennsylvania Press, 1972).

See also the following entries:
> BOYCOTT
> NATIONAL WOODWORK MANUFACTURES ASSOCIATION V. NATIONAL LABOR RELATIONS BOARD
> UNFAIR LABOR PRACTICES (UNIONS)

secondary strike, strike against an employer because it is doing business with another employer whose workers are on strike.

second career: *see* CAREER CHANGE.

SEIU: *see* LABOR ORGANIZATION, Service employees' International Union.

selection: *see* PERSONNEL SELECTION.

Selection Consulting Center: *see* TEST PUBLISHERS.

Selection Guidelines: *see* UNIFORM GUIDELINES ON EMPLOYEE SELECTION.

selection interview: *see* INTERVIEW.

selection out, euphemism for terminating an employee from a training program or employment.

selection procedure, according to the "Uniform Guidelines on Employee Selection," a selection procedure is

> any measure, combination of measures, or procedures used as a basis for any employment decision. Selection procedures include the full range of assessment techniques from traditional paper and pencil tests, performance tests, training programs, or probationary periods and physical, educational, and work experience requirements through informal or casual interviews and unscored application forms.

See also UNIFORM GUIDELINES ON EMPLOYEE SELECTION.

selection ratio, number of job applicants selected compared to the number of job applicants who were available.

self-actualization, apex of Abraham Maslow's needs hierarchy, where an individual theoretically reaches self-fulfillment and becomes all that he or she is capable of becoming. The importance of the concept of self-actualization was established long before Maslow gave it voice. The 19th century poet, Robert Browning, described its essence when he said "a man's reach should exceed his grasp, or what's a heaven for?" Maslow's needs hierarchy was originally presented in "A Theory of Human Motivation," *Psychological Review* (July 1943). For a technique to measure self-actualization, *see* Charles Bonjean and Gary Vance, "A Short Form Measure of Self-Actualization," *Journal of Applied Behavioral Science* (July–August–September 1968).

self-appraisal, performance evaluation technique in which the employee takes the initiative in appraising his/her own performance. *See* Kenneth S. Teel, "Self-Appraisal Revisited," *Personnel Journal* (July 1978).

Self-Directed Search (SDS), vocational interest inventory commonly used in vocational guidance and counseling. Administration, scoring and interpretation is performed by the individual. Consists of two booklets, the Assessment Booklet (for evaluation of individual's abilities and interest) and an Occupation Finder (a listing of 95 percent of all job types). TIME: Untimed. AUTHOR: John L. Holland, PUBLISHER: Consulting Psychologists Press, Inc. (*see* TEST PUBLISHERS).

self-employed, members of the workforce who work for themselves—in their own trade or business—as opposed to wage earners who are in the employ of others.

Self-Employed Individuals Tax Retirement Act of 1962: *see* KEOGH PLAN.

self-employment tax, means by which persons who work for themselves are provided social security coverage. Each self-employed person must pay self-employment tax on part or all of his or her income to help finance social security benefits, which are payable to self-employed persons as well as wage earners.

self-fulfilling prophecy, causing something to happen by believing it will. If a manager or teacher believes that his or her employees or students are not capable, they will eventually live up or down to the manager's or teacher's expectations. For a case study of how a manager's expectations about employee performance become a self fulfilling prophecy, *see* J. Sterling Livingston, "Pygmalion in Management," *Harvard Business Review* (July–August 1969).

self-report inventory: *see* PERSONALITY INVENTORY.

semiskilled workers, employees whose jobs are confined to well established work routines, usually requiring a considerable degree of manipulative ability and a limited exercise of independent judgment.

senior civil service, as recommended by the Hoover Commission of the 1950s, the federal government should establish a senior civil service "consisting of career administrators selected from all agencies of the Government solely on the basis of demonstrated competence to fill positions requiring a high degree of managerial competence." The senior civil service concept was only realized when the Civil Service Reform Act of 1978 created the Senior Executive Service.

Senior Executive Service (SES), federal government's top management corps, established by the Civil Service Reform Act of 1978.
The SES includes managers at GS 16 through Executive Level IV or their equiva-

lents in the executive branch. The large majority of SES executives are career managers; there is a 10 percent, government-wide ceiling on the number who may be non-career. In addition, about 45 percent of SES positions are career-reserved; that is, they can be filled only by career executives. *See* "All You Ever Wanted to Know About SES," *Civil Service Journal* (April–June 1979).
See also CIVIL SERVICE REFORM ACT OF 1978.

seniority, social mechanism that gives priority to the individuals who are the most senior—have the longest service—in an organization. Seniority is often used to determine which employees will be promoted, subjected to layoff, or given/denied other employment advantages. For a legal analysis, *see* Barry A. Friedman, "Seniority Systems and the Law," *Personnel Journal* (July 1976). For contractual provisions, *see* Winston L. Tillery, "Seniority Administration in Major Agreements, "*Monthly Labor Review* (December 1972).
See also the following entries:
BENEFIT SENIORITY
COMPETITIVE SENIORITY
DEPARTMENTAL SENIORITY
DOVETAIL SENIORITY
INTERNATIONAL BROTHERHOOD OF TEAMSTERS V. UNITED STATES
INVERSE SENIORITY
RETROACTIVE SENIORITY
SUPERSENIORITY
TRANS WORLD AIRLINES V. HARDISON

Senn v. Tile Layer's Protective Union, 301 U.S. 468 (1937), U.S. Supreme Court case, which held that a state anti-injunction law supporting peaceful picketing was constitutional.

sensitivity training: *see* LABORATORY TRAINING and BRADFORD, LELAND P.

separation, termination of an individual's employment for whatever reason.

separation interview: *see* EXIT INTERVIEW.

separation pay: *see* SEVERANCE PAY.

separation rate, ratio of the number of separations per hundred employees over a specified time span.

series of classes, all classes of positions involving the same kind of work, but which may vary as to the level of difficulty and responsibility and have differing grade and salary ranges. The classes in a series either have differing titles (*e.g.*, assistant accountant, associate accountant, senior accountant) or numerical designations (*e.g.*, Accountant I, Accountant II, Accountant III). Be wary of numerical designations, however. There is no uniformity in their use; an Accountant I could be either the most junior or most senior level.

See also POSITION CLASSIFICATION.

Service Employees' International Union: *see* LABOR ORGANIZATION.

service fee, money (usually the equivalent of union dues) that non-union members of an agency shop bargaining unit pay the union for negotiating and administering the collective bargaining agreement.

SES: *see* SENIOR EXECUTIVE SERVICE.

SET: *see* SHORT EMPLOYMENT TEST.

set: *see* POPULATION.

set-up time, time during the normal work day when a worker's machine is being set up (usually by the machine's operator) prior to commencing production. Union contracts frequently provide time standards for set-up operations.

70-percent syndrome: *see* CUTTING SCORE.

706 agency, state and local fair employment practices agency named for Section 706(c) of Title VII of the Civil Rights Act of 1964, which requires aggrieved individuals to submit claims to state or local fair employment practices agencies before they are eligible to present their cases to the federal government's Equal Employment Opportunity Commission. State and local agencies that have the ability to provide the same protections provided by Title VII as would the EEOC are termed 706 agencies. The EEOC maintains a list of the 706 agencies that it formally recognizes.

sever: *see* FIRE.

severance pay, also called DISMISSAL PAY, SEPARATION PAY, and TERMINATION PAY, lump-sum payment by an employer to an employee who has been permanently separated from the organization because of a work force reduction, the introduction of labor-saving machinery, or for any reason other than "cause." The amount of a severance payment is usually determined by a schedule based on years of service and earnings. About 40 percent of all union contracts contain provisions for severance pay.

Country	TYPICAL SEVERANCE PAYMENTS TO EXECUTIVES IN THE U.S. AND 13 OTHER COUNTRIES EXPRESSED AS A PERCENTAGE OF ANNUAL CASH INCOME	
	% Payment if income is $45,000	% Payment if income is $20,000
Belgium	300	200
Italy	280	190
Spain	250	250
Japan	250	200
Venezuela	135	135
Mexico	105	107
W. Germany	100	50
Britain	100	50
Brazil	90	90
France	80	80
Netherlands	50	50
Sweden	50	50
U.S.	50	33
Canada	35	35

Source: John Costello, "What Managers are Paid if they are Terminated," *Nation's Business* (August 1977).

Eligible federal government employees have severance pay computed on the basis of one week's salary for each year of the first 10 years of service and 2 week's salary for each year of service after 10 years. For employees over age 40, an age adjustment allowance is added to the basic allowance by computing 10 percent of the basic allowance of each year over age 40. The total severance pay that a federal employee may receive is limited to one year's pay at the rate of pay received immediately prior to separation.

See also NOLDE BROTHERS, INC. V. LOCAL NO. 358, BAKERY WORKERS.

sex differential, also RACE DIFFERENTIAL, lower than "regular" wage rate paid by an employer to female and/or black employees. Such differentials were paid before the advent of current equal employment opportunity laws and are now illegal.

sex discrimination, any disparate or unfavorable treatment of an individual in an employment situation because of his or her sex. The Civil Rights Act of 1964 makes sex discrimination illegal except where a bona fide occupational qualification is involved. For a legal analysis, *see* Jerri D. Gilbreath, "Sex Discrimination and Title VII of the Civil Rights Act," *Personnel Journal* (January 1977). *See also* Paul Osterman, "Sex Discrimination in Professional Employment: A

Case Study," *Industrial and Labor Relations Review* (July 1979).

See also the following entries:

CITY OF LOS ANGELES, DEPARTMENT OF
    WATER & POWER V. MANHART
DISCRIMINATION
GOESAERT V. CLEARY
PITTSBURGH PRESS CO. V. THE PITTSBURGH
    COMMISSION ON HUMAN RELATIONS
PREGNANCY DISCRIMINATION ACT OF 1978
SCHLESINGER V. BALLARD

sexist, person or organization that consciously or unconsciously practices sex discrimination.

sex plus, situation where an employer does not discriminate against all males or all females, but discriminates against a subset of either sex. *Phillips* v. *Martin Marietta*, 400 U.S. 542 (1971), is the U.S. Supreme Court case, that dealt with the "sex plus" criterion for evaluating applicants for employment. Martin Marietta had a policy of hiring both sexes for a particular job but refused to hire any women with pre-school-aged children. The court found this "sex plus" policy to be in violation of Title VII of the Civil Rights Act of 1964.

sexual harassment, exists whenever an individual in a position to control or influence another's job, career, or grade uses such power to gain sexual favors or punish the refusal of such favors. Sexual harassment on the job varies from inappropriate sexual innuendo to coerced sexual relations. *See* Kerri Weisel, "Title VII: Legal Protection Against Sexual Harassment," *Washington Law Review* (December 1977); Lin Farley, *The Sexual Harassment of Women on the Job* (N.Y.: McGraw-Hill, 1979); Patricia A. Somers and Judith Clementson-Mohr, "Sexual Extortion in the Workplace," *The Personnel Administrator* (April 1979); Catharine A. MacKinnon, *Sexual Harassment of Working Women* (New Haven, Conn.: Yale University Press, 1979).

SFAAW: *see* LABOR ORGANIZATION, Stove, Furnace and Allied Appliance Workers' International Union of North America.

Shakespeare, William (1564-1616), English writer who created now classic studies in personnel management and organizational behavior. His more famous works include:

MacBeth—the story of a ruthless workaholic who allows his too ambitious wife to egg him on to the top, only to find that he can't hack it when up against a "C" section rival.

Romeo and Juliet—illustrates the dysfunctional aspects of a breakdown in communications between two competing paternalistic organizations. This situation is only temporarily rectified when informal inter-organizational communications are established at the employee level—unfortunately with poisonous results.

Hamlet—poignant case study of a sensitive young executive who fails to move up in the organizational hierarchy because of his inability to make decisions.

Othello—minority employee makes it to the top, only to find that jealousy at the office leads to murder.

King Lear—chief executive of a family business learns the perils of early retirement.

Shanker, Albert (1928-), became president of the United Federation of Teachers in New York City in 1964 and president of the American Federation of Teachers in 1974.

shape-up, a declining method of hiring—long common in the maritime industry—which had men line up at the beginning of each day so that they could be selected (or rejected) for work.

Shaw, Lemuel (1781-1861), chief justice of the Supreme Judicial Court of Massachusetts from 1830 to 1860 who wrote a landmark decision, in the case of *Commonwealth* v. *Hunt*, 4 Metcalf, 45 Mass., III (1842), which held that it was not a criminal act of conspiracy for a combination of employees or a union to refuse to work for an employer who hires nonunion labor. This decision established the legality of the right to strike for higher wages. For a biography, *see* Leonard W. Levy, *Law of the Commonwealth and Chief Justice Shaw* (Cambridge, Mass.: Harvard University Press, 1957).

sheepskin psychosis: *see* CREDENTIALISM.

Sheet Metal Workers' International Association: *see* LABOR ORGANIZATION.

sheltered workshop, places of employment that offer a controlled, noncompetitive environment for persons unable to compete in the regular world of work because of physical or mental disabilities. For a history, *see* Nathan Nelson, *Workshops for the Handicapped in the United States: An Historical and Developmental Perspective* (Springfield, Ill.: Charles C. Thomas, 1971).

See also WAGNER–O'DAY ACT.

Shelton* v. *Tucker, 364 U.S. 479 (1960), U.S. Supreme Court case, which dealt with the questions of whether public employees could have membership in subversive organizations, organizations with illegal objectives, and unions. Their right to join the latter was upheld. With regard to the former, it was held that there could be no general answer. Rather, each case has to be judged on the basis of whether a public employee actually supports an organization's illegal aims, because, as the Supreme Court expressed it, "Those who join an organization but do not share its unlawful purposes and who do not participate in its unlawful activities surely pose no threat, either as citizens or as public employees." Consequently, it is incumbent upon public employers seeking to dismiss employees for membership in subversive organizations or those with illegal purposes to prove that the employees actually shared in the subversive organization's objectionable aims and activities.

Sherbert v. Verner, 374 U.S. 398 (1963), U.S. Supreme Court case, which held it was unconstitutional to disqualify a person for unemployment compensation benefits solely because that person refused to accept employment that would require working on Saturday contrary to his or her religious belief.

Sheridan Psychological Services, Inc.: see TEST PUBLISHERS.

Sherman Antitrust Act of 1890, also called SHERMAN ACT, federal statute that held "every contract, combination in the form of trust or otherwise, or conspiracy, in restraint of trade or commerce . . . , is hereby declared to be illegal." While the statute was directed at industrial monopolies, the courts used the act punitively against the budding union movement. Subsequent legislation (the Clayton Act of 1914) exempted unions from the Sherman Act prohibitions on the restraint of trade.
See also the following entries:
LAWLOR V. LOEWE
UNITED MINE WORKERS V. PENNINGTON
UNITED STATES V. HUTCHESON

shift, fixed: see FIXED SHIFT.

shift, split: see BROKEN TIME.

shift premium, also called SHIFT DIFFERENTIAL, extra compensation paid as an inducement to accept shift work.

shift work, formal tour of duty that is mostly outside of "normal" daytime business hours. According to Richard A. Edwards, in "Shift Work: Performance and Satisfaction," *Per-*

sonnel Journal (November 1975), an examination of the research on the efficiency of night or shift workers seems to indicate that it is "a physiological fact of life that night shift workers will never perform with the same efficiency as the other two shifts."

Shoe and Allied Craftsmen, Brotherhood of: see LABOR ORGANIZATION.

Shoe Workers of America, United: see LABOR ORGANIZATION.

Shoe Workers' Union, Boot and: see LABOR ORGANIZATION.

shop committee, group of union members in the same organizational unit who have been selected to speak for the union membership on any of a variety of issues.

shop steward: see STEWARD.

Short Employment Test (SET), three tests that measure verbal, numerical and clerical abilities of applicants for clerical positions. Developed to supplement tests being used by member banks of the American Bankers Association in their selection of clerical workers. TIME: 15/20 minutes. AUTHORS: G. K. Bennett and Marjorie Gelink. PUBLISHER: Psychological Corporation (*see* TEST PUBLISHERS).

Short Tests of Clerical Ability, series of tests for job applicants in various clerical areas used for employment selection and placement in business and industry settings. Test series includes: Short Occupational Knowledge Test for Bookkeepers, Short Occupational Knowledge Test for Office Machine Operators, and Short Occupational Knowledge Test for Secretaries. TIME: 10/15 minutes each test. AUTHORS: Bruce A. Campbell and Suellen O. Johnson. PUBLISHER: Science Research Associates, Inc. (*see* TEST PUBLISHERS).

showing of interest, evidence of membership—the requirement that a union must show that it has adequate support from employees in a proposed bargaining unit before a representation election can be held. A "showing of interest" is usually demonstrated by signed authorization cards.

Shultz, George P. (1920-   ), Secretary of Labor from 1969 to 1970, director of the Office and Management and Budget from 1970 to 1972, and Secretary of the Treasury from 1972 to 1974.

sick leave, leave of absence, usually with

pay, granted to employees who cannot attend work because of illness. *See* Charles N. Weaver, "Influence of Sex, Salary and Age on Seasonal Use of Sick leave," *Personnel Journal* (August 1970); Maureen Heneghan and Sigmund G. Ginsberg," Use of Sick Leave," *Personnel Administration* (September–October 1970).

sick-leave bank, arrangement that allows employees to pool some of their paid sick-leave days in a common fund so that they may draw upon that fund if extensive illness uses up their remaining paid time off. Sick-leave banks have tended to discourage absenteeism; because, with everyone jointly owning days in the bank, there is some psychological pressure on workers not to use their sick-leave unless they are really sick.

Sidell, William (1915-   ), became president of the United Brotherhood of Carpenters and Joiners of America in 1972.

Siderographers, International Association of: *see* LABOR ORGANIZATION.

significance, also called STATISTICAL SIGNIFICANCE, degree to which one can be confident in the reliability of a statistical measure. For example, a confidence level of .05 means that the statistical finding would occur by chance in only one sample out of every twenty.

silver-circle rate, higher than standard pay rate based upon length of service.

Simon, Herbert A. (1916-   ), awarded the Noble Prize for Economics in 1978 for his pioneering work in management decision making, Simon is best known to the personnel world for his equally impressive contributions to our understanding of organizational behavior. Major works include: *Administrative Behavior* (N.Y.: Macmillan, 1947); *Public Administration*, with D. Smithburg and V. Thompson (N.Y.: Knopf, 1950); *Models of Man: Social and Rational* (N.Y.: John Wiley, 1958); *The New Science of Management Decision* (N.Y.: Harper & Row, 1960); *The Shape of Automation for Men and Management* (N.Y.: Harper & Row, 1965); *Human Problem Solving*, with Allen Newell (Englewood Cliffs, N.J.: Prentice-Hall, 1972). *See also* PROVERBS OF ADMINISTRATION and SATISFICING.

simulation: *see* GAMING SIMULATION.

***Sinclair Refining* v. *Atkinson:* see** BOYS MARKET V. RETAIL CLERKS' LOCAL 770.

sinecure, any position for which a salary is extracted but little or no work is expected. This was originally an ecclesiastical term, which meant a church office that did not require the care of souls. Sinecure is Latin for "without care."

Siney, John (1831-1880), president of the first national miner's union, the Miners' National Association. For a biography, *see* Edward Pinkowski, *John Siney: The Miners Martyr* (Philadelphia: Sunshine Press, 1963).

single rate: *see* FLAT RATE.

SIT: *see* SLOSSON INTELLIGENCE TEST.

sit-down strike, also STAY-IN STRIKE, any work stoppage during which the strikers remain at their work stations and refuse to leave the employer's premises in order to forestall the employment of strikebreakers. This kind of strike gained widespread publicity in the 1930s as a tactic of the unions in the rubber and automobile industries. A sit-down strike that lasts for a substantial period of time is then called a *stay-in strike*. For a history, *see* Daniel Nelson (ed.), "The Beginning of the Sit-Down Era: The Reminiscences of Rex Murray," *Labor History* (Winter 1974); Sidney Fine, *Sit-Down: The General Motors Strike of 1936-1937* (Ann Arbor: University of Michigan Press, 1969).

In 1939, the U.S. Supreme Court in *National Labor Relations Board* v. *Fansteel Metallurgical Corp.*, 306 U.S. 240 (1939), ruled that the right to strike did not extend to the use of sit-down strikes and that employees discharged under such circumstances had no reinstatement rights under the National Labor Relations (Wagner) Act of 1935. The Court held that a sit-down strike

> was an illegal seizure of the buildings in order to prevent their use by the employer in a lawful manner and thus by acts of force and violence to compel the employer to submit. When the employees resorted to that sort of compulsion they took a position outside the protection of the statute and accepted the risk of the termination of their employment upon grounds aside from the exercise of the legal rights which the statute was designed to conserve....

situational management: *see* CONTINGENCY MANAGEMENT.

SIU: *see* LABOR ORGANIZATION, Seafarers' International Union of North America.

SIU-AGLIW: *see* LABOR ORGANIZATION, Atlantic Gulf, Lakes and Inland Waters District, under Seafarers' International Union of North America.

SIU-IBPAW: *see* LABOR ORGANIZATION, Pottery and Allied Workers, International Brotherhood of Sailors' Union of the, under Seafarers' International Union of North America.

SIU-IUPW: *see* LABOR ORGANIZATION, International Union of Petroleum and Industrial Workers, under Seafarers' International Union of North America.

SIU-MCS: *see* LABOR ORGANIZATION, Marine Cooks and Stewards' Union, under Seafarers' International Union of North America.

SIU-MFOW: *see* LABOR ORGANIZATION, Pacific Coast Marine Firemen, Oilers, Watertenders and Wipers Association, under Seafarers' International Union of North America.

SIU-SUP: *see* LABOR ORGANIZATION, Sailors' Union of the Pacific, under Seafarers' International Union of North America.

Sixteen Personality Factor Questionnaire (16PF), assesses sixteen basic personality dimensions (*i.e.*, practical vs. imaginative, relaxed vs. tense, introversion vs. extraversion, trusting vs. suspicious, humble vs. assertive, emotionally stable vs. affected by feelings, etc. Designed for use with individuals age 16 and over. TIME: Varies. AUTHORS: R. B. Cattell, H. W. Eber, and M. M. Tatsuoka. PUBLISHER: Institute for Personality and Ability Testing (*see* TEST PUBLISHERS).

skewness, tendency of a distribution to depart from symmetry or balance around the mean. If the scores tend to cluster at the lower end of the distribution, the distribution is said to be positively skewed; if they tend to cluster at the upper end of the distribution, the distribution is said to be negatively skewed.

skill differential, differences in wage rates paid to workers employed in occupational categories requiring varying levels of skill.

skilled labor, workers who, having trained for a relatively long time, have mastered jobs of considerable skill requiring the exercise of substantial independent judgment. According to an *Industry Week* survey reported in the August 29, 1977, issue, the skilled laborers most in demand are: machine operators, mechanics, welders, and electricians. *See* W. Franke and D. Sokel, *The Shortage of Skilled*

and Technical Workers (Lexington, Mass.: Lexington Books, 1970).

skills, physical or manipulative activities requiring knowledge for their execution.

skills survey, also called SKILLS INVENTORY, comprehensive collection and examination of data on the workforce to determine the composition and level of employees' skills, knowledges, and abilities so that they can be more fully utilized and/or developed to fill the staffing needs of an organization. A skills survey or inventory may at times be the process of collecting data and at other times the product as represented by a collection of data in a variety of forms. To be effective, skills data must also be arranged in such a manner that the information gathered can be readily accessible for management use.

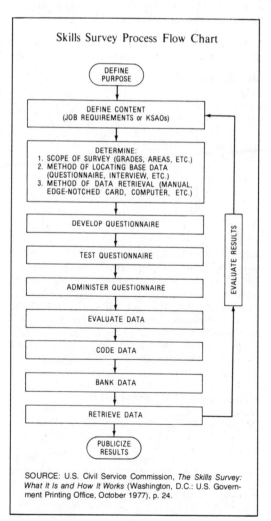

SOURCE: U.S. Civil Service Commission, *The Skills Survey: What It Is and How It Works* (Washington, D.C.: U.S. Government Printing Office, October 1977), p. 24.

Skinner, B. F. (1904-   ), full name FREDERIC BURRHUS SKINNER, one of the most influential of behavioral psychologists, inventor of the teaching machine, and generally considered to be the "father" of programmed instruction. Major works include: *Waldon Two* (N.Y.: Macmillan 1948, 1966); *Science and Human Behavior* (N.Y.: Free Press, 1953, 1965); *The Technology of Teaching* (N.Y.: Appleton-Century-Crofts, 1968); *Beyond Freedom and Dignity* (N.Y.: Knopf, 1971).

Sleeping Car Porters, Brotherhood of: *see* LABOR ORGANIZATION.

slide-rule discipline, approach to discipline that eliminates supervisory discretion and sets very specific quantitative standards as the consequences of specific violations. For example, a discipline policy based on this concept might hold that any employee who is late for work more than four times in a 30-day period would be "automatically" suspended for three days.

Sloan Management Review, professional management journal of the Alfred P. Sloan School of Management at the Massachusetts Institute of Technology. It is published three times each academic year (Fall, Winter, and Spring) and has as its principal goal the exchange of information between academic and business communities.

> *Sloan Management Review*
> Alfred P. Sloan School of Management
> Massachusetts Institute of Technology
> Cambridge, MA 02139

Slosson Educational Publications: *see* TEST PUBLISHERS.

Slosson Intelligence Test (SIT), brief intelligence test that is individually and verbally administered. Scores correlate highly with tests that normally take one hour or more. Items are based in part upon the Stanford-Binet Intelligence Scale, Third Revision and the Gesell Developmental Schedules. TIME: 10/30 minutes. AUTHOR: Richard L. Slosson. PUBLISHER: Slosson Educational Publications (*see* TEST PUBLISHERS).

slot, position in an organization.

slowdown, deliberate reduction of output by employees. Such efforts are usually designed to bring economic pressure upon an employer without incurring the costs of a strike. *See* Richard S. Hammett, Joel Seidman, and Jack London, "The Slowdown as a Union Tactic," *Journal of Political Economy* (April 1957).

SLU: *see* LABOR ORGANIZATION, Southern Labor Union.

small-group research, also GROUP, study of small groups. A *group* consists of a number of individuals who interact with each other in a particular social setting. Generally, groups are classified as "small" when each member can at least take personal cognizance of all other members. This distinguishes small groups from social units that are so large that it is impossible for each member to be aware of all others. For the pioneering concepts of small-group research, *see* George C. Homans, *The Human Group* (N.Y.: Harcourt, Brace Jovanovich, 1950); Robert T. Golembiewski *The Small Group: An Analysis of Research Concepts and Operations* (Chicago: University of Chicago Press, 1962); A. Paul Hare, *Handbook of Small Group Research* (N.Y.: The Free Press, 2nd ed., 1976).

See also GROUP DYNAMICS and ORGANIZATION DEVELOPMENT.

Small Parts Dexterity Test, Crawford: *see* CRAWFORD SMALL PARTS DEXTERITY TEST.

Smith Act: *see* ALIEN REGISTRATION ACT OF 1940.

Smith–Hughes Act of 1917, federal vocational educational act that established the principles of federal financial aid and cooperation with the states in promoting public vocational education.

Smith v. Arkansas State Highway Employees, Local 1315, 60 L. Ed. 2d 360 (1979), U.S Supreme Court case, which held that the Arkansas State Highway Commission's refusal to consider a Highway Department employee's grievance, when submitted by a union rather than by the employee, did not violate 1st Amendment rights.

smorgasbord benefits plan: *see* CAFETERIA BENEFITS PLAN.

SMW: *see* LABOR ORGANIZATION, Sheet Metal Workers' International Association.

social audit, defined by Raymond A. Bauer and Dan H. Fenn, Jr., in "What *is* a Corporate Social Audit?" *Harvard Business Review* (January–February 1973), as "a commitment to systematic assessment of and reporting on some meaningful, definable domain of a company's activities that have social impact."

social insurance, any benefit program that a state makes available to the members of its society in time of need and as a matter of right.

social reference group: *see* REFERENCE GROUP.

social security, once defined by Britain's Lord Beveridge as "a job when you can work and an income when you can't." In the United States, social security is the popular name for the Old Age, Survivors, and Disability Insurance (OASDI) system established by the Social Security Act of 1935. At first, social security only covered private sector employees upon retirement. In 1939, the law was changed to pay survivors when the worker died, as well as certain dependents when the worker retired. In the 1950s, coverage was extended to include most self-employed persons, most state and local employees, household and farm employees, members of the armed forces, and members of the clergy. Today, almost all U.S. jobs are covered by social security.

Disability insurance was added in 1954 to give workers protection against loss of earnings due to total disability. The social security program was expanded again in 1965 with the enactment of Medicare, which assured hospital and medical insurance protection to people 65 and over. Since 1973, Medicare coverage has been available to people under 65 who have been entitled to disability checks for 2 or more consecutive years and to people with permanent kidney failure who need dialysis or kidney transplants. Amendments enacted in 1972 provide that social security benefits will increase automatically with the cost of living. *See* Alicia H. Munnell, *The Future of Social Security* (Washington D.C.: The Brookings Institution, 1977); Robert M. Ball, *Social Security: Today and Tomorrow* (N.Y.: Columbia University Press, 1978); Martha Derthick, *Policymaking for Social Security* (Washington, D.C.: The Brookings Institution, 1979).

See also OLD AGE, SURVIVORS, AND DISABILITY INSURANCE and HELVERING V. DAVIS.

Social Security Act of 1935, federal statute that, as amended, is the foundation of the nation's social insurance program. For histories, *see* Edwin E. White, *The Development of the Social Security Act* (Madison: University of Wisconsin Press, 1963); Roy Lubove, *The Struggle for Social Security: 1900-1935* (Cambridge, Mass.: Harvard University Press, 1968); J. Douglas Brown, *An American Philosophy of Social Security: Evolution and Issues* (Princeton: Princeton University Press, 1972).

See also OLD AGE, SURVIVORS, AND DISABILITY INSURANCE and UNEMPLOYMENT INSURANCE.

Society for Personnel Administration: *see* INTERNATIONAL PERSONNEL MANAGEMENT ASSOCIATION.

Society for the Advancement of Management (SAM), formed in 1912 by colleagues of Frederick W. Taylor as a professional society dedicated to the discussion and promotion of

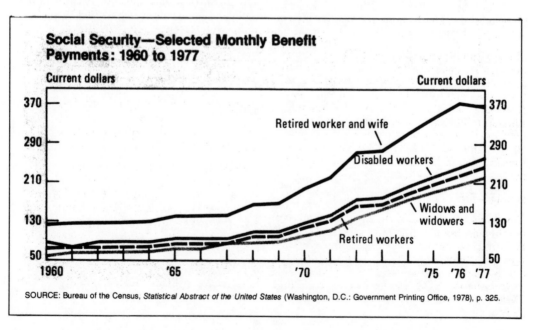

SOURCE: Bureau of the Census, *Statistical Abstract of the United States* (Washington, D.C.: Government Printing Office, 1978), p. 325.

scientific management, SAM is now a peer training organization "devoted to helping managers develop professionally through communication and interaction with other managers."

Society for the Advancement of Management
135 West 50th Street
New York, NY 10020
(212) 586-8100

sociogram, diagram showing the interactions between members of a group. Typically, it has circles representing people and arrows extending from those circles pointing out the other people (circles) that are liked, disliked, etc.

sociology, occupational: *see* OCCUPATIONAL SOCIOLOGY.

sociology of work: *see* OCCUPATIONAL SOCIOLOGY.

sociometry, technique for discovering the patterns of interpersonal relationships that exist within a group. A sociometric analysis typically has each member of the group express his or her choices for or against other members of the group. A common question on such surveys is "who should be the leader of the group?" The ensuing preference and rejection patterns can be used to construct sociograms or social maps. For the pioneering work in sociometric methodologies, *see* J. L. Moreno, "Contributions of Sociometry to Research Methodology in Sociology," *American Sociological Review* (June 1947); J. L. Moreno (ed.), *The Sociometry Reader* (Glencoe, Ill.: The Free Press, 1960). For an evalu-

ation of its usefulness, *see* B. J. Speroff, "Sociometry: A Key to the Informal Organization," *Personnel Journal* (February 1968).

socio-technical systems, concept that a work group is neither a technical nor a social system, but an interdependent socio-technical system. Research on this concept was pioneered in the early 1950s by the Tavistock Institute of Human Relations in London. For accounts by the original researchers, *see* F. E. Emery and E. L. Trist, "Socio-Technical Systems," C. W. Churchman and M. Verhulst (eds.), *Management Science, Models, and Techniques* (London: Pergamon, 1960), Vol II; Fred E. Emery, "Characteristics of Socio-Technical Systems," Louis E. Davis and James C. Taylor (eds.), *Design of Jobs* (Baltimore: Penguin Books, 1972). *See also* Thomas G. Cummings and Suresh Srivastva, *Management of Work: A Socio-Technical Systems Approach* (Kent State University Press, 1977).

Socrates (470-399 B.C.), ancient Greek philosopher who established the intellectual foundations of modern employment testing when he asserted that "The unexamined life is not worth living."

soldier, in the industrial world, to malinger, to shrink one's duty, to feign illness, or to make a pretense of working. The usage comes from naval history. In earlier centuries, soldiers aboard ship did not have duties as arduous as those of the regular ship's company. So the sailors made soldiering synonymous with loafing and other nonproductive activities.

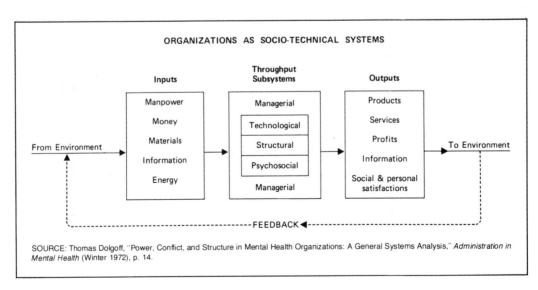

ORGANIZATIONS AS SOCIO-TECHNICAL SYSTEMS

SOURCE: Thomas Dolgoff, "Power, Conflict, and Structure in Mental Health Organizations: A General Systems Analysis," *Administration in Mental Health* (Winter 1972), p. 14.

South Carolina Labor Council, AFL–CIO: *see* AMERICAN FEDERATION OF LABOR–CONGRESS OF INDUSTRIAL ORGANIZATIONS.

South Dakota State Federation of Labor: *see* AMERICAN FEDERATION OF LABOR–CONGRESS OF INDUSTRIAL ORGANIZATIONS.

Southern Labor Union: *see* LABOR ORGANIZATION.

Spanish Speaking Program, also HISPANIC EMPLOYMENT PROGRAM, federal government program established on November 5, 1970 to call attention to the needs of the Spanish-speaking in federal employment. It is an integral part of the government's total EEO effort and is designed to assure equal employment opportunity for the Spanish-speaking in all aspects of federal employment. In March 1978, the name of the Spanish Speaking Program was changed to the Hispanic Employment Program. *See* Office of the Spanish Speaking Program, U.S. Civil Service Commission, *Spanish Speaking Program: A Guidebook for Coordinators* (Washington, D.C.: U.S. Government Printing Office, 1975).

span of control, extent of a manager's responsibility. The span of control has usually been expressed as the number of subordinates that a manager should supervise. Sir Ian Hamilton, *The Soul and Body of an Army* (London: Edward Arnold & Co., 1921), is generally credited with having first asserted that the "average human brain finds its effective scope in handling from three to six other brains." A. V. Graicunas took a mathematical approach to the concept and demonstrated, in "Relationship in Organization," Luther Gulick and Lyndall Urwick (eds.), *Papers on the Science of Administration* (N.Y.: Institute of Public Administration, 1937), that as the number of subordinates reporting to a manager increases arithmetically, the number of possible interpersonal interactions increased geometrically. Building upon Graicunas' work, Lyndall F. Urwick boldly asserts, in "The Manager's Span of Control," *Harvard Business Review* (May–June 1956), that "no superior can supervise directly the work of more than five or, at the most, six subordinates whose work interlocks." Studies on the concept of span of control abound but there is no consensus on an "ideal" span.

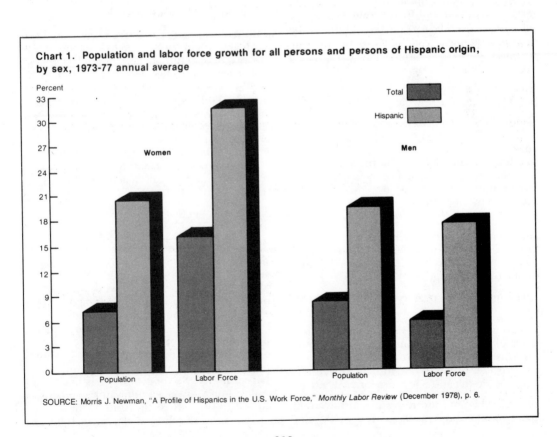

Chart 1. Population and labor force growth for all persons and persons of Hispanic origin, by sex, 1973-77 annual average

SOURCE: Morris J. Newman, "A Profile of Hispanics in the U.S. Work Force," *Monthly Labor Review* (December 1978), p. 6.

spatial relations, measure of an individual's ability for rapid and dexterous manipulation of pieces and parts relative to one another (*i.e.,* perceiving geometric relationships).

Spearman-Brown Formula, formula for determining the relationship between the reliability of a test and its length.

specification, also called JOB SPECIFICATION and CLASS SPECIFICATION, written description of the duties and responsibilities of a class of positions. Specifications usually include: the title of the position; a general statement of the nature of the work; examples of typical tasks; the minimum requirements and qualifications for the position; the knowledges, skills, and abilities essential for satisfactory performance; and the assigned salary range.

Specifications are designed to highlight those aspects of a position that are significant for classification purposes. They are descriptive, not restrictive. They are not expected to include all of the possible duties that might make up an individual position.

See also POSITION CLASSIFICATION.

speededness, appropriateness of a test in terms of the length of time allotted. For most purposes, a good test will make full use of the examination period but not be so speeded that an examinee's rate of work will have an undue influence on the score received.

speed rating, performance rating that compares the speed with which an employee performs specific tasks against an observer's standard or norm.

speed test, term loosely applied to any test that few can complete within the alloted time or, more technically, a test consisting of a large number of relatively easy items so that a high score depends on how fast an examinee can work within a time limit.

speed-up, also STRETCH-OUT, terms referring to any effort by employers to obtain an increase in productivity without a corresponding increase in wages.

speed-up boy, derogatory term for an "efficiency expert."

spiral-omnibus test, test in which the various kinds of tasks are distributed throughout the test (instead of being grouped together) and are in cycles of increasing difficulty. There is only one timing and one score for such a test.

split commission, awarding of partial credit and compensation to each of several sales

persons when each is directly involved in completing a sale. The normal commission is divided among the recipients.

split-dollar life insurance, also called SUPPLEMENTAL LIFE INSURANCE, life insurance for employees paid for by an employer. In the event of the covered employee's death, the employer totally recovers the paid premiums from the benefit sum with the remainder distributed to the employee's beneficiaries. *See* Robert B. Morley, "New Uses of Supplemental Life Insurance," *The Personnel Administrator* (May 1975).

split-half reliability, measure of the reliability of a test obtained by correlating scores on one half of a test with scores on the other half and correcting for the reduced size.

split labor market, according to Edna Bonacich, in "A Theory of Ethnic Antagonism: The Split Labor Market," *American Sociological Review* (October 1972), "to be split, a labor market must contain at least two groups of workers whose price of labor differs for the same work, or would differ if they did the same work."

split shift: *see* BROKEN TIME.

split-the-difference, collective bargaining tactic in which both sides agree to a settlement half way between their bargaining positions. For a lesson on strategy, *see* Roger L. Bowlby and William R. Schriver, "Bluffing and the 'Split-the-Difference' Theory of Wage Bargaining," *Industrial and Labor Relations Review* (January 1978).

Sprading, Abe L. (1885-1970), president of the Amalgamated Association of Street, Electric Railway and Motor Coach Employees of America from 1946 to 1959.

SSI: *see* SUPPLEMENTAL SECURITY INCOME.

staffing, one of the most basic functions of management and usually considered synonymous with employment—that is, the process of hiring people to perform work for the organization. Staffing defines the organization by translating its objectives and goals into a specific work plan. It structures the responsibilities of the organization's human resources into a work system by establishing who will perform what function, and have what authority. Staffing must also make the employment, advancement, and compensation processes satisfy the criteria of equity and due process while at the same time re-

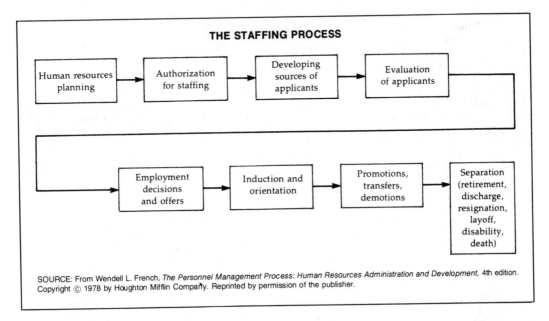

THE STAFFING PROCESS

Human resources planning → Authorization for staffing → Developing sources of applicants → Evaluation of applicants

→ Employment decisions and offers → Induction and orientation → Promotions, transfers, demotions → Separation (retirement, discharge, resignation, layoff, disability, death)

SOURCE: From Wendell L. French, *The Personnel Management Process: Human Resources Administration and Development*, 4th edition. Copyright © 1978 by Houghton Mifflin Company. Reprinted by permission of the publisher.

lating their processes to the overall organizational structure in order to ensure their relevance. Staffing is the essence of the personnel management process.

staffing dynamics, phrase used by those who are not content with calling turnover turnover.

staffing plan, planning document that minimally (1) lists an organization's projected personnel needs by occupation and grade level and (2) identifies how these needs will be met.

staffing program planning, determination by organization personnel management of the numbers and kinds of personnel management actions necessary during each stage of the planning period to staff the workforce required in management's program plan.

staff organization, those segments of a larger organization that provide support services and have no direct responsibilities for line operations or production. Personnel administration has traditionally been a staff function. *See* Ernest Dale and Lyndall F. Urwick, *Staff in Organization* (N.Y.: McGraw-Hill, 1960).

Stahl, O. Glenn (1910-   ), until his retirement in 1969, the director of the Bureau of Policies and Standards, U.S. Civil Service Commission, and the author of one of the leading texts on public personnel administration. Major works include: *The Personnel Job of Government Managers* (Chicago: International Personnel Management Association,

1971); *Public Personnel Administration* (N.Y.: Harper & Row, 7th ed., 1976).

Stakhanovite, decidedly dated term for a ratebuster. Alexei Stakhanov was a Russian miner who regularly exceeded his production quota. During Stalin's regime, he was a well published example of the "ideal" Russian worker. Rumor has it that Stakhanov increased his production output on secret orders from the Communist Party. For his efforts, he was promoted from worker to commissar and even awarded the Order of Lenin.

standard, employment: *see* EMPLOYMENT STANDARD.

standard allowance, established amount of time by which the normal time for employees to complete their tasks is increased in order to compensate for the expected amount of personal and/or unavoidable delays.

standard deviation, measure of the variability of a distribution about its mean or average. In distributions of test scores, for example, a low standard deviation would indicate a tendency of scores to cluster about the mean; a high standard deviation would indicate a wide variation in scores. In a normal distribution, approximately 68 percent of the cases lie between +1 S.D. and −1 S.D. from the mean and approximately 96 percent of the cases between +2 S.D. and −2 S.D. from the mean.

standard error of measurement, number expressed in score units that serves as another

Standard Federal Regions

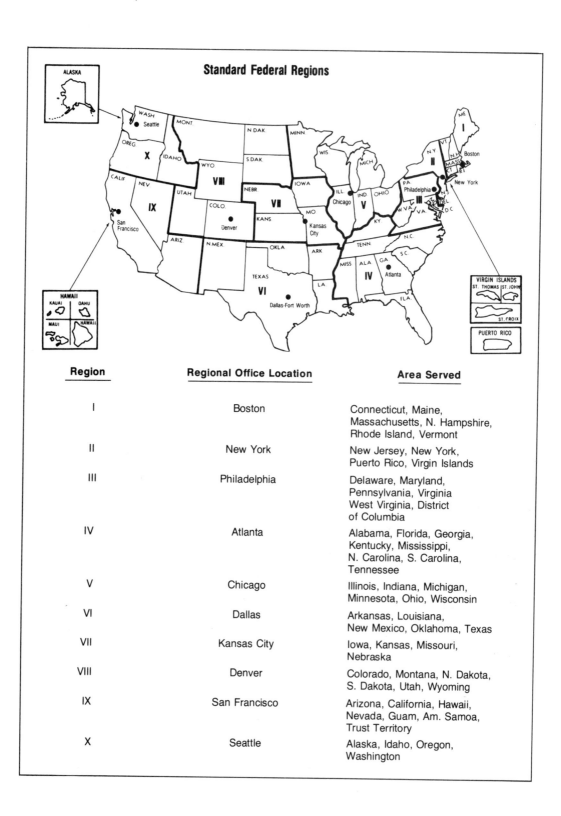

Region	Regional Office Location	Area Served
I	Boston	Connecticut, Maine, Massachusetts, N. Hampshire, Rhode Island, Vermont
II	New York	New Jersey, New York, Puerto Rico, Virgin Islands
III	Philadelphia	Delaware, Maryland, Pennsylvania, Virginia West Virginia, District of Columbia
IV	Atlanta	Alabama, Florida, Georgia, Kentucky, Mississippi, N. Carolina, S. Carolina, Tennessee
V	Chicago	Illinois, Indiana, Michigan, Minnesota, Ohio, Wisconsin
VI	Dallas	Arkansas, Louisiana, New Mexico, Oklahoma, Texas
VII	Kansas City	Iowa, Kansas, Missouri, Nebraska
VIII	Denver	Colorado, Montana, N. Dakota, S. Dakota, Utah, Wyoming
IX	San Francisco	Arizona, California, Hawaii, Nevada, Guam, Am. Samoa, Trust Territory
X	Seattle	Alaska, Idaho, Oregon, Washington

index of test reliability. It can be interpreted as indicating the probability that if an error of measurement of a test is 20 points, there are approximately 2 chances out of 3 that an individual's "true score" will be within ± 20 points of his/her "obtained score" on the test. Similarly, the chances are approximately 96 out of 100 that his/her "true score" will be within ± 40 points of his/her "obtained score."

standard federal regions geographic subdivisions of the U.S. established to achieve more uniformity in the location and geographic jurisdiction of federal field offices as a basis for promoting more systematic coordination among agencies and among federal–state–local governments and for securing management improvements and economies through greater interagency and intergovernmental cooperation. Boundaries were drawn and regional office locations designed for 10 regions, and agencies are required to adopt the uniform system when changes are made or new offices established.

Standard Form 171, the federal government's "Personal Qualifications Statement" and its universal employment application.

standard hour, the normally expected amount of work to be done in an hour.

standard-hour plan, incentive plan that rewards an employee by a percent premium that equals the percent by which performance beats the standard.

standardization, specification of consistent procedures to be followed in administering, scoring, and interpreting tests.

standardized test, any objective test given under constant conditions and/or any test for which a set of norms is available.

standard of living, measure of the material affluence enjoyed by a nation or by an individual.

standard rate: *see* FLAT RATE.

standards: *see* CLASSIFICATION STANDARDS.

standard score, any transformed test score, in terms of which raw scores are expressed for convenience and ease of interpretation.

standards of conduct, an organization's formal guidelines for ethical behavior. For example, the standards of conduct for National Aeronautics and Space Administration employees require that

each NASA employee will refrain from any use of his official position which is motivated by, or has the appearance of being motivated by, the desire for private gain for himself or other persons. He must conduct himself in such a manner that there is not the slightest suggestion of the extracting of private advantage from his Government employment.

See also ETHICS and CODE OF ETHICS.

standards of performance, statements that tell an employee how well he or she must perform a task to be considered a satisfactory employee. Standards cover how much, how accurately, in what time period, or in what manner, the various job tasks are to be performed. The performance standards, whether written or unwritten, will specify the minimum level of performance at which an employee must work in order to attain a satisfactory performance rating. Written performance standards are usually required only when an employee is warned that he or she may receive an unsatisfactory rating.

Stanford University Press: *see* TEST PUBLISHERS.

starvation wages: *see* LIVING WAGE.

State, County, and Municipal Employees, American Federation of: *see* LABOR ORGANIZATION.

state of the art, level of development in a given scientific or technological field at a given time, usually the present.

static system: *see* DYNAMIC SYSTEM.

statistical inference, use of information observed in a sample to make predictions about a larger population.

statistical significance: *see* SIGNIFICANCE.

statistical validation, also called CRITERION RELATED VALIDATION, validation that involves definition of what is to be measured (*i.e.*, criterion) by some systematic method based upon observations of the job behavior of individuals. Possible measures of the knowledges, skills, abilities, and other employee characteristics are then obtained for individuals. Through statistical means, the strength of the relationship between the criterion and the measures is evaluated (validity).

If the criterion has been defined rationally through a careful empirical analysis of job duties, job-relatedness of the appraisal procedure is considered to be present. If the criterion has not been defined in this way, job-relatedness is inferred but not assured.

See also VALIDATION and VALIDITY.

statistics, any gathered numerical data and any of the processes of analyzing and of making inferences from the data. While there are innumerable works on the collection and interpretation of statistics, the classic work on statistical presentation is: Darrell Huff, *How to Lie with Statistics* (N.Y.: W. W. Norton & Co., 1954). This work is valuable for those who would lie, those who would not, and those who would like not to be lied to.

See also DISRAELI, BENJAMIN.

status, abstraction of one's relative position or ranking within an organization or society.

status symbols, visible signs of an individual's social status or importance in an organization. Status symbols are a significant element of the psychic compensation of every job. Under varying circumstances almost anything can be a status symbol—a private secretary, a key to the executive washroom, an assigned parking space, wood as opposed to metal office furniture, etc. For an account of the relentless search for greater status, *see* Vance Packard, *The Status Seekers* (N.Y.: David McKay Co., 1959).

stay-in strike: *see* SIT-DOWN STRIKE.

Steelworkers of America, United: *see* LABOR ORGANIZATION.

Steelworkers' Trilogy, three decisions of the U.S. Supreme Court, which held that: (1) a labor–management dispute could not be judged to be nonarbitrable unless the parties specifically excluded the subject from the arbitration process; (2) the role of the federal courts is limited when the parties have agreed to submit all questions of contract interpretation to an arbitrator; and (3) the interpretation of a collective bargaining agreement is a question for the arbitrator and the courts do not have the right to overrule the arbitrator because of his interpretation.

The trilogy cases are, respectively: *United Steelworkers of America* v. *Warrior and Gulf Navigation Co.*, 363 U.S. 574 (1960); *United Steelworkers of America* v. *American Manufacturing Co.*, 363 U.S. 564 (1960); and *United Steelworkers of America* v. *Enterprise Wheel and Car Corp.*, 363 U.S. 593 (1960).

step bonus, feature of wage incentive plans that call for a substantial increase in incentive payments when the quantity and/or quality of output reaches a specified level.

Stephens, Uriah Smith (1821-1882), Grand Master Workman of the Knights of Labor from its founding in 1869 to 1879.

step increases: *see* INCREMENT.

steward, also called SHOP STEWARD and UNION STEWARD, local union's most immediate representative in a plant or department. Usually elected by fellow employees (but sometimes appointed by the union leadership), the shop steward handles grievances, collects dues, solicits new members, etc. A shop steward usually continues to work at his or her regular job and handles union matters on a part-time basis, frequently on the employer's time. According to the *AFL-CIO Manual for Shop Stewards* (July 1978),

> it is important that the steward understands his relationship with management. Although the foreman, forelady or supervisor exercises certain authority over him in his role as a worker in the department, when they meet to discuss grievances the steward acts as an official representative of the union and, therefore, has equal status. He has every right to be expected to be treated as an equal as well as the right to express himself fully on the problem under discussion.

See Allan N. Nash, *The Union Steward: Duties, Rights, and Status* (Ithaca, N.Y.: New York State School of Industrial and Labor Relations, Cornell University, 1977).

steward chief, union representative who supervises the activities of a group of shop stewards.

stint-plan wage system, system that assigns a definite output as an employee's day's work; and, if the work is completed in less than normal time, the employee is credited with a full day's work and allowed to go home.

Stock Acquisition Plan, Executive: *see* EXECUTIVE STOCK ACQUISITION PLAN.

Stockberger, Warner W.: *see* STOCKBERGER ACHIEVEMENT AWARD.

Stockberger Achievement Award, established in 1948 to honor the memory of Dr. Warner W. Stockberger (1872-1944), a pioneer and leader in federal personnel administration. Dr. Stockberger was the first director of personnel of the U.S. Department of Agriculture and in 1937, served as the first president of the Society for Personnel Administration. The purpose of the award is to recognize and honor a person in public or private life who has made an outstanding contribution toward the improvement of public management at any level of government. The award is presented annually (for the preceding year) by the International Personnel Management Association (successor to the Society for Personnel Administration) and is claimed to be its highest honor.

Past Recipients

1978 Alan K. Campbell
1977 Emery E. Olson
1976 Esther C. Lawton
1975 Winston W. Crouch
1974 F. Arnold McDermott
1973 Franklin K. DeWald
1972 Elmer B. Staats
1971 Robert E. Hampton
1970 Charles F. Mullally
1969 Kenneth O. Warner
1968 Carl Barnes
1967 Morris K. Udall
1966 Robert H. Willey
1965 Arthur J. Goldberg
1964 Warren B. Irons
1963 Dale Yoder
1962 Rensis Likert
1961 O. Glenn Stahl
1960 Rogert W. Jones
1959 Albert H. Aronson
1958 Marion B. Folsom
1957 John W. Macy, Jr.
1956 James P. Mitchell
1955 Harold W. Dodds
1954 Leonard D. White
1953 T. Roy Reid
1952 Robert Ramspeck
1951 Gordon R. Clapp
1950 Frederick M. Davenport
1949 Ismar Baruch
1948 Arthur S. Fleming

stock-option plan, any of a variety of plans that allow employees to purchase shares of the company's stock at a future date at a price that is significantly lower than the stock's market value. If the price of the stock rises, the employee would find it profitable to exercise his option and buy the stock at a discount unavailable on the open market. Stock options tend to be limited to those key managers who can significantly influence the success of the company. As such they have a certain status value. For the studies of various plans, see Donald R. Simpson, "Stock Options," Milton L. Rock (ed.), *Handbook of Wage and Salary Administration* (N.Y.: McGraw-Hill, 1972); V. Henry Rothschild II and Jack B. Salwen, "Stock Option Plans in Transition," *Conference Board Record* (June 1973); Fred O. Nwokobia, "Profit-Related Stock Options: Immunizing Grants Against

the Market," *Compensation Review* (Third Quarter 1975).

stoop labor, farm work involving the picking of crops that grow close to or into the ground.

Stove, Furnace and Allied Appliance Workers' International Union of North America: *see* LABOR ORGANIZATION.

straight commission, method of compensating sales employees by solely paying them a percentage of the value of the goods they sell.

straight salary, method of compensating sales employees by solely paying them a fixed salary without regard to the dollar value of the sales that they generate within a specified time period.

stranger laboratory, laboratory experience for individuals from differing organizations.

stranger pickets, workers who picket an employee who has never employed them.
See also AMERICAN FEDERATION OF LABOR V. SWING.

straw boss, colloquial term for a supervisor who has no real authority, power or status with which to back up his orders.

stress, engineering term applied to humans in reference to any condition or situation that forces the body to respond to it. Prolonged stress can overtax an individual's emotional and/or physical ability to cope with it. The pioneering work on "stress on the whole person" was done by Hans Seyle, *The Stress of Life* (N.Y.: McGraw-Hill, rev. ed., 1976). *Also see* David E. Morrison, "Stress and the Public Administrator," *Public Administration Review* (July–August 1977).
See also the following entries:

MID-CAREER CRISIS
NERVOUS BREAKDOWN
OCCUPATIONAL NEUROSIS

stress interview, interview in which the interviewer deliberately creates a stressful situation for the interviewee in order to see how the interviewee might behave under such pressure. Common tactics used to induce stress include: critically questioning the opinions of the interviewee, frequent interruptions of interviewee's answers to possibly hostile questions, silence on the part of the interviewer for an extended period, etc.

stretch-out: *see* SPEED-UP.

strike, also called WALKOUT, mutual agreement among workers (whether members of a union or not) to a temporary work stoppage in

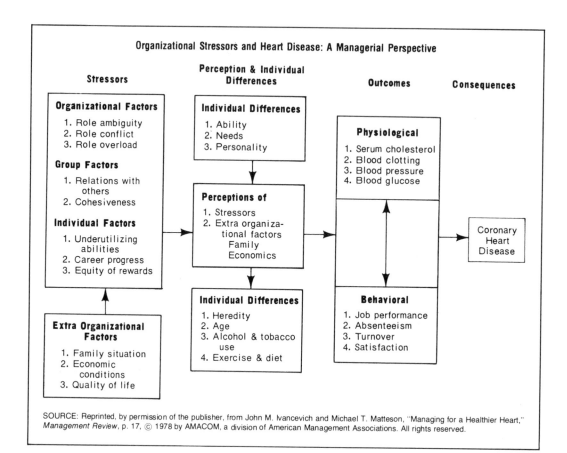

Organizational Stressors and Heart Disease: A Managerial Perspective

SOURCE: Reprinted, by permission of the publisher, from John M. Ivancevich and Michael T. Matteson, "Managing for a Healthier Heart," *Management Review*, p. 17, © 1978 by AMACOM, a division of American Management Associations. All rights reserved.

order to obtain or resist a change in their working conditions. The term is thought to have nautical origins, because sailors would stop work by striking or taking down their sails. A strike or potential strike is considered an essential element of the collective bargaining process. Many labor leaders would claim that collective bargaining can never be more than a charade without the right to strike. According to the Bureau of Labor Statistics, the United States suffered 5,648 strikes in 1976, involving more than 2.4 million workers. For a defense of the right to strike, *see* T. Kennedy, "Freedom to Strike Is in the Public Interest," *Harvard Business Review* (July–August 1970). To prepare for a strike, *see* Lee T. Paterson and John Liebert, *Management Strike Handbook* (Chicago: International Personnel Management Associations, 1974). For alternatives, *see* Theore E. Kheel *et al.*, "Exploring Alternatives to the Strike," *Monthly Labor Review* (September 1973).

See also the following entries:

APEX HOSIERY CO. V. LEADER

BATTERTON V. FRANCIS
BLUE FLU
BUFFALO FORGE V. UNITED STEELWORKERS
ECONOMIC STRIKE
GENERAL STRIKE
GRADUAL PRESSURE STRIKE
ILLEGAL STRIKE
JURISDICTIONAL STRIKE
NATIONAL LABOR RELATIONS BOARD V. ALLIS-CHALMERS
NATIONAL LABOR RELATIONS BOARD V. GRANITE STATE JOINT BOARD, TEXTILE WORKERS
NATIONAL LABOR RELATIONS BOARD V. MACKAY RADIO & TELEGRAPH COMPANY
NEW YORK TELEPHONE CO. V. NEW YORK STATE DEPARTMENT OF LABOR
POSITIVE STRIKE
QUICKIE STRIKE
RECOGNITION STRIKE
RED RASH
SECONDARY STRIKE
SHAW, LEMUEL
SIT-DOWN STRIKE
SYMPATHY STRIKE
UNFAIR LABOR PRACTICES (UNIONS)
WILDCAT STRIKE
WORK STOPPAGE
WORK TO RULE

STATES GRANTING PUBLIC EMPLOYEES RIGHT TO STRIKE

Presently, eight states grant public employees the limited right to strike. These states and their provisions are:

1. Alaska. Public employees are divided into three classes:
- *Class 1*—Essential employees (police, firefighters, guards and hospital workers) have no right to strike. Contract negotiation impasses are resolved through binding arbitration.
- *Class 2*—Employees whose services can be stopped for short periods of time have a limited right to strike if a majority of those within the bargaining unit vote by secret ballot to do so. Limits are determined by interests of health, safety, and welfare of the public.
- *Class 3*—All other public employees have the right to strike if a majority of those in the unit vote by secret ballot to do so.

2. Hawaii. Contract negotiation impasses for firefighters are resolved through binding arbitration. Other employees have the right to strike if the following criteria are met:
- the Law's impasse procedures of factfinding and mediation have been followed,
- sixty days have elapsed since the factfinding panel has made its report public, and
- the union has given ten days notice of its intent to strike to the Public Employment Relations Board (PERB) and the employer.

PERB may impose procedures, such as binding arbitration to resolve the dispute if the strike endangers the public health or safety.

3. Minnesota. Except for essential employees, the right to strike exists if the employer refuses to accept the union request for binding arbitration of the negotiation impasse or refuses to accept the arbitration award.

4. Montana. Nurses are permitted to strike if no other health care facility strike exists within a 150 mile radius and if the union gives the employer a 30 day notice. The State Supreme Court has also ruled that public employees have the right to strike.

5. Oregon. Negotiation impasses involving police, firefighters and guards are resolved through binding arbitration. Other employees have the right to strike if the following conditions are met:
- the Law's impasse procedures of factfinding and mediation have been followed,
- sixty days have elapsed since the factfinding panel has made its report public, and
- the union has given ten days notice of its intent to strike to the Board and the employer.

6. Pennsylvania. Strikes by police, firefighters, guards and court employees are prohibited. Negotiation impasses are resolved through binding arbitration. All other employees are permitted to strike after the impasse procedures of factfinding and mediation have been utilized and unless the strike creates a clear and present danger or threat to the health, safety or welfare of the public.

7. Vermont. Municipal employees have the right to strike if:
- thirty days have elapsed since the parties received the factfinder's report, and
- the strike does not endanger the health, safety, or welfare of the public.

8. Wisconsin. Strikes by state employees, police, or firefighters are prohibited. Municipal employees may strike if:
- both parties withdraw their final offers before binding arbitration begins, and
- ten days notice is given.

SOURCE: "Strikes in the Public Sector," *Midwest Monitor: A Digest of Current Literature and Developments in Public Sector Labor Relations* (January/February 1979).

---

strike authorization, also called STRIKE VOTE, formal vote by union members that (if passed) invests the union leadership with the right to call a strike without additional consultation with the union membership.

strike benefits, payments by a union to its striking members or to nonmembers who are out on strike in support of the union. The U.S. Supreme Court has held, in *United States* v. *Allen Kaiser*, 363 U.S. 299 (1960), that, for tax purposes, strike benefits are to be considered as gifts and thus not taxable as part of a worker's gross income. *See* Sheldon M. Kline, "Strike Benefits of National Unions," *Monthly Labor Review* (March 1975);

John Gennard, *Financing Strikers* (N.Y.: John Wiley, 1977).

strike-bound, any organization that is being struck by its employees and/or attempting to function in spite of the strike.

strikebreaker, person who accepts a position vacated by a worker on strike or a worker who continues to work while others are on strike. The Labor–Management Relations (Taft–Hartley) Act of 1947 guarantees a strikebreaker's right to work and makes it illegal for unions to attempt to prohibit strikebreakers from crossing picket lines.

See also the following entries:

AMERICAN STEEL FOUNDRIES V. TRI-CITY
   CENTRAL TRADES COUNCIL
ANTI-STRIKEBREAKER ACT OF 1936
NOBLE
SCAB

strike counselors: *see* UNION COUNSELORS.

strike duty, tasks assigned to union members by the union leadership during the course of a strike (for example, picketing, distributing food, preventing violence, creating violence, etc.).

strike fund, monies reserved by a union to be used during a strike to cover costs such as strike benefits or legal fees. Strike funds are not necessarily separate from a union's general fund. The amount of strike funds available may mean the success or failure of a strike.

strike notice, formal notice of an impending work stoppage that is presented by a union to an employer or to an appropriate government agency.

strike pay, union payments to union members as partial compensation for income loss during a strike.

strike vote: *see* STRIKE AUTHORIZATION.

stroking, also POSITIVE STROKING and NEGATIVE STROKING. Eric Berne, in *Games People Play: The Psychology of Human Relationships* (N.Y.: Grove Press, 1964), took the intimate physical act of stroking and developed its psychological analogy in conversation. All of human intercourse can be viewed from the narrow perspective of the giving and receiving of physical and psychological strokes. In an organizational context, *positive stroking* consists of the laying of kind words on employees. *Negative stroking* involves using less than kinds words—being critical. See Thomas C. Clary, "Motivation Through Positive Stroking," *Public Personnel Management* (March–April 1973).
   See also MOTIVATION.

Strong–Campbell Interest Inventory (SCII), vocational interest inventory that allows individuals to compare their preferences with reference groups in a large range of occupations; helps the test taker identify a general section of the occupational world for more intensive study. This inventory is a 1974 revision of the Strong–Vocational Interest Blank (SVIB) that combined the men's and women's scales to reduce or remove sex bias and is widely used in vocational and/or career counseling. TIME: Untimed-approximately 30/40 minutes. AUTHORS: Edward K. Strong and David P. Campbell. PUBLISHER: Stanford University Press (*see* TEST PUBLISHERS).

Strong Vocational Interest Blank (SVIB), paper-and-pencil vocational inventory used primarily for vocational counseling at the high school and college student level for career choice and in personnel counseling. There are separate scales for men and women. Usage has been replaced by the SCII which integrated the two scales (nondiscriminatory). TIME: 30/60 minutes. AUTHORS: E. K. Strong, Jr., D. P. Campbell, R. F. Berdie, K. E. Clark. PUBLISHER: Stanford University Press (*see* TEST PUBLISHERS).

struck work, products produced by strikebreakers.

structural unemployment, unemployment resulting from changes in technology, consumption patterns or government policies—a mismatch between available labor and demand for skills. Structural unemployment can be said to be an inherent part of a dynamic economic system. The "cure" for structural unemployment is worker retraining. *See* Eleanor G. Gilpatrick, *Structural Unemployment And Aggregate Demand* (Baltimore: The Johns Hopkins University Press, 1966).

structured role playing, role-play exercise or simulation in which the players receive oral or written instruction giving them cues as to their roles.

SUB: *see* SUPPLEMENTAL UNEMPLOYMENT BENEFIT.

subemployment, concept that tries to capture two major dimensions of labor market functioning that produce, and reproduce poverty—the lack of opportunity for work and substandard wage employment. *See* T. Vietorisz, R. Mier, and J. Giblin, "Subemployment: Exclusion and Inadequacy Indexes," *Monthly Labor Review* (May 1975).

subsistence allowance, payments for an employee's reasonable expenses (meals, lodging, transportation, etc.) while traveling on behalf of his employer.

subsistence theory of wages: *see* IRON LAW OF WAGES.

subordinate rating, evaluation of an organizational superior by someone of lesser rank.

substandard rate, wage rate below established occupational, prevailing, or legal levels.

subsystem, one of the various parts of a larger system.

Suffridge, James Arthur (1909-   ), president of the Retail Clerks International Protective Association from 1944 to 1947 and again from 1955 to 1968. For biographical information, *see* Michael Harrington, *The Retail Clerks* (N.Y.: John Wiley, 1962).

Sugarman, Jule M. (1927-   ), vice-chairman of the U.S. Civil Service Commission from 1977 to its demise in 1979. He then became deputy director of the Office of Personnel Management.

Sugarman v. Dougall, 413 U.S. 634 (1973), U.S. Supreme Court case, which held that a ban on the employment of resident aliens by a state was unconstitutional, because it encompassed positions that had little, if any, relation to a legitimate state interest in treating aliens differently from citizens. However, the court also stated that alienage might be rea-sonably taken into account with regard to specific positions.

See also the following entries:
AMBACH V. NORWICK
CITIZENSHIP, U.S.
FOLEY V. CONNELIE
HAMPTON V. MOW SUN WONG

suggestion system, formal effort to encourage employees to make recommendations that would improve the operations of their organizations. *See* Charles Foos, "How to Administer A Suggestion System," *Management Review* (August 1968); Edward H. Downey and Walter L. Balk, *Employee Innovation and Government Productivity: A Study of Suggestion Systems in the Public Sector* (Chicago: International Personnel Management Association, 1976). For a history, *see* Stanley J. Seimer, *Suggestion Plans in American Industry* (Syracuse, N.Y.: Syracuse University Press, 1959).

See also SCANLON PLAN.

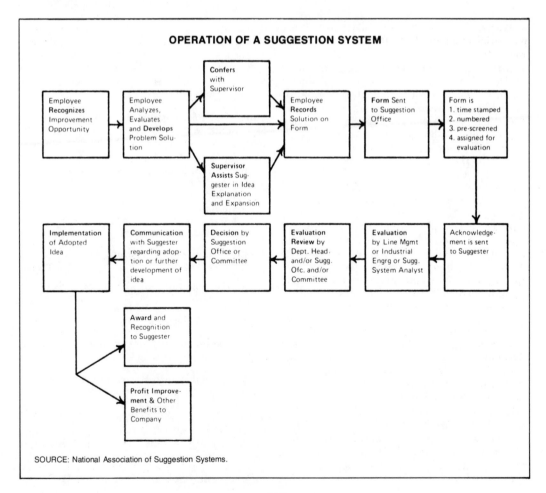

OPERATION OF A SUGGESTION SYSTEM

SOURCE: National Association of Suggestion Systems.

Summer Employment Program: *see* UNITED STATES EMPLOYMENT SERVICE.

sunshine bargaining, also called GOLDFISH-BOWL BARGAINING, collective bargaining sessions open to the press and public. This process is more likely to be used in public sector negotiations (in response to the assertion that since the spending of public funds are the essence of the negotiations, the negotiating process should be open to public scrutiny).

superannuated rate, pay rate below the prevailing rate that is paid to older employees who are in need or are needed because of a labor shortage. A ratio for superannuated workers is sometimes provided for in union agreements. The lower rate is justified on the theory that these older, otherwise retired, workers are not as productive as younger employees. Some superannuated rate policies may be in violation of age discrimination laws.

supergrades, federal government executives in grades GS-16, 17, and 18.

supernumerary income, that portion of a worker's income which is not needed for the essentials of everyday life and consequently available for luxuries and other optional spending. *See* Fabian Linden, "Supernumerary Income: A Statistical Measure of Consumer Affluence," *Conference Board Record* (April 1968).

superseniority, also called SYNTHETIC SENIORITY, seniority that supercedes ordinary seniority, which is dependent on an individual's length of service. Because a union may be detrimentally affected if its key union officials are subject to layoffs, union contracts often grant them superseniority. This synthetic seniority is designed to ensure continued representation for workers remaining following a reduction in force. Superseniority also provides an advantage to management since established lines of communication with the union and its members continues without interruption. Sometimes union contracts provide for superseniority for special categories of employees (such as the aged or physically handicapped and key personnel essential if production is to be maintained). *See* Max S. Wortman, "Superseniority—Myth or Reality?" *Labor Law Journal* (April 1967); George K. Leonard, "Practical Applications of Superseniority," *Labor Law Journal* (January 1975).

supervision, directing the performance of one or more workers towards the accomplishment of organizational goals. *See* Robert M. Fulmer, *Supervision: Principles of Professional Management* (Beverly Hills, Calif.: Glencoe Press, 1976).

Supervision: The Magazine of Industrial Relations and Operating Management, monthly that covers all aspects of supervisor-employee relations.

> *Supervision: The Magazine of Industrial Relations and Operating Management*
> National Research Bureau, Inc.
> 424 North Third Street
> Burlington, IA 52601

supervisor, according to Section 2(11) of the National Labor Relations Act, as amended, the term "supervisor" means

> any individual having authority, in the interest of the employer, to hire, transfer, suspend, lay off, recall, promote, discharge, assign, reward, or discipline other employees, or responsibly to direct them, or to adjust their grievances, or effectively to recommend such action, if in connection with the foregoing the exercise of such authority is not of a merely routine or clerical nature, but requires the use of independent judgment.

See also HANNA MINING CO. V. DISTRICT 2, MARINE ENGINEERS.

Supervisory Management, monthly magazine that deals with all aspects of supervisory management.

> *Supervisory Management*
> American Management Associations
> 135 West 50th St
> New York, NY 10020
>
> **Subscriptions:**
> P.O. Box 319
> Saranac Lake, NY 12983

supplemental compensation, executive: *see* EXECUTIVE SUPPLEMENTAL COMPENSATION.

supplemental compensation: *see* BONUS.

supplemental dental insurance: *see* SUPPLEMENTAL MEDICAL INSURANCE.

supplemental life insurance: *see* SPLIT-DOLLAR LIFE INSURANCE.

supplemental medical insurance, also SUPPLEMENTAL DENTAL INSURANCE, fringe benefit usually offered only to top management, whereby all expenses from medical and/or dental care not covered by the general medical/dental policy offered by the company are reimbursable.

Supplemental Security Income (SSI), federal

program that assures a minimum monthly income to needy people with limited income and resources who are 65 or older, blind, or disabled. Eligibility is based on income and assets. Although the program is administered by the Social Security Administration, it is financed from general revenues, not from social security contributions.

supplemental unemployment benefit (SUB), payments to laid off workers from private unemployment insurance plans that are supplements to state unemployment insurance compensation. The first SUB plan was negotiated by the Ford Motor Company and the United Auto Workers in 1955. By 1973, about 29 percent of the members of major unions worked under contracts containing SUB plans. There are two basic SUB plans—the individual account and the pooled fund. With the former, contributions are credited to each employee's account and a terminated employee may take his benefits with him. With the latter, benefits are paid from a common fund and individual employees have no vested rights should they leave the company. For the history of SUB, see Joseph M. Becker, *Guaranteed Income for the Unemployed: The Story of SUB* (Baltimore: Johns Hopkins Press, 1968). For a financial analysis, see Emerson H. Beier, "Financing Supplemental Unemployment Benefits," *Monthly Labor Review* (November 1969).

Survey Research Center: see INSTITUTE FOR SOCIAL RESEARCH.

survivors benefits, totality of the benefits that are paid upon the death of an employee to his/her legal survivors. Employees are frequently required to make a decision at the time of retirement whether or not to take a reduced pension that allows for survivors benefits.

suspension, removing an individual from employment for a specified period. Suspensions, by their nature temporary, are disciplinary acts—more severe than a reprimand yet less severe than a discharge.

SVIB: see STRONG VOCATIONAL INTEREST BLANK.

sweat shop, work sites where employees worked long hours for low wages usually under unsanitary conditions. While sweat shop conditions have been mostly eliminated in the United States because of the union movement and labor legislation, the term is still used informally to refer to various working conditions that employees might find distasteful. For a description of real sweat shops, see Leon Stein, ed., *Out of the Sweat Shop: The Struggle for Industrial Democracy* (N.Y.: Quadrangle, 1977).

sweetheart agreement, also called SWEETHEART CONTRACT, expressions for any agreement between an employer and a union or union official that benefits them but not the workers. Incidences of employer bribes to labor officials in order to gain their agreement to substandard or "sweetheart" contracts are well known to American labor history.

sweetheart clause, that portion of a union contract that makes a general policy statement about the harmonious manner in which both sides will live up to the spirit and letter of the agreement.

sweetheart contract: see SWEETHEART AGREEMENT.

sweet pay: see WELL PAY.

swing shift, extra shift of workers in an organization operating on a continuous or seven-day basis. The swing crew rotates among the various shifts to compensate for those employees who are absent, sick, on vacation, etc.

Sylvis, William H. (1828-1869), credited with "inventing" the union membership card, he led the Iron-Molders' International Union during its most successful period and was a founder and president of the National Labor Union.

sympathy strike, also called SYMPATHETIC STRIKE, strike by one union undertaken solely to support the aims of another union in an effort to exert indirect pressure upon an employer. The Labor–Management Relations (Taft–Hartley) Act of 1947 made sympathy strikes illegal.

synectics, originally a Greek word, meaning the joining together of different and apparently irrelevant elements, it is now used to describe an experimental process of observing and recording the unrestrained exchange of ideas among a group in order to methodically develop new ideas, solve problems and/or make discoveries. As an effort to induce creativity, it is akin to brainstorming. See William J. J. Gordon, *Synectics: The Development of Creative Capacity* (N.Y.: Harper & Row, 1961).

synthetic basic-motion times, time standards

for fundamental motions and groups of motions.

synthetic seniority: *see* SUPERSENIORITY.

synthetic time study, time study, not dependent upon direct observation, in which time elements are obtained from other sources of time data.

synthetic validity, also called INDIRECT VALIDITY, inferring validity by means of a systematic analysis of a job and its elements, obtaining test validity for the various elements, then combining the elemental validities into a whole synthetic validity. *See* M. J. Balma, "The Development of Processes for Indirect or Synthetic Validity," *Personnel Psychology* Vol. 12 (1959).

system, any organized collection of parts that is united by prescribed interactions and designed for the accomplishment of a specific goal or general purpose. According to William Exton, Jr., in *The Age of Systems: The Human Dilemma* (N.Y.: American Management Association, 1972), the term system

> represents the principle of functional combination of resources to produce intended result of effects. The combination may be great or small, simple or enormously complex, active or potential, solitary or parallel, new or old, static or dynamic. The intended effect may be fixed or otherwise, unique or repetitive or continuous, geographically or spacially defined or unlimited in territorial scope, physical or symbolic, tangible or intangible.

system, career: *see* CAREER SYSTEM.

System 4, Rensis Likert's term for a participative–democratic managerial style. *See* his *The Human Organization* (N.Y.: McGraw-Hill, 1967).

systemic discrimination, use of employment practices (recruiting methods, selection tests, promotion policies, etc.) that have the unintended effect of excluding or limiting the employment prospects of women and minorities. Because of court interpretations of Title VII of the Civil Rights Act of 1964, all such systemic discrimination despite its "innocence," must be eliminated where it cannot be shown that such action would place an unreasonable burden on the employer or that such practices can not be replaced by other practices which would not have such an adverse effect.

systemism, belief that systems can actually be designed and managed to achieve their expressed goals. For the counter-arguments that "systems in general work poorly or not at all," *see* John Gall, *"Systematics: How Systems Work and Especially How They Fail* (N.Y.: Quadrangle, 1975).

systems analysis, methodologically rigorous collection, manipulation, and evaluation of organizational data in order to determine the best way to improve the functioning of the organization (the system) and to aid a decisionmaker in selecting a preferred choice among alternatives. According to David I. Cleland and William R. King, in *Management: A Systems Approach* (N.Y.: McGraw-Hill, 1972),

> systems analysis is a way of reaching decisions which contrasts with intuition-based and unsystematic approaches; the techniques of systems analysis help to make a complex problem understandable and manageable in the sense of offering possible strategies and solutions and establishing, to the maximum extent practical, criteria for selecting the best solution.

systems analyst, specialist in systems analysis.

systems approach, also called SYSTEMS PHILOSOPHY. The systems approach or philosophy can help a manager cope with complex situations by providing an analytical framework which conceives of an enterprise as a set of objects with a given set of relationships and attributes all connected to each other and their environment in such a way as to form an entirety. Because both organizations (as well as the whole world) are constantly changing, approaches to dealing with such systems must necessarily have a corresponding evolution. According to C. West Churchman, in *The Systems Approach* (N.Y.: Delacorte Press, 1968),

> we must admit that the problem—the appropriate approach to systems—is not solved, but this is a very mild way of putting the matter. This is not an unsolved problem in the sense in which certain famous mathematical problems are unsolved. It's not as though we can expect that next year or a decade from now someone will find the correct systems approach and all deception will disappear. This, in my opinion, is not in the nature of systems. What is in the nature of systems is a continuing perception and deception, a continuing re-viewing of the world, of the whole system, and of its components. The essence of the systems approach, therefore, is confusion as well as enlightenment. The two are inseparable aspects of human living.

systems management, according to Richard A. Johnson, Fremont E. Kast and James E. Rosenzweig, in *The Theory and Management of Systems* (N.Y.: McGraw-Hill, 3rd ed., 1973), systems management

involves the application of systems theory to managing organizational systems or subsystems. It can refer to management of a particular function or to projects or programs within a larger organization. An important point is that systems theory is a vital ingredient in the managerial process. It involves recognizing a general model of input–transformation–output with identifiable flows of material, energy, and information. It also emphasizes the interrelationships among subsystems as well as the suprasystem to which a function, project, or organization belongs.

systems philosophy: *see* SYSTEMS APPROACH.

systems theory: *see* GENERAL SYSTEMS THEORY.

T

TA: *see* TRANSACTIONAL ANALYSIS.

Taft–Hartley Act: *see* LABOR–MANAGEMENT RELATIONS ACT OF 1947.

take-home pay, also called NET PAY, employee's wages minus deductions that are either required (such as taxes) or requested (such as savings bonds).

tall organization: *see* FLAT ORGANIZATION.

tardiness, reporting to work later than the scheduled time.

target, expected earnings under a piece-rate wage system. The earnings target is usually set at a fixed percentage, 10 to 15 percent, above the base rate.

task, unit of work.

task analysis, identifying the various elements essential to the accomplishment of a task.

task-and-bonus plan, wage incentive plan paying a specific percent of the base wage rate (in addition to the base wage rate) when a specified level of production is maintained or exceeded for a specified period of time.

task force, also called INTERDISCIPLINARY TEAM, temporary organizational unit charged with accomplishing a specific mission. Committees tend to be chiefly concerned with the assessment of information in order to reach a conclusion. In contrast a task group, task force, or interdisciplinary team is aggressively oriented. According to Lawrence W. Bass, in *Management By Task Forces: A Manual on the Operation of Interdisciplinary Teams* (Mt. Airy, Md.: Lomond Books, 1975), the great benefit of task forces is the great improvement that they bring about in information transfer.

> The members develop needed information in their respective spheres. They communicate their findings and conclusions to their colleagues on a timely schedule in order that the others may take them into consideration in carrying out their own missions. Their contacts are frequent and mutually helpful. They participate in discussions to dovetail their common and individual progress toward main objectives. They are an integrated community.

See also WORK GROUP.

task group: *see* WORK GROUP.

TAT: *see* THEMATIC APPERCEPTION TEST.

tax deferred annuity, also called TAX SHELTERED ANNUITY, annuity whose employee contributions are not subject to taxes at the time that the contributions are made. Contributions are later taxed as they are paid out after retirement when the annuitant is presumably in a lower tax bracket.

tax equalization policy, program that has an employer deduct from the salary of employees sent overseas the amount of taxes that would have been due if they had resided in the United States. In return, the employer assumes the total burden of both U.S. and host nation income taxes.

taxes, employment/payroll: *see* EMPLOYMENT TAXES.

Tax Reduction Act Employee Stock Ownership Plan (TRASOP), varient of Employee Stock Ownership Plans (ESOP's) that takes advantage of the Tax Reduction Act of 1975 and the Tax Reform Act of 1976, which sought to stimulate the adoption of ESOP's by offering additional investment tax credit to corporate sponsors. *See* Paul E. Burke, "TRASOPs: The Beautiful Benefit," *Personnel Journal* (March 1978).

tax-reimbursement allowance, additional money paid to an employee assigned overseas to compensate for the additional taxes that must be paid (both U.S. and foreign) in excess of what would have been paid had the employee remained in the United States.

tax sheltered annuity: *see* TAX DEFERRED ANNUITY.

Taylor, Frederick W. (1856-1915), originally an engineer, is now considered the "father of scientific management." He did pioneering work on time-and-motion studies and led the search for the "one best way" of accomplishing any given task. Major works include: *Shop Management* (N.Y.: Harper & Bros., 1903); *The Principles of Scientific Management* (N.Y.: Harper & Bros., 1911). For biographies, *see* Frank Barkley Copley, *Frederick W. Taylor: Father of Scientific Management* (N.Y.: Harper & Bros., 1923; reprinted by Augustus M. Kelley, 1969), 2 volumes; Subhir Kakar, *Frederick Taylor: A Study in Personality and Innovation* (Cambridge: Mass.: M.I.T. Press, 1970).
See also SCIENTIFIC MANAGEMENT.

Taylor Differential Piece-Rate Plan, also DIFFERENTIAL PIECE RATE PLAN, incentive plan where different piece rates are established for substandard, standard, and higher than standard production.

Taylorism, term used to describe the "scientific management" advocated by Frederick W. Taylor.

Taylor Law, in full PUBLIC EMPLOYEES' FAIR EMPLOYMENT ACT, New York State's law governing the unionization of state, county, and municipal employees. It grants all public employees the right to organize and be recognized, provides for a Public Employment Relations Board for the resolution of impasses, prohibits strikes, and provides a schedule of penalties for both striking individuals and their unions. The Taylor Law owes its name to George W. Taylor, a University of Pennsylvania Wharton School professor, who chaired the Governor's Committee on Public Employee Relations that recommended the enacting legislation in 1966.

TDA: *see* LABOR ORGANIZATION, Train Dispatchers Association, American.

tea break: *see* COFFEE BREAK.

Teachers, American Federation of: *see* LABOR ORGANIZATION.

Teachers Insurance and Annuity Association (TIAA), manages portable pension plans for professional employees of colleges and universities.

TIAA
730 Third Ave.

New York, NY 10017
(212) 490-9000

Tead, Ordway (1891-1973), pioneer in applying psychology to industry and co-author of one of the first personnel management texts. Major works include: *Instincts in Industry* (Boston: Houghton Mifflin, 1918); *Personnel Administration: Its Principles and Practice*, with Henry C. Metcalf (N.Y.: McGraw-Hill, 1920); *The Art of Leadership* (N.Y.: McGraw-Hill, 1935); *The Art of Administration* (N.Y.: McGraw-Hill, 1951); *Administration: Its Purpose and Performance* (N.Y.: Harper & Bros. 1959).

team building, any planned and managed change involving a group of people in order to improve communications and working relationships. Team building is most effective when used as a part of a long-range strategy for organizational and personal development. *See* Richard Beckhard, "Optimizing Team-Building Efforts," *Journal of Contemporary Business* (Summer 1972); Thomas H. Patten, Jr., and Lester E. Dorey, "Long-Range Results of a Team Building OD Effort," *Public Personnel Management* (January–February 1977).

Teamsters, Chauffeurs, Warehousemen and Helpers of America, International Brotherhood of: *see* LABOR ORGANIZATION.

Teamsters, Local 695 v. Vogt, 354 U.S. 284 (1957), U.S. Supreme Court case, which held that a state, in enforcing a public policy, may constitutionally enjoin peaceful picketing aimed at preventing effectuation of that policy.

Teamsters v. United States: *see* INTERNATIONAL BROTHERHOOD OF TEAMSTERS V. UNITED STATES.

Technical Engineers, International Federation of Professional and: *see* LABOR ORGANIZATION.

Technicians, Association of Civilian: *see* LABOR ORGANIZATION.

technological unemployment, unemployment that results from the displacement of workers by machinery or by the introduction of more efficient methods of production.

Telegraph Workers, United: *see* LABOR ORGANIZATION.

Television and Radio Artists, American Federation of: *see* LABOR ORGANIZATION, under Actors and Artistes of America, Associated.

Temperament Survey, Guilford–Zimmerman: *see* GUILFORD–ZIMMERMAN TEMPERAMENT SURVEY.

temporary appointment: *see* APPOINTMENT.

temporary restraining order: *see* INJUNCTION.

Tennessee State Labor Council: *see* AMERICAN FEDERATION OF LABOR–CONGRESS OF INDUSTRIAL ORGANIZATIONS.

tenure, period of time that one occupies a position. In the academic world and in some government jurisdictions, to have "tenure" means that an individual may continue in his or her position until retirement, subject, of course, to adequate behavior and the continued viability of the organization.
See also PERRY V. SINDERMAN.

term appointment: *see* APPOINTMENT.

terminal arbitration, arbitration that is called for as the final step in a grievance procedure.

terminate: *see* FIRE.

termination contract, agreement between an employer and a new employee that provides for salary continuation for the employee in the event of termination. The length of time that compensation continues to be paid typically varies from six months to two years. *See* Frank R. Beaudine, "The Termination Contract as a Recessionary Employment Tool," *Personnel Journal* (June 1975)

termination pay: *see* SEVERANCE PAY.

term life insurance, temporary insurance that offers protection for a limited number of years and has no cash value.

test anxiety, nervousness that an examinee experiences before and during the administration of a test. For a study concluding that test anxiety is, except for extremes, inversely correlated with test performance, *see* C. S. Berkely and C. F. Sproule, "Test Anxiety and Test Unsophistication: The Effects and Cures," *Public Personnel Management* (January 1973).

test fidelity, extent to which a test represents the actual duties of a job.

testmanship, art of doing better on an examination without actually cheating. While there

---

PERCENTAGE OF FACULTY MEMBERS WITH TENURE, 1978-79

	Universities	Other Four-year Institutions	Two-year Institutions	All Institutions
Professors	97.0	94.9	97.2	95.8
Men	97.1	94.9	97.0	95.9
Women	95.6	94.6	98.1	95.2
Associate Professors	83.0	91.2	92.2	82.7
Men	83.2	81.5	93.5	83.0
Women	81.5	79.9	89.1	81.6
Assistant Professors	17.9	31.4	59.7	30.3
Men	16.6	30.5	62.3	29.1
Women	21.1	33.0	55.6	32.7
Instructors	5.2	7.8	18.3	9.3
Men	5.1	8.2	19.4	9.7
Women	5.2	7.5	17.2	8.9
Lecturers	4.1	0.5	9.5	2.9
Men	4.9	0.7	7.9	3.4
Women	2.9	0.2	10.5	2.3
No Academic Rank	1.4	29.3	78.1	75.5
Men	2.0	32.0	81.7	79.0
Women	0.0	23.8	71.1	68.7
All Ranks	63.4	60.5	72.4	63.5
Men	68.8	65.8	77.1	68.5
Women	39.0	45.3	63.8	48.7

SOURCE: National Center for Education Statistics.

are a great number of test preparation books available, the one by the author of the classic *How to Lie with Statistics* might seem to have much to commend it. See Darrell Huff, *Score: The Strategy of Taking Tests* (N.Y.: Appleton-Century-Crofts, 1961). Huff contends that, *"Test-taking is an art and can be learned like any other."*

Test of Mental Maturity, California: *see* CALIFORNIA TEST OF MENTAL MATURITY.

Test of Mental Maturity, California Short Form: *see* CALIFORNIA SHORT FORM TEST OF MENTAL MATURITY.

test publishers, are listed in current edition of O. K. Buros (ed.), *The Mental Measurements Yearbook* (Highland Park, N.J.: Gryphon Press). *See also* selective listing "TEST PUBLISHERS" in box near this entry.

test–retest reliability, measure of the reliability obtained by giving individuals the same

test for a second time after an interval and correlating the sets of scores.

tests and testing: *see* entries listed below (asterisk identifies commercially available tests commonly used in employment selection and placement):

*ADVANCED PERSONNEL TEST (APT)
*ADAPTABILITY TEST, THE
*BENNETT MECHANICAL COMPREHENSION TEST (BMCT)
*BERNREUTER PERSONALITY INVENTORY
*CALIFORNIA OCCUPATIONAL PREFERENCE SURVEY (COPSYSTEM)
*CALIFORNIA PSYCHOLOGICAL INVENTORY
*CALIFORNIA SHORT FORM TEST OF MENTAL MATURITY (CTMM/SF)
*CALIFORNIA TEST OF MENTAL MATURITY (CTMM)
*CATTELL CULTURE FAIR INTELLIGENCE TEST
*CONCEPT MASTERY TEST (CMR)
CONFIDENCE TESTING
*COOPERATIVE SCHOOL AND COLLEGE ABILITY TESTS (SCAT)

TEST PUBLISHERS

American Guidance Services, Inc.
Publisher's Building
Circle Pines, MN 55014

Bobbs-Merrill Company, Inc. (The)
4300 West 62nd Street
Indianapolis, IN 46268

California Test Bureau
CTB/McGraw-Hill
Del Monte Research Park
Monterey, CA 93940

Consulting Psychologists Press, Inc.
577 College Avenue
Palo Alto, CA 94306

Educational and Industrial Testing Service
P. O. Box 7234
San Diego, CA 92107

Follett Educational Corporation
1010 West Washington Blvd.
Chicago, IL 60607

Harcourt, Brace, Jovanovich, Inc.
757 Third Avenue
New York, NY 10017

Houghton Mifflin Company
110 Tremont Street
Boston, MA 02107

Industrial Psychology Inc.
515 Madison Avenue
New York, NY 10022

McCann Associates, Inc.
2763 Philmont Avenue
Huntington Valley, PA 19006

Merit Employment Assessment Services, Inc.
P. O. Box 193
Flossmoor, IL 60422

Psychological Corporation (The)
304 East 45th Street
New York, NY 10017

Research Psychologists Press, Inc.
13 Greenwich Avenue
Goshen, NY 10924

Science Research Associates, Inc.
259 East Erie Street
Chicago, IL 60611

Selection Consulting Center
5777 Madison Avenue, Suite 820
Sacramento, CA 95841

Sheridan Psychological Services, Inc.
P. O. Box 837
Beverly Hills, CA 90213

Slosson Educational Publications
140 Pine Street
East Aurora, NY 14052

Stanford University Press
Stanford, CA 94305

William, Lynde, and Williams
153 East Erie Street
Painesville, OH 44077

Wonderlic, E.F., and Associates
Box 7
Northfield, IL 60093

*CRAWFORD SMALL PARTS DEXTERITY TEST
CREATIVITY TEST
CRITERION-REFERENCED TEST
CULTURE-FAIR TEST
*DAVIS READING TEST
*DIFFERENTIAL APTITUDE TESTS (DAT)
DEXTERITY TEST
DIAGNOSTIC TEST
*EDWARDS PERSONAL PREFERENCE SCHEDULE (EPPS)
EMPLOYMENT TESTING
*EYSENCK PERSONALITY INVENTORY (EPI)
*FIRO B
*FLANAGAN APTITUDE CLASSIFICATION TEST (FACT)
*FLANAGAN INDUSTRIAL TEST (FIT)
FREE-RESPONSE TEST
*FUNDAMENTAL ACHIEVEMENT SERIES (FAS)
*GORDON OCCUPATIONAL CHECK LIST (GOCL)
*GUILFORD-ZIMMERMAN TEMPERAMENT SURVEY (GZTS)
*HALL OCCUPATIONAL ORIENTATION INVENTORY (HOOI)
HANDS-ON TEST
INDIVIDUAL TEST
INTELLIGENCE TEST
INTEREST TEST
*JOB TESTS PROGRAM
*KUDER GENERAL INTEREST SURVEY (KGIS)
*KUDER OCCUPATIONAL INTEREST SURVEY (KOIS)
*KUDER PREFERENCE RECORD
*MILLER ANALOGIES TEST (MAT)
*MINNESOTA CLERICAL TEST (MCT)
*MINNESOTA MULTIPHASIC PERSONALITY INVENTORY (MMPI)
*MINNESOTA RATE OF MANIPULATION TEST
*MINNESOTA SPATIAL RELATIONS TEST
*MINNESOTA VOCATIONAL INTEREST INVENTORY (MVII)
*MULTIPLE-APTITUDE TESTS (MAT)
MULTIPLE-CHOICE TEST
NORM-REFERENCED TEST
*OHIO VOCATIONAL INTEREST SURVEY (OVIS)
*OTIS-LENNON MENTAL ABILITY TEST (OLMAT)
PERFORMANCE TEST
*PERSONALITY RESEARCH FORM (PRF)
PERSONALITY TEST
*PERSONNEL TESTS FOR INDUSTRY (PTI)
POST-TEST
POWER TEST
PRE-TEST
PROFICIENCY TEST
PSYCHOLOGICAL TEST
*PURDUE PEGBOARD TEST
QUALIFYING TEST
RANKING TEST
*REVISED MINNESOTA PAPER FORM BOARD TEST
RORSCHACH TEST
*SELF-DIRECTED SEARCH (SDS)
*SHORT EMPLOYMENT TEST (SET)
*SHORT TESTS OF CLERICAL ABILITY
*SIXTEEN PERSONALITY FACTOR QUESTIONNAIRE (16PF)

*SLOSSON INTELLIGENCE TEST (SIT)
SPEED TEST
SPIRAL-OMNIBUS TEST
STANDARDIZED TEST
*STRONG-CAMPBELL INTEREST INVENTORY (SCII)
*STRONG VOCATIONAL INTEREST BLANK (SVIB)
TEST ANXIETY
TEST FIDELITY
TESTMANSHIP
TEST PUBLISHERS
TEST–RETEST RELIABILITY
TOWER AMENDMENT
*TYPING TEST FOR BUSINESS (TTB)
*VOCATIONAL PREFERENCE INVENTORY (VPI)
*WATSON GLASER CRITICAL THINKING APPRAISAL (WGCT)
*WECHSLER ADULT INTELLIGENCE SCALE (WAIS)
*WECHSLER-BELLVUE INTELLIGENCE SCALE (WBIS)
*WESMAN PERSONNEL CLASSIFICATION TEST (WPCT)
*WESTERN PERSONNEL TESTS
*WLW CULTURE FAIR INVENTORY (CFI)
*WLW PERSONAL ATTITUDE INVENTORY
*WONDERLIC PERSONNEL TEST (WPT)
*WORK VALUES INVENTORY (WVI)

Texas and New Orleans Railway v. Brotherhood of Railway and Steamship Clerks, 281 U.S. 548 (1930), U.S. Supreme Court case, which denied a company the option of bargaining with its "company union" and required it to bargain with the self-organized union of its employees.

Texas State AFL–CIO: *see* AMERICAN FEDERATION OF LABOR–CONGRESS OF INDUSTRIAL ORGANIZATIONS.

Textile Workers of America, United: *see* LABOR ORGANIZATION.

Textile Workers Union of America: *see* LABOR ORGANIZATION.

Textile Workers v. Darlington Manufacturing Company, also called DARLINGTON CASE, 380 U.S. 263 (1965), U.S. Supreme court case, which held that while an employer had an absolute right to terminate his entire business for any reason, he does not have the right to close or move part of his business if he is motivated by anti-union bias. *See* Sherman F. Dallas and Beverly K. Schaffer, "Whatever Happened to the Darlington Case?" *Labor Law Journal* (January 1973); Robert A. Bedolis, "The Supreme Court's Darlington Mills Opinion," *The Conference Board Record* (June 1965).

Textile Workers v. Lincoln Mills 353 U.S. 448 (1957), U.S. Supreme Court case, which held that the arbitration clause in a collective bargaining agreement is the *quid pro quo* given by the employer in return for the non-strike clause agreed to by a union.

T-Group: *see* LABORATORY TRAINING.

T-Group, family: *see* FAMILY T-GROUP.

Theatrical Stage Employees and Moving Picture Machine Operators of the United States and Canada, International Alliance of: *see* LABOR ORGANIZATION.

Thematic Apperception Test (TAT), projective test that uses a standard set of pictures and calls for the subject to reveal his or her personality by making up stories about them. Variations of the TAT have been successfully used for vocational counseling and executive selection, as well as for determining attitudes toward labor problems, minority groups, and authority. *See* P. C. Cummin, "TAT Correlates of Executive Performance," *Journal of Applied Psychology* (February 1967).

Theory X and Theory Y, contrasting sets of assumptions made by managers about human behavior that Douglas McGregor distilled and labeled in *The Human Side of Enterprise* (N.Y.: McGraw-Hill, 1960).
Theory X holds that:

1. The average human being has an inherent dislike of work and will avoid it if possible.
2. Because of this human characteristic of dislike of work, most people must be coerced, controlled, directed, or threatened with punishment to get them to put forth adequate effort toward the achievement of organizational objectives.
3. The average human being prefers to be directed, wishes to avoid responsibility, has relatively little ambition, wants security above all.

Theory X assumptions are essentially a restatement of the premises of the scientific management movement, not a flattering picture of the average citizen of modern industrial society. While McGregor's portrait can be criticized for implying greater pessimism concerning the nature of man on the part of managers than is perhaps warranted, Theory X is all the more valuable as a memorable theoretical construct because it serves as such a polar opposite of Theory Y. (McGregor would later deny that the theories were polar opposites and assert that they were "simply different cosmologies.")
Theory Y holds that:

1. The expenditure of physical and mental effort in work is as natural as play or rest.

The average human being does not inherently dislike work. Depending upon controllable conditions, work may be a source of satisfaction (and will be voluntarily performed) or a source of punishment (and will be avoided if possible).
2. External control and the threat of punishment are not the only means for bringing about effort toward organizational objectives. Men and women will exercise self-direction and self-control in the service of objectives to which they are committed.
3. Commitment to objectives is a function of the rewards associated with their achievement. The most significant of such rewards (*e.g.*, the satisfaction of ego and self-actualization needs) can be direct products of effort directed toward organizational objectives.
4. The average human being learns, under proper conditions, not only to accept but to seek responsibility. Avoidance of responsibility, lack of ambition, and emphasis on security are generally consequences of experience, not inherent human characteristics.
5. The capacity to exercise a relatively high degree of imagination, ingenuity, and creativity in the solution of organizational problems is widely, not narrowly, distributed in the population.
6. Under the conditions of modern industrial life, the intellectual potentialities of the average human being are only partially utilized.

While McGregor admitted that the assumptions of Theory Y were not finally validated, he found them "far more consistent with the existing knowledge in the social sciences than are the assumptions of Theory X." A central motif in both Theory X and Theory Y is control. With Theory X, control comes down from management via strict supervision. Theory Y, on the contrary, assumes that employees will be internally rather than externally controlled. Such internal control presumably comes from an inward motivation to perform effectively.

therblig, basic elements of work motions first classified by the "inventor" of motion study, Frank G. Gilbreth. Therbligs (Gilbreth spelled backward) came in 17 varieties and remain the foundation of the science of motion study. The basic therbligs, as modified by the Society for the Advancement of Management, are: search, select, grasp, reach, move, hold, release, position, pre-position, inspect, assemble, disassemble, use, unavoidable delay, avoidable delay, plan, and rest to overcome fatigue.

think tank, colloquial term that refers to an organization or organizational segment whose sole function is research. Some of the better known "think tanks" include: The RAND Corporation, The Hudson Institute, and The Stanford Research Institute. For a complete account, see Paul Dickson, *Think Tanks* (N.Y.: Atheneum, 1971).

third-party allegations of discrimination, allegations of discrimination in employment brought by third parties—that is, groups or individuals not alleging discrimination against themselves and not seeking relief on their own behalf. The purpose of third-party procedures is to permit organizations with an interest in furthering equal opportunity to call attention to equal employment opportunity problems that appear to require correction or remedial action and that are unrelated to individual complaints of discrimination.

third sector, all those organizations that fit neither in the public sector (government) nor the private sector (business). Theodore Levitt, in *The Third Sector: New Tactics for a Responsive Society* (N.Y.: Amacom Press, 1973), defines the third sector as comprising "those organizations which have risen to institutionalize activism in order to meet problems ignored by the other two sectors." For a symposium, see Michael E. McGill and Leland M. Wooton, (eds.), "Management in the Third Sector," *Public Administration Review* (September–October 1975).

Thornhill v. Alabama: see PICKETING.

threshold effect, total impression a job applicant makes by his or her bearing, dress, manners, etc., as he or she "comes through the door."

throughput, middle step in data processing or a system's operation; it comes after input and before output.

Thurstone Scale, attitude scale created by Louis L. Thurstone that has judges rate the favorability of statements, then has subjects select those statements with which they agree. See L. L. Thurston and E. J. Chave, *The Measurement of Attitude* (Chicago: University of Chicago Press, 1929).

Thurstone Test of Mental Alertness (TTMA), test of mental ability used in screening personnel applicants in business and industry, particularly sales and clerical jobs. Consists of 126 verbal and quantitative items in alternate order and ascending difficulty. TIME: 20 minutes. AUTHOR: Thelma G. and L. L. Thurstone. PUBLISHER: Science Research Associates, Inc. (*see* TEST PUBLISHERS).

TIAA: *see* TEACHERS INSURANCE AND ANNUITY ASSOCIATION.

Tile, Marble and Terrazzo Finishers and Shopmen International Union: *see* LABOR ORGANIZATION.

time, broken: *see* BROKEN TIME.

time card, most basic payroll form on which is recorded, either manually or by means of a mechanical time clock, the hours that an employee has worked during a particular pay period. For an analysis, see E. B. Helin, "Sophisticating the Antiquated Time Card," *Personnel Journal* (June 1971).

time horizon, that distance into the future to which a planner looks when seeking to evaluate the consequences of a proposed action. See Ronald J. Ebert and DeWayne Piehl, "Time Horizon: A Concept for Management," *California Management Review* (Summer 1973).

time-sharing, simultaneous use of a central computer by two or more remote users, each of whom has direct and individual use of the central computer through the use of a terminal. The first commercial computer time-sharing services began in 1965.

time study, according to Benjamin W. Niebel, in *Motion and Time Study*, (Homewood, Ill.: Richard D. Irwin, 6th ed., 1976),

time study involves the technique of establishing an allowed time standard to perform a given task, based upon measurement of the work content of the prescribed method, with due allowance for fatigue and for personal and unavoidable delays. The time study analyst has several techniques that can be used to establish a standard: stopwatch time study, standard data, fundamental motion data, work sampling, and estimates based upon historical data.

See also the following entries:

GILBRETH, FRANK BUNKER AND LILLIAN MOLLER
MOTION STUDY
SYNTHETIC TIME STUDY
THERBLIG
WORK SAMPLING

timetable: *see* GOAL.

time wage rate, any pay structure providing for wage payments in terms of an hourly, weekly, or monthly time interval. This is in contrast to a piece-rate structure where an employee is paid only for the amount that he or she produces.

title, also called CLASS TITLE, the "label" used to officially designate a class. It is descriptive of the work performed and its relative level.

titles, in addition to their use as formal job descriptions, are useful management tools (and cheap, too). The appropriate title can provide incalculable psychic income and a decided advantage when dealing with the outside world. A sales representative may be more effective as a vice president for sales. A secretary may be more effective as an administrative assistant. Some housewives are even slightly more content to be known as domestic engineers. Shakespeare's Juliet was wrong. A rose by any other name would not necessarily smell as sweet; sometimes it smells better!

Title VII, in the context of equal employment opportunity, almost invariably refers to Title VII of the Civil Rights Act of 1964 (as amended)—the backbone of the nation's EEO effort (*see Appendix 1*). It prohibits employment discrimination because of race, color, religion, sex, or national origin and created the Equal Employment Opportunity Commission as its enforcement vehicle. The federal courts have relied heavily upon Title VII in mandating remedial action on the part of employers.

See also the following entries:

BROWN V. GENERAL SERVICES ADMINISTRATION
CITY OF LOS ANGELES, DEPARTMENT OF WATER & POWER V. MANHART
CONSTRUCTIVE DISCHARGE THEORY
DISCRIMINATION
HAZELWOOD SCHOOL DISTRICT V. UNITED STATES
INTERNATIONAL BROTHERHOOD OF TEAMSTERS V. UNITED STATES
MAKE WHOLE
NATIONAL ORIGIN DISCRIMINATION
PREGNANCY DISCRIMINATION ACT OF 1978
RELIGIOUS DISCRIMINATION
RETROACTIVE SENIORITY
706 AGENCY
SEX PLUS
SEXUAL HARASSMENT
SYSTEMIC DISCRIMINATION
TOWER AMENDMENT

title-structure change, elimination of a title by substitution of a more appropriate title without any change in duties or responsibilities of the position involved.

TMTF: *see* LABOR ORGANIZATION, Tile,

Marble and Terrazzo Finishers and Shopmen International Union.

Tobacco Workers International Union: *see* LABOR ORGANIZATION.

Tobin, Maurice J. (1901-1953), Secretary of Labor from 1948 to 1953.

tokenism, in the context of Equal Employment Opportunity, an insincere EEO effort by which a few minority group members are hired in order to satisfy government affirmative action mandates or the demands of pressure groups.

Tool Craftsmen, International Association of: *see* LABOR ORGANIZATION.

Tool, Die and Mold Makers, International Union of: *see* LABOR ORGANIZATION.

tool-handling time, that time during the normal work day that the worker devotes to tending to the tools that are the necessary instruments of his or her work.

Torcaso* v. *Watkins, 367 U.S. 488 (1961), U.S. Supreme Court case, which held that a state requirement of a declaration of a belief in God as a qualification for office was unconstitutional because it invades one's freedom of belief and religion guaranteed by the 1st Amendment and protected by the 14th Amendment from infringement by the states.

total labor force: *see* LABOR FORCE.

totem-pole ranking, rank ordering of employees, usually for purposes of evaluation, where each is placed above or below another with no more than one individual per rank.
See also LOW MAN ON THE TOTEM POLE.

Totten, Ashley Leopold (1884-1963), one of the founders of the Brotherhood of Sleeping Car Porters in 1925 and secretary-treasurer of that union for more than 30 years. For biographical information, *see* Brailsford R. Brazeral, *The Brotherhood of Sleeping Car Porters: Its Origin and Development* (N.Y.: Harper & Bros. 1946).

tour of duty, hours that an employee is scheduled to work.

Tower Amendment, portion of Title VII of the Civil Rights Act of 1964 that was introduced by Senator John Tower of Texas during Senate debate on the act. The Tower Amendment, Section 703 (h), had the effect of establishing, in legal terms, the right of an employer to give "professionally developed ability tests" as long as they were not intentionally discriminatory. The amendment reads as follows:

Nor shall it be an unlawful employment practice for an employer to give and to act upon the results of any professionally developed ability test provided that such test, its administration or action upon the results is not designed, intended or used to discriminate because of race, color, religion, sex, or national origin.

Toys, Playthings, Novelties and Allied Products of the United States and Canada, International Union of Dolls: *see* LABOR ORGANIZATION.

track record, athletic metaphor for an individual's history of performance in any given field or endeavor.

Trademark Society, Inc.: *see* LABOR ORGANIZATION.

trade union: *see* CRAFT UNION.

Train Dispatchers Association, American: *see* LABOR ORGANIZATION.

trainee rate: *see* BEGINNER'S RATE.

trainerless laboratory, laboratory training experience conducted by the participants themselves.

training, organized effort to increase the capabilities of individuals and modify their behavior in order to achieve previously determined objectives. For texts, *see* I. L. Goldstein, *Training: Program Development and Design* (Monterey, Calif.: Brooks/Cole, 1974); Kenneth T. Byers (ed.), *Employee Training and Development in the Public Sector* (Chicago: International Personnel Management Association, rev. ed., 1974); Robert L. Craig (ed.), *Training and Development Handbook* (N.Y.: McGraw-Hill, 2nd ed., 1976); Dugan Laird, *Approaches To Training and Development* (Reading, Mass.: Addison-Wesley, 1978).

See also the following entries:

AMERICAN SOCIETY FOR TRAINING AND DEVELOPMENT
COLD-STORAGE TRAINING
IN-SERVICE TRAINING
JOINT TRAINING
LABORATORY TRAINING
NATIONAL TRAINING LABORATORIES INSTITUTE FOR APPLIED BEHAVIORAL SCIENCE
POST-ENTRY TRAINING
RADIUS CLAUSE
ROLE
VERTICAL TRAINING
VESTIBULE TRAINING
VOCATIONAL TRAINING

Training and Development Journal, monthly journal of the American Society for Training and Development, Inc. Articles written both by practitioners and academics emphasize all phases of training and organization development. Selections tend to be more practical than theoretical.

Training and Development Journal
Editorial Address:
Editor, ASTD
P.O. Box 5307
6414 Odana Road
Madison, WI 53705
Subscriptions and Advertising Address:
ASTD
P.O. Box 5307
Madison, WI 53705

training by objectives, much as a management by objectives system establishes objectives and breaks down all subordinate activity into subdivisions that contribute to the overall objectives, "training by objectives" allows employees to establish their own developmental goals (compatible with organizational goals) and direct their activities toward these goals. For the most comprehensive treatment of this concept, *see* George S. Odiorne, *Training by Objectives: An Economic Approach To Management Training* (N.Y.: The MacMillan Company, 1970).

training demand, also TRAINING NEED, expressed preferences for training programs by individuals. *Training need* reflects some form of skill deficit that is directly related to job performance. If an organization's sole criterion for initiating a training program is demand, the danger will persist that what is demanded is not necessarily what is needed. *See* Richard A. Morano, "Determining Organizational Training Needs," *Personnel Psychology* (Winter 1973); Richard F. Fraser, John W. Gore and Chester C. Cotton, "A System for Determining Training Needs," *Personnel Journal* (December 1978).

training evaluation, also TRAINING MEASUREMENT, determination of the extent to which a training program is justified by its results. *Training measurement* must precede training evaluation, because it reveals the changes that may have occurred as a result of training. The essential question is whether or not a training effort has met its objective. Annual reports frequently boast of the number of employees trained during the preceding year but such "facts" should be looked upon with great suspicion. It is a common mistake to assume that the number of people who have been subjected to training is equal to

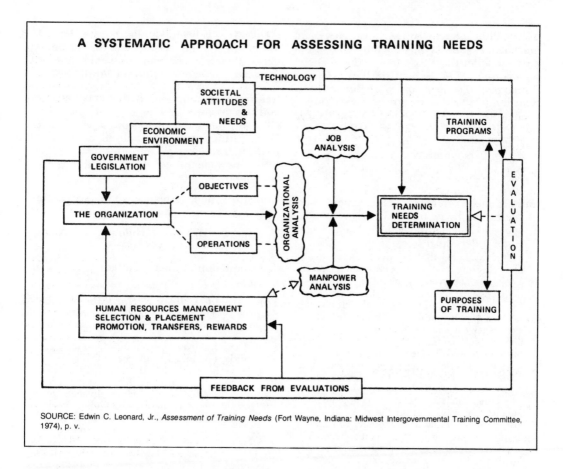

A SYSTEMATIC APPROACH FOR ASSESSING TRAINING NEEDS

SOURCE: Edwin C. Leonard, Jr., *Assessment of Training Needs* (Fort Wayne, Indiana: Midwest Intergovernmental Training Committee, 1974), p. v.

the number who have been trained. No statement of training accomplishment can confidently be made unless it is supported by sophisticated measures of evaluation. *See* Irwin L. Goldstein, *Training: Program Development and Evaluation* (Monterey, Calif.: Brooks/Cole, 1974); Richard Morano, "Measurement and Evaluation of Training," *Training and Development Journal* (July 1975); Donald Kirkpatrick, *Evaluating Training Programs* (Madison, Wis.: American Society for Training and Development, 1975).

training measurement: *see* TRAINING EVALUATION.

training need: *see* TRAINING DEMAND.

Training: The Magazine of Human Resources Development, monthly trade magazine dealing with all aspects of training and human resource development. Articles tend to be written by practitioners in order to help managers of training development functions use the behavioral sciences to solve human performance problems.

Training: The Magazine of Human Resources Development
731 Hennepin Avenue
Minneapolis, MN 55403

transactional analysis (TA), approach to psychotherapy first developed by Eric Berne. Transactional analysis defines the basic unit of social intercourse as a "transaction." There are three "ego states" from which transactions emanate—that of a "parent," an "adult," or a "child." The transactions between individuals can be classified as complementary, crossed, simple or ulterior, based upon the response that an individual receives to a "transactional stimulus"—any action that consciously or unconsciously acknowledges the presence of other individuals. The transactional analysis framework has become a popular means of helping managers to assess the nature and effectiveness of their interpersonal behavior. By striving for more adult-to-adult transactions, managers may eliminate many of the "games people play." For the first published account, *see* Eric Berne, "Transactional Analysis: A New and Effective Method of Group Therapy," *American Journal of Psychotherapy* (October 1958). For the best seller that made transactional analysis a household term, *see* Eric Berne, *Games People Play: The Psychology of Human Relationships* (N.Y.: Grove Press, 1964). For a general treatment, *see* Thomas A. Harris, *I'm OK–You're OK* (N.Y.: Harper & Row, 1969). For an application to personnel, *see* A. J. Tasca, "Personnel Management: A T/A Perspective," *Personnel Journal* (November 1974).

transactional avoidance, "management theory" described by Norman A. Parker, in "The Tongue-in-Cheek Approach To Management Theories," *Personnel Journal* (July 1978):

> The psychologists have put a lot of time into analyzing relationships between people. They have observed that many of these relationships, or transactions, take place between two people playing combinations of roles as parent, child or adult. The conclusion usually reached is that in a work situation, the optimal transaction is conducted by two people playing the role of adult. This is nice if you can get everyone involved to agree to act like an adult. Unfortunately, such is not always the case. Some days, when the planets are right, two people might interact that way. Most of the time there is just too much going on to bother. You then have the transactor making a real college try to be "OK," while the transactee is sucking his or her thumb or acting like a wounded parent. What this leads to is ambivalence in the transaction process, and that is bad and almost incurable. Transactional Avoidance, however, neatly side-steps all the pitfalls.
>
> The basic concept of Transactional Avoidance was devised by an exhermit. His thesis is that in any kind of confrontation, somebody usually loses and therefore any avoidance of transaction is a plus. The elements of the technique involves free delegation of everything, and since almost everyone is familiar with the rudiments of delegation, there is no long learning process involved. The originator of this system refuses to teach any classes and little has been published on this promising concept.

transcendental meditation, technique utilizing biofeedback, which seeks to expand an individual's intellectual growth and consciousness. For the methodology, *see* Robert B. Kory, *The Transcendental Meditation Program for Business People* (N.Y.: AMACOM, 1976).

transfer, also called LATERAL TRANSFER, job reassignment in which the employee retains approximately the same pay, status, and responsibility as in his or her previous assign-

ment. *See* Edward J. Bardi and Jack L. Simonetti, "The Game of Management Chess-Policies and Perils of Management Transfers," *Personnel Journal* (April 1977).

transfer of training, theory that knowledge or abilities acquired in one area aids the acquisition of knowledge or abilities in other areas. When prior learning is helpful, it is called *positive transfer*. When prior learning inhibits new learning, it is called *negative transfer*.

Transit Union, Amalgamated: *see* LABOR ORGANIZATION.

Transport Workers Union of America: *see* LABOR ORGANIZATION.

Transportation Union, United: *see* LABOR ORGANIZATION.

Trans World Airlines* v. *Hardison, 432 U.S. 63 (1977), U.S. Supreme Court case, which ruled

> that an employer is not required to arrange Saturdays off for an employee so that he may observe his Sabbath, if in doing so the employer would incur more than minimal costs - such as overtime pay for a replacement. The Court also ruled that, if employees' work schedules are determined on the basis of seniority, an employer is not required to violate the seniority privileges of others so that an employee can observe a Saturday Sabbath.

trashcan hypothesis, assertion that the personnel department is the dumping ground of management. According to Dalton E. McFarland, in *Cooperation and Conflict in Personnel Administration*, (New York: American Foundation for Management Research, 1962),

> in the assignment of functions to employee relations executives, chief executives or members of organizing committees have no systematic basis for determining the degree of appropriateness of the function for this department. Consequently, they view the personnel department as a dumping ground for a broad array of functions having little to do with the major goals of personnel administration. These decisions have a potential for weakening the performance of major employee relations functions. Personnel executives dislike this extension of their duties and the resulting thinning out of time and available resources.

TRASOP: *see* TAX REDUCTION ACT EMPLOYEE STOCK OWNERSHIP PLAN.

Treasury Employees Union, National: *see* LABOR ORGANIZATION.

Tree Fruits ruling: *see* LABOR BOARD V. FRUIT PACKERS.

Triangle Shirtwaist Factory Fire, fire that focused national attention on the need for adequate safety regulations in factories. On March 25, 1911, 146 people died in a fire in the Triangle Shirtwaist Factory "sweatshop." For a history, *see* Leon Stein, *Triangle Fire* (Phila.: J. B. Lippincott Co., 1967).

trilogy cases: *see* STEELWORKER'S TRILOGY.

TRSOC: *see* LABOR ORGANIZATION, Trademark Society, Inc.

true-false item, test question that calls for the examinee to indicate whether a given statement is true or false.

true score, score entirely free of measurement errors. True scores are hypothetical values never obtained in actual testing, which always involves some measurement error. A true score is sometimes defined as the average score that would result from an infinite series of measurements with the same or exactly equivalent tests, assuming no practice or change in the examinee during the testings.

Truitt Manufacturing decision: *see* NATIONAL LABOR RELATIONS BOARD V. TRUITT MANUFACTURING.

trusteeship, also called UNION TRUSTEESHIP, situation whereby a labor organization (usually a national or international union) suspends the authority of a subordinate organization (usually a local union) and takes control of the subordinate organization's assets and administrative apparatus. Trusteeships are commonly authorized by the constitutions of international unions in order to prevent and, if necessary, remedy corruption and mismanagement by local union officials. Title III of the Labor–Management Reporting and Disclosure (Landrum–Griffin) Act of 1959 prescribes the conditions under which union trusteeships may be established and continued. *See* Daniel L. Shneidman, "Union Trusteeships and Section 304 (a) of the Landrum–Griffin Act," *Labor Law Journal* (June 1963).

TTB: *see* TYPING TEST FOR BUSINESS.

TTMA: *see* THURSTONE TEST OF MENTAL ALERTNESS.

tuition aid, also TUITION REFUND, training program that partially or fully reimburses employees for the expenses of taking job related part-time courses at local colleges or universities. For an analysis, *see* Richard A. Kaimann and Daniel Robey, "Tuition Refund—Asset or Liability?" *Personnel Journal* (August 1976). *See also* Milwaukee Personnel Department Training Unit, "Tuition Reimbursement in Employee Productivity and OD: A Survey," *Public Personnel Management* (May–June 1977).

turkey farm, also called TURKEY OFFICE and TURKEY DIVISION, government office having little work and slight, if any, responsibility. Government managers frequently find it easier to place troublesome or incompetent employees on turkey farms rather than go through the hassle of adverse action proceedings.

Turner, J. C. (1916-   ), became president of the International Union of Operating Engineers in 1975.

turnover, movement of individuals into, through, and out of an organization. Turnover can be statistically defined as the total number (or percentage) of separations that occurs over a given time period. The turnover rate is an important indicator of the morale and health of an organization. For analysis of turnover, *see* James L. Price, *The Study of Turnover* (Ames, Iowa: Iowa State University Press, 1977); Barrie O. Pettman (ed.), *Labour Turnover and Retention* (N.Y.: Halsted Press, John Wiley and Sons, 1975).

See also STAFFING DYNAMICS and WORK PREVIEW.

TWIU: *see* LABOR ORGANIZATION, Tobacco Workers International Union.

Two-Factor Theory: *see* MOTIVATION–HYGIENE THEORY.

TWU: *see* LABOR ORGANIZATION, Transport Workers Union of America.

Typing Test for Business (TTB), used in employment screening of applicants for typing positions. Five tests measure typing skills in straight copy, letters, revised manuscript, numbers, and tables. A 2-minute practice period is allowed for warmup and machine familiarization. TIME: 30/40 minutes. AUTHORS: J. E. Doppelt, A. D. Hartman, F. B. Krawchick. PUBLISHER: Psychological Corporation (*see* TEST PUBLISHERS).

Typographical Union, International: *see* LABOR ORGANIZATION.

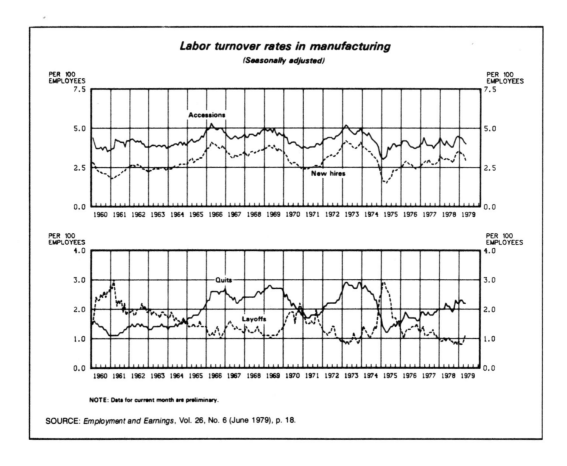

Labor turnover rates in manufacturing

(Seasonally adjusted)

NOTE: Data for current month are preliminary.

SOURCE: *Employment and Earnings*, Vol. 26, No. 6 (June 1979), p. 18.

U

UAW: *see* LABOR ORGANIZATION, Automobile, Aerospace and Agricultural Implement Workers of America, International Union, United.

UBCW: *see* LABOR ORGANIZATION, Brick and Clay Workers of America, United.

UCLEA: *see* UNIVERSITY AND COLLEGE LABOR EDUCATION ASSOCIATION.

UE: *see* LABOR ORGANIZATION, Electrical, Radio and Machine Workers of America, United.

UFW: *see* LABOR ORGANIZATION, Farm Workers of America, United.

UFWA: *see* LABOR ORGANIZATION, Furniture Workers of America, United.

UGCW: *see* LABOR ORGANIZATION, Glass and Ceramic Workers of North America, United.

UGW: *see* LABOR ORGANIZATION, Garment Workers of America, United.

UIU: *see* LABOR ORGANIZATION, Upholsterers' International Union of North America.

UJH: *see* LABOR ORGANIZATION, Horseshoers of the United States and Canada, International Union of Journeymen.

UMW: *see* LABOR ORGANIZATION, Mine Workers of America, United.

unaffiliated union, union not affiliated with the AFL-CIO.

unassembled examination, examination in which applicants are rated solely on their education, experience, and other requisite qualifications as shown in the formal application and on any supporting evidence that may be required.

unauthorized strike: *see* WILDCAT STRIKE.

unclassified positions: *see* EXCEPTED POSITIONS.

underachievement: *see* OVERACHIEVEMENT.

underemployment, those workers who are involuntarily working less than a normal work week and those who are situated in jobs that do not make efficient use of their skills and educational backgrounds. Examples of the latter would include a Ph. D. driving a taxi or an engineer working as a file clerk.

understudy, individual who is engaged in on-the-job training under the direction of a journeyman or an individual who is specifically hired to replace someone planning to retire.

underutilization, in the context of equal employment opportunity, occurs when there are fewer minorities or women in a particular job classification than would be reasonably expected by their general availability.

undocumented workers: *see* ILLEGAL ALIENS.

unemployed, experienced: *see* EXPERIENCED UNEMPLOYED.

unemployed, hard-core: *see* HARD-CORE UNEMPLOYED.

unemployed, hidden: *see* DISCOURAGED WORKERS.

unemployment, persons able and willing to work who are actively (but unsuccessfully) seeking to work at the prevailing wage rate are among the unemployed. The unemployment rate is probably the most significant indicator of the health of the economy. U.S. economists tend to consider an unemployment rate of about four percent of the total labor force as "full employment." Unemployment statistics are compiled monthly by the Bureau of Labor Statistics. These figures are obtained by surveys of a sample of all U.S. households. The Bureau of the Census,

341

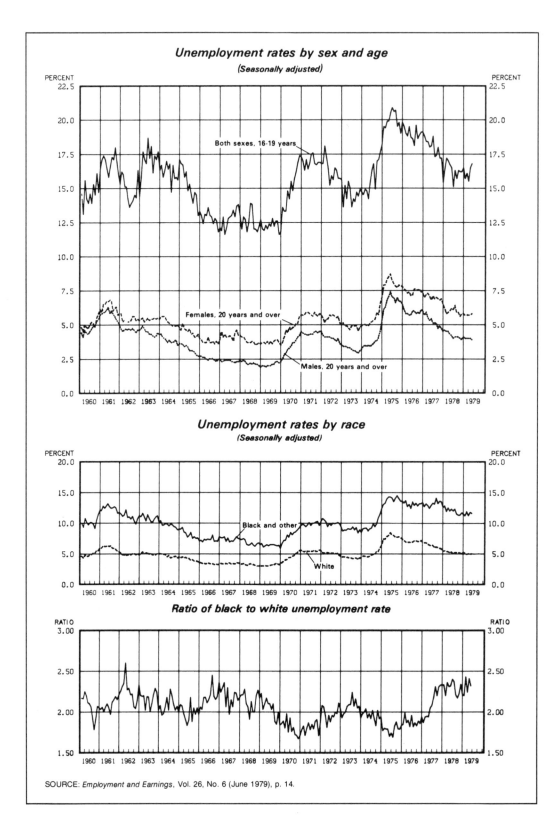

Unemployment rates by sex and age
(Seasonally adjusted)

Both sexes, 16-19 years

Females, 20 years and over

Males, 20 years and over

Unemployment rates by race
(Seasonally adjusted)

Black and other

White

Ratio of black to white unemployment rate

SOURCE: *Employment and Earnings*, Vol. 26, No. 6 (June 1979), p. 14.

which actually conducts the surveys, defines an unemployed person as a civilian over sixteen years old who, during a given week, was available to work but had none, and (1) had been actively seeking employment during the past month, or (2) was waiting to be recalled from a layoff, or (3) was waiting to report to a new job within 30 days. For the most comprehensive history on the concept of unemployment, *see* John A. Garraty, *Unemployment In History: Economic Thought and Public Policy* (N.Y.: Harper & Row, 1978).

See also the following entries:

FRICTIONAL UNEMPLOYMENT
PHANTOM UNEMPLOYMENT
PHILLIPS CURVE
RESIDUAL UNEMPLOYMENT
SEASONAL UNEMPLOYMENT
STRUCTURAL UNEMPLOYMENT
TECHNOLOGICAL UNEMPLOYMENT

unemployment benefits, also called UNEMPLOYMENT COMPENSATION, specific payments available to workers from the various state unemployment insurance programs. Unemployment benefits are available as a matter of right (without a means test) to unemployed workers who have demonstrated their attachment to the labor force by a specified amount of recent work and/or earnings in covered employment. To be eligible for benefits, the worker must be ready, able, and willing to work and must be registered for work at a public employment office. A worker who meets these eligibility conditions may still be denied benefits if he or she is disqualified for an act that would indicate the worker is responsible for his or her own unemployment.

A worker's monetary benefit rights are determined on the basis of employment in covered work over a prior reference period (called the "base period"). Under all state laws, the weekly benefit amount—that is, the amount payable for a week of total unemployment—varies with the worker's past wages within certain minimum and maximum limits. In most of the states, the formula is designed to compensate for a fraction of the usual weekly wage (normally about 50 percent), subject to specified dollar maximums.

The requirements for getting unemployment insurance benefits are generally as follows:

1. The worker must register for work at a public employment office and file a claim for benefits.
2. He or she must have worked previously on a job covered by the state law. This usually includes jobs in factories, mines, offices, or other places of private industry and commerce.
3. He or she must have a prescribed amount of employment or earnings in covered employment during a specified "base period," generally a year, prior to the time benefits are claimed.
4. He or she must be able to work. In general, unemployment insurance benefits are not payable to workers who are sick or unable to work for any other reason, although a few states continue to pay the benefits (within the legal limits) to workers who became ill after they had established their claims, so long as no offer of suitable work is refused.
5. The worker must be available for work and must be ready and willing to take a suitable job if one is offered.
6. The worker must not have:
   a. quit his or her job voluntarily without good cause. (In some states, the law says "without good cause attributable to the employer" or "connected with the work.")
   b. been discharged for misconduct in connection with his or her work.
   c. refused or failed, without good cause, to apply for or accept an offer of suitable work. (What is "suitable" work is generally decided by the state. However, under federal law, no worker may be denied benefits for refusing to accept a new job under substandard labor conditions, where a labor dispute is involved, or where the worker would be required to join a company union or to resign from or refrain from joining any bona fide labor organization.)
   d. become unemployed because of a stoppage of work as the result of a labor dispute, in which he or she is interested or participating, that occurred at the establishment where the worker was last employed.

See also the following entries:

NEW YORK TELEPHONE CO. V. NEW YORK STATE DEPARTMENT OF LABOR
SHERBERT V. VERNER
SUPPLEMENTAL UNEMPLOYMENT BENEFITS

unemployment compensation: *see* UNEMPLOYMENT BENEFITS.

unemployment insurance, programs designed to provide cash benefits to regularly employed members of the labor force who become involuntarily unemployed and who are able and willing to accept suitable jobs.

The first unemployment insurance law in the United States was passed by Wisconsin in 1932 and served as a forerunner for the un-

Unemployment Insurance Under State Laws, Jan. 1, 1978[3]

Jurisdiction	Average Weekly Benefit Paid for Total Unemployment 1976 [1]	Maximum Weekly Benefits [2]	Average Weekly Wages in Covered Employment 1976 [1]	Basic Maximum Weekly Benefit as a Percentage of Average Weekly Wages — Now	Basic Maximum Weekly Benefit as a Percentage of Average Weekly Wages — 1939	Regular Duration of Benefits by Weeks [4]	Percentage of Claimants Who Exhausted Benefits 1976 [1]	Average Employer Tax Rate, 1976 (Estimated) Percentage of Taxable Payrolls	Percentage of Total Payrolls
United States	$75		$204				38%	2.5%	1.2%
Alabama	67	$ 90	180	50%	87%	11-26	32	1.9	1.0
Alaska	82	90-120	494	18	41	14-28	21	3.7	2.0
Arizona	73	85	191	44	61	12-26	40	1.5	.9
Arkansas	63	100	162	61 ⁵	95	10-26	34	2.2	1.2
California	71	104	214	48	50	12-26	35	3.5	2.0
Colorado	85	121	197	61 ⁵	62	7-26	53	1.7	.7
Connecticut	79	116-174	214	54 ⁵	56	26	33	3.0	1.5
Delaware	84	140	222	63 ⁵	58	17-26	42	2.7	.9
District of Columbia	99	148	233	63 ⁵	59	17-34	48	2.7	1.0
Florida	64	82	182	45	81	10-26	50	2.1	1.1
Georgia	69	90	183	49	87	9-26	43	1.3	.8
Hawaii	85	120	184	65 ⁵	85	26	44	3.0	2.0
Idaho	70	110	181	60 ⁵	82	10-26	28	1.7	1.2
Illinois	92	115-138	225	51 ⁵	56	26	43	2.0	.8
Indiana	64	74-124	211	35	58	4-26	36	1.8	.8
Iowa	87	124	186	66 ⁵	67	10-39	36	2.2	1.4
Kansas	70	109	182	59 ⁵	66	10-26	33	2.2	1.0
Kentucky	67	94	189	49 ⁵	69	15-26	33	2.5	1.3
Louisiana	69	120	197	60 ⁵	90	12-28	37	1.9	.9
Maine	63	86-129	167	51 ⁵	74	11-26	31	3.2	1.7
Maryland	73	89	204	43	65	26	19	2.2	1.0
Massachusetts	77	108-162	196	55 ⁵	57	9-30	43	4.2	1.8
Michigan	88	97-136	248	39	53	11-26	39	3.6	1.8
Minnesota	81	122	199	61 ⁵	62	13-26	42	1.9	1.0
Mississippi	51	80	160	50	97	12-26	29	1.8	.9
Missouri	73	85	198	42	61	8-26	37	2.7	1.1
Montana	66	104	174	59 ⁵	60	13-26	39	2.3	1.2
Nebraska	68	90	176	51	66	17-26	39	2.7	1.2
Nevada	74	94	198	47 ⁵	57	11-26	49	3.2	1.9
New Hampshire	65	95	171	55	70	26	11	2.6	1.3
New Jersey	78	104	221	47 ⁵	55	15-26	50	3.4	1.5
New Mexico	60	83	173	47 ⁵	73	18-30	33	1.8	.9
New York	74	115	229	50	51	26	45	3.4	1.3
North Carolina	64	105	167	62 ⁵	89	13-26	26	1.4	.6
North Dakota	70	115	174	66 ⁵	69	18-26	27	2.0	.8
Ohio	85	102-161	220	46 ⁵	54	20-26	31	2.3	1.0
Oklahoma	61	101	186	54 ⁵	61	10-26	47	1.7	.8
Oregon	69	112	202	55 ⁵	53	9-26	27	3.3	2.0
Pennsylvania	87	133-141	206	64 ⁵	60	30	29	2.9	1.2
Puerto Rico	43	60	127	47 ⁵	—	20	78	3.0	3.0
Rhode Island	72	106-126	174	60 ⁵	70	12-26	42	4.0	2.0
South Carolina	64	111	167	66 ⁵	99	10-26	30	2.1	1.1
South Dakota	66	96	153	62 ⁵	69	10-26	30	1.0	.5
Tennessee	61	95	176	53	78	12-26	36	1.6	.7
Texas	55	63	195	32	65	9-26	39	.6	.3
Utah	74	119	181	65 ⁵	70	10-36	32	1.7	1.0
Vermont	69	102	168	60 ⁵	66	26	32	2.2	1.1
Virginia	69	110	181	60	74	12-26	33	1.0	.5
Washington	76	119	219	55 ⁵	57	8-30	40	3.0	1.8
West Virginia	59	139	210	66 ⁵	59	26	22	2.0	.8
Wisconsin	85	133	198	67	65	1-34	40	2.1	1.0
Wyoming	72	111	201	55 ⁵	78	11-26	24	2.0	.9

¹ Calendar Year—latest data available.
² Where two figures are shown, the larger includes maximum dependents' allowances.
³ Includes benefit legislation enacted in 1977 with an effective date in 1978.
⁴ Where two figures are shown, the lower represents the shortest possible duration. In most States this is the entitlement of a claimant with minimum weekly benefits and minimum qualifying wages. But in six States a higher than minimum weekly benefit amount may result in shorter duration where the distribution of earnings is concentrated in the high quarter.
⁵ Maximum weekly benefit is determined as a specified percentage of average weekly covered wages and is computed annually, or in a few States, semi-annually. The base year used for setting the maximum is not necessarily calendar 1977. This explains why the percentage figures in the fifth column may vary slightly from the statutory percentages.

employment insurance provisions of the Social Security Act of 1935. Unlike the old-age provisions of the social security legislation, which are administered by the federal government alone, the unemployment insurance system was made federal–state in character.

The Social Security Act provided an inducement to the states to enact unemployment insurance laws by means of a tax offset. A uniform national tax was imposed on the payrolls of industrial and commercial employers who in 20 weeks or more in a calendar year had eight workers or more. Employers who paid a tax to a state with an approved unemployment insurance law could credit (offset) the state tax against the national tax (up to 90 percent of the federal levy). Thus, employers in states without an unemployment insurance law would not have an advantage in competing with similar businesses in states with such a law, because they would still be subject to the federal payroll tax. Furthermore, their employees would not be eligible for benefits. In addition, the Social Security Act authorized grants to states to meet the full costs of administering the state systems. By July 1937, all 48 states, the territories of Alaska and Hawaii, and the District of Columbia had passed unemployment insurance laws. Much later, Puerto Rico adopted its own unemployment insurance program, which was incorporated into the federal-state system in 1961.

Federal law provides that a state unemployment insurance program has to meet certain requirements if employers are to get their offset against the federal tax and if the state is to receive federal grants for administration. These requirements are intended to assure that a state participating in the program has a sound and genuine unemployment insurance system, fairly administered, and financially secure. One of these requirements is that all contributions collected under the state laws be deposited in the unemployment trust fund in the U.S. Treasury. The fund is invested as a whole, but each state has a separate account to which its deposits and its share of interest on investments are credited. Aside from certain broad federal standards, each state has responsibility for the content and development of its unemployment insurance law. The state itself decides what the amount and duration of benefits shall be and, with minor limitations, what the coverage and contributions rates shall be, and what the eligibility requirements and disqualification provisions shall be. The states also directly administer the laws—

collecting contributions, maintaining wage records (where applicable), taking claims, determining eligibility, and paying benefits to unemployed workers. For a history, see William Haber & Merrill G. Murray, *Unemployment Insurance in the American Economy: An Historical Review and Analysis* (Homewood, Ill.: Richard D. Irwin, 1966). For a critique, see Martin S. Feldstein, "Unemployment Insurance: Time for Reform," *Harvard Business Review* (March–April 1975).

unfair labor practices (employers). The National Labor Relations (Wagner) Act of 1935 specifically forbade certain actions—unfair labor practices—by employers. These prohibitions, which serve to protect the right of employees to organize themselves in labor unions, are:

Section 8(a) (1) forbids an employer "to interfere with, restrain, or coerce employees." Any prohibited interference by an employer with the rights of employees to organize, to form, join, or assist a labor organization, to bargain collectively, or to refrain from any of these activities, constitutes a violation of this section. This is a broad prohibition on employer interference, and an employer violates this section whenever it commits any of the other employer unfair labor practices. In consequence, whenever a violation of Section 8 (a) (2), (3), (4), or (5) is committed, a violation of Section 8 (a) (1) is also found. This is called a "derivative violation" of Section 8 (a) (1).

Section 8(a) (2) makes it unlawful for an employer "to dominate or interfere with the formation or administration of any labor organization or contribute financial or other support to it." This section not only outlaws "company unions" that are dominated by the employer, but also forbids an employer to contribute money to a union it favors or to give a union improper advantages that are denied to rival unions.

Section 8(a) (3) makes it an unfair labor practice for an employer to discriminate against employees "in regard to hire or tenure of employment or any term or condition of employment" for the purpose of encouraging or discouraging membership in a labor organization. In general, the act makes it illegal for an employer to discriminate in employment because of an employee's union or other group activity within the protection of the Act. A banding together of employees, even in the absence of a formal organization, may constitute a labor organization for purposes of Section 8 (a) (3). It also prohibits discrimination because an employee has refrained from taking part in such union or group activity except where a valid union-shop agreement is in effect. Discrimination within the meaning of the act would include such action as refusing to hire, discharging, demoting, assigning to a less desirable shift or job, or withholding benefits.

Section 8(a) (4) makes it an unfair labor practice for an employer "to discharge or otherwise discriminate against an employee because he has filed charges or given testimony under this Act." This provision guards the right of employees to seek the protection of the act by using the processes of the NLRB. Like the previous section, it forbids an employer to discharge, lay off, or engage in other forms of discrimination in working conditions against employees who have filed charges with the NLRB, given affidavits to NLRB investigators, or testified at an NLRB hearing. Violations of this section are in most cases also violations of Section 8 (a) (3).

Section 8(a) (5) makes it illegal for an employer to refuse to bargain in good faith about wages, hours, and other conditions of employment with the representative selected by a majority of the employees in a unit appropriate for collective bargaining. A bargaining representative seeking to enforce its right concerning an employer under this section must show that it has been designated by a majority of the employees, that the unit is appropriate, and that there has been both a demand that the employer bargain and a refusal by the employer to do so.

See also the following entries:

BOULWAREISM
MASTRO PLASTICS CORP. V. NATIONAL LABOR
   RELATIONS BOARD
WILLIAM E. ARNOLD CO. V. CARPENTERS
   DISTRICT COUNCIL OF JACKSONVILLE

unfair labor practices (unions). Twelve years after the passage of the National Labor Relations Act, the Congress became convinced that both employees and employers needed additional legal protections against unfair labor practices of unions. So the Labor–Management Relations (Taft–Hartley) Act of 1947 amended the National Labor Relations Act to include the following major prohibitions:

Section 8(b) (1) (A) forbids a labor organization or its agents "to restrain or coerce employees." The section also provides that it is not intended to "impair the rights of a labor organization to prescribe its own rules" concerning membership in the labor organization. A union may violate this section by coercive conduct of its officers or agents, of pickets on a picket line endorsed by the union, or of strikers who engage in coercion in the presence of union representatives who do not repudiate the conduct. Unlawful coercion may consist of acts specifically directed at an employee such as phys-

ical assaults, threats of violence, and threats to affect an employee's job status. Coercion also includes other forms of pressure against employees such as acts of a union while representing employees as their exclusive bargaining agent. A union that is a statutory bargaining representative owes a duty of fair representation to all the employees it represents. It may exercise a wide range of reasonable discretion in carrying out the representative function, but it violates Section 8 (b) (1) (A) if, while acting as the employees' statutory bargaining representative, it takes or withholds action in connection with their employment because of their union activities or for any irrelevant or arbitrary reason such as an employee's race or sex.

Section 8(b) (1) (B) prohibits a labor organization from restraining or coercing an employer in the selection of a bargaining representative. The prohibition applies regardless of whether the labor organization is the majority representative of the employees in the bargaining unit.

Section 8(b) (2) makes it an unfair labor practice for a labor organization to cause an employer to discriminate against an employee. (Section 8(a) (3) prohibits an employer from discriminating against an employee in regard to wages, hours, and other conditions of employment for the purpose of encouraging or discouraging membership in a labor organization.)

Section 8(b) (3) makes it illegal for a labor organization to refuse to bargain in good faith with an employer about wages, hours, and other conditions of employment if it is the representative of that employer's employees. This section imposes on labor organizations the same duty to bargain in good faith that is imposed on employers by Section 8(a) (5).

Section 8(b) (4) prohibits a labor organization from engaging in a strike, or to induce or encourage a strike, work stoppage, or a refusal to perform services by "any individual employed by any person engaged in commerce or in an industry affecting commerce" in order to foster a secondary boycott, a strike against certification, a jurisdictional strike, or a "hot cargo" agreement.

Section 8(b) (5) makes it illegal for a union to charge employees covered by an authorized union-security agreement a membership fee in an amount the NLRB "finds excessive or discriminatory under all the circumstances."

Section 8(b) (6) forbids a labor organization "to cause or attempt to cause an employer to pay or deliver or agree to pay or deliver any money or other thing of value, in the nature of an exaction, for services which are not performed or not to be performed."

Section 8(b) (7) prohibits a labor organization that is not currently certified as the employees' representative from picketing or threatening to picket with an object of obtaining recognition by the employer (recognitional picketing) or acceptance by his or her employees as their representative (organizational picketing).

See also BOOSTER LODGE NO. 405, MACHINISTS V. NATIONAL LABOR RELATIONS BOARD and WILLIAM E. ARNOLD CO. V. CARPENTERS DISTRICT COUNCIL OF JACKSONVILLE.

unfair list, list of companys (or their products) that a union considers hostile to the interests of labor.

Uniform Guidelines on Employee Selection, guidelines adopted in 1978 by the four federal agencies most concerned with employee selection processes: the Equal Employment Opportunity Commission, the Civil Service Commission, the Department of Justice, and the Department of Labor. The guidelines are designed to assist employers, labor organizations, employment agencies, and licensing and certification boards to comply with requirements of federal law prohibiting employment practices that discriminate on grounds of race, color, religion, sex, or national origin. For the guidelines and clarifying questions and answers, *see Appendices 2 and 3*.

See also SELECTION PROCEDURE.

union: *see* list under LABOR ORGANIZATION. *See also* the following entries:

    BONA FIDE UNION
    BREAD-AND-BUTTER UNIONS
    BUSINESS UNIONS
    CENTRAL LABOR UNION
    CLOSED UNION
    COMPANY UNION
    CRAFT UNION
    GENERAL LABOR UNION
    INDEPENDENT UNION
    INDUSTRIAL UNION
    INTERNATIONAL UNION
    LOCAL INDEPENDENT UNION
    LOCAL INDUSTRIAL UNION
    LOCAL UNION
    MULTICRAFT UNION
    NATIONAL UNION
    OPEN UNION
    UNAFFILIATED UNION
    WHITE-COLLAR UNION

union counselors, also called STRIKE COUNSELORS, under ordinary circumstances, a union member who has volunteered to take a training course on the work of his or her community's social agencies. Training completed, the counselor serves as a referral agent in the local union, supplying information about the location, specific services, eligibility requirements, and application procedures to fellow union members who seek help in resolving some personal or family problem. In the event of a strike, the counselor advises strikers how they may best avail themselves of their community's social welfare programs. *See* Armand J. Thiebolt, Jr., and Ronald M. Cowin, *Welfare and Strikes: The Use of Public Funds to Support Strikers* (Philadelphia: The Wharton School of the University of Pennsylvania, 1972).

union dues: *see* DUES.

union hiring hall: *see* HIRING HALL.

unionism, dual: *see* DUAL UNIONISM.

union label, any imprint attached to an item that indicates that it was made by union labor. Unions naturally encourage their members and the public to buy only those products bearing a union label. *See* Monroe M. Bird and James W. Robinson, "The Effectiveness of the Union Label and 'Buy Union' Campaigns," *Industrial and Labor Relations Review* (July 1972).

UNION LABEL

One of the world's most famous union labels is that of the International Ladies Garment Workers Union.

Union Labor Report, information service published by the Bureau of National Affairs, Inc., for union officials at all levels. Covers the rights of unions, shop problems, union administration, equal employment opportunities, organizing, bargaining, elections, NLRB procedures, the rights of strikers, and wages and hours.

Union of Professional Airmen: *see* LABOR ORGANIZATION, under Air Line Pilots Association.

union organizer: *see* ORGANIZER.

union scale: *see* JOURNEYMAN PAY.

union security, generally, any agreement between an employer and a union that requires every employee in the bargaining unit, as a condition of employment, to be a member of the union or to pay a specified sum to the union for its bargaining services. *See* Patricia N. Blair, "Union Security Agreement in Public Employment," *Cornell University Law Review* (January 1975).

union-security clause, provision in a collective bargaining agreement that seeks to protect the union by providing for a constant flow of funds by any of a variety of means. Union-security clauses typically provide for such things as the checkoff, the closed shop, the union shop, the agency shop, preferential hiring, etc.

union shop, union-security provision found in some collective bargaining agreements that requires all employees to become members of the union within a specified time (usually 30 days) after being hired (or after the provision is negotiated) and to remain members of the union as a condition of employment.
See also MODIFIED UNION SHOP.

union steward: *see* STEWARD.

union trusteeship: *see* TRUSTEESHIP.

unit: *see* BARGAINING UNIT.

unit, employer: *see* EMPLOYER UNIT.

United Airlines v. *Evans*, 431 U.S. 553 (1977), U.S. Supreme Court case that limited an employer's liability for prior violations under Title VII. The court ruled that an employee who was illegally discriminated against after Title VII took effect could lose her right to retroactive seniority if she fails to file charges within the specified period (now 180 days) after the violation occurred. For an analysis, *see* Stephen L. Swanson, "The Effect of the Supreme Court's Seniority Decisions," *Personnel Journal* (December 1977).

United Airlines v. *McMann*, 434 U.S. 192 (1977), U.S. Supreme Court case, which upheld the Age Discrimination in Employment Act of 1967. The court held that the law, designed to protect the rights of workers age 40 to 65, does not prohibit "bona fide" retirement plans that require involuntary termination before the age of 65. However, the act's 1978 amendments overturned the court's decision.

United Allied Workers International Union: *see* LABOR ORGANIZATION, Allied Workers International Union, United.

United Association of Journeymen and Apprentices of the Plumbing and Pipe Fitting Industry of the United States and Canada: *see* LABOR ORGANIZATION, Plumbing and Pipe Fitting Industry of the United States and Canada, United Association of Journeymen and Apprentices of the.

United Brick and Clay Workers of America, The: *see* LABOR ORGANIZATION, Brick and Clay Workers of America, The United.

United Brotherhood of Carpenters and Joiners of America: *see* LABOR ORGANIZATION, Carpenters and Joiners of America, United Brotherhood of.

United Cement, Lime and Gypsum Workers International Union: *see* LABOR ORGANIZATION, Cement, Lime and Gypsum Workers International Union, United.

United Electrical, Radio, and Machine Workers of America: *see* LABOR ORGANIZATION, Electrical, Radio, and Machine Workers of America, United.

United Farm Workers of America: *see* LABOR ORGANIZATION, Farm Workers of America, United.

United Food and Commercial Workers International Union: *see* LABOR ORGANIZATION, Food and Commercial Workers International Union, United.

United Furniture Workers of America: *see* LABOR ORGANIZATION, Furniture Workers of America, United.

United Garment Workers of America: *see* LABOR ORGANIZATION, Garment Workers of America, United.

United Glass and Ceramic Workers of North America: *see* LABOR ORGANIZATION, Glass and Ceramic Workers of North America, United.

United Hatters, Cap and Millinery Workers International Union: *see* LABOR ORGANIZATION, Hatters, Cap and Millinery Workers International Union, United.

United Mine Workers of America: *see* LABOR ORGANIZATION, Mine Workers of America, United.

United Mine Workers v. Pennington, 381 U.S. 657 (1965), U.S. Supreme Court case, which held that pattern bargaining may leave both employers and unions liable for damages under the Sherman Anti-Trust Act of 1890 if it can be shown that the parties who wrote the pattern setting contract conspired to impose it on others. *See* Herman A. Gray, "Pennington and the 'Favored Nation' Clause," *Labor Law Journal* (November 1965).

United Paperworkers International Union: *see* LABOR ORGANIZATION, Paperworkers International Union, United.

United Public Workers v. Mitchell: *see* UNITED STATES CIVIL SERVICE COMMISSION V. NATIONAL ASSOCIATION OF LETTER CARRIERS.

United Retail Workers Union: *see* LABOR ORGANIZATION, Retail Workers Union, United.

United Rubber, Cork, Linoleum and Plastic Workers of America: *see* LABOR ORGANIZATION, Rubber, Cork, Linoleum and Plastic Workers of America, United.

United Shoe Workers of America: *see* LABOR ORGANIZATION, Shoe Workers of America, United.

United Slate, Tile and Composition Roofers, Damp and Waterproof Workers Association: *see* LABOR ORGANIZATION, Roofers, Damp and Waterproof Workers Association, United Slate, Tile and Composition.

United States Civil Service Commission, the central personnel agency of the United States from 1883 to 1978. It was abolished by the Civil Service Reform Act of 1978.

See also CIVIL SERVICE REFORM ACT OF 1978, OFFICE OF PERSONNEL MANAGEMENT, and MERIT SYSTEMS PROTECTION BOARD.

United States Civil Service Commission v. National Association of Letter Carriers 413 U.S. 548 (1973), U.S. Supreme Court case, which upheld the Hatch Act's limitations on the political activities of federal employees.

The *Letter Carriers* decision reaffirmed an earlier court ruling, *United Public Workers v. Mitchell*, 330 U.S. 75 (1947), which had held that the ordinary citizen rights of federal employees could be abridged by Congress in the interest of increasing or maintaining the efficiency of the federal service.

In the 1972 case, *National Association of Letter Carriers* v. *United States Civil Service Commission*, the Court of Appeals for the District of Columbia Circuit declared the Hatch Act to be unconstitutional because its vague and "overboard" language made it impossible to determine what it prohibited. When this case was appealed to the Supreme Court, the court reasoned that, despite some ambiguities, an ordinary person using ordinary common sense could ascertain and comply with the regulations involved. It also argued that its decision did nothing more than to confirm the judgment of history that political neutrality was a desirable, or even essential, feature of public employment in the United States.

United States Code, official lawbooks that contain all federal Laws.

United States Conference of Mayors, an organization of city governments founded in 1933. It is a national forum through which this country's larger cities express their concerns and actively work to meet U.S. urban needs. By limiting membership and participation to the 750 cities with over 30,000 population and by concentrating on questions of federal–city relationships, the Conference seeks to become a focus for urban political leadership.

> *United States Conference of Mayors*
> 1620 Eye Street, N.W.
> Washington, DC 20006
> (202) 293-7300

United States court of appeals: *see* COURT OF APPEALS.

United States district court: *see* DISTRICT COURT.

United States Employment Services (USES), federal agency within the U.S. Department of Labor, which provides assistance to states and territories in establishing and maintaining a system of over 2,400 local public employment offices. Established by the Wagner–Peyser Act of 1933, the USES is responsible for providing job placement and other employment services to unemployed individuals and other jobseekers, providing employers and workers with job development, placement, recruitment and similar assistance including employment, counseling, and special services to youth, women, older workers, and handicapped persons, and related supportive services. The USES is also responsible for the development of state and local information on employment and unemployment, and on occupational demand and supply necessary for the planning and operation of job training and vocational education programs throughout the country.

The USES develops policies and procedures to provide a complete placement service to workers and employers in rural areas. Migrant and seasonal farmworkers receive assistance to help them maintain year-round employment through the federal–state employment services interstate clearance system. The USES is responsible for insuring that, in the interstate recruitment of farm and woods workers, applicable standards and regulations relating to housing, transportation, wages, and other conditions are met.

The USES provides special assistance to youth between 16 and 22 years of age through its cooperative school program and through specialized youth staff in local offices. The *Cooperative School Program* is a part of the overall youth program and is aimed at easing the transition from school to work by offering placement counseling and job finding services to prospective dropouts, graduates, and job-ready youth. Another youth service is the *Summer Employment Program,* through which school youths are referred to private and public summer jobs. In addition, special cooperative programs are developed with the Office of Personnel Management, the National Alliance of Businessmen, and local prime sponsors under the Comprehensive Employment and Training Act for the referral of primarily disadvantaged youth to summer jobs and/or training opportunities in federal establishments, with private employers, or to specially funded job or training opportunities.

Other USES services include: certifying aliens who seek to immigrate to the United States for employment; providing employment services and adjustment assistance to U.S. workers adversely affected by foreign imports under the Trade Act of 1974; issuing *Exemplary Rehabilitation Certificates* to qualified persons discharged from the armed services under conditions other than honorable; providing job search guidance and aptitude-testing services to workers; giving specialized recruitment assistance to employers; providing labor market information to other federal or state agencies to meet various program responsibilities and to the public on state and local employment conditions; providing guidance, counseling, referral, and placement in apprenticeship opportunities through *Apprenticeship Information Centers* located in selected state employment service offices; reviewing rural industrialization loan and grant certification applications under the Rural Development Act of 1972; maintaining an occupational research program for the compilation of the *Dictionary of Occupational Titles;* and providing bonding assistance to individuals who have been unable to obtain it on their own.

United States Reports, official record of cases decided by the U.S. Supreme Court. When cases are cited, *United States Reports* is abbreviated to "U.S." For example, the legal citation for the case of *Pickering* v. *Board of Education* is 391 U.S. 563 (1968). This means that the case will be found on page 563 of volume 391 of the *United States Reports* and that it was decided in 1968.

United States Statutes at Large, bound volumes, issued annually, containing all public and private laws and concurrent resolutions enacted during a session of Congress, reorganization plans, proposed and ratified amendments to the Constitution, and presidential proclamations.

United States v. Allen Kaiser: *see* STRIKE BENEFITS.

United States v. Archie Brown: *see* CLEANSING PERIOD.

United States v. Darby Lumber, 312 U.S. 100 (1941), U.S. Supreme Court case that upheld the Fair Labor Standards Act of 1938, which established minimum wages and maximum hours for workers in businesses engaged in, or producing goods for, interstate commerce.

United States v. Hutcheson, 312 U.S. 219 (1941), U.S. Supreme Court case, which held that criminal liability could not be imposed, under the Sherman Antitrust Act of 1890, on a union that calls for picketing and/or a boycott against an employer because of a jurisdictional dispute with another union.

United Steelworkers of America: *see* LABOR ORGANIZATION, Steelworkers of America, United.

United Steelworkers of America v. American Manufacturing Co., 363 U.S. 564 (1960), U.S. Supreme Court case, which held that the role of the federal courts is limited when the parties have agreed to submit all questions of contract interpretation to an arbitrator.
See also STEELWORKERS' TRILOGY.

United Steelworkers of America v. Enterprise Wheel and Car Corp., 363 U.S. 593 (1960), U.S. Supreme Court case, which held that the interpretation of a collective bargaining agreement is a question for an arbitrator and the courts do not have the right to overrule an arbitrator because of his interpretation.

See also STEELWORKERS' TRILOGY.

United Steelworkers of America v. Warrior and Gulf Navigation Co., 363 U.S. 574 (1960), U. S. Supreme Court case, which held that a labor–management dispute could not be judged to be nonarbitrable unless the parties specifically excluded the subject from the arbitration process.

See also ARBITRABILITY and STEELWORKERS' TRILOGY.

United Steelworkers of America v. Weber, et al., 61 L.Ed.2d 480 (1979), decided together with KAISER ALUMINUM & CHEMICAL CORP. V. WEBER, ET AL., U.S. Supreme Court decision that upheld an affirmative action program giving blacks preference in selection of employees for a training program.

In 1974, the United Steelworkers of America and Kaiser Aluminum & Chemical Corporation entered into a master collective bargaining agreement covering terms and conditions of employment at 15 Kaiser plants. The agreement included an affirmative action plan designed to eliminate conspicuous racial imbalances in Kaiser's then almost exclusively white craft work forces. It reserved 50 percent of the openings in in-plant, craft-training programs for blacks until the percentage of black craft workers in a plant became commensurate with the percentage of blacks in the local labor force. This litigation arose from the operation of the affirmative action plan at one of Kaiser's plants, where, prior to 1974, only 1.83 percent of the skilled craft workers were black even though the local work force was approximately 39 percent black. Pursuant to the national agreement, Kaiser, rather than continuing its practice of hiring trained outsiders, established a training program to train its production workers to fill craft openings. Trainees were selected on the basis of seniority, with the proviso that at least 50 percent of the trainees were to be black until the percentage of black skilled craft workers in the plant approximated the percentage of blacks in the local labor force. During the plan's first year of operation, seven black and six white craft trainees were selected from the plant's production work force. The most junior black trainee had less seniority than several white production workers whose bids for admission were rejected. Thereafter, Brian Weber, one of those white production workers, instituted a class action in a federal district court. The suit alleged that because the affirmative action program had resulted in junior black employees receiving training in preference to more senior white employees, Weber and other similarly situated white employees had been discriminated against in violation of Title VII of the Civil Rights Act of 1964 (which makes it unlawful to discriminate because of race in hiring and in the selection of apprentices for training programs).

The district court ruled in favor of Weber. The court of appeals affirmed, holding that all employment preferences based upon race—including those preferences incidental to bona fide affirmative action plans—violated Title VII's prohibition against racial discrimination in employment. The U.S. Supreme Court reversed the lower court rulings. Justice Brennan, in delivering the majority opinion of the court, stated that "the only question before us is the narrow statutory issue of whether Title VII *forbids* private employers and unions from voluntarily agreeing upon bona fide affirmative action plans that accord racial preferences. . . ." The court concluded "that Congress did not intend to limit traditional business freedom to such a degree as to prohibit all voluntary, race-conscious affirmative action." Brennan went on to add that, because Kaiser's preferential scheme was legal, it was unnecessary to "define in detail the line of demarcation between permissible and impermissible affirmative action plans."

See also the following entries:
AFFIRMATIVE ACTION
CIVIL RIGHTS ACT OF 1964
REGENTS OF THE UNIVERSITY OF CALIFORNIA V. ALLAN BAKKE
REVERSE DISCRIMINATION
TITLE VII

United Telegraph Workers: *see* LABOR ORGANIZATION, Telegraph Workers, United.

United Textile Workers of America: *see* LABOR ORGANIZATION, Textile Workers of America, United.

United Transportation Union: *see* LABOR ORGANIZATION, Transportation Union, United.

unit labor cost: *see* LABOR COSTS.

unit seniority: *see* DEPARTMENTAL SENIORITY.

unity of command, concept that each individual in an organization should be accountable to only a single superior.

unity of direction, concept that there should be only one head and one plan for each organizational segment.

universe: *see* POPULATION.

University and College Labor Education Association (UCLEA), an organization of universities and colleges with regular and continuing programs to provide labor education/labor studies for workers and their organizations.

UCLEA
% Bureau of Labor Education
128 College Avenue
Orono, ME 04473

University of Michigan Business Review, published six times a year to provide its business readership with concise articles on research and applications in management techniques, economic analysis and commentary, business implications of public policy and survey articles in the various business specialities.

University of Michigan Business Review
Graduate School of Business Administration
The University of Michigan
Ann Arbor, MI 48109

University Professors, American Association of: *see* LABOR ORGANIZATION.

unobstrusive measures, measures taken without the subject being aware that he or she is being observed. *See* Eugene J. Webb, *et al.*, *Unobstrusive Measures: Nonreactive Research in the Social Sciences* (Chicago: Rand McNally, 1966).

unpatterned interview: *see* PATTERNED INTERVIEW.

unskilled workers, employees whose jobs are confined to manual operations limited to the performance of relatively simple duties requiring only the slightest exercise of independent judgement.

unstructured role playing, role-play exercise or simulation in which the players are not given specific information on the character of their roles.

Upholsterers' International Union of North America: *see* LABOR ORGANIZATION.

UPIU: *see* LABOR ORGANIZATION, Paperworkers International Union, United.

Upjohn Institute for Employment Research, private, nonprofit organization founded in 1945 to foster "research into the causes and effects of unemployment and to study and in-

vestigate the feasibility and methods of insuring against unemployment and devise ways and means of preventing and alleviating the distress and hardship caused by unemployment"

Upjohn Institute for Employment Research
300 South Westnedge Avenue
Kalamazoo, MI 49007
(616) 343-5541

up-or-out system, career system that terminates individuals who do not qualify themselves for the next higher level of the system within a specified time period. The U.S. military officer corps and Foreign Service are two examples of up-or-out systems.

upward-mobility program, systematic management effort that focuses on the development and implementation of specific career opportunities for lower-level employees who are in positions or occupational series which do not enable them to realize their full work potential. An upward-mobility program is usually just one aspect of an organization's overall EEO effort. *See* Thomas E. Diggin, "Upward Mobility—TECOM puts it all Together," *Public Personnel Management* (May–June 1974); Gary Gemmill, "Reward Mapping and Upward Mobility," *Management of Personnel Quarterly* (Winter 1970).

URW: *see* LABOR ORGANIZATION, Rubber, Cork, Linoleum and Plastic Workers of America, United.

Urwick, Lyndall F. (1891-   ), one of the prioneers of the classical school of organization theory. Major works include: *Papers on the Science of Administration*, with Luther Gulick (N.Y.: Institute of Public Administration, 1937); *Scientific Principles of Organization* (N.Y.: American Management Association, 1938); *The Elements of Administration* (N.Y.: Harper & Bros., 1944); *The Pattern of Management* (Minneapolis: University of Minnesota Press, 1956); *Staff in Organization*, with Ernest Dale (N.Y.: McGraw-Hill, 1960).

U.S.: *see* UNITED STATES REPORTS.

USA: *see* LABOR ORGANIZATION, Steelworkers of America, United.

Usery, W. J., Jr. (1923-   ), Secretary of Labor from 1976 to 1977.

Usery v. Turner Elkhorn Mining Co., 428 U.S. 1 (1976), U.S. Supreme Court case, which upheld that portion of the Federal Coal Mine Health and Safety Act of 1969 making coal mine operators liable for benefits to former miners (and their dependents) who have suffered from black-lung disease (pneumoconiosis).

USES: *see* UNITED STATES EMPLOYMENT SERVICE.

USW: *see* LABOR ORGANIZATION, Shoe Workers of America, United.

UTAH-PEA: *see* LABOR ORGANIZATION, Utah Public Employees Association.

Utah Public Employees Association: *see* LABOR ORGANIZATION.

Utah State AFL–CIO: *see* AMERICAN FEDERATION OF LABOR–CONGRESS OF INDUSTRIAL ORGANIZATIONS.

Utility Workers Union of America: *see* LABOR ORGANIZATION.

Utility Workers of New England, Inc., Brotherhood of: *see* LABOR ORGANIZATION.

UTU: *see* LABOR ORGANIZATION, Transportation Union, United.

UTW: *see* LABOR ORGANIZATION, Telegraph Workers, United.

UTWA: *see* LABOR ORGANIZATION, Textile Workers of America, United.

UWNE: *see* LABOR ORGANIZATION, Utility Workers of New England, Inc., Brotherhood of.

UWU: *see* LABOR ORGANIZATION, Utility Workers Union of America.

V

vacancy, available position for which an organization is actively seeking to recruit a worker.

vacating an award, court's setting aside of an arbitration award.

vacation pay, pay for specified periods of time off work. The vacation or leave time that an employee earns frequently varies with length of service.

valence, in Victor H. Vroom's "Expectancy Theory of Motivation," the value an employee places on an incentive or reward. For a full account of Vroom's theory, *see* his *Work and Motivation* (N.Y.: John Wiley & Sons, 1964). For a test of it, *see* Robert Pritchard, Philip DeLeo, and Clarence VonBergen, Jr., "The Field Experimental Test of Expectancy—Valence Incentive Motivation Techniques," *Organizational Behavior and Human Performance* (April 1976).

See also EXPECTANCY THEORY.

validation, process of investigation by which the validity of a particular type of test use is estimated. What is important here is to identify an ambiguity in the term "to validate," which is responsible for much confusion in the area of employment testing. To validate in ordinary language may mean to mark with an indication of official approval. In this sense, it is also possible to "invalidate" or to indicate official disapproval. In the technical vocabulary of employment testing, to validate is to investigate, to conduct research. Thus, in validating a test (more properly, in validating a use of a test), one is conducting an inquiry. In this context, the term "invalidating" has no meaning at all.

See also the following entries:
CONSENSUAL VALIDATION
CRITERION RELATED VALIDATION
CROSS VALIDATION
DIFFERENTIAL VALIDATION
STATISTICAL VALIDATION
VALIDITY

validity, extent to which a test measures what it is supposed to measure or the accuracy of inferences drawn from test scores.

See also the following entries:
CONCURRENT VALIDITY
CONSTRUCT VALIDITY
CONTENT VALIDITY
CONVERGENT VALIDITY
CURRICULAR VALIDITY
DISCRIMINANT VALIDITY
EMPIRICAL VALIDITY
FACE VALIDITY
ITEM VALIDITY
OPERATIONAL VALIDITY
PREDICTIVE VALIDITY
RATIONAL VALIDITY
SYNTHETIC VALIDITY
VALIDATION

validity coefficient, correlation coefficient that estimates the relationship between scores on a test (or test battery) and the criterion.

Vance v. Bradley, 59 L. Ed. 2d 171 (1979), U.S. Supreme Court case, which held that requiring officers of the U.S. Foreign Service to retire at age 60 did not violate the equal protection component of the due process clause of the Fifth Amendment, even though other federal employees do not face mandatory retirement at such an early age.

variable, any factor or condition subject to measurement, alteration, and/or control.

variable, contextual: *see* CONTEXTUAL VARIABLE.

variable annuity, also called ASSET-LINKED ANNUITY, annuity that varies with the value of assets. In an effort to protect the purchasing power of a pensioner, some pension plans link benefit accruals to the value of an associated asset portfolio. Upon retirement, the pensioner may have the option of continuing to receive asset-linked benefits or to convert total benefits to a conventional fixed-income annuity.

variable life insurance, form of life insurance whose death benefit is dependent upon the performance of investments in a common portfolio.

variance, difference between an expected or standard value and an actual one.

variance analysis: *see* ANALYSIS OF VARIANCE.

Variety Artists, American Guild of: *see* LABOR ORGANIZATION, under Actors and Artistes of America, Associated.

velvet ghetto, organizational unit (such as a public relations department) that is overloaded with women in response to an affirmative action program and in compensation for their scarcity in other professional or management categories. For a discussion, *see* "PR: 'The Velvet Ghetto' of Affirmative Action," *Business Week* (May 8, 1978).

Vermont State Labor Council AFL–CIO: *see* AMERICAN FEDERATION OF LABOR–CONGRESS OF INDUSTRIAL ORGANIZATIONS.

Vermont State Employees Association, Inc.: *see* LABOR ORGANIZATION.

vertical communication: *see* COMMUNICATION.

vertical loading: *see* JOB LOADING.

vertical occupational mobility: *see* OCCUPATIONAL MOBILITY.

vertical training, simultaneous training of people who work together, irrespective of their status in the organization.

vertical union: *see* INDUSTRIAL UNION.

vertical work group, work group containing individuals whose positions differ in rank, prestige, and level of skill.

vested benefit: *see* VESTING.

vestibule training, training that prepares a new employee for an occupation after acceptance for employment but before the assumption of the new job's duties. For example, rookie training for new police.

vesting, granting an employee the right to a pension at normal retirement age even if the employee leaves the organization before the age of normal retirement. A vested benefit is usually based on accrued pension credit, as opposed to the pension for which the employee would have been eligible had he/she remained in the organization until retirement.

See also DEFERRED FULL VESTING, DEFERRED GRADED VESTING, and IMMEDIATE FULL VESTING.

veteran, disabled: *see* DISABLED VETERAN.

veterans preference. The modern concept of veterans preference dates from 1865, when Congress, toward the end of the Civil War, affirmed that "persons honorably discharged from the military or naval service by reason of disability resulting from wounds or sickness incurred in the line of duty, shall be preferred for appointments to civil offices, provided they are found to possess the business capacity necessary for the proper discharge of the duties of such offices." The 1865 law was superceded in 1919, when preference was extended to all "honoraly discharged" veterans, their widows, and to wives of disabled veterans. The Veterans Preference Act of 1944 expanded the scope of veterans preference by providing for a five-point bonus on federal examination scores for all honorably separated veterans (except for those with a service-connected disability who are entitled to a 10 point bonus). Veterans also received other advantages in federal employment (such as protections against arbitrary dismissal and preference in the event of a reduction-in-force).

All states and many other jurisdictions have veterans preference laws of varying intensity. New Jersey, for an extreme example, offers veterans absolute preference: if a veteran passes an extrance examination, he/she must be hired no matter what his/her score before nonveterans can be hired. Veterans competing with each other are rank ordered, and all disabled veterans receive preference over other veterans. Veterans preference laws have been criticized because they have allegedly made it difficult for government agencies to hire and promote more women and minorities. Although the original version of the Civil Service Reform Act of 1978 sought to limit veterans preference in the federal service, the final version contained a variety of new provisions *strengthening* veterans preference.

See also PERSONNEL ADMINISTRATOR OF MASSACHUSETTS V. FEENEY and MILITARY SERVICE.

Veterans Readjustment Assistance Act of 1974, federal statute that required contractors with federal contracts of $10,000 or more to establish program to take "affirmative action" to employ and advance in employment all disabled veterans (with 30% or more disability) and other veterans for the first 48 months after discharge.

See also LABOR-MANAGEMENT SERVICES ADMINISTRATION.

veterans reemployment rights, reemployment rights program, under provisions of Chapter 43 of Title 38, U.S. Code, for men and women who leave their jobs to perform training or service in the armed forces. The Office of Veterans Reemployment Rights of the Labor–Management Services Administration of the U.S. Department of Labor has responsibility for the program. In general terms, to be entitled to reemployment rights a veteran must leave a position (other than a temporary position) with a private employer, the federal government, or a state or local government for the purpose of entering the armed forces, voluntarily or involuntarily. The employer is generally obligated to reemploy the veteran within a reasonable time after he/she makes application for the position he/she would have occupied if he/she had remained on the job instead of entering military service.

See also FOSTER V. DRAVO CORP.

Vietnam Era Veterans Readjustment Act of 1974: *see* VETERANS READJUSTMENT ACT OF 1974.

Virginia State AFL–CIO: *see* AMERICAN FEDERATION OF LABOR–CONGRESS OF INDUSTRIAL ORGANIZATIONS.

vocational behavior, total realm of human actions and interactions related to the work environment, including preparation for work, participation in the workforce, and retirement. For a text, *see* Donald G. Zytowski, *Vocational Behavior: Readings in Theory and Research*, (New York: Holt, Rinehart and Winston, Inc., 1968).

vocational counseling, any professional assistance given to an individual preparing to enter the workforce concerning the choice of occupation.

Vocational Education Act of 1963, federal statute that authorized federal grants to states to assist them to maintain, extend, and improve existing programs of vocational education; to develop new programs of vocational education; and to provide part-time employment for youths who need the earnings from such employment to continue their vocational training on a full-time basis.

See also SMITH-HUGHES ACT OF 1917.

vocational maturity, term, premised upon the belief that vocational behavior is a develop-mental process, which implies a comparison of an individual's chronological and vocational ages. For a model of vocational maturity, *see* John O. Crites "Career Development Processes: A Model of Vocational Maturity," Edwin Herr (ed.), *Vocational Guidance and Human Development* (Boston, Houghton Mifflin Co., 1974).

vocational maturity quotient, ratio of vocational maturity to chronological age.

Vocational Preference Inventory (VPI), personality inventory designed to measure a broad range of information about the subject's interpersonal relations, interests, values, self-conception, coping behavior and identification. Consists of 160 occupational titles to which an individual indicates likes or dislikes. TIME: 15/30 minutes. AUTHOR: John L. Holland. PUBLISHER: Consulting Psychologists Press, Inc. (*see* TEST PUBLISHERS).

vocational psychology, scientific study of vocational behavior and development. According to John O. Crites, in *Vocational Psychology* (N.Y.: McGraw-Hill, 1969):

> Historically the field of vocational psychology grew out of the practice of vocational guidance. It seems desirable to differentiate between them, however, if vocational psychology is to become firmly established as the science of vocational behavior and development—unconfounded with the purposes and procedures of vocational guidance, which is still largely an art. There is one important area of overlap (approximately 10 percent) which should be mentioned. To the extent that vocational guidance, as a stimulus or treatment condition, is functionally related to vocational behavior, then it falls within the purview of vocational psychology as a field of study.

vocational rehabilitation, restoration of the handicapped to the fullest physical, mental, social, vocational and economic usefulness of which they are capable. See Ronald W. Conley, *The Economics of Vocational Rehabilitation* (Baltimore: John Hopkins Press, 1965).

Vocational Rehabilitation Act of 1973, federal statute that requires federal contractors with contracts in excess of $2,500 to "take affirmative action to employ and advance in employment qualified handicapped individuals." The act also established within the federal government an Interagency Committee on Handicapped Employees whose purpose is "(1) to provide a focus for Federal and other employment of handicapped individuals, and to review, on a periodic basis, in cooperation with the Civil Service Commission [now Office of Personnel Management], the adequacy of hiring, placement, and advancement practices with respect to handicapped individuals, by each department, agency, and instrumentality in the executive branch of Government, and to insure that the special needs of such individuals are being met; and (2) to consult with the Civil Service Commission to assist the Commission to carry out its responsibilities" in implementing affirmative action programs for the handicapped.

vocational training, formal preparation for a particular business or trade.

voice stress analyzer: *see* LIE DETECTOR.

voluntary arbitration, arbitration agreed to by two parties in the absence of any legal or contractual requirement.

voluntary bargaining items, those items over which collective bargaining is neither mandatory nor illegal.

voluntary demotion: *see* DEMOTION.

Von Bertalanffy, Ludwig: *see* BERTALANFFY, LUDWIG VON.

VPI: *see* VOCATIONAL PREFERENCE INVENTORY.

Vroom, Victor H. (1932-   ), industrial psychologist and a leading authority on organizational motivation and leadership. His major work on expectancy theory is *Work and Motivation* (N.Y.: John Wiley, 1964).
    See also VALENCE.

VT-SEA: *see* LABOR ORGANIZATION, Vermont State Employees Association.

W

WA: *see* LABOR ORGANIZATION, Watchmen's Association, Independent.

wage, guaranteed annual: *see* GUARANTEED ANNUAL WAGE.

wage, living: *see* LIVING WAGE.

wage-and-price controls, a government's formal efforts to control inflation by regulating the wages and prices of its economic system. For accounts of the wage-and-price controls of the 1971 to 1974 period, *see* George P. Shultz and Kenneth W. Dam, "Reflections on Wage and Price Controls," *Industrial and Labor Relations Review* (January 1977); Robert A. Kagan, *Regulatory Justice: Implementing a Wage-Price Freeze* (N.Y.: Basic Books, 1978).

See also FRY V. UNITED STATES.

Wage and Price Stability, Council on: *see* COUNCIL ON WAGE AND PRICE STABILITY.

wage and salary administration, according to Herbert G. Zollitsch and Adolph Langsner, in *Wage and Salary Administration* (Cincinnati, Ohio: South-Western Publishing Co., 2nd ed., 1970), wage and salary administration "may be thought of as the planning, organizing, and controlling of those activities that relate to the direct and indirect payments made to employees for the work they perform or the services they render."

wage and salary survey: *see* WAGE SURVEY.

Wage and Tax Statement: *see* FORM W-2.

wage arbitration, referral of a wage dispute to an arbitrator.

ASPECTS OF A FORMAL WAGE AND SALARY PROGRAM

Technique	Objective
Job information	To determine job facts as a necessary step in job evaluation (as well as in employment, management development, organizational studies, and general supervision). Job facts may be recorded in job questionnaires or job descriptions.
Job evaluation	To determine relative job worth.
Job pricing	To translate relative job worth into money.
Individual pay increases	To reward employees for higher productivity and better job performance and/or to reflect increases in pay levels in the labor market.
Communications	To give supervisors the information they need to carry out the program and gain its acceptance.
Administrative procedures and practices	To resolve individual problems, keep the program current and operating efficiently, and provide general guidance to managers.
Union participation	To meet the requirements of collective bargaining.
Controls	To insure reasonably consistent and equitable application of the wage and salary program and to maintain control over costs.

SOURCE: Reprinted, by permission of the publisher, from Robert E. Sibson, Compensation, p. 165, © 1974 by AMACOM, a division of American Management Associations. All rights reserved.

wage area, national and/or regional areas selected on the basis of population size, employment, location, or other criteria for wage surveys. *See* James N. Houff, "Improving Area Wage Survey Indexes," *Monthly Labor Review* (January 1973).

wage assignment, voluntary transfer of earned wages to a third party to pay debts, buy savings bonds, pay union dues, etc.

wage compression: *see* SALARY COMPRESSION.

wage criteria, those external and internal standards or factors that determine the internal pay structure of an organization. According to David W. Belcher, in *Compensation Administration* (Englewood Cliffs, N.J.: Prentice-Hall, 1974),

wage criteria may be used by organizations and unions to rationalize positions taken as well as to arrive at these positions. Also, strictly applying the various criteria would in many situations result in conflicting decisions. For example, if the cost of living is up 10 percent and ability to pay is down 10 percent, comparable wages in the area justify a 5 percent increase, and comparable wages in the industry call for a 5 percent decrease, what change in wage level is justified?

wage differentials, differences in wages paid for identical or similar work that are justified because of differences in work schedules, hazards, cost of living, or other factors. *See* Orel R. Winjum, "Negotiated Wage Rate Differentials," *Personnel Journal* (August 1971).

wage drift, concept that explains the gap between basic wage rates and actual earnings, which tend to be higher because of overtime, bonuses, and other monetary incentives.

Wage Earner Plan, title of Chapter 13 of the Bankruptcy Act, which allows anyone who is employed to get an extension of time to pay off debts in lieu of bankruptcy if the employee submits all earnings to court jurisdiction until all creditors have been paid. For details, *see* Irving L. Berg, "The Wage Earner Plan as an Alternative to Bankruptcy," *Personnel Journal* (March 1971).

wage floor, minimum wage established by contract or law.

wage increase, deferred: *see* DEFERRED WAGE INCREASE.

wage inequity: *see* COGNITIVE DISSONANCE.

wage garnishment: *see* GARNISHMENT.

wage parity: *see* PARITY.

wage–price freeze: *see* WAGE-AND-PRICE CONTROLS.

wage progression, progressively higher wage rates that can be earned in the same job. Progression takes place on the basis of length of service, merit, or other criteria.

wage range: *see* PAY RANGE.

wage reopener clause: *see* REOPENER CLAUSE.

wages, also SALARY, as defined by J. D. Dunn and Frank M. Rachel, in *Wage and Salary Administration: Total Compensation Systems* (N.Y.: McGraw-Hill, 1971):

The remuneration (pay) received by an employee (or group of employees) for services rendered during a specific period of time—hour, day, week, or month. Traditionally, the term "wages" has been used to denote the pay of a factory employee or any employee on an hourly rate, and "salary" has been used to denote the pay of an administrative, professional, clerical, or managerial employee on a weekly, monthly, or annual time basis.

See also the following entries:

BARGAINING THEORY OF WAGES
BOOTLEG WAGES
COMPETITIVE WAGES
GRADUATED WAGES
INDIRECT WAGES
IRON LAW OF WAGES
REAL WAGES
LIVING WAGE
PAY
SALARY

Wages and Hours Act: *see* FAIR LABOR STANDARDS ACT.

wage survey, also called WAGE AND SALARY SURVEY, and AREA WAGE SURVEY, formal effort to gather data on compensation rates and/or ranges for comparable jobs within an area, industry, or occupation. Wage surveys on both a national and regional basis are available from such organizations as the American Management Association, the International Personnel Management Association, and the International City Management Association. *See* Bruce R. Ellig, "Salary Surveys: Design to Application," *The Personnel Administrator* (October 1977); James N. Houff, "Improving Area Wage Survey Indexes," *Monthly Labor Review* (January 1973).

See also COMMUNITY WAGE SURVEY.

wage tax, any tax on wages and salaries

levied by a government. Many cities have wage taxes that force suburban commuters to help pay for the services provided to the region by the central city.

Wagner Act: *see* NATIONAL LABOR RELATIONS ACT OF 1935.

Wagner Acts, Baby: *see* BABY WAGNER ACTS.

Wagner–Connery Act: *see* NATIONAL LABOR RELATIONS ACT OF 1935.

Wagner–O'Day Act, federal statute, provides that sheltered workshops serving blind and severely handicapped persons shall receive special preference in bidding on federal government contracts for products and services.

Wagner–Peyser Act of 1933, federal statute that established the U.S. Employment Service in the Department of Labor to assist in the development of a cooperative nationwide system of public employment offices.

WAIS: *see* WECHSLER ADULT INTELLIGENCE SCALE.

walk-around pay, pay for workers who "walk around" with federal inspectors. Occupational Safety and Health Administration inspectors must sometimes be accompanied on their plant inspections.

walkout: *see* STRIKE.

Walsh–Healey Public Contracts Act of 1936, federal statute establishing basic labor standards for work done on U.S. government contracts exceeding $10,000 in value.

Warehouse Industrial International Union: *see* LABOR ORGANIZATION.

warm-up effect, adjustment process that takes place at the start of work. The warm-up period is over when the work curve reaches its first peak.

Washington Public Employees Association: *see* LABOR ORGANIZATION.

Washington State Labor Council, AFL–CIO: *see* AMERICAN FEDERATION OF LABOR–CONGRESS OF INDUSTRIAL ORGANIZATIONS.

Washington v. *Davis*, 426 U.S. 229 (1976), U.S Supreme Court case, which held that although the Due Process Clause of the 5th Amendment prohibits the government from invidious discrimination, it does not follow that a law or other official act is unconstitutional *solely* because it has a racially dispro-

portionate impact. The court ruled that, under the Constitution (as opposed to Title VII of the Civil Rights Act of 1964), there must be discriminatory purpose or intent—adverse impact alone is insufficient. *See* Carl F. Goodman, "Public Employment and the Supreme Court's 1975–76 Term," *Public Personnel Management* (September–October 1976).

WASH-PEA: *see* LABOR ORGANIZATION, Washington Public Employees Association.

wash up: *see* CLEAN-UP TIME.

Watchmen's Association, Independent: *see* LABOR ORGANIZATION.

Watch Workers Union, American: *see* LABOR ORGANIZATION.

Watson–Glaser Critical Thinking Appraisal (WGCT), instrument that provides a measure or analysis of critical thinking abilities. Scores indicate strengths and weaknesses in areas such as inference, assumption, deduction, interpretation, and arguments. Used in a variety of educational assessment situations, selection processes, and research situations. TIME: 50/60 minutes. AUTHORS: Goodwin Watson and Edward M. Glaser. PUBLISHER: Harcourt, Brace, Jovanovich, Inc. (*see* TEST PUBLISHERS).

Watts, Glenn E. (1920-   ), elected president of the Communications Workers of America in 1974.

WBIS: *see* WECHSLER–BELLVUE INTELLIGENCE SCALE.

Weber, Joseph N. (1866-1950), president of the American Federation of Musicians from 1900 to 1940. His union grew from 6,000 to 170,000 members under his leadership.

Weber, Max (1864-1920), German sociologist who produced an analysis of bureaucracy that is still the most influential statement—the point of departure for all further analyses—on the subject. For a biography, *see* Reinhard Bendix, *Max Weber: An Intellectual Portrait* (Garden City, N.Y.: Doubleday, 1960)

Weber decision: *see* UNITED STEELWORKERS OF AMERICA V. WEBER, ET AL.

Wechsler Adult Intelligence Scale (WAIS), widely used test for general intelligence designed for persons ranging in age from 16 to over 75. Consists of six verbal and five performance tests. Revision of Wechsler–Bellvue Intelligence Scale. TIME: 40/60 minutes.

Notice To Employees Working on Government Contracts

This establishment is performing Government contract work subject to the—

Service Contract Act
or
Public Contracts Act

During the period of performance on the contract the following requirements must be observed:

Minimum Wages

Your rate must be at least $2.65 an hour effective January 1, 1978; $2.90 an hour effective January 1, 1979; $3.10 an hour effective January 1, 1980; and $3.35 an hour effective January 1, 1981. A higher rate may be required for both *Service* and *Supply* contracts if a wage determination applies. (A higher rate may also be required for *Service* contracts if a predecessor contractor has paid a higher rate for your classification pursuant to a collective bargaining agreement.) Such higher rates for *Service* contracts will be posted as an attachment to this Notice.

Fringe Benefits

Service contract wage determinations may require fringe benefit payments (or a cash equivalent). *Supply* contracts do not require fringe benefits.

Overtime Pay

You must be paid 1½ times your basic rate of pay for all hours worked over 8 in a day or 40 in a week, whichever is greater. There are some exceptions.

Safety and Health

The work must be performed under conditions that are sanitary, and not hazardous or dangerous to the employees' health and safety.

No person under 16 years of age may be employed on a *Supply* Contract.

Information

Further information on the wage provisions of the Service Contract Act or the Walsh-Healey Public Contracts Act may be obtained from the Wage and Hour Division. Information relating to the safety and health provisions may be obtained from the Occupational Safety and Health Administration. Offices are located in principal cities. Check your telephone directory under U.S. Government, Department of Labor, Wage and Hour Division or the Occupational Safety and Health Administration.

U.S. Department of Labor
Employment Standards Administration
Wage and Hour Division
Washington, D.C. 20210

AUTHOR: David Wechsler. PUBLISHER: Psychological Corporation (*see* TEST PUBLISHERS).

Wechsler–Bellvue Intelligence Scale (WBIS), published in 1939, one of the first general intelligence tests designed for adults. Measures general comprehension, arithmetic abilities, vocabulary and other general informational items. Replaced by Wechsler Adult Intelligence Scale (WAIS). TIME: 40/60 minutes. AUTHOR: David Wechsler. PUBLISHER: Psychological Corporation (*see* TEST PUBLISHERS).

weighted application blank, weights or numeric values can be placed on the varying responses to application blank items. After a job analysis determines the knowledges, skills, and abilities necessary to perform the duties of a position, corresponding personal characteristics can be elicited. Applicants who score highest on the weighted application blank would be given first consideration. *See* H. M. Trice, "The Weighted Application Blank—A Caution," *The Personnel Administrator* (May–June 1964).

***Weingarten* decision:** *see* NATIONAL LABOR RELATIONS BOARD V. J. WEINGARTEN, INC.

welfare funds, employer contributions, agreed to during collective bargaining, to a common fund to provide welfare benefits to the employees of all of the contributing employers.

well pay, also called SWEET PAY, incentive payments to workers who are neither "sick" nor late over a specified time period. In some companies, well pay is called "sweet pay" for "Stay at Work, Earn Extra Pay."

Wesman Personnel Classification Test (WPCT), general intelligence test used primarily in selection and placement of personnel in business and industry. Composed of verbal and numerical subtests that are summed for a total score. TIME: 25/35 minutes. AUTHOR: Alexander G. Wesman. PUBLISHER: Psychological Corporation (*see* TEST PUBLISHERS).

West Coast Hotel* v. *Parrish, 300 U.S. 379 (1937), U.S. Supreme Court case, which upheld the minimum wage law of the State of Washington, by declaring that a minimum wage law did not violate the freedom of contract provided by the Due Process Clause of the 14th Amendment. This case overruled the court's earlier decision, *Adkins* v. *Children's Hospital*, 261 U.S. 525 (1923), which held unconstitutional a federal law establishing minimum wages for women and children in the District of Columbia.

Western Personnel Test, short measure of mental abilities designed for use in business and industry. Measures such things as number series, word meanings, arithmetic reasoning, and sentence arrangement. TIME: 5-10 minutes. AUTHORS: R. L. Gunn and M. P. Manson. PUBLISHER: Psychological Corporation (*see* TEST PUBLISHERS).

Western States Service Station Employees Union: *see* LABOR ORGANIZATION.

West Virginia Labor Federation, AFL–CIO: *see* AMERICAN FEDERATION OF LABOR–CONGRESS OF INDUSTRIAL ORGANIZATIONS.

W. E. Upjohn Institute for Employment Research: *see* UPJOHN INSTITUTE FOR EMPLOYMENT RESEARCH.

WGA: *see* LABOR ORGANIZATION, Writers Guild of America.

WGCT: *see* WATSON–GLASER CRITICAL THINKING APPRAISAL.

Wharton, Arthur O. (1873-1944), president of the International Association of Machinists from 1926 to 1939. For biographical information, *see* Mark Perlman, *The Machinists: A New Study in American Trade Unionism* (Cambridge, Mass.: Harvard University Press, 1961).

"When in charge, ponder. When in trouble, delegate. When in doubt, mumble.": *see* INTERNATIONAL ASSOCIATION OF PROFESSIONAL BUREAUCRATS.

whipsawing: *see* WHIPSAW STRIKE.

whipsaw strike, strike stratagem that uses one struck employer as an example to others in order to encourage them to accede to union demands without the necessity of additional strikes.

whistle blower, individual who believes the public interest overrides the interests of their organization and publicly "blows the whistle" if their organization is involved in corrupt, illegal, fraudulent or harmful activity. For accounts of famous whistle blowers, *see* Ralph Nader, Peter J. Petkas, and Kate Blackwell (eds.), *Whistle Blowing: The Report of the Conference on Professional Responsibility* (N.Y.: Grossman Publishers, 1972); Charles Peters and Taylor Branch (eds.), *Blowing The Whistle: Dissent in the Public Interest* (N.Y.: Praeger Publishers, 1972); Kenneth D. Walters, "Your Employees' Right to Blow the Whistle," *Harvard Business Review* (July–August 1975).

White Collar Report, weekly report concerning clerical, technical, scientific, professional, and other white collar employees published by the Bureau of National Affairs, Inc. Covers organizing activities, salaries and fringe benefits, collective bargaining, equal employment opportunity activities, court and board decisions.

white-collar unions, general term for a union whose members are more likely to wear street clothes and sit at a desk than wear work clothes and stand at a lathe. *See* Adolf Sturmthal, *White-Collar Trade Unions: Contemporary Developments in Industrialized Societies* (Urbana, Ill.: University of Illinois Press, 1966); George Sayers Bain, *The Growth of White-Collar Unionism* (N.Y.: Oxford University Press, 1970); Everett M. Kassalow, "White-Collar Unions and the Work Humanization Movement," *Monthly Labor Review* (May 1977). For a house history of the Office and Professional Employees International Union (OPEIU), *see* Joseph E. Finley, *White Collar Union: The Story of the OPEIU and Its People* (N.Y.: Octagon Books, 1975).

white-collar workers, employee whose job requires slight physical effort and allows him/her to wear ordinary clothes. *See* C. Wright Mills, *White Collar: The American Middle Class* (N.Y.: Oxford University Press, 1951); J. M. Pennings, "Work Value Systems of White-Collar Workers," *Administrative Science Quarterly* (December 1970); Carl Dean Snyder, *White Collar Workers and the UAW* (Urbana, Ill.: University of Illinois Press, 1973).
See also BLUE-COLLAR WORKERS for employment statistics.

Whitney, Alexander Fell (1873-1949), president of the Brotherhood of Railroad Trainmen from 1928 until his death. For biographical information, *see* Joel I. Seidman, *The Brotherhood of Railroad Trainmen: The Internal Political Life of a National Union* (N.Y.: John Wiley, 1962).

Whitten Amendment, amendment to the federal government's Classification Act, which states that federal employees may only be permanently appointed to one grade within a 52-week period and may be promoted no more than one grade at a time.

whole-job ranking, job evaluation method that simply ranks jobs as a whole. For example, a small organization might rank one person president, another as bookkeeper, two others as stock clerks, etc.

whole-man concept, philosophic attitude that management should be concerned with an employee's physical and mental health both on and off the job.

Whyte, William Foote (1914-   ), sociologist and one of the foremost authorities on human relations in industry. His work has often emphasized the impact of technology upon managerial behavior. Major works include: *Street Corner Society* (Chicago: University of Chicago Press, 1943); *Human Relations in the Restaurant Industry* (N.Y.: McGraw-Hill, 1948); *Pattern for Industrial Peace* (N.Y.: Harper & Row, 1951); *Money and Motivation* (N.Y.: Harper & Row, 1955); *Men at Work* (Homewood, Ill.: Richard D. Irwin, 1961).

wildcat strike, also called UNAUTHORIZED STRIKE and OUTLAW STRIKE, work stoppage not sanctioned by union leadership and usually contrary to an existing labor contract. Unless it can be shown unfair employer practices were the direct cause of the wildcat strike, the union could be libel for damages in a breach of contract suit by management. Garth L. Mangum, in "Taming Wildcat Strikes," *Harvard Business Review* (April–May 1960), holds that "wildcat strikes are management's responsibility—they continue as long as the participants find them profitable; cease when management, through disciplinary action, makes them unrewarding." For an analysis of how wildcat strikes are treated by the courts, *see* Evan J. Spelfogel, "Wildcat Strikes and Minority Concerted Activity—Discipline, Damage Suits and Injunctions," *Labor Law Journal* (September 1973). *See also* Jeanne M. Brett and Stephen B. Goldberg, "Wildcat Strikes in Bituminous Coal Mining," *Industrial and Labor Relations Review* (July 1979).
See also NONSUABILITY CLAUSE.

Wiley & Sons v. Livingston: see JOHN WILEY & SONS V. LIVINGSTON.

Williams, Whiting (1878-   ), was the personnel director of a steel company when he quit in order to become a blue-collar "industrial laborer" in order to study working conditions. His subsequent books were the first

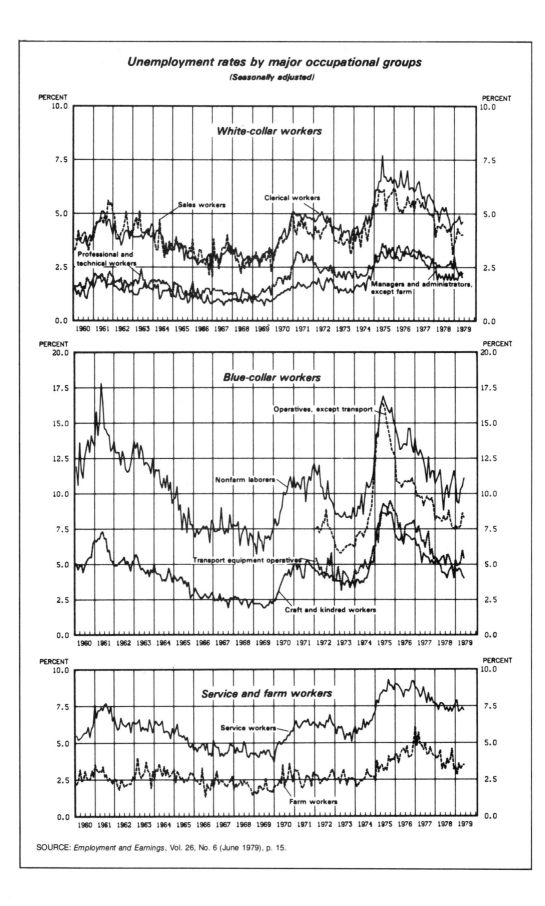

Unemployment rates by major occupational groups
(Seasonally adjusted)

White-collar workers

Sales workers

Clerical workers

Professional and technical workers

Managers and administrators, except farm

Blue-collar workers

Operatives, except transport

Nonfarm laborers

Transport equipment operatives

Craft and kindred workers

Service and farm workers

Service workers

Farm workers

SOURCE: *Employment and Earnings*, Vol. 26, No. 6 (June 1979), p. 15.

major studies demonstrating that worker performance was significantly influenced by emotion and attitude. His impressionistic conclusions were later empirically validated by the Hawthorne experiments. Major works include: *What's on the Worker's Mind* (N.Y.: Charles Scribner's Sons, 1920); *Mainsprings of Men* (N.Y.: Charles Scribner's Sons, 1925).

William E. Arnold Co.* v. *Carpenters District Council of Jacksonville, 417 U.S. 12 (1974), U.S. Supreme Court case, which held that when an activity in question is arguably both an unfair labor practice prohibited by the National Labor Relations Act and a breach of a collective bargaining agreement, the National Labor Relations Board's authority "is not exclusive and does not destroy the jurisdiction" of appropriate courts.

William, Lynde, and Williams: *see* TEST PUBLISHERS.

Williams–Steiger Act: *see* OCCUPATIONAL SAFETY AND HEALTH ACT OF 1970.

Wilson, William Bauchop (1862-1934), appointed by President Woodrow Wilson, in 1913 to be the first secretary of the U.S. Department of Labor.

Wilson* v. *New: *see* ADAMSON ACT OF 1916.

WIN: *see* WORK INCENTIVE PROGRAM.

wink, unit of time equal to 1/2000 of a minute, which is used in motion-and-time study.

Winpisinger, William W. (1924-   ), president of the International Association of Machinists and Aerospace workers.

Wirtz, W. Willard (1912-   ), Secretary of Labor from 1962 to 1969.

Wisconsin State AFL–CIO: *see* AMERICAN FEDERATION OF LABOR–CONGRESS OF INDUSTRIAL ORGANIZATIONS.

withholding tax, those federal, state, or local taxes that were withheld by employers from the paychecks of their employees and paid directly to the taxing jurisdiction.

WLW Culture Fair Inventory (CFI), 30-item, nonverbal test that measures reasoning and spatial ability. The test was developed for use in industrial job placement. TIME: 30/45 minutes. AUTHORS: B. O. Murray, L. C. Steckle, R. W. Henderson. PUBLISHER: William, Lynde, and Williams (*see* TEST PUBLISHERS).

WLW Personal Attitude Inventory, 64-item,

self-report inventory that measures such factors as emotional stability, friendliness, aggressiveness, humility and insight, reliability and leadership ability. TIME: 20 minutes. AUTHOR: Robert W. Henderson. PUBLISHER: William, Lynde, and Williams (*see* TEST PUBLISHERS).

Wobblies, slang term for members of the Industrial Workers of the World, a radical union that was founded in 1905 and saw its greatest strength before World War I.
See also INDUSTRIAL WORKERS OF THE WORLD.

Wolkomir, Nathan T. (1909-   ), elected president of the National Federation of Federal Employees in 1964.

Women's Bureau, agency of the U.S. Department of Labor that is responsible for formulating standards and policies to promote the welfare of wage earning women, improve their working conditions, increase their efficiency, advance their opportunities for professional employment, and investigate and report on all matters pertinent of the welfare of women in industry. The Women's Bureau has regional offices established in 10 areas throughout the United States.

Wonderlic, E. F., and Associates: *see* TEST PUBLISHERS.

Wonderlic Personnel Test (WPT), 50-item timed measure of adult intelligence (an abridged adaptation of the Otis Self-Administering Test of Mental Ability) used in the screening of individuals for lower-level positions in business and industry (*i.e.,* bookkeeper, cashier, clerk, police, warehouseman, technician, utility lineman). Because performance on this test is closely related to the amount and quality of education an individual has completed, it tends to discriminate against educationally disadvantaged minority group members. This was so noted by the Supreme Court in *Griggs* v. *Duke Power Company.* As a result of this ruling, the Wonderlic Personnel Test now offers separate norms for blacks in areas of education, age, sex, and geographical regions. TIME: 12 minutes. AUTHOR: E. F. Wonderlic. PUBLISHER: E. F. Wonderlic and Associates (*see* TEST PUBLISHERS).

Woodcock, Leonard Freel (1911-   ), president of the United Automobile, Aerospace and Agricultural Implement Workers of America from 1970 until 1977, when he was appointed by President Jimmy Carter to be head of the U.S. Liaison Office in Peking, People's Republic of China.

Woodworkers of America, International: *see* LABOR ORGANIZATION.

work, according to Mark Twain, in *The Adventures of Tom Sawyer*, "Work consists of whatever a body is obliged to do, and play consists of whatever a body is not obliged to do." For an exhaustive survey of the nature of work, *see* Report of a Special Task Force to the Secretary of HEW, *Work in America* (Cambridge, Mass.: The MIT Press, 1973).

See also the following entries:

    BESPOKE WORK
    DEAD WORK
    FAT WORK
    OUT-OF-TITLE WORK

work-activities centers, centers planned and designed exclusively to provide therapeutic activities for handicapped clients whose physical or mental impairment is so severe as to make their productive capacity inconsequential. The Secretary of Labor is authorized by the Fair Labor Standards Act to allow the employment of handicapped persons in work activities centers at less than the minimum wage.

workaholic, word first used by Wayne Oates, in his *Confessions of a Workaholic: The Facts About Work Addiction* (N.Y.: World Publishing, 1971), to describe the addiction, the compulsion or the uncontrollable need to work incessantly. A workaholic is a person whose involvement in his/her work is so excessive that his/her health, personal happiness, interpersonal relations and social functioning are adversely affected. *See* Wayne E. Oates, *Workaholics, Make Laziness Work for You* (Garden City. N.Y.: Doubleday 1978).

work curve, also called OUTPUT CURVE, graphic presentation of an organization's or individual's productivity over a specified period of time.

workday, basic: *see* BASIC WORKDAY.

work design: *see* JOB DESIGN.

work disability: *see* DISABILITY.

workers *see* EMPLOYEE. *See also* following entries:

    BLUE-COLLAR WORKERS
    DISADVANTAGED WORKERS
    DISCOURAGED WORKERS
    DISPLACED EMPLOYEE
    EXEMPT EMPLOYEE
    FULL-TIME WORKERS

    GUEST WORKER
    HOURLY-RATE WORKERS
    ILLEGAL ALIENS
    ITINERANT WORKER
    PINK-COLLAR JOBS
    PRODUCTION WORKERS
    SEMISKILLED WORKERS
    UNSKILLED WORKERS
    WHITE-COLLAR WORKERS

workers' compensation: *see* WORKMEN'S COMPENSATION.

workers' councils, also called WORKS COUNCILS, any of a variety of joint labor–management bodies serving as vehicles for the resolution of problems of mutual interest. Workers' councils are usually associated with concepts of industrial democracy and are found mostly in Europe. *See* Erland Waldenstrom, "Works Councils: The Need to be Involved," *Columbia Journal of World Business* (May–June 1968).

work ethic: *see* PROTESTANT ETHIC.

workfare, any public welfare program that requires welfare payment recipients to work (work + welfare = workfare) or enroll in a formal job-training program.

workforce planning, determination by organization management of the numbers, kinds, and costs of the workers needed to carry out each stage of the organization's program plan.

work group, also called WORKING GROUP and TASK GROUP, task unit within a larger organizational social system charged with the responsibility for making a specific contribution to the goals of the larger organization. *See* Maxine Bucklow, "A New Role for the Work Group," *Administrative Science Quarterly* (June 1966); J. Stephen Heinen and Eugene Jacobson, "A Model of Task Group Development in Complex Organizations and a Strategy of Implementation," *Academy of Management Review* (October 1976); David G. Bowers and Doris L. Hausser, "Work Group Types and Intervention Effects in Organizational Development," *Administrative Science Quarterly* (March 1977).

work group, horizontal: *see* HORIZONTAL WORK GROUP.

work-in, form of protest demonstration in which a group of employees report to work as usual but refuse to follow their normal routines.

Work Incentive Program (WIN), federal programs authorized by the Social Security Amendments of 1967 and 1971. It is jointly

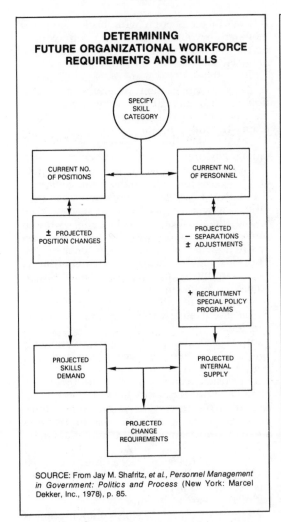

DETERMINING
FUTURE ORGANIZATIONAL WORKFORCE
REQUIREMENTS AND SKILLS

SOURCE: From Jay M. Shafritz, *et al.*, *Personnel Management in Government: Politics and Process* (New York: Marcel Dekker, Inc., 1978), p. 85.

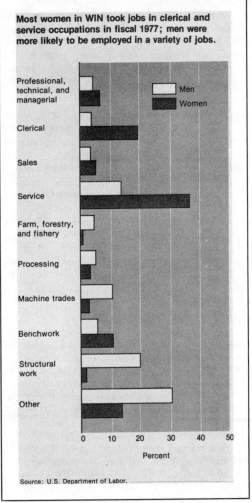

Most women in WIN took jobs in clerical and service occupations in fiscal 1977; men were more likely to be employed in a variety of jobs.

Source: U.S. Department of Labor.

administered by the Departments of Labor and Health, Education, and Welfare, and is designed to help persons receiving Aid to Families with Dependent Children (AFDC) become self-supporting. The 1971 amendment shifted the program emphasis from training to immediate employment.

All AFDC applicants and recipients are required (unless exempt by law) to register with the WIN sponsor (usually the state employment agency) for employment and manpower services as a condition of eligibility. WIN utilizes existing employment-related training programs and WIN-funded activities—both directed toward ultimate placements in unsubsidized jobs. In preparation for this, WIN offers such manpower services as on-the-job training for the job-ready, or public service employment arranged by prior agreement with public or private non-

profit organizations for individuals for whom unsubsidized jobs are not available. Manpower services are supplemented by necessary supportive social services, including day care for children, which are provided by or through a separate administrative unit of the welfare agency.

The Revenue Act of 1971 provides employers with an incentive in the form of a tax credit for hiring WIN registrants. As an alternative, a welfare tax credit is also available to employers of WIN registrants under related legislation.

working certificate: *see* WORKING PAPERS.

working class, all who work. When the term is used politically, it tends to exclude managers, professionals, and anyone who is not at the lower end of the educational and economic scales. For an analytical description, *see* Andrew Levison, *The Working-Class Majority* (N.Y.: Coward, McCann & Geoghegan, Inc., 1974). For a social history of the American working class, see: Herbert G. Gutman, *Work, Culture, and Society in Industrializing America* (N.Y.: Alfred A. Knopf, 1976).

working conditions, those factors, both physical and psychological, which comprise an employee's work environment. Included are such things as arrangement of office and factory equipment, salary or wages, fringe benefits, supervision, work routine, fair employment practices, health and safety precautions, length of work day, and relationship with co-workers. *See* Neal Q. Herrick and Robert P. Quinn, "The Working Conditions Survey as a Source of Social Indicators," *Monthly Labor Review* (April 1971); Robert P. Quinn, *et al.*, "Evaluating Working Conditions in America," *Monthly Labor Review* (November 1973).

working group: *see* WORK GROUP.

working hours, flexible: *see* FLEXI-TIME.

working papers, also called WORKING CERTIFICATE and WORK PERMIT, federal certificate of age showing that a minor is above the oppressive child-labor age applicable to the occupation in which he/she would be employed. Such proof of age is required under the provisions of the Fair Labor Standards Act and the Walsh–Healey Public Contracts Act. Working papers are issued by a designee of the administrator of the Wage and Hour Division of the U.S. Department of Labor.

working permit: *see* WORKING PAPERS.

work measurement, any method used to establish an equitable relationship between the volume of work performed and the human resources devoted to its accomplishment. Concerned with both volume and time a work measurement program is basically a means of setting standards to determine just what constitutes a fair day's work. For a presentation of methods, *see* Robert I. Stevens and Walter J. Bieber, "Work Measurement Techniques" *Journal of Systems Management* (February 1977).

See also MOTION STUDY and TIME STUDY.

workmen's compensation, also called WORKERS' COMPENSATION and INDUSTRIAL ACCIDENT INSURANCE, designed to provide cash benefits and medical care when a worker is injured in connection with his/her job and monetary payments to his/her survivors if he/she is killed on the job, was the first form of social insurance to develop widely in the United States. There are now 54 different workers' compensation programs in operation. Each of the 50 states and Puerto Rico has its own workmen's compensation program. In addition, there are three federal workers' compensation programs, covering federal government and private employees in the District of Columbia, and longshoremen and harbor workers throughout the country.

Before the passage of workmen's compensation laws, an injured employee ordinarily had to file suit against his/her employer and prove that the injury was due to the employer's negligence in order to recover damages. The enactment of workmen's compensation laws introduced the principle that a worker incurring an occupational injury would be compensated regardless of fault or blame in the accident and with a minimum of delay and legal formality. In turn, the employer's liability was limited, because workmen's compensation benefits became the exclusive remedy for work-related injuries.

The usual condition for entitlement to benefits is that the injury or death "arises out of and in the course of employment." Most programs exclude injuries due to the employee's intoxication, willful misconduct, or gross negligence. Although virtually limited to injuries or diseases traceable to industrial "accidents" initially, the scope of the laws has broadened over the years to cover occupational diseases as well.

In most states, workmen's compensation is paid for entirely by employers who either purchase insurance coverage or self insure—that is, assume total financial liability for the work accidents of their employees.

The Occupational Health and Safety Act of 1970 created the National Commission on State Workmen's Compensation Laws to evaluate the various state workmen's compensation programs. The commission reported that "the evidence compels us to conclude that state workmen's compensation laws are in general neither adequate nor equitable," *Report of the National Commission on State Workman's Compensation Laws* (Washington, D.C.: U.S. Government Printing Office, 1972). For critiques of present programs, *see* Daniel M. Kasper, "For A Better Worker's Compensation System," *Harvard Business Review* (March–April 1977); Robert J. Paul, "Workers' Compensation—An Adequate Employee Benefit?"

Workers' Compensation Under State Laws, January 1, 1978

Compulsory Law ★ (Others Elective)	Exemptions: Firms Employing Less Than	Exemptions: Other Groups	Maximum Medical Care	Waiting Period: No Benefit Payment for First (In Number of Days)	Waiting Period: Unless Time Off Exceeds (In Number of Days)	Jurisdiction	Temporary Total Disability: Intended Benefit as a % of Weekly Wage	Temporary Total Disability: Actual Maximum Weekly Benefit Allowed	Temporary Total Disability: Benefit Limitations: Duration (In Weeks)	Temporary Total Disability: Benefit Limitations: Amount	Permanent Total Disability: Weekly Benefit Allowed	Permanent Total Disability: Benefit Limitations: Duration (In Weeks)	Permanent Total Disability: Benefit Limitations: Amount	Death Benefits: Funeral Allowance All Cases	Death Benefits: Payment in Cases of No Dependency	Death Benefits: Survivors Benefits: Maximum Weekly Benefit	Death Benefits: Survivors Benefits: Benefit Limitations: Time	Death Benefits: Survivors Benefits: Benefit Limitations: Amount
★	3	Farm, Domestic, Casual	Full	3	21	Alabama †	66⅔%	$ 120	300		$ 120	Duration of disability		$1,000	$ 100 SIF*	$ 120	500 weeks	
★	0	Harvest or Transient help	2 years	3	28	Alaska †	66⅔	552	No limitations		552	Duration of disability		1,000	10,000 SIF	552	W, C-19	No limit
★	0	Domestic	Full	7	14	Arizona	66⅔	154	No limitations		154	Duration of disability		1,000	1,150 SIF	81-154	W, C-18	No limit
★	3	Farm, Domestic	Full	7	14	Arkansas	66⅔	87	450	$37,800	87	Duration of disability		750	500 SIF	87	W, C-25	No limit
★	0	Domestic, Casual, Nonprofit, Athletes	Full	3	21	California	66⅔	154	240		154	Duration of disability		1,000	No payment	154		$50,000 $55,000
★	0	Domestic, Casual	$20,000	3	14	Colorado †	66⅔	161	No limitations		161	Duration of disability		1,000	15,000 SIF	161	W, C-21	No limit
★	0	Outworkers, Casual	Full	3	7	Connecticut †	66⅔	147-221	No limitations		147-221	Duration of disability		1,500	No payment	147-221	W, C-18	No limit
★	0	Domestic	Full	3	7	Delaware †	66⅔	144	No limitations		144	Duration of disability		700	No payment	144-173	W, C-25	No limit
★	0	Farm, Domestic, Casual	Full	3	14	District of Columbia †	66⅔	367	No limitations		367	Duration of disability		1,000	5,000 SIF	367	W, C-23	No limit
★	0	Farm, Domestic	Full	7	14	Florida †	60	119	350		119	Duration of disability		1,000	No payment	84-112	W, C-22	50,000
★	3	Farm, Domestic, Casual	$5,000	7	28	Georgia	66⅔	95	No limitations		95	Duration of disability		750	No payment	95	400 weeks	32,500
★	0	Domestic	Full	2	5	Hawaii †	66⅔	179	No limitations		179	Duration of disability		1,500	8,775 SIF	134-179	W, C-22	312 x SAWW
★	0	Farm, Domestic, Casual	Full	5	14	Idaho †	60	99-148	52	Thereafter 60% of State wage	99-148	Reduced benefit for life		750	No payment	74-99	500 weeks	49,500
★	Firms with less than $1,000 annual payroll.		Full	3	14	Illinois †	66⅔	304	No limitations		304	Duration of disability		1,750	400 SIF	304	W, C-25	$250,000 or 20 yrs. whichever is greater
★	0	Farm, Domestic, Casual	Full	7	21	Indiana	66⅔	120	500	60,000	120	500	60,000	1,500	No payment	120	500 weeks	60,000
★	0		Full	3	14	Iowa †	80	247	No limitations		247	Duration of disability		1,000	100 SIF	247	W, C-25	No limit
★	Firms with less than $10,000 annual payroll.	Farm, Casual	Full	7	21	Kansas †	66⅔	121		50,000	121	Duration of disability		2,000	5,000 SIF	121	W, C-23	50,000
★	0	Farm, Domestic	Full	7	14	Kentucky †	66⅔	104	No limitations		104	Duration of disability		1,500	No payment	104	W, C-22	No limit
★	0	Covers only specified hazardous work	Full	7	42	Louisiana †	66⅔	130	No limitations		130	Duration of disability		1,500	No payment	130	W, C-23	No limit
★	0	Farm, Domestic, Casual	Full	3	14	Maine †	66⅔	221	No limitations		221	Duration of disability		1,000	100 x SAWW	221	W, C-23	No limit
★	0	Farm	Full	3	14	Maryland †	66⅔	188	No limitations		188	Duration of disability		1,200	550 SIF	188	W, C-23	No limit if W dependent
★	0	Domestic, Casual, Athletes	Full	5	6	Massachusetts	66⅔	150 +	$6 for each dependent	37,500	150 +	$6 for each dependent Duration of disability		1,000	1,000 SIF	55 + 6 for each child	W, C-18	No limit unless W self supporting
★	3	Farm, Domestic	Full	7	14	Michigan	66⅔	127-156	No limitations		127-156	Duration of disability		1,500	No payment	127-150	500 weeks	
★	0	Domestic, Casual, Athletes	Full	3	10	Minnesota	66⅔	197	No limitations		197	Duration of disability		1,000	5,000 SIF	197	W, C-21	No limit
★	5	Farm, Domestic, Public	Full	5	14	Mississippi	66⅔	91	450	40,950	91	450	40,950	1,000	500 SIF	91	450 weeks	40,950
★	6	Farm, Domestic	Full	3	28	Missouri	66⅔	95	400		95	Duration of disability		2,000	No payment	95	W, C-22	
★	0	Domestic, Casual	Full	7	7	Montana †	66⅔	174	No limitations		174	Duration of disability		1,100	1,000 SIF	174	W, C-25	No limit
★	0	Farm, Domestic, Casual	Full	7	42	Nebraska	66⅔	140	No limitations		140	Duration of disability		1,000	No payment	140	W, C-25	No limit
★	0	Farm, Domestic, Casual	Full	5	5	Nevada †	66⅔	198	No limitations		198	Duration of disability		1,200	No payment	198	W, C-22	No limit
★	0	Domestic, Casual	Full	3	7	New Hampshire †	66⅔	169	No limitations		169	Duration of disability		1,200	500 SIF	169	W-400 weeks C-18	
	0	Casual	Full	7	7	New Jersey †	66⅔	138	300		138	450	Board may extend	750	No payment	138	W, C-18	After 450 wks. any earnings deducted
★	4	Farm, Domestic, Casual	Full	7	28	New Mexico †	66⅔	153	600 x SAWW		153	600 x SAWW		1,500	1,000	153		600 x SAWW
★	0	Farm	Full	7	14	New York	66⅔	125	No limitations		125	Duration of disability		750	1,000 SIF	125	W, C-18	No limit
★	4	Farm, Domestic, Casual, some saw mills & loggers	Full	7	28	North Carolina †	66⅔	168	No limitations		158	Duration of disability		500	No payment	158	W, C-18	No limit
★	0	Farm, Domestic, Casual	Full	5	5	North Dakota †	66⅔	171 +	$5 for each child No limitations		171 +	$5 for each child Duration of disability		1,000	No payment	75 + 7 for each child	W, C-18	No limit
★	0		Full	7	21	Ohio †	66⅔	198	No limitations		198	Duration of disability		1,200	No payment	198	W, C-25	No limit
★	2	Clerical, Farm	Full	3	5	Oklahoma	66⅔	60	300		50	500		None	1,000	Lump sum payment		14,000 25,000
★	0	Domestic, Casual	Full	3	14	Oregon †	66⅔	214	No limitations		214-239	Duration of disability		1,000	No payment	107-214	W, C-23	No limit
★	0	Casual	Full	7	14	Pennsylvania †	66⅔	199	No limitations		199	Duration of disability		1,500	No payment	199	W, C-23	No limit
★	0	Domestic, Casual	Full	3	10	Puerto Rico	66⅔	45	312		29	Duration of disability		300	No payment	29	W, C-25	No limit
★	4	Farm, Domestic, Casual	Full	3	14	Rhode Island †	66⅔	176 +	$6 for each dependent No limitations	Not to exceed 80% of ee's amt	176 +	$6 for each dependent Duration of disability	Not to exceed 80% of ee's amt	1,800	750 SIF	176 + 6 for each child	W, C-23	
	4	Farm, Domestic, Casual, saw mills & loggers	10 weeks	7	14	South Carolina †	66⅔	160	500	40,000	160	500	40,000	400	No payment	160	W-500 weeks C-18	40,000
★	0	Farm (unless using machines), Domestic, Casual	Full	7	7	South Dakota †	66⅔	130	No limitations		130	Duration of disability		2,000	500 SIF	130 + 50/mo. each child	W, C-25	No limit
★	5	Farm, Domestic, Casual, Public	Full	7	14	Tennessee	66⅔	100	No limitations		100	400	Thereafter $15 weekly to $40,000	750	150 SIF	100	W, C-22	40.000
	0	Farm, Domestic, Casual	Full	7	28	Texas	66⅔	91	401		91	401		1,250	32,760 SIF	91	W, C-25	
★	0	Farm, Domestic, Casual	Full	3	14	Utah †	66⅔	183	312		156	312		1,000	15,600 SIF	156	312 weeks	
★	0	Casual	Full	3	7	Vermont †	66⅔	170 +	$5 for each child No limitations		170	330		500	500 SIF	170	W, C-18	No limit
★	3	Domestic, Casual	Full	7	21	Virginia †	66⅔	175	500 x SAWW		175	500 x SAWW		1,000	No payment	175		500 x SAWW
★	0	Domestic, Casual	Full	3	14	Washington †	60-75	163	No limitations		163	Duration of disability		1,000	10,000 SIF	163	W, C-23	No limit
★	0	Farm, Domestic	Full	3	14	West Virginia †	66⅔	208	208		208	Duration of disability		1,500	No payment	208	W, C-23	No limit
★	0	Domestic, Casual	Full	3	7	Wisconsin †	66⅔	189	No limitations		189	Duration of disability		750	80% of death benefits otherwise payable (to State Treasury)	189	400 weeks	
★	0	Clerical, Farm, Domestic, Casual	$880	3	8	Wyoming †	66⅔	190	No limitations		127		30,000	1,100	500 SIF	127	W, C-19	25,000

† Maximum Benefit Adjusted Annually SAWW means State Average Weekly Wage "W" means payment to widow until death or remarriage "C" means payment to children until age specified Lower benefit amount applies to single worker, higher amounts for dependents * SIF: indicates special fund or second injury fund

Academy of Management Review (October 1976).

See also MOUNTAIN TIMBER COMPANY V. WASHINGTON and HAWKINS V. BLEAKLY.

work motivation: *see* MOTIVATION.

work permit: *see* WORKING PAPERS.

work premium, also called PREMIUM PAY, extra compensation for work that is considered unpleasant, hazardous, or inconvenient. Overtime is the most obvious example of a work premium. *See* Janice Neipert Hedges, "Long Workweeks and Premium Pay," *Monthly Labor Review* (April 1976).

work preview, also called JOB SAMPLE and JOB PREVIEW, management technique for presenting prospective employees with realistic information about the particular job that they are considering. *See* Michael A. Raphael, "Work Previews Can Reduce Turnover and Improve Performance," *Personnel Journal* (February 1975); John P. Wanous, "A Job Preview Makes Recruiting More Effective," *Harvard Business Review* (September–October 1975).

work-ready, term used to describe a handicapped person who, if given employment, would be able to perform adequately on the job without being a burden to others.

Work Related Abstracts, monthly that seeks to abstract the significant and the informative from over 250 management, labor, government, professional, and university periodicals.

> *Work Related Abstracts*
> Information Coordinators, Inc.
> 1435-37 Randolph Street
> Detroit, MI 48226

work relief: *see* RELIEF.

work restructuring: *see* JOB RESTRUCTURING.

work rules, formal regulations prescribing both on-the-job behavior and working conditions. Work rules are usually incorporated into a collective bargaining agreement at the insistence of the union in order to restrict management's ability to unilaterally set production standards and/or reassign employees. The union's goal is to maximize and protect the jobs available to its members, protect their health and safety, and to maintain stable work assignments for union members. *See* Joseph B. Wollenberger, "Acceptable Work Rules and Penalties: A Company Guide," *Personnel* (July–August 1963).

work sampling, also called JOB SAMPLING, technique used to discover the proportions of total time devoted to the various components of a job. Data obtained from work sampling can be used to establish allowances applicable to a job, to determine machine utilization, and to provide the criteria for production standards. While this same information can be obtained by time-study procedures, work sampling—dependent as it is upon the laws of probability—will usually provide the information faster and at less cost. For a text on the technique, *see* Ralph M. Barnes, *Work Sampling*, 2nd edition (N.Y.: John Wiley & Sons, 1966).

Work sampling is also used to describe a performance test designed to be a miniature replica of behavior required on-the-job, which attempts to measure how well an employee will perform in the particular occupation. Such tests are considered a more precise device for measuring particular occupational abilities than simple motor skills or verbal ability tests. *See* James J. Asher and James A. Sciarrino, "Realistic Work Sample Tests: A Review," *Personnel Psychology* (Winter 1974); Michael K. Mount, Paul M. Muchinsky, and Lawrence M. Hanser, "The Predictive Validity of a Work Sample: A Laboratory Study," *Personnel Psychology* (Winter 1977); Donald J. Schwartz, "A Job Sampling Approach to Merit System Examining," *Personnel Psychology* (Summer 1977).

works councils: *see* WORKERS' COUNCILS.

worksharing, procedure for dividing the available work (or hours of work) among all eligible employees as an alternative to layoffs during slow periods. Three types of worksharing procedures may be identified—reduction in hours (by far the most common), division of work, and rotation of employment. *Reduction in hours*, as its name implies, requires that weekly hours of work be reduced below normal (non-overtime) schedules, usually within stated limits, to spread the work. The second procedure—*division of work*—is normally found in agreements covering employees on piecework or incentive systems, and emphasizes earnings rather than hours of work (although reduced hours may also occur). All available work is divided equally among eligible employees; under some conditions, faster workers may work somewhat fewer hours than slower ones for the same pay. The last procedure—*rotation of employment* (or layoff)—provides that short, specific periods of layoff be rotated equally among all employees, in contrast to the more common practice of laying off junior employees for longer or indefinite periods. Worksharing provisions are often part of a union contract. *See* Bureau of Labor Statistics, U.S. Department of Labor, *Major Collective Bargaining Agreements: Layoff, Recall and Worksharing Procedures* (Wash. D.C.: U.S. Government Printing Office, Bulletin 1425-13, 1972). Nancy J. McNeff, *et al.*, "Alternatives to Employee Layoffs: Work Sharing and Prelayoff Consultation," *Personnel* (January–February 1978).

See also JOB SHARING.

work station, specific location and immediate surrounding area in which a job is performed.

work stoppage, according to both the U.S. Departments of Commerce and Labor, a work stoppage is a concerted and complete withholding of services by employees that lasts for at least one workday or one work shift.

work to rule, work slowdown in which all of the formal work rules are so scrupulously obeyed that productivity suffers considerably. Those working to rule seek to place pressure on management without losing pay by going on strike. Work-to-rule protests are particularly popular in the public sector where most formal strikes are illegal.

work values, importance that employees place on the various aspects of work such as pay, prestige, security, responsibility, etc. *See* Stephen Wollock, et al., "Development of the Survey of Work Values," *Journal of Applied Psychology,* vol. 55, no. 4 (1971); Charles L. Hughes and Vincent S. Flowers, "Shaping Personnel Strategies to Disparate Value Systems," *Personnel* (March–April 1973).

Work Values Inventory (WVI), test used as an aid in understanding the value structure of the individual. Consists of 45 items with 15 scales that include altruism, creativity, independence, security, achievement, prestige, supervisory relations, way of life, etc. TIME: 10-20 minutes. AUTHOR: Donald E. Super. PUBLISHER: Houghton Mifflin Company (*see* TEST PUBLISHERS).

workweek, expected or actual period of employment for a "normal" week, usually expressed in number of hours. According to the Fair Labor Standards Act, a workweek is a period of 168 hours during 7 consecutive 24-hour periods. It may begin on any day of the week and any hour of the day established by the employer. For purposes of minimum wage and overtime payment, each workweek stands alone, and there can be no averaging of two or more workweeks (except for hospital or nursing home employees on an "8-and-80" schedule or seamen on U.S. vessels). Employee coverage, compliance with wage payment requirements, and the application of most exemptions are determined on a workweek basis.

See also the following entries:
BASIC WORKWEEK
4-DAY WORKWEEK
GUARANTEED WORKWEEK

WPCT: *see* WESMAN PERSONNEL CLASSIFICATION TEST.

WPPW: *see* LABOR ORGANIZATION, Pulp and Paper Workers, Association of Western.

WPT: *see* WONDERLIC PERSONNEL TEST.

wrap-up clause: *see* ZIPPER CLAUSE.

Writers Guild of America: *see* LABOR ORGANIZATION.

writ of certiorari: *see* CERTIORARI.

writ of mandamus: *see* MANDAMUS.

WSSS: *see* LABOR ORGANIZATION, Western States Service Station Employees Union.

W-2 Form: *see* FORM W-2.

Wurf, Jerry (1919-   ), president of the American Federation of State, County, and Municipal Employees (AFSCME) since 1964. For biographical accounts, *see* Fred C. Shapiro, "How Jerry Wurf Walks on Water," *The New York Times Magazine* (April 11, 1976); K. Bode, "Crying Wurf," *The New Republic* (July 2, 1977).

WVI: *see* WORK VALUES INVENTORY.

WV-PEA: *see* LABOR ORGANIZATION, West Virginia Public Employees Association.

WWML: *see* LABOR ORGANIZATION, Lathers International Union, The Wood, Wire and Metal.

Wyoming State AFL–CIO: *see* AMERICAN FEDERATION OF LABOR–CONGRESS OF INDUSTRIAL ORGANIZATIONS.

Wyoming State Employees Association: *see* LABOR ORGANIZATION.

WY-SEA: *see* LABOR ORGANIZATION, Wyoming State Employees Association.

Y

Yablonski, Joseph A. (1910-1969), called JOCK YABLONSKI, unsuccessfully challenged W. A. "Tony" Boyle for the presidency of the United Mine Workers in 1969. Subsequently, Yablonski, his wife, and daughter were shot by three gunmen hired by Boyle, who was later convicted of three counts of first degree murder. For an account, *see* Brit Hume, *Death and the Mines: Rebellion and Murder in the United Mine Workers* (N.Y.: Grossman, 1971).

Year Book of Labour Statistics, annual summary of the principal labor statistics from about 180 countries or territories that is published by International Labour Office, Geneva, Switzerland.

year-end bonus: *see* NONPRODUCTION BONUS.

yellow-dog contract, any agreement (written or oral) between an employer and an employee that calls for the employee to resign from, or refrain from joining, a union. In the early part of this century, this was a common tactic used by employers wary of union influences. The Norris–LaGuardia Act of 1932 made yellow-dog contracts illegal.

Yerkes, Robert M. (1876-1956), president of the American Psychological Association in 1918 and one of the team of psychologists who produced the famous Army Alpha and Army Beta intelligence tests first used by the United States Army during World War I.

Z

Zagoria, Sam (1919-   ), former member of the National Labor Relations Board, who became director of the Labor–Management Relations Service (established by the National League of Cities, the U.S. Conference of Mayors, and the National Association of Counties) in 1970. He is the editor of *Public Workers and Public Unions* (Englewood Cliffs, N.J.: Prentice-Hall, 1972).

Zander, Arnold Scheuer (1901-   ), organized and became the first president of the American Federation of State, County, and Municipal Employees. For biographical information, *see* Leo Kramer, *Labor's Paradox: The American Federation of State, County, and Municipal Employees, AFL–CIO* (N.Y.: John Wiley, 1962).

zero-defects program, formal effort at quality assuredness aimed at eliminating human errors during production. *See* George E. Fouch, "Motivation for Quality-Zero Defects Program," *Industrial Quality Control* (November 1965).

Z score, another way of referring to a standard score.

zipper clause, also called WRAP-UP CLAUSE, portion of a collective bargaining contract that specifically states the written agreement is complete and anything not contained in it is not agreed to. A typical zipper clause might read: "This contract is complete in itself and sets forth all the terms and conditions of the agreement between the parties hereto." The main purpose of the zipper or wrap-up clause is to prevent either party from demanding a renewal of negotiations during the life of the contract. It also serves to limit the freedom of a grievance arbitrator because his rulings must be based solely on the written agreement's contents.

zone of acceptance, also called ACCEPTANCE THEORY OF AUTHORITY, concept that authority stems from the bottom up, based on the extent to which individuals are willing to hold in abeyance their own critical faculties and accept the directives of their organizational superiors. The "zone of acceptance" itself is a theoretical range of tolerance within which organizational members will accept orders without question. A pioneering analysis of this concept is "The Role of Authority," Chapter VII of Herbert Simon's *Administrative Behavior* (N.Y.: The Free Press, 1947). Note that Simon's concept admittedly built upon Chester I. Barnard's concept of the "zone of indifference."

zone of indifference, concept that comes from Chester I. Barnard's *The Functions of the Executive* (Cambridge, Mass.: Harvard University Press, 1938). According to Barnard:

> If all the orders for actions reasonably practicable be arranged in the order of their acceptability to the person affected, it may be conceived that there are a number which are clearly unacceptable, that is, which certainly will not be obeyed; there is another group somewhat more or less on the neutral line, that is, either barely acceptable or barely unacceptable; and a third group unquestionably acceptable. This last group lies within the "zone of indifference." The person affected will accept orders lying within this zone and is relatively indifferent as to what the order is so far as the question of authority is concerned.

zone of uncertainty, range or zone of test scores within which it cannot truly be said that differing scores actually represent differing levels of attainment.

Appendix 1

Title VII of the Civil Rights
Act of 1964 as Amended by
The Equal Employment Opportunity
Act of 1972

Appendix 1
Title VII of the Civil Rights
Act of 1964 as Amended by
The Equal Employment Opportunity
Act of 1972*

AN ACT

To enforce the constitutional right to vote, to confer jurisdiction upon the district courts of the United States to provide injunctive relief against discrimination in public accommodations, to authorize the Attorney General to institute suits to protect constitutional rights in public facilities and public education, to extend the Commission on Civil Rights, to prevent discrimination in federally assisted programs, to establish a Commission on Equal Employment Opportunity, and for other purposes.

DEFINITIONS

Section 701. For the purposes of this title—

(a) The term "person" includes one or more individuals, *governments, governmental agencies, political subdivisions,* labor unions, partnerships, associations, corporations, legal representatives, mutual companies, joint-stock companies, trusts, unincorporated organizations, trustees, trustees in bankruptcy, or receivers.

(b) The term "employer" means a person engaged in an industry affecting commerce who has *fifteen* or more employees for each working day in each of twenty or more calendar weeks in the current or preceding calendar year, and

any agent of such a person, but such term does not include (1) the United States, a corporation wholly owned by the Government of the United States, an Indian tribe, or *any department or agency of the District of Columbia subject by statute to procedures of the competitive service (as defined in section 2102 of title 5 of the United States Code),* or (2) a bona fide private membership club (other than a labor organization) which is exempt from taxation under section 501(c) of the Internal Revenue Code of 1954, *except that during the first year after the date of enactment of the Equal Employment Opportunity Act of 1972, persons having fewer than twenty-five employees (and their agents) shall not be considered employers.*

(c) The term "employment agency" means any person regularly undertaking with or without compensation to procure employees for an employer or to procure for employees opportunities to work for an employer and includes an agent of such a person.

(d) The term "labor organization" means a labor organization engaged in an industry affecting commerce, and any agent of such an organization, and includes any organization of any kind, any agency, or employee representation

*Source: Committee Print of the Subcommittee on Labor of the Committee on Labor and Public Welfare, U.S. Senate (Washington: U.S. Government Printing Office, 1972). Amendments made by the EEO Act of 1972 (P.L. 92-261) are printed in italics.

committee, group, association, or plan so engaged in which employees participate and which exists for the purpose, in whole or in part, of dealing with employers concerning grievances, labor disputes, wages, rates of pay, hours, or other terms or conditions of employment, and any conference, general committe, joint or system board, or joint council so engaged which is subordinate to a national or international labor organization.

(e) A labor organization shall be deemed to be engaged in an industry affecting commerce if (1) it maintains or operates a hiring hall or hiring office which procures employees for an employer or procures for employees opportunities to work for an employer, or (2) the number of its members (or, where it is a labor organization composed of other labor organizations or their representatives, if the aggregate number of the members of such other labor organization) is (A) *twenty-five* or more during the first year after the *date of enactment of the Equal Employment Opportunity Act of 1972, or (B) fifteen* or more thereafter, and such labor organization—

(1) is the certified representative of employees under the provisions of the National Labor Relations Act, as amended, or the Railway Labor Act, as amended;

(2) although not certified, is a national or international labor organization or a local labor organization recognized or acting as the representative of employees of an employer or employers engaged in an industry affecting commerce; or

(3) has chartered a local labor organization or subsidiary body which is representing or actively seeking to represent employees of employers within the meaning of paragraph (1) or (2); or

(4) has been chartered by a labor organization representing or actively seeking to represent employees within the meaning of paragraph (1) or (2) as the local or subordinate body through which such employees may enjoy membership or become affiliated with such labor organization; or

(5) is a conference, general committee, joint or system board, or joint council sub-ordinate to a national or international labor organization, which includes a labor organization engaged in an industry affecting commerce within the meaning of any of the preceding paragraphs of this subsection.

(f) The term "employee" means an individual employed by an employer, *except that the term 'employee' shall not include any person elected to public office in any State or political subdivision of any State by the qualified voters thereof, or any person chosen by such officer to be on such officer's personal staff, or an appointee on the policymaking level or an immediate adviser with respect to the exercise of the constitutional or legal powers of the office. The exemption set forth in the preceding sentence shall not include employees subject to the civil service laws of a State government, governmental agency or political subdivision.*

(g) The term "commerce" means trade, traffic, commerce, transportation, transmission, or communication among the several States; or between a State and any place outside thereof; or within the District of Columbia, or a possession of the United States; or between points in the same State but through a point outside thereof.

(h) The term "industry affecting commerce" means any activity, business, or industry in commerce or in which a labor dispute would hinder or obstruct commerce or the free flow of commerce and includes any activity or industry "affecting commerce" within the meaning of the Labor-Management Reporting and Disclosure Act of 1959, *and further includes any governmental industry, business, or activity.*

(i) The term "State" includes a State of the United States, the District of Columbia, Puerto Rico, the Virgin Islands, American Samoa, Guam, Wake Island, the Canal Zone, and Outer Continental Shelf lands defined in the Outer Continental Shelf Lands Act.

(j) The term "religion" includes all aspects of religious observance and

practice, as well as belief, unless an employer demonstrates that he is unable to reasonably accommodate to an employee's or prospective employee's, religious observance or practice without undue hardship on the conduct of the employer's business.

EXEMPTION

Section 702. This title shall not apply to an employer with respect to the employment of aliens outside any State, or to a religious corporation, association, *educational institution,* or society with respect to the employment of individuals of a particular religion to perform work connected with the carrying on by such corporation, association, *educational institution,* or society of its *activities.*

DISCRIMINATION BECAUSE OF RACE, COLOR, RELIGION, SEX, OR NATIONAL ORIGIN

Section 703. (a) It shall be an unlawful employment practice for an employer—

(1) to fail or refuse to hire or to discharge any individual, or otherwise to discriminate against any individual with respect to his compensation, terms, conditions, or privileges of employment, because of such individual's race, color, religion, sex, or national origin; or

(2) to limit, segregate, or classify his employees *or applicants for employment* in any way which would deprive or tend to deprive any individual of employment opportunities or otherwise adversely affect his status as an employee, because of such individual's race, color, religion, sex, or nataional origin.

(b) It shall be an unlawful employment practice for an employment agency to fail or refuse to refer for employment, or otherwise to discriminate against, any individual because of his race, color, religion, sex or national origin, or to classify or refer for employment any individual on the basis of his race, color, religion, sex, or national origin.

(c) It shall be an unlawful employment practice for a labor organization—

(1) to exclude or to expel from its membership, or otherwise to discriminate against, any individual because of his race, color, religion, sex, or national origin;

(2) to limit, segregate, or classify its membership, *or applicants for membership* or to classify or fail or refuse to refer for employment any individual, in any way which would deprive or tend to deprive any individual of employment opportunities, or would limit such employment opportunities or otherwise adversely affect his status as an employee or as an applicant for employment, because of such individual's race, color, religion, sex, or national origin; or

(3) to cause or attempt to cause an employer to discriminate against an individual in violation of this section.

(d) It shall be an unlawful employment practice for any employer, labor organization, or joint labor-management committee controlling apprenticeship or other training or retraining, including on-the-job training programs to discriminate against any individual because of his race, color, religion, sex, or national origin in admission to, or employment in, any program established to provide apprenticeship or other training.

(e) Notwithstanding any other provision of this title, (1) it shall not be an unlawful employment practice for an employer to hire and employ employees, for an employment agency to classify, or refer for employment any individual, for a labor organization to classify its membership or to classify or refer for employment any individual, or for an employer, labor organization, or joint labor-management committee controlling apprenticeship or other training or retraining programs to admit or employ any individual in any such program, on the basis of his religion, sex, or national origin in those certain instances where religion, sex, or national origin is a bona fide occupational qualification reasonably necessary to the normal operation of that particular business or enterprise, and (2) it shall not be an unlawful employment practice for a school, college, university, or other educational institution or institution of learning to hire and employ employees of a particular religion if such school, college, university, or other educational institution or institution of learning is, in whole or in substantial part, owned, supported, controlled, or managed by a particular religion or by a particular religious corporation, association, or society, or if the curriculum of such school, college, university, or other educational institution or institution of learning is directed toward the propagation of a particular religion.

(f) As used in this title, the phrase "unlawful employment practice" shall not be deemed to include any action or measure taken by an employer, labor organization, joint labor-management committee, or employment agency with respect to an individual who is a member of the Communist Party of the United States or of any other organization required to register as a Communist-action or Communist-front organization by final order of the Subversive Activities Control Board pursuant to the Subversive Activities Control Act of 1950.

(g) Notwithstanding any other provision of this title, it shall not be an unlawful employment practice for an employer to fail or refuse to hire and employ any individual for any position, for an employer to discharge any individual from any position, or for an employment agency to fail or refuse to refer any individual for employment in any position, or for a labor organization to fail or refuse to refer any individual for employment in any position, if—

(1) the occupancy of such position, or access to the premises in or upon which any part of the duties of such position is performed or is to be performed, is subject to any requirement imposed in the interest of the national security of the United States under any security program in effect pursuant to or administered under any statute of the United States or any Executive order of the President; and

(2) such individual has not fulfilled or has ceased to fulfill that requirement.

(h) Notwithstanding any other provision of this title, it shall not be an unlawful employment practice for an employer to apply different standards of compensation, or different terms, conditions, or privileges of employment pursuant to a bona fide seniority or merit system, or a system which measures earnings by quantity or quality of production or to employees who work in different locations, provided that such differences are not the result of an intention to discriminate because of race, color, religion, sex, or national origin, nor shall it be an unlawful employment practice for an employer to give and to act upon the results of any professionally developed ability test provided that such test, its administration or action upon the results is not designed, intended or used to discriminate because of race, color, religion, sex or national origin. It shall not be an unlawful employment practice under this title for any employer to differentiate upon the basis of sex in determining the amount of the wages or compensation paid or to be paid to employees of such employer if such differentiation is authorized by the provisions of section 6(d) of the Fair Labor Standards Act of 1938, as amended (29 U.S.C. 206(d)).

(i) Nothing contained in this title shall apply to any business or enterprise on or near an Indian reservation with respect to any publicly announced employment practice of such business or enterprise under which a preferential treatment is given to any individual because he is an Indian living on or near a reservation.

(j) Nothing contained in this title shall be interpreted to require any employer, employment agency, labor organization, or joint labor-management committee subject to this title to grant preferential treatment to any individual or to any group because of the race, color, religion, sex, or national origin of such individual or group on account of an imbalance which may exist with respect to the total number or percentage of persons of any race, color, religion, sex, or national origin employed by any employer, referred or classified for employment by any employment agency or labor organization, admitted to membership or classified by any labor organization, or admitted to, or employed in, any apprenticeship or other training program, in comparison with the total number or percentage of persons of such race, color, religion, sex, or national origin in any community, State, section, or other area, or in the available work force in any community, State, section, or other area.

OTHER UNLAWFUL EMPLOYMENT PRACTICES

Section 704. (a) It shall be an unlawful employment practice for an employer to discriminate against any of his employees or applicants for employment, for an employment agency, or joint labor-management committee controlling apprenticeship or other training or retraining, including on-the-job training programs, to discriminate against any individual, or for a labor organization to discriminate against any member thereof or applicant for membership, because he has opposed any practice made an unlawful employment practice by this title, or because he has made a charge, testified, assisted, or participated in any manner in an investigation, proceeding, or hearing under this title.

(b) It shall be an unlawful employment practice for an employer, labor organization, employment agency, or joint labor-management committee controlling apprenticeship or other training or retraining, including on-the-job training programs, to print or publish or cause to be printed or published any notice or advertisement relating to

employment by such an employer or membership in or any classification or referral for employment by such a labor organization, or relating to any classification or referral for employment by such an employment agency, or relating to admission to, or employment in, any program established to provide apprenticeship or other training by such a joint labor-management committee indicating any preference, limitation, specification, or discrimination, based on race, color, religion, sex or national origin, except that such a notice or advertisement may indicate a preference, limitation, specification, or discrimination based on religion, sex, or national origin when religion, sex, or national origin is a bona fide occupational qualification for employment.

EQUAL EMPLOYMENT OPPORTUNITY COMMISSION

Section 705. (a) There is hereby created a Commission to be known as the Equal Employment Opportunity Commission, which shall be composed of five members, not more than three of whom shall be members of the same political party. Members of the Commission shall be appointed by the President by and with the advice and consent of the Senate for a term of five years. Any individual chosen to fill a vacancy shall be appointed only for the unexpired term of the member whom he shall succeed, and all members of the Commission shall continue to serve until their successors are appointed and qualified, except that no such member of the Commission shall continue to serve (1) for more than sixty days when the Congress is in session unless a nomination to fill such vacancy shall have been submitted to the Senate, or (2) after the adjournment sine die of the session of the Senate in which such nomination was submitted. The President shall designate one member to serve as Chairman of the Commission, and one member to serve as Vice Chairman. The Chairman shall be responsible on behalf of the Commission for the administrative operations of the Commission, and *except as provided in subsection (b),* shall appoint, in accordance with the *provisions of title 5, United States Code, governing appointments in the competitive service, such officers, agents, attorneys, hearing examiners, and employees as he deems necessary to assist it in the performance of its functions and to fix their compensation in accordance with the provisions of chapter 51 and subchapter III of chapter 53 of title 5, United States Code, relating to classification and General Schedule pay rates: Provided, that assignment, removal, and compensation of hearing examiners shall be in accordance with sections 3105, 3344, 5362, and 7521 of title 5, United States Code.*

(b) (1) There shall be a General Counsel of the Commission appointed by the President, by and with the advice and consent of the Senate, for a term of four years. The General Counsel shall have responsibility for the conduct of litigation as provided in sections 706 and 707 of this title. The General Counsel shall have such other duties as the Commission may prescribe or as may be provided by law and shall concur with the Chairman of the Commission on the appointment and supervision of regional attorneys. The General Counsel of the Commission on the effective date of this Act shall continue in such position and perform the functions specified in this subsection until a successor is appointed and qualified.

(2) Attorneys appointed under this section may, at the direction of the Commission, appear for and represent the Commission in any case in court, provided that the Attorney General shall conduct all litigation to which the Commission is a party in the Supreme Court pursuant to this title.

(c) A vacancy in the Commission shall not impair the right of the remaining members to exercise all the powers of the Commission and three members thereof shall constitute a quorum.

(d) The Commission shall have an official seal which shall be judicially noticed.

(e) The Commission shall at the close of each fiscal year report to the Congress and to the President concerning the action it has taken; the names, salaries, and duties of all individuals in its employ and the moneys it has disbursed; and shall make such further reports on the cause of and means of eliminating discrimination and such recommendations for further legislation as may appear desirable.

(f) The principal office of the Commission shall be in or near the District of Columbia, but it may meet or exercise any or all its powers at any other place. The Commission may establish such regional or State offices as it deems necessary to accomplish the purpose of this title.

(g) The Commission shall have power—

(1) to cooperate with and, with their consent, utilize regional, State, local, and other agencies, both public and private, and individuals;

(2) to pay to witnesses whose depositions are taken or who are summoned before the Commission or any of its agents the same witness and mileage fees as are paid to witnesses in the courts of the United States:

(3) to furnish to persons subject to this title such technical assistance as they may request to further their compliance with this title or an order issued thereunder;

(4) upon the request of (i) any employer, whose employees or some of them, or (ii) any labor organization, whose members or some of them, refuse or threaten to refuse to cooperate in effectuating the provisions of this title, to assist in such effectuation by conciliation or such other remedial action as is provided by this title;

(5) to make such technical studies as are appropriate to effectuate the purposes and

policies of this title and to make the results of such studies available to the public;

(6) to *intervene* in a civil action brought *under section 706 by an aggrieved party against a respondent other than a government, governmental agency, or political subdivision.*

(h) The Commission shall, in any of its educational or promotional activities, cooperate with other departments and agencies in the performance of such educational and promotional activities.

(i) All officers, agents, attorneys, and employees of the Commission shall be subject to the provisions of section 9 of the Act of August 2, 1939, as amended (the Hatch Act), notwithstanding any exemption contained in such section.

PREVENTION OF UNLAWFUL EMPLOYMENT PRACTICES

Section 706. *(a) The Commission is empowered, as hereinafter provided, to prevent any person from engaging in any unlawful employment practice as set forth in section 703 or 704 of this title.*

(b) Whenever a *charge is filed by or on behalf of a* person claiming to be aggrieved, or by a member of the Commission, *alleging* that an employer, employment agency, labor *organization, or joint labor-management committee controlling apprenticeship or other training or retraining, including on-the-job training programs, has en*gaged in an unlawful employment practice, the Commission shall *serve a notice of the charge (including the date, place and circumstances of the alleged unlawful employment practice) on* such employer, employment agency, labor *organization, or joint labor-management committee (hereinafter referred to as the "respondent") within ten days, and shall make an investigation thereof. Charges shall be in writing under oath or affirmation and shall contain such information and be in such form as the Commission requires. Charges* shall not

be made public by the Commission. If the Commission *determines* such investigation that there is *not* reasonable cause to believe that the charge is true, *it shall dismiss the charge and promptly notify the person claiming to be aggrieved and the respondent of its action. In determining whether reasonable cause exists, the Commission shall accord substantial weight to final findings and orders made by State or local authorities in proceedings commenced under State or local law pursuant to the requirements of subsections (c) and (d). If the Commission determines after such investigation that there is reasonable cause to believe that the charge is true,* the Commission shall endeavor to eliminate any such alleged unlawful employment practice by informal methods of conference, consiliation, and persuasion. Nothing said or done during and as a part of such *informal* endeavors may be made public by the Commission, *its officers or employees, or used as evidence in a subsequent proceeding* without the written consent of the *persons concerned. Any person* who *makes* public information in violation of this subsection shall be fined not more than $1,000 or imprisoned for not more than one *year, or both. The Commission shall make its determination on reasonable cause as promptly as possible and, so far as practicable, not later than one hundred and twenty days from the filing of the charge or, where applicable under subsection (c) or (d) from the date upon which the Commission is authorized to take action with respect to the charge.*

(c) In the case of an alleged unlawful employment practice occuring in a State, or political subdivision of a State, which has a State or local law prohibiting the unlawful employment practice alleged and establishing or authorizing a State or local authority to grant or seek relief from such practice or to institute criminal proceedings with respect thereto upon receiving notice thereof, no charge may be filed under subsec-

tion (a) by the person aggrieved before the expiration of sixty days after proceedings have been commenced under the State or local law, unless such proceedings have been earlier terminated, provided that such sixty-day period shall be extended to one hundred and twenty days during the first year after the effective date of such State or local law. If any requirement for the commencement of such proceedings is imposed by a State or local authority other than a requirement of the filing of a written and signed statement of the facts upon which the proceeding is based, the proceeding shall be deemed to have been commenced for the purposes of this subsection at the time such statement is sent by registered mail to the appropriate State or local authority.

(d) In the case of any charge filed by a member of the Commission alleging an unlawful employment practice occurring in a State or political subdivision of a State which has a State or local law prohibiting the practice alleged and establishing or authorizing a State or local authority to grant or seek relief from such practice or to institute criminal proceedings with respect thereto upon receiving notice thereof, the Commission shall, before taking any action with respect to such charge, notify the appropriate State or local officials and, upon request, afford them a reasonable time, but not less than sixty days (provided that such sixty-day period shall be extended to one hundred and twenty days during the first year after the effective date of such State or local law), unless a shorter period is requested, to act under such State or local law to remedy the practice alleged.

(e) A charge under this section shall be filed within one hundred and eighty days after the alleged unlawful employment practice occurred and notice of the charge (including the date, place and circumstances of the alleged unlawful employment practice) shall be served upon the person against whom such charge is made within ten days

thereafter, except that in a case of an unlawful employment practice with respect to which the person aggrieved has initially instituted proceedings with a State or local agency with authority to grant or seek relief from such practice or to institute criminal proceedings with respect thereto upon receiving notice thereof, such charge shall be filed by or on behalf of the person aggrieved within three hundred days after the alleged unlawful employment practice occurred, or within thirty days after receiving notice that the State or local agency has terminated the proceedings under the State or local law, whichever is earlier, and a copy of such charge shall be filed by the Commission with the State or local agency.

(f) (1) If within thirty days after a charge is filed with the Commission or within thirty days after expiration of any period of reference under subsection (c) or (d), the Commission has been unable to secure from the respondent a conciliation agreement acceptable to the Commission, the Commission may bring a civil action against any respondent not a government, governmental agency, or political subdivision named in the charge. In the case of a respondent which is a government, governmental agency, or political subdivision, if the Commission has been unable to secure from the respondent a conciliation agreement acceptable to the Commission, the Commission shall take no further action and shall refer the case to the Attorney General who may bring a civil action against such respondent in the appropriate United States district court. The person or persons aggrieved shall have the right to intervene in a civil action brought by the Commission or the Attorney General in a case involving a government, governmental agency, or political subdivision. If a charge filed with the Commission pursuant to subsection (b) is dismissed by the Commission, or if within one hundred and eighty days from the filing of such charge or the expiration of any period of reference under subsection (c) or (d), whichever is later, the Commission has not filed a civil action under this section or the Attorney General has notified a civil action in a case involving a government, governmental agency, or political subdivision, or the Commission has not entered into a conciliation agreement to which the person aggrieved is a party, the Commission, or the Attorney General in a case involving a government, governmental agency, or political subdivision, shall so notify the person aggrieved and within ninety days after the giving of such notice a civil action may be brought against the respondent named in the charge (A) by the person claiming to be aggrieved, or (B) if such charge was filed by a member of the Commission, by any person whom the charge alleges was aggrieved by the alleged unlawful employment practice. Upon application by the complainant and in such circumstances as the court may deem just, the court may appoint an attorney for such complainant and may authorize the commencement of the action without the payment of fees, costs, or security. Upon timely application, the court may, in its discretion, permit the Commission, or the Attorney General in a case involving a government, governmental agency, or political subdivision, to intervene in such civil action upon certification that the case is of general public importance. Upon request, the court may, in its discretion, stay further proceedings for not more than sixty days pending the termination of State or local proceedings described in subsections (c) or (d) of this section or further efforts of the Commission to obtain voluntary compliance.

(2) Whenever a charge is filed with the Commission and the Commission concludes on the basis of a preliminary investigation that prompt judicial action is necessary to carry out the purposes of this Act, the Commission, or the Attorney General in a case involving a government, governmental agency, or polit-

ical subdivision, may bring an action for appropriate temporary or preliminary relief pending final disposition of such charge. Any temporary restraining order or other order granting preliminary or temporary relief shall be issued in accordance with rule 65 of the Federal Rules of Civil Procedure. It shall be the duty of a court having jurisdiction over proceedings under this section to assign cases for hearing at the earliest practicable date and to cause such cases to be in every way expedited.

(3) Each United States district court and each United States court of a place subject to the jurisdiction of the United States shall have jurisdiction of actions brought under this title. Such an action may be brought in any judicial district in the State in which the unlawful employment practice is alleged to have been committed, in the judicial district in which the employment records relevant to such practice are maintained and administered, or in the judicial district in which the aggrieved person would have worked but for the alleged unlawful employment practice, but if the respondent is not found within any such district, such an action may be brought within the judicial district in which the respondent has his principal office. For purposes of sections 1404 and 1406 of title 28 of the United States Code, the judicial district in which the respondent has his principal office shall in all cases be considered a district in which the action might have been brought.

(4) It shall be the duty of the chief judge of the district (or in his absence, the acting chief judge) in which the case is pending immediately to designate a judge in such district to hear and determine the case. In the event that no judge in the district is available to hear and determine the case, the chief judge of the district, or the acting chief judge, as the case may be, shall certify this fact to the chief judge of the circuit (or in his absence, the acting chief judge) who shall then designate a district or circuit

judge of the circuit to hear and determine the case.

(5) It shall be the duty of the judge designated pursuant to this subsection to assign the case for hearing at the earliest practicable date and to cause the case to be in every way expedited. If such judge has not scheduled the case for trial within one hundred and twenty days after issue has been joined, that judge may appoint a master pursuant to rule 53 of the Federal Rules of Civil Procedure.

(g) If the court finds that the respondent has intentionally engaged in or is intentionally engaging in an unlawful employment practice charged in the complaint, the court may enjoin the respondent from engaging in such unlawful employment practice, and order such affirmative action as may be appropriate, which may include, but is not limited to, reinstatement or hiring of employees, with or without back pay (payable by the employer, employment agency, or labor organization, as the case may be, responsible for the unlawful employment practice), or any other equitable relief as the court deems appropriate. Back pay liability shall not accrue from a date more than two years prior to the filing of a charge with the Commission. Interim earnings or amounts earnable with reasonable diligence by the person or persons discriminated against shall operate to reduce the back pay otherwise allowable. No order of the court shall require the admission or reinstatement of an individual as a member of a union, or the hiring, reinstatement, or promotion of an individual as an employee, or the payment to him of any back pay, if such individual was refused admission, suspended, or expelled, or was refused employment or advancement or was suspended or discharged for any reason other than discrimination on account of race, color, religion, sex, or national origin or in violation of section 704(a).

(h) The provisions of the Act entitled "An Act to amend the Judicial Code and to define and limit the jurisdiction of courts sitting in equity, and for other purposes," approved March 23, 1932 (29 U.S.C. 101-115), shall not apply with respect to civil actions brought under this section.

(i) In any case in which an employer, employment agency, or labor organization fails to comply with an order of a court issued in a civil action brought under *this section*, the Commission may commence proceedings to compel compliance with such order.

(j) Any civil action brought under *this section* and any proceedings brought under subsection (i) shall be subject to appeal as provided in sections 1291 and 1292, title 28, United States Code.

(k) In any action or proceeding under this title the court, in its discretion, may allow the prevailing party, other than the Commission or the United States, a reasonable attorney's fee as part of the costs, and the Commission and the United States shall be liable for costs the same as a private person.

Section 707. (a) Whenever the Attorney General has reasonable cause to believe that any person or group of persons is engaged in a pattern or practice of resistance to the full enjoyment of any of the rights secured by this title, and that the pattern or practice is of such a nature and is intended to deny the full exercise of the rights herein described, the Attorney General may bring a civil action in the appropriate district court of the United States by filing with it a complaint (1) signed by him (or in his absence the Acting Attorney General), (2) setting forth facts pertaining to such pattern or practice, and (3) requesting such relief, including an application for a permanent or temporary injunction, restraining order or other order against the person or persons responsible for such pattern or practice, as he deems necessary to insure the full enjoyment of the rights herein described.

(b) The district courts of the United States shall have and shall exercise jurisdiction of proceedings instituted

385

pursuant to this section, and in any such proceeding the Attorney General may file with the clerk of such court a request that a court of three judges be convened to hear and determine the case. Such request by the Attorney General shall be accompanied by a certificate that, in his opinion, the case is of general public importance. A copy of the certificate and request for a three-judge court shall be immediately furnished by such clerk to the chief judge of the circuit (or in his absence, the presiding circuit judge of the circuit) in which the case is pending. Upon receipt of such request it shall be the duty of the chief judge of the circuit or the presiding circuit judge, as the case may be, to designate immediately three judges in such circuit, of whom at least one shall be a circuit judge and another of whom shall be a district judge of the court in which the proceeding was instituted, to hear and determine such case, and it shall be the duty of the judges so designated to assign the case for hearing at the earliest practicable date, to participate in the hearing and determination thereof, and to cause the case to be in every way expedited. An appeal from the final judgment of such court will lie to the Supreme Court.

In the event the Attorney General fails to file such a request in any such proceeding, it shall be the duty of the chief judge of the district (or in his absence, the acting chief judge) in which the case is pending immediately to designate a judge in such district to hear and determine the case. In the event that no judge in the district is available to hear and determine the case, the chief judge of the district, or the acting chief judge, as the case may be, shall certify this fact to the chief judge of the circuit (or in his absence, the acting chief judge) who shall then designate a district or circuit judge of the circuit to hear and determine the case.

It shall be the duty of the judge designated pursuant to this section to assign the case for hearing at the earliest prac-ticable date and to cause the case to be in every way expedited.

(c) Effective two years after the date of enactment of the Equal Employment Opportunity Act of 1972, the functions of the Attorney General under this section shall be transferred to the Commission, together with such personnel, property, records, and unexpended balances of appropriations, allocations, and other funds employed, used, held, available, or to be made available in connection with such functions unless the President submits, and neither House of Congress vetoes, a reorganization plan pursuant to chapter 9, of title 5, United States Code, inconsistent with the provisions of this subsection. The Commission shall carry out such functions in accordance with subsection (d) and (e) of this section.

(d) Upon the transfer of functions provided for in subsection (c) of this section, in all suits commenced pursuant to this section prior to the date of such transfer, proceedings shall continue without abatement, all court orders and decrees shall remain in effect, and the Commission shall be substituted as a party for the United States of America, the Attorney General, or the Acting Attorney General, as appropriate.

(e) Subsequent to the date of enactment of the Equal Employment Opportunity Act of 1972, the Commission shall have authority to investigate and act on a charge of a pattern or practice of discrimination, whether filed by or on behalf of a person claiming to be aggrieved or by a member of the Commission. All such actions shall be conducted in accordance with the procedures set forth in section 706 of this Act.

EFFECT ON STATE LAWS

Section 708. Nothing in this title shall be deemed to exempt or relieve any person from any liability, duty, penalty, or punishment provided by any present or future law of any State or political subdivision of a State, other than any such law which purports to require or permit the doing of any act which would be an unlawful employment practice under this title.

INVESTIGATIONS, INSPECTIONS, RECORDS, STATE AGENCIES

Section 709. (a) In connection with any investigation of a charge filed under section 706, the Commission or its designated 'representative shall at all reasonable times have access to, for the purposes of examination, and the right to copy any evidence of any person being investigated or proceeded against that relates to unlawful employment practices covered by this title and is relevant to the charge under investigation.

(b) The Commission may cooperate with State and local agencies charged with the administration of State fair employment practices laws and, with the consent of such agencies, may, for the purpose of carrying out its functions and duties under this title and within the limitation of funds appropriated specifically for such purpose, *engage in and contribute to the cost of research and other projects of mutual interest undertaken by such agencies, and* utilize the services of such agencies and their employees, and, notwithstanding any other provision of law, *pay by advance or reimbursement* such agencies and their employees for services rendered to assist the Commission in carrying out this title. In furtherance of such cooperative efforts, the Commission may enter into written agreements with such State or local agencies and such agreements may include provisions under which the Commission shall refrain from processing a charge in any cases or class of cases specified in such agreements or under which the Commission shall relieve any person or class of persons in such State or locality from requirements imposed under this section. The Commission shall rescind any such agreement whenever it determines that the agreement no longer serves the interest of effective enforcement of this title.

(c) *Every* employer, employment agency, and labor organization subject to this title shall (1) make and keep such records relevant to the determinations of whether unlawful employment practices have been or are being committed, (2) preserve such records for such periods, and (3) make such reports therefrom, as the Commission shall prescribe by regulation or order, after public hearing, as reasonable, necessary, or appropriate for the enforcement of this title or the regulations or orders thereunder. The Commission shall, by regulation, require each employer, labor organization, and joint labor-management committee subject to this title which controls an apprenticeship or other training program to maintain such records as are reasonably necessary to carry out the purpose of this title, including, but not limited to, a list of applicants who wish to participate in such program, including the chronological order in which applications were received, and *to* furnish to the Commission upon request, a detailed description of the manner in which persons are selected to participate in the apprenticeship or other training program. Any employer, employment agency, labor organization, or joint labor-management committee which believes that the application to it of any regulation or order issued under this section would result in undue hardship may apply to the Commission for an exemption from the application of such regulation or order, *and, if such application for an exemption is denied,* bring a civil action in the United States district court for the district where such records are kept. If the Commission or the court, as the case may be, finds that the application of the regulation or order to the employer, employment agency, or labor organization in question would impose an undue hardship, the Commission or the court, as the case may be, may grant appropriate relief. *If any person required* to comply with the provisions of this subsection fails or refuses to do so, the United States district court for the district in which such person is found, resides, or transacts business, shall, upon application of the Commission, or the Attorney General in a case involving a government, governmental agency or political subdivision, have jurisdiction to issue to such person an order requiring him to comply.

(d) In prescribing requirements pursuant to subsection (c) of this section, the Commission shall consult with other interested State and Federal agencies and shall endeavor to coordinate its requirements with those adopted by such agencies. The Commission shall furnish upon request and without cost to any State or local agency charged with the administration of a fair employment practice law information obtained pursuant to subsection (c) of this section from any employer, employment agency, labor organization, or joint labor-management committee subject to the jurisdiction of such agency. Such information shall be furnished on condition that it not be made public by the recipient agency prior to the institution of a proceeding under State or local law involving such information. If this condition is violated by a recipient agency, the Commission may decline to honor subsequent requests pursuant to this subsection.

(e) It shall be unlawful for any officer or employee of the Commission to make public in any manner whatever any information obtained by the Commission pursuant to its authority under this section prior to the institution of any proceeding under this title involving such information. Any officer or employee of the Commission who shall make public in any manner whatever any information in violation of this subsection shall be guilty of a misdemeanor and upon conviction thereof, shall be fined not more than $1,000, or imprisoned not more than one year.

INVESTIGATORY POWERS

Section 710. For the purpose of all hearings and investigations conducted by the Commission or its duly authorized agents or agencies, section 11 of the National Labor Relations Act (49 Stat. 455; 29 U.S.C. 161) shall apply.

NOTICES TO BE POSTED

Section 711. (a) Every employer, employment agency, and labor organization, as the case may be, shall post and keep posted in conspicuous places upon its premises where notices to employees, applicants for employment, and members are customarily posted a notice to be prepared or approved by the Commission setting forth excerpts from, or summaries of, the pertinent provisions of this title and information pertinent to the filing of a complaint.

(b) A willful violation of this section shall be punishable by a fine of not more than $100 for each separate offense.

VETERANS' PREFERENCE

Section 712. Nothing contained in this title shall be construed to repeal or modify any Federal, State, territorial, or local law creating special rights or preference for veterans.

RULES AND REGULATIONS

Section 713. (a) The Commission shall have authority from time to time to issue, amend, or rescind suitable procedural regulations to carry out the provisions of this title. Regulations issued under the section shall be in conformity with the standards and limitations of the Administrative Procedure Act.

(b) In any action or proceeding based on any alleged unlawful employment practice, no person shall be subject to any liability or punishment for or on account of (1) the commission by such person of an unlawful employment practice if he pleads and proves that the act or omission complained of was in good faith, in conformity with, and in reliance on any written interpretation or opinion of the Commission, or (2) the failure of such person to publish and file any information required by any provision of this title if he pleads and proves that he failed to publish and file such information in good faith, in conformity with the instructions of the Commission issued under this title regarding the filing of such information. Such a defense, if established, shall be a bar to the action or proceeding, notwithstanding that (A) after such act or omission, such interpretation or opinion is modified or rescinded or is determined by judicial authority to be invalid or of no legal effect, or (B) after publishing or filing the description and annual reports, such publication or filing is determined by judicial authority not to be in conformity with the requirements of this title.

FORCIBLY RESISTING THE COMMISSION OR ITS REPRESENTATIVES

Section 714. The provisions of *sections 111 and 1114* title 18, United States Code, shall apply to officers, agents, and employees of the Commission in the performance of their official duties. *Notwithstanding the provisions of section 111 and 1114 of title 18, United States Code, whoever in violation of the provisions of section 1114 of such title kills a person while engaged in or on account of the performance of his official functions under this Act shall be punished by imprisonment for any term of years or for life.*

EQUAL EMPLOYMENT OPPORTUNITY COORDINATING COUNCIL

Section 715. *There shall be established an Equal Employment Opportunity Coordinating Council (hereinafter referred to in this section as the Council) composed of the Secretary of Labor, the Chairman of the Equal Employment Opportunity Commission, the Attorney General, the Chairman of the United States Civil Service Commission, and the Chairman of the United States Civil Rights Commission, or their respective delegates. The Council shall have the responsibility for developing and implementing agreements, policies and practices designed to maximize effort, promote efficiency, and eliminate conflict, competition, duplication and inconsistency among the operations, functions and jurisdictions of the various departments, agencies and branches of the Federal government responsible for the implementation and enforcement of equal employment opportunity legislation, orders, and policies. On or before July 1 of each year, the Council shall transmit to the President and to the Congress a report of its activities, together with such recommendations for legislative or administrative changes as it concludes are desirable to further promote the purposes of this section.*

EFFECTIVE DATE

Section 716. (a) This title shall become effective one year after the date of its enactment.

(b) Notwithstanding subsection (a), sections of this title other than sections 703, 704, 706, and 707 shall become effective immediately.

(c) The President shall, as soon as feasible after the enactment of this title, convene one or more conferences for the purpose of enabling the leaders of groups whose members will be affected by this title to become familiar with the rights afforded and obligations imposed by its provisions, and for the purpose of making plans which will result in the fair and effective administration of this title when all of its provisions become effective. The President shall invite the participation in such conference or conferences of (1) the members of the President's Committee on Equal Employment Opportunity, (2) the members of the Commission on Civil Rights, (3) representatives of State and local agencies engaged in furthering equal employment opportunity, (4) representatives of private agencies engaged in furthering equal employment opportunity, (4) representatives of private agencies engaged in furthering equal employment opportunity, and (5) representatives of employers, labor organizations, and employment agencies who will be subject to this title.

NONDISCRIMINATION IN FEDERAL GOVERNMENT EMPLOYMENT

Section 717. *(a) All personnel actions affecting employees or applicants for employment (except with regard to aliens employed outside the limits of the United States) in military departments as defined in section 102 of title 5, United States Code, in executive agencies (other than the General Accounting Office) as defined in section 105 of title 5, United States Code (including employees and applicants for employment who are paid from nonappropriated funds), in the United States Postal Service and the Postal Rate Commission, in those units of the Government of the District of Columbia having positions in the competitive service, and in those units of the legislative and judicial branches of the Federal Government having positions in the competitive service, and in the Library of Congress shall be made free from any discrimination based on race, color, religion, sex, or national origin.*

(b) Except as otherwise provided in this subsection, the Civil Service Commission shall have authority to enforce the provisions of subsection (a) through appropriate remedies, including reinstatement or hiring of employees with or without back pay, as will effectuate the policies of this section, and shall issue

such rules, regulations, orders, and instructions as it deems necessary and appropriate to carry out its responsibilities under this section. The Civil Service Commission shall—

(1) be responsible for the annual review and approval of a national and regional equal employment opportunity plan which each department and agency and each appropriate unit referred to in subsection (a) of this section shall submit in order to maintain an affirmative program of equal employment opportunity for all such employees and applicants for employment;

(2) be responsible for the review and evaluation of the operation of all agency equal employment opportunity programs, periodically obtaining and publishing (on at least a semiannual basis) progress reports from each such department, agency, or unit; and

(3) consult with and solicit the recommendations of interested individuals, groups, and organizations relating to equal employment opportunity.

The head of each such department, agency or unit shall comply with such rules, regulations, orders, and instructions which shall include a provision that an employee or applicant for employment shall be notified of any final action taken on any complaint of discrimination filed by him thereunder. The plan submitted by each department, agency, and unit shall include, but not be limited to—

(1) provision for the establishment of training and education programs designed to provide a maximum opportunity for employees to advance so as to perform at their highest potential; and

(2) a description of the qualifications in terms of training and experience relating to equal employment opportunity for the principal and operating officials of each such department, agency, or unit responsible for carrying out the equal employment opportunity program and of the allocation of personnel and resources proposed by such department, agency, or unit to carry out its equal employment opportunity program.

With respect to employment in the Library of Congress, authorities granted in this subsection to the Civil Service

Commission shall be exercised by the Librarian of Congress.

(c) Within thirty days of receipt of notice of final action taken by a department, agency, or unit referred to in subsection 717(a), or by the Civil Service Commission upon an appeal from a decision or order of such department, agency, or unit on a complaint of discrimination based on race, color, religion, sex, or national origin, brought pursuant to subsection (a) of this section, Executive Order 11478 or any succeeding Executive orders, or after one hundred and eighty days from the filing of the initial charge with the department, agency, or unit or with the Civil Service Commission on appeal from a decision or order of such department, agency, or unit until such time as final action may be taken by a department, agency, or unit, an employee or applicant for employment, if aggrieved by the final disposition of his complaint, or by the failure to take final action on his complaint, may file a civil action as provided in section 706, in which civil action the head of the department, agency, or unit, as appropriate, shall be the defendant.

(d) The provisions of section 706(f) through (k), as applicable, shall govern civil actions brought hereunder.

(e) Nothing contained in this Act shall relieve any Government agency or official of its or his primary responsibility to assure nondiscrimination in employment as required by the Constitution and statutes or of its or his responsibilities under Executive Order 11478 relating to equal employment opportunity in the Federal Government.

SPECIAL PROVISIONS WITH RESPECT TO DENIAL, TERMINATION, AND SUSPENSION OF GOVERNMENT CONTRACTS

Section 718. No Government contract, or portion thereof, with any employer, shall be denied, withheld, terminated, or suspended, by any agency or officer of the United States under any equal employment opportunity law or order, where such employer has an affirmative action plan which has previously been accepted by the Government for the same facility within the past twelve months without first according such employer full hearing and adjudication under the provision of title 5, United States Code, section 554, and the following pertinent sections: Provided, that if such employer has deviated substantially from such previously agreed to affirmative action plan, this section shall not apply: Provided further, that for the purposes of this section an affirmative action plan shall be deemed to have been accepted by the Government at the time the appropriate compliance agency has accepted such plan unless within forty-five days thereafter the Office of Federal Contract Compliance has disapproved such plan.

Appendix 2

Adoption by Four Agencies
of Uniform Guidelines on
Employee Selection
Procedures (1978)

[6570-06]

Title 29—Labor

CHAPTER XIV—EQUAL EMPLOYMENT OPPORTUNITY COMMISSION

PART 1607—UNIFORM GUIDELINES ON EMPLOYEE SELECTION PROCEDURES (1978)

Title 5—Administrative Personnel

CHAPTER I—CIVIL SERVICE COMMISSION

PART 300—EMPLOYMENT (GENERAL)

Title 28—Judicial Administration

CHAPTER I—DEPARTMENT OF JUSTICE

PART 50—STATEMENTS OF POLICY

Title 41—Public Contracts and Property Management

CHAPTER 60—OFFICE OF FEDERAL CONTRACT COMPLIANCE PROGRAMS, DEPARTMENT OF LABOR

PART 60-3—UNIFORM GUIDELINES ON EMPLOYEE SELECTION PROCEDURES (1978)

Adoption of Employee Selection Procedures

AGENCIES: Equal Employment Opportunity Commission, Civil Service Commission, Department of Justice and Department of Labor.

ACTION: Adoption of uniform guidelines on employee selection procedures as final rules by four agencies.

SUMMARY: This document sets forth the uniform guidelines on employee selection procedures adopted by the Equal Employment Opportunity Commission, Civil Service Commission, Department of Justice, and the Department of Labor. At present two different sets of guidelines exist. The guidelines are intended to establish a uniform Federal position in the area of prohibiting discrimination in employment practices on grounds of race, color, religion, sex, or national origin. Cross reference documents are published at 5 CFR 300.103(c) (Civil Service Commission), 28 CFR 50.14 (Department of Justice), 29 CFR Part 1607 (Equal Employment Opportunity Commission), and 41 CFR Part 60-3 (Department of Labor) elsewhere in this issue.

EFFECTIVE DATE: September 25, 1978.

FOR FURTHER INFORMATION CONTACT:

Doris Wooten, Associate Director, Donald J. Schwartz, Staff Psychologist, Office of Federal Contract Compliance Programs, Room C-3324, Department of Labor, 200 Constitution Avenue NW., Washington, D.C. 20210, 202-523-9426.

Peter C. Robertson, Director, Office of Policy Implementation, Equal Employment Opportunity Commission, 2401 E Street NW., Washington, D.C. 20506, 202-634-7060.

David L. Rose, Chief, Employment Section, Civil Rights Division, Department of Justice, 10th Street and Pennsylvania Avenue NW., Washington, D.C. 20530, 202-739-3831.

A. Diane Graham, Director, Federal Equal Employment Opportunity, Civil Service Commission, 1900 E Street NW., Washington, D.C. 20415, 202-632-4420.

H. Patrick Swygert, General Counsel, Civil Service Commission, 1900 E Street NW., Washington, D.C. 20415, 202-632-4632.

SUPPLEMENTARY INFORMATION:

AN OVERVIEW OF THE 1978 UNIFORM GUIDELINES ON EMPLOYEE SELECTION PROCEDURES

I. BACKGROUND

One problem that confronted the Congress which adopted the Civil Rights Act of 1964 involved the effect of written preemployment tests on equal employment opportunity. The use of these test scores frequently denied employment to minorities in many cases without evidence that the tests were related to success on the job. Yet employers wished to continue to use such tests as practical tools to assist in the selection of qualified employees. Congress sought to strike a balance which would proscribe discrimination, but otherwise permit the use of tests in the selection of employees. Thus, in title VII, Congress authorized the use of "any professionally developed ability test provided that such test, its administration or action upon the results is not designed, intended or used to discriminate * * *".[1]

At first, some employers contended that, under this section, they could use any test which had been developed by a professional so long as they did not intend to exclude minorities, even if such exclusion was the consequence of the use of the test. In 1966, the Equal Employment Opportunity Commission (EEOC) adopted guidelines to advise employers and other users what the law and good industrial psycholo-

gy practice required.[1] The Department of Labor adopted the same approach in 1968 with respect to tests used by Federal contractors under Executive Order 11246 in a more detailed regulation. The Government's view was that the employer's intent was irrelevant. If tests or other practices had an adverse impact on protected groups, they were unlawful unless they could be justified. To justify a test which screened out a higher proportion of minorities, the employer would have to show that it fairly measured or predicted performance on the job. Otherwise, it would not be considered to be "professionally developed."

In succeeding years, the EEOC and the Department of Labor provided more extensive guidance which elaborated upon these principles and expanded the guidelines to emphasize all selection procedures. In 1971 in *Griggs* v. *Duke Power Co.*,[2] the Supreme Court announced the principle that employer practices which had an adverse impact on minorities and were not justified by business necessity constituted illegal discrimination under title VII. Congress confirmed this interpretation in the 1972 amendments to title VII. The elaboration of these principles by courts and agencies continued into the mid-1970's,[4] but differences between the EEOC and the other agencies (Justice, Labor, and Civil Service Commission) produced two different sets of guidelines by the end of 1976.

With the advent of the Carter administration in 1977, efforts were intensified to produce a unified government position. The following document represents the result of that effort. This introduction is intended to assist those not familiar with these matters to understand the basic approach of the uniform guidelines. While the guidelines are complex and technical, they are based upon the principles which have been consistently upheld by the courts, the Congress, and the agencies.

The following discussion will cite the sections of the Guidelines which embody these principles.

II. ADVERSE IMPACT

The fundamental principle underlying the guidelines is that employer policies or practices which have an adverse impact on employment opportunities of any race, sex, or ethnic group are illegal under title VII and the Executive order unless justified by business necessity.[5] A selection procedure

---

[1]See 35 U.S.L.W. 2137 (1966).

[2]401 U.S. 424 (1971).

[4]See, e.g., *Albermarle Paper Co.* v. *Moody*, 422 U.S. 405 (1975).

[5]*Griggs*, note 3, supra; uniform guidelines on employee selection procedures (1978), section 3A, (hereinafter cited by section number only).

---

[1]Section 703(h), 42 U.S.C. 2000e(2)(h).

Appendix 2: Uniform Selection Guidelines

which has no adverse impact generally does not violate title VII or the Executive order.[6] This means that an employer may usually avoid the application of the guidelines by use of procedures which have no adverse impact.[7] If adverse impact exists, it must be justified on grounds of business necessity. Normally, this means by validation which demonstrates the relation between the selection procedure and performance on the job.

The guidelines adopt a "rule of thumb" as a practical means of determining adverse impact for use in enforcement proceedings. This rule is known as the "⅘ths" or "80 percent" rule.[8] It is not a legal definition of discrimination, rather it is a practical device to keep the attention of enforcement agencies on serious discrepancies in hire or promotion rates or other employment decisions. To determine whether a selection procedure violates the "⅘ths rule", an employer compares its hiring rates for different groups.[9] But this rule of thumb cannot be applied automatically. An employer who has conducted an extensive recruiting campaign may have a larger than normal pool of applicants, and the "⅘ths rule" might unfairly expose it to enforcement proceedings.[10] On the other hand, an employer's reputation may have discouraged or "chilled" applicants of particular groups from applying because they believed application would be futile. The application of the "⅘ths" rule in that situation would allow an employer to evade scrutiny because of its own discrimination.[11]

III. IS ADVERSE IMPACT TO BE MEASURED BY THE OVERALL PROCESS?

In recent years some employers have eliminated the overall adverse impact of a selection procedure and employed sufficient numbers of minorities or women to meet this "⅘th's rule of thumb". However, they might continue use of a component which does have an adverse impact. For example, an employer might insist on a minimum passing score on a written test which is not job related and which has an adverse impact on minorities.[12] However, the employer might compensate for this adverse impact by hiring a sufficient proportion of minorities who do meet its standards, so that its overall hiring is on a par with or higher than the applicant flow. Employers have argued that as long as their "bottom line" shows no overall

adverse impact, there is no violation at all, regardless of the operation of a particular component of the process.

Employee representatives have argued that rights under equal employment opportunity laws are individual, and the fact that an employer has hired some minorities does not justify discrimination against other minorities. Therefore, they argue that adverse impact is to be determined by examination of each component of the selection procedure, regardless of the "bottom line." This question has not been answered definitively by the courts. There are decisions pointing in both directions.

These guidelines do not address the underlying question of law. They discuss only the exercise of prosecutorial discretion by the Government agencies themselves.[13] The agencies have decided that, generally, their resources to combat discrimination should be used against those respondents whose practices have restricted or excluded the opportunities of minorities and women. If an employer is appropriately including all groups in the work-force, it is not sensible to spend Government time and effort on such a case, when there are so many employers whose practices do have adverse effects which should be challenged. For this reason, the guidelines provide that, in considering whether to take enforcement action, the Government will take into account the general posture of the employer concerning equal employment opportunity, including its affirmative action plan and results achieved under the plan.[14] There are some circumstances where the government may intervene even though the "bottom line" has been satisfied. They include the case where a component of a selection procedure restricts promotional opportunities of minorities or women who were discriminatorily assigned to jobs, and where a component, such as a height requirement, has been declared unlawful in other situations.[15]

What of the individual who is denied the job because of a particular component in a procedure which otherwise meets the "bottom line" standard? The individual retains the right to proceed through the appropriate agencies, and into Federal court.[16]

IV. WHERE ADVERSE IMPACT EXISTS: THE BASIC OPTIONS

Once an employer has established that there is adverse impact, what

steps are required by the guidelines? As previously noted, the employer can modify or eliminate the procedure which produces the adverse impact, thus taking the selection procedure from the coverage of these guidelines. If the employer does not do that, then it must justify the use of the procedure on grounds of "business necessity."[17] This normally means that it must show a clear relation between performance on the selection procedure and performance on the job. In the language of industrial psychology, the employer must validate the selection procedure. Thus the bulk of the guidelines consist of the Government's interpretation of standards for validation.

V. VALIDATION: CONSIDERATION OF ALTERNATIVES

The concept of validation as used in personnel psychology involves the establishment of the relationship between a test instrument or other selection procedure and performance on the job. Federal equal employment opportunity law has added a requirement to the process of validation. In conducting a validation study, the employer should consider available alternatives which will achieve its legitimate business purpose with lesser adverse impact.[18] The employer cannot concentrate solely on establishing the validity of the instrument or procedure which it has been using in the past.

This same principle of using the alternative with lesser adverse impact is applicable to the manner in which an employer uses a valid selection procedure.[19] The guidelines assume that there are at least three ways in which an employer can use scores on a selection procedure: (1) To screen out of consideration those who are not likely to be able to perform the job successfully; (2) to group applicants in accordance with the likelihood of their successful performance on the job; and (3) to rank applicants, selecting those with the highest scores for employment.[20]

The setting of a "cutoff score" to determine who will be screened out may have an adverse impact. If so, an employer is required to justify the initial cutoff score by reference to its need for a trustworthy and efficient work force.[21] Similarly, use of results for

---

[6] *Furnco* v. *Waters*, 98 S.Ct. 2943 (1978).
[7] Section 6.
[8] Section 4D.
[9] Section 16R (definition of selection rate).
[10] Section 4D (special recruiting programs).
[11] *Ibid* (user's actions have discouraged applicants).
[12] See, e.g., *Griggs* v. *Duke Power Co.*, 401 U.S. 424 (1971).

[13] Section 4C.
[14] Section 4E.
[15] Section 4C.
[16] The processing of individual cases is excluded from the operation of the bottom line concept by the definition of "enforcement action," section 16I. Under section 4C, where adverse impact has existed, the employer must keep records of the effect of each component for 2 years after the adverse effect has dissipated.

[17] A few practices may be used without validation even if they have adverse impact. See, e.g., *McDonnell Douglas* v. *Green*, 411 U.S. 792 (1973) and section 6B.
[18] *Albemarle Paper Co.* v. *Moody*, 422 U.S. 405 (1975); *Robinson* v. *Lorillard Corp.*, 444 F. 2d 791 (4th Cir. 1971).
[19] Sections 3B; 5G.
[20] *Ibid.*
[21] See sections 3B; 5H. See also sections 14B(6) (criterion-related validity); 14C(9) (content validity); 14D(1) (construct validity).

---

grouping or for rank ordering is likely to have a greater adverse effect than use of scores solely to screen out unqualified candidates. If the employer chooses to use a rank order method, the evidence of validity must be sufficient to justify that method of use.[22]

VI. TESTING FOR HIGHER LEVEL JOBS

Normally, employers test for the job for which people are hired. However, there are situations where the first job is temporary or transient, and the workers who remain are promoted to work which involves more complex activities. The guidelines restrict testing for higher level jobs to users who promote a majority of the employees who remain with them to the higher level job within a reasonable period of time.[23]

VII. HOW IS VALIDATION TO BE CONDUCTED

Validation has become highly technical and complex, and yet is constantly changing as a set of concepts in industrial psychology. What follows here is a simple introduction to a highly complex field. There are three concepts which can be used to validate a selection procedure. These concepts reflect different approaches to investigating the job relatedness of selection procedures and may be interrelated in practice. They are (1) criterion-related validity,[24] (2) content validity,[25] and (3) construct validity.[26] In criterion-related validity, a selection procedure is justified by a statistical relationship between scores on the test or other selection procedure and measures of job performance. In content validity, a selection procedure is justified by showing that it representatively samples significant parts of the job, such as a typing test for a typist. Construct validity involves identifying the psychological trait (the construct) which underlies successful performance on the job and then devising a selection procedure to measure the presence and degree of the construct. An example would be a test of "leadership ability." The guidelines contain technical standards and documentation requirements for the application of each of the three approaches.[27] One of the problems which the guidelines attempt to meet is the "borderline" be-

tween "content validity" and "construct validity." The extreme cases are easy to understand. A secretary, for example, may have to type. Many jobs require the separation of important matters which must be handled immediately from those which can be handled routinely. For the typing function, a typing test is appropriate. It is justifiable on the basis of content validity because it is a sample of an important or critical part of the job. The second function can be viewed as involving a capability to exercise selective judgment in light of the surrounding circumstances, a mental process which is difficult to sample.

In addressing this situation, the guidelines attempt to make it practical to validate the typing test by a content strategy,[28] but do not allow the validation of a test measuring a construct such as "judgment" by a content validity strategy.

The bulk of the guidelines deals with questions such as those discussed in the above paragraphs. Not all such questions can be answered simply, nor can all problems be addressed in the single document. Once the guidelines are issued, they will have to be interpreted in light of changing factual, legal, and professional circumstances.

VIII. SIMPLIFICATION OF REPORTING AND RECORDKEEPING REQUIREMENTS

The reporting and recordkeeping provisions which appeared in the December 30 draft which was published for comment have been carefully reviewed in light of comments received and President Carter's direction to limit paperwork burdens on those regulated by Government to the minimum necessary for effective regulation. As a result of this review, two major changes have been made in the documentation requirements of the guidelines:

(1) A new section 15A(1) provides a simplified recordkeeping option for employers with fewer than 100 employees;

(2) Determinations of the adverse impact of selection procedures need not be made for groups which constitute less than 2 percent of the relevant labor force.

Also, the draft has been changed to make clear that users can assess adverse impact on an annual basis rather than on a continuing basis.

Analysis of comments. The uniform guidelines published today are based upon the proposition that the Federal Government should speak to the public and to those whom it regulates with one voice on this important subject; and that the Federal Government ought to impose upon itself obligations for equal employment opportunity which are at least as demanding as

those it seeks to impose on others. These guidelines state a uniform Federal position on this subject, and are intended to protect the rights created by title VII of the Civil Rights Act of 1964, as amended, Executive Order 11246, as amended, and other provisions of Federal law. The uniform guidelines are also intended to represent "professionally acceptable methods" of the psychological profession for demonstrating whether a selection procedure validly predicts or measures performance for a particular job. *Albemarle Paper Co.* v. *Moody*, 442 U.S. 405, 425. They are also intended to be consistent with the decisions of the Supreme Court and authoritative decisions of other appellate courts.

Although the development of these guidelines preceded the issuance by President Jimmy Carter of Executive Order 12044 designed to improve the regulatory process, the spirit of his Executive order was followed in their development. Initial agreement among the Federal agencies was reached early in the fall of 1977, and the months from October 1977 until today have been spent in extensive consultation with civil rights groups whose clientele are protected by these guidelines; employers, labor unions, and State and local governments whose employment practices are affected by these guidelines; State and local government antidiscrimination agencies who share with the Federal Government enforcement responsibility for discriminatory practices; and appropriate members of the general public. For example, an earlier draft of these guidelines was circulated informally for comment on October 28, 1977, pursuant to OMB Circular A-85. Many comments were received from representatives of State and local governments, psychologists, private employers, and civil rights groups. Those comments were taken into account in the draft of these guidelines which was published for comment December 30, 1977, 42 FR 66542.

More than 200 organizations and individuals submitted written comments on the December 30, 1977, draft. These comments were from representatives of private industry, public employers, labor organizations, civil rights groups, the American Psychological Association and components thereof, and many individual employers, psychologists, and personnel specialists. On March 3, 1978, notice was given of a public hearing and meeting to be held on April 10, 1978, 43 FR 9131. After preliminary review of the comments, the agencies identified four issues of particular interest, and invited testimony particularly on those issues, 43 FR 11812 (March 21, 1978). In the same notice the agencies published questions and answers on four

---

[22] Sections 5G, 14B(6); 14C(9); 14D(1).

[23] Section 5I.

[24] Sections 5B, (General Standards); 14B (Technical Standards); 15B (Documentation); 16F (Definition).

[25] Sections 5B (General Standards); 14C (Technical Standards); 15C (Documentation); 16D (Definition).

[26] Sections 5B (General Standards); 14D (Technical Standards); 15D (Documentation); 16E (Definition).

[27] Technical standards are in section 14; documentation requirements are in section 15.

[28] Section 14C.

Appendix 2: Uniform Selection Guidelines

issues of concern to the commenters. The questions and answers were designed to clarify the intent of the December 30, 1977, draft, so as to provide a sharper focus for the testimony at the hearing.

At a full day of testimony on April 10, 1978, representatives of private industry, State and local governments, labor organizations, and civil rights groups, as well as psychologists, personnel specialists, and others testified at the public hearing and meeting. The written comments, testimony, and views expressed in subsequent informal consultations have been carefully considered by the four agencies. We set forth below a summary of the comments, and the major issues raised in the comments and testimony, and attempt to explain how we have resolved those issues.

The statement submitted by the American Psychological Association (A.P.A.) stated that "these guidelines represent a major step forward and with careful interpretation can provide a sound basis for concerned professional work." Most of the A.P.A. comments were directed to clarification and interpretation of the present language of the proposal. However, the A.P.A. recommended substantive change in the construct validity section and in the definition of work behavior.

Similarly, the Division of Industrial and Organizational Psychology (division 14) of the A.P.A. described the technical standards of the guidelines as "superior" in terms of congruence with professional standards to "most previous orders and guidelines but numerous troublesome aspects remain." Division 14 had substantial concerns with a number of the provisions of the general principles of the draft.

Civil rights groups generally found the uniform guidelines far superior to the FEA guidelines, and many urged their adoption, with modifications concerning ranking and documentation. Others raised concerns about the "bottom line" concept and other provisions of the guidelines.

The Ad Hoc Group on Employee Selection Procedures representing many employers in private industry supported the concept of uniform guidelines, but had a number of problems with particular provisions, some of which are described below. The American Society for Personnel Administration (ASPA) and the International Personnel Management Association, which represents State and local governments, generally took the same position as the ad hoc group. Major industrial unions found that the draft guidelines were superior to the FEA guidelines, but they perceived them to be inferior to the EEOC guidelines. They challenged particularly the

bottom line concept and the construct validity section.

The building trade unions urged an exclusion of apprenticeship programs from coverage of the guidelines. The American Council on Education found them inappropriate for employment decisions concerning faculty at institutions of higher education. Other particular concerns were articulated by organizations representing the handicapped, licensing and certifying agencies, and college placement offices.

General Principles

1. *Relationship between validation and elimination of adverse impact, and affirmative action.* Federal equal employment opportunity law generally does not require evidence of validity for a selection procedure if there is no adverse impact; e.g., *Griggs* v. *Duke Power Co.*, 401 U.S. 424. Therefore, a user has the choice of complying either by providing evidence of validity (or otherwise justifying use in accord with Federal law), or by eliminating the adverse impact. These options have always been present under Federal law, 29 CFR 1607.3; 41 CFR 60-3.3(a); and the Federal Executive Agency Guidelines, 41 FR 51734 (November 23, 1976). The December 30 draft guidelines, however, clarified the nature of the two options open to users.

Psychologists expressed concern that the December 30 draft of section 6A encouraged the use of invalid procedures as long as there is no adverse impact. Employers added the concern that the section might encourage the use of illegal procedures not having an adverse impact against the groups who have historically suffered discrimination (minorities, women), even if they have an adverse impact on a different group (whites, males).

Section 6A was not so intended, and we have revised it to clarify the fact that illegal acts purporting to be affirmative action are not the goal of the agencies or of the guidelines; and that any employee selection procedure must be lawful and should be as job related as possible. The delineation of examples of alternative procedures was eliminated to avoid the implication that particular procedures are either prescribed or are necessarily appropriate. The basic thrust of section 6A, that elimination of adverse impact is an alternative to validation, is retained.

The inclusion of excerpts from the 1976 Equal Employment Opportunity Coordinating Council Policy Statement on Affirmative Action in section 13B of the December 30 draft was criticized as not belonging in a set of guidelines for the validation of selection procedures. Section 13 has been revised. The general statement of

policy in support of voluntary affirmative action, and the reaffirmation of the policy statement have been retained, but this statement itself is now found in the appendix to the guidelines.

2. *The "bottom line" (section 4C).* The guidelines provide that when the overall selection process does not have an adverse impact the Government will usually not examine the individual components of that process for adverse impact or evidence of validity. The concept is based upon the view that the Federal Government should not generally concern itself with individual components of a selection process, if the overall effect of that process is nonexclusionary. Many commenters criticized the ambiguity caused by the word "generally" in the December 30 draft of section 4C which provided, "the Federal enforcement agencies * * * generally will not take enforcement action based upon adverse impact of any component" of a process that does not have an overall adverse impact. Employer groups stated the position that the "bottom line" should be a rule prohibiting enforcement action by Federal agencies with respect to all or any part of a selection process where the bottom line does not show adverse impact. Civil rights and some labor union representatives expressed the opposing concerns that the concept may be too restrictive, that it may be interpreted as a matter of law, and that it might allow certain discriminatory conditions to go unremedied.

The guidelines have been revised to clarify the intent that the bottom line concept is based upon administrative and prosecutorial discretion. The Federal agencies cannot accept the recommendation that they never inquire into or take enforcement action with respect to any component procedure unless the whole process of which it is a part has an adverse impact. The Federal enforcement agencies believe that enforcement action may be warranted in unusual circumstances, such as those involving other discriminatory practices, or particular selection procedures which have no validity and have a clear adverse impact on a national basis. Other unusual circumstances may warrant a high level agency decision to proceed with enforcement actions although the "bottom line" has been satisfied. At the same time the agencies adhere to the bottom line concept of allocating resources primarily to those users whose overall selection processes have an adverse impact. See overview, above, part III.

3. *Investigation of alternative selection procedures and alternative methods of use (section 3B).* The December 30 draft included an obligation on the user, when conducting a validity

397

study, to investigate alternative procedures and uses, in order to determine whether there are other procedures which are substantially equally valid, but which have less adverse impact. The American Psychological Association stated:

"We would concur with the drafters of the guidelines that it is appropriate in the determination of a selection strategy to consider carefully a variety of possible procedures and to think carefully about the question of adverse impact with respect to each of these procedures. Nevertheless, we feel it appropriate to note that a rigid enforcement of these sections, particularly for smaller employers, would impose a substantial and expensive burden on these employers."

Since a reasonable consideration of alternatives is consistent with the underlying principle of minimizing adverse impact consistent with business needs, the provision is retained.

Private employer representatives challenged earlier drafts of these guidelines as being inconsistent with the decision of the Supreme Court in *Albemarle Paper Co.* v. *Moody*, 422 U.S. 405. No such inconsistency was intended. Accordingly, the first sentence of section 3B was revised to paraphrase the opinion in the *Albemarle* decision, so as to make it clear that section 3B is in accord with the principles of the *Albemarle* decision.

Section 3B was further revised to clarify the intent of the guidelines that the obligation to investigate alternative procedures is a part of conducting a validity study, so that alternative procedures should be evaluated in light of validity studies meeting professional standards, and that section 3B does not impose an obligation to search for alternatives if the user is not required to conduct a validity study.

Just as, under section 3B of the guidelines, a user should investigate alternative selection procedures as a part of choosing and validating a procedure, so should the user investigate alternative uses of the selection device chosen to find the use most appropriate to his needs. The validity study should address the question of what method of use (screening, grouping, or rank ordering) is appropriate for a procedure based on the kind and strength of the validity evidence shown, and the degree of adverse impact of the different uses.

4. *Establishment of cutoff scores and rank ordering.* Some commenters from civil rights groups believed that the December 30 draft guidelines did not provide sufficient guidance as to when it was permissible to use a selection procedure on a ranking basis rather than on a pass-fail basis. They also objected to section 5G in terms of setting cutoff scores. Other comments noted a lack of clarity as to how the determi-

nation of a cutoff score or the use of a procedure for ranking candidates relates to adverse impact.

As we have noted, users are not required to validate procedures which do not have an adverse impact. However, if one way of using a procedure (e.g., for ranking) results in greater adverse impact than another way (e.g., pass/fail), the procedure must be validated for that use. Similarly, cutoff scores which result in adverse impact should be justified. If the use of a validated procedure for ranking results in greater adverse impact than its use as a screening device, the evidence of validity and utility must be sufficient to warrant use of the procedures as a ranking device.

A new section 5G has been added to clarify these concepts. Section 5H (formerly section 5G) addresses the choice of a cutoff score when a procedure is to be used for ranking.

5. *Scope: Requests for exemptions for certain classes of users.* Some employer groups and labor organizations (e.g., academic institutions, large public employers, apprenticeship councils) argued that they should be exempted from all or some of the provisions of these guidelines because of their special needs. The intent of Congress as expressed in Federal equal employment opportunity law is to apply the same standards to all users, public and private.

These guidelines apply the same principles and standards to all employers. On the other hand, the nature of the procedures which will actually meet those principles and standards may be different for different employers, and the guidelines recognize that fact. Accordingly, the guidelines are applicable to all employers and other users who are covered by Federal equal employment opportunity law.

Organizations of handicapped persons objected to excluding from the scope of these guidelines the enforcement of laws prohibiting discrimination on the basis of handicap, in particular the Rehabilitation Act of 1973, sections 501, 503, and 504. While this issue has not been addressed in the guidelines, nothing precludes the adoption of the principles set forth in these guidelines for other appropriate situations.

Licensing and certification boards raised the question of the applicability of the guidelines to their licensing and certification functions. The guidelines make it clear that licensing and certification are covered "to the extent" that licensing and certification may be covered by Federal equal employment opportunity law.

Voluntary certification boards, where certification is not required by law, are not users as defined in section 16 with respect to their certifying

functions and therefore are not subject to these guidelines. If an employer relies upon such certification in making employment decisions, the employer is the user and must be prepared to justify, under Federal law, that reliance as it would any other selection procedure.

6. *The "Four-Fifths Rule of Thumb" (section 4D).* Some representatives of employers and some professionals suggest that the basic test for adverse impact should be a test of statistical significance, rather than the four-fifths rule. Some civil rights groups, on the other hand, still regard the four-fifths rule as permitting some unlawful discrimination.

The Federal agencies believe that neither of these positions is correct. The great majority of employers do not hire, promote, or assign enough employees for most jobs to warrant primary reliance upon statistical significance. Many decisions in day-to-day life are made on the basis of information which does not have the justification of a test of statistical significance. Courts have found adverse impact without a showing of statistical significance. *Griggs* v. *Duke Power Co.*, supra; *Vulcan Society of New York* v. *CSC of N.Y.*, 490 F. 2d 387, 393 (2d Cir. 1973); *Kirkland* v. *New York St. Dept. of Corr. Serv.*, 520 F. 2d 420, 425 (2d Cir. 1975).

Accordingly, the undersigned believe that while the four-fifths rule does not define discrimination and does not apply in all cases, it is appropriate as a rule of thumb in identifying adverse impact.

Technical Standards

7. *Criterion-related validity (section 14B).* This section of the guidelines found general support among the commenters from the psychological profession and, except for the provisions concerning test fairness (sometimes mistakenly equated with differential prediction or differential validity), generated relatively little comment.

The provisions of the guidelines concerning criterion-related validity studies call for studies of fairness of selection procedures where technically feasible.

Section 14B(8). Some psychologists and employer groups objected that the concept of test fairness or unfairness has been discredited by professionals and pointed out that the term is commonly misused. We recognize that there is serious debate on the question of test fairness; however, it is accepted professionally that fairness should be examined where feasible. The A.P.A. standards for educational and psychological tests, for example, direct users to explore the question of fairness on finding a difference in group performances (section E9, pp. 43-44). Similarly the concept of test fairness is one which is closely related to the basic thrust of Federal equal employment opportunity law; and that concept was endorsed by the Supreme Court in *Albemarle Paper Co. v. Moody*, 422 U.S. 405.

Accordingly, we have retained in the guidelines the obligation upon users to investigate test fairness where it is technically feasible to do so.

8. *Content validity*. The Division of Industrial and Organizational Psychology of A.P.A. correctly perceived that the provisions of the draft guidelines concerning content validity, with their emphasis on observable work behaviors or work products, were "greatly concerned with minimizing the inferential leap between test and performance." That division expressed the view that the draft guidelines neglected situations where a knowledge, skill or ability is necessary to an outcome but where the work behavior cannot be replicated in a test. They recommended that the section be revised.

We believe that the emphasis on observable work behaviors or observable work products is appropriate; and that in order to show content validity, the gap between the test and performance on the job should be a small one. We recognize, however, that content validity may be appropriate to support a test which measures a knowledge, skill, or ability which is a necessary prerequisite to the performance of the job, even though the test might not be close enough to the work behavior to be considered a work sample, and the guidelines have been revised appropriately. On the other hand, tests of mental processes which are not directly observable and which may be difficult to determine on the basis of observable work behaviors or work products should not be supported by content validity.

Thus, the Principles for the Validation and Use of Personnel Selection Procedures (Division of Industrial and Organizational Psychology, American Psychological Association, 1975, p. 10), discuss the use of content validity to support tests of "specific items of knowledge, or specific job skills," but call attention to the inappropriateness of attempting to justify tests for traits or constructs on a content validity basis.

9. *Construct validity (section 14D)*. Business groups and professionals expressed concern that the construct validity requirements in the December 30 draft were confusing and technically inaccurate. As section 14D indicates, construct validity is a relatively new procedure in the field of personnel selection and there is not yet substantial guidance in the professional literature as to its use in the area of employment practices. The provisions on construct

validity have been revised to meet the concerns expressed by the A.P.A. The construct validity section as revised clarifies what is required by the Federal enforcement agencies at this stage in the development of construct validity. The guidelines leave open the possibility that different evidence of construct validity may be accepted in the future, as new methodologies develop and become incorporated in professional standards and other professional literature.

10. *Documentation (section 15)*. Commenters stated that the documentation section did not conform to the technical requirements of the guidelines or was otherwise inadequate. Section 15 has been clarified and two significant changes have been made to minimize the recordkeeping burden. (See overview, part VIII.)

11. *Definitions (section 16)*. The definition of work behavior in the December 30, 1977 draft was criticized by the A.P.A. and others as being too vague to provide adequate guidance to those using the guidelines who must identify work behavior as a part of any validation technique. Other comments criticized the absence or inadequacies of other definitions, expecially "adverse impact." Substantial revisions of and additions to this section were therefore made.

UNIFORM GUIDELINES ON EMPLOYEE SELECTION PROCEDURES (1978)

NOTE.—These guidelines are issued jointly by four agencies. Separate official adoptions follow the guidelines in this part IV as follows: Civil Service Commission, Department of Justice, Equal Employment Opportunity Commission, Department of Labor.

For official citation see section 18 of these guidelines.

TABLE OF CONTENTS

GENERAL PRINCIPLES

Appendix 2: Uniform Selection Guidelines

(c) General Considerations in Fairness Investigations
(d) When Unfairness Is Shown
(e) Technical Feasibility of Fairness Studies
(f) Continued Use of Selection Procedures When Fairness Studies not Feasible

C. Technical Standards for Content Validity Studies
(1) Appropriateness of Content Validity Studies
(2) Job Analysis for Content Validity
(3) Development of Selection Procedure
(4) Standards For Demonstrating Content Validity
(5) Reliability
(6) Prior Training or Experience
(7) Training Success
(8) Operational Use
(9) Ranking Based on Content Validity Studies

D. Technical Standards For Construct Validity Studies
(1) Appropriateness of Construct Validity Studies
(2) Job Analysis For Construct Validity Studies
(3) Relationship to the Job
(4) Use of Construct Validity Study Without New Criterion-Related Evidence
(a) Standards for Use
(b) Determination of Common Work Behaviors

DOCUMENTATION OF IMPACT AND VALIDITY EVIDENCE

15. Documentation of Impact and Validity Evidence

A. Required Information
(1) Simplified Recordkeeping for Users With Less Than 100 Employees
(2) Information on Impact
(a) Collection of Information on Impact
(b) When Adverse Impact Has Been Eliminated in The Total Selection Process
(c) When Data Insufficient to Determine Impact
(3) Documentation of Validity Evidence
(a) Type of Evidence
(b) Form of Report
(c) Completeness

B. Criterion-Related Validity Studies
(1) User(s), Location(s), and Date(s) of Study
(2) Problem and Setting
(3) Job Analysis or Review of Job Information
(4) Job Titles and Codes
(5) Criterion Measures
(6) Sample Description
(7) Description of Selection Procedure
(8) Techniques and Results
(9) Alternative Procedures Investigated
(10) Uses and Applications
(11) Source Data
(12) Contact Person
(13) Accuracy and Completeness

C. Content Validity Studies
(1) User(s), Location(s), and Date(s) of Study
(2) Problem and Setting
(3) Job Analysis—Content of the Job
(4) Selection Procedure and its Content
(5) Relationship Between Selection Procedure and the Job
(6) Alternative Procedures Investigated
(7) Uses and Applications
(8) Contact Person
(9) Accuracy and Completeness

D. Construct Validity Studies
(1) User(s), Location(s), and Date(s) of Study
(2) Problem and Setting
(3) Construct Definition
(4) Job Analysis
(5) Job Titles and Codes
(6) Selection Procedure
(7) Relationship to Job Perfromance
(8) Alternative Procedures Investigated
(9) Uses and Applications
(10) Accuracy and Completeness
(11) Source Data
(12) Contact Person

E. Evidence of Validity from Other Studies
(1) Evidence from Criterion-Related Validity Studies
(a) Job Information
(b) Relevance of Criteria
(c) Other Variables
(d) Use of the Selection Procedure
(e) Bibliography
(2) Evidence from Content Validity Studies
(3) Evidence from Construct Validity Studies

F. Evidence of Validity from Cooperative Studies

G. Selection for Higher Level Jobs

H. Interim Use of Selection Procedures

DEFINITIONS

16. Definitions

APPENDIX

17. Policy Statement on Affirmative Action (see Section 13B)
18. Citations

GENERAL PRINCIPLES

SECTION 1. *Statement of purpose.*—A. *Need for uniformity—Issuing agencies.* The Federal government's need for a uniform set of principles on the question of the use of tests and other selection procedures has long been recognized. The Equal Employment Opportunity Commission, the Civil Service Commission, the Department of Labor, and the Department of Justice jointly have adopted these uniform guidelines to meet that need, and to apply the same principles to the Federal Government as are applied to other employers.

B. *Purpose of guidelines.* These guidelines incorporate a single set of principles which are designed to assist employers, labor organizations, employment agencies, and licensing and certification boards to comply with requirements of Federal law prohibiting employment practices which discriminate on grounds of race, color, religion, sex, and national origin. They are designed to provide a framework for determining the proper use of tests and other selection procedures. These guidelines do not require a user to conduct validity studies of selection procedures where no adverse impact results. However, all users are encouraged to use selection procedures which are valid, especially users operating under merit principles.

C. *Relation to prior guidelines.* These guidelines are based upon and supersede previously issued guidelines on employee selection procedures. These guidelines have been built upon court decisions, the previously issued guidelines of the agencies, and the practical experience of the agencies, as well as the standards of the psychological profession. These guidelines are intended to be consistent with existing law.

SEC. 2. *Scope.*—A. *Application of guidelines.* These guidelines will be applied by the Equal Employment Opportunity Commission in the enforcement of title VII of the Civil Rights Act of 1964, as amended by the Equal Employment Opportunity Act of 1972 (hereinafter "Title VII"); by the Department of Labor, and the contract compliance agencies until the transfer of authority contemplated by the President's Reorganization Plan No. 1 of 1978, in the administration and enforcement of Executive Order 11246, as amended by Executive Order 11375 (hereinafter "Executive Order 11246"); by the Civil Service Commission and other Federal agencies subject to section 717 of Title VII; by the Civil Service Commission in exercising its responsibilities toward State and local governments under section 208(b)(1) of the Intergovernmental-Personnel Act; by the Department of Justice in exercising its responsibilities under Federal law; by the Office of Revenue Sharing of the Department of the Treasury under the State and Local Fiscal Assistance Act of 1972, as amended; and by any other Federal agency which adopts them.

B. *Employment decisions.* These guidelines apply to tests and other selection procedures which are used as a basis for any employment decision. Employment decisions include but are not limited to hiring, promotion, demotion, membership (for example, in a labor organization), referral, retention, and licensing and certification, to the extent that licensing and certification may be covered by Federal equal employment opportunity law. Other selection decisions, such as selection for training or transfer, may also be considered employment decisions if they lead to any of the decisions listed above.

C. *Selection procedures.* These guidelines apply only to selection procedures which are used as a basis for making employment decisions. For example, the use of recruiting procedures designed to attract members of a particular race, sex, or ethnic group, which were previously denied employment opportunities or which are currently underutilized, may be necessary to bring an employer into compliance with Federal law, and is frequently an essential element of any effective af-

Appendix 2: Uniform Selection Guidelines

firmative action program; but recruitment practices are not considered by these guidelines to be selection procedures. Similarly, these guidelines do not pertain to the question of the lawfulness of a seniority system within the meaning of section 703(h), Executive Order 11246 or other provisions of Federal law or regulation, except to the extent that such systems utilize selection procedures to determine qualifications or abilities to perform the job. Nothing in these guidelines is intended or should be interpreted as discouraging the use of a selection procedure for the purpose of determining qualifications or for the purpose of selection on the basis of relative qualifications, if the selection procedure had been validated in accord with these guidelines for each such purpose for which it is to be used.

D. *Limitations.* These guidelines apply only to persons subject to Title VII, Executive Order 11246, or other equal employment opportunity requirements of Federal law. These guidelines do not apply to responsibilities under the Age Discrimination in Employment Act of 1967, as amended, not to discriminate on the basis of age, or under sections 501, 503, and 504 of the Rehabilitation Act of 1973, not to discriminate on the basis of handicap.

E. *Indian preference not affected.* These guidelines do not restrict any obligation imposed or right granted by Federal law to extend a preference in employment to Indians living on or near an Indian reservation in connection with employment opportunities on or near an Indian reservation.

SEC. 3. *Discrimination defined: Relationship between use of selection procedures and discrimination.—A. Procedure having adverse impact constitutes discrimination unless justified.* The use of any selection procedure which has an adverse impact on the hiring, promotion, or other employment or membership opportunities of members of any race, sex, or ethnic group will be considered to be discriminatory and inconsistent with these guidelines, unless the procedure has been validated in accordance with these guidelines, or the provisions of section 6 below are satisfied.

B. *Consideration of suitable alternative selection procedures.* Where two or more selection procedures are available which serve the user's legitimate interest in efficient and trustworthy workmanship, and which are substantially equally valid for a given purpose, the user should use the procedure which has been demonstrated to have the lesser adverse impact. Accordingly, whenever a validity study is called for by these guidelines, the user should include, as a part of the validity study, an investigation of suitable alternative selection procedures and suitable alternative methods of using the selection procedure which have as little adverse impact as possible, to determine the appropriateness of using or validating them in accord with these guidelines. If a user has made a reasonable effort to become aware of such alternative procedures and validity has been demonstrated in accord with these guidelines, the use of the test or other selection procedure may continue until such time as it should reasonably be reviewed for currency. Whenever the user is shown an alternative selection procedure with evidence of less adverse impact and substantial evidence of validity for the same job in similar circumstances, the user should investigate it to determine the appropriateness of using or validating it in accord with these guidelines. This subsection is not intended to preclude the combination of procedures into a significantly more valid procedure, if the use of such a combination has been shown to be in compliance with the guidelines.

SEC. 4. *Information on impact.—A. Records concerning impact.* Each user should maintain and have available for inspection records or other information which will disclose the impact which its tests and other selection procedures have upon employment opportunities of persons by identifiable race, sex, or ethnic group as set forth in subparagraph B below in order to determine compliance with these guidelines. Where there are large numbers of applicants and procedures are administered frequently, such information may be retained on a sample basis, provided that the sample is appropriate in terms of the applicant population and adequate in size.

B. *Applicable race, sex, and ethnic groups for recordkeeping.* The records called for by this section are to be maintained by sex, and the following races and ethnic groups: Blacks (Negroes), American Indians (including Alaskan Natives), Asians (including Pacific Islanders), Hispanic (including persons of Mexican, Puerto Rican, Cuban, Central or South American, or other Spanish origin or culture regardless of race), whites (Caucasians) other than Hispanic, and totals. The race, sex, and ethnic classifications called for by this section are consistent with the Equal Employment Opportunity Standard Form 100, Employer Information Report EEO-1 series of reports. The user should adopt safeguards to insure that the records required by this paragraph are used for appropriate purposes such as determining adverse impact, or (where required) for developing and monitoring affirmative action programs, and that such records are not used improperly. See sections 4E and 17(4), below.

C. *Evaluation of selection rates. The "bottom line."* If the information called for by sections 4A and B above shows that the total selection process for a job has an adverse impact, the individual components of the selection process should be evaluated for adverse impact. If this information shows that the total selection process does not have an adverse impact, the Federal enforcement agencies, in the exercise of their administrative and prosecutorial discretion, in usual circumstances, will not expect a user to evaluate the individual components for adverse impact, or to validate such individual components, and will not take enforcement action based upon adverse impact of any component of that process, including the separate parts of a multipart selection procedure or any separate procedure that is used as an alternative method of selection. However, in the following circumstances the Federal enforcement agencies will expect a user to evaluate the individual components for adverse impact and may, where appropriate, take enforcement action with respect to the individual components: (1) where the selection procedure is a significant factor in the continuation of patterns of assignments of incumbent employees caused by prior discriminatory employment practices, (2) where the weight of court decisions or administrative interpretations hold that a specific procedure (such as height or weight requirements or no-arrest records) is not job related in the same or similar circumstances. In unusual circumstances, other than those listed in (1) and (2) above, the Federal enforcement agencies may request a user to evaluate the individual components for adverse impact and may, where appropriate, take enforcement action with respect to the individual component.

D. *Adverse impact and the "four-fifths rule."* A selection rate for any race, sex, or ethnic group which is less than four-fifths (⅘) (or eighty percent) of the rate for the group with the highest rate will generally be regarded by the Federal enforcement agencies as evidence of adverse impact, while a greater than four-fifths rate will generally not be regarded by Federal enforcement agencies as evidence of adverse impact. Smaller differences in selection rate may nevertheless constitute adverse impact, where they are significant in both statistical and practical terms or where a user's actions have discouraged applicants disproportionately on grounds of race, sex, or ethnic group. Greater differences in selection rate may not constitute adverse impact where the differences are based on small numbers and are not statistically significant, or where special recruiting or other programs cause the pool of minority or female candidates to be atypical of the normal pool of applicants from that group. Where the user's evidence concerning the impact of a selection procedure indicates adverse impact but is based upon numbers which are too small to be reliable, evidence concerning the impact of the procedure over a longer period of time and/or evidence concerning the impact which the selection procedure had when used in the same manner in similar circumstances elsewhere may be considered in determining adverse impact. Where the user has not maintained data on adverse impact as required by the documentation section of applicable guidelines, the Federal enforcement agencies may draw an inference of adverse impact of the selection process from the failure of the user to maintain such data, if the user has an underutilization of a group in the job category, as compared to the group's representation in the relevant labor market or, in the case of jobs filled from within, the applicable work force.

E. *Consideration of user's equal employment opportunity posture.* In carrying out their obligations, the Federal enforcement agencies will consider the general posture of the user with respect to equal employment opportunity for the job or group of jobs in question. Where a user has adopted an affirmative action program, the Federal enforcement agencies will consider the provisions of that program, including the goals and timetables which the user has adopted and the progress which the user has made in carrying out that program and in meeting the goals and timetables. While such affirmative action programs may in design and execution be race, color, sex, or ethnic conscious, selection procedures under such programs should be based upon the ability or relative ability to do the work.

Sec. 5. *General standards for validity studies.*—A. *Acceptable types of validity studies.* For the purposes of satisfying these guidelines, users may rely upon criterion-related validity studies, content validity studies or construct validity studies, in accordance with the standards set forth in the technical standards of these guidelines, section 14 below. New strategies for showing the validity of selection procedures will be evaluated as they become accepted by the psychological profession.

B. *Criterion-related, content, and construct validity.* Evidence of the validity of a test or other selection procedure by a criterion-related validity study should consist of empirical data demonstrating that the selection procedure is predictive of or significantly correlated with important elements of job performance. See section 14B

below. Evidence of the validity of a test or other selection procedure by a content validity study should consist of data showing that the content of the selection procedure is representative of important aspects of performance on the job for which the candidates are to be evaluated. See section 14C below. Evidence of the validity of a test or other selection procedure through a construct validity study should consist of data showing that the procedure measures the degree to which candidates have identifiable characteristics which have been determined to be important in successful performance in the job for which the candidates are to be evaluated. See section 14D below.

C. *Guidelines are consistent with professional standards.* The provisions of these guidelines relating to validation of selection procedures are intended to be consistent with generally accepted professional standards for evaluating standardized tests and other selection procedures, such as those described in the Standards for Educational and Psychological Tests prepared by a joint committee of the American Psychological Association, the American Educational Research Association, and the National Council on Measurement in Education (American Psychological Association, Washington, D.C., 1974) (hereinafter "A.P.A. Standards") and standard textbooks and journals in the field of personnel selection.

D. *Need for documentation of validity.* For any selection procedure which is part of a selection process which has an adverse impact and which selection procedure has an adverse impact, each user should maintain and have available such documentation as is described in section 15 below.

E. *Accuracy and standardization.* Validity studies should be carried out under conditions which assure insofar as possible the adequacy and accuracy of the research and the report. Selection procedures should be administered and scored under standardized conditions.

F. *Caution against selection on basis of knowledges, skills, or ability learned in brief orientation period.* In general, users should avoid making employment decisions on the basis of measures of knowledges, skills, or abilities which are normally learned in a brief orientation period, and which have an adverse impact.

G. *Method of use of selection procedures.* The evidence of both the validity and utility of a selection procedure should support the method the user chooses for operational use of the procedure, if that method of use has a greater adverse impact than another method of use. Evidence which may be sufficient to support the use of a selec-

tion procedure on a pass/fail (screening) basis may be insufficient to support the use of the same procedure on a ranking basis under these guidelines. Thus, if a user decides to use a selection procedure on a ranking basis, and that method of use has a greater adverse impact than use on an appropriate pass/fail basis (see section 5H below), the user should have sufficient evidence of validity and utility to support the use on a ranking basis. See sections 3B, 14B (5) and (6), and 14C (8) and (9).

H. *Cutoff scores.* Where cutoff scores are used, they should normally be set so as to be reasonable and consistent with normal expectations of acceptable proficiency within the work force. Where applicants are ranked on the basis of properly validated selection procedures and those applicants scoring below a higher cutoff score are appropriate in light of such expectations have little or no chance of being selected for employment, the higher cutoff score may be appropriate, but the degree of adverse impact should be considered.

I. *Use of selection procedures for higher level jobs.* If job progression structures are so established that employees will probably, within a reasonable period of time and in a majority of cases, progress to a higher level, it may be considered that the applicants are being evaluated for a job or jobs at the higher level. However, where job progression is not so nearly automatic, or the time span is such that higher level jobs or employees' potential may be expected to change in significant ways, it should be considered that applicants are being evaluated for a job at or near the entry level. A "reasonable period of time" will vary for different jobs and employment situations but will seldom be more than 5 years. Use of selection procedures to evaluate applicants for a higher level job would not be appropriate:

(1) If the majority of those remaining employed do not progress to the higher level job;

(2) If there is a reason to doubt that the higher level job will continue to require essentially similar skills during the progression period; or

(3) If the selection procedures measure knowledges, skills, or abilities required for advancement which would be expected to develop principally from the training or experience on the job.

J. *Interim use of selection procedures.* Users may continue the use of a selection procedure which is not at the moment fully supported by the required evidence of validity, provided: (1) The user has available substantial evidence of validity, and (2) the user has in progress, when technically feasible, a study which is designed to produce the additional evidence required by these guidelines within a reasonable time. If such a study is not technically feasible, see section 6B. If the study does not demonstrate validity, this provision of these guidelines for interim use shall not constitute a defense in any action, nor shall it relieve the user of any obligations arising under Federal law.

K. *Review of validity studies for currency.* Whenever validity has been shown in accord with these guidelines for the use of a particular selection procedure for a job or group of jobs, additional studies need not be performed until such time as the validity study is subject to review as provided in section 3B above. There are no absolutes in the area of determining the currency of a validity study. All circumstances concerning the study, including the validation strategy used, and changes in the relevant labor market and the job should be considered in the determination of when a validity study is outdated.

SEC. 6. *Use of selection procedures which have not been validated.*—A. *Use of alternate selection procedures to eliminate adverse impact.* A user may choose to utilize alternative selection procedures in order to eliminate adverse impact or as part of an affirmative action program. See section 13 below. Such alternative procedures should eliminate the adverse impact in the total selection process, should be lawful and should be as job related as possible.

B. *Where validity studies cannot or need not be performed.* There are circumstances in which a user cannot or need not utilize the validation techniques contemplated by these guidelines. In such circumstances, the user should utilize selection procedures which are as job related as possible and which will minimize or eliminate adverse impact, as set forth below.

(1) *Where informal or unscored procedures are used.* When an informal or unscored selection procedure which has an adverse impact is utilized, the user should eliminate the adverse impact, or modify the procedure to one which is a formal, scored or quantified measure or combination of measures and then validate the procedure in accord with these guidelines, or otherwise justify continued use of the procedure in accord with Federal law.

(2) *Where formal and scored procedures are used.* When a formal and scored selection procedure is used which has an adverse impact, the validation techniques contemplated by these guidelines usually should be followed if technically feasible. Where the user cannot or need not follow the validation techniques anticipated by these guidelines, the user should

either modify the procedure to eliminate adverse impact or otherwise justify continued use of the procedure in accord with Federal law.

SEC. 7. *Use of other validity studies.*—A. *Validity studies not conducted by the user.* Users may, under certain circumstances, support the use of selection procedures by validity studies conducted by other users or conducted by test publishers or distributors and described in test manuals. While publishers of selection procedures have a professional obligation to provide evidence of validity which meets generally accepted professional standards (see section 5C above), users are cautioned that they are responsible for compliance with these guidelines. Accordingly, users seeking to obtain selection procedures from publishers and distributors should be careful to determine that, in the event the user becomes subject to the validity requirements of these guidelines, the necessary information to support validity has been determined and will be made available to the user.

B. *Use of criterion-related validity evidence from other sources.* Criterion-related validity studies conducted by one test user, or described in test manuals and the professional literature, will be considered acceptable for use by another user when the following requirements are met:

(1) *Validity evidence.* Evidence from the available studies meeting the standards of section 14B below clearly demonstrates that the selection procedure is valid;

(2) *Job similarity.* The incumbents in the user's job and the incumbents in the job or group of jobs on which the validity study was conducted perform substantially the same major work behaviors, as shown by appropriate job analyses both on the job or group of jobs on which the validity study was performed and on the job for which the selection procedure is to be used; and

(3) *Fairness evidence.* The studies include a study of test fairness for each race, sex, and ethnic group which constitutes a significant factor in the borrowing user's relevant labor market for the job or jobs in question. If the studies under consideration satisfy (1) and (2) above but do not contain an investigation of test fairness, and it is not technically feasible for the borrowing user to conduct an internal study of test fairness, the borrowing user may utilize the study until studies conducted elsewhere meeting the requirements of these guidelines show test unfairness, or until such time as it becomes technically feasible to conduct an internal study of test fairness and the results of that study can be acted upon. Users obtaining selection procedures from publishers should

consider, as one factor in the decision to purchase a particular selection procedure, the availability of evidence concerning test fairness.

C. *Validity evidence from multiunit study.* If validity evidence from a study covering more than one unit within an organization statisfies the requirements of section 14B below, evidence of validity specific to each unit will not be required unless there are variables which are likely to affect validity significantly.

D. *Other significant variables.* If there are variables in the other studies which are likely to affect validity significantly, the user may not rely upon such studies, but will be expected either to conduct an internal validity study or to comply with section 6 above.

SEC. 8. *Cooperative studies.*—A. *Encouragement of cooperative studies.* The agencies issuing these guidelines encourage employers, labor organizations, and employment agencies to cooperate in research, development, search for lawful alternatives, and validity studies in order to achieve procedures which are consistent with these guidelines.

B. *Standards for use of cooperative studies.* If validity evidence from a cooperative study satisfies the requirements of section 14 below, evidence of validity specific to each user will not be required unless there are variables which are likely to affect validity significantly.

SEC. 9. *No assumption of validity.*—A. *Unacceptable substitutes for evidence of validity.* Under no circumstances will the general reputation of a test or other selection procedures, its author or its publisher, or casual reports of it's validity be accepted in lieu of evidence of validity. Specifically ruled out are: assumptions of validity based on a procedure's name or descriptive labels; all forms of promotional literature; data bearing on the frequency of a procedure's usage; testimonial statements and credentials of sellers, users, or consultants; and other nonempirical or anecdotal accounts of selection practices or selection outcomes.

B. *Encouragement of professional supervision.* Professional supervision of selection activities is encouraged but is not a substitute for documented evidence of validity. The enforcement agencies will take into account the fact that a thorough job analysis was conducted and that careful development and use of a selection procedure in accordance with professional standards enhance the probability that the selection procedure is valid for the job.

SEC. 10. *Employment agencies and employment services.*—A. *Where selection procedures are devised by agency.* An employment agency, including private employment agencies and State employment agencies, which agrees to a request by an employer or labor organization to device and utilize a selection procedure should follow the standards in these guidelines for determining adverse impact. If adverse impact exists the agency should comply with these guidelines. An employment agency is not relieved of its obligation herein because the user did not request such validation or has requested the use of some lesser standard of validation than is provided in these guidelines. The use of an employment agency does not relieve an employer or labor organization or other user of its responsibilities under Federal law to provide equal employment opportunity or its obligations as a user under these guidelines.

B. *Where selection procedures are devised elsewhere.* Where an employment agency or service is requested to administer a selection procedure which has been devised elsewhere and to make referrals pursuant to the results, the employment agency or service should maintain and have available evidence of the impact of the selection and referral procedures which it administers. If adverse impact results the agency or service should comply with these guidelines. If the agency or service seeks to comply with these guidelines by reliance upon validity studies or other data in the possession of the employer, it should obtain and have available such information.

SEC. 11. *Disparate treatment.* The principles of disparate or unequal treatment must be distinguished from the concepts of validation. A selection procedure—even though validated against job performance in accordance with these guidelines—cannot be imposed upon members of a race, sex, or ethnic group where other employees, applicants, or members have not been subjected to that standard. Disparate treatment occurs where members of a race, sex, or ethnic group have been denied the same employment, promotion, membership, or other employment opportunities as have been available to other employees or applicants. Those employees or applicants who have been denied equal treatment, because of prior discriminatory practices or policies, must at least be afforded the same opportunities as had existed for other employees or applicants during the period of discrimination. Thus, the persons who were in the class of persons discriminated against during the period the user followed the discriminatory practices should be allowed the opportunity to qualify under less stringent selection procedures previously followed, unless the user demonstrates that the increased standards are required by business necessity. This section does not prohibit

a user who has not previously followed merit standards from adopting merit standards which are in compliance with these guidelines; nor does it preclude a user who has previously used invalid or unvalidated selection procedures from developing and using procedures which are in accord with these guidelines.

SEC. 12. *Retesting of applicants.* Users should provide a reasonable opportunity for retesting and reconsideration. Where examinations are administered periodically with public notice, such reasonable opportunity exists, unless persons who have previously been tested are precluded from retesting. The user may however take reasonable steps to preserve the security of its procedures.

SEC. 13. *Affirmative action.*—A. *Affirmative action obligations.* The use of selection procedures which have been validated pursuant to these guidelines does not relieve users of any obligations they may have to undertake affirmative action to assure equal employment opportunity. Nothing in these guidelines is intended to preclude the use of lawful selection procedures which assist in remedying the effects of prior discriminatory practices, or the achievement of affirmative action objectives.

B. *Encouragement of voluntary affirmative action programs.* These guidelines are also intended to encourage the adoption and implementation of voluntary affirmative action programs by users who have no obligation under Federal law to adopt them; but are not intended to impose any new obligations in that regard. The agencies issuing and endorsing these guidelines endorse for all private employers and reaffirm for all governmental employers the Equal Employment Opportunity Coordinating Council's "Policy Statement on Affirmative Action Programs for State and Local Government Agencies" (41 FR 38814, September 13, 1976)." That policy statement is attached hereto as appendix, section 17.

TECHNICAL STANDARDS

SEC. 14. *Technical standards for validity studies.* The following minimum standards, as applicable, should be met in conducting a validity study. Nothing in these guidelines is intended to preclude the development and use of other professionally acceptable techniques with respect to validation of selection procedures. Where it is not technically feasible for a user to conduct a validity study, the user has the obligation otherwise to comply with these guidelines. See sections 6 and 7 above.

A. *Validity studies should be based on review of information about the job.* Any validity study should be

based upon a review of information about the job for which the selection procedure is to be used. The review should include a job analysis except as provided in section 14B(3) below with respect to criterion-related validity. Any method of job analysis may be used if it provides the information required for the specific validation strategy used.

B. *Technical standards for criterion-related validity studies.*—(1) *Technical feasibility.* Users choosing to validate a selection procedure by a criterion-related validity strategy should determine whether it is technically feasible (as defined in section 16) to conduct such a study in the particular employment context. The determination of the number of persons necessary to permit the conduct of a meaningful criterion-related study should be made by the user on the basis of all relevant information concerning the selection procedure, the potential sample and the employment situation. Where appropriate, jobs with substantially the same major work behaviors may be grouped together for validity studies, in order to obtain an adequate sample. These guidelines do not require a user to hire or promote persons for the purpose of making it possible to conduct a criterion-related study.

(2) *Analysis of the job.* There should be a review of job information to determine measures of work behavior(s) or performance that are relevant to the job or group of jobs in question. These measures or criteria are relevant to the extent that they represent critical or important job duties, work behaviors or work outcomes as developed from the review of job information. The possibility of bias should be considered both in selection of the criterion measures and their application. In view of the possibility of bias in subjective evaluations, supervisory rating techniques and instructions to raters should be carefully developed. All criterion measures and the methods for gathering data need to be examined for freedom from factors which would unfairly alter scores of members of any group. The relevance of criteria and their freedom from bias are of particular concern when there are significant differences in measures of job performance for different groups.

(3) *Criterion measures.* Proper safeguards should be taken to insure that scores on selection procedures do not enter into any judgments of employee adequacy that are to be used as criterion measures. Whatever criteria are used should represent important or critical work behavior(s) or work outcomes. Certain criteria may be used without a full job analysis if the user can show the importance of the criteria to the particular employment con-

text. These criteria include but are not limited to production rate, error rate, tardiness, absenteeism, and length of service. A standardized rating of overall work performance may be used where a study of the job shows that it is an appropriate criterion. Where performance in training is used as a criterion, success in training should be properly measured and the relevance of the training should be shown either through a comparsion of the content of the training program with the critical or important work behavior(s) of the job(s), or through a demonstration of the relationship between measures of performance in training and measures of job performance. Measures of relative success in training include but are not limited to instructor evaluations, performance samples, or tests. Criterion measures consisting of paper and pencil tests will be closely reviewed for job relevance.

(4) *Representativeness of the sample.* Whether the study is predictive or concurrent, the sample subjects should insofar as feasible be representative of the candidates normally available in the relevant labor market for the job or group of jobs in question, and should insofar as feasible include the races, sexes, and ethnic groups normally available in the relevant job market. In determining the representativeness of the sample in a concurrent validity study, the user should take into account the extent to which the specific knowledges or skills which are the primary focus of the test are those which employees learn on the job.

Where samples are combined or compared, attention should be given to see that such samples are comparable in terms of the actual job they perform, the length of time on the job where time on the job is likely to affect performance, and other relevant factors likely to affect validity differences; or that these factors are included in the design of the study and their effects identified.

(5) *Statistical relationships.* The degree of relationship between selection procedure scores and criterion measures should be examined and computed, using professionally acceptable statistical procedures. Generally, a selection procedure is considered related to the criterion, for the purposes of these guidelines, when the relationship between performance on the procedure and performance on the criterion measure is statistically significant at the 0.05 level of significance, which means that it is sufficiently high as to have a probability of no more than one (1) in twenty (20) to have occurred by chance. Absence of a statistically significant relationship between a selection procedure and job performance should not necessarily discourage

other investigations of the validity of that selection procedure.

(6) *Operational use of selection procedures.* Users should evaluate each selection procedure to assure that it is appropriate for operational use, including establishment of cutoff scores or rank ordering. Generally, if other factors reman the same, the greater the magnitude of the relationship (e.g., coorelation coefficient) between performance on a selection procedure and one or more criteria of performance on the job, and the greater the importance and number of aspects of job performance covered by the criteria, the more likely it is that the procedure will be appropriate for use. Reliance upon a selection procedure which is significantly related to a criterion measure, but which is based upon a study involving a large number of subjects and has a low correlation coefficient will be subject to close review if it has a large adverse impact. Sole reliance upon a single selection instrument which is related to only one of many job duties or aspects of job performance will also be subject to close review. The appropriateness of a selection procedure is best evaluated in each particular situation and there are no minimum correlation coefficients applicable to all employment situations. In determining whether a selection procedure is appropriate for operational use the following considerations should also be taken into account: The degree of adverse impact of the procedure, the availability of other selection procedures of greater or substantially equal validity.

(7) *Overstatement of validity findings.* Users should avoid reliance upon techniques which tend to overestimate validity findings as a result of capitalization on chance unless an appropriate safeguard is taken. Reliance upon a few selection procedures or criteria of successful job performance when many selection procedures or criteria of performance have been studied, or the use of optimal statistical weights for selection procedures computed in one sample, are techniques which tend to inflate validity estimates as a result of chance. Use of a large sample is one safeguard: cross-validation is another.

(8) *Fairness.* This section generally calls for studies of unfairness where technically feasible. The concept of fairness or unfairness of selection procedures is a developing concept. In addition, fairness studies generally require substantial numbers of employees in the job or group of jobs being studied. For these reasons, the Federal enforcement agencies recognize that the obligation to conduct studies of fairness imposed by the guidelines generally will be upon users or groups of users with a large number of persons in a a job class, or test developers;

and that small users utilizing their own selection procedures will generally not be obligated to conduct such studies because it will be technically infeasible for them to do so.

(a) *Unfairness defined.* When members of one race, sex, or ethnic group characteristically obtain lower scores on a selection procedure than members of another group, and the differences in scores are not reflected in differences in a measure of job performance, use of the selection procedure may unfairly deny opportunities to members of the group that obtains the lower scores.

(b) *Investigation of fairness.* Where a selection procedure results in an adverse impact on a race, sex, or ethnic group identified in accordance with the classifications set forth in section 4 above and that group is a significant factor in the relevant labor market, the user generally should investigate the possible existence of unfairness for that group if it is technically feasible to do so. The greater the severity of the adverse impact on a group, the greater the need to investigate the possible existence of unfairness. Where the weight of evidence from other studies shows that the selection procedure predicts fairly for the group in question and for the same or similar jobs, such evidence may be relied on in connection with the selection procedure at issue.

(c) *General considerations in fairness investigations.* Users conducting a study of fairness should review the A.P.A. Standards regarding investigation of possible bias in testing. An investigation of fairness of a selection procedure depends on both evidence of validity and the manner in which the selection procedure is to be used in a particular employment context. Fairness of a selection procedure cannot necessarily be specified in advance without investigating these factors. Investigation of fairness of a selection procedure in samples where the range of scores on selection procedures or criterion measures is severely restricted for any subgroup sample (as compared to other subgroup samples) may produce misleading evidence of unfairness. That factor should accordingly be taken into account in conducting such studies and before reliance is placed on the results.

(d) *When unfairness is shown.* If unfairness is demonstrated through a showing that members of a particular group perform better or poorer on the job than their scores on the selection procedure would indicate through comparison with how members of other groups perform, the user may either revise or replace the selection instrument in accordance with these guidelines, or may continue to use the selection instrument operationally

405

with appropriate revisions in its use to assure compatibility between the probability of successful job performance and the probability of being selected.

(e) *Technical feasibility of fairness studies.* In addition to the general conditions needed for technical feasibility for the conduct of a criterion-related study (see section 16, below) an investigation of fairness requires the following:

(i) An adequate sample of persons in each group available for the study to achieve findings of statistical significance. Guidelines do not require a user to hire or promote persons on the basis of group classifications for the purpose of making it possible to conduct a study of fairness; but the user has the obligation otherwise to comply with these guidelines.

(ii) The samples for each group should be comparable in terms of the actual job they perform, length of time on the job where time on the job is likely to affect performance, and other relevant factors likely to affect validity differences; or such factors should be included in the design of the study and their effects identified.

(f) *Continued use of selection procedures when fairness studies not feasible.* If a study of fairness should otherwise be performed, but is not technically feasible, a selection procedure may be used which has otherwise met the validity standards of these guidelines, unless the technical infeasibility resulted from discriminatory employment practices which are demonstrated by facts other than past failure to conform with requirements for validation of selection procedures. However, when it becomes technically feasible for the user to perform a study of fairness and such a study is otherwise called for, the user should conduct the study of fairness.

C. *Technical standards for content validity studies.*—(1) *Appropriateness of content validity studies.* Users choosing to validate a selection procedure by a content validity strategy should determine whether it is appropriate to conduct such a study in the particular employment context. A selection procedure can be supported by a content validity strategy to the extent that it is a representative sample of the content of the job. Selection procedures which purport to measure knowledges, skills, or abilities may in certain circumstances be justified by content validity, although they may not be representative samples, if the knowledge, skill, or ability measured by the selection procedure can be operationally defined as provided in section 14C(4) below, and if that knowledge, skill, or ability is a necessary prerequisite to successful job performance.

A selection procedure based upon inferences about mental processes cannot be supported solely or primarily on the basis of content validity. Thus, a content strategy is not appropriate for demonstrating the validity of selection procedures which purport to measure traits or constructs, such as intelligence, aptitude, personality, commonsense, judgment, leadership, and spatial ability. Content validity is also not an appropriate strategy when the selection procedure involves knowledges, skills, or abilities which an employee will be expected to learn on the job.

(2) *Job analysis for content validity.* There should be a job analysis which includes an analysis of the important work behavior(s) required for successful performance and their relative importance and, if the behavior results in work product(s), an analysis of the work product(s). Any job analysis should focus on the work behavior(s) and the tasks associated with them. If work behavior(s) are not observable, the job analysis should identify and analyze those aspects of the behavior(s) that can be observed and the observed work products. The work behavior(s) selected for measurement should be critical work behavior(s) and/or important work behavior(s) constituting most of the job.

(3) *Development of selection procedures.* A selection procedure designed to measure the work behavior may be developed specifically from the job and job analysis in question, or may have been previously developed by the user, or by other users or by a test publisher.

(4) *Standards for demonstrating content validity.* To demonstrate the content validity of a selection procedure, a user should show that the behavior(s) demonstrated in the selection procedure are a representative sample of the behavior(s) of the job in question or that the selection procedure provides a representative sample of the work product of the job. In the case of a selection procedure measuring a knowledge, skill, or ability, the knowledge, skill, or ability being measured should be operationally defined. In the case of a selection procedure measuring a knowledge, the knowledge being measured should be operationally defined as that body of learned information which is used in and is a necessary prerequisite for observable aspects of work behavior of the job. In the case of skills or abilities, the skill or ability being measured should be operationally defined in terms of observable aspects of work behavior of the job. For any selection procedure measuring a knowledge, skill, or ability the user should show that (a) the selection procedure measures and is a representative sample of that knowl-

edge, skill, or ability; and (b) that knowledge, skill, or ability is used in and is a necessary prerequisite to performance of critical or important work behavior(s). In addition, to be content valid, a selection procedure measuring a skill or ability should either closely approximate an observable work behavior, or its product should closely approximate an observable work product. If a test purports to sample a work behavior or to provide a sample of a work product, the manner and setting of the selection procedure and its level and complexity should closely approximate the work situation. The closer the content and the context of the selection procedure are to work samples or work behaviors, the stronger is the basis for showing content validity. As the content of the selection procedure less resembles a work behavior, or the setting and manner of the administration of the selection procedure less resemble the work situation, or the result less resembles a work product, the less likely the selection procedure is to be content valid, and the greater the need for other evidence of validity.

(5) *Reliability.* The reliability of selection procedures justified on the basis of content validity should be a matter of concern to the user. Whenever it is feasible, appropriate statistical estimates should be made of the reliability of the selection procedure.

(6) *Prior training or experience.* A requirement for or evaluation of specific prior training or experience based on content validity, including a specification of level or amount of training or experience, should be justified on the basis of the relationship between the content of the training or experience and the content of the job for which the training or experience is to be required or evaluated. The critical consideration is the resemblance between the specific behaviors, products, knowledges, skills, or abilities in the experience or training and the specific behaviors, products, knowledges, skills, or abilities required on the job, whether or not there is close resemblance between the experience or training as a whole and the job as a whole.

(7) *Content validity of training success.* Where a measure of success in a training program is used as a selection procedure and the content of a training program is justified on the basis of content validity, the use should be justified on the relationship between content of the training program and the content of the job.

(8) *Operational use.* A selection procedure which is supported on the basis of content validity may be used for a job if it represents a critical work behavior (i.e., a behavior which is necessary for performance of the job) or

work behaviors which constitute most of the important parts of the job.

(9) *Ranking based on content validity studies.* If a user can show, by a job analysis or otherwise, that a higher score on a content valid selection procedure is likely to result in better job performance, the results may be used to rank persons who score above minimum levels. Where a selection procedure supported solely or primarily by content validity is used to rank job candidates, the selection procedure should measure those aspects of performance which differentiate among levels of job performance.

D. *Technical standards for construct validity studies.*— (1) *Appropriateness of construct validity studies.* Construct validity is a more complex strategy than either criterion-related or content validity. Construct validation is a relatively new and developing procedure in the employment field, and there is at present a lack of substantial literature extending the concept to employment practices. The user should be aware that the effort to obtain sufficient empirical support for construct validity is both an extensive and arduous effort involving a series of research studies, which include criterion related validity studies and which may include content validity studies. Users choosing to justify use of a selection procedure by this strategy should therefore take particular care to assure that the validity study meets the standards set forth below.

(2) *Job analysis for construct validity studies.* There should be a job analysis. This job analysis should show the work behavior(s) required for successful performance of the job, or the groups of jobs being studied, the critical or important work behavior(s) in the job or group of jobs being studied, and an identification of the construct(s) believed to underlie successful performance of these critical or important work behaviors in the job or jobs in question. Each construct should be named and defined, so as to distinguish it from other constructs. If a group of jobs is being studied the jobs should have in common one or more critical or important work behaviors at a comparable level of complexity.

(3) *Relationship to the job.* A selection procedure should then be identified or developed which measures the construct identified in accord with subparagraph (2) above. The user should show by empirical evidence that the selection procedure is validly related to the construct and that the construct is validly related to the performance of critical or important work behavior(s). The relationship between the construct as measured by the selection procedure and the related work behavior(s) should be supported by

empirical evidence from one or more criterion-related studies involving the job or jobs in question which satisfy the provisions of section 14B above.

(4) *Use of construct validity study without new criterion-related evidence.*—(a) *Standards for use.* Until such time as professional literature provides more guidance on the use of construct validity in employment situations, the Federal agencies will accept a claim of construct validity without a criterion-related study which satisfies section 14B above only when the selection procedure has been used elsewhere in a situation in which a criterion-related study has been conducted and the use of a criterion-related validity study in this context meets the standards for transportability of criterion-related validity studies as set forth above in section 7. However, if a study pertains to a number of jobs having common critical or important work behaviors at a comparable level of complexity, and the evidence satisfies subparagraphs 14B (2) and (3) above for those jobs with criterion-related validity evidence for those jobs, the selection procedure may be used for all the jobs to which the study pertains. If construct validity is to be generalized to other jobs or groups of jobs not in the group studied, the Federal enforcement agencies will expect at a minimum additional empirical research evidence meeting the standards of subparagraphs section 14B (2) and (3) above for the additional jobs or groups of jobs.

(b) *Determination of common work behaviors.* In determining whether two or more jobs have one or more work behavior(s) in common, the user should compare the observed work behavior(s) in each of the jobs and should compare the observed work product(s) in each of the jobs. If neither the observed work behavior(s) in each of the jobs nor the observed work product(s) in each of the jobs are the same, the Federal enforcement agencies will presume that the work behavior(s) in each job are different. If the work behaviors are not observable, then evidence of similarity of work products and any other relevant research evidence will be considered in determining whether the work behavior(s) in the two jobs are the same.

DOCUMENTATION OF IMPACT AND VALIDITY EVIDENCE

SEC. 15. *Documentation of impact and validity evidence.*—A. *Required information.* Users of selection procedures other than those users complying with section 15A(1) below should maintain and have available for each job information on adverse impact of the selection process for that job and, where it is determined a selection

process has an adverse impact, evidence of validity as set forth below.

(1) *Simplified recordkeeping for users with less than 100 employees.* In order to minimize recordkeeping burdens on employers who employ one hundred (100) or fewer employees, and other users not required to file EEO-1, et seq., reports, such users may satisfy the requirements of this section 15 if they maintain and have available records showing, for each year:

(a) The number of persons hired, promoted, and terminated for each job, by sex, and where appropriate by race and national origin;

(b) The number of applicants for hire and promotion by sex and where appropriate by race and national origin; and

(c) The selection procedures utilized (either standardized or not standardized).

These records should be maintained for each race or national origin group (see section 4 above) constituting more than two percent (2%) of the labor force in the relevant labor area. However, it is not necessary to maintain records by race and/or national origin (see § 4 above) if one race or national origin group in the relevant labor area constitutes more than ninety-eight percent (98%) of the labor force in the area. If the user has reason to believe that a selection procedure has an adverse impact, the user should maintain any available evidence of validity for that procedure (see sections 7A and 8).

(2) *Information on impact.*—(a) Collection of information on impact. Users of selection procedures other than those complying with section 15A(1) above should maintain and have available for each job records or other information showing whether the total selection process for that job has an adverse impact on any of the groups for which records are called for by sections 4B above. Adverse impact determinations should be made at least annually for each such group which constitutes at least 2 percent of the labor force in the relevant labor area or 2 percent of the applicable workforce. Where a total selection process for a job has an adverse impact, the user should maintain and have available records or other information showing which components have an adverse impact. Where the total selection process for a job does not have an adverse impact, information need not be maintained for individual components except in circumstances set forth in subsection 15A(2)(b) below. If the determination of adverse impact is made using a procedure other than the "four-fifths rule," as defined in the first sentence of section 4D above, a justification, consistent with section 4D above, for

the procedure used to determine adverse impact should be available.

(b) *When adverse impact has been eliminated in the total selection process.* Whenever the total selection process for a particular job has had an adverse impact, as defined in section 4 above, in any year, but no longer has an adverse impact, the user should maintain and have available the information on individual components of the selection process required in the preceding paragraph for the period in which there was adverse impact. In addition, the user should continue to collect such information for at least two (2) years after the adverse impact has been eliminated.

(c) *When data insufficient to determine impact.* Where there has been an insufficient number of selections to determine whether there is an adverse impact of the total selection process for a particular job, the user should continue to collect, maintain and have available the information on individual components of the selection process required in section 15(A)(2)(a) above until the information is sufficient to determine that the overall selection process does not have an adverse impact as defined in section 4 above, or until the job has changed substantially.

(3) *Documentation of validity evidence.*—(a) *Types of evidence.* Where a total selection process has an adverse impact (see section 4 above) the user should maintain and have available for each component of that process which has an adverse impact, one or more of the following types of documentation evidence:

(i) Documentation evidence showing criterion-related validity of the selection procedure (see section 15B, below).

(ii) Documentation evidence showing content validity of the selection procedure (see section 15C, below).

(iii) Documentation evidence showing construct validity of the selection procedure (see section 15D, below).

(iv) Documentation evidence from other studies showing validity of the selection procedure in the user's facility (see section 15E, below).

(v) Documentation evidence why a validity study cannot or need not be performed and why continued use of the procedure is consistent with Federal law.

(b) *Form of report.* This evidence should be compiled in a reasonably complete and organized manner to permit direct evaluation of the validity of the selection procedure. Previously written employer or consultant reports of validity, or reports describing validity studies completed before the issuance of these guidelines are acceptable if they are complete in regard to the documentation requirements contained in this section, or if they satisfied requirements of guidelines which were in effect when the validity study was completed. If they are not complete, the required additional documentation should be appended. If necessary information is not available the report of the validity study may still be used as documentation, but its adequacy will be evaluated in terms of compliance with the requirements of these guidelines.

(c) *Completeness.* In the event that evidence of validity is reviewed by an enforcement agency, the validation reports completed after the effective date of these guidelines are expected to contain the information set forth below. Evidence denoted by use of the word "(Essential)" is considered critical. If information denoted essential is not included, the report will be considered incomplete unless the user affirmatively demonstrates either its unavailability due to circumstances beyond the user's control or special circumstances of the user's study which make the information irrelevant. Evidence not so denoted is desirable but its absence will not be a basis for considering a report incomplete. The user should maintain and have available the information called for under the heading "Source Data" in sections 15B(11) and 15D(11). While it is a necessary part of the study, it need not be submitted with the report. All statistical results should be organized and presented in tabular or graphic form to the extent feasible.

B. *Criterion-related validity studies.* Reports of criterion-related validity for a selection procedure should include the following information:

(1) *User(s), location(s), and date(s) of study.* Dates and location(s) of the job analysis or review of job information, the date(s) and location(s) of the administration of the selection procedures and collection of criterion data, and the time between collection of data on selection procedures and criterion measures should be provided (Essential). If the study was conducted at several locations, the address of each location, including city and State, should be shown.

(2) *Problem and setting.* An explicit definition of the purpose(s) of the study and the circumstances in which the study was conducted should be provided. A description of existing selection procedures and cutoff scores, if any, should be provided.

(3) *Job analysis or review of job information.* A description of the procedure used to analyze the job or group of jobs, or to review the job information should be provided (Essential). Where a review of job information results in criteria which may be used without a full job analysis (see section 14B(3)), the basis for the selection of these criteria should be reported (Essential). Where a job analysis is required a complete description of the work behavior(s) or work outcome(s), and measures of their criticality or importance should be provided (Essential). The report should describe the basis on which the behavior(s) or outcome(s) were determined to be critical or important, such as the proportion of time spent on the respective behaviors, their level of difficulty, their frequency of performance, the consequences of error, or other appropriate factors (Essential). Where two or more jobs are grouped for a validity study, the information called for in this subsection should be provided for each of the jobs, and the justification for the grouping (see section 14B(1)) should be provided (Essential).

(4) *Job titles and codes.* It is desirable to provide the user's job title(s) for the job(s) and the corresponding job title(s) and code(s) from U.S. Employment Service's Dictionary of Occupational Titles.

(5) *Criterion measures.* The bases for the selection of the criterion measures should be provided, together with references to the evidence considered in making the selection of criterion measures (essential). A full description of all criteria on which data were collected and means by which they were observed, recorded, evaluated, and quantified, should be provided (essential). If rating techniques are used as criterion measures, the appraisal form(s) and instructions to the rater(s) should be included as part of the validation evidence, or should be explicitly described and available (essential). All steps taken to insure that criterion measures are free from factors which would unfairly alter the scores of members of any group should be described (essential).

(6) *Sample description.* A description of how the research sample was identified and selected should be included (essential). The race, sex, and ethnic composition of the sample, including those groups set forth in section 4A above, should be described (essential). This description should include the size of each subgroup (essential). A description of how the research sample compares with the relevant labor market or work force, the method by which the relevant labor market or work force was defined, and a discussion of the likely effects on validity of differences between the sample and the relevant labor market or work force, are also desirable. Descriptions of educational levels, length of service, and age are also desirable.

(7) *Description of selection procedures.* Any measure, combination of measures, or procedure studied should be completely and explicitly described or attached (essential). If commercial-

ly available selection procedures are studied, they should be described by title, form, and publisher (essential). Reports of reliability estimates and how they were established are desirable.

(8) *Techniques and results.* Methods used in analyzing data should be described (essential). Measures of central tendency (e.g., means) and measures of dispersion (e.g., standard deviations and ranges) for all selection procedures and all criteria should be reported for each race, sex, and ethnic group, which constitutes a significant factor in the relevant labor market (essential). The magnitude and direction of all relationships between selection procedures and criterion measures investigated should be reported for each relevant race, sex, and ethnic group and for the total group (essential). Where groups are too small to obtain reliable evidence of the magnitude of the relationship, need not be reported separately. Statements regarding the statistical significance of results should be made (essential). Any statistical adjustments, such as for less then perfect reliability or for restriction of score range in the selection procedure or criterion should be described and explained; and uncorrected correlation coefficients should also be shown (essential). Where the statistical technique categorizes continuous data, such as biserial correlation and the phi coefficient, the categories and the bases on which they were determined should be described and explained (essential). Studies of test fairness should be included where called for by the requirements of section 14B(8) (essential). These studies should include the rationale by which a selection procedure was determined to be fair to the group(s) in question. Where test fairness or unfairness has been demonstrated on the basis of other studies, a bibliography of the relevant studies should be included (essential). If the bibliography includes unpublished studies, copies of these studies, or adequate abstracts or summaries, should be attached (essential). Where revisions have been made in a selection procedure to assure compatability between successful job performance and the probability of being selected, the studies underlying such revisions should be included (essential). All statistical results should be organized and presented by relevant race, sex, and ethnic group (essential).

(9) *Alternative procedures investigated.* The selection procedures investigated and available evidence of their impact should be identified (essential). The scope, method, and findings of the investigation, and the conclusions reached in light of the findings, should be fully described (essential).

(10) *Uses and applications.* The methods considered for use of the selection procedure (e.g., as a screening device with a cutoff score, for grouping or ranking, or combined with other procedures in a battery) and available evidence of their impact should be described (essential). This description should include the rationale for choosing the method for operational use, and the evidence of the validity and utility of the procedure as it is to be used (essential). The purpose for which the procedure is to be used (e.g., hiring, transfer, promotion) should be described (essential). If weights are assigned to different parts of the selection procedure, these weights and the validity of the weighted composite should be reported (essential). If the selection procedure is used with a cutoff score, the user should describe the way in which normal expectations of proficiency within the work force were determined and the way in which the cutoff score was determined (essential).

(11) *Source data.* Each user should maintain records showing all pertinent information about individual sample members and raters where they are used, in studies involving the validation of selection procedures. These records should be made available upon request of a compliance agency. In the case of individual sample members these data should include scores on the selection procedure(s), scores on criterion measures, age, sex, race, or ethnic group status, and experience on the specific job on which the validation study was conducted, and may also include such things as education, training, and prior job experience, but should not include names and social security numbers. Records should be maintained which show the ratings given to each sample member by each rater.

(12) *Contact person.* The name, mailing address, and telephone number of the person who may be contacted for further information about the validity study should be provided (essential).

(13) *Accuracy and completeness.* The report should describe the steps taken to assure the accuracy and completeness of the collection, analysis, and report of data and results.

C. *Content validity studies.* Reports of content validity for a selection procedure should include the following information:

(1) *User(s), location(s) and date(s) of study.* Dates and location(s) of the job analysis should be shown (essential).

(2) *Problem and setting.* An explicit definition of the purpose(s) of the study and the circumstances in which the study was conducted should be provided. A description of existing selection procedures and cutoff scores, if any, should be provided.

(3) *Job analysis—Content of the job.* A description of the method used to analyze the job should be provided (essential). The work behavior(s), the associated tasks, and, if the behavior results in a work product, the work products should be completely described (essential). Measures of criticality and/or importance of the work behavior(s) and the method of determining these measures should be provided (essential). Where the job analysis also identified the knowledges, skills, and abilities used in work behavior(s), an operational definition for each knowledge in terms of a body of learned information and for each skill and ability in terms of observable behaviors and outcomes, and the relationship between each knowledge, skill, or ability and each work behavior, as well as the method used to determine this relationship, should be provided (essential). The work situation should be described, including the setting in which work behavior(s) are performed, and where appropriate, the manner in which knowledges, skills, or abilities are used, and the complexity and difficulty of the knowledge, skill, or ability as used in the work behavior(s).

(4) *Selection procedure and its content.* Selection procedures, including those constructed by or for the user, specific training requirements, composites of selection procedures, and any other procedure supported by content validity, should be completely and explicitly described or attached (essential). If commercially available selection procedures are used, they should be described by title, form, and publisher (essential). The behaviors measured or sampled by the selection procedure should be explicitly described (essential). Where the selection procedure purports to measure a knowledge, skill, or ability, evidence that the selection procedure measures and is a representative sample of the knowledge, skill, or ability should be provided (essential).

(5) *Relationship between the selection procedure and the job.* The evidence demonstrating that the selection procedure is a representative work sample, a representative sample of the work behavior(s), or a representative sample of a knowledge, skill, or ability as used as a part of a work behavior and necessary for that behavior should be provided (essential). The user should identify the work behavior(s) which each item or part of the selection procedure is intended to sample or measure (essential). Where the selection procedure purports to sample a work behavior or to provide a sample of a work product, a comparison should be provided of the manner, setting, and the level of complexity of the selection procedure with those of

the work situation (essential). If any steps were taken to reduce adverse impact on a race, sex, or ethnic group in the content of the procedure or in its administration, these steps should be described. Establishment of time limits, if any, and how these limits are related to the speed with which duties must be performed on the job, should be explained. Measures of central tend- ency (e.g., means) and measures of dispersion (e.g., standard deviations) and estimates of realibility should be reported for all selection procedures if available. Such reports should be made for relevant race, sex, and ethnic subgroups, at least on a statistically reliable sample basis.

(6) *Alternative procedures investigated.* The alternative selection procedures investigated and available evidence of their impact should be identified (essential). The scope, method, and findings of the investigation, and the conclusions reached in light of the findings, should be fully described (essential).

(7) *Uses and applications.* The methods considered for use of the selection procedure (e.g., as a screening device with a cutoff score, for grouping or ranking, or combined with other procedures in a battery) and available evidence of their impact should be described (essential). This description should include the rationale for choosing the method for operational use, and the evidence of the validity and utility of the procedure as it is to be used (essential). The purpose for which the procedure is to be used (e.g., hiring, transfer, promotion) should be described (essential). If the selection procedure is used with a cutoff score, the user should describe the way in which normal expectations of proficiency within the work force were determined and the way in which the cutoff score was determined (essential). In addition, if the selection procedure is to be used for ranking, the user should specify the evidence showing that a higher score on the selection procedure is likely to result in better job performance.

(8) *Contact person.* The name, mailing address, and telephone number of the person who may be contacted for further information about the validity study should be provided (essential).

(9) *Accuracy and completeness.* The report should describe the steps taken to assure the accuracy and completeness of the collection, analysis, and report of data and results.

D. *Construct validity studies.* Reports of construct validity for a selection procedure should include the following information:

(1) *User(s), location(s), and date(s) of study.* Date(s) and location(s) of the job analysis and the gathering of other evidence called for by these guidelines should be provided (essential).

(2) *Problem and setting.* An explicit definition of the purpose(s) of the study and the circumstances in which the study was conducted should be provided. A description of existing selection procedures and cutoff scores, if any, should be provided.

(3) *Construct definition.* A clear definition of the construct(s) which are believed to underlie successful performance of the critical or important work behavior(s) should be provided (essential). This definition should include the levels of construct performance relevant to the job(s) for which the selection procedure is to be used (essential). There should be a summary of the position of the construct in the psychological literature, or in the absence of such a position, a description of the way in which the definition and measurement of the construct was developed and the psychological theory underlying it (essential). Any quantitative data which identify or define the job constructs, such as factor analyses, should be provided (essential).

(4) *Job analysis.* A description of the method used to analyze the job should be provided (essential). A complete description of the work behavior(s) and, to the extent appropriate, work outcomes and measures of their criticality and/or importance should be provided (essential). The report should also describe the basis on which the behavior(s) or outcomes were determined to be important, such as their level of difficulty, their frequency of performance, the consequences of error or other appropriate factors (essential). Where jobs are grouped or compared for the purposes of generalizing validity evidence, the work behavior(s) and work product(s) for each of the jobs should be described, and conclusions concerning the similarity of the jobs in terms of observable work behaviors or work products should be made (essential).

(5) *Job titles and codes.* It is desirable to provide the selection procedure user's job title(s) for the job(s) in question and the corresponding job title(s) and code(s) from the United States Employment Service's dictionary of occupational titles.

(6) *Selection procedure.* The selection procedure used as a measure of the construct should be completely and explicitly described or attached (essential). If commercially available selection procedures are used, they should be identified by title, form and publisher (essential). The research evidence of the relationship between the selection procedure and the construct, such as factor structure, should be included (essential). Measures of central tendency, variability and reliability of

the selection procedure should be provided (essential). Whenever feasible, these measures should be provided separately for each relevant race, sex and ethnic group.

(7) *Relationship to job performance.* The criterion-related study(ies) and other empirical evidence of the relationship between the construct measured by the selection procedure and the related work behavior(s) for the job or jobs in question should be provided (essential). Documentation of the criterion-related study(ies) should satisfy the provisions of section 15B above or section 15E(1) below, except for studies conducted prior to the effective date of these guidelines (essential). Where a study pertains to a group of jobs, and, on the basis of the study, validity is asserted for a job in the group, the observed work behaviors and the observed work products for each of the jobs should be described (essential). Any other evidence used in determining whether the work behavior(s) in each of the jobs is the same should be fully described (essential).

(8) *Alternative procedures investigated.* The alternative selection procedures investigated and available evidence of their impact should be identified (essential). The scope, method, and findings of the investigation, and the conclusions reached in light of the findings should be fully described (essential).

(9) *Uses and applications.* The methods considered for use of the selection procedure (e.g., as a screening device with a cutoff score, for grouping or ranking, or combined with other procedures in a battery) and available evidence of their impact should be described (essential). This description should include the rationale for choosing the method for operational use, and the evidence of the validity and utility of the procedure as it is to be used (essential). The purpose for which the procedure is to be used (e.g., hiring, transfer, promotion) should be described (essential). If weights are assigned to different parts of the selection procedure, these weights and the validity of the weighted composite should be reported (essential). If the selection procedure is used with a cutoff score, the user should describe the way in which normal expectations of proficiency within the work force were determined and the way in which the cutoff score was determined (essential).

(10) *Accuracy and completeness.* The report should describe the steps taken to assure the accuracy and completeness of the collection, analysis, and report of data and results.

(11) *Source data.* Each user should maintain records showing all pertinent

410

information relating to its study of construct validity.

(12) *Contact person.* The name, mailing address, and telephone number of the individual who may be contacted for further information about the validity study should be provided (essential).

E. *Evidence of validity from other studies.* When validity of a selection procedure is supported by studies not done by the user, the evidence from the original study or studies should be compiled in a manner similar to that required in the appropriate section of this section 15 above. In addition, the following evidence should be supplied:

(1) *Evidence from criterion-related validity studies.—a. Job information.* A description of the important job behavior(s) of the user's job and the basis on which the behaviors were determined to be important should be provided (essential). A full description of the basis for determining that these important work behaviors are the same as those of the job in the original study (or studies) should be provided (essential).

b. *Relevance of criteria.* A full description of the basis on which the criteria used in the original studies are determined to be relevant for the user should be provided (essential).

c. *Other variables.* The similarity of important applicant pool or sample characteristics reported in the original studies to those of the user should be described (essential). A description of the comparison between the race, sex and ethnic composition of the user's relevant labor market and the sample in the original validity studies should be provided (essential).

d. *Use of the selection procedure.* A full description should be provided showing that the use to be made of the selection procedure is consistent with the findings of the original validity studies (essential).

e. *Bibliography.* A bibliography of reports of validity of the selection procedure for the job or jobs in question should be provided (essential). Where any of the studies included an investigation of test fairness, the results of this investigation should be provided (essential). Copies of reports published in journals that are not commonly available should be described in detail or attached (essential). Where a user is relying upon unpublished studies, a reasonable effort should be made to obtain these studies. If these unpublished studies are the sole source of validity evidence they should be described in detail or attached (essential). If these studies are not available, the name and address of the source, an adequate abstract or summary of the validity study and data, and a contact person in the source organization should be provided (essential).

(2) *Evidence from content validity studies.* See section 14C(3) and section 15C above.

(3) *Evidence from construct validity studies.* See sections 14D(2) and 15D above.

F. *Evidence of validity from cooperative studies.* Where a selection procedure has been validated through a cooperative study, evidence that the study satisfies the requirements of sections 7, 8 and 15E should be provided (essential).

G. *Selection for higher level job.* If a selection procedure is used to evaluate candidates for jobs at a higher level than those for which they will initially be employed, the validity evidence should satisfy the documentation provisions of this section 15 for the higher level job or jobs, and in addition, the user should provide: (1) a description of the job progression structure, formal or informal; (2) the data showing how many employees progress to the higher level job and the length of time needed to make this progression; and (3) an identification of any anticipated changes in the higher level job. In addition, if the test measures a knowledge, skill or ability, the user should provide evidence that the knowledge, skill or ability is required for the higher level job and the basis for the conclusion that the knowledge, skill or ability is not expected to develop from the training or experience on the job.

H. *Interim use of selection procedures.* If a selection procedure is being used on an interim basis because the procedure is not fully supported by the required evidence of validity, the user should maintain and have available (1) substantial evidence of validity for the procedure, and (2) a report showing the date on which the study to gather the additional evidence commenced, the estimated completion date of the study, and a description of the data to be collected (essential).

DEFINITIONS

SEC. 16. *Definitions.* The following definitions shall apply throughout these guidelines:

A. *Ability.* A present competence to perform an observable behavior or a behavior which results in an observable product.

B. *Adverse impact.* A substantially different rate of selection in hiring, promotion, or other employment decision which works to the disadvantage of members of a race, sex, or ethnic group. See section 4 of these guidelines.

C. *Compliance with these guidelines.* Use of a selection procedure is in compliance with these guidelines if such use has been validated in accord with these guidelines (as defined below), or if such use does not result in adverse

impact on any race, sex, or ethnic group (see section 4, above), or, in unusual circumstances, if use of the procedure is otherwise justified in accord with Federal law. See section 6B, above.

D. *Content validity.* Demonstrated by data showing that the content of a selection procedure is representative of important aspects of performance on the job. See section 5B and section 14C.

E. *Construct validity.* Demonstrated by data showing that the selection procedure measures the degree to which candidates have identifiable characteristics which have been determined to be important for successful job performance. See section 5B and section 14D.

F. *Criterion-related validity.* Demonstrated by empirical data showing that the selection procedure is predictive of or significantly correlated with important elements of work behavior. See sections 5B and 14B.

G. *Employer.* Any employer subject to the provisions of the Civil Rights Act of 1964, as amended, including State or local governments and any Federal agency subject to the provisions of section 717 of the Civil Rights Act of 1964, as amended, and any Federal contractor or subcontractor or federally assisted construction contractor or subcontractor covered by Executive Order 11246, as amended.

H. *Employment agency.* Any employment agency subject to the provisions of the Civil Rights Act of 1964, as amended.

I. *Enforcement action.* For the purposes of section 4 a proceeding by a Federal enforcement agency such as a lawsuit or an administrative proceeding leading to debarment from or withholding, suspension, or termination of Federal Government contracts or the suspension or withholding of Federal Government funds; but not a finding of reasonable cause or a conciliation process or the issuance of right to sue letters under title VII or under Executive Order 11246 where such finding, conciliation, or issuance of notice of right to sue is based upon an individual complaint.

J. *Enforcement agency.* Any agency of the executive branch of the Federal Government which adopts these guidelines for purposes of the enforcement of the equal employment opportunity laws or which has responsibility for securing compliance with them.

K. *Job analysis.* A detailed statement of work behaviors and other information relevant to the job.

L. *Job description.* A general statement of job duties and responsibilities.

M. *Knowledge.* A body of information applied directly to the performance of a function.

N. *Labor organization.* Any labor organization subject to the provisions of the Civil Rights Act of 1964, as amended, and any committee subject thereto controlling apprenticeship or other training.

O. *Observable.* Able to be seen, heard, or otherwise perceived by a person other than the person performing the action.

P. *Race, sex, or ethnic group.* Any group of persons identifiable on the grounds of race, color, religion, sex, or national origin.

Q. *Selection procedure.* Any measure, combination of measures, or procedure used as a basis for any employment decision. Selection procedures include the full range of assessment techniques from traditional paper and pencil tests, performance tests, training programs, or probationary periods and physical, educational, and work experience requirements through informal or casual interviews and unscored application forms.

R. *Selection rate.* The proportion of applicants or candidates who are hired, promoted, or otherwise selected.

S. *Should.* The term "should" as used in these guidelines is intended to connote action which is necessary to achieve compliance with the guidelines, while recognizing that there are circumstances where alternative courses of action are open to users.

T. *Skill.* A present, observable competence to perform a learned psychomoter act.

U. *Technical feasibility.* The existence of conditions permitting the conduct of meaningful criterion-related validity studies. These conditions include: (1) An adequate sample of persons available for the study to achieve findings of statistical significance; (2) having or being able to obtain a sufficient range of scores on the selection procedure and job performance measures to produce validity results which can be expected to be representative of the results if the ranges normally expected were utilized; and (3) having or being able to devise unbiased, reliable and relevant measures of job performance or other criteria of employee adequacy. See section 14B(2). With respect to investigation of possible unfairness, the same considerations are applicable to each group for which the study is made. See section 14B(8).

V. *Unfairness of selection procedure.* A condition in which members of one race, sex, or ethnic group characteristically obtain lower scores on a selection procedure than members of another group, and the differences are not reflected in differences in measures of job performance. See section 14B(7).

W. *User.* Any employer, labor organization, employment agency, or licensing or certification board, to the extent it may be covered by Federal equal employment opportunity law, which uses a selection procedure as a basis for any employment decision. Whenever an employer, labor organization, or employment agency is required by law to restrict recruitment for any occupation to those applicants who have met licensing or certification requirements, the licensing or certifying authority to the extent it may be covered by Federal equal employment opportunity law will be considered the user with respect to those licensing or certification requirements. Whenever a State employment agency or service does no more than administer or monitor a procedure as permitted by Department of Labor regulations, and does so without making referrals or taking any other action on the basis of the results, the State employment agency will not be deemed to be a user.

X. *Validated in accord with these guidelines or properly validated.* A demonstration that one or more validity study or studies meeting the standards of these guidelines has been conducted, including investigation and, where appropriate, use of suitable alternative selection procedures as contemplated by section 3B, and has produced evidence of validity sufficient to warrant use of the procedure for the intended purpose under the standards of these guidelines.

Y. *Work behavior.* An activity performed to achieve the objectives of the job. Work behaviors involve observable (physical) components and unobservable (mental) components. A work behavior consists of the performance of one or more tasks. Knowledges, skills, and abilities are not behaviors, although they may be applied in work behaviors.

APPENDIX

17. *Policy statement on affirmative action* (see section 13B). The Equal Employment Opportunity Coordinating Council was established by act of Congress in 1972, and charged with responsibility for developing and implementing agreements and policies designed, among other things, to eliminate conflict and inconsistency among the agencies of the Federal Government responsible for administering Federal law prohibiting discrimination on grounds of race, color, sex, religion, and national origin. This statement is issued as an initial response to the requests of a number of State and local officials for clarification of the Government's policies concerning the role of affirmative action in the overall equal employment opportunity program. While the Coordinating Council's adoption of this statement expresses only the views of the signatory agencies concerning this important subject, the principles set forth below should serve as policy guidance for other Federal agencies as well.

(1) Equal employment opportunity is the law of the land. In the public sector of our society this means that all persons, regardless of race, color, religion, sex, or national origin shall have equal access to positions in the public service limited only by their ability to do the job. There is ample evidence in all sectors of our society that such equal access frequently has been denied to members of certain groups because of their sex, racial, or ethnic characteristics. The remedy for such past and present discrimination is twofold.

On the one hand, vigorous enforcement of the laws against discrimination is essential. But equally, and perhaps even more important are affirmative, voluntary efforts on the part of public employers to assure that positions in the public service are genuinely and equally accessible to qualified persons, without regard to their sex, racial, or ethnic characteristics. Without such efforts equal employment opportunity is no more than a wish. The importance of voluntary affirmative action on the part of employers is underscored by title VII of the Civil Rights Act of 1964, Executive Order 11246, and related laws and regulations—all of which emphasize voluntary action to achieve equal employment opportunity.

As with most management objectives, a systematic plan based on sound organizational analysis and problem identification is crucial to the accomplishment of affirmative action objectives. For this reason, the Council urges all State and local governments to develop and implement results oriented affirmative action plans which deal with the problems so identified.

The following paragraphs are intended to assist State and local governments by illustrating the kinds of analyses and activities which may be appropriate for a public employer's voluntary affirmative action plan. This statement does not address remedies imposed after a finding of unlawful discrimination.

(2) Voluntary affirmative action to assure equal employment opportunity is appropriate at any stage of the employment process. The first step in the construction of any affirmative action plan should be an analysis of the employer's work force to determine whether percentages of sex, race, or ethnic groups in individual job classifications are substantially similar to the percentages of those groups available in the relevant job market who possess the basic job-related qualifications.

When substantial disparities are found through such analyses, each element of the overall selection process should be examined to determine which elements operate to exclude persons on the basis of sex, race, or ethnic group. Such elements include, but are not limited to, recruitment, testing, ranking certification, interview, recommendations for selection, hiring, promotion, etc. The examination of each element of the selection process should at a minimum include a determination of its validity in predicting job performance.

(3) When an employer has reason to believe that its selection procedures have the exclusionary effect described in paragraph 2 above, it should initiate affirmative steps to remedy the situation. Such steps, which in design and execution may be race, color, sex, or ethnic "conscious," include, but are not limited to, the following:

(a) The establishment of a long-term goal, and short-range, interim goals and timetables for the specific job classifications, all of which should take into account the availability of basically qualified persons in the relevant job market;

(b) A recruitment program designed to attract qualified members of the group in question;

(c) A systematic effort to organize work and redesign jobs in ways that provide opportunities for persons lacking "journeyman" level knowledge or skills to enter and, with appropriate training, to progress in a career field;

(d) Revamping selection instruments or procedures which have not yet been validated in order to reduce or eliminate exclusionary effects on particular groups in particular job classifications;

(e) The initiation of measures designed to assure that members of the affected group who are qualified to perform the job are included within the pool of persons from which the selecting official makes the selection;

(f) A systematic effort to provide career advancement training, both classroom and on-the-job, to employees locked into dead end jobs; and

(g) The establishment of a system for regularly monitoring the effectiveness of the particular affirmative action program, and procedures for making timely adjustments in this program where effectiveness is not demonstrated.

(4) The goal of any affirmative action plan should be achievement of genuine equal employment opportunity for all qualified persons. Selection under such plans should be based

upon the ability of the applicant(s) to do the work. Such plans should not require the selection of the unqualified, or the unneeded, nor should they require the selection of persons on the basis of race, color, sex, religion, or national origin. Moreover, while the Council believes that this statement should serve to assist State and local employers, as well as Federal agencies, it recognizes that affirmative action cannot be viewed as a standardized program which must be accomplished in the same way at all times in all places.

Accordingly, the Council has not attempted to set forth here either the minimum or maximum voluntary steps that employers may take to deal with their respective situations. Rather, the Council recognizes that under applicable authorities, State and local employers have flexibility to formulate affirmative action plans that are best suited to their particular situations. In this manner, the Council believes that affirmative action programs will best serve the goal of equal employment opportunity.

Respectfully submitted,

HAROLD R. TYLER, Jr.,
Deputy Attorney General and Chairman of the Equal Employment Coordinating Council.

MICHAEL H. MOSKOW,
Under Secretary of Labor.

ETHEL BENT WALSH,
Acting Chairman, Equal Employment Opportunity Commission.

ROBERT E. HAMPTON,
Chairman, Civil Service Commission.

ARTHUR E. FLEMMING,
Chairman, Commission on Civil Rights.

Because of its equal employment opportunity responsibilities under the State and Local Government Fiscal Assistance Act of 1972 (the revenue sharing act), the Department of Treasury was invited to participate in the formulation of this policy statement; and it concurs and joins in the adoption of this policy statement.

Done this 26th day of August 1976.

RICHARD ALBRECHT,
General Counsel,
Department of the Treasury.

Section 18. *Citations.* The official title of these guidelines is "Uniform

Guidelines on Employee Selection Procedures (1978)". The Uniform Guidelines on Employee Selection Procedures (1978) are intended to establish a uniform Federal position in the area of prohibiting discrimination in employment practices on grounds of race, color, religion, sex, or national origin. These guidelines have been adopted by the Equal Employment Opportunity Commission, the Department of Labor, the Department of Justice, and the Civil Service Commission.

The official citation is:
"Section ——, Uniform Guidelines on Employee Selection Procedure (1978); 43 FR —— (August 25, 1978)."

The short form citation is:
"Section ——, U.G.E.S.P. (1978); 43 FR —— (August 25, 1978)."

When the guidelines are cited in connection with the activities of one of the issuing agencies, a specific citation to the regulations of that agency can be added at the end of the above citation. The specific additional citations are as follows:

Equal Employment Opportunity Commission
    29 CFR Part 1607
Department of Labor
Office of Federal Contract Compliance Programs
    41 CFR Part 60-3
Department of Justice
    28 CFR 50.14
Civil Service Commission
    5 CFR 300.103(c)

Normally when citing these guidelines, the section number immediately preceding the title of the guidelines will be from these guidelines series 1-18. If a section number from the codification for an individual agency is needed it can also be added at the end of the agency citation. For example, section 6A of these guidelines could be cited for EEOC as follows: "Section 6A, Uniform Guidelines on Employee Selection Procedures (1978); 43 FR ——, (August 25, 1978); 29 CFR Part 1607, section 6A."

ELEANOR HOLMES NORTON,
Chair, Equal Employment Opportunity Commission.

ALAN K. CAMPBELL,
Chairman,
Civil Service Commission.

RAY MARSHALL,
Secretary of Labor.

GRIFFIN B. BELL,
Attorney General.

Appendix 3

Adoption of Questions and
Answers to Clarify and
Provide a Common
Interpretation of the
Uniform Guidelines on
Employee Selection
Procedures

Title 29—Labor

CHAPTER XIV—EQUAL EMPLOYMENT OPPORTUNITY COMMISSION

PART 1607—UNIFORM GUIDELINES ON EMPLOYEE SELECTION PROCEDURES (1978)

Title 5—Administrative Personnel

OFFICE OF PERSONNEL MANAGEMENT

PART 300—EMPLOYMENT (GENERAL)

Title 28—Judicial Administration

CHAPTER I—DEPARTMENT OF JUSTICE

PART 50—STATEMENTS OF POLICY

Title 31—Money and Finance: Treasury

CHAPTER I—MONETARY OFFICES: DEPARTMENT OF THE TREASURY

PART 51—FISCAL ASSISTANCE TO STATE AND LOCAL GOVERNMENTS

Title 41—Public Contracts and Property Management

CHAPTER 60—OFFICE OF FEDERAL CONTRACT COMPLIANCE PROGRAMS, DEPARTMENT OF LABOR

PART 60-3—UNIFORM GUIDELINES ON EMPLOYEE SELECTION PROCEDURES (1978)

Adoption of Questions and Answers To Clarify and Provide a Common Interpretation of the Uniform Guidelines on Employee Selection Procedures

AGENCIES: Equal Employment Opportunity Commission, Office of Personnel Management, Department of Justice, Department of Labor and Department of Treasury.

ACTION: Adoption of questions and answers designed to clarify and provide a common interpretation of the Uniform Guidelines on Employee Selection Procedures.

SUMMARY: The Uniform Guidelines on Employee Selection Procedures were issued by the five Federal agencies having primary responsibility for the enforcement of Federal equal employment opportunity laws, to establish a uniform Federal government position. See 43 FR 38290, et seq. (Aug. 25, 1978) and 43 FR 40223 (Sept. 11, 1978). They became effective on September 25, 1978, The issuing agencies recognize the need for a common interpretation of the Uniform Guidelines, as well as the desirability of providing additional guidance to employers and other users, psychologists, and investigators, compliance officers and other Federal enforcement personnel. These Questions and Answers are intended to address that need and to provide such guidance.

EFFECTIVE DATE: March 2, 1979.

FOR FURTHER INFORMATION CONTACT:

A. Diane Graham, Assistant Director, Affirmative Employment Programs, Office of Personnel Management, 1900 E Street, NW., Washington, D.C. 20415, 202/632-4420.

James Hellings, Special Assistant to the Assistant Director, Intergovernmental Personnel Programs, Office of Personnel Management, 1900 E Street, NW., Washington, D.C. 20415, 202/632-6248.

Kenneth A. Millard, Chief, State and Local Section, Personnel Research and Development Center, Office of Personnel Management, 1900 E St., NW., Washington, D.C. 20415, 202-632-6238.

Peter C. Robertson, Director, Office of Policy Implementation, Equal Employment Opportunity Commission, 2401 E Street, NW., Washington, D.C. 20506, 202/634-7060.

David L. Rose, Chief, Employment Section, Civil Rights Division, Department of Justice, 10th Street and Pennsylvania Avenue, NW., Washington, D.C. 20530, 202/633-3831.

Donald J. Schwartz, Psychologist, Office of Federal Contract Compliance Programs, Room C-3324, Department of Labor, 200 Constitution Avenue, NW., Washington, D.C. 20210, 202/523-9426.

Herman Schwartz, Chief Counsel, Office of Revenue Sharing, Department of the Treasury, 2401 E Street, NW., Washington, D.C. 20220, 202/634-5182.

James O. Taylor, Jr., Research Psychologist, Office of Systemic Programs, Equal Employment Opportunity Commission, 2401 E St., NW., Washington, D.C. 20506, 202/254-3036.

INTRODUCTION

The problems addressed by the Uniform Guidelines on Employee Selection Procedures (43 FR 38290 et seq., August 25, 1978) are numerous and important, and some of them are complex. The history of the development of those Guidelines is set forth in the introduction to them (43 FR 38290-95). The experience of the agencies has been that a series of answers to commonly asked questions is helpful in providing guidance not only to employers and other users, but also to psychologists and others who are called upon to conduct validity studies, and to investigators, compliance officers and other Federal personnel who have enforcement responsibilities.

The Federal agencies which issued the Uniform Guidelines—the Departments of Justice and Labor, the Equal Employment Opportunity Commission, the Civil Service Commission (which has been succeeded in relevant part by the Office of Personnel Management), and the Office of Revenue Sharing, Treasury Department—recognize that the goal of a uniform position on these issues can best be achieved through a common interpretation of the same guidelines. The following Questions and Answers are part of such a common interpretation. The material included is intended to interpret and clarify, but not to modify, the provisions of the Uniform Guidelines. The questions selected are commonly asked questions in the field and those suggested by the Uniform Guidelines themselves and by the extensive comments received on the various sets of proposed guidelines prior to their adoption. Terms are used in the questions and answers as they are defined in the Uniform Guidelines.

The agencies recognize that additional questions may be appropriate for similar treatment at a later date, and contemplate working together to provide additional guidance in interpreting the Uniform Guidelines. Users and other interested persons are invited to submit additional questions.

ELEANOR HOLMES NORTON,
Chair, Equal Employment Opportunity Commission.

ALAN K. CAMPBELL,
Director, Office of Personnel Management.

DREW S. DAYS III,
Assistant Attorney General, Civil Rights Division, Department of Justice.

WELDEN ROUGEAU,
Director, Office of Federal Contract Compliance, Department of Labor.

KENT A. PETERSON,
Acting Deputy Director, Office of Revenue Sharing.

I. PURPOSE AND SCOPE

1. Q. What is the purpose of the Guidelines?

A. The guidelines are designed to aid in the achievement of our nation's

416

goal of equal employment opportunity without discrimination on the grounds of race, color, sex, religion or national origin. The Federal agencies have adopted the Guidelines to provide a uniform set of principles governing use of employee selection procedures which is consistent with applicable legal standards and validation standards generally accepted by the psychological profession and which the Government will apply in the discharge of its responsibilities.

2. Q. What is the basic principle of the Guidelines?

A. A selection process which has an adverse impact on the employment opportunities of members of a race, color, religion, sex, or national origin group (referred to as "race, sex, and ethnic group," as defined in Section 16P) and thus disproportionately screens them out is unlawfully discriminatory unless the process or its component procedures have been validated in accord with the Guidelines, or the user otherwise justifies them in accord with Federal law. See Sections 3 and 6.[1] This principle was adopted by the Supreme Court unanimously in *Griggs* v. *Duke Power Co.*, 401 U.S. 424, and was ratified and endorsed by the Congress when it passed the Equal Employment Opportunity Act of 1972, which amended Title VII of the Civil Rights Act of 1964.

3. Q. Who is covered by the Guidelines?

A. The Guidelines apply to private and public employers, labor organizations, employment agencies, apprenticeship committees, licensing and certification boards (see Question 7), and contractors or subcontractors, who are covered by one or more of the following provisions of Federal equal employment opportunity law: Title VII of the Civil Rights Act of 1964, as amended by the Equal Employment Opportunity Act of 1972 (hereinafter Title VII); Executive Order 11246, as amended by Executive Orders 11375 and 12086 (hereinafter Executive Order 11246); the State and Local Fiscal Assistance Act of 1972, as amended; Omnibus Crime Control and Safe Streets Act of 1968, as amended; and the Intergovernmental Personnel Act of 1970, as amended. Thus, under Title VII, the Guidelines apply to the Federal Government with regard to Federal employment. Through Title VII they apply to most private employers who have 15 or more employees for 20 weeks or more a calendar year, and to most employment agencies, labor organizations and apprenticeship committees. They apply to state and local governments which employ 15 or more employees, or which receive revenue sharing funds, or which receive funds from the Law Enforcement Assistance Administration to impose and strengthen law enforcement and criminal justice, or which receive grants or other federal assistance under a program which requires maintenance of personnel standards on a merit basis. They apply through Executive Order 11246 to contractors and subcontractors of the Federal Government and to contractors and subcontractors under federally-assisted construction contracts.

4. Q. Are college placement officers and similar organizations considered to be users subject to the Guidelines?

A. Placement offices may or may not be subject to the Guidelines depending on what services they offer. If a placement office uses a selection procedure as a basis for any employment decision, it is covered under the definition of "user". Section 16. For example, if a placement office selects some students for referral to an employer but rejects others, it is covered. However, if the placement office refers all interested students to an employer, it is not covered, even though it may offer office space and provision for informing the students of job openings. The Guidelines are intended to cover all users of employee selection procedures, including employment agencies, who are subject to Federal equal employment opportunity law.

5. Q. Do the Guidelines apply only to written tests?

A. No. They apply to all selection procedures used to make employment decisions, including interviews, review of experience or education from application forms, work samples, physical requirements, and evaluations of performance. Sections 2B and 16Q, and see Question 6.

6. Q. What practices are covered by the Guidelines?

A. The Guidelines apply to employee selection procedures which are used in making employment decisions, such as hiring, retention, promotion, transfer, demotion, dismissal or referral. Section 2B. Employee selection procedures include job requirements (physical, education, experience), and evaluation of applicants or candidates on the basis of application forms, interviews, performance tests, paper and pencil tests, performance in training programs or probationary periods, and any other procedures used to make an employment decision whether administered by the employer or by an employment agency. See Section 2B.

7. Q. Do the Guidelines apply to the licensing and certification functions of state and local governments?

A. The Guidelines apply to such functions to the extent that they are covered by Federal law. Section 2B. The courts are divided on the issue of such coverage. The Government has taken the position that at least some kinds of licensing and certification which deny persons access to employment opportunity may be enjoined in an action brought pursuant to Section 707 of the Civil Rights Act of 1964, as amended.

8. Q. What is the relationship between Federal equal employment opportunity law, embodied in these Guidelines, and State and Local government merit system laws or regulations requiring rank ordering of candidates and selection from a limited number of the top candidates?

A. The Guidelines permit ranking where the evidence of validity is sufficient to support that method of use. State or local laws which compel rank ordering generally do so on the assumption that the selection procedure is valid. Thus, if there is adverse impact and the validity evidence does not adequately support that method of use, proper interpretation of such a state law would require validation prior to ranking. Accordingly, there is no necessary or inherent conflict between Federal law and State or local laws of the kind described.

Under the Supremacy Clause of the Constitution (Art. VI, Cl. 2), however, Federal law or valid regulation overrides any contrary provision of state or local law. Thus, if there is any conflict, Federal equal opportunity law prevails. For example, in *Rosenfeld* v. *So. Pacific Co.*, 444 F. 2d 1219 (9th Cir., 1971), the court held invalid state protective laws which prohibited the employment of women in jobs entailing long hours or heavy labor, because the state laws were in conflict with Title VII. Where a State or local official believes that there is a possible conflict, the official may wish to consult with the State Attorney General, County or City attorney, or other legal official to determine how to comply with the law.

II. ADVERSE IMPACT, THE BOTTOM LINE AND AFFIRMATIVE ACTION

9. Q. Do the Guidelines require that only validated selection procedures be used?

A. No. Although validation of selection procedures is desirable in personnel management, the Uniform Guidelines require users to produce evidence of validity only when the selection procedure adversely affects the opportunities of a race, sex, or ethnic group

---

[1] Section references throughout these questions and answers are to the sections of the *Uniform Guidelines on Employee Selection Procedures* (herein referred to as "Guidelines") that were published by the Equal Employment Opportunity Commission, the Civil Service Commission, the Department of Labor, and the Department of Justice on Aug. 25, 1978, 43 FR 38290. The Uniform Guidelines were adopted by the Office of Revenue Sharing of the Department of Treasury on September 11, 1978. 43 FR 40223.

FEDERAL REGISTER, VOL. 44, NO. 43—FRIDAY, MARCH 2, 1979

for hire, transfer, promotion, retention or other employment decision. If there is no adverse impact, there is no validation requirement under the Guidelines. Sections 1B and 3A. See also, Section 6A.

10. Q. What is adverse impact?

A. Under the Guidelines adverse impact is a substantially different rate of selection in hiring, promotion or other employment decision which works to the disadvantage of members of a race, sex or ethnic group. Sections 4D and 16B. See Questions 11 and 12.

11. Q. What is a substantially different rate of selection?

A. The agencies have adopted a rule of thumb under which they will generally consider a selection rate for any race, sex, or ethnic group which is less than four-fifths (4/5ths) or eighty percent (80%) of the selection rate for the group with the highest selection rate as a substantially different rate of selection. See Section 4D. This "4/5ths" or "80%" rule of thumb is not intended as a legal definition, but is a practical means of keeping the attention of the enforcement agencies on serious discrepancies in rates of hiring, promotion and other selection decisions.

For example, if the hiring rate for whites other than Hispanics is 60%, for American Indians 45%, for Hispanics 48%, and for Blacks 51%, and each of these groups constitutes more than 2% of the labor force in the relevant labor area (see Question 16), a comparison should be made of the selection rate for each group with that of the highest group (whites). These comparisons show the following impact ratios: American Indians 45/60 or 75%; Hispanics 48/60 or 80%; and Blacks 51/60 or 85%. Applying the 4/5ths or 80% rule of thumb, on the basis of the above information alone, adverse impact is indicated for American Indians but not for Hispanics or Blacks.

12. Q. How is adverse impact determined?

A. Adverse impact is determined by a four step process.

(1) calculate the rate of selection for each group (divide the number of persons selected from a group by the number of applicants from that group).

(2) observe which group has the highest selection rate.

(3) calculate the impact ratios, by comparing the selection rate for each group with that of the highest group (divide the selection rate for a group by the selection rate for the highest group).

(4) observe whether the selection rate for any group is substantially less (i.e., usually less than 4/5ths or 80%) than the selection rate for the highest group. If it is, adverse impact is indicated in most circumstances. See Section 4D.

For example:

Applicants	Hires	Selection rate Percent hired
80 White	48	48/80 or 60%
40 Black	12	12/40 or 30%

A comparison of the black selection rate (30%) with the white selection rate (60%) shows that the black rate is 30/60, or one-half (or 50%) of the white rate. Since the one-half (50%) is less than 4/5ths (80%) adverse impact is usually indicated.

The determination of adverse impact is not purely arithmetic however; and other factors may be relevant. See, Section 4D.

13. Q. Is adverse impact determined on the basis of the overall selection process or for the components in that process?

A. Adverse impact is determined first for the overall selection process for each job. If the overall selection process has an adverse impact, the adverse impact of the individual selection procedure should be analyzed. For any selection procedures in the process having an adverse impact which the user continues to use in the same manner, the user is expected to have evidence of validity satisfying the Guidelines. Sections 4C and 5D. If there is no adverse impact for the overall selection process, in most circumstances there is no obligation under the Guidelines to investigate adverse impact for the components, or to validate the selection procedures used for that job. Section 4C. But see Question 25.

14. Q. The Guidelines designate the "total selection process" as the initial basis for determining the impact of selection procedures. What is meant by the "total selection process"?

A. The "total selection process" refers to the combined effect of all selection procedures leading to the final employment decision such as hiring or promoting. For example, appraisal of candidates for administrative assistant positions in an organization might include initial screening based upon an application blank and interview, a written test, a medical examination, a background check, and a supervisor's interview. These in combination are the total selection process. Additionally, where there is more than one route to the particular kind of employment decision, the total selection process encompasses the combined results of all routes. For example, an employer may select some applicants for a particular kind of job through appropriate written and performance tests. Others may be selected through an internal upward mobility program, on the basis

of successful performance in a directly related trainee type of position. In such a case, the impact of the total selection process would be the combined effect of both avenues of entry.

15. Q. What is meant by the terms "applicant" and "candidate" as they are used in the Uniform Guidelines?

A. The precise definition of the term "applicant" depends upon the user's recruitment and selection procedures. The concept of an applicant is that of a person who has indicated an interest in being considered for hiring, promotion, or other employment opportunities. This interest might be expressed by completing an application form, or might be expressed orally, depending upon the employer's practice.

The term "candidate" has been included to cover those situations where the initial step by the user involves consideration of current employees for promotion, or training, or other employment opportunities, without inviting applications. The procedure by which persons are identified as candidates is itself a selection procedure under the Guidelines.

A person who voluntarily withdraws formally or informally at any stage of the selection process is no longer an applicant or candidate for purposes of computing adverse impact. Employment standards imposed by the user which discourage disproportionately applicants of a race, sex or ethnic group may, however, require justification. Records should be kept for persons who were applicants or candidates at any stage of the process.

16. Q. Should adverse impact determinations be made for all groups regardless of their size?

A. No. Section 15A(2) calls for annual adverse impact determinations to be made for each group which constitutes either 2% or more of the total labor force in the relevant labor area, or 2% or more of the applicable workforce. Thus, impact determinations should be made for any employment decision for each group which constitutes 2% or more of the labor force in the relevant labor area. For hiring, such determination should also be made for groups which constitute more than 2% of the applicants; and for promotions, determinations should also be made for those groups which constitute at least 2% of the user's workforce. There are record keeping obligations for all groups, even those which are less than 2%. See Question 86.

17. Q. In determining adverse impact, do you compare the selection rates for males and females, and blacks and whites, or do you compare selection rates for white males, white females, black males and black females?

A. The selection rates for males and females are compared, and the selection rates for the race and ethnic groups are compared with the selection rate of the race or ethnic group with the highest selection rate. Neutral and objective selection procedures free of adverse impact against any race, sex or ethnic group are unlikely to have an impact against a subgroup. Thus there is no obligation to make comparisons for subgroups (e.g., white male, white female, black male, black female). However, there are obligations to keep records (see Question 87), and any apparent exclusion of a subgroup may suggest the presence of discrimination.

18. Q. Is it usually necessary to calculate the statistical significance of differences in selection rates when investigating the existence of adverse impact?

A. No. Adverse impact is normally indicated when one selection rate is less than 80% of the other. The federal enforcement agencies normally will use only the 80% (⅘ths) rule of thumb, except where large numbers of selections are made. See Questions 20 and 22.

19. Q. Does the ⅘ths rule of thumb mean that the Guidelines will tolerate up to 20% discrimination?

A. No. The ⅘ths rule of thumb speaks only to the question of adverse impact, and is not intended to resolve the ultimate question of unlawful discrimination. Regardless of the amount of difference in selection rates, unlawful discrimination may be present, and may be demonstrated through appropriate evidence. The ⅘ths rule merely establishes a numerical basis for drawing an initial inference and for requiring additional information.

With respect to adverse impact, the Guidelines expressly state (section 4D) that differences in selection rates of less than 20% may still amount to adverse impact where the differences are significant in both statistical and practical terms. See Question 20. In the absence of differences which are large enough to meet the ⅘ths rule of thumb or a test of statistical significance, there is no reason to assume that the differences are reliable, or that they are based upon anything other than chance.

20. Q. Why is the ⅘ths rule called a rule of thumb?

A. Because it is not intended to be controlling in all circumstances. If, for the sake of illustration, we assume that nationwide statistics show that use of an arrest record would disqualify 10% of all Hispanic persons but only 4% of all whites other than Hispanic (hereafter non-Hispanic), the selection rate for that selection procedure is 90% for Hispanics and 96% for non-Hispanics. Therefore, the ⅘ rule of thumb would not indicate the presence of adverse impact (90% is approximately 94% of 96%). But in this example, the information is based upon nationwide statistics, and the sample is large enough to yield statistically significant results, and the difference (Hispanics are 2½ times as likely to be disqualified as non-Hispanics) is large enough to be practically significant. Thus, in this example the enforcement agencies would consider a disqualification based on an arrest record alone as having an adverse impact. Likewise, in *Gregory* v. *Litton Industries*, 472 F. 2d 631 (9th Cir., 1972), the court held that the employer violated Title VII by disqualifying persons from employment solely on the basis of an arrest record, where that disqualification had an adverse impact on blacks and was not shown to be justified by business necessity.

On the other hand, a difference of more than 20% in rates of selection may not provide a basis for finding adverse impact if the number of persons selected is very small. For example, if the employer selected three males and one female from an applicant pool of 20 males and 10 females, the ⅘ths rule would indicate adverse impact (selection rate for women is 10%; for men 15%; 10/15 or 66⅔% is less than 80%), yet the number of selections is too small to warrant a determination of adverse impact. In these circumstances, the enforcement agency would not require validity evidence in the absence of additional information (such as selection rates for a longer period of time) indicating adverse impact. For recordkeeping requirements, see Section 15A(2)(c) and Questions 84 and 85.

21. Q. Is evidence of adverse impact sufficient to warrant a validity study or an enforcement action where the numbers involved are so small that it is more likely than not that the difference could have occurred by chance? For example:

Applicants	Not hired	Hired	Selection rate percent hired
80 White	64	16	20
20 Black	17	3	15
White Selection Rate.....			20
Black Selection Rate			15
15 divided by 20 = 75% (which is less than 80%).			

A. No. If the numbers of persons and the difference in selection rates are so small that it is likely that the difference could have occurred by chance, the Federal agencies will not assume the existence of adverse impact, in the absence of other evidence. In this example, the difference in selection rates is too small, given the small number of black applicants, to constitute adverse impact in the absence of other information (see Section 4D). If only one more black had been hired instead of a white the selection rate for blacks (20%) would be higher than that for whites (18.7%). Generally, it is inappropriate to require validity evidence or to take enforcement action where the number of persons and the difference in selection rates are so small that the selection of one different person for one job would shift the result from adverse impact against one group to a situation in which that group has a higher selection rate than the other group.

On the other hand, if a lower selection rate continued over a period of time, so as to constitute a pattern, then the lower selection rate would constitute adverse impact, warranting the need for validity evidence.

22. Q. Is it ever necessary to calculate the statistical significance of differences in selection rates to determine whether adverse impact exists?

A. Yes. Where large numbers of selections are made, relatively small differences in selection rates may nevertheless constitute adverse impact if they are both statistically and practically significant. See Section 4D and Question 20. For that reason, if there is a small difference in selection rates (one rate is more than 80% of the other), but large numbers of selections are involved, it would be appropriate to calculate the statistical significance of the difference in selection rates.

23. Q. When the ⅘th rule of thumb shows adverse impact, is there adverse impact under the Guidelines?

A. There usually is adverse impact, except where the number of persons selected and the difference in selection rates are very small. See Section 4D and Questions 20 and 21.

24. Q. Why do the Guidelines rely primarily upon the ⅘ths rule of thumb, rather than tests of statistical significance?

A. Where the sample of persons selected is not large, even a large real difference between groups is likely not to be confirmed by a test of statistical significance (at the usual .05 level of significance). For this reason, the Guidelines do not rely primarily upon a test of statistical significance, but use the ⅘ths rule of thumb as a practical and easy-to-administer measure of whether differences in selection rates are substantial. Many decisions in day-to-day life are made without reliance upon a test of statistical significance.

25. Q. Are there any circumstances in which the employer should evaluate components of a selection process, even though the overall selection process results in no adverse impact?

A. Yes, there are such circumstances: (1) Where the selection procedure is a significant factor in the continuation of patterns of assignments of incumbent employees caused by prior discriminatory employment practices. Assume, for example, an employer who traditionally hired blacks as employees for the "laborer" department in a manufacturing plant, and traditionally hired only whites as skilled craftsmen. Assume further that the employer in 1962 began to use a written examination not supported by a validity study to screen incumbent employees who sought to enter the apprenticeship program for skilled craft jobs. The employer stopped making racial assignments in 1972. Assume further that for the last four years, there have been special recruitment efforts aimed at recent black high school graduates and that the selection process, which includes the written examination, has resulted in the selection of black applicants for apprenticeship in approximately the same rates as white applicants.

In those circumstances, if the written examination had an adverse impact, its use would tend to keep incumbent black employees in the laborer department, and deny them entry to apprenticeship programs. For that reason, the enforcement agencies would expect the user to evaluate the impact of the written examination, and to have validity evidence for the use of the written examination if it has an adverse impact.

(2) Where the weight of court decisions or administrative interpretations holds that a specific selection procedure is not job related in similar circumstances.

For example, courts have held that because an arrest is not a determination of guilt, an applicant's arrest record by itself does not indicate inability to perform a job consistent with the trustworthy and efficient operation of a business. Yet a no arrest record requirement has a nationwide adverse impact on some minority groups. Thus, an employer who refuses to hire applicants solely on the basis of an arrest record is on notice that this policy may be found to be discriminatory. *Gregory* v. *Litton Industries*, 472 F. 2d 631 (9th Cir., 1972) (excluding persons from employment solely on the basis of arrests, which has an adverse impact, held to violate Title VII). Similarly, a minimum height requirement disproportionately disqualifies women and some national origin groups, and has been held not to be job related in a number of cases. For example, in *Dothard* v. *Rawlinson*, 433 U.S. 321 (1977), the Court held that height and weight requirements not shown to be job related were violative of Title VII. Thus an employer using a minimum height requirement should have evidence of its validity.

(3) In addition, there may be other circumstances in which an enforcement agency may decide to request an employer to evaluate components of a selection process, but such circumstances would clearly be unusual. Any such decision will be made only at a high level in the agency. Investigators and compliance officers are not authorized to make this decision.

26. Q. Does the bottom line concept of Section 4C apply to the administrative processing of charges of discrimination filed with an issuing agency, alleging that a specific selection procedure is discriminatory?

A. No. The bottom line concept applies only to enforcement actions as defined in Section 16 of the Guidelines. Enforcement actions include only court enforcement actions and other similar proceedings as defined in Section 16I. The EEOC administrative processing of charges of discrimination (investigation, finding of reasonable cause/no cause, and conciliation) required by Section 706(b) of Title VII are specifically exempted from the bottom line concept by the definition of an enforcement action. The bottom line concept is a result of a decision by the various enforcement agencies that, as a matter of prosecutorial discretion, they will devote their limited enforcement resources to the most serious offenders of equal employment opportunity laws. Since the concept is not a rule of law, it does not affect the discharge by the EEOC of its statutory responsibilities to investigate charges of discrimination, render an administrative finding on its investigation, and engage in voluntary conciliation efforts. Similarly, with respect to the other issuing agencies, the bottom line concept applies not to the processing of individual charges, but to the initiation of enforcement action.

27. Q. An employer uses one test or other selection procedure to select persons for a number of different jobs. Applicants are given the test, and the successful applicants are then referred to different departments and positions on the basis of openings available and their interests. The Guidelines appear to require assessment of adverse impact on a job-by-job basis (Section 15A(2)(a)). Is there some way to show that the test as a whole does not have adverse impact even though the proportions of members of each race, sex or ethnic group assigned to different jobs may vary?

A. Yes, in some circumstances. The Guidelines require evidence of validity only for those selection procedures which have an adverse impact, and which are part of a selection process which has an adverse impact. If the test is administered and used in the same fashion for a variety of jobs, the impact of that test can be assessed in

the aggregate. The records showing the results of the test, and the total number of persons selected, generally would be sufficient to show the impact of the test. If the test has no adverse impact, it need not be validated.

But the absence of adverse impact of the test in the aggregate does not end the inquiry. For there may be discrimination or adverse impact in the assignment of individuals to, or in the selection of persons for, particular jobs. The Guidelines call for records to be kept and determinations of adverse impact to be made of the overall selection process on a job by job basis. Thus, if there is adverse impact in the assignment or selection procedures for a job even though there is no adverse impact from the test, the user should eliminate the adverse impact from the assignment procedure or justify the assignment procedure.

28. Q. The Uniform Guidelines apply to the requirements of Federal law prohibiting employment practices which discriminate on the grounds of race, color, religion, sex or national origin. However, records are required to be kept only by sex and by specified race and ethnic groups. How can adverse impact be determined for religious groups and for national origin groups other than those specified in Section 4B of the Guidelines?

A. The groups for which records are required to be maintained are the groups for which there is extensive evidence of continuing discriminatory practices. This limitation is designed in part to minimize the burden on employers for recordkeeping which may not be needed.

For groups for which records are not required, the person(s) complaining may obtain information from the employer or others (voluntarily or through legal process) to show that adverse impact has taken place. When that has been done, the various provisions of the Uniform Guidelines are fully applicable.

Whether or not there is adverse impact, Federal equal employment opportunity law prohibits any deliberate discrimination or disparate treatment on grounds of religion or national origin, as well as on grounds of sex, color, or race.

Whenever "ethnic" is used in the Guidelines or in these Questions and Answers, it is intended to include national origin and religion, as set forth in the statutes, executive orders, and regulations prohibiting discrimination. See Section 16P.

29. Q. What is the relationship between affirmative action and the requirements of the Uniform Guidelines?

A. The two subjects are different, although related. Compliance with the Guidelines does not relieve users of their affirmative action obligations, including those of Federal contractors and subcontractors under Executive Order 11246. Section 13.

The Guidelines encourage the development and effective implementation of affirmative action plans or programs in two ways. First, in determining whether to institute action against a user on the basis of a selection procedure which has adverse impact and which has not been validated, the enforcement agency will take into account the general equal employment opportunity posture of the user with respect to the job classifications for which the procedure is used and the progress which has been made in carrying out any affirmative action program. Section 4E. If the user has demonstrated over a substantial period of time that it is in fact appropriately utilizing in the job or group of jobs in question the available race, sex or ethnic groups in the relevant labor force, the enforcement agency will generally exercise its discretion by not initiating enforcement proceedings based on adverse impact in relation to the applicant flow. Second, nothing in the Guidelines is intended to preclude the use of selection procedures, consistent with Federal law, which assist in the achievement of affirmative action objectives. Section 13A. See also, Questions 30 and 31.

30. Q. When may a user be race, sex or ethnic-conscious?

A. The Guidelines recognize that affirmative action programs may be race, sex or ethnic conscious in appropriate circumstances, (See Sections 4E and 13; See also Section 17, Appendix). In addition to obligatory affirmative action programs (See Question 29), the Guidelines encourage the adoption of voluntary affirmative action programs. Users choosing to engage in voluntary affirmative action are referred to EEOC's Guidelines on Affirmative Action (44 F.R. 4422, January 19, 1979). A user may justifiably be race, sex or ethnic-conscious in circumstances where it has reason to believe that qualified persons of specified race, sex or ethnicity have been or may be subject to the exclusionary effects of its selection procedures or other employment practices in its work force or particular jobs therein. In establishing long and short range goals, the employer may use the race, sex, or ethnic classification as the basis for such goals (Section 17(3) (a)).

In establishing a recruiting program, the employer may direct its recruiting activities to locations or institutions which have a high proportion of the race, sex, or ethnic group which has been excluded or underutilized (section 17(3) (b)). In establishing the pool of qualified persons from which final

selections are to be made, the employer may take reasonable steps to assure that members of the excluded or underutilized race, sex, or ethnic group are included in the pool (Section 17(3) (e)).

Similarly, the employer may be race, sex or ethnic-conscious in determining what changes should be implemented if the objectives of the programs are not being met (Section 17(3) (g)).

Even apart from affirmative action programs a user may be race, sex or ethnic-conscious in taking appropriate and lawful measures to eliminate adverse impact from selection procedures (Section 6A).

31. Q. Section 6A authorizes the use of alternative selection procedures to eliminate adverse impact, but does not appear to address the issue of validity. Thus, the use of alternative selection procedures without adverse impact seems to be presented as an option in lieu of validation. Is that its intent?

A. Yes. Under Federal equal employment opportunity law the use of any selection procedure which has an adverse impact on any race, sex or ethnic group is discriminatory unless the procedure has been properly validated, or the use of the procedure is otherwise justified under Federal law. *Griggs* v. *Duke Power Co.*, 401 U.S. 424 (1971); Section 3A. If a selection procedure has an adverse impact, therefore, Federal equal employment opportunity law authorizes the user to choose lawful alternative procedures which eliminate the adverse impact rather than demonstrating the validity of the original selection procedure.

Many users, while wishing to validate all of their selection procedures, are not able to conduct the validity studies immediately. Such users have the option of choosing alternative techniques which eliminate adverse impact, with a view to providing a basis for determining subsequently which selection procedures are valid and have as little adverse impact as possible.

Apart from Federal equal employment opportunity law, employers have economic incentives to use properly validated selection procedures. Nothing in Section 6A should be interpreted as discouraging the use of properly validated selection procedures; but Federal equal employment opportunity law does not require validity studies to be conducted unless there is adverse impact. See Section 2C.

III. GENERAL QUESTIONS CONCERNING VALIDITY AND THE USE OF SELECTION PROCEDURES

32. Q. What is "validation" according to the Uniform Guidelines?

A. Validation is the demonstration of the job relatedness of a selection procedure. The Uniform Guidelines

recognize the same three validity strategies recognized by the American Psychological Association:

(1) Criterion-related validity—a statistical demonstration of a relationship between scores on a selection procedure and job performance of a sample of workers.

(2) Content validity—a demonstration that the content of a selection procedure is representative of important aspects of performance on the job.

(3) Construct validity—a demonstration that (a) a selection procedure measures a construct (something believed to be an underlying human trait or characteristic, such as honesty) and (b) the construct is important for successful job performance.

33. Q. What is the typical process by which validity studies are reviewed by an enforcement agency?

A. The validity study is normally requested by an enforcement officer during the course of a review. The officer will first determine whether the user's data show that the overall selection process has an adverse impact, and if so, which component selection procedures have an adverse impact. See Section 15A(3). The officer will then ask for the evidence of validity for each procedure which has an adverse impact. See Sections 15B, C, and D. This validity evidence will be referred to appropriate personnel for review. Agency findings will then be communicated to the user.

34. Q. Can a user send its validity evidence to an enforcement agency before a review, so as to assure its validity?

A. No. Enforcement agencies will not review validity reports except in the context of investigations or reviews. Even in those circumstances, validity evidence will not be reviewed without evidence of how the selection procedure is used and what impact its use has on various race, sex, and ethnic groups.

35. Q. May reports of validity prepared by publishers of commercial tests and printed in test manuals or other literature be helpful in meeting the Guidelines?

A. They may be. However, it is the user's responsibility to determine that the validity evidence is adequate to meet the Guidelines. See Section 7, and Questions 43 and 66. Users should not use selection procedures which are likely to have an adverse impact without reviewing the evidence of validity to make sure that the standards of the Guidelines are met.

The following questions and answers (36–81) assume that a selection procedure has an adverse impact and is part of a selection process that has an adverse impact.

Appendix 3: Guidelines Questions and Answers

36. Q. How can users justify continued use of a procedure on a basis other than validity?

A. Normally, the method of justifying selection procedures with an adverse impact and the method to which the Guidelines are primarily addressed, is validation. The method of justification of a procedure by means other than validity is one to which the Guidelines are not addressed. See Section 6B. In *Griggs* v. *Duke Power Co.*, 401 U.S. 424, the Supreme Court indicated that the burden on the user was a heavy one, but that the selection procedure could be used if there was a "business necessity" for its continued use; therefore, the Federal agencies will consider evidence that a selection procedure is necessary for the safe and efficient operation of a business to justify continued use of a selection procedure.

37. Q. Is the demonstration of a rational relationship (as that term is used in constitutional law) between a selection procedure and the job sufficient to meet the validation requirements of the Guidelines?

A. No. The Supreme Court in *Washington* v. *Davis*, 426 U.S. 229 (1976) stated that different standards would be applied to employment discrimination allegations arising under the Constitution than would be applied to employment discrimination allegations arising under Title VII. The *Davis* case arose under the Constitution, and no Title VII violation was alleged. The Court applied a traditional constitutional law standard of "rational relationship" and said that it would defer to the "seemingly reasonable acts of administrators and executives." However, it went on to point out that under Title VII, the appropriate standard would still be an affirmative demonstration of the relationship between the selection procedure and measures of job performance by means of accepted procedures of validation and it would be an "insufficient response to demonstrate some rational basis" for a selection procedure having an adverse impact. Thus, the mere demonstration of a rational relationship between a selection procedure and the job does not meet the requirement of Title VII of the Civil Rights Act of 1964, or of Executive Order 11246, or the State and Local Fiscal Assistance Act of 1972, as amended (the revenue sharing act) or the Omnibus Crime Control and Safe Streets Act of 1968, as amended, and will not meet the requirements of these Guidelines for a validity study. The three validity strategies called for by these Guidelines all require evidence that the selection procedure is related to successful performance on the job. That evidence may be obtained through local validation or through validity studies done elsewhere.

38. Q. Can a user rely upon written or oral assertions of validity instead of evidence of validity?

A. No. If a user's selection procedures have an adverse impact, the user is expected to produce evidence of the validity of the procedures as they are used. Thus, the unsupported assertion by anyone, including representatives of the Federal government or State Employment Services, that a test battery or other selection procedure has been validated is not sufficient to satisfy the Guidelines.

39. Q. Are there any formal requirements imposed by these Guidelines as to who is allowed to perform a validity study?

A. No. A validity study is judged on its own merits, and may be performed by any person competent to apply the principles of validity research, including a member of the user's staff or a consultant. However, it is the user's responsibility to see that the study meets validity provisions of the Guidelines, which are based upon professionally accepted standards. See Question 42.

40. Q. What is the relationship between the validation provisions of the Guidelines and other statements of psychological principles, such as the *Standards for Educational and Psychological Tests*, published by the American Psychological Association (Wash., D.C., 1974) (hereinafter "American Psychological Association *Standards*")?

A. The validation provisions of the Guidelines are designed to be consistent with the generally accepted standards of the psychological profession. These Guidelines also interpret Federal equal employment opportunity law, and embody some policy determinations of an administrative nature. To the extent that there may be differences between particular provisions of the Guidelines and expressions of validation principles found elsewhere, the Guidelines will be given precedence by the enforcement agencies.

41. Q. When should a validity study be carried out?

A. When a selection procedure has adverse impact on any race, sex or ethnic group, the Guidelines generally call for a validity study or the elimination of adverse impact. See Sections 3A and 6, and Questions 9, 31, and 36. If a selection procedure has adverse impact, its use in making employment decisions without adequate evidence of validity would be inconsistent with the Guidelines. Users who choose to continue the use of a selection procedure with an adverse impact until the procedure is challenged increase the risk that they will be found to be engaged in discriminatory practices and will be liable for back pay awards, plaintiffs' attorneys' fees, loss of Federal contracts, subcontracts or grants, and the like. Validation studies begun on the eve of litigation have seldom been found to be adequate. Users who choose to validate selection procedures should consider the potential benefit from having a validation study completed or well underway before the procedures are administered for use in employment decisions.

42. Q. Where can a user obtain professional advice concerning validation of selection procedures?

A. Many industrial and personnel psychologists validate selection procedures, review published evidence of validity and make recommendations with respect to the use of selection procedures. Many of these individuals are members or fellows of Division 14 (Industrial and Organizational Psychology) or Division 5 (Evaluation and Measurement) of the American Psychological Association. They can be identified in the membership directory of that organization. A high level of qualification is represented by a diploma in Industrial Psychology awarded by the American Board of Professional Psychology.

Individuals with the necessary competence may come from a variety of backgrounds. The primary qualification is pertinent training and experience in the conduct of validation research.

Industrial psychologists and other persons competent in the field may be found as faculty members in colleges and universities (normally in the departments of psychology or business administration) or working as individual consultants or as members of a consulting organization.

Not all psychologists have the necessary expertise. States have boards which license and certify psychologists, but not generally in a specialty such as industrial psychology. However, State psychological associations may be a source of information as to individuals qualified to conduct validation studies. Addresses of State psychological associations or other sources of information may be obtained from the American Psychological Association, 1200 Seventeenth Street, NW., Washington, D.C. 20036.

43. Q. Can a selection procedure be a valid predictor of performance on a job in a certain location and be invalid for predicting success on a different job or the same job in a different location?

A. Yes. Because of differences in work behaviors, criterion measures, study samples or other factors, a selection procedure found to have validity in one situation does not necessarily have validity in different circumstances. Conversely, a selection procedure not found to have validity in one situation may have validity in different circumstances. For these reasons, the Guidelines requires that certain standards be satisfied before a user may rely upon findings of validity in another situation. Section 7 and Section 14D. See also, Question 66. Cooperative and multi-unit studies are however encouraged, and, when those standards of the Guidelines are satisfied, validity evidence specific to each location is not required. See Section 7C and Section 8.

44. Q. Is the user of a selection procedure required to develop the procedure?

A. No. A selection procedure developed elsewhere may be used. However, the user has the obligation to show that its use for the particular job is consistent with the Guidelines. See Section 7.

45. Q. Do the Guidelines permit users to engage in cooperative efforts to meet the Guidelines?

A. Yes. The Guidelines not only permit but encourage such efforts. Where users have participated in a cooperative study which meets the validation standards of these Guidelines and proper account has been taken of variables which might affect the applicability of the study to specific users, validity evidence specific to each user will not be required. Section 8.

46. Q. Must the same method for validation be used for all parts of a selection process?

A. No. For example, where a selection process includes both a physical performance test and an interview, the physical test might be supported on the basis of content validity, and the interview on the basis of a criterion-related study.

47. Q. Is a showing of validity sufficient to assure the lawfulness of the use of a selection procedure?

A. No. The use of the selection procedure must be consistent with the validity evidence. For example, if a research study shows only that, at a given passing score the test satisfactorily screens out probable failures, the study would not justify the use of substantially different passing scores, or of ranked lists of those who passed. See Section 5G. Similarly, if the research shows that a battery is valid when a particular set of weights is used, the weights actually used must conform to those that were established by the research.

48. Q. Do the Guidelines call for a user to consider and investigate alternative selection procedures when conducting a validity study?

A. Yes. The Guidelines call for a user, when conducting a validity study, to make a reasonable effort to become aware of suitable alternative selection procedures and methods of

use which have as little adverse impact as possible, and to investigate those which are suitable. Section 3B.

An alternative procedure may not previously have been used by the user for the job in question and may not have been extensively used elsewhere. Accordingly, the preliminary determination of the suitability of the alternative selection procedure for the user and job in question may have to be made on the basis of incomplete information. If on the basis of the evidence available, the user determines that the alternative selection procedure is likely to meet its legitimate needs, and is likely to have less adverse impact than the existing selection procedure, the alternative should be investigated further as a part of the validity study. The extent of the investigation should be reasonable. Thus, the investigation should continue until the user has reasonably concluded that the alternative is not useful or not suitable, or until a study of its validity has been completed. Once the full validity study has been completed, including the evidence concerning the alternative procedure, the user should evaluate the results of the study to determine which procedure should be used. See Section 3B and Question 50.

49. Q. Do the Guidelines call for a user continually to investigate "suitable alternative selection procedures and suitable alternative methods of using the selection procedure which have as little adverse impact as possible"?

A. No. There is no requirement for continual investigation. A reasonable investigation of alternatives is called for by the Guidelines as a part of any validity study. Once the study is complete and validity has been found, however, there is generally no obligation to conduct further investigations, until such time as a new study is called for. See, Sections 3B and 5K. If a government agency, complainant, civil rights organization or other person having a legitimate interest shows such a user an alternative procedure with less adverse impact and with substantial evidence of validity for the same job in similar circumstances, the user is obliged to investigate only the particular procedure which has been presented. Section 3B.

50. Q. In what circumstances do the Guidelines call for the use of an alternative selection procedure or an alternative method of using the procedure?

A. The alternative selection procedure (or method of use) should be used when it has less adverse impact and when the evidence shows that its validity is substantially the same or greater for the same job in similar circumstances. Thus, if under the original selection procedure the selection rate for black applicants was only one

half (50 percent) that of the selection rate for white applicants, whereas under the alternative selection procedure the selection rate for blacks is two-thirds (67 percent) that of white applicants, the new alternative selection procedure should be used when the evidence shows substantially the same or greater validity for the alternative than for the original procedure. The same principles apply to a new user who is deciding what selection procedure to institute.

51. Q. What are the factors to be considered in determining whether the validity for one procedure is substantially the same as or greater than that of another procedure?

A. In the case of a criterion-related validity study, the factors include the importance of the criteria for which significant relationships are found, the magnitude of the relationship between selection procedure scores and criterion measures, and the size and composition of the samples used. For content validity, the strength of validity evidence would depend upon the proportion of critical and/or important job behaviors measured, and the extent to which the selection procedure resembles actual work samples or work behaviors. Where selection procedures have been validated by different strategies, or by construct validity, the determination should be made on a case by case basis.

52. Q. The Guidelines require consideration of alternative procedures and alternative methods of use, in light of the evidence of validity and utility and the degree of adverse impact of the procedure. How can a user know that any selection procedure with an adverse impact is lawful?

A. The Uniform Guidelines (Section 5G) expressly permit the use of a procedure in a manner supported by the evidence of validity and utility, even if another method of use has a lesser adverse impact. With respect to consideration of alternative selection procedures, if the user made a reasonable effort to become aware of alternative procedures, has considered them and investigated those which appear suitable as a part of the validity study, and has shown validity for a procedure, the user has complied with the Uniform Guidelines. The burden is then on the person challenging the procedure to show that there is another procedure with better or substantially equal validity which will accomplish the same legitimate business purposes with less adverse impact. Section 3B. See also, *Albemarle Paper Co. v. Moody*, 422 U.S. 405.

53. Q. Are the Guidelines consistent with the decision of the Supreme Court in *Furnco Construction Corp. v. Waters*, —— U.S. ——, 98 S. Ct. 2943 (1978) where the Court stated: "Title

VII • • • does not impose a duty to adopt a hiring procedure that maximizes hiring of minority employees."

A. Yes. The quoted statement in *Furnco* v. *Waters* was made on a record where there was no adverse impact in the hiring process, no different treatment, no intentional discrimination, and no contractual obligations under E.O. 11246. Section 3B of the Guidelines is predicated upon a finding of adverse impact. Section 3B indicates that, when two or more selection procedures are available which serve a legitimate business purpose with substantially equal validity, the user should use the one which has been demonstrated to have the lesser adverse impact. Part V of the Overview of the Uniform Guidelines, in elaborating on this principle, states: "Federal equal employment opportunity law has added a requirement to the process of validation. In conducting a validation study, the employer should consider available alternatives which will achieve its legitimate purpose with lesser adverse impact."

Section 3B of the Guidelines is based on the principle enunciated in the Supreme Court decision in *Albemarle Paper Co.* v. *Moody*, 422 U.S. 405 (1975) that, even where job relatedness has been proven, the availability of other tests or selection devices which would also serve the employer's legitimate interest in "efficient and trustworthy workmanship" without a similarly undesirable racial effect would be evidence that the employer was using its tests merely as a pretext for discrimination.

Where adverse impact still exists, even though the selection procedure has been validated, there continues to be an obligation to consider alternative procedures which reduce or remove that adverse impact if an opportunity presents itself to do so without sacrificing validity. Where there is no adverse impact, the *Furnco* principle rather than the *Albemarle* principle is applicable.

IV. TECHNICAL STANDARDS

54. Q. How does a user choose which validation strategy to use?

A. A user should select a validation strategy or strategies which are (1) appropriate for the type of selection procedure, the job, and the employment situation, and (2) technically and administratively feasible. Whatever method of validation is used, the basic logic is one of prediction; that is, the presumption that level of performance on the selection procedure will, on the average, be indicative of level of performance on the job after selection. Thus, a criterion-related study, particularly a predictive one, is often regarded as the closest to such an ideal.

See American Psychological Association *Standards*, pp. 26-27.

Key conditions for a criterion-related study are a substantial number of individuals for inclusion in the study, and a considerable range of performance on the selection and criterion measures. In addition, reliable and valid measures of job performance should be available, or capable of being developed. Section 14B(1). Where such circumstances exist, a user should consider use of the criterion-related strategy.

Content validity is appropriate where it is technically and administratively feasible to develop work samples or measures of operationally defined skills, knowledges, or abilities which are a necessary prerequisite to observable work behaviors. Content validity is not appropriate for demonstrating the validity of tests of mental processes or aptitudes or characteristics; and is not appropriate for knowledges, skills or abilities which an employee will be expected to learn on the job. Section 14C(1)

The application of a construct validity strategy to support employee selection procedures is newer and less developed than criterion-related or content validity strategies. Continuing research may result in construct validity becoming more widely used. Because construct validity represents a generalization of findings, one situation in which construct validity might hold particular promise is that where it is desirable to use the same selection procedures for a variety of jobs. An overriding consideration in whether or not to consider construct validation is the availability of an individual with a high level of expertise in this field.

In some situations only one kind of validation study is likely to be appropriate. More than one strategy may be possible in other circumstances, in which case administrative considerations such as time and expense may be decisive. A combination of approaches may be feasible and desirable.

55. Q. Why do the Guidelines recognize only content, construct and criterion-related validity?

A. These three validation strategies are recognized in the Guidelines since they represent the current professional consensus. If the professional commmunity recognizes new strategies or substantial modifications of existing strategies, they will be considered and, if necessary, changes will be made in the Guidelines. Section 5A.

56. Q. Why don't the Uniform Guidelines state a preference for criterion-related validity over content or construct validity?

A. Generally accepted principles of the psychological profession support the use of criterion-related, content or

construct validity strategies as appropriate. American Psychological Association *Standards*, E, pp. 25-26. This use was recognized by the supreme Court in *Washington* v. *Davis*, 426 U.S. 229, 247, fn. 13. Because the Guidelines describe the conditions under which each validity strategy is inappropriate, there is no reason to state a general preference for any one validity strategy.

57. Q. Are the Guidelines intended to restrict the development of new testing strategies, psychological theories, methods of job analysis or statistical techniques?

A. No. The Guidelines are concerned with the validity and fairness of selection procedures used in making employment decisions, and are not intended to limit research and new developments. See Question 55.

58. Q. Is a full job analysis necessary for all validity studies?

A. It is required for all content and construct studies, but not for all criterion-related studies. See Sections 14A and 14B(2). Measures of the results or outcomes of work behaviors such as production rate or error rate may be used without a full job analysis where a review of information about the job shows that these criteria are important to the employment situation of the user. Similarly, measures such as absenteeism, tardiness or turnover may be used without a full job analysis if these behaviors are shown by a review of information about the job to be important in the specific situation. A rating of overall job performance may be used without a full job analysis only if the user can demonstrate its appropriateness for the specific job and employment situation through a study of the job. The Supreme Court held in *Albemarle Paper Co.* v. *Moody*, 422 U.S. 405 (1975), that measures of overall job performance should be carefully developed and their use should be standardized and controlled.

59. Q. Section 5J on interim use requires the user to have available substantial evidence of validity. What does this mean?

A. For purposes of compliance with 5J, "substantial evidence" means evidence which may not meet all the validation requirements of the Guidelines but which raises a strong inference that validity pursuant to these standards will soon be shown. Section 5J is based on the proposition that it would not be an appropriate allocation of Federal resources to bring enforcement proceedings against a user who would soon be able to satisfy fully the standards of the Guidelines. For example, a criterion-related study may have produced evidence which meets almost all of the requirements of the Guidelines with the exception that the gathering of the data of test fairness is still in progress and the fairness study has not yet produced results. If the correlation coefficient for the group as a whole permits the strong inference that the selection procedure is valid, then the selection procedure may be used on an interim basis pending the completion of the fairness study.

60. Q. What are the potential consequences to a user when a selection procedure is used on an interm basis?

A. The fact that the Guidelines permit interim use of a selection procedure under some conditions does not immunize the user from liability for back pay, attorney fees and the like, should use of the selection procedure later be found to be in violation of the Guidelines. Section 5J. For this reason, users should take steps to come into full compliance with the Guidelines as soon as possible. It is also appropriate for users to consider ways of minimizing adverse impact during the period of interim use.

61. Q. Must provisions for retesting be allowed for job-knowledge tests, where knowledge of the test content would assist in scoring well on it the second time?

A. The primary intent of the provision for retesting is that an applicant who was not selected should be given another chance. Particularly in the case of job-knowledge tests, security precautions may preclude retesting with the same test after a short time. However, the opportunity for retesting should be provided for the same job at a later time, when the applicant may have acquired more of the relevant job knowledges.

62 Q. Under what circumstances may a selection procedure be used for ranking?

A. Criterion-related and construct validity strategies are essentially empirical, statistical processes showing a relationship between performance on the selection procedure and performance on the job. To justify ranking under such validity strategies, therefore, the user need show mathematical support for the proposition that persons who receive higher scores on the procedure are likely to perform better on the job.

Content validity, on the other hand, is primarily a judgmental process concerned with the adequacy of the selection procedure as a sample of the work behaviors. Use of a selection procedure on a ranking basis may be supported by content validity if there is evidence from job analysis or other empirical data that what is measured by the selection procedure is associated with differences in levels of job performance. Section 14C(9); see also Section 5G.

Any conclusion that a content validated procedure is appropriate for

ranking must rest on an inference that higher scores on the procedure are related to better job performance. The more closely and completely the selection procedure approximates the important work behaviors, the easier it is to make such an inference. Evidence that better performance on the procedure is related to greater productivity or to performance of behaviors of greater difficulty may also support such an inference.

Where the content and context of the selection procedure are unlike those of the job, as, for example, in many paper-and-pencil job knowledge tests, it is difficult to infer an association between levels of performance on the procedure and on the job. To support a test of job knowledge on a content validity basis, there must be evidence of a specific tie-in between each item of knowledge tested and one or more work behaviors. See Question 79. To justify use of such a test for ranking, it would also have to be demonstrated from empirical evidence either that mastery of more difficult work behaviors, or that mastery of a greater scope of knowledge corresponds to a greater scope of important work behaviors.

For example, for a particular warehouse worker job, the job analysis may show that lifting a 50-pound object is essential, but the job analysis does not show that lifting heavier objects is essential or would result in significantly better job performance. In this case a test of ability to lift 50 pounds could be justified on a content validity basis for a pass/fail determination. However, ranking of candidates based on relative amount of weight that can be lifted would be inappropriate.

In another instance, a job analysis may reflect that, for the job of machine operator, reading of simple instructions is not a major part of the job but is essential. Thus, reading would be a critical behavior under the Guidelines. See Section 14C(8), since the job analysis in this example did not also show that the ability to read such instructions more quickly or to understand more complex materials would be likely to result in better job performance, a reading test suported by content validity alone should be used on a pass/fail rather than a ranking basis. In such circumstances, use of the test for ranking would have to be supported by evidence from a criterion-related (or construct) validity study.

On the other hand, in the case of a person to be hired for a typing pool, the job analysis may show that the job consists almost entirely of typing from manuscript, and that productivity can be measured directly in terms of finished typed copy. For such a job,

typing constitutes not only a critical behavior, but it constitutes most of the job. A higher score on a test which measured words per minute typed, with adjustments for errors, would therefore be likely to predict better job performance than a significantly lower score. Ranking or grouping based on such a typing test would therefore be appropriate under the Guidelines.

63. Q. If selection procedures are administered by an employment agency or a consultant for an employer, is the employer relieved of responsibilities under the Guidelines?

A. No. The employer remains responsible. It is therefore expected that the employer will have sufficient information available to show: (a) What selection procedures are being used on its behalf; (b) the total number of applicants for referral by race, sex and ethnic group; (c) the number of persons, by race, sex and ethnic group, referred to the employer; and (d) the impact of the selection procedures and evidence of the validity of any such procedure having an adverse impact as determined above.

A. CRITERION-RELATED VALIDITY

64. Q. Under what circumstances may success in training be used as a criterion in criterion-related validity studies?

A. Success in training is an appropriate criterion when it is (1) necessary for successful job performance or has been shown to be related to degree of proficiency on the job and (2) properly measured. Section 14B(3). The measure of success in training should be carefully developed to ensure that factors which are not job related do not influence the measure of training success. Section 14B(3).

65. Q. When may concurrent validity be used?

A. A concurrent validity strategy assumes that the findings from a criterion-related validity study of current employees can be applied to applicants for the same job. Therefore, if concurrent validity is to be used, differences between the applicant and employee groups which might affect validity should be taken into account. The user should be particularly concerned with those differences between the applicant group and current employees used in the research sample which are caused by work experience or other work related events or by prior selection of employees and selection of the sample. See Section 14B(4).

66. Q. Under what circumstances can a selection procedure be supported (on other than an interim basis) by a criterion-related validity study done elsewhere?

A. A validity study done elsewhere may provide sufficient evidence if four conditions are met (Sec. 7B):

1. The evidence from the other studies clearly demonstrates that the procedure was valid in its use elsewhere.

2. The job(s) for which the selection procedure will be used closely matches the job(s) in the original study as shown by a comparison of major work behaviors as shown by the job analyses in both contexts.

3. Evidence of fairness from the other studies is considered for those groups constituting a significant factor in the user's labor market. Section 7B(3). Where the evidence is not available the user should conduct an internal study of test fairness, if technically feasible. Section 7B(3).

4. Proper account is taken of variables which might affect the applicability of the study in the new setting, such as performance standards, work methods, representativeness of the sample in terms of experience or other relevant factors, and the currency of the study.

67. Q. What does "unfairness of a selection procedure" mean?

A. When a specific score on a selection procedure has a different meaning in terms of expected job performance for members of one race, sex or ethnic group than the same score does for members of another group, the use of that selection procedure may be unfair for members of one of the groups. See section 16V. For example, if members of one group have an average score of 40 on the selection procedure, but perform on the job as well as another group which has an average score of 50, then some uses of the selection procedure would be unfair to the members of the lower scoring group. See Question 70.

68. Q. When should the user investigate the question of fairness?

A. Fairness should be investigated generally at the same time that a criterion-related validity study is conducted, or as soon thereafter as feasible. Section 14B(8).

69. Q. Why do the Guidelines require that users look for evidence of unfairness?

A. The consequences of using unfair selection procedures are severe in terms of discriminating against applicants on the basis of race, sex or ethnic group membership. Accordingly, these studies should be performed routinely where technically feasible and appropriate, whether or not the probability of finding unfairness is small. Thus, the Supreme Court indicated in *Albemarle Paper Co. v. Moody*, 422 U.S. 405, that a validation study was "materially deficient" because, among other reasons, it failed to investigate fairness where it was not shown to be unfeasible to do so. Moreover,

the American Psychological Association *Standards* published in 1974 call for the investigation of test fairness in criterion-related studies wherever feasible (pp. 43–44).

70. Q. What should be done if a selection procedure is unfair for one or more groups in the relevant labor market?

A. The Guidelines discuss three options. See Section 14B(8)(d). First, the selection instrument may be replaced by another validated instrument which is fair to all groups. Second, the selection instrument may be revised to eliminate the sources of unfairness. For example, certain items may be found to be the only ones which cause the unfairness to a particular group, and these items may be deleted or replaced by others. Finally, revisions may be made in the method of use of the selection procedure to ensure that the probability of being selected is compatible with the probability of successful job performance.

The Federal enforcement agencies recognize that there is serious debate in the psychological profession on the question of test fairness, and that information on that concept is developing. Accordingly, the enforcement agencies will consider developments in this field in evaluating actions occasioned by a finding of test unfairness.

71. Q. How is test unfairness related to differential validity and to differential prediction?

A. Test unfairness refers to use of selection procedures based on scores when members of one group characteristically obtain lower scores than members of another group, and the differences are not reflected in measures of job performance. See Sections 16V and 14B(8)(a), and Question 67.

Differential validity and test unfairness are conceptually distinct. Differential validity is defined as a situation in which a given instrument has significantly different validity coefficients for different race, sex or ethnic groups. Use of a test may be unfair to some groups even when differential validity is not found.

Differential prediction is a central concept for one definition of test unfairness. Differential prediction occurs when the use of the same set of scores systematically overpredicts or underpredicts job performance for members of one group as compared to members of another group.

Other definitions of test unfairness which do not relate to differential prediction may, however, also be appropriately applied to employment decisions. Thus these Guidelines are not intended to choose between fairness models as long as the model selected is appropriate to the manner in which the selection procedure is used.

72. Q. What options does a user have if a criterion-related study is appropriate but is not feasible because there are not enough persons in the job?

A. There are a number of options the user should consider, depending upon the particular facts and circumstances, such as:

1. Change the procedure so as to eliminate adverse impact (see Section 6A);

2. Validate a procedure through a content validity strategy, if appropriate (see Section 14C and Questions 54 and 74);

3. Use a selection procedure validated elsewhere in conformity with the Guidelines (see Sections 7–8 and Question 66);

4. Engage in a cooperative study with other facilities or users (in cooperation with such users either bilaterally or through industry or trade associations or governmental groups), or participate in research studies conducted by the state employment security system. Where different locations are combined, care is needed to insure that the jobs studied are in fact the same and that the study is adequate and in conformity with the Guidelines (see Sections 8 and 14 and Question 45).

5. Combine essentially similar jobs into a single study sample. See Section 14B(1).

B. CONTENT VALIDITY

73. Q. Must a selection procedure supported by content validity be an actual "on the job" sample of work behaviors?

A. No. The Guidelines emphasize the importance of a close approximation between the content of the selection procedure and the observable behaviors or products of the job, so as to minimize the inferential leap between performance on the selection procedure and job performance. However, the Guidelines also permit justification on the basis of content validity of selection procedures measuring knowledges, skills, or abilities which are not necessarily samples of work behaviors if: (1) The knowledge, skill, or ability being measured is operationally defined in accord with Section 14C(4); and (2) that knowledge, skill, or ability is a prerequisite for critical or important work behaviors. In addition users may justify a requirement for training, or for experience obtained from prior employment or volunteer work, on the basis of content validity, even though the prior training or experience does not duplicate the job. See Section 14B(6).

74. Q. Is the use of a content validity strategy appropriate for a procedure measuring skills or knowledges which are taught in training after initial employment?

Appendix 3: Guidelines Questions and Answers

A. Usually not. The Guidelines state (Section 14C(1)) that content validity is not appropriate where the selection procedure involves knowledges, skills, or abilities which the employee will be expected to learn "on the job". The phrase "on the job" is intended to apply to training which occurs after hiring, promotion or transfer. However, if an ability, such as speaking and understanding a language, takes a substantial length of time to learn, is required for successful job performance, and is not taught to those initial hires who possess it in advance, a test for that ability may be supported on a content validity basis.

75. Q. Can a measure of a trait or construct be validated on the basis of content validity?

A. No. Traits or constructs are by definition underlying characteristics which are intangible and are not directly observable. They are therefore not appropriate for the sampling approach of content validity. Some selection procedures, while labeled as construct measures, may actually be samples of observable work behaviors. Whatever the label, if the operational definitions are in fact based upon observable work behaviors, a selection procedure measuring those behaviors may be appropriately supported by a content validity strategy. For example, while a measure of the construct "dependability" should not be supported on the basis of content validity, promptness and regularity of attendance in a prior work record are frequently inquired into as a part of a selection procedure, and such measures may be supported on the basis of content validity.

76. Q. May a test which measures what the employee has learned in a training program be justified for use in employment decisions on the basis of content validity?

A. Yes. While the Guidelines (Section 14C(1)) note that content validity is not an appropriate strategy for knowledges, skills or abilities which an employee "will be expected to learn on the job", nothing in the Guidelines suggests that a test supported by content validity is not appropriate for determining what the employee has learned on the job, or in a training program. If the content of the test is relevant to the job, it may be used for employment decisions such as retention or assignment. See Section 14C(7).

77. Q. Is a task analysis necessary to support a selection procedure based on content validity?

A. A description of all tasks is not required by the Guidelines. However, the job analysis should describe all important work behaviors and their relative importance and their level of difficulty. Sections 14C(2) and 15C(3). The

job analysis should focus on observable work behaviors and, to the extent appropriate, observable work products, and the tasks associated with the important observable work behaviors and/or work products. The job analysis should identify how the critical or important work behaviors are used in the job, and should support the content of the selection procedure.

78. Q. What is required to show the content validity of a paper-and-pencil test that is intended to approximate work behaviors?

A. Where a test is intended to replicate a work behavior, content validity is established by a demonstration of the similarities between the test and the job with respect to behaviors, products, and the surrounding environmental conditions. Section 14B(4).

Paper-and-pencil tests which are intended to replicate a work behavior are most likely to be appropriate where work behaviors are performed in paper and pencil form (e.g., editing and bookkeeping). Paper-and-pencil tests of effectiveness in interpersonal relations (e.g., sales or supervision), or of physical activities (e.g., automobile repair) or ability to function properly under danger (e.g., firefighters) generally are not close enough approximations of work behaviors to show content validity.

The appropriateness of tests of job knowledge, whether or not in pencil and paper form, is addressed in Question 79.

79. Q. What is required to show the content validity of a test of a job knowledge?

A. There must be a defined, well recognized body of information, and knowledge of the information must be prerequisite to performance of the required work behaviors. The work behavior(s) to which each knowledge is related should be identified on an item by item basis. The test should fairly sample the information that is actually used by the employee on the job, so that the level of difficulty of the test items should correspond to the level of difficulty of the knowledge as used in the work behavior. See Section 14C(1) and (4).

80. Q. Under content validity, may a selection procedure for entry into a job be justified on the grounds that the knowledges, skills or abilities measured by the selection procedure are prerequisites to successful performance in a training program?

A. Yes, but only if the training material and the training program closely approximate the content and level of difficulty of the job and if the knowledges, skills or abilities are not those taught in the training program. For example, if training materials are at a level of reading difficulty substantially in excess of the reading difficulty of

materials used on the job, the Guidelines would not permit justification on a content validity basis of a reading test based on those training materials for entry into the job.

Under the Guidelines a training program itself is a selection procedure if passing it is a prerequisite to retention or advancement. See Section 2C and 14C(17). As such, the content of the training program may only be justified by the relationship between the program and critical or important behaviors of the job itself, or through a demonstration of the relationship between measures of performance in training and measures of job performance.

Under the example given above, therefore, where the requirements in the training materials exceed those on the job, the training program itself could not be validated on a content validity basis if passing it is a basis for retention or promotion.

C. CONSTRUCT VALIDITY

81. Q. In Section 5, "General Standards for Validity Studies," construct validity is identified as no less acceptable than criterion-related and content validity. However, the specific requirements for construct validity, in Section 14D, seem to limit the generalizability of construct validity to the rules governing criterion-related validity. Can this apparent inconsistency be reconciled?

A. Yes. In view of the developing nature of construct validation for employment selection procedures, the approach taken concerning the generalizability of construct validity (section 14D) is intended to be a cautious one. However, construct validity may be generalized in circumstances where transportability of tests supported on the basis of criterion-related validity would not be appropriate. In establishing transportability of criterion-related validity, the jobs should have substantially the same major work behaviors. Section 7B(2). Construct validity, on the other hand, allows for situations where only some of the important work behaviors are the same. Thus, well-established measures of the construct which underlie particular work behaviors and which have been shown to be valid for some jobs may be generalized to other jobs which have some of the same work behaviors but which are different with respect to other work behaviors. Section 14D(4).

As further research and professional guidance on construct validity in employment situations emerge, additional extensions of construct validity for employee selection may become generally accepted in the profession. The agencies encourage further research and professional guidance with respect to the appropriate use of construct validity.

V. RECORDS AND DOCUMENTATION

82. Q. Do the Guidelines have simplified recordkeeping for small users (employers who employ one hundred or fewer employees and other users not required to file EEO-1, et seq. reports)?

A. Yes. Although small users are fully covered by Federal equal employment opportunity law, the Guidelines have reduced their record-keeping burden. See option in Section 15A(1). Thus, small users need not make adverse impact determinations nor are they required to keep applicant data on a job-by-job basis. The agencies also recognize that a small user may find that some of its validation strategies are not feasible. See Question 54. If a small user has reason to believe that its selection procedures have adverse impact and validation is not feasible, it should consider other options. See Sections 7A and 8 and Questions 31, 36, 45, 66, and 72.

83. Q. Is the requirement in the Guidelines that users maintain records of the race, national origin, and sex of employees and applicants constitutional?

A. Yes. For example, the United States Court of Appeals for the First Circuit rejected a challenge on constitutional and other grounds to the Equal Employment Opportunity Commission regulations requiring State and local governmental units to furnish information as to race, national origin and sex of employees. *United States* v. *New Hampshire*, 539 F. 2d 277 (1st Cir. 1976), *cert. denied*, sub nom. *New Hampshire* v. *United States*, 429 U.S. 1023. The Court held that the recordkeeping and reporting requirements promulgated under Title VII of the Civil Rights Act of 1964, as amended, were reasonably necessary for the Federal agency to determine whether the state was in compliance with Title VII and thus were authorized and constitutional. The same legal principles apply to recordkeeping with respect to applicants.

Under the Supremacy Clause of the Constitution, the Federal law requiring maintenance of records identifying race, sex and national origin overrides any contrary provision of State law. See Question 8.

The agencies recognize, however, that such laws have been enacted to prevent misuse of this information. Thus, employers should take appropriate steps to ensure proper use of all data. See Question #88.

84. Q. Is the user obliged to keep records which show whether its selection processes have an adverse impact on race, sex, or ethnic groups?

A. Yes. Under the Guidelines users are obliged to maintain evidence indicating the impact which their selection processes have on identifiable race, sex or ethnic groups. Sections 4 A and B. If the selection process for a job does have an adverse impact on one or more such groups, the user is expected to maintain records showing the impact for the individual procedures. Section 15A(2).

85. Q. What are the recordkeeping obligations of a user who cannot determine whether a selection process for a job has adverse impact because it makes an insufficient number of selections for that job in a year?

A. In such circumstances the user should collect, maintain, and have available information on the impact of the selection process and the component procedures until it can determine that adverse impact does not exist for the overall process or until the job has changed substantially. Section 15A(2)(c).

86. Q. Should applicant and selection information be maintained for race or ethnic groups constituting less than 2% of the labor force and the applicants?

A. Small employers and other small users are not obliged to keep such records. Section 15A(1). Employers with more than 100 employees and other users required to file EEO-1 et seq. reports should maintain records and other information upon which impact determinations could be made, because section 15A2 requires the maintenance of such information for "any of the groups for which records are called for by section 4B above." See also, Section 4A.

No user, regardless of size, is required to make adverse impact determinations for race or ethnic groups constituting less than 2% of the labor force and the applicants. See Question 16.

87. Q. Should information be maintained which identifies applicants and persons selected both by sex and by race or ethnic group?

A. Yes. Although the Federal agencies have decided not to require computations of adverse impact by subgroups (white males, black males, white females, black females—see Question 17), the Guidelines call for record keeping which allows identification of persons by sex, combined with race or ethnic group, so as to permit the identification of discriminatory practices on any such basis. Section 4A and 4B.

88. Q. How should a user collect data on race, sex or ethnic classifications for purposes of determining the impact of selection procedures?

A. The Guidelines have not specified any particular procedure, and the enforcement agencies will accept different procedures that capture the necessary information. Where applications are made in person, a user may maintain a log or applicant flow chart based upon visual observation, identifying the number of persons expressing an interest, by sex and by race or national origin; may in some circumstances rely upon personal knowledge of the user; or may rely upon self-identification. Where applications are not made in person and the applicants are not personally known to the employer, self-identification may be appropriate. Wherever a self-identification form is used, the employer should advise the applicant that identification by race, sex and national origin is sought, not for employment decisions, but for record-keeping in compliance with Federal law. Such self-identification forms should be kept separately from the application, and should not be a basis for employment decisions; and the applicants should be so advised. See Section 4B.

89. Q. What information should be included in documenting a validity study for purposes of these Guidelines?

A. Generally, reports of validity studies should contain all the information necessary to permit an enforcement agency to conclude whether a selection procedure has been validated. Information that is critical to this determination is denoted in Section 15 of the Guidelines by the word "(essential)".

Any reports completed after September 25, 1978, (the effective date of the Guidelines) which do not contain this information will be considered incomplete by the agencies unless there is good reason for not including the information. Users should therefore prepare validation reports according to the format of Section 15 of the Guidelines, and should carefully document the reasons if any of the information labeled "(essential)" is missing.

The major elements for all types of validation studies include the following:

When and where the study was conducted.

A description of the selection procedure, how it is used, and the results by race, sex, and ethnic group.

How the job was analyzed or reviewed and what information was obtained from this job analysis or review.

The evidence demonstrating that the selection procedure is related to the job. The nature of this evidence varies, depending upon the strategy used.

What alternative selection procedures and alternative methods of using the selection procedure were studied and the results of this study.

The name, address and telephone number of a contact person who can

Appendix 3: Guidelines Questions and Answers

provide further information about the study.

The documentation requirements for each validation strategy are set forth in detail in Section 15 B, C, D, E, F, and G. Among the requirements for each validity strategy are the following:

1. *Criterion-Related Validity*

A description of the criterion measures of job performance, how and why they were selected, and how they were used to evaluate employees.

A description of the sample used in the study, how it was selected, and the size of each race, sex, or ethnic group in it. •

A description of the statistical methods used to determine whether scores on the selection procedure are related to scores on the criterion measures of job performance, and the results of these statistical calculations.

2. *Content Validity*

The content of the job, as identified from the job analysis.

The content of the selection procedure.

The evidence demonstrating that the content of the selection procedure is a representative sample of the content of the job.

3. *Construct Validity*

A definition of the construct and how it relates to other constructs in the psychological literature.

The evidence that the selection procedure measures the construct.

The evidence showing that the measure of the construct is related to

work behaviors which involve the construct.

90. Q. Although the records called for under "Source Data", Section 15B(11) and section 15D(11), are not listed as "Essential", the Guidelines state that each user should maintain such records, and have them available upon request of a compliance agency. Are these records necessary? Does the absence of complete records preclude the further use of research data compiled prior to the issuance of the Guidelines?

A. The Guidelines require the maintenance of these records in some form "as a necessary part of the study." Section 15A(3)(c). However, such records need not be compiled or maintained in any specific format. The term "Essential" as used in the Guidelines refers to information considered essential to the validity report. Section 15A(3)(b). The Source Data records need not be included with reports of validation or other formal reports until and unless they are specifically requested by a compliance agency. The absence of complete records does not preclude use of research data based on those records that are available. Validation studies submitted to comply with the requirements of the Guidelines may be considered inadequate to the extent that important data are missing or there is evidence that the collected data are inaccurate.

[FR Doc. 79-6323 Filed 3-1-79; 8:45 am]

FEDERAL REGISTER, VOL. 44, NO. 43—FRIDAY, MARCH 2, 1979

About the Author

Jay M. Shafritz is on the faculty of the Graduate School of Public Affairs of the University of Colorado at Denver. Previously, he was on the faculties of the University of Houston at Clear Lake City, the State University of New York at Albany, and Rennselaer Polytechnic Institute.

Dr. Shafritz is the author of *Position Classification: A Behavioral Analysis for the Public Service* (1973), *Public Personnel Management: The Heritage of Civil Service Reform* (1975); co-author of *State Government Productivity: The Environment for Improvement* (1976), *Personnel Management in Government: Politics and Process* (1978); and co-editor of *Classics of Public Administration* (1978), *Government Budgeting: Theory, Process and Politics* (1978), *Classics of Organization Theory* (1978), *Program Evaluation in the Public Sector* (1979).